Lecture Notes in Computer Science 7148

Commenced Publication in 1973
Founding and Former Series Editors:
Gerhard Goos, Juris Hartmanis, and Jan van Leeuwen

Lecture Notes in Computer Science 7148

Viktor Kuncak Andrey Rybalchenko (Eds.)

Verification, Model Checking, and Abstract Interpretation

13th International Conference, VMCAI 2012
Philadelphia, PA, USA, January 22-24, 2012
Proceedings

Springer

Volume Editors

Viktor Kuncak
Swiss Federal Institute of Technology Lausanne (EPFL)
IC IIF LARA INR 318, Station 14, 1015 Lausanne, Switzerland
E-mail: viktor.kuncak@epfl.ch

Andrey Rybalchenko
Technische Universität München, Institut für Informatik
Boltzmannstr. 3, 85748 Munich, Germany
E-mail: rybal@in.tum.de

ISSN 0302-9743 e-ISSN 1611-3349
ISBN 978-3-642-27939-3 e-ISBN 978-3-642-27940-9
DOI 10.1007/978-3-642-27940-9
Springer Heidelberg Dordrecht London New York

Library of Congress Control Number: 2011945036

CR Subject Classification (1998): F.3.1, F.3.2, D.2.4, F.4.1, D.1-3

LNCS Sublibrary: SL 1 – Theoretical Computer Science and General Issues

Typesetting: Camera-ready by author, data conversion by Scientific Publishing Services, Chennai, India

Printed on acid-free paper

Springer is part of Springer Science+Business Media (www.springer.com)

Preface

This volume contains the proceedings of the 13th International Conference on Verification, Model Checking, and Abstract Interpretation (VMCAI 2012), held in Philadelphia, Pennsylvania, USA, during January 22–24, 2012. VMCAI 2012 was the 13th in a series of meetings. Previous editions of the conference were held in Port Jefferson 1997, Pisa 1998, Venice 2002, New York 2003, Venice 2004, Paris 2005, Charleston 2006, Nice 2007, San Francisco 2008, Savannah 2009, Madrid 2010, and Austin 2011.

VMCAI provides a forum for researchers from the communities of verification, model checking, and abstract interpretation. The conference showcases state-of-the-art research in each of those areas and facilitates interaction, cross-fertilization, and advancement of hybrid methods that span multiple areas. The topics covered in the conference include program verification, model checking, abstract interpretation static analysis, deductive methods, program certification, debugging techniques, abstract domains, type systems, optimization. Papers may address any programming paradigm, including concurrent, constraint, functional, imperative, logic and object-oriented programming.

This year, 70 papers were submitted to VMCAI. Each submission was reviewed by at least three Program Committee members, and on average each paper was reviewed by 3.22 committee members. After carefully deliberating over the relevance and quality of each paper, the Program Committee chose to accept 26 papers for presentation at the conference.

This year's edition continued the VMCAI tradition of inviting distinguished speakers to give talks and tutorials. The program included talks by Alex Aiken, Rajeev Alur, Ahmed Bouajjani, Ranjit Jhala, and Tobias Nipkow.

The quality of the conference crucially depends on the hard work the Program Committee and subreviewers put into the paper selection process; we thank them greatly for their efforts. Our thanks also go to the Steering Committee members for helpful advice, in particular to David Schmidt and Lenore Zuck for their invaluable efforts in the conference organization. VMCAI 2012 was co-located with POPL 2012 and held in co-operation with ACM (Association for Computing Machinery). We thank Matthew Might, who served as our interface to the POPL organizers, and ACM for help with the local arrangements. Finally, we are grateful to Andrei Voronkov, whose EasyChair system eased the submission and paper selection process, and greatly simplified the compilation of the proceedings.

January 2012

Viktor Kuncak
Andrey Rybalchenko

Organization

Program Committee

Josh Berdine	Microsoft Research, UK
Nikolaj Bjørner	Microsoft Research, USA
Bor-Yuh Evan Chang	University of Colorado at Boulder, USA
Wei-Ngan Chin	National University of Singapore
Radhia Cousot	CNRS / École Normale Supérieure, France
Sophia Drossopoulou	Imperial College London, UK
Philippa Gardner	Microsoft Research and Imperial College London, UK
Patricia Hill	University of Parma, Italy
Marieke Huisman	University of Twente, The Netherlands
Radu Iosif	Verimag/CNRS/University of Grenoble, France
Daniel Kroening	Computing Laboratory, Oxford University, UK
Viktor Kuncak	EPFL, Switzerland
Barbara König	Universität Duisburg-Essen, Germany
Francesco Logozzo	Microsoft Research, USA
Rupak Majumdar	UCLA, USA
Greg Morrisett	Harvard University, USA
Corina Pasareanu	CMU/NASA Ames Research Center, USA
Andreas Podelski	University of Freiburg, Germany
Sriram Rajamani	Microsoft Research, India
Andrey Rybalchenko	Technische Universität München, Germany
Mooly Sagiv	Tel-Aviv University, Israel
Sriram Sankaranarayanan	University of Colorado at Boulder, USA
Helmut Veith	Vienna University of Technology, Austria
Heike Wehrheim	University of Paderborn, Germany
Eran Yahav	Technion, Israel
Lenore Zuck	University of Illinois in Chicago, USA

Additional Reviewers

Berger, Martin
Besova, Galina
Beyer, Dirk
Blom, Stefan
Bouaziz, Mehdi
Bruggink, Sander
Calvanese, Diego
Chakarov, Aleksandar
Chaki, Sagar
Chatterjee, Krishnendu
Costea, Andreea
Cox, Arlen
Craciun, Florin
Dang, Thao
David, Cristina
De Moura, Leonard
Doyen, Laurent
Fehnker, Ansgar
Feo, Sergio
Feo-Arenis, Sergio
Feret, Jérôme

Gotsman, Alexey
Gurov, Dilian
Hoffmann, Joerg
Hülsbusch, Mathias
Jacobs, Swen
Jobstmann, Barbara
Katoen, Joost-Pieter
Kinder, Johannes
Knottenbelt, William
Komuravelli, Anvesh
Konecny, Filip
Konnov, Igor
Kuperstein, Michael
Lal, Akash
Laviron, Vincent
Le, Duy Khanh
Le, Quang Loc
Le, Ton Chanh
Lewis, Matt
Malkis, Alexander
Maric, Filip
Martel, Matthieu
Massé, Damien
Mauborgne, Laurent
Mereacre, Alexandru
Meshman, Yuri
Nickovic, Dejan
Nori, Aditya
Partush, Nimrod
Piskac, Ruzica
Popeea, Corneliu
Rinetzky, Noam
Rival, Xavier
Rozier, Kristin Yvonne
Rungta, Neha
Sangnier, Arnaud
Seghir, Mohamed Nassim
Sharma, Asankhaya
Shoham, Sharon
Simacek, Jiri
Simaitis, Aistis
Smith, Gareth
Stoelinga, Marielle
Stückrath, Jan
Suter, Philippe
Tautschnig, Michael
Timm, Nils
Timmer, Mark
Tobin-Hochstadt, Sam
Van Glabbeek, Robert
Veanes, Margus
Vojnar, Tomas
Wonisch, Daniel
Wright, Adam
Zaharieva, Marina
Zuleger, Florian

Table of Contents

Abstract Domains for Automated Reasoning about List-Manipulating Programs with Infinite Data*

Ahmed Bouajjani[1], Cezara Drăgoi[2], Constantin Enea[1], and Mihaela Sighireanu[1]

[1] LIAFA, Univ Paris Diderot & CNRS
{abou,cenea,sighirea}@liafa.jussieu.fr
[2] IST Austria
cezarad@ist.ac.at

Abstract. We describe a framework for reasoning about programs with lists carrying integer numerical data. We use abstract domains to describe and manipulate complex constraints on configurations of these programs mixing constraints on the shape of the heap, sizes of the lists, on the multisets of data stored in these lists, and on the data at their different positions. Moreover, we provide powerful techniques for automatic validation of Hoare-triples and invariant checking, as well as for automatic synthesis of invariants and procedure summaries using modular inter-procedural analysis. The approach has been implemented in a tool called CELIA and experimented successfully on a large benchmark of programs.

1 Introduction

Reasoning about heap-manipulating programs can be quite complex and its automatization is a real challenge both from the theoretical and the practical point of view. Indeed, the specification of such a program (consider for instance a sorting algorithm), includes in general various types of constraints, for instance constraints on the structure of the heap (i.e., being a list, acyclic, etc.), on the (unbounded) sizes of the different parts of the heap (i.e., equality of the lengths of two lists), on the (muti)sets of elements stored in different parts of the heap (i.e., equality between the multisets of data stored in two different lists), as well as on the relations existing between the data (potentially ranging over infinite domains) stored in the heap (i.e., sortedness of a list).

For example, the procedure `quicksort` given in Fig. 1 sorts the input list pointed to by the variable `a`. The specification of `quicksort` includes (1) the sortedness of the output list pointed to by `res`, expressed by the formula:

$$\forall y_1, y_2.\ 0 \leq y_1 \leq y_2 < \mathtt{len}(\mathtt{res}) \Rightarrow \mathtt{data}(\mathtt{res}, y_1) \leq \mathtt{data}(\mathtt{res}, y_2) \qquad (1)$$

where y_1 and y_2 are interpreted as integers and used to refer to positions in the list pointed to by `res`, $\mathtt{len}(\mathtt{res})$ denotes the length of this list, and $\mathtt{data}(\mathtt{res}, y_1)$ denotes the integer stored in the element of `res` at position y_1, and (2) the preservation property saying that input and output lists have the same (multisets of) elements. This property is expressed by the equation

$$\mathtt{ms}(\mathtt{a}^0) = \mathtt{ms}(\mathtt{res}) \qquad (2)$$

* This work was partly supported by the French National Research Agency (ANR) project Veridyc (ANR-09-SEGI-016).

V. Kuncak and A. Rybalchenko (Eds.): VMCAI 2012, LNCS 7148, pp. 1–22, 2012.

```
typedef struct list {
      struct list *next;
      int data;
      } list;

void split(list *a, int v, list **sm, list **gr){
  list *x=a;
  while (x != NULL){
    if (x->data <= v){
      ...
      /* adds the element pointed
      to by x to sm */
    }
    else{
      ...
      /* adds the element pointed
      to by x to gr */
    }
    x = x->next;
  } }
```

```
list* quicksort(list* a){
  list *left,*right,*pivot,*res,*start;
  int d;
  if (a == NULL || a->next == NULL)
    copy(a,res);
  else {
    d = a->data;
    alloc(&pivot,1);
    pivot->data = d;
    start = a->next;

    split(start,d,&left,&right);

    left = quicksort(left);
    right = quicksort(right);

    res = concat(left,pivot,right);
  }
  return res;
}
```

Fig. 1. The `quicksort` algorithm on singly-linked lists

where $\mathtt{ms}(\mathtt{a}^0)$ (resp. $\mathtt{ms}(\mathtt{res})$) denotes the multiset of integers stored in the list pointed to by a at the beginning of the procedure (resp. res at the end of the procedure).

Therefore, reasoning on the correctness of such programs requires designing formal frameworks where such kind of constraints (and their combinations) can be manipulated, i.e., expressed, proved valid, and synthesized.

From the expressiveness point of view, multi-sorted logics interpreted on labelled graphs over infinite alphabets can be naturally considered in this context. As said above, such a logic should allow expressing (1) structural properties on graphs using reachability predicates, as well as (2) constraints on (multi)sets of reachable elements: constraints on their sizes using some arithmetics like Presburger arithmetics for instance, equality/inclusion constraints on the multisets of data they are carrying, etc., and also (3) constraints on the data attached to the different nodes in the graph using some theory on the considered type of data, for instance in the case of integers, it would be possible to consider again Presburger arithmetics to express data constraints.

Given such an expressive specification language, the challenge then is to provide algorithmic techniques allowing to carry out automatically correctness proofs of programs w.r.t. some specifications. (Here we consider partial correctness proofs, i.e., checking safety properties.) This task is not trivial since of course the considered problem is undecidable in general for the considered class of programs and specifications. Nevertheless, our aim is to provide sound techniques that are powerful enough to handle most of the cases that arise in practice.

A first objective is to provide automatic support for pre/post-condition reasoning, assuming that we are given a program together with annotations specifying assumptions and requirements on the configurations at its different control points, including loop invariants and procedure specifications. The aim is to automatize each step in the correction proof using algorithms for checking the validity of Hoare triples, i.e., given a program statement s, a pre-condition ϕ and a post-condition ψ, check that starting from any configuration satisfying ϕ, executing s always leads to a configuration satisfying ψ. Phrased in the logic-based framework mentioned above, this corresponds to checking whether the formula $\mathtt{post}(\phi, St) \Rightarrow \psi$ is valid, where $\mathtt{post}(\phi, St)$ is supposed to be a formula that characterizes the set of all immediate successors of ϕ after executing St. Therefore, we need to have (1) procedures for computing effectively the formula $\texttt{post}(\phi, St)$ for any given St and ϕ, and (2) algorithms for deciding entailments between two formulas in order to check that $\texttt{post}(\phi, St) \Rightarrow \psi$ holds.

Beyond that, a more ambitious objective is to provide algorithms for automatic synthesis of invariants and procedure summaries (i.e., assertions specifying the relations between the inputs and outputs of the procedures). This allows to augment the degree of automation since the user would not need to provide all the necessary annotations for the correctness proof, which is usually cumbersome and quite complex. Instead, he would be able to rely on synthesis techniques that can discover automatically the missing assertions (e.g., strong enough loop invariants) to complete the proof.

To achieve these goals, several problems must be faced. First, we must be able to decide the validity of the manipulated formulas. The problem is that it is very hard to define classes of formulas for which this is possible and that are expressive enough to cover relevant program properties such as those mentioned above, mixing complex constraints on the shape, sizes, and data. In fact, in many cases, the needed assertions are expressed using formulas that are outside the known decidable logics.

As for assertion synthesis, the additional problem is that the space of assertions is infinite, and it is hard to discover the relevant properties that hold for all possible configurations at some point in the program. Especially, it is important to have clever techniques for the generation of universally quantified formulas that capture such properties that may involve in general quite intricate relations between elements of the heap. Naive procedures would not be able to generate accurate enough assertions.

In this work, we propose an approach for addressing these issues based on the framework of abstract interpretation [12]. We focus on the case of (sequential) programs manipulating dynamic linked lists carrying integer numerical data.

First, we consider that constraints are expressed as elements of abstract domains, the latter being equipped with appropriate meet, join, and entailment operations. These operations correspond to approximations of the logical operations of conjunction, disjunction, and logical implication in the sense that the meet (resp. join) under-approximates conjunction (resp. over-approximates disjunction), and the entailment is a sound approximation of logical implication, i.e., if the entailment holds, then necessarily the implication holds also. In addition to these operations, abstract transformers are introduced allowing to define an over-approximation of $\texttt{post}(\phi, St)$, for every statement St and constraint ϕ in the considered abstract domain. Therefore, validating Hoare triples in this framework amounts to checking an entailment between two elements of some abstract domain. Notice that entailment checking in this context does not need to be complete in general. But then, the difficulty is of course in the design of the abstract domains (and the associated operations mentioned above) so that they allow expressing the kind of constraints that are needed for reasoning about significant classes of programs, and they offer powerful mechanisms for computing abstract post-images and for checking entailment that are accurate enough to be successful and efficient in practice.

Furthermore, invariant synthesis and procedure summary generation can naturally be done in this framework using intra/inter-procedural analyses. These analyses are defined as fixpoint computations using the abstract domains mentioned above. However, an additional, and quite delicate, issue that must be addressed in this case is how to guarantee termination while ensuring accuracy of the analyses. In particular, quite elaborate extrapolation (or widening) techniques are needed to generate universally quantified formulas that combine ordering and data constraints. Another important issue to address is scalability of the analyses. A natural approach for tackling this issue is to design modular inter-procedural analyses where the analysis of each procedure call is performed locally, by considering only the part of the heap that is accessible by the variables of the procedure. Then, a delicate problem arises which is how to maintain the relations that might exist between the elements of the local heap before and after the procedure call and the rest of the elements in the heap.

We propose in this paper abstract domains allowing to reason about the various kind of constraints that we have mentioned above, i.e., constraints on the shape of the heap, on the lengths of the lists starting at some locations, on the multisets of the data in these lists, and on the values of the data at different positions on these lists. We show that the proposed domains allow to reason accurately about complex constraints, in particular, our entailment checking techniques allow to establish the validity of formulas that are beyond the capabilities of the existing tools, including the currently most advanced SMT solvers such as CVC3 [2] and Z3 [15].

Moreover, we propose modular inter-procedural analysis techniques allowing to generate automatically invariants as well as procedure summaries. We show that in order to be accurate, modular reasoning requires nontrivial combinations of abstract analyses using different domains, in particular the domain of universally quantified formulas and the domain of multiset constraints. We have implemented the abstract domains and the techniques described in the paper in a tool called CELIA, and we have carried out a large set of experimentations showing the strength and the efficiency of our approach.

2 Programs

We consider a class of strongly typed sequential programs which manipulate singly linked lists. We suppose that all manipulated lists have the same type, i.e., pointer to a record called `list` consisting of one pointer field `next` and one data field `data` of integer type. The generalization to records with several data fields is straightforward.

Syntax: Let *PVar* be a set of variables of type pointer to `list` (*PVar* includes the constant `NULL`) and *DVar* a set of variables interpreted as integers. A *program* is defined by a set of procedures, each of them defined by a tuple $P = (\mathbf{fpi}, \mathbf{fpo}, \mathbf{loc}, G)$, where $\mathbf{loc} \subseteq PVar \cup DVar$ is the vector of local variables, $\mathbf{fpi} \subseteq \mathbf{loc}$ and $\mathbf{fpo} \subseteq \mathbf{loc}$ are the vectors of formal input, resp. output, parameters, and G is an *intra-procedural control flow graph* (CFG, for short). The edges of the CFG are labeled by (1) statements of the form p`=new`, p`=`q, p`->next=`q, p`->data=`dt, and $\mathbf{y}$`=`$Q(\mathbf{x})$, where $p, q \in PVar$, dt is a term representing an integer, Q is a procedure name, and $\mathbf{y}, \mathbf{x} \subseteq PVar \cup DVar$, (2) boolean conditions on data built using predicates over $\mathbb{Z}$, (3) boolean conditions on pointers of the form p`==`q, where $p, q \in PVar$, or (4) statements `assert` φ and `assume` φ, where φ is a formula in the logic SL3 defined in Section 3. The semantics assumes a garbage collector and consequently, the statement `free` is useless. We assume a call-by-value semantics for the procedure input parameters and that each procedure has its own set of local variables. We forbid pointers to procedures and pointer arithmetic.

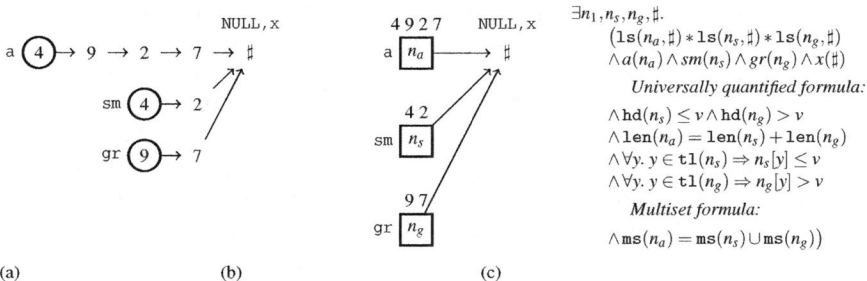

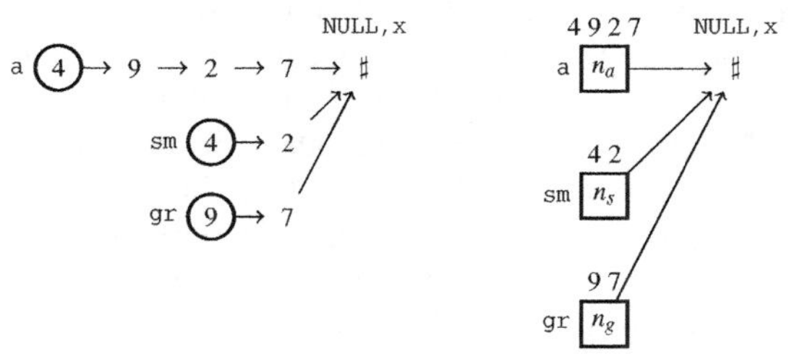

$$\exists n_1, n_s, n_g, \sharp.\ (\mathtt{ls}(n_a,\sharp) * \mathtt{ls}(n_s,\sharp) * \mathtt{ls}(n_g,\sharp) \wedge a(n_a) \wedge sm(n_s) \wedge gr(n_g) \wedge x(\sharp)$$

Universally quantified formula:

$$\wedge\, \mathtt{hd}(n_s) \leq v \wedge \mathtt{hd}(n_g) > v$$
$$\wedge\, \mathtt{len}(n_a) = \mathtt{len}(n_s) + \mathtt{len}(n_g)$$
$$\wedge\, \forall y.\ y \in \mathtt{tl}(n_s) \Rightarrow n_s[y] \leq v$$
$$\wedge\, \forall y.\ y \in \mathtt{tl}(n_g) \Rightarrow n_g[y] > v$$

Multiset formula:

$$\wedge\, \mathtt{ms}(n_a) = \mathtt{ms}(n_s) \cup \mathtt{ms}(n_g))$$

(a) (b) (c)

Fig. 2. Heap (a), heap decomposition (b), and SL3 (c) representations of a program configuration in the procedure `split`

Semantics: A program configuration consists of a valuation of the variables interpreted as integers and a configuration of the allocated memory. The latter is represented by a labeled directed graph where nodes represent list elements and edges represent values of the field `next` (every node has exactly one successor). The constant `NULL` is represented by the distinguished node $\sharp$. Nodes are labeled with values of the field `data` and program pointer variables. Such a representation is called a *heap*. For example, the valuation $[v \leftarrow 6]$ and the graph in Fig. 2(a) represents a program configuration of the procedure `split` from Fig. 1.

Definition 1 (Heap). *A heap over PVar and DVar is a tuple $H = (N,S,V,L,D)$ where: (1) N is a finite set of nodes which contains a distinguished node $\sharp$, (2) $S : N \rightharpoonup N$ is a successor partial function s.t. only $S(\sharp)$ is undefined, (3) $V : PVar \to N$ is a function associating nodes to pointer variables s.t. $V(\mathtt{NULL}) = \sharp$, (4) $L : N \rightharpoonup \mathbb{Z}$ is a partial function associating nodes to integers s.t. only $L(\sharp)$ is undefined, and (5) $D : DVar \to \mathbb{Z}$ is a valuation for the data variables.*

Definition 2 (Simple/Crucial node). *A node labeled with a pointer variable or which has at least 2 predecessors is called* crucial. *Otherwise, it's called a* simple node. □

For example, the circled nodes in Fig. 2(a) are crucial nodes. All the other nodes are simple. Since the semantics we consider is based on garbage collection, the heaps do not contain garbage, i.e., all the nodes of the graph are reachable from nodes labeled with pointer variables.

The *intra-procedural semantics* is defined by a mapping δ which associates to each control point c in the program a set of heaps over *PVar* and *DVar*, representing the set of program configurations reachable at c. As usual, the mapping δ is obtained as the least fixed point of a system of recursive equations. For any statement *St* and any set of heaps $\mathcal{H}$ over *PVar* and *DVar*, $\mathtt{post}_c(\mathcal{H}, St)$ denotes the concrete post-condition operator.

We consider an *inter-procedural semantics* based on relations between program configurations. To have a compositional semantics, we follow the approach of *local heap semantics* introduced in [29], where at each procedure call, the callee has access only to the part of the heap that is reachable from its actual parameters, called the *local heap*. For example, in Fig. 3(a), the local heap for the procedure call `quicksort(left)` contains only the nodes reachable from the node labeled by `left`. This approach simplifies the semantics since it avoids the representation of the call stack in the program configurations. However, its use is delicate because the nodes in the local heap of the callee may be shared with the local heaps of other procedures. If during the call these nodes become locally unreachable or deleted, the local heaps of the other procedures must also be updated accordingly. To solve this problem, [29] proposes to maintain for each procedure call the nodes of the local heap from which the shared paths start, but which are not pointed to by the procedure parameters. These nodes are called *cut-points*. Notice that, in general, the number of cut-points may be unbounded. However, there is a significant class of programs for which cut-points are never generated during the execution. This class, called *cut-point free programs* [30], includes programs such as sorting algorithms, traversal of lists, insertion, deletion, etc. In this paper, we consider cut-point free programs and we focus on the problems induced by data manipulation.

For any procedure $P = (\mathbf{fpi}, \mathbf{fpo}, \mathbf{loc}, G)$ and any control point c in P, we consider relations between a program configuration at the entry point of P and a program configuration at c. These relations are represented using a double vocabulary $\mathbf{loc} \cup \mathbf{loc}^0$, where $\mathbf{loc}^0 = \{v^0 \mid v \in \mathbf{loc}\}$ denote the values of the variables in $\mathbf{loc}$ at the entry point of P. A relation associated to P at c is represented by a heap over $\mathbf{loc} \cup \mathbf{loc}^0$ consisting of a valuation for the integer variables in $(\mathbf{loc} \cap DVar) \cup (\mathbf{loc} \cap DVar)^0$ and a graph which is the union of two sub-graphs: G^0 represents the local heap at the entry point of P and G represents the local heap at the control point c. For example, a relation associated to `quicksort` at line 33 is represented by the valuation $[d^0 \leftarrow 0, d \leftarrow 6]$ and the graph in Figure 3(a) (we suppose that integer variables are initialized to 0). The subgraph containing only the nodes reachable from the node labeled by $\mathtt{a}^0$ represents the input configuration while the rest of the graph represents the configuration at line 33.

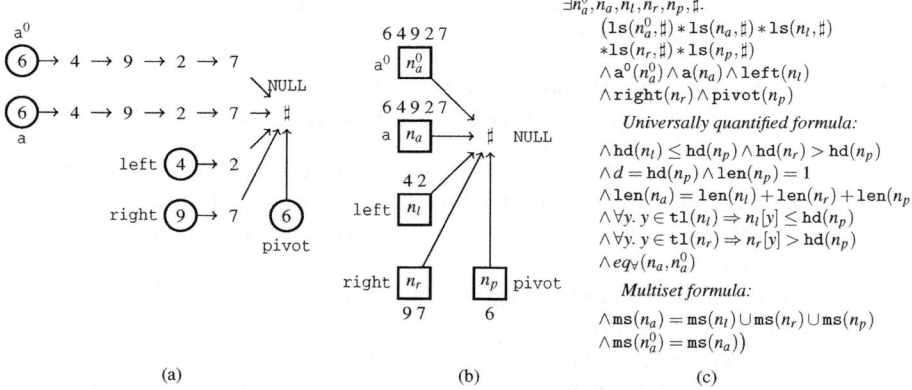

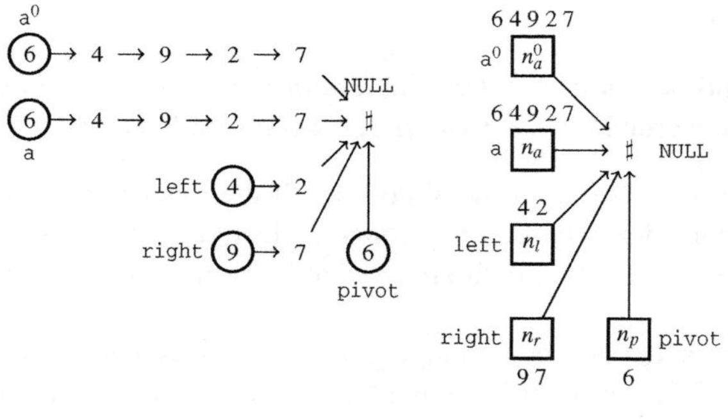

$\exists n_a^0, n_a, n_l, n_r, n_p, \sharp.$
$(\mathtt{ls}(n_a^0,\sharp) * \mathtt{ls}(n_a,\sharp) * \mathtt{ls}(n_l,\sharp)$
$* \mathtt{ls}(n_r,\sharp) * \mathtt{ls}(n_p,\sharp)$
$\wedge\, \mathtt{a}^0(n_a^0) \wedge \mathtt{a}(n_a) \wedge \mathtt{left}(n_l)$
$\wedge\, \mathtt{right}(n_r) \wedge \mathtt{pivot}(n_p)$

Universally quantified formula:

$\wedge\, \mathtt{hd}(n_l) \leq \mathtt{hd}(n_p) \wedge \mathtt{hd}(n_r) > \mathtt{hd}(n_p)$
$\wedge\, d = \mathtt{hd}(n_p) \wedge \mathtt{len}(n_p) = 1$
$\wedge\, \mathtt{len}(n_a) = \mathtt{len}(n_l) + \mathtt{len}(n_r) + \mathtt{len}(n_p)$
$\wedge\, \forall y.\ y \in \mathtt{tl}(n_l) \Rightarrow n_l[y] \leq \mathtt{hd}(n_p)$
$\wedge\, \forall y.\ y \in \mathtt{tl}(n_r) \Rightarrow n_r[y] > \mathtt{hd}(n_p)$
$\wedge\, eq_\forall(n_a, n_a^0)$

Multiset formula:

$\wedge\, \mathtt{ms}(n_a) = \mathtt{ms}(n_l) \cup \mathtt{ms}(n_r) \cup \mathtt{ms}(n_p)$
$\wedge\, \mathtt{ms}(n_a^0) = \mathtt{ms}(n_a))$

(c)

Fig. 3. Heap (a), heap decomposition (b), and SL3 (c) representations of a relation between program configurations in the procedure `quicksort`

The inter-procedural semantics is defined by a mapping ρ which associates to each control point c in the CFG of a procedure P a set of heaps over $\mathbf{loc} \cup \mathbf{loc}^0$. The mapping ρ is obtained as the least fixed point of a system of recursive equations [13,33]. The extension of the postcondition operator $\mathtt{post}_c$ over relations is also denoted by $\mathtt{post}_c$.

3 Specification Logic

We introduce hereafter *Singly-Linked List Logic* (SL3, for short) whose models are heaps. Its definition is based on a *decomposition* of heaps obtained as follows. Given a heap H, its decomposition $\overline{H}$ is defined by (1) keeping only some nodes from H but at least all the crucial nodes, (2) adding an edge between any two nodes which are reachable in H, and (3) labeling every node n with a sequence, which contains the integers on the path from H starting in n and ending in its successor in the new graph $\overline{H}$. The valuation for the program integer variables is unchanged. For example, Fig. 2(b), resp. Fig. 3(b), gives a decomposition for the heap in Fig. 2(a), resp. Fig. 3(a).

Syntax of SL3: Formulas in SL3 describe heap decompositions. Let *NVar* be a set of *node variables* interpreted as nodes of the decomposition. An SL3 formula is a disjunction of formulas of the form $\exists N.\ \varphi_G \wedge \varphi_P \wedge \varphi_D$, $N \subseteq NVar$, without free node variables:

- φ_G defines the edges of the decomposition; it contains a set of atomic formulas of the form $\mathtt{ls}(n,m)$ denoting an edge between the nodes n and m, which are connected using the $*$ operator (notation borrowed from separation logic [28]). The operator $*$ states that there is no sharing between the list segments represented by the edges of the decomposition;
- φ_P is a conjunction of formulas of the form $x(n)$ with $x \in PVar$ and $n \in NVar$, expressing the fact that x labels the node n;
- φ_D, called a *data formula*, is a first-order formula that describes the integer variables and the integer sequences labeling the nodes of the decomposition.

Syntax of Data Formulas: In the following, the sequence of integers labeling the node n is denoted also by n. The formula φ_D has the following form:

$$\Big(E \wedge \bigwedge_{G(\mathbf{y}) \in \mathcal{G}} \forall \mathbf{y}.\ G(\mathbf{y}) \Rightarrow U(\mathbf{y})\Big) \quad \wedge \quad \Big(\bigwedge_{i} t_1^i = t_2^i\Big), \text{ where}$$

- E is a Presburger formula, called *existential constraint*, which characterizes the first elements of the sequences labeling the nodes of the decomposition (denoted by $\mathtt{hd}(n)$), the lengths of the integer sequences (denoted by $\mathtt{len}(n)$), and the values of the variables from *DVar*,
- $\mathbf{y}$ is a set of *position variables* interpreted as integers representing positions in the sequences labeling the nodes of the decomposition,
- $\mathcal{G}$ is a set of guards $G(\mathbf{y})$, which are conjunctions of (1) formulas that associate vectors of position variables with sequences ($\mathbf{y} \in \mathtt{tl}(n)$ means that the position variables from the vector $\mathbf{y}$ are interpreted as positions in the tail of the sequence n) and (2) a conjunction of linear constraints over the position variables that may use terms of the form $\mathtt{len}(n)$,

- $U(\mathbf{y})$ is a Presburger formula over terms of the form y, $n[y]$, denoting the integer at position y in the sequence n, $\mathtt{len}(n)$, and $\mathtt{hd}(n)$. A term $n[y]$ appears in $U(\mathbf{y})$ only if the guard $G(\mathbf{y})$ contains a constraint $\mathbf{y} \in \mathtt{tl}(n)$ with $y \in \mathbf{y}$. This restriction is used to avoid undefined terms. For instance, if n denotes a sequence of length 2 then the term $n[y]$ with y interpreted as 3 is undefined,
- t_1^i, t_2^i are multiset terms of the form $u_1 \cup \cdots \cup u_s$ ($s \geq 1$ and $\cup$ is the union of multisets) where basic terms u_i are of the form (1) $\mathtt{mhd}(n)$ (resp. d) representing the singleton containing the first integer of the sequence labeling n (resp. the value of d), or (2) $\mathtt{mtl}(n)$ representing the multiset containing all the integers of the sequence n except the first one. As a shorthand, $\mathtt{mhd}(n) \cup \mathtt{mtl}(n)$ is denoted by $\mathtt{ms}(n)$.

For example, the formula from Fig. 2(c) describes the decomposition from Fig. 2(b). Analogously, the formula from Fig. 3(c) describes the decomposition from Fig. 3(b), where the equality of sequences is described by:

$$eq_{\forall}(n,n^0) := \mathtt{hd}(n) = \mathtt{hd}(n^0) \wedge \mathtt{len}(n) = \mathtt{len}(n^0) \wedge \forall y_1, y_2.\ (y_1 \in \mathtt{tl}(n) \wedge y_2 \in \mathtt{tl}(n^0) \wedge y_1 = y_2) \Rightarrow n[y_1] = n^0[y_2] \quad (3)$$

Semantics of SL3: For simplicity, we assume that any two distinct node variables represent two distinct nodes in the decomposition. Given a decomposition $\overline{H}$ and an SL3 formula φ, $\overline{H}$ satisfies φ if there exists a disjunct ψ of φ, which is of the form $\exists N.\ \varphi_G \wedge \varphi_P \wedge \varphi_D$, and an interpretation I of the node variables in ψ as nodes in $\overline{H}$ s.t. (1) $(I(n), I(m))$ is an edge in $\overline{H}$ iff φ_G contains the formula $\mathtt{ls}(n,m)$, (2) $I(n)$ is labeled with $x \in PVar$ iff φ_P contains the atomic formula $x(n)$, and (3) the integer data in $\overline{H}$ satisfies the properties given by φ_D. Then, a heap H satisfies an SL3 formula φ if there exists a decomposition $\overline{H}$ of H that satisfies φ. The set of heaps satisfying an SL3 formula φ is denoted by $[\varphi]$.

Fragments of SL3: The fragment of SL3 which contains formulas without multiset constraints is denoted by SL3$^{\mathbb{U}}$ while the fragment of SL3 which describes the integer data using only multiset constraints is denoted by SL3$^{\mathbb{M}}$. An SL3 formula is called *succinct* if it describes heap decompositions that do not contain simple nodes.

4 Reasoning about Programs without Procedure Calls

In this section, we present solutions based on abstraction for checking and synthesizing assertions for programs without procedure calls.

4.1 Pre/Post Condition Reasoning

We describe a framework for pre/post-condition reasoning when the annotations are given in SL3. In general, the difficulty is to check entailments of the form $\mathtt{post}(\varphi_{pre}, St) \Rightarrow \varphi_{post}$, where $\mathtt{post}(\varphi_{pre}, St)$ is an SL3 formula that models exactly (over-approximates) the set of heaps $\mathtt{post}_c([\varphi_{pre}], St)$. In the following, we consider only entailments where the heap decompositions described by φ_{post} do not contain simple nodes, i.e., φ_{post} is succinct. This implies that the invariants and the post-conditions we can check must satisfy this restriction, which is usually the case in practice.

As a running example, we consider the problem of checking an invariant for the `while` loop in the procedure `split` from Fig. 1. This invariant, denoted by *Inv*, contains several disjuncts. Two of them, denoted by ψ_1 and ψ_2, are pictured in Fig. 4(c) and Fig. 4(d); the sub-formula that describes the edges and the labeling with pointer variables of the heap decomposition is represented by a graph. The disjuncts of *Inv* not represented in Fig. 4(c) are similar, i.e., they consider the cases where `x`, `sm`, or `gr` point to `NULL`. Instead of checking the validity of $\texttt{post}(Inv, St) \Rightarrow Inv$, where St is the body of the loop, we consider the problem of checking the simpler entailment $(\psi_1^p \vee \psi_2^p) \Rightarrow (\psi_1 \vee \psi_2)$, where ψ_1^p and ψ_2^p are given in Fig. 4(a) and Fig. 4(b), respectively (ψ_1^p is a sub-formula of $\texttt{post}(\psi_1, St)$ while ψ_2^p is a sub-formula of $\texttt{post}(\psi_2, St)$).

Let φ and φ' be two SL3 formulas and consider the problem of checking the validity of the entailment $\varphi \Rightarrow \varphi'$. To efficiently handle the disjunction, we check if for any disjunct ψ of φ there exists a disjunct ψ' of φ' such that $\psi \Rightarrow \psi'$. For example, $(\psi_1^p \vee \psi_2^p) \Rightarrow (\psi_1 \vee \psi_2)$ is valid if $\psi_1^p \Rightarrow \psi_1$ and $\psi_2^p \Rightarrow \psi_2$. This approach is complete only if both SL3 formulae φ and φ' are succinct and if any two disjuncts of φ' describe non-isomorphic heap decompositions (the isomorphism ignores the integer sequences).

Next, to check an entailment of the form $\psi \Rightarrow \psi'$, where ψ is of the form $\exists N.\ \varphi_G \wedge \varphi_P \wedge \varphi_D$ and ψ' is of the form $\exists N'.\ \varphi'_G \wedge \varphi'_P \wedge \varphi'_D$, a first approach is to check that the labeled graphs described by ψ and ψ' are isomorphic and that φ_D entails φ'_D. This check is complete only if both ψ and ψ' are succinct. Then, the entailment between φ_D and φ'_D is valid if (1) the existential constraint of φ_D implies the existential constraint of φ'_D, (2) the right part of any universally quantified implication in φ'_D is implied by the right part of an universally quantified implication in φ_D having a similar guard, and (3) the multiset constraints in φ_D imply the multiset constraints in φ'_D. A sufficient condition to test the validity of $\sqsubseteq_{\mathbb{M}}$ is: for every multiset equality in φ'_D of the form $t_1 = t_2$, φ_D contains the multiset equalities $t_1 = t_1^1 \cup t_1^2 \cdots \cup t_1^p$, $t_2 = t_2^1 \cup t_2^2 \cdots \cup t_2^p$, and for any $1 \leq i \leq p$, $t_1^i = t_2^i$. The approximation for the entailment that we obtain in this way is denoted by $\sqsubseteq$. For example, in Fig. 4, $\psi_2^p \sqsubseteq \psi_2$ and consequently, $\psi_2^p \Rightarrow \psi_2$.

The operator $\texttt{fold}^{\#}$: To prove entailments of the form $\psi \Rightarrow \psi'$, where ψ is not succinct, we define an operator $\texttt{fold}^{\#}$, which computes a succinct SL3 formula that over-approximates ψ (i.e., it eliminates the existential node variables in ψ which represent simple nodes). The extension of $\texttt{fold}^{\#}$ to SL3 formulas is defined by $\texttt{fold}^{\#}(\bigvee_i \psi_i) = \bigvee_i \texttt{fold}^{\#}(\psi_i)$. Clearly, if $\texttt{fold}^{\#}(\psi) \sqsubseteq \psi'$ then $\psi \Rightarrow \psi'$. Such entailments arise naturally when checking loop invariants. Even if we consider a succinct invariant *Inv*, the post-condition operator `post` will unfold the structures and introduce simple nodes. Consequently, *Inv* describes heap decompositions that are not isomorphic to heap decompositions in $\texttt{post}(Inv, St)$ and $\texttt{post}(Inv, St) \sqsubseteq Inv$ does not hold. However, it may happen that $\texttt{fold}^{\#}(\texttt{post}(Inv, St)) \sqsubseteq Inv$ which is enough to prove $\texttt{post}(Inv, St) \Rightarrow Inv$. In the running example, we have that $\texttt{fold}^{\#}(\psi_1^p) \Rightarrow \psi_1$ which implies $\psi_1^p \Rightarrow \psi_1$.

Let ψ be the disjunct of some SL3 formula. In general, $\texttt{fold}^{\#}(\psi)$ is defined such that every maximal path $n_0, n_1, \ldots, n_{k-1}, n_k$ in the graph described by ψ between two crucial nodes n_0 and n_k is replaced by one edge between n_0 and n_k and the integer sequence labeling n_0 in the models of $\texttt{fold}^{\#}(\psi)$ is the concatenation of the integer sequences labeling n_0, n_1,…,n_{k-1} in ψ. For example, $\texttt{fold}^{\#}(\psi_1^p)$ is defined such that the paths n_a, n'_x, n_x and $n'_g, n_g, \sharp$ are replaced by an edge from n_a to n_x and an edge from n'_g to $\sharp$,

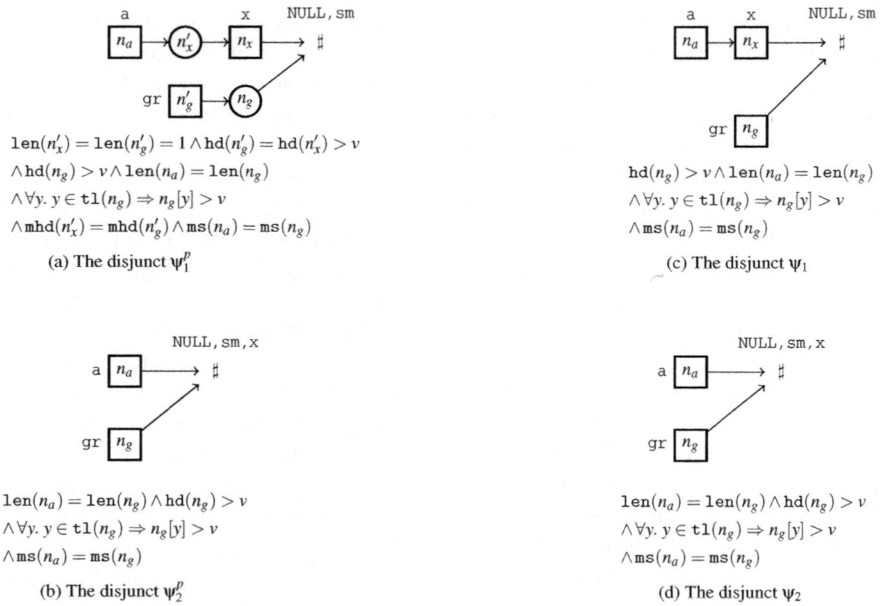

Fig. 4. Checking the invariant for the loop in the procedure `split`

respectively. Also, the sequences labeling n_a and n'_g in $\mathtt{fold}^\#(\psi_1^p)$ are the concatenation of the sequences labeling n_a, n'_x and n'_g, n_g, respectively. The multiset constraints are handled independently of the other constraints. Thus, $\mathtt{fold}^\#(\psi_1^p)$ contains the multiset constraint $\mathtt{ms}(n_a) = \mathtt{ms}(n'_g)$, which is obtained by (1) applying an inference rule in ψ_1^p that infers the constraint $\mathtt{ms}(n'_x) \cup \mathtt{ms}(n_a) = \mathtt{ms}(n'_g) \cup \mathtt{ms}(n_g)$ (the hypotheses of the inference rule are $\mathtt{mhd}(n'_x) = \mathtt{mhd}(n'_g)$, $\mathtt{ms}(n_a) = \mathtt{ms}(n_g)$, and $\mathtt{len}(n'_x) = \mathtt{len}(n'_g) = 1$) and (2) substituting $\mathtt{ms}(n'_x) \cup \mathtt{ms}(n_a)$ with $\mathtt{ms}(n_a)$ and $\mathtt{ms}(n'_g) \cup \mathtt{ms}(n_g)$ with $\mathtt{ms}(n'_g)$.

The other type of constraints are computed as follows. The properties of the sequences labeling n_a in the models of $\mathtt{fold}^\#(\psi_1^p)$ are easy to obtain because there are no universal formulas that describe the sequences labeling n_a and n'_x in ψ_1^p. We have to update only the length constraints, i.e., substitute $\mathtt{len}(n_a)$ by $\mathtt{len}(n_a) - \mathtt{len}(n'_x)$ and project out the term $\mathtt{len}(n'_x)$. Then, the properties of the sequences labeling n'_g in the models of ψ_1^p are obtained as follows:

- We update the length constraints as in the previous case, i.e., we substitute $\mathtt{len}(n_g)$ by $\mathtt{len}(n_g) - \mathtt{len}(n'_g)$ and project out the term $\mathtt{len}(n'_g)$.
- The universal formula that describes n'_g in $\mathtt{fold}^\#(\psi_1^p)$ has the same guard as the one describing n_g in ψ_1^p. It is obtained by taking into consideration that the tail of n'_g in $\mathtt{fold}^\#(\psi_1^p)$ is the concatenation between the head and the tail of n_g in ψ_1^p. Thus, we obtain a formula of the form $\forall y.\ y \in \mathtt{tl}(n'_g) \Rightarrow (U_1 \vee U_2)$, where U_1 is the property of $\mathtt{hd}(n_g)$ and U_2 is the property of $\mathtt{tl}(n_g)$. The formula U_1 is $E\left[\mathtt{hd}(n_g) \leftarrow n'_g[y]\right]$, where E is the existential constraint of ψ_1^p, and U_2 is obtained from the right part of $\forall y.\ y \in \mathtt{tl}(n_g) \Rightarrow n_g[y] > v$ by substituting $n_g[y]$ with $n'_g[y]$, i.e., U_2 is $n'_g[y] > v$.

The relation Closure: In the example above, the input given to $\texttt{fold}^{\#}$ contains only universally-quantified implications over one position variable. When these implications contain at least two position variables, the computation of the universally-quantified implications describing the concatenations is more involved. Let us consider the following formula expressing the fact that the sequences labeling n_1 and n_2 are sorted:

$$\psi_3 := \exists n_1, n_2.\ \big(\texttt{ls}(n_1,n_2) * \texttt{ls}(n_2,\sharp) \wedge x(n_1) \wedge \texttt{sorted}(n_1) \wedge \texttt{less}(n_1) \wedge \texttt{sorted}(n_2) \wedge \texttt{less}(n_1)\big)$$
$$\texttt{sorted}(n) := \forall y_1, y_2.\ ([y_1,y_2] \in \texttt{tl}(n) \wedge y_1 \leq y_2) \Rightarrow n[y_1] \leq n[y_2]$$
$$\texttt{less}(n) := \forall y.\ [y] \in \texttt{tl}(n) \Rightarrow \texttt{hd}(n) \leq n[y].$$

In $\texttt{fold}^{\#}(\psi_3)$, the sequence labeling n_1 should be the concatenation of the sequences labeling n_1 and n_2 in ψ_3 (n_2 represents a simple node in ψ_3). The universal formulas describing this sequence should have the same guards as the formulas in ψ_3, i.e., $G_1(y_1,y_2) = [y_1,y_2] \in \texttt{tl}(n_1) \wedge y_1 \leq y_2$ and $G_2(y) = y \in \texttt{tl}(n_1)$. In the following, we focus on the first guard. An approach similar to the one used for guards of the form $y \in \texttt{tl}(n)$ could take the union of the properties expressed using the guard $G_1(y_1,y_2)$ on each sequence (n_1 and n_2) and define it as a property of the concatenation. Unfortunately, this definition is unsound. The formula $\forall y_1,y_2.\ G_1(y_1,y_2) \Rightarrow n_1[y_1] \leq n_1[y_2]$ is not implied by ψ because the concatenation of two sorted words is not always sorted.

The definition of $\texttt{fold}^{\#}$ is based on a relation between guards and sets of guards, called Closure (see [1] for more details). If we go back to the formula ψ then $\texttt{sorted}(n_1) \wedge \texttt{less}(n_1)$ characterizes the data values in the first part of the concatenation and $\texttt{sorted}(n_2) \wedge \texttt{less}(n_2)$ characterizes the data values in the second part. But, out of two positions in the concatenation, one might be in n_1 (different from the first element of n_1) and the other one in n_2. Therefore, to define a sound $\texttt{fold}^{\#}$ operator, we need a universally-quantified implication having as guard $G_3(y_1,y_2) = y_1 \in \texttt{tl}(n_1) \wedge y_2 \in \texttt{tl}(n_2)$. In fact, $\texttt{Closure}(G_1(y_1,y_2))$ is the set of guards $\{G_1(y_1,y_2), G_2(y), G_3(y_1,y_2)\}$. The operator $\texttt{fold}^{\#}$ combines universal formulas with guards from $\texttt{Closure}(G_1(y_1,y_2))$ in order to compute the formula of the form $\forall y_1,y_2.\ G_1(y_1,y_2) \Rightarrow U$ (see [5,1] for more details). If these formulas are not present in the input formula then $\texttt{fold}^{\#}$ over-approximates it to *true*.

4.2 Invariant Synthesis

We consider a static analysis for programs with singly-linked lists based on *abstract interpretation* [12]. We define in [5] a generic abstract domain whose elements represent sets of heaps. Two important instances are $\mathcal{A}_{\mathbb{HS}}(k,\mathcal{A}_{\mathbb{U}})$ and $\mathcal{A}_{\mathbb{HS}}(k,\mathcal{A}_{\mathbb{M}})$ (the parameter k may be omitted). The elements of $\mathcal{A}_{\mathbb{HS}}(k,\mathcal{A}_{\mathbb{U}})$ are $\mathsf{SL3}^{\mathbb{U}}$ formulas and the elements of $\mathcal{A}_{\mathbb{HS}}(k,\mathcal{A}_{\mathbb{M}})$ are $\mathsf{SL3}^{\mathbb{M}}$ formulas. The conjunctions of universally-quantified implications from $\mathsf{SL3}^{\mathbb{U}}$ formulas are elements of an abstract domain denoted by $\mathcal{A}_{\mathbb{U}}$ and the conjunctions of equalities between multiset terms from $\mathsf{SL3}^{\mathbb{M}}$ formulas are elements of an abstract domain denoted by $\mathcal{A}_{\mathbb{M}}$. The elements of $\mathcal{A}_{\mathbb{HS}}(k,\mathcal{A}_{\mathbb{U}})$ and $\mathcal{A}_{\mathbb{HS}}(k,\mathcal{A}_{\mathbb{M}})$ are also called *abstract heap sets*. The abstract values satisfy the following restrictions: (1) any two disjuncts describe non-isomorphic heap decompositions and (2) any disjunct describes a heap decomposition with at most k simple nodes. Also, $\mathcal{A}_{\mathbb{HS}}(k,\mathcal{A}_{\mathbb{U}})$ has another two parameters which restrict the form of the universally-quantified formula describing the integer sequences. The first parameter is a set of guards $\mathbb{P}$, also called *guard patterns*, and the second one is a numerical abstract domain $\mathcal{A}_{\mathbb{Z}}$ (such as the *Octagons* abstract domain [24], the *Polyhedra* abstract domain [14], etc.). Then, the formulas belonging to $\mathcal{A}_{\mathbb{HS}}(k, \mathcal{A}_{\mathbb{U}})$ are disjunctions of formulas of the form:

$$\exists N. \left(\varphi_G \wedge \varphi_P \wedge E \wedge \bigwedge_{G(\mathbf{y}) \in \mathbb{P}(N)} \forall \mathbf{y}.\, G(\mathbf{y}) \Rightarrow U(\mathbf{y}) \right),$$

where (1) $\mathbb{P}(N)$ is a set of guards obtained from $\mathbb{P}$ by substituting all node variables with elements of N and (2) E and $U(\mathbf{y})$ are elements of the numerical abstract domain $\mathcal{A}_{\mathbb{Z}}$. The order relation between elements of $\mathcal{A}_{\mathbb{HS}}(k, \mathcal{A}_{\mathbb{U}})$ (resp. $\mathcal{A}_{\mathbb{HS}}(k, \mathcal{A}_{\mathbb{M}})$) is exactly $\sqsubseteq$ restricted to $\mathsf{SL3}^{\mathbb{U}}$ (resp. $\mathsf{SL3}^{\mathbb{M}}$) formulas. If we ignore integer data, the number of heap decompositions without garbage and with at most k simple nodes is bounded. Consequently, the lattice $\mathcal{A}_{\mathbb{HS}}(k, \mathcal{A}_{\mathbb{M}})$ is finite and there is no need to define a widening operator. The lattice $\mathcal{A}_{\mathbb{HS}}(k, \mathcal{A}_{\mathbb{U}})$ is infinite due to the numerical abstract domain $\mathcal{A}_{\mathbb{Z}}$. We define a widening operator which is parametrized by the widening operator of $\mathcal{A}_{\mathbb{Z}}$.

Unfolding/Folding: The analysis over these abstract domains iterates the following two steps: (1) unfolding the structures in order to reveal the properties of some internal nodes in the lists, which makes necessary to introduce some simple nodes and then, (b) folding the structures, in order to keep the graphs finite, by eliminating the simple nodes and in the same time collecting the informations on these nodes using a formula that speaks about data sequences. To terminate, the widening operator is applied.

```
void initEven(list* head) {
   list *headi = head;
   int i = 0;
   while(headi != NULL) {
      headi->data = 2*i;
      headi = headi->next;
      i++;
   }
}
```

Fig. 5.

We define sound abstract transformers for the statements in the class of programs we consider. The statements that dereference the `next` pointer field (`x=y->next` and `x->next=y`) introduce simple nodes. The folding step is applied every time the number of simple nodes becomes greater than k. It consists in applying the operator $\texttt{fold}^{\#}$ described in Sec. 4.1. In particular, this is the crucial step that allows to generate universally quantified properties from a number of relations between a finite (bounded) number of nodes. To make the operator $\texttt{fold}^{\#}$ precise, we should consider abstract domains $\mathcal{A}_{\mathbb{HS}}(k, \mathcal{A}_{\mathbb{U}})$ parametrized by sets of guard patterns $\mathbb{P}$ which are closed under the relation `Closure`, i.e., they include $\texttt{Closure}(G)$, for any G in $\mathbb{P}$.

We illustrate the unfold/fold mechanism on the procedure `initEven` from Fig. 5. We analyze this program using the abstract domain $\mathcal{A}_{\mathbb{HS}}(1, \mathcal{A}_{\mathbb{U}})$ parametrized by (1) a set of guard patterns consisting of one element $y \in \texttt{tl}(n)$ and (2) the *Polyhedra* abstract domain. The analysis begins to unroll the loop of the procedure starting from the first SL3 formula given in Fig. 6. This formula represents the set of all heaps that consist of a path between a vertex labeled by `head` and `headi`, and the distinguished node $\sharp$.

Every symbolic execution of the statement `headi=headi->next` in the loop generates a formula with two disjuncts: the first one corresponds to the case when `headi` points to `NULL` (the list traversal ends) and the second one unfolds the structure, i.e., introduces a new node which is pointed to by `headi`. The formulas obtained after unrolling once and thrice the loop are given in Fig. 6. An edge starting in some node n and labeled by 1 means that the formula contains the constraint $\texttt{len}(n) = 1$. Also, a node n labeled by some integer v means that the formula contains the constraint $\texttt{hd}(n) = v$.

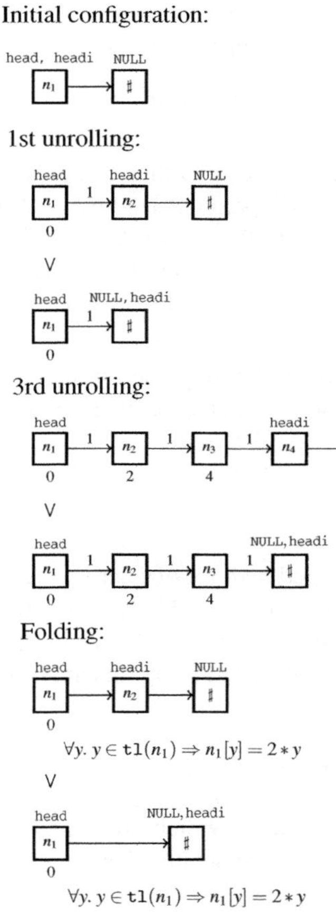

Fig. 6.

The size of the list pointed to by head is potentially unbounded, so the size of the graphs grows at each unrolling. In order to guarantee termination, the analysis manipulates graphs that contain at most one simple node (i.e., $k = 1$). Notice that after the third unrolling of the loop, the graphs contain two simple nodes. To keep the size of the abstract heaps bounded, the analysis eliminates these nodes but, before that, it collects the information that the unrolling of the loop revealed about them. This step is called folding the structure and consists in applying $\texttt{fold}^{\#}$. We obtain a universal formula that describes the data properties of the nodes that have been eliminated. Because the analysis is parametrized by the pattern $\forall y.\ y \in \texttt{tl}(n)$, $\texttt{fold}^{\#}$ generates a universally quantified formula of the form $\forall y.\ y \in \texttt{tl}(n_1) \Rightarrow U$. To this, it searches for all possible instantiations of the variable y that satisfy the pattern, in this case the nodes labeled by 2 and 4, and it applies the join in the numerical abstract domain between the constraints on these nodes, i.e., $\texttt{dt}(y) = 2$ and $\texttt{dt}(y) = 4$. The resulting formula is given in Fig. 6.

The unfolding and folding steps are repeated until the analysis reaches a fixed point. To ensure the convergence of the fixed point computation, apart from bounding the size of the graphs, we use the widening operator of the numerical abstract domain $\mathcal{A}_{\mathbb{Z}}$. In the considered example, widening makes the length constraints converge to the fact that the list pointed to by head is greater than or equal to one. Consequently, the universally quantified formula from Fig. 6 is generalized to the entire list.

4.3 A Sound Decision Procedure Based on Abstraction

In Sec. 4.1, we have shown that for any φ and φ' two $\mathsf{SL3}^{\mathbb{U}}$ formulas, the entailment $\varphi \Rightarrow \varphi'$ is valid if for any disjunct ψ' of φ' there exists a disjunct ψ of φ such that $\texttt{fold}^{\#}(\psi) \sqsubseteq \psi'$. Notice that $\texttt{fold}^{\#}(\psi) \sqsubseteq \psi'$ holds only if ψ' contains universally-quantified implications having the same guards as some universally-quantified implications in ψ. For example, the entailment $\psi_4 \Rightarrow \psi_5$ in Fig. 7 is valid but $\psi_4 \not\sqsubseteq \psi_5$ (because ψ_4 is succinct there is no need to apply the operator $\texttt{fold}^{\#}$). This happens because ψ_4 does not contain an universally-quantified implication having as guard $[y_1, y_2] \in \texttt{tl}(n_1) \wedge y_2 = y_1 + 1$.

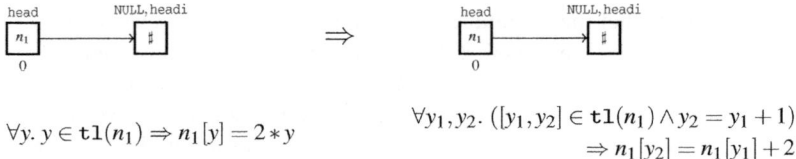

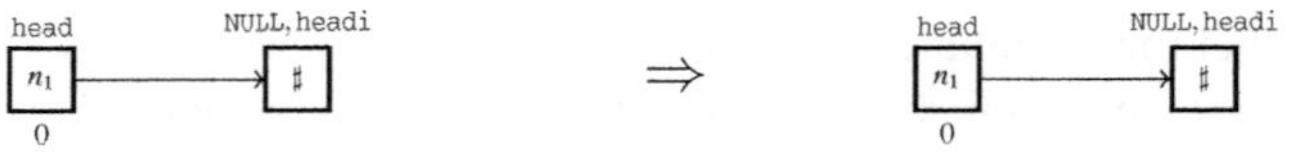

$\forall y.\ y \in \mathtt{tl}(n_1) \Rightarrow n_1[y] = 2 * y$

$\forall y_1, y_2.\ ([y_1, y_2] \in \mathtt{tl}(n_1) \wedge y_2 = y_1 + 1) \Rightarrow n_1[y_2] = n_1[y_1] + 2$

Fig. 7. An entailment between two formulas denoted by ψ_4 and ψ_5

The operator $\mathtt{convert}_{\mathbb{P}}$**:** In order to increase the precision of entailment checking between $\mathsf{SL3}^{\mathbb{U}}$ formulas, we define an operator $\mathtt{convert}_{\mathbb{P}}$ [6], parametrized by a set of guard patterns $\mathbb{P}$. For any $\mathsf{SL3}^{\mathbb{U}}$ formula φ, $\mathtt{convert}_{\mathbb{P}}(\varphi)$ is an $\mathsf{SL3}^{\mathbb{U}}$ formula equivalent to φ which contains universally-quantified implications having as guards constraints from $\mathbb{P}$. Therefore, for any φ and φ' two $\mathsf{SL3}^{\mathbb{U}}$ formulas, if $\mathtt{convert}_{\mathbb{P}}(\varphi) \sqsubseteq \varphi'$ then $\varphi \Rightarrow \varphi'$. The operator $\mathtt{convert}_{\mathbb{P}}$ is defined as follows:

- We consider a program containing several `while` loops that traverse the list segments constrained by φ. For example, in the case of ψ_4, we consider the program:

```
list *headi = head;
while (headi != NULL)
  headi = headi->next;
```

- The program is analyzed using $\mathcal{A}_{\mathbb{HS}}(k, \mathcal{A}_{\mathbb{U}})$ parametrized by a set of guard patterns $\mathbb{P}' = \mathbb{P} \cup \mathbb{P}_\varphi \cup \mathtt{Closure}(\mathbb{P} \cup \mathbb{P}_\varphi)$, where $\mathbb{P}_\varphi$ are the patterns in φ. The precondition is exactly φ. We denote by $\varphi_{\mathbb{P}}$ the postcondition (i.e., the formula describing the configurations reachable at the end of the program) synthesized using this analysis.
- $\mathtt{convert}_{\mathbb{P}}(\varphi)$ is the conjunction of φ and $\varphi_{\mathbb{P}}$.

The formula $\mathtt{convert}_{\mathbb{P}}(\varphi)$ is equivalent to φ because, by definition, $\varphi_{\mathbb{P}}$ is implied by φ. For example, $\mathtt{convert}_{\mathbb{P}_1}(\psi_1)$, where $\mathbb{P}_1$ consists of $y \in \mathtt{tl}(n_1)$, $[y_1, y_2] \in \mathtt{tl}(n_1) \wedge y_2 = y_1 + 1$, and the closure of these two patterns, is a formula which contains both universally quantified implications from Fig. 7 (see [6] for more details). The fact that $\mathtt{convert}_{\mathbb{P}_1}(\psi_1) \sqsubseteq \psi_2$ proves that $\psi_1 \Rightarrow \psi_2$ is valid.

5 Reasoning about Programs with Procedure Calls

In this section, we extend the pre/post condition reasoning framework and the static analysis from the previous section to (recursive) programs with procedure calls.

5.1 Pre/Post Condition Reasoning

We assume that, besides loop invariants, each procedure is annotated by a precondition and a postcondition. Following the local heap semantics, they describe only the part of the heap relevant to the procedure. The precondition describes heaps where all nodes are reachable from the input parameters and the postcondition describes relations between the input and the output configurations, i.e., heaps over the double vocabulary $\mathbf{loc} \cup \mathbf{loc}^0$.

The validity of Hoare triples corresponding to procedure calls can be checked as follows. Let P be a procedure annotated by a precondition φ_{pre} and a postcondition φ_{post}

and let $\{\varphi_1\}P(\mathbf{ai},\mathbf{ao})\{\varphi_2\}$, be a Hoare triple, where **ai**, resp. **ao**, are the input, resp. output, actual parameters (the validity of Hoare triples corresponding to $q = P(\mathbf{ai},\mathbf{ao})$ is checked in a similar manner). This Hoare triple is valid if (1) for any heap H modeled by φ_1, the sub-graph of H containing all the nodes reachable from the actual input parameters **ai** satisfies φ_{pre} and (2) $\mathtt{post}(\varphi, P(\mathbf{ai},\mathbf{ao})) \Rightarrow \varphi_2$. The first condition holds if the entailment $local(\varphi_1) \Rightarrow \varphi_{pre}[\gamma]$ is valid, where $local(\varphi_1)$ is a sub-formula of φ_1 describing only nodes reachable from the actual parameters in **ai** and γ is a substitution that replaces formal parameters with actual parameters. For example, consider the Hoare triple in Fig. 10 for the first recursive call of the procedure `quicksort` in Fig. 1. The sub-formula $local(\varphi_1)$, where φ_1 is the formula in the left of Fig. 10, is $\mathtt{ls}(n_l,\sharp) \wedge \mathtt{left}(n_l) \wedge \mathtt{hd}(n_l) \leq \mathtt{hd}(n_p) \wedge \forall y.\ y \in \mathtt{tl}(n_l) \Rightarrow n_l[y] \leq \mathtt{hd}(n_p)$. Clearly, it implies the precondition of `quicksort`, which states that the input list is acyclic.

Then, $\mathtt{post}(\varphi_1, P(\mathbf{ai},\mathbf{ao}))$ is a disjunction of formulas obtained by combining a disjunct ψ_1 of φ_1 and a disjunct ψ_{post} of φ_{post} s.t. the decomposition of the input heap in ψ_{post} is isomorphic to the decomposition of the local heap in ψ_1 (the isomorphism is denoted by h). Thus, (1) we replace in ψ_1 the sub-formula that describes the local heap (without integer data) with the sub-formula that describes the output heap in ψ_{post} (without integer data), (2) we redirect all edges ending in nodes labeled by actual parameters (from ψ_1) to the nodes labeled by the corresponding formal parameters (from ψ_{post}), and (3) integer data is described by a formula of the form $\sigma = \exists N_0.\ (\varphi_D \wedge \varphi_{D,post}[h])$, where φ_D (resp. $\varphi_{D,post}$) is the sub-formula of ψ_1 (resp. ψ_{post}) that describes integer data and N_0 is the set of variables denoting nodes from the input heap in ψ_{post} (the isomorphism h is used as a substitution for node variables). Notice that the logic SL3 is extended by allowing existential quantification over node variables in the part that describes the integer data. For example, given the postcondition of `quicksort` in Fig. 9(b) and the formula φ_1 in the left of Fig. 10, $\varphi = \mathtt{post}(\varphi_1, \mathtt{left} = \mathtt{quicksort(left)})$ is the formula in Fig. 11 ($\varphi_{D,\mathtt{qst}}$ is given in Fig. 9).

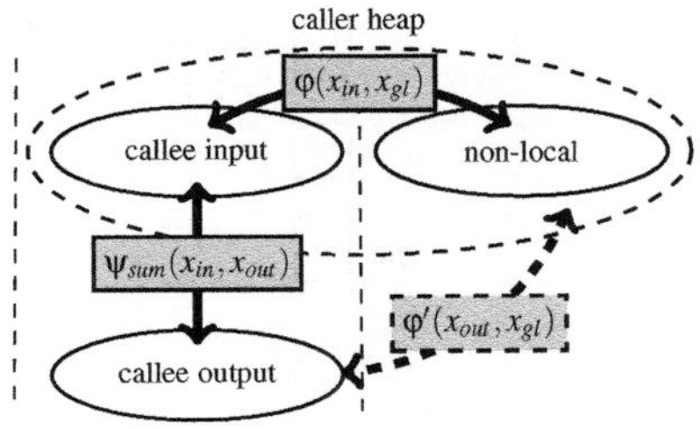

Fig. 8. Relation between caller and callee local heaps

The approach based on local heaps can be too weak for proving the validity of Hoare triples corresponding to procedure calls. Elements in the local heap of the callee are linked at the call point to external elements by some data relation, φ, and the procedure is annotated by some postcondition ψ_{sum} that relates the input heap with the output heap. This situation is depicted in Fig. 8. The problem is how to recover the link φ' between the elements in the callee output heap and the external elements in the caller heap.

Annotations in SL3$^{\mathbb{U}}$ for `quicksort`: For the procedure `quicksort`, annotations in SL3$^{\mathbb{U}}$ are not sufficient to prove that it outputs a sorted list. This procedure takes the first element `d` of the input list `a` as the pivot, splits the tail of `a` into two lists `left` and `right`, where all the elements of `left`, resp. `right`, are smaller, resp. greater, than `d`, and then performs two recursive calls on the lists `left` and `right`, before composing the results, together with `d`, into a sorted list.

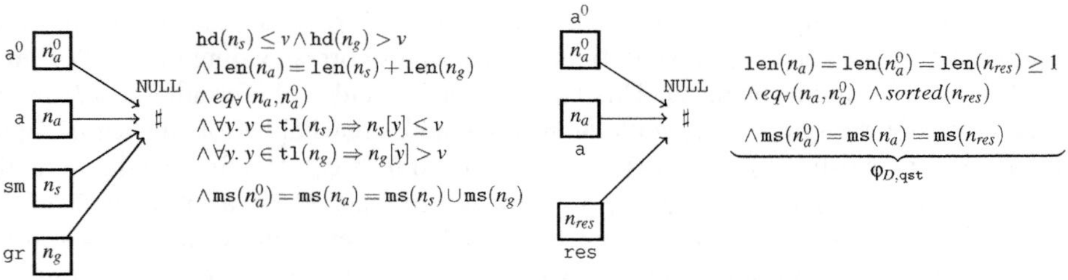

(a) The postcondition of `split` (b) The postcondition of `quicksort`

Fig. 9. Postconditions for `split` and `quicksort`

Assume that the $\mathsf{SL3}^{\mathbb{U}}$ postcondition of `split`, resp. `quicksort`, is the formula in Fig. 9(a), resp. Fig. 9(b), without the multiset constraints. We show that the approach based on local heaps can not be used to prove the validity of the Hoare triple given in Fig.10; for the moment, we ignore the multiset constraints in φ_D. When computing $\varphi' = \mathtt{post}(\varphi'_1, \mathtt{left} = \mathtt{quicksort(left)})$, where φ'_1 is the formula in the left of Fig.10 without the multiset equalities, the constraint that all the elements of `left` are less than or equal to the pivot is lost. The only constraint over the list pointed to by `left` in φ' is that the list is sorted. The reason for this is twofold: (1) the annotations of `quicksort` describe only the input and the output list and they don't refer to other variables from the context of the call (i.e., they don't contain the property that all the elements of the input list are less than or equal to the pivot) and (2) the postcondition of `quicksort` contains no relation between the elements of the input and the output list because $\mathsf{SL3}^{\mathbb{U}}$ cannot express the fact that a list is a permutation of another list.

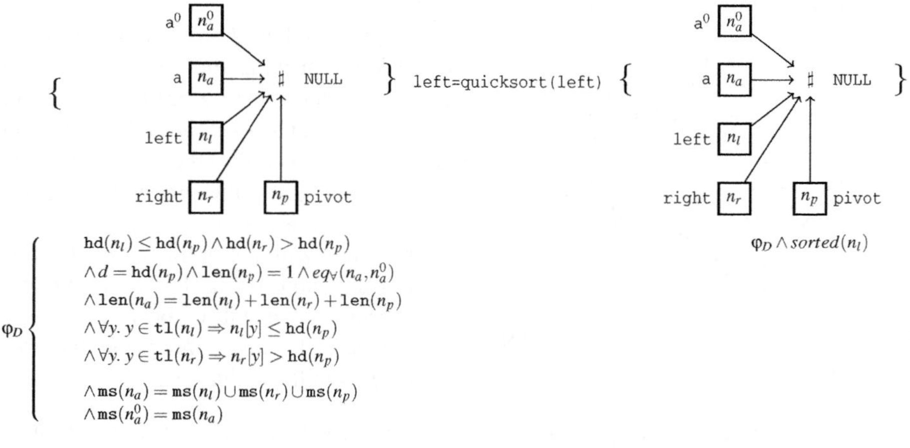

Fig. 10. A Hoare triple in SL3 for the first recursive call in `quicksort`

Combining Universal Formulas and Multiset Constraints: To be able to prove that `quicksort` outputs a sorted list, we must consider annotations with formulas from the full SL3. That is, the list segments are now described by universally-quantified formulas *and* multiset constraints. The new postcondition for `split`, resp. `quicksort`, is the one in Fig. 9(a), resp. Fig. 9(b). Now, the difficulty is to reason in the combined theory.

With the new annotations, we have to check the validity of the Hoare triple from Fig.10 (multiset constraints are now taken into consideration). The crucial point in proving the validity of $\texttt{post}(\varphi_1, \texttt{left} = \texttt{quicksort}(\texttt{left})) \Rightarrow \varphi_2$, where φ_2 is the formula in the right of Fig.10, is to prove that the data constraints in Fig. 11 imply that all the elements of the sequence n_{res} (the new value of the list pointed to by `left`) are smaller than or equal to $\texttt{hd}(n_p)$, i.e.,

$$\begin{aligned}\exists n_l.\ \Big(\texttt{hd}(n_l) \leq \texttt{hd}(n_p) \wedge \forall y.\ y \in \texttt{tl}(n_l) \Rightarrow n_l[y] \leq \texttt{hd}(n_p) \wedge \texttt{ms}(n_{res}) = \texttt{ms}(n_l)\Big) \\ \Rightarrow \Big(\texttt{hd}(n_{res}) \leq \texttt{hd}(n_p) \wedge \forall y.\ y \in \texttt{tl}(n_{res}) \Rightarrow n_{res}[y] \leq \texttt{hd}(n_p)\Big).\end{aligned} \quad (4)$$

In words, if the sequences n_l and n_{res} have the same multisets of elements and all elements of n_l are less than the pivot then, the latter also holds about the elements of n_{res}. Notice that the operator $\sqsubseteq$ from Sec. 4.1 is not precise enough to prove this entailment.

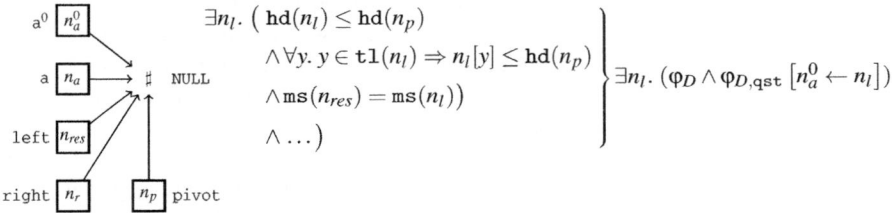

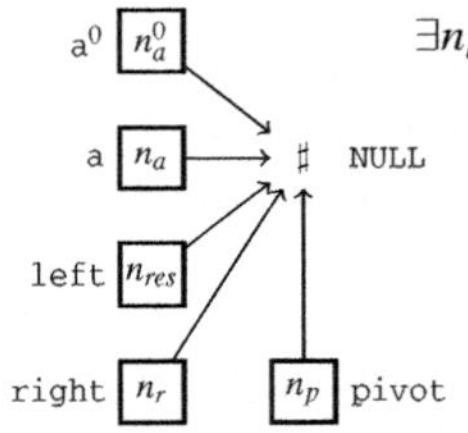

$$\left.\begin{aligned}\exists n_l.\ (\ &\texttt{hd}(n_l) \leq \texttt{hd}(n_p) \\ &\wedge \forall y.\ y \in \texttt{tl}(n_l) \Rightarrow n_l[y] \leq \texttt{hd}(n_p) \\ &\wedge \texttt{ms}(n_{res}) = \texttt{ms}(n_l)) \\ &\wedge \ldots)\end{aligned}\right\} \exists n_l.\ (\varphi_D \wedge \varphi_{D,\texttt{qst}}\ [n_a^0 \leftarrow n_l])$$

Fig. 11. The formula $\varphi = \texttt{post}(\varphi_1, \texttt{left} = \texttt{quicksort}(\texttt{left}))$

We define an operator called `stregthen` [6] which can be used to prove such implications. It considers the same program as in $\texttt{convert}_{\mathbb{P}}$, consisting of a sequence of loops that traverse the list segments. Then, it performs an analysis of this program using a partially reduced product [11] between the domain of abstract heap sets with universal formulas, $\mathcal{A}_{\mathbb{HS}}(\mathcal{A}_{\mathbb{U}})$, and the domain of abstract heap sets with multiset constraints, $\mathcal{A}_{\mathbb{HS}}(\mathcal{A}_{\mathbb{M}})$. The elements of this product are pairs from $\mathcal{A}_{\mathbb{HS}}(\mathcal{A}_{\mathbb{U}}) \times \mathcal{A}_{\mathbb{HS}}(\mathcal{A}_{\mathbb{M}})$. Almost all the abstract transformers are defined by $F^{\#}(A_1, A_2) = (F^{\#}_{\mathbb{U}}(A_1), F^{\#}_{\mathbb{M}}(A_2))$, for any $(A_1, A_2) \in \mathcal{A}_{\mathbb{HS}}(\mathcal{A}_{\mathbb{U}}) \times \mathcal{A}_{\mathbb{HS}}(\mathcal{A}_{\mathbb{M}})$, where $F^{\#}_{\mathbb{U}}$ is the abstract transformer in $\mathcal{A}_{\mathbb{HS}}(\mathcal{A}_{\mathbb{U}})$ and $F^{\#}_{\mathbb{M}}$ is the abstract transformer in $\mathcal{A}_{\mathbb{HS}}(\mathcal{A}_{\mathbb{M}})$. The only exception is the abstract transformer for `p=q->next`, denoted by $G^{\#}$, which is defined by $G^{\#}(A_1, A_2) = \sigma(G^{\#}_{\mathbb{U}}(A_1), G^{\#}_{\mathbb{M}}(A_2))$, where σ is a partial reduction operator that transfers information between the two abstract elements. To check the validity of $\varphi \Rightarrow \varphi_2$, the analysis starts from a precondition defined as a pair $(\varphi_{\mathbb{U}}, \varphi_{\mathbb{M}})$, where $\varphi_{\mathbb{U}}$ is obtained from φ by removing all multiset constraints and $\varphi_{\mathbb{M}}$ is obtained from φ by removing all universally-quantified implications. The output of `stregthen` is the conjunction between the input formula and the postcondition synthesized by the analysis. In this case, applying `stregthen` on the formula φ, we obtain $\varphi \wedge \texttt{hd}(n_l) \leq \texttt{hd}(n_p) \wedge \forall y.\ y \in \texttt{tl}(n_l) \Rightarrow n_l[y] \leq \texttt{hd}(n_p)$. Now, the fact that $\varphi \sqsubseteq \varphi_2$ holds proves the validity of $\varphi \Rightarrow \varphi_2$ which implies the validity of the Hoare triple from Fig. 10.

5.2 Synthesis of Procedure Summaries

For programs with procedure calls, we define a compositional analysis such that the summary of a procedure is computed only once and then reused whenever the procedure is called. Again, in order to solve the problems raised by the use of local heaps, we strengthen the analysis in the domain of universally-quantified formulas with the analysis in the domain of multiset constraints. Thus, we define an abstract domain which is a partial reduced product between $\mathcal{A}_{\mathbb{HS}}(\mathcal{A}_{\mathbb{U}})$ and $\mathcal{A}_{\mathbb{HS}}(\mathcal{A}_{\mathbb{M}})$. The partial reduction operator is exactly `strengthen` and it is used in the abstract transformers for procedure returns and `assert` statements. The analysis over this partial reduced product is able for instance to synthesize the expected summary for the procedure `quicksort`.

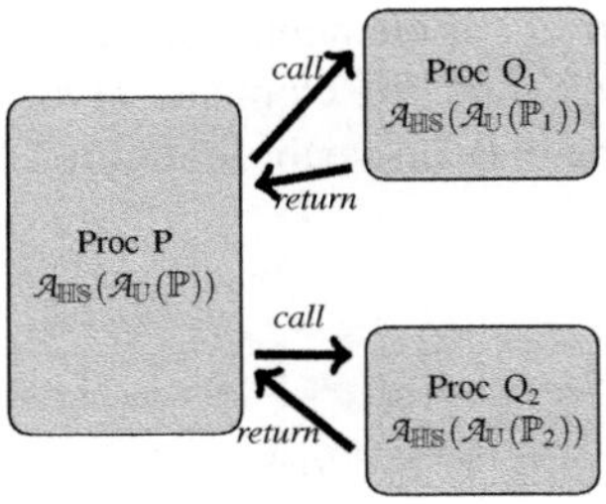

Fig. 12.

Another problem that we address for the design of a compositional analysis is due to the use of patterns for guards of universally-quantified implications. Indeed, the analysis of different procedures may need to use different sets of patterns and therefore, it is important to be able to localize the choice of these patterns to each procedure. Otherwise, it would be necessary to use a set of patterns that includes the union of all the sets that are used during the whole analysis. This would obviously make the analysis inefficient.

Consequently, during the analysis, at procedure calls and returns, we need to switch from an abstract domain of formulas parametrized by some set of patterns, say $\mathbb{P}$, to an abstract domain parametrized by another set of patterns $\mathbb{P}_1$ or $\mathbb{P}_2$ as shown in Figure 12 ($\mathcal{A}_{\mathbb{HS}}(\mathcal{A}_{\mathbb{U}}(\mathbb{P}))$ denotes the domain of abstract heap sets with universally-quantified implications parametrized by the set of patterns $\mathbb{P}$). This transformation is defined using the operator $\texttt{convert}_{\mathbb{P}}$ (see [6] for more details).

6 Experimental Results

We have implemented the inter-procedural analysis in a tool called CELIA [9]. CELIA is a plugin of the FRAMA-C platform [8], thus taking as input annotated C programs. CELIA instantiates the generic module FIXPOINT (`http://gforge.inria.fr/`) of fixpoint computation over control-flow graphs with the implementation of the abstract domains $\mathcal{A}_{\mathbb{HS}}(\mathcal{A}_{\mathbb{U}})$ and $\mathcal{A}_{\mathbb{HS}}(\mathcal{A}_{\mathbb{M}})$ and their abstract transformers. The implementation of the $\mathcal{A}_{\mathbb{HS}}(\mathcal{A}_{\mathbb{U}})$ domain considers the patterns $y \in \texttt{tl}(w)$, $(y_1, y_2) \in \texttt{tl}(w) \wedge y_1 \leq y_2$, $(y_1, y_2) \in \texttt{tl}(w) \wedge y_2 = y_1 + 1$, and $y_1 \in \texttt{tl}(w_1) \wedge y_2 \in \texttt{tl}(w_2) \wedge y_1 = y_2$ and it is generic on the numerical domain $\mathcal{A}_{\mathbb{Z}}$ used to represent data and length constraints. For this, we use the APRON platform [21] to access domains like octagons or polyhedra.

Benchmark: We have applied CELIA to a benchmark of C programs which is available on the web site of CELIA. The benchmark includes the basic functions that are used in usual libraries on singly-linked lists, for example the GTK `gslist` library which is part of the Linux distribution. These functions belong to several classes: (1) (recursive) functions performing elementary operations on list: adding/deleting the first/last element, initializing a list of some length, (2) (recursive) functions performing a traversal of one resp. two lists, without modifying their structures, but modifying their data, (3) functions computing from one resp. two input lists some output parameters of type list or integer, and (4) sorting algorithms on lists. The benchmark also contains programs which do several calls of the above functions on lists. For example, we handle some programs manipulating chaining hash tables. For that, we use abstraction techniques (slicing, unfolding fixed-size arrays) available through the Frama-C platform.

We have used CELIA for checking equivalence between sorting algorithms. The `strengthen` operation plays an essential role. Let P_1 and P_2 be two sorting procedures working on two input lists I_1 and I_2, and producing two outputs O_1 and O_2. The equivalence of P_1 and P_2 is reduced to the validity of the implication

$$\begin{aligned}\big(equal(I_1,I_2) \wedge\ sorted(O_1) \wedge \mathtt{ms}(I_1) = \mathtt{ms}(O_1)\\ \wedge\ sorted(O_2) \wedge \mathtt{ms}(I_2) = \mathtt{ms}(O_2)\big)\\ \Rightarrow equal(O_1, O_2),\end{aligned} \tag{5}$$

where *equal* and *sorted* are expressed by universally quantified implications as in SL3. Our techniques are able to find that this formula is indeed valid. For instance, this entailment and the one in (4) can not be proved using SMT solvers like CVC3 [2] and Z3 [15] (the multiset equality of two sequences $\mathtt{ms}(n_1) = \mathtt{ms}(n_2)$ is rewritten as $\exists m.\, permutation(m) \wedge \forall i.\; n_1[m[i]] = n_2[i]$, where $permutation(m)$ expresses the fact that the sequence m defines a permutation).

7 Conclusions and Related Work

The paper presents a logic-based framework the verification and the analysis of programs with lists and data. It introduces a family of abstract domains whose elements are first-order formulas that describe the shape/size of the allocated memory and the scalar data stored in the list cells. The latter is characterized using universal formulas or multiset constraints. The elements of these abstract domains can be used as annotations within pre/post-condition reasoning. In this context, we introduce sound procedures for checking the validity of Hoare triples. Then, we define an accurate inter-procedural analysis that is able to automatically synthesize invariants and procedure summaries. This analysis is compositional and it is based on unfolding/folding the program data structures. The precision is obtained using partial reduction operators, which allow to combine analyses over different abstract domains. Overall, our framework allows to combine smoothly pre-post condition reasoning with assertion synthesis.

Related Work: Assertion synthesis for programs with dynamic data structures has been addressed using different approaches, like constraint solving, e.g. [3], abstract interpretation, e.g., [7,13,20,16,17,18,19,25,32,30,31,34], Craig interpolants, e.g. [22], and automata-theoretic techniques, e.g. [4].

Several works [20,16,25] consider invariant synthesis for programs with unidimensional arrays of integers. The class of invariants they can generate is included in the one handled by our approach using $\mathcal{A}_{\mathbb{HS}}(\mathcal{A}_{\mathbb{U}})$. These techniques are based on an automatically generated finite partitioning of the array indices. We consider a larger class of programs for which these techniques can not be applied. The analysis introduced in

[25] for programs with arrays can synthesize invariants on multisets of the elements in array fragments. This technique differs from ours based on the domain $\mathcal{A}_{\mathbb{HS}}(\mathcal{A}_{\mathbb{M}})$ by the fact that it can not be applied directly to programs with dynamic lists.

In [19], a synthesis technique for universally quantified formulas is presented. Our technique differs from this one by the type of user guiding information. Indeed, the quantified formulas in [19] are of the form $\forall \mathbf{y}.\ F_1 \Rightarrow F_2$, where F_2 must be given by the user. In contrast, our approach fixes the formulas in left hand side of the implication and synthesizes the right hand side. The two approaches are in principle incomparable.

Shape analysis [32] allows to synthesize invariants describing the allocated memory. The invariants are expressed in a three-valued first-order logic, and they may combine shape and data constraints. However, the basic (instrumentation) predicates used in these invariants need to be defined by the user. More recent work [10,23] improve on this approach by defining frameworks for combining abstract domains for shape and data constraints. The approaches defined in these works still require that basic predicates describing shape and data are provided by the user. In our approach, relevant parts of the data constraints are discovered automatically by the analysis, the user must provide only some of the guard patterns. On the other hand, [32,23] can handle a more general class of data structures than singly-linked lists. Boolean heap abstraction [26,27] is a symbolic shape analysis sharing the concepts underlying three-valued shape analysis [32]. It also allows to generate some kind of universally quantified invariants combining shape and data constraints. In addition, [27] defines a CEGAR technique allowing to discover new predicates on the heap objects that are part of the invariant. However, in order to generate accurate invariants, the approach proposed in [27] needs a suitable initial set of predicates on the data in the heap, whereas in our approach such kind of predicates are not required from the user.

Concerning the approaches based on abstract interpretation which can handle procedure calls, most of them [7,13,18,30,31] focus on shape properties and do not consider constraints on sizes or data. The approach in [30] can synthesize procedure summaries that describe data if the instrumentation predicates which guide the abstraction speak about data. Providing patterns is simpler than providing instrumentation predicates on data because patterns contain only constraints between (universally-quantified) positions (in the left-hand-side of the implication) and no constraints on data. Actually, patterns are in many cases simple (ordering/equality constraints) and can be discovered using natural heuristics based on the program syntax or proposed by the user, whereas constraints on data can be more complex. Our approach allows to discover (maybe unpredictable) data constraints for given guard patterns. The analysis in [18] combines a numerical abstract domain with a shape analysis. It is not restricted by the class of data structures but the generated assertions describe only the shape and the size of the heap.

References

1. Drăgoi, C.: Automated verification of heap-manipulating programs with infinite data. PhD thesis, University Paris Diderot - Paris 7 (2011)
2. Barrett, C., Tinelli, C.: CVC3. In: Damm, W., Hermanns, H. (eds.) CAV 2007. LNCS, vol. 4590, pp. 298–302. Springer, Heidelberg (2007)

3. Beyer, D., Henzinger, T.A., Majumdar, R., Rybalchenko, A.: Invariant Synthesis for Combined Theories. In: Cook, B., Podelski, A. (eds.) VMCAI 2007. LNCS, vol. 4349, pp. 378–394. Springer, Heidelberg (2007)
4. Bouajjani, A., Bozga, M., Habermehl, P., Iosif, R., Moro, P., Vojnar, T.: Programs with Lists Are Counter Automata. In: Ball, T., Jones, R.B. (eds.) CAV 2006. LNCS, vol. 4144, pp. 517–531. Springer, Heidelberg (2006)
5. Bouajjani, A., Drăgoi, C., Enea, C., Rezine, A., Sighireanu, M.: Invariant Synthesis for Programs Manipulating Lists with Unbounded Data. In: Touili, T., Cook, B., Jackson, P. (eds.) CAV 2010. LNCS, vol. 6174, pp. 72–88. Springer, Heidelberg (2010)
6. Bouajjani, A., Dragoi, C., Enea, C., Sighireanu, M.: On inter-procedural analysis of programs with lists and data. In: Proc. of PLDI, pp. 578–589 (2011)
7. Calcagno, C., Distefano, D., O'Hearn, P.W., Yang, H.: Compositional shape analysis by means of bi-abduction. In: Proc. of POPL, pp. 289–300 (2009)
8. CEA. Frama-C Platform, `http://frama-c.com`
9. Celia plugin, `http://www.liafa.jussieu.fr/celia`
10. Chang, B.-Y.E., Rival, X.: Relational inductive shape analysis. In: Proc. of POPL, pp. 247–260 (2008)
11. Cousot, P., Cousot, R.: Systematic design of program analysis frameworks. In: Proc. of POPL, pp. 269–282 (1979)
12. Cousot, P., Cousot, R.: Abstract interpretation: A unified lattice model for static analysis of programs by construction or approximation of fixpoints. In: Proc. of POPL, pp. 238–252 (1977)
13. Cousot, P., Cousot, R.: Static determination of dynamic properties of recursive procedures. In: Proc. of IFIP Conf. on Formal Description of Programming Concepts, pp. 237–277 (1977)
14. Cousot, P., Halbwachs, N.: Automatic discovery of linear restraints among variables of a program. In: Proc. of POPL, pp. 84–96 (1978)
15. de Moura, L., Bjørner, N.: Z3: An Efficient SMT Solver. In: Ramakrishnan, C.R., Rehof, J. (eds.) TACAS 2008. LNCS, vol. 4963, pp. 337–340. Springer, Heidelberg (2008)
16. Gopan, D., Reps, T.W., Sagiv, S.: A framework for numeric analysis of array operations. In: Proc. of POPL, pp. 338–350 (2005)
17. Gotsman, A., Berdine, J., Cook, B.: Interprocedural Shape Analysis with Separated Heap Abstractions. In: Yi, K. (ed.) SAS 2006. LNCS, vol. 4134, pp. 240–260. Springer, Heidelberg (2006)
18. Gulwani, S., Lev-Ami, T., Sagiv, M.: A combination framework for tracking partition sizes. In: Proc. of POPL, pp. 239–251 (2009)
19. Gulwani, S., McCloskey, B., Tiwari, A.: Lifting abstract interpreters to quantified logical domains. In: POPL, pp. 235–246 (2008)
20. Halbwachs, N., Péron, M.: Discovering properties about arrays in simple programs. In: PLDI, pp. 339–348 (2008)
21. Jeannet, B., Miné, A.: APRON: A Library of Numerical Abstract Domains for Static Analysis. In: Bouajjani, A., Maler, O. (eds.) CAV 2009. LNCS, vol. 5643, pp. 661–667. Springer, Heidelberg (2009)
22. Jhala, R., McMillan, K.L.: Array Abstractions from Proofs. In: Damm, W., Hermanns, H. (eds.) CAV 2007. LNCS, vol. 4590, pp. 193–206. Springer, Heidelberg (2007)
23. McCloskey, B., Reps, T., Sagiv, M.: Statically Inferring Complex Heap, Array, and Numeric Invariants. In: Cousot, R., Martel, M. (eds.) SAS 2010. LNCS, vol. 6337, pp. 71–99. Springer, Heidelberg (2010)
24. Miné, A.: The octagon abstract domain. Higher-Order and Symbolic Computation 19(1), 31–100 (2006)

25. Perrelle, V., Halbwachs, N.: An Analysis of Permutations in Arrays. In: Barthe, G., Hermenegildo, M. (eds.) VMCAI 2010. LNCS, vol. 5944, pp. 279–294. Springer, Heidelberg (2010)
26. Podelski, A., Wies, T.: Boolean Heaps. In: Hankin, C., Siveroni, I. (eds.) SAS 2005. LNCS, vol. 3672, pp. 268–283. Springer, Heidelberg (2005)
27. Podelski, A., Wies, T.: Counterexample-guided focus. In: Proc. of POPL, pp. 249–260 (2010)
28. Reynolds, J.C.: Separation logic: A logic for shared mutable data structures. In: Proc. of LICS. IEEE Computer Society (2002)
29. Rinetzky, N., Bauer, J., Reps, T.W., Sagiv, S., Wilhelm, R.: A semantics for procedure local heaps and its abstractions. In: Proc. of POPL, pp. 296–309 (2005)
30. Rinetzky, N., Sagiv, M., Yahav, E.: Interprocedural Shape Analysis for Cutpoint-Free Programs. In: Hankin, C., Siveroni, I. (eds.) SAS 2005. LNCS, vol. 3672, pp. 284–302. Springer, Heidelberg (2005)
31. Rival, X., Chang, B.-Y.E.: Calling context abstraction with shapes. In: Proc. of POPL, pp. 173–186 (2011)
32. Sagiv, S., Reps, T.W., Wilhelm, R.: Parametric shape analysis via 3-valued logic. ACM Trans. Program. Lang. Syst. 24(3), 217–298 (2002)
33. Sharir, M., Pnueli, A.: Two approaches to interprocedural data flow analysis. In: Program Flow Analysis: Theory and Applications, pp. 189–234. Prentice-Hall (1981)
34. Vafeiadis, V.: Shape-Value Abstraction for Verifying Linearizability. In: Jones, N.D., Müller-Olm, M. (eds.) VMCAI 2009. LNCS, vol. 5403, pp. 335–348. Springer, Heidelberg (2009)

Software Verification with Liquid Types*

Ranjit Jhala

University of California, San Diego
jhala@cs.ucsd.edu

Abstract. Traditional software verification algorithms work by using a combination of Floyd-Hoare Logics, Model Checking and Abstract Interpretation, to check and infer suitable program invariants. However, these techniques are problematic in the presence of complex but ubiquitous constructs like generic data structures, first-class functions. We observe that modern type systems are capable of the kind of analysis needed to analyze the above constructs, and we use this observation to develop Liquid Types, a new static verification technique which combines the complementary strengths of Floyd-Hoare logics, Model Checking, and Types. As a result, we demonstrate how liquid types can be used to statically verify properties ranging from memory safety to data structure correctness, in higher-order languages like ML. This presentation is based on joint work with Patrick Rondon and Ming Kawaguchi.

* This work was supported by NSF grants CCF-0644361, CNS-0720802, CCF-0702603, and gifts from Microsoft Research.

V. Kuncak and A. Rybalchenko (Eds.): VMCAI 2012, LNCS 7148, p. 23, 2012.

Teaching Semantics with a Proof Assistant: No More LSD Trip Proofs

Tobias Nipkow

Institut für Informatik, Technische Universität München

Abstract. We describe a course on the semantics of a simple imperative programming language and on applications to compilers, type systems, static analyses and Hoare logic. The course is entirely based on the proof assistant Isabelle and includes a compact introduction to Isabelle. The overall aim is to teach the students how to write correct and readable proofs.

1 Introduction

A perennial challenge for both students and teachers of theoretical informatics courses are proofs and how to teach them. Scott Aaronson [1] characterizes the situation very well:

> I still remember having to grade hundreds of exams where the students started out by assuming what had to be proved, or filled page after page with gibberish in the hope that, somewhere in the mess, they might accidentally have said something correct.
>
> ... innumerable examples of "parrot proofs" — NP- completeness reductions done in the wrong direction, arguments that look more like LSD trips than coherent chains of logic ...

One could call it the London underground phenomenon:

Students MIND THE GAP Proofs

I do not want to play the blame game but want to suggest a way to bridge this gap with the help of a proof assistant. The underlying assumptions are that

- the above mentioned "LSD trip proofs" are the result of insufficient practice and that
- proof assistants lead to abundant practice because they are addictive like video games:

V. Kuncak and A. Rybalchenko (Eds.): VMCAI 2012, LNCS 7148, pp. 24–38, 2012.

Let me explain the analogy between proof assistants and video games. The main advantage of a proof assistant is that it gives the students immediate feedback. Incorrect proofs are rejected right away.[1] Such rejections are an insult and challenge for motivated students. They will persist in their struggle to convince the machine, chasing that elusive `No subgoals`, Isabelle's equivalent of `You have reached the next level of World of Proofcraft`. Of course many students need the additional motivation that the homework they struggle with actually counts towards their final grade.

This is in contrast to the usual system of homework that is graded by a teaching assistant and returned a week later, long after the student struggled with it, and at a time when the course has moved on. This delay significantly reduces the impact that any feedback scribbled on the homework may have. Of course, a proof assistant does not replace a teaching assistant, who can explain *why* a proof is wrong and what to do about it. This is why lab sessions in the presence of teaching assistants are still essential.

The rest of the paper describes a new programming language semantics course based on the proof assistant Isabelle/HOL [14], where "semantics" really means "semantics and applications", for example compilers and program analyses. All of the material of the course (Isabelle theories, slides, lecture notes) are freely available at `http://www.in.tum.de/~nipkow/semantics`.

2 Course History and Format

Fifteen years ago I formalized parts of Winskel's textbook [23], which I was teaching from, in Isabelle/HOL. The longer term vision was a "Mechanized Semantics Textbook" [11,12] as I called it. Although I used the growing collection of semantics theories in Isabelle in my courses, I did not teach Isabelle in my semantics courses and certainly did not require the students to write Isabelle proofs. I felt that the proof language available at the time was not suitable for expressing proofs at an abstract enough level for use in a semantics (as opposed to a proof assistant) course. Predictably, the students' ability to write proofs did not improve

[1] And a fair number of (morally) correct ones, too, because they lack the details the proof assistant unfortunately tends to require.

as a result. It was Christian Urban who first taught a semantics course at TUM based on Isabelle/HOL. He focused on λ-calculus and employed Nominal Isabelle/HOL [18] to deal with variable binding. He in turn was inspired by the Software Foundations course by Benjamin Pierce [17] who teaches Coq and selected areas of both imperative languages and λ-calculus. At this point Isabelle had acquired a readable proof language, which overcame my earlier reluctance to teach Isabelle in a semantics course. I designed a new semantics course and finally made the "Mechanized Semantics Textbook" (in the form of Isabelle theories) the basis of the new course. It is this new course that I report on.

2.1 Format

It is a graduate level course in the theory section of the curriculum. There are a number of alternative courses, for example Logic, Automata Theory, and Algorithms. The Semantics course typically attracts 15–20 students, most of them master students. There are 3 full lecture hours per week, and 1.5 hours of lab sessions, over 15 weeks. In the lab sessions, led by teaching assistants, the students are asked to solve exercises and the solutions are discussed at the end. In addition, there is a homework sheet every one or two weeks. The course is worth 8 ECTS points, with 30 ECTS points being the average workload per semester.

The whole course is based on the proof assistant Isabelle. It is used in the lectures, the lab sessions and in the homework. The homework is the heart and soul of the course. Hence 40% of the final grade is based on the homework. The exam, which contributes 60% to the final grade, is independent of Isabelle and focuses on semantics and informal proofs.

2.2 Prerequisites

Because this is a graduate level course (although advanced undergraduates take it, too), we expect that the students have some background in logical notation, proofs, and functional programming.

Logic. We expect some basic familiarity with logical notation from introductory mathematics courses, typically a discrete math course. We assume that the students are able to read and understand simple formulas of predicate logic involving functions, sets and relations. They should have been exposed to mathematical proofs, including induction, but we do not expect that they can write such proofs themselves (reliably).

Functional Programming. We assume that the students have had some exposure to functional programming, to the extent that they know about ML-style datatypes, recursive functions and pattern matching.[2]

[2] At TUM, a functional programming course is mandatory for informatics undergraduates.

3 Aims and Principles

This section explains the general aims and principles underlying the course; to a large extent they are generic and independent of the semantics content.

3.1 No More LSD Trip Proofs!

Next to semantics, this is the central aim of the course. Programming language semantics and its applications deal with complex objects, for example compilers. Analyzing such tools requires precise proofs. Graduate level informatics students who specialize in this area must understand the underlying proof principles and must be able to construct such proofs, both informally on paper and with the help of a machine.

We believe we have largely reached this aim. The students obtained on average 88% of the homework points, an unprecedented percentage that is due to the video game effect of a proof assistant described in the introduction together with the 40% incentive. In fact, any system where students can immediately tell how much of the homework they have solved successfully without having to hand it in will create a strong incentive to maximize the number of points obtained.

3.2 Teach Semantics, Not Proof Assistants

More precisely:

> Teach a Semantics course with the help of a proof assistant,
> not a Proof Assistant course with semantics examples.

The Semantics dog should wag the proof assistant tail, not the other way around. We believe we have reached that goal. Only approximately one quarter of the semester is dedicated to the proof assistant, the remaining three quarters are dedicated to semantics. Neither did we have to make any compromises on the semantics front. The material is no simpler than what we had covered in the past.

3.3 Teach Proofs, Not Proof Scripts

Most theorem provers provide a scripting language for writing proofs. Such proofs are sequences of commands to the prover that, in their entirety, are hard or impossible to read for the human, unless he executes them in the proof assistant. In Isabelle they look like this, where ... elides some basic proof methods:

apply(...)
apply(...)
⋮

Such proofs are for machines, not for humans. They lack the information what is being proved at each point, and they lack structure. They do not convey ideas. They are like assembly language programs. Luckily, Isabelle has a higher-level proof language *Isar* [21] that is inspired by the proof language of Mizar [8] (see [22] for a comparison). Mizar has no low-level scripting language. Hence the "Teach proofs, not proof scripts" principle is really due to Mizar.

As an example we show an Isar proof of Cantor's theorem, where f is a function from a type to its powerset and ... are again suitable proof methods:

lemma $\neg surj\ f$
proof
  assume $surj\ f$
  hence $\exists a.\ \{x \mid x \notin f\ x\} = f\ a$ **by** ...
  hence *False* **by** ...
qed

This is the proof language used for most of the course. It is close to the informal language of mathematics and allows a smooth transition in the presentation style during the course: from Isar proofs on the machine to more traditional proofs on the blackboard (see Section 3.5).

3.4 Teach Proofs, Not Logic

Of course this is not a new idea, mathematicians have been doing this successfully for a long time. To be provocative: proof systems like natural deduction belong in logic courses, where the fine structure of logic is studied. But for students who already have some exposure to logical notation and proof (see Section 2.2), single step proofs in some proof system are a straightjacket. Application-oriented courses—remember, we are trying to teach Semantics, not logic— should reason *modulo logic*: if the student believes that A together with B implies C, he should be able to just write

from A **and** B **have** C **by** *hammer*

where *hammer* is some suitable proof method of the underlying proof assistant. Isar allows exactly that, and Isabelle offers a number of automatic hammers for this purpose, in particular the connection to powerful external automatic provers [4]. The motto is: Do not let logic dominate your thinking, let automatic provers take care of logic.

If *hammer* fails, the user has to refine the proof. This is exactly the Mizar approach. Of course there is a problem: how to figure out what intermediate step might help the proof assistant to see reason, or how to figure out that the claimed deduction is not valid? For the second alternative, Isabelle offers tools for counterexample search [4]. For the first alternative (and also the second!), we have to admit that proof scripts are an excellent way to home in on gaps in a proof. Hence we actually teach apply-scripts, but only in small doses. We also teach a bit of natural deduction, but in disguise: not as inference rules but as Isar text patterns. See Section 4.

3.5 Do Not Let the Proof Assistant Dominate Your Presentation

In the beginning of the course, when introducing the proof assistant, it is essential to demonstrate the interaction with the proof assistant in class for long periods. But even then, we intersperse these demos with slides that introduce or summarize *concepts* and go beyond what the interaction with the system will tell you. Moreover, displaying an Isabelle file with a video projector is never as pleasing to the eye as a separate presentation of the same material, say some function definitions, as LaTeXed slides. Isabelle's LaTeX generation facility and its "antiquotations" allow us to transfer material from Isabelle files to slides automatically without having to type it in a second time.

During the second part of the course, the Semantics part, we gradually move to conventional presentations based on slides and the blackboard, although we never completely abandon Isabelle. We believe that slides (with animations) and especially the blackboard are better suited to explain many concepts and proofs than an Isabelle demo is. When moving to the blackboard for developing proofs, we initially stick closely to Isar to phrase these proofs. As the students become more comfortable with Isar, we begin taking more and more liberties on the blackboard, moving towards informal proofs. The aim is to strengthen the students' ability to bridge the gap between formal and informal proofs.

3.6 Executability Matters

Most students' intuition is greatly enhanced by executable models. As it turns out, most of our formalizations are naturally executable. This is obvious for recursive functions but less so for inductively defined predicates. In fact, students at first do not think of inductive predicates as executable, unless they have a Prolog background. It is an important insight that, for example, inductively defined operational semantics is executable because of the dataflow from the initial to the final state. It is exactly with this application in mind that we made inductive predicates executable in Isabelle [3,2], subject to a mode analysis. This unique feature of Isabelle permits us to execute most of the models in our course, no matter whether they are recursive or inductive or mixtures thereof.

4 Teaching Isabelle

In this and the next section we describe the technical content of the course: first the introduction to Isabelle and proofs, and then the actual semantics and applications part.

Following our principle that the proof assistant should only be a means to an end, namely teaching semantics, we introduce only as much of Isabelle as is necessary for the semantics material. This enables us to cover the material in about 4 weeks, just over a quarter of the semester. The details of this approach can be found elsewhere [13].

We follow the Isabelle tutorial [14] in making functional programming the entry road to theorem proving. HOL includes a functional language, just like other proof assistants do. We assume that the students have had some exposure to functional programming (see Section 2.2) and introduce HOL as a combination of programming and logic, starting with booleans, natural numbers and lists. Students who lack a functional programming background usually manage to pick up the principles from those examples. To start with, our only formulas are equations. After week 1, students can write examples like this:

datatype *tree* = *Node tree nat tree* | *Tip*

fun *mirror* :: *tree* ⇒ *tree* **where**
mirror (*Node l n r*) = *Node* (*mirror r*) *n* (*mirror l*) |
mirror Tip = *Tip*

lemma *mirror* (*mirror t*) = *t*
apply(*induct t*)
apply *auto*
done

Contrary to our motto "Teach proofs, not proof scripts" we introduce proof scripts after all. One reason is their succinctness: the syntax is minimal, which is important at this early stage where students are easily confused by all the new syntax. At the same time the students are taught what the corresponding informal proofs look like.

Week 2 offers a first taste of semantics. Week 1 has been an uphill struggle for the students. It is important show them that they can already model a number of interesting notions on a simple level. We introduce arithmetic and boolean expressions, their evaluation, constant folding optimization, and a compiler from arithmetic expressions to a stack machine. Of course we also prove that optimizer and compiler preserve the semantics.

Week 3 introduces logic beyond equality. We assume that the students are able to read and understand simple formulas of predicate logic (recall Section 2.2) and we merely explain how to write them in HOL. They are also introduced to Isabelle's array of automatic proof tools, in particular *Sledgehammer* [4], Isabelle's link to the automatic first-order provers E, SPASS, Vampire and Z3. Sledgehammer soon becomes the students' best friend in their battle with proofs. Since not all proofs are automatic, we also explain a limited amount of single step reasoning with apply-scripts, as motivated in Section 3.4. Inductive definitions are introduced as the last important modeling tool.

Week 4 is dedicated to the structured proof language Isar (see Section 3.3). In addition to Isar itself we also teach a number of useful proof patterns that correspond to natural deduction rules, for example

show $\neg$ *P*
proof
  assume *P*
  ⋮
  show *False* ...
qed

Although Isabelle's automation subsumes single natural deduction steps, such patterns can improve readability of proofs if used selectively.

5 Semantics

The course concentrates on a single imperative language IMP as you can find it in traditional textbooks by Winskel [23] and Nielson and Nielson [9,10]. In fact, we cover material similar to that by the Nielsons. There are two choices here. Concentrating on a single language permits us to cover many aspects and applications of semantics such as compilers, type systems, Hoare logic, static analyses and abstract interpretation. Concentrating on an imperative language builds on standard background knowledge of the students and emphasizes the relevance of semantics to mainstream computer science, thus facilitating the motivation of the students. We give a sketchy overview of the material. It was developed jointly with Gerwin Klein and more details can be found in the Isabelle distribution and in print [6].

5.1 IMP

IMP is the *de facto* standard imperative language in semantics courses. It contains arithmetic expressions (type *aexp*), boolean expressions (type *bexp*), and commands (type *com*). Commands are defined as the following datatype:

datatype *com* = *SKIP*
  | *vname* ::= *aexp*
  | *com*; *com*
  | *IF bexp THEN com ELSE com*
  | *WHILE bexp DO com*

Variable names (type *vname*) are strings. The state of an IMP program is a function from *vname* to *int*. Arithmetic and boolean expressions are evaluated by recursively defined functions. The only arithmetic operator in *aexp* is + and the only comparison operator in *bexp* is <. Commands are given both a big and a small step semantics and their equivalence is proved:

$$(c,s) \Rightarrow t \longleftrightarrow (c,s) \rightarrow\!* (SKIP,t)$$

where $\Rightarrow$ is the big step and $\rightarrow$ the small step semantics.

5.2 Compiler

We compile to a simple stack machine with the following instructions:

datatype *instr* = *LOADI int* | *LOAD vname* | *STORE vname* | *ADD*
| *JMP int* | *JMPLESS int* | *JMPGE int*

All jumps are relative. The compilation function *ccomp* is defined by recursion over the syntax. We prove that it preserves the semantics:

$ccomp\ c \vdash (0,\ s,\ stk) \rightarrow* (isize\ (ccomp\ c),\ t,\ stk) \longleftrightarrow (c,\ s) \Rightarrow t$

The left-hand side describes the execution of the stack machine.

We have intentionally refrained from considering infinite executions as well. Leroy's elegant treatment [7] opens a whole new can of worms, coinductive definitions, which Isabelle knows about, but the students do not.

5.3 Typed IMP

We modify IMP by allowing both integer and real variables and values. There are no coercions and the semantics gets stuck when trying to add an integer and a real value. A type system for expressions is introduced and it is shown that the type systems fits the small step semantics, i.e. that well typed programs enjoy progress and preservation.

5.4 Static Analyses

We consider two iteration-free static analyses: definite assignment analysis as in Java and live variable analysis. Iterative analyses are considered later in the context of abstract interpretation.

Definite assignment analysis is defined as an inductive predicate D of type $vname\ set \Rightarrow com \Rightarrow vname\ set \Rightarrow bool$ that resembles a Hoare triple: the two sets represent the set of variables definitely initialized before and after the command. Soundness of the analysis w.r.t. a semantics that detects access of uninitialized variables is proved.

Live variable analysis is performed by a recursive function L that computes the set of variables live before a command given those that are live after the command. As mentioned above, the analysis is not iterative, it trades precision for efficiency:

$L\ (WHILE\ b\ DO\ c)\ X = vars\ b \cup X \cup L\ c\ X$

We also define a recursive optimization function *bury* that turns all assignments to dead variables into *SKIP*. Here are two of the defining equations:

$bury\ (x ::= a)\ X = (\textsf{if}\ x \in X\ \textsf{then}\ x ::= a\ \textsf{else}\ SKIP)$
$bury\ (c_1;\ c_2)\ X = bury\ c_1\ (L\ c_2\ X);\ bury\ c_2\ X$

We show that *bury* is sound: the big step transitions of c and *bury* c agree if the states are compared w.r.t. live variables only.

5.5 Security Type Systems

As a second and non-standard example of a type system we consider two versions of the Volpano-Smith-Irvine [20] security type system. First an executable one (following Section 3.6):

$$l \vdash \mathit{SKIP} \qquad \frac{\mathit{sec\text{-}aexp}\ a \leq \mathit{sec}\ x \qquad l \leq \mathit{sec}\ x}{l \vdash x ::= a} \qquad \frac{l \vdash c_1 \qquad l \vdash c_2}{l \vdash c_1;\ c_2}$$

$$\frac{\mathit{max}\ (\mathit{sec\text{-}bexp}\ b)\ l \vdash c_1 \qquad \mathit{max}\ (\mathit{sec\text{-}bexp}\ b)\ l \vdash c_2}{l \vdash \mathit{IF}\ b\ \mathit{THEN}\ c_1\ \mathit{ELSE}\ c_2} \qquad \frac{\mathit{max}\ (\mathit{sec\text{-}bexp}\ b)\ l \vdash c}{l \vdash \mathit{WHILE}\ b\ \mathit{DO}\ c}$$

And then the standard one based on a subsumption rule:

$$\frac{\mathit{sec\text{-}bexp}\ b \leq l \qquad l \vdash' c_1 \qquad l \vdash' c_2}{l \vdash' \mathit{IF}\ b\ \mathit{THEN}\ c_1\ \mathit{ELSE}\ c_2} \qquad \frac{\mathit{sec\text{-}bexp}\ b \leq l \qquad l \vdash' c}{l \vdash' \mathit{WHILE}\ b\ \mathit{DO}\ c}$$

$$\frac{l \vdash' c \qquad l' \leq l}{l' \vdash' c}$$

The first three rules for $\vdash'$ agree with the ones for $\vdash$ and have been omitted. We prove non-interference and the equivalence of the two systems.

5.6 Hoare Logic

We consider the standard partial correctness system and model assertions semantically as predicates on states. Soundness and completeness are proved. A verification condition generator (assuming loop-annotated programs) is defined and its soundness and completeness is proved. The details can already be found in the "Mechanized Semantics Textbook" [11].

5.7 Abstract Interpretation

We develop a generic abstract interpreter for IMP commands annotated with abstract states. Every command, except sequential composition, is annotated with the abstract state P after the command. The syntax is $\mathit{SKIP}\ \{P\}$, $x ::= a\ \{P\}$, $\mathit{IF}\ b\ \mathit{THEN}\ c_1\ \mathit{ELSE}\ c_2\ \{P\}$ and $\{I\}\ \mathit{WHILE}\ b\ \mathit{DO}\ c\ \{P\}$. The post-states P refer to the very end of each command, not to the end of the *ELSE* branch or the loop body. The I in $\{I\}\ \mathit{WHILE}\ b\ \mathit{DO}\ c\ \{P\}$ is the loop invariant. Starting from a program where all annotations are $\bot$ (annotations are in fact lifted abstract states, i.e. either $\mathit{Up}\ S$ or $\bot$), the abstract interpreter iterates a step function that maps annotated commands to annotated commands, changing only the annotations. Each step corresponds to the synchronous execution of one computation step at all points in the command. This corresponds to a Jacobi iteration on the corresponding dataflow equations.

Rather than go into the technical details, we explain the abstract interpreter by means of a worked example, interval analysis. An abstract state is a list of pairs (x,*ivl*) of variable names x and intervals *ivl*. An interval is of the form $\{i\ldots j\}$ where i and j are integers. Infinite lower or upper bounds are simply dropped. For example, $\{1\ldots\}$ is the set of all positive integers. We consider the iterated application of the step function to this program:

$''x'' ::= N\ 7\ \{\bot\};$
$\{\bot\}$
$\mathit{WHILE}\ \mathit{Less}\ (V\ ''x'')\ (N\ 100)\ \mathit{DO}\ ''x'' ::= \mathit{Plus}\ (V\ ''x'')\ (N\ 1)\ \{\bot\}$
$\{\bot\}$

The first iteration tells us that x has value 7 after the assignment:

$''x'' ::= N\ 7\ \{\mathit{Up}\ [(''x'', \{7\ldots 7\})]\};$
$\{\bot\}$
$\mathit{WHILE}\ \mathit{Less}\ (V\ ''x'')\ (N\ 100)\ \mathit{DO}\ ''x'' ::= \mathit{Plus}\ (V\ ''x'')\ (N\ 1)\ \{\bot\}$
$\{\bot\}$

The next step merely initializes the invariant:

$''x'' ::= N\ 7\ \{\mathit{Up}\ [(''x'', \{7\ldots 7\})]\};$
$\{\mathit{Up}\ [(''x'', \{7\ldots 7\})]\}$
$\mathit{WHILE}\ \mathit{Less}\ (V\ ''x'')\ (N\ 100)\ \mathit{DO}\ ''x'' ::= \mathit{Plus}\ (V\ ''x'')\ (N\ 1)\ \{\bot\}$
$\{\bot\}$

One more step propagates the invariant to the end of the loop body:

$''x'' ::= N\ 7\ \{\mathit{Up}\ [(''x'', \{7\ldots 7\})]\};$
$\{\mathit{Up}\ [(''x'', \{7\ldots 7\})]\}$
$\mathit{WHILE}\ \mathit{Less}\ (V\ ''x'')\ (N\ 100)$
$\mathit{DO}\ ''x'' ::= \mathit{Plus}\ (V\ ''x'')\ (N\ 1)\ \{\mathit{Up}\ [(''x'', \{8\ldots 8\})]\}$
$\{\bot\}$

In the next step, an ordinary join of $\{7\ldots 7\}$ and $\{8\ldots 8\}$ would result in the new invariant $\{7\ldots 8\}$ and it would take many iterations until the actual invariant $\{7\ldots 100\}$ is reached. Therefore we extend the abstract interpreter with widening and obtain the new invariant $\{7\ldots\}$ instead:

$''x'' ::= N\ 7\ \{\mathit{Up}\ [(''x'', \{7\ldots 7\})]\};$
$\{\mathit{Up}\ [(''x'', \{7\ldots\})]\}$
$\mathit{WHILE}\ \mathit{Less}\ (V\ ''x'')\ (N\ 100)$
$\mathit{DO}\ ''x'' ::= \mathit{Plus}\ (V\ ''x'')\ (N\ 1)\ \{\mathit{Up}\ [(''x'', \{8\ldots 8\})]\}$
$\{\bot\}$

For simplicity, widening is used at any point, not just for invariants. This means that when $\{7\ldots\}$ is pushed through the loop body it is first restricted to $\{7..99\}$, then incremented to $\{8\ldots 100\}$) and then widened with the previous $\{8\ldots 8\}$ to $\{8\ldots\}$. The post-state $\{100\ldots\}$ is obtained by a backwards analysis of the loop condition:

```
''x'' ::= N 7 {Up [(''x'', {7...7})]};
{Up [(''x'', {7...})]}
WHILE Less (V ''x'') (N 100)
DO ''x'' ::= Plus (V ''x'') (N 1) {Up [(''x'', {8...})]}
{Up [(''x'', {100...})]}
```

This is a post-fixed point and it is time to improve the result with narrowing. This time the post-state of the loop body is the result of narrowing $\{8..100\}$ with the old $\{8...\}$, which yields $\{8...100\}$.

```
''x'' ::= N 7 {Up [(''x'', {7...7})]};
{Up [(''x'', {7...})]}
WHILE Less (V ''x'') (N 100)
DO ''x'' ::= Plus (V ''x'') (N 1) {Up [(''x'', {8...100})]}
{Up [(''x'', {100...})]}
```

Next time $\{8...100\}$ narrows the invariant $\{7...\}$ to $\{7...100\}$:

```
''x'' ::= N 7 {Up [(''x'', {7...7})]};
{Up [(''x'', {7...100})]}
WHILE Less (V ''x'') (N 100)
DO ''x'' ::= Plus (V ''x'') (N 1) {Up [(''x'', {8...100})]}
{Up [(''x'', {100...})]}
```

Backwards analysis of the loop condition turns the invariant into the post-state $\{100...100\}$:

```
''x'' ::= N 7 {Up [(''x'', {7...7})]};
{Up [(''x'', {7...100})]}
WHILE Less (V ''x'') (N 100)
DO ''x'' ::= Plus (V ''x'') (N 1) {Up [(''x'', {8...100})]}
{Up [(''x'', {100...100})]}
```

We have reached a fixed point and terminate.

The main advantage of this approach to abstract interpretation is its extreme concreteness and intuitiveness: the above example snapshots are the direct results of running the iterated step function. The abstract interpretation process is truly animated. In the presenece of widening/narrowing, the above iteration strategy is not optimal as Cachera and Pichardie [5] point out. They formalize a *denotational* abstract interpreter that is more precise (at least for the given examples, and possibly in general). From a teaching perspective we prefer the annotated commands approach because the student can see the results at intermediate stages by iterating the step function; a denotational approach yields the final result directly.

6 Conclusion

We have only taught the course 1 1/2 times so far. Hence it is difficult to draw definitive conclusions. But the overall tendency is very positive:

- The students earned 88% of the possible homework points, an unusually high number, especially considering that much of the homework consisted of proofs. We strongly conjecture that this is due to the use of a proof assistant (see Section 3.1) combined with the fact that the homework accounted for 40% of the final grade. One attempt at cheating was discovered. With more students than the current 15–20, plagiarism would become more of an issue.
- In the final exam, the results were significantly above average, both compared to previous editions of the course and to other theory courses. However, a comparison of the different exams is difficult because of differences like oral versus written. The final exam complemented the homework in that the exam concentrated on the semantics material, did not involve the proof assistant, but required the students to give informal proof sketches.
- The overall written feedback from the course was positive. The only negative comments concerned the amount of time the students spent on their homework ("too time consuming"). Looking at the overall departmental course evaluation statistics, only the database course was more demanding in terms of the amount of time the students invested (according to their own estimate). Unfortunately, this reflects the state of the art of proof assistants.

In summary: there were no more LSD trip proofs, the students had mastered both formal and informal proofs[3] and had a better understanding of the semantics material. Teaching Isabelle required the first quarter of the semester. We believe that this initial investment did not just improve the students' understanding of the logical foundations, it also allowed us to cover the semantics material more quickly than normally because of the solid and uniform foundations that could be taken for granted.

I concur with Pierce's assessment that this form of semantics course is the way of the future. There are many other courses out there that use proof assistants in some form or another (for example, Leroy's summer school course `http://cristal.inria.fr/~xleroy/courses/Eugene-2011/`), but there are few published accounts. Exceptions are ACL2 and DrScheme based courses in functional programming and software engineering [15,16,19] where automatic program verification and refutation is the focus and less the interactive construction of proofs. It will be interesting to see how much proof assistants will have an impact on teaching beyond the usual suspects of programming languages, formal methods and logic.

Acknowledgments. Gerwin Klein has been a long term collaborator on this project. Sascha Böhme, Alex Krauss, Brian Huffman and Peter Lammich helped to run this course. All of them helped to debug this paper.

[3] Of course we should not forget that many of the proofs in this area follow standard patterns.

References

1. Aaronson, S.: Teaching statement (2007), http://www.scottaaronson.com/teaching.pdf
2. Berghofer, S., Bulwahn, L., Haftmann, F.: Turning Inductive into Equational Specifications. In: Berghofer, S., Nipkow, T., Urban, C., Wenzel, M. (eds.) TPHOLs 2009. LNCS, vol. 5674, pp. 131–146. Springer, Heidelberg (2009)
3. Berghofer, S., Nipkow, T.: Executing Higher Order Logic. In: Callaghan, P., Luo, Z., McKinna, J., Pollack, R. (eds.) TYPES 2000. LNCS, vol. 2277, pp. 24–40. Springer, Heidelberg (2002)
4. Blanchette, J.C., Bulwahn, L., Nipkow, T.: Automatic Proof and Disproof in Isabelle/HOL. In: Tinelli, C., Sofronie-Stokkermans, V. (eds.) FroCos 2011. LNCS, vol. 6989, pp. 12–27. Springer, Heidelberg (2011)
5. Cachera, D., Pichardie, D.: A Certified Denotational Abstract Interpreter. In: Kaufmann, M., Paulson, L.C. (eds.) ITP 2010. LNCS, vol. 6172, pp. 9–24. Springer, Heidelberg (2010)
6. Klein, G.: Interactive proof: Applications to semantics. In: Proc. Summer School Marktoberdorf 2011 (to appear, 2012)
7. Leroy, X.: Coinductive Big-Step Operational Semantics. In: Sestoft, P. (ed.) ESOP 2006. LNCS, vol. 3924, pp. 54–68. Springer, Heidelberg (2006)
8. Naumowicz, A., Korniłowicz, A.: A Brief Overview of Mizar. In: Berghofer, S., Nipkow, T., Urban, C., Wenzel, M. (eds.) TPHOLs 2009. LNCS, vol. 5674, pp. 67–72. Springer, Heidelberg (2009)
9. Nielson, H.R., Nielson, F.: Semantics with Applications. Wiley (1992)
10. Nielson, H.R., Nielson, F.: Semantics with Applications. An Appatizer. Springer, Heidelberg (2007)
11. Nipkow, T.: Winskel is (Almost) Right: Towards a Mechanized Semantics Textbook. In: Chandru, V., Vinay, V. (eds.) FSTTCS 1996. LNCS, vol. 1180, pp. 180–192. Springer, Heidelberg (1996)
12. Nipkow, T.: Winskel is (almost) right: Towards a mechanized semantics textbook. Formal Aspects of Computing 10, 171–186 (1998)
13. Nipkow, T.: Interactive proof: Introduction to Isabelle/HOL. In: Proc. Summer School Marktoberdorf 2011 (to appear, 2012)
14. Nipkow, T., Paulson, L.C., Wenzel, M.T.: Isabelle/HOL. LNCS, vol. 2283. Springer, Heidelberg (2002)
15. Page, R.: Engineering software correctness. J. Functional Programming 17(6), 675–686 (2007)
16. Page, R., Eastlund, C., Felleisen, M.: Functional programming and theorem proving for undergraduates: A progress report. In: Proc. 2008 International Workshop on Functional and Declarative Programming in Education, FDPE 2008, pp. 21–30. ACM (2008)
17. Pierce, B.C.: Lambda, the ultimate TA: using a proof assistant to teach programming language foundations. In: Proc. 14th ACM SIGPLAN International Conference on Functional Programming, ICFP 2009, pp. 121–122. ACM (2009)
18. Urban, C.: Nominal techniques in Isabelle/HOL. J. Automated Reasoning 40, 327–356 (2008)

19. Vaillancourt, D., Page, R., Felleisen, M.: ACL2 in DrScheme. In: Manolios, P., Wilding, M. (eds.) Proc. Sixth International Workshop on the ACL2 Theorem Prover and its Applications, pp. 107–116. ACM (2006)
20. Volpano, D., Smith, G., Irvine, C.: A sound type system for secure flow analysis. Journal of Computer Security 4(2-3), 167–187 (1996)
21. Wenzel, M.: Isabelle/Isar — A Versatile Environment for Human-Readable Formal Proof Documents. PhD thesis, Institut für Informatik, Technische Universität München (2002)
22. Wenzel, M., Wiedijk, F.: A comparison of Mizar and Isar. J. Automated Reasoning, 389–411 (2002)
23. Winskel, G.: The Formal Semantics of Programming Languages. MIT Press (1993)

WHALE: An Interpolation-Based Algorithm for Inter-procedural Verification

Aws Albarghouthi[1], Arie Gurfinkel[2], and Marsha Chechik[1]

[1] Department of Computer Science, University of Toronto, Canada
[2] Software Engineering Institute, Carnegie Mellon University, USA

Abstract. In software verification, Craig interpolation has proven to be a powerful technique for computing and refining abstractions. In this paper, we propose an interpolation-based software verification algorithm for checking safety properties of (possibly recursive) sequential programs. Our algorithm, called WHALE, produces inter-procedural proofs of safety by exploiting interpolation for guessing function summaries by generalizing under-approximations (i.e., finite traces) of functions. We implemented our algorithm in LLVM and applied it to verifying properties of low-level code written for the pacemaker challenge. We show that our prototype implementation outperforms existing state-of-the-art tools.

1 Introduction

In the software verification arena, software model checking has emerged as a powerful technique both for proving programs correct and for finding bugs. Given a program P and a safety property φ to be verified, e.g., an assertion in the code, a model checker either finds an execution of P that refutes φ or computes an invariant that proves that P is correct w.r.t. φ.

Traditionally [3], software model checkers rely on computing a finite abstraction of the program, e.g., a Boolean program, and using classical model checking algorithms [8] to explore the abstract state space. Due to the over-approximating nature of these abstractions, the found counterexamples may be spurious. Counterexample-guided abstraction refinement (CEGAR) techniques [7] help detect these and refine the abstraction to eliminate them. This loop continues until a real counterexample is found or a proof of correctness, in the form of a program invariant, is computed.

More recently, a new class of software model checking algorithms has emerged. They construct program invariants by generalizing from finite paths through the control flow graph of the program. The most prominent of these are *interpolation-based algorithms* [27,26,16], introduced by McMillan in [27] and inspired by the success of *Craig interpolants* [9] for image-approximation in symbolic model checking [25]. In general, interpolation-based software model checking techniques extract interpolants from refutation proofs of infeasible program paths. The interpolants form an inductive sequence of Hoare triples that prove safety of a given program path, and potentially others.

V. Kuncak and A. Rybalchenko (Eds.): VMCAI 2012, LNCS 7148, pp. 39–55, 2012.

Interpolation-based techniques avoid the expensive abstraction step of their traditional CEGAR-based counterparts and, due to their reliance on examining program paths for deriving invariants, are better suited for bug finding [26]. Yet, so far, interpolation-based techniques have been limited to intra-procedural analysis [27], restricted to non-recursive programs with bounded loops [26], or not modular in terms of generated proofs [16].

In this paper, we present WHALE: an inter-procedural interpolation-based software model checking algorithm that produces modular safety proofs of (recursive) sequential programs. Our key insight is to use interpolation to compute a function summary by generalizing from an under-approximation of a function, thus avoiding the need to fully expand the function and resulting in modular proofs of correctness. The use of interpolants allows us to produce concise summaries that eliminate facts irrelevant to the property in question. We also show how the power of SMT solvers can be exploited in our setting by encoding a path condition over multiple (or all) inter-procedural paths of a program in a single formula. We have implemented a prototype of WHALE using the LLVM compiler infrastructure [23] and verified properties of low-level C code written for the pacemaker grand challenge.

The rest of this paper is organized as follows: In Sec. 2, we illustrate WHALE on an example. In Sec. 3, we present background and notation used in the rest of the paper. In Sec. 4, we introduce inter-procedural reachability graphs. In Sec. 5, we present the algorithm. In Sec. 6, we discuss our implementation and present our experimental results. Finally, in Sec. 7 and Sec. 8, we discuss related work, sketch future research directions, and conclude the paper.

2 Motivating Example

In this section, we use WHALE to prove that `mc91` in Fig. 1, a variant of the famous McCarthy 91 function [24], always returns a value ≥ 91, i.e., `mc91(p)` $\geq$ 91 for all values of p.

WHALE works by iteratively constructing a forest of *Abstract Reachability Graphs* (ARGs) (we call it an *iARG*) with one ARG for the main function, and one ARG for each function call inside each ARG. Each ARG $\mathcal{A}_i$ is associated with some function F_k, an expression G_i over the arguments of F_k, called the *guard*, and an expression S_i over the arguments and the return variables of F_k, called the *summary*. Intuitively, WHALE uses ARG $\mathcal{A}_i$ to show that function F_k behaves according to S_i, assuming the arguments satisfy G_i and assuming all other functions behave according to their corresponding ARGs in the iARG. A node v in an ARG $\mathcal{A}_i$ corresponds to a control location ℓ_v and is labeled by an expression e_v over program variables. WHALE maintains the invariant that e_v is an over-approximation of the states reachable from the states in G_i, at the entry point of F_k, along the path to v. It is always sound to let e_v be *true*. We now apply WHALE to `mc91` in Fig. 1, producing ARGs `A` (starting with `A`$_1$), with `G` and `S` as their guards and summaries, respectively.

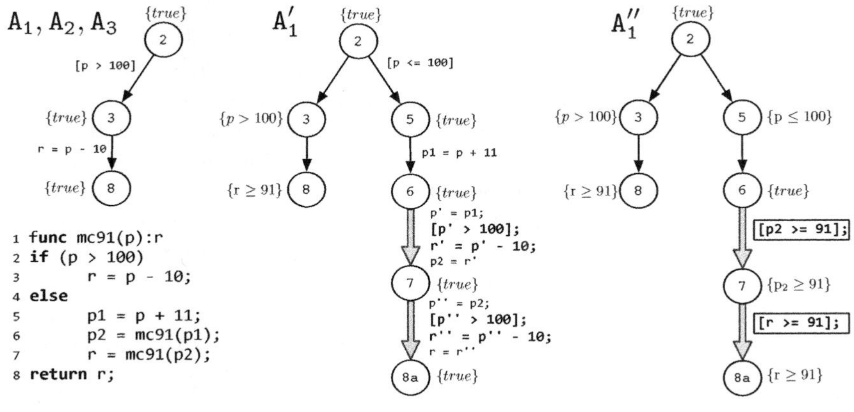

Fig. 1. Applying WHALE to mc91

Step 1. For each ARG in Fig. 1, the number inside a node v is the location ℓ_v and the expression in braces is e_v. For our property, mc91(p) ≥ 91, the guard G_1 is *true*, and the summary S_1 is $r \geq 91$. The single path of A_1 is a potential counterexample: it reaches the return statement (line 8), and node 8 is labeled *true* (which does not imply the summary $r \geq 91$). To check for feasibility of the computed counterexample, WHALE checks satisfiability of the corresponding *path formula* $\pi = true \wedge (p > 100) \wedge (r = p - 10) \wedge (r < 91)$ obtained by conjoining the guard, all of the conditions and assignments on the path, and the negation of the summary. Here, π is unsatisfiable. Hence, the counterexample is infeasible, and the ARG labeling can be strengthened to exclude it.

Step 2. Like [27], WHALE uses interpolants to strengthen the labels. For a pair of formulas (A, B) s.t. $A \wedge B$ is unsatisfiable, *an interpolant* $\hat{A}$ is a formula in the common vocabulary of A and B s.t. $A \Rightarrow \hat{A}$ and $\hat{A} \Rightarrow \neg B$. Intuitively, $\hat{A}$ is a weakening of A that is inconsistent with B. Each node v in the infeasible counterexample is labeled by an interpolant obtained by letting A be the part of the path formula for the path from root to v, and B be the rest of the path formula. The new labeling is shown in Fig. 1 in ARG A'_1.

Step 3. Next, the second path through mc91 is added to A'_1 and has to be checked for feasibility. This path has two recursive calls that need to be represented in the path formula. For each call statement, WHALE creates a new *justifying* ARG, in order to keep track of the under-approximation of the callee used in the proof of the caller and to construct the proof that the callee behaves according to a given specification.

Let A_2 and A_3 be the ARGs justifying the first and the second calls, respectively. For simplicity of presentation, assume that A_2 and A_3 have been unrolled and are identical to A_1 in Fig. 1. The path formula π for the path 2, 5, ..., 8a is constructed by under-approximating the callees by inlining them with the justifying ARGs (shown by bold labels on the grey call edges in A'_1). Specifically, $\pi = true \wedge (p \leq 100) \wedge (p_1 = p + 11) \wedge U_1 \wedge U_2 \wedge (r < 91)$, where U_1 and U_2

represent the under-approximations of the called functions on edges (6,7) and (7,8), respectively. This path formula is unsatisfiable and thus the counterexample is infeasible. Again, interpolants are used to strengthen node labels, as shown in ARG $\mathtt{A}_1''$. Furthermore, the interpolants are also used to generalize the under-approximations of the callees by taking the interpolant of the pair (A, B), where A is the path formula of the under-approximation and B is the rest of the path formula. The resulting interpolant $\hat{A}$ is a specification of the callee that is weaker than its under-approximation, but strong enough to exclude the infeasible counterexample. For example, to generalize the under-approximation U_1, we set A to U_1 and B to $true \wedge (p \leq 100) \wedge (p_1 = p + 11) \wedge U_2 \wedge (r < 91)$. The resulting generalizations, which happen to be $r \geq 91$ for both calls, are shown on the call edges in ARG $\mathtt{A}_1''$ with variables renamed to suit the call context.

Step 4. At this point, all intra-procedural paths of `mc91` have been examined. Hence, $\mathtt{A}_1''$ is a proof that the body of `mc91` returns $r \geq 91$ assuming that the first call returns $r \geq 91$ and that the second one returns $r \geq 91$ whenever $p \geq 91$. To discharge the assumptions, WHALE sets guards and summaries for the ARGs $\mathtt{A}_2$ and $\mathtt{A}_3$ as follows: $\mathtt{G}_2 = true$, $\mathtt{S}_2 = r \geq 91$, $\mathtt{G}_3 = p \geq 91$ and $\mathtt{S}_3 = r \geq 91$, and can continue to unroll them following steps 1-3 above. However, in this example, the assumptions on recursive calls to `mc91` are weaker than what was established about the body of `mc91`. Thus, we conclude that the ARGs $\mathtt{A}_2$ and $\mathtt{A}_3$ are *covered* by $\mathtt{A}_1''$ and do not need to be expanded further, finishing the analysis. Intuitively, the termination condition is based on the Hoare proof rule for recursive functions [19] (see Sec. 3).

In practice, WHALE only keeps track of guards, summaries, and labels at entry and exit nodes. Other labels can be derived from those when needed.

To summarize, WHALE explores the program by unwinding its control flow graph. Each time a possible counterexample is found, it is checked for feasibility and, if needed, the labels are strengthened using interpolants. If the counterexample is inter-procedural, then an under-approximation of the callee is used for the feasibility check, and interpolants are used to guess a summary of the called function. WHALE attempts to verify the summary in a similar manner, but if the verification is unsuccessful, it generates a counterexample which is used to refine the under-approximation used by the caller and to guess a new summary.

3 Preliminaries

In this section, we present the notation used in the rest of the paper.

Program Syntax. We divide program statements into simple statements and function calls. A *simple statement* is either an assignment statement `x = exp` or a conditional statement `assume(`Q`)`, where `x` is a program variable, and `exp` and Q are an expression and a Boolean expression over program variables, respectively. We write $[\![T]\!]$ for the standard semantics of a simple statement T.

$$\frac{P' \Rightarrow P\ \{P\}T\{Q\}\ Q \Rightarrow Q'}{\{P'\}T\{Q'\}} \quad \frac{(P' \wedge \boldsymbol{p} = \boldsymbol{a}) \Rightarrow P\ \{P\}B_F\{Q\}\ (Q \wedge \boldsymbol{p}, \boldsymbol{r} = \boldsymbol{a}, \boldsymbol{b}) \Rightarrow Q'}{\{P'\}\boldsymbol{b} = F(\boldsymbol{a})\{Q'\}} \quad \frac{\{P\}\boldsymbol{b} = F(\boldsymbol{a})\{Q\} \vdash \{P\}B_F\{Q\}}{\{P\}\boldsymbol{b} = F(\boldsymbol{a})\{Q\}}$$

Fig. 2. Three Rules of Hoare Logic

Functions are declared as `func foo` $(p_1, \ldots, p_n) : r_1, \ldots, r_k \quad B_{\texttt{foo}}$, defining a function with name `foo`, n parameters $\mathcal{P} = \{p_1, \ldots, p_n\}$, k return variables $\mathcal{R} = \{r_1, \ldots, r_k\}$, and body $B_{\texttt{foo}}$. We assume that a function never modifies its parameters. The return value of a function is the valuation of all return variables at the time when the execution reaches the exit location. Functions are called using syntax $b_1, \ldots, b_k =$ `foo` $(a_1, \ldots, a_n)$, interpreted as a call to `foo`, passing *values* of local variables $a_1, \ldots, a_n$ as parameters $p_1, \ldots, p_n$, respectively, and storing the *values* of the return variables $r_1, \ldots, r_k$ in local variables $b_1, \ldots, b_k$, respectively. The variables $\{a_i\}_{i=1}^n$ and $\{b_i\}_{i=1}^k$ are assumed to be disjoint. Moreover, for all $i, j \in [1, n]$, s.t. $i \neq j$, $a_i \neq a_j$. That is, there are no duplicate elements in $\{a_i\}_{i=1}^n$. The same holds for the set $\{b_i\}_{i=1}^k$.

Program Model. A *program* $P = (F_1, F_2, \ldots, F_n)$ is a list of n functions. Each *function* $F = (\mathcal{L}, \Delta, \mathsf{en}, \mathsf{ex}, \mathcal{P}, \mathcal{R}, \mathsf{Var})$ is a tuple where $\mathcal{L}$ is a finite set of control locations, Δ is a finite set of actions, $\mathsf{en}, \mathsf{ex} \in \mathcal{L}$ are designated entry and exit locations, respectively, and $\mathcal{P}$, $\mathcal{R}$ and Var are sets of parameter, return and local variables, respectively (we use no global variables). An *action* $(\ell_1, T, \ell_2) \in \Delta$ is a tuple where $\ell_1, \ell_2 \in \mathcal{L}$ and T is a program statement over $\mathsf{Var} \cup \mathcal{P} \cup \mathcal{R}$. We assume that the control flow graph (CFG) represented by $(\mathcal{L}, \Delta)$ is a directed acyclic graph (DAG) (and loops are modeled by tail-recursion). Execution starts in the first function in the program. For a function $F = (\mathcal{L}, \Delta, \mathsf{en}, \mathsf{ex}, \mathcal{P}, \mathcal{R}, \mathsf{Var})$, we write $\mathcal{L}(F)$ for $\mathcal{L}$, $\Delta(F)$ for Δ, etc. We write $\boldsymbol{p}_i$ and $\boldsymbol{r}_i$ to denote vectors of parameter and return variables of F_i.

Floyd-Hoare Logic. A *Hoare Triple* [20] $\{P\}T\{Q\}$ where T is a program statement and P and Q are propositional formulas, indicates that if P is true of program variables before executing T, and T terminates, then Q is true after T completes. P and Q are called the *pre-* and the *postcondition*, respectively.

We make use of three proof rules shown in Fig. 2. The first is the *rule of consequence*, indicating that a precondition of a statement can be strengthened whereas its postcondition can be weakened. The second is the *rule of function instantiation* where B_F is a body of a function F with parameters $\boldsymbol{p}$ and returns $\boldsymbol{r}$. It explicates the conditions under which F can be called with actual parameters $\boldsymbol{a}$, returning $\boldsymbol{b}$, and with P' and Q' as pre- and postconditions, respectively. For this rule, we assume that P is over the set of variables $\boldsymbol{p}$ and Q is over the variables $\boldsymbol{p}$ and $\boldsymbol{r}$. The third is the *rule of recursion*, indicating that a recursive function F satisfies the pre-/postconditions (P, Q) if the body of F satisfies (P, Q) *assuming* that all recursive calls satisfy (P, Q). For two sets of triples X and Y, $X \vdash Y$ indicates that Y can be proven from X (i.e., X is weaker than Y). We also say $\vdash X$ to mean that X is valid, i.e., that it follows from the axioms.

4 Inter-procedural Reachability Graphs

In this section, we introduce *Abstract Reachability Graphs* (ARGs) that extend the notion of an Abstract Reachability Tree (ART) [17] to DAGs. At a high level, an ARG represents an exploration of the state space of a function, while making assumptions about the behavior of other functions it calls. We then define a forest of ARGs, called an *Inter-procedural Abstract Reachability Graph* (iARG), to represent exploration of the state space of a program with multiple functions.

Abstract Reachability Graphs (ARGs). Let $F = (\mathcal{L}, \Delta, \mathsf{en}, \mathsf{ex}, \mathcal{P}, \mathcal{R}, \mathsf{Var})$ be a function. A *Reachability Graph* (RG) of F is a tuple $(V, E, \epsilon, \nu, \tau)$ where

- (V, E, ϵ) is a DAG rooted at $\epsilon \in V$,
- $\nu : V \to \mathcal{L}$ is a *node map*, mapping nodes to control locations s.t. $\nu(\epsilon) = \mathsf{en}$ and $\nu(v) = \mathsf{ex}$ for every leaf node v,
- and $\tau : E \to \Delta$ is an *edge map*, mapping edges to program actions s.t. for every edge $(u, v) \in E$ there exists $(\nu(u), \tau(u, v), \nu(v)) \in \Delta$.

We write $V^{\mathsf{e}} = \{v \in V \mid \nu(v) = \mathsf{ex}\}$ for all leaves (*exit nodes*) in V. We call an edge e, where $\tau(e)$ is a call statement, a *call-edge*. We assume that call edges are ordered in some linearization of a topological order of (V, E).

An *Abstract Reachability Graph* (ARG) $\mathcal{A}$ of F is a tuple (U, ψ, G, S), where

- U is reachability graph of F,
- ψ is a *node labelling* that labels the root and leaves of U with formulas over program variables,
- G is a formula over $\mathcal{P}$ called a *guard*,
- and S is a formula over $\mathcal{P} \cup \mathcal{R}$ called a *summary*.

For example, ARG $\mathtt{A}_1$ is given in Fig. 1 with a guard $\mathtt{G}_1 = \mathit{true}$, a summary $\mathtt{S}_1 = r \leq 91$, and with ψ shown in braces.

An ARG $\mathcal{A}$ is *complete* iff for every path in F there is a corresponding path in $\mathcal{A}$. Specifically, $\mathcal{A}$ is complete iff every node $v \in V$ has a successor for every action $(\nu(v), T, \ell) \in \Delta$, i.e., there exists an edge $(v, w) \in E$ s.t. $\nu(w) = \ell$ and $\tau(v, w) = T$. It is *safe* iff for every leaf $v \in V$, $\psi(v) \Rightarrow S$. For example, in Fig. 2, ARG $\mathtt{A}_1''$ is safe and complete, ARG $\mathtt{A}_1'$ is complete but not safe, and other ARGs are neither safe nor complete.

Inter-procedural ARGs. An *Inter-procedural Abstract Reachability Graph* (iARG) $\mathcal{A}(P)$ of a program $P = (F_1, \ldots, F_n)$ is a tuple $(\sigma, \{\mathcal{A}_1, \ldots, \mathcal{A}_k\}, R^{\mathcal{J}}, R^{\mathcal{C}})$, where

- $\sigma : [1, k] \to [1, n]$ maps ARGs to corresponding functions, i.e., $\mathcal{A}_i$ is an ARG of $F_{\sigma(i)}$,
- $\{\mathcal{A}_1, \ldots, \mathcal{A}_k\}$ is a set of ARGs,
- $R^{\mathcal{J}}$ is an acyclic *justification relation* between ARGs s.t. $(\{\mathcal{A}_1, \ldots, \mathcal{A}_k\}, R^{\mathcal{J}})$ is the *justification tree* of $\mathcal{A}(P)$ rooted at $\mathcal{A}_1$,
- and $R^{\mathcal{C}}$ is a *covering relation* between ARGs. Informally, if $(\mathcal{A}_i, \mathcal{A}_j) \in R^{\mathcal{J}}$ then there is a call-edge in $\mathcal{A}_i$ that is *justified* (expanded) by $\mathcal{A}_j$.

Require: $\mathcal{A}_i$ is uncovered and incomplete
func EXPANDARG (ARG $\mathcal{A}_i$) :
    replace U_i with a supergraph U_i',
        where U_i is the unwinding of $\mathcal{A}_i$
    RESET($\mathcal{A}_i$)

Require: $\mathcal{A}_i \not\sqsubseteq_{\mathcal{J}} \mathcal{A}_j$, $\sigma(i) = \sigma(j)$,
    $\mathcal{A}_i$ and $\mathcal{A}_j$ are uncovered,
    $\{G_j\}B_{F_{\sigma(i)}}\{S_j\} \vdash \{G_i\}B_{F_{\sigma(i)}}\{S_i\}$
func COVERARG (ARGs $\mathcal{A}_i$ and $\mathcal{A}_j$) :
    $R^{\mathcal{C}} \leftarrow R^{\mathcal{C}} \setminus \{(\mathcal{A}_l, \mathcal{A}_i) \mid (\mathcal{A}_l, \mathcal{A}_i) \in R^{\mathcal{C}}\}$
    $R^{\mathcal{C}} \leftarrow R^{\mathcal{C}} \cup \{(\mathcal{A}_i, \mathcal{A}_j)\}$

func RESET (ARG $\mathcal{A}_i$) :
    $\forall v \cdot \psi_i(v) \leftarrow true$
    for all $\{\mathcal{A}_j \mid \exists e \in E_i \cdot \mathcal{J}(e) = \mathcal{A}_j\}$ **do**
        $G_j \leftarrow true\,;\, S_j \leftarrow true$
        RESET($\mathcal{A}_j$)

func UPDATE (ARG $\mathcal{A}_i$, g, s) :
    $G_i \leftarrow G_i \wedge g\,;\, S_i \leftarrow S_i \wedge s$
    RESET($\mathcal{A}_i$)

Require: $\mathcal{A}_i$ is uncovered, $\nu(v) = \mathsf{ex}(F_{\sigma(i)})$, $\psi_i(v) \not\Rightarrow S_i$
func REFINEARG (vertex v in $\mathcal{A}_i$) :
    $cond \leftarrow G_i \wedge \text{IDAGCOND}(\mathcal{A}_i, \{v\}) \wedge \neg S_i$
    if $cond$ is UNSAT **then**
        $g_0, s_0, g_1, s_1, \ldots, s_m, s_{m+1} \leftarrow \text{STITP}(cond)$
        $\psi_i(v) \leftarrow \psi_i(v) \wedge S_i\,;\, \psi_i(\epsilon_i) \leftarrow \psi_i(\epsilon_i) \wedge g_0$
        let $e_1, \ldots, e_m$ be topologically ordered sequence
            of all call-edges in $\mathcal{A}_i$ that can reach v
        for all $e_k = (u, w) \in e_1, \ldots, e_m$ **do**
            UPDATE($\mathcal{J}(e_k)$, GUARD(g_k), SUM(s_k))
    else
        if $i = 1$ **then** Terminate with "UNSAFE"
        $R^{\mathcal{C}} \leftarrow R^{\mathcal{C}} \setminus \{(\mathcal{A}_l, \mathcal{A}_i) \mid (\mathcal{A}_l, \mathcal{A}_i) \in R^{\mathcal{C}}\}$
        for all $\{\mathcal{A}_j \mid (\mathcal{A}_j, \mathcal{A}_i) \in R^{\mathcal{J}}\}$ **do** RESET($\mathcal{A}_j$)

Require: $\mathcal{A}_i$ is uncovered, safe, and complete
func UPDATEGUARD (ARG $\mathcal{A}_i$) :
    $G_i \leftarrow \psi(\epsilon_i)$

Fig. 3. The WHALE Algorithm. The function STITP is used to compute interpolants and is defined later in this section.

The justification tree corresponds to a partially unrolled call-graph. We write $\mathcal{A}_i \sqsubseteq_{\mathcal{J}} \mathcal{A}_j$ for the ancestor relation in the justification tree. Given two nodes $u, v \in V_i$, an inter-procedural (u, v)-path in $\mathcal{A}_i$ is a (u, v)-path in $\mathcal{A}_i$ in which every call-edge e is expanded, recursively, by a trace in an ARG $\mathcal{A}_j$, where $(\mathcal{A}_i, \mathcal{A}_j) \in R^{\mathcal{J}}$. For convenience, we assume that $\sigma(1) = 1$, and use a subscript to refer to components of an $\mathcal{A}_i$ in $\mathcal{A}(P)$, e.g., ψ_i is the node labelling of $\mathcal{A}_i$.

An ARG $\mathcal{A}_i$ is *directly covered* by $\mathcal{A}_j$ iff $(\mathcal{A}_i, \mathcal{A}_j) \in R^{\mathcal{C}}$. $\mathcal{A}_i$ is *covered* by $\mathcal{A}_j$ iff $\mathcal{A}_j \sqsubseteq_{\mathcal{J}} \mathcal{A}_i$ and $\mathcal{A}_j$ is directly covered by another ARG. $\mathcal{A}_i$ is covered iff it is covered by some $\mathcal{A}_j$; otherwise, it is *uncovered*. A covering relation $R^{\mathcal{C}}$ is *sound* iff for all $(\mathcal{A}_i, \mathcal{A}_j) \in R^{\mathcal{C}}$:

- $\mathcal{A}_i$ and $\mathcal{A}_j$ are mapped to the same function F_l, i.e., $\sigma(i) = \sigma(j) = l$;
- $i \neq j$ and $\mathcal{A}_i$ is not an ancestor of $\mathcal{A}_j$, i.e., $\mathcal{A}_i \not\sqsubseteq_{\mathcal{J}} \mathcal{A}_j$;
- the specification of $\mathcal{A}_j$ is stronger than that of $\mathcal{A}_i$, i.e., $\{G_j\}\boldsymbol{r} = F_l(\boldsymbol{p})\{S_j\} \vdash \{G_i\}\boldsymbol{r} = F_l(\boldsymbol{p})\{S_i\}$;
- and $\mathcal{A}_j$ is uncovered.

For example, for ARGs in Fig. 1, $(\mathtt{A}_3, \mathtt{A}_1'') \in R^{\mathcal{C}}$, and $\mathtt{A}_1''$ is uncovered. $\mathtt{A}_3$ is left incomplete, since the validity of its guard and summary follow from the validity of the guard and summary of $\mathtt{A}_1''$: $\{true\}B_{\mathtt{mc91}}\{r \geq 91\} \vdash \{p \geq 91\}B_{\mathtt{mc91}}\{r \geq 91\}$ where $(true, r \geq 91)$ and $(p \geq 91, r \geq 91)$ are the guard and summary pairs of $\mathtt{A}_1''$ and $\mathtt{A}_3$, respectively. An iARG $\mathcal{A}(P)$ is *safe* iff $\mathcal{A}_1$ is safe. It is *complete* iff every uncovered ARG $\mathcal{A}_i \in \mathcal{A}(P)$ is complete.

5 The Whale Algorithm

In this section, we provide a detailed exposition of WHALE. We begin with an overview of its basic building blocks.

Overview. Given a program $P = (F_1, \ldots F_n)$ and a pair of formulas (G, S), our goal is to decide whether $\vdash \{G\}B_{F_1}\{S\}$. WHALE starts with an iARG $\mathcal{A}(P) = (\sigma, \{\mathcal{A}_1\}, R^{\mathcal{J}}, R^{\mathcal{C}})$ where $\sigma(1) = 1$, and $R^{\mathcal{J}}$ and $R^{\mathcal{C}}$ are empty relations. $\mathcal{A}_1$ has one vertex v and $\nu(v) = \mathsf{en}(F_1)$. The guard G_1 and summary S_1 are set to G and S, respectively. In addition to the iARG, WHALE maintains a map $\mathcal{J}$ from call-edges to ARGs and an invariant that $(\mathcal{A}_i, \mathcal{A}_j) \in R^{\mathcal{J}}$ iff there exists $e \in E_i$ s.t. $\mathcal{J}(e) = \mathcal{A}_j$.

WHALE is an extension of IMPACT [27] to inter-procedural programs. Its three main operations (shown in Fig. 3), EXPANDARG, COVERARG, and REFINEARG, correspond to their counterparts of IMPACT. EXPANDARG adds new paths to explore; COVERARG ensures that there is no unnecessary exploration, and REFINEARG checks for presence of counterexamples and guesses guards and summaries. All operations maintain soundness of $R^{\mathcal{C}}$. WHALE terminates either when REFINEARG finds a counterexample, or when none of the operations are applicable. In the latter case, the iARG is complete. We show at the end of this section that this also establishes the desired result: $\vdash \{G_1\}B_{F_1}\{S_1\}$.

EXPANDARG adds new paths to an ARG $\mathcal{A}_i$ if it is incomplete, by replacing an RG U_i with a supergraph U_i'. Implicitly, new ARGs are created to justify any new call edges, as needed, and are logged in the justification map $\mathcal{J}$. A new ARG $\mathcal{A}_j$ is initialized with a $G_j = S_j = \mathit{true}$ and $V_j = \{v\}$, where v is an entry node. The paths can be added one-at-a-time (as in IMPACT and in the example in Sec. 2), all-at-once (by adding a complete CFG), or in other ways. Finally, all affected labels are reset to *true*

COVERARG covers an ARG $\mathcal{A}_i$ by $\mathcal{A}_j$. Its precondition maintains the soundness of $R^{\mathcal{C}}$. Furthermore, we impose a total order, $\prec$, on ARGs s.t. $\mathcal{A}_i \sqsubset \mathcal{A}_j$ implies $\mathcal{A}_i \prec \mathcal{A}_j$, to ensure that COVERARG is not applicable indefinitely. Note that once an ARG is covered, all ARGs it covers are uncovered (line 5).

REFINEARG is the core of WHALE. Given an exit node v of some unsafe ARG $\mathcal{A}_i$, it checks whether there exists an inter-procedural counterexample in $\mathcal{A}(P)$, i.e., an inter-procedural (ϵ_i, v)-path that satisfies the guard G_i and violates the summary S_i. This is done using IDAGCOND to construct a condition *cond* that is satisfiable iff there is a counterexample (line 16). If *cond* is SAT and $i = 1$, then there is a counterexample to $\{G_1\}\, B_{F_1}\, \{S_1\}$, and WHALE terminates (line 24). If *cond* is SAT and $i \neq 1$, the guard and the summary of $\mathcal{A}_i$ are invalidated, all ARGs covered by $\mathcal{A}_i$ are uncovered, and all ARGs used to justify call edges of $\mathcal{A}_i$ are reset (lines 25-26). If *cond* is UNSAT, then there is no counterexample in the current iARG. However, since the iARG represents only a partial unrolling of the program, this does not imply that the program is safe. In this case, REFINEARG uses interpolants to *guess* guards and summaries of functions called from $\mathcal{A}_i$ (lines 17-22) which can be used to replace their under-approximations without introducing new counterexamples.

The two primary distinctions between WHALE and IMPACT are in constructing a set of formulas to represent an ARG and in using interpolants to guess function summaries from these formulas. We describe these below.

Inter-procedural DAG Condition. A *DAG condition* of an ARG $\mathcal{A}$ is a formula φ s.t. every satisfying assignment to φ corresponds to an execution through $\mathcal{A}$, and vice versa. A naive way to construct it is to take a disjunction of all the *path conditions* of the paths in the DAG. An *inter-procedural DAG condition* of an ARG $\mathcal{A}$ in an iARG $\mathcal{A}(P)$ (computed by the function iDAGCOND) is a formula φ whose every satisfying assignment corresponds to an inter-procedural execution through $\mathcal{A}_i$ in $\mathcal{A}(P)$ and vice versa.

We assume that $\mathcal{A}_i$ is in Static Single Assignment (SSA) form [10] (i.e., every variable is assigned at most once on every path). iDAGCOND uses the function DAGCOND to compute a DAG condition[1]:

$$\text{DAGCOND}(\mathcal{A}_i, X) \triangleq C \wedge D, \text{ where}$$

$$C = c_{\epsilon_i} \wedge \bigwedge_{v \in V_i'} \{c_v \Rightarrow \bigvee \{c_w \mid (v,w) \in E_i\}\}$$

$$D = \bigwedge_{(v,w) \in E_i'} \{(c_v \wedge c_w) \Rightarrow [\![\tau_i(v,w)]\!] \mid \tau_i(v,w) \text{ is simple}\}, \quad (1)$$

c_i are Boolean variables for nodes of $\mathcal{A}_i$ s.t. a variable c_v corresponds to node v, and $V_i' \subseteq V_i$ and $E_i' \subseteq E_i$ are sets of nodes and edges, respectively, that can reach a node in the set of exit nodes X. Intuitively, C and D encode all paths through $\mathcal{A}_i$ and the corresponding path condition, respectively. DAGCOND ignores call statements which (in SSA) corresponds to replacing calls by non-deterministic assignments.

Example 1. Consider computing DAGCOND($\mathtt{A}_1'$, $\{8, 8a\}$) for the ARG $\mathtt{A}_1'$ in Fig. 1, where c_8 and c_{8a} represent the two exit nodes, on the left and on the right, respectively. Then, $C = c_2 \wedge (c_2 \Rightarrow (c_3 \vee c_5)) \wedge (c_3 \Rightarrow c_8) \wedge (c_5 \Rightarrow c_6) \wedge (c_6 \Rightarrow c_7) \wedge (c_7 \Rightarrow c_{8a})$ and $D = (c_2 \wedge c_3 \Rightarrow p \leq 100) \wedge (c_3 \wedge c_8 \Rightarrow r = p - 10) \wedge (c_2 \wedge c_5 \Rightarrow p \leq 100) \wedge (c_5 \wedge c_6 \Rightarrow p_1 = p + 11)$. Any satisfying assignment to $C \wedge D$ represents an execution through 2,3,8 or 2,5,. . . ,8, where the call statements on edges (6,7) and (7,8) set p_2 and r non-deterministically.

The function iDAGCOND($\mathcal{A}_i, X$) computes an inter-procedural DAG condition for a given ARG and a set X of exit nodes of $\mathcal{A}_i$ by using DAGCOND and interpreting function calls. A naive encoding is to inline every call-edge e with the justifying ARG $\mathcal{J}(e)$, but this results in a monolithic formula which hinders interpolation in the next step of REFINEARG. Instead, we define it as follows:

$$\text{iDAGCOND}(\mathcal{A}_i, X) \triangleq \text{DAGCOND}(\mathcal{A}_i, X) \wedge \bigwedge_{k=1}^{m} \mu_k, \text{ where}$$

$$\mu_k \triangleq (c_{v_k} \wedge c_{w_k}) \Rightarrow ((\boldsymbol{p}_{\sigma(j)}, \boldsymbol{r}_{\sigma(j)} = \boldsymbol{a}, \boldsymbol{b}) \wedge \text{iDAGCOND}(\mathcal{A}_j, V_j^e)), \quad (2)$$

m is the number of call-edges in $\mathcal{A}_i$, $e = (v_k, w_k)$ is the kth call-edge[2], $\mathcal{A}_j = \mathcal{J}(e)$, and $\tau(e)$ is $\boldsymbol{b} = F_{\sigma(j)}(\boldsymbol{a})$. Intuitively, μ_k is the under-approximation of the kth

[1] In practice, we use a more efficient encoding described in [14].

[2] Recall, call-edges are ordered in some linearization of a topological order of RG U_i.

call-edge e in $\mathcal{A}_i$ by the traces in the justifying ARG $\mathcal{A}_j = \mathcal{J}(e)$. Note that iDAGCOND always terminates since the justification relation is acyclic.

Example 2. Following Example 1, iDAGCOND($\mathtt{A}'_1, \{8, 8a\}$) is $(C \wedge D) \wedge \mu_1 \wedge \mu_2$, where $C \wedge D$ are as previously defined, and μ_1, μ_2 represent constraints on the edges (6, 7) and (7, 8). Here, $\mu_1 = (c_6 \wedge c_7) \Rightarrow ((p' = p_1 \wedge p_2 = r') \wedge$ DAGCOND($\mathtt{A}_2, \{8\}$)), i.e., if an execution goes through the edge (6,7), then it has to go through the paths of $\mathtt{A}_2$ – the ARG justifying this edge. Using primed variables avoids name clashes between the locals of the caller and the callee.

Lemma 1. *Given an iARG $\mathcal{A}(P)$, an ARG $\mathcal{A}_i \in \mathcal{A}(P)$, and a set of exit nodes X, there exists a total onto map from satisfying assignments of* iDAGCOND($\mathcal{A}_i, X$) *to inter-procedural (ϵ_i, X)-executions in $\mathcal{A}(P)$.*[3]

A corollary to Lemma 1 is that for any pair of formulas G and S, $G \wedge$ iDAGCOND($\mathcal{A}_i, X$) $\wedge S$ is UNSAT iff there does not exist an execution in $\mathcal{A}_i$ that starts at ϵ_i in a state satisfying G and ends in a state $v \in X$ satisfying S.

Guessing Guards and Summaries. Our goal now is to show how under-approximations of callees in formulas produced by iDAGCOND can be generalized. First, we define a function

$$\text{SPECCOND}(\mathcal{A}_i, X, I) \triangleq \text{DAGCOND}(\mathcal{A}_i, X) \wedge \bigwedge_{k=1}^{m} \mu_k,$$

where $I = \{(q_k, t_k)\}_{k=1}^m$ is a sequence of formulas over program variables, $\mu_k = (c_{v_k} \wedge c_{w_k}) \Rightarrow ((\boldsymbol{p}_{\sigma(j)}, \boldsymbol{r}_{\sigma(j)} = \boldsymbol{a}, \boldsymbol{b}) \wedge (q_k \Rightarrow t_k))$, and the rest is as in the definition of iDAGCOND. SPECCOND is similar to iDAGCOND, except that it takes a sequence of pairs of formulas (pre- and postconditions) that act as specifications of the called functions on the call-edges $\{e_k\}_{k=1}^m$ along the paths to X in $\mathcal{A}_i$. Every satisfying assignment of SPECCOND($\mathcal{A}_i, X, I$) corresponds to an execution through $\mathcal{A}_i$ ending in X, where each call-edge e_k is interpreted as `assume`($q_k \Rightarrow t_k$).

Lemma 2. *Given an iARG $\mathcal{A}(P)$, an ARG $\mathcal{A}_i \in \mathcal{A}(P)$, a set of exit nodes X, and a sequence of formulas $I = \{(q_k, t_k)\}_{k=1}^m$, there exists a total and onto map from satisfying assignments of* SPECCOND($\mathcal{A}_i, X, I$) *to (ϵ_i, X)-executions in $\mathcal{A}_i$, where each call-edge e_k is interpreted as* `assume`($q_k \Rightarrow t_k$).

Given an UNSAT formula $\Phi = G_i \wedge$ iDAGCOND($\mathcal{A}_i, X$) $\wedge \neg S_i$, the goal is to find a sequence of pairs of formulas $I = \{(q_k, t_k)\}_k$ s.t. $G_i \wedge$SPECCOND($\mathcal{A}_i, X, I$)$\wedge \neg S_i$ is UNSAT, and for every t_k, iDAGCOND($\mathcal{A}_j, V_j^e$) $\Rightarrow t_k$, where $\mathcal{A}_j = \mathcal{J}(e_k)$. That is, we want to *weaken* the under-approximations of callees in Φ, while keeping Φ UNSAT. For this, we use interpolants.

We require a stronger notion of interpolants than usual: Let $\Pi = \varphi_0 \wedge \cdots \wedge \varphi_{n+1}$ be UNSAT. A sequence of formulas $g_0, s_0, \ldots, g_{n-1}, s_{n-1}, g_n$ is a *state/-transition interpolant sequence* of Π, written STITP(Π), iff:

[3] Proofs are available at [1].

1. $\varphi_0 \Rightarrow g_0$,
2. $\forall i \in [0, n] \cdot \varphi_{i+1} \Rightarrow s_i$,
3. $\forall i \in [0, n] \cdot (g_i \wedge s_i) \Rightarrow g_{i+1}$,
4. and $g_n \wedge \varphi_{n+1}$ is UNSAT.

We call g_i and s_i the state- and transition-interpolants, respectively. STITP(Π) can be computed by a repeated application of current SMT-interpolation algorithms [6] on the same resolution proof:

$$g_i = \textsc{Itp}(\bigwedge_{j=0}^{i} \varphi_j, \bigwedge_{j=i+1}^{n+1} \varphi_j, pf) \qquad s_i = \textsc{Itp}(\varphi_i, \bigwedge_{j=0}^{i-1} \varphi_j \wedge \bigwedge_{j=i+1}^{n+1} \varphi_j, pf),$$

where *pf* is a fixed resolution proof and ITP(A, B, pf) is a Craig interpolant of (A, B) from *pf*. The proof of correctness of the above computation is similar to that of Theorem 6.6 of [6].

Recall that REFINEARG (Fig. 3), on line 16, computes a formula $cond = G_i \wedge \varphi \wedge \bigwedge_{k=1}^{m} \mu_k \wedge \neg S_i$ using IDAGCOND for ARG $\mathcal{A}_i$ and an exit node v, where μ_k is an under-approximation representing the call-edge $e_k = (u_k, w_k)$. For simplicity of presentation, let $\tau(e_k)$ be $\boldsymbol{b}_k = F_k(\boldsymbol{a}_k)$. Assume *cond* is UNSAT and let $g_0, s_0, \ldots, s_m, g_{m+1}$ be state/transition interpolants for *cond*. By definition, each s_k is an over-approximation of μ_k that keeps *cond* UNSAT. Similarly, g_0 is an over-approximation of G_i that keeps *cond* UNSAT, and g_k, where $k \neq 0$, is an over-approximation of the executions of $\mathcal{A}_i$ assuming that all call statements on edges $e_k, \ldots, e_m$ are non-deterministic. This is due to the fact that $(G_i \wedge \varphi \wedge \mu_1 \wedge \cdots \wedge \mu_{j-1}) \Rightarrow g_j$. Note that $g_0, s_0, \ldots, s_m, g_{m+1}$ are also state/transition interpolants for the formula $G_i \wedge \varphi \wedge (g_1 \Rightarrow s_1) \wedge \cdots \wedge (g_m \Rightarrow s_m) \wedge \neg S_i$. The goal (lines 18–22) is to use the sequence $\{(g_k, s_k)\}_{k=1}^{m}$ to compute a sequence $I = \{(q_k, t_k)\}_{k=1}^{m}$ s.t. $G_i \wedge \textsc{SpecCond}(\mathcal{A}_i, \{v\}, I) \wedge \neg S_i$ is UNSAT. By definition of an interpolant, s_k is over the variables $\boldsymbol{a}_k$, $\boldsymbol{b}_k$, c_{u_k}, and c_{w_k}, whereas t_k has to be over $\boldsymbol{p}_k$ and $\boldsymbol{r}_k$, to represent a summary of F_k. Similarly, g_k is over $\boldsymbol{a}_k$, $\boldsymbol{b}_k$, c_{u_j}, and c_{w_j} for all $j \geq k$, whereas q_k has to be over $\boldsymbol{p}_k$ to represent a guard on the calling contexts. This transformation is done using the following functions:

$$\textsc{Sum}(s_k) \triangleq s_k[c_{u_k}, c_{w_k} \leftarrow \top][\boldsymbol{a}_k, \boldsymbol{b}_k \leftarrow \boldsymbol{p}_k, \boldsymbol{r}_k]$$

$$\textsc{Guard}(g_k) \triangleq \exists Q \cdot g_k[c_u \leftarrow (u_k \sqsubseteq u) \mid u \in V_i][\boldsymbol{a}_k \leftarrow \boldsymbol{p}_k],$$

where the notation $\varphi[x \leftarrow y]$ stands for a formula φ with all occurrences of x replaced by y, $w \sqsubseteq u$ means that a node u is reachable from w in $\mathcal{A}_i$, and Q is the set of all variables in g_k except for $\boldsymbol{a}_k$.

Given a transition interpolant s_k, SUM(s_k) is an over-approximation of the set of reachable states by the paths in $\mathcal{J}(u_k, w_k)$. GUARD(g_k) sets all (and only) successor nodes of u_k to true, thus restricting g_k to executions reaching the call-edge (u_k, w_k); furthermore, all variables except for the arguments $\boldsymbol{a}_k$ are existentially quantified, effectively over-approximating the set of parameter values with which the call on (u_k, w_k) is made.

Lemma 3. *Given an ARG $\mathcal{A}_i \in \mathcal{A}(P)$, and a set of exit nodes X, let $\Phi = G_i \wedge$ IDAGCOND$(\mathcal{A}_i, X) \wedge \neg S_i$ be UNSAT and let $g_0, s_0, \ldots, s_m, g_{m+1}$ be* STITP(Φ). *Then, $G_i \wedge \textsc{SpecCond}(\mathcal{A}_i, X, \{(\textsc{Guard}(g_k), \textsc{Sum}(s_k))\}_{k=1}^{m}) \wedge \neg S_i$ is UNSAT.*

Example 3. Let $cond = true \wedge \varphi \wedge \mu_1 \wedge \mu_2 \wedge (r < 91)$, where $true$ is the guard of $\mathtt{A}'_1$, φ is $C \wedge D$ from Example 1, μ_1 and μ_2 are as defined in Example 2, and $(r < 91)$ is the negation of the summary of $\mathtt{A}'_1$. A possible sequence of state/transition interpolants for $cond$ is $g_0, s_0, g_1, s_1, g_2, s_2, g_3$, where $g_1 = (r < 91 \Rightarrow (c_6 \wedge c_7 \wedge c_{8a}))$, $s_1 = ((c_6 \wedge c_7) \Rightarrow p_2 \geq 91)$, $g_2 = (r < 91 \Rightarrow (c_7 \wedge c_{8a} \wedge p_2 \geq 91))$, and $s_2 = ((c_7 \wedge c_{8a}) \Rightarrow r \geq 91)$. Hence, GUARD$(g_1) = \exists r \cdot r < 91$ (since all c_u, where node u is reachable from node 6, are set to true), SUM$(s_1) = r \geq 91$ (since r is the return variable of `mc91`), GUARD$(g_2) = p \geq 91$, and SUM$(s_2) = r \geq 91$.

REFINEARG uses (GUARD(g_k), SUM(s_k)) of each edge e_k to strengthen the guard and summary of its justifying ARG $\mathcal{J}(e_k)$. While GUARD(g_k) may have existential quantifiers, it is not a problem for iDAGCOND since existentials can be skolemized. However, its may be a problem for deciding the precondition of COVERARG. In practice, we eliminate existentials using interpolants by observing that for a complete ARG $\mathcal{A}_i$, $\psi_i(\epsilon_i)$ is a quantifier-free safe over-approximation of the guard. Once an ARG $\mathcal{A}_i$ is complete, UPDATEGUARD in Fig. 3 is used to update G_i with its quantifier-free over-approximation. Hence, an expensive quantifier elimination step is avoided.

Soundness and Completeness. By Lemma 1 and Lemma 2, WHALE maintains an invariant that every complete, safe and uncovered ARG $\mathcal{A}_i$ means that its corresponding function satisfies its guard and summary *assuming* that all other functions satisfy the corresponding guards and summaries of all ARGs in the current iARG. Formally, let Y and Z be two sets of triples defined as follows:

$$Y \triangleq \{\{G_j\}\, \boldsymbol{b} = F_{\sigma(j)}\, (\boldsymbol{a})\{S_j\} \mid \mathcal{A}_j \in \mathcal{A}(P) \text{ is uncovered or directly covered}\}$$
$$Z \triangleq \{\{G_i\}\, B_{F_{\sigma(i)}}\, \{S_i\} \mid \mathcal{A}_i \in \mathcal{A}(P) \text{ is safe, complete, and uncovered}\}$$

WHALE maintains the invariant $Y \vdash Z$. Furthermore, if the algorithm terminates, every uncovered ARG is safe and complete, and every directly covered ARG is justified by an uncovered one. This satisfies the premise of Hoare's (generalized) proof rule for mutual recursion and establishes soundness of WHALE.

WHALE is complete for Boolean programs, under the restriction that the three main operations are scheduled fairly (specifically, COVERARG is applied infinitely often). The key is that WHALE only uses interpolants over program variables in a current scope. For Boolean programs, this bounds the number of available interpolants. Therefore, all incomplete ARGs are eventually covered.

Theorem 1. WHALE *is sound. Under fair scheduling, it is also complete for Boolean programs.*

6 Implementation and Evaluation

We have built a prototype implementation of WHALE using the LLVM compiler infrastructure [23] as a front-end. For satisfiability checking and interpolant generation, we use the MATHSAT4 SMT solver [5]. The implementation and examples reported here are available at [1].

	WHALE			WOLVERINE 0.5	BLAST 2.5			
Program	**#ARGs**	**#Refine**	**Time**	**Time**	**Time (B1)**	**Time (B2)**	**#Preds (B1)**	**#Preds (B2)**
ddd1.c	5	3	**0.43**	4.01	4.64	1.71	15	8
ddd2.c	5	3	**0.59**	5.71	5.29	2.65	16	10
ddd3.c	6	5	**20.19**	30.56	48	20.32	25	16
ddd1err.c	5	1	**0.16**	3.82	0.42	1.00	25	8
ddd2err.c	5	1	**0.28**	5.72	0.44	0.96	5	8
ddd3err.c	5	11	126.4	**17.25**	TO	43.11	TO	37
ddd4err.c	6	1	5.73	**1.76**	24.51	CR	19	CR

Fig. 4. A comparison between WHALE, BLAST, and WOLVERINE. Time is in seconds.

Our implementation of WHALE is a particular heuristic determinization of the three operations described in Sec. 5: A FIFO queue is used to schedule the processing of ARGs. Initially, the queue contains only the main ARG $\mathcal{A}_1$. When an ARG is picked up from the queue, we first try to cover it with another ARG, using COVERARG. In case it is still uncovered, we apply UPDATEARG and REFINEARG until they are no longer applicable, or until REFINEARG returns a counterexample. Every ARG created by UPDATEARG or modified by RESET is added to the processing queue. Furthermore, we use several optimizations not reported here. In particular, we merge ARGs of same the function. The figures reported in this section are for the number of combined ARGs and do not represent the number of function calls considered by the analysis.

Our goal in evaluating WHALE is two-fold: (1) to compare effectiveness of our interpolation-based approach against traditional predicate abstraction techniques, and (2) to compare our inter-procedural analysis against intra-procedural interpolation-based algorithms. For (1), we compared WHALE with BLAST [4]. For (2), we compared WHALE with WOLVERINE [22], a recent software model checker that implements IMPACT algorithm [27] (it inlines functions and, thus, does not handle recursion).

For both evaluations, we used non-recursive low-level C programs written for the pacemaker grand challenge[4]. Pacemakers are devices implanted in a human's body to monitor heart rate and send electrical signals (paces) to the heart when required. We wrote test harnesses to simulate the pacemaker's interaction with the heart on one of the most complex pacemaker operation modes (DDD). The major actions of a pacemaker are sensing and pacing. Periodically, a pacemaker suspends its sensing operation and then turns it back on. The properties we checked involved verifying correct sequences of toggling sensing operations, e.g., that sensing is not suspended for more than two time steps, where we measured time steps by the number of interrupts the pacemaker receives.

Fig. 4 summarizes the results of our experiments. BLAST was run in two configurations, B1 and B2[5]. WOLVERINE was run in its default (optimal) configuration. For WHALE, we show the number of ARGs created and the number

[4] Detailed information on the pacemaker challenge is available at `http://www.cas.mcmaster.ca/wiki/index.php/Pacemaker`.

[5] B1 is `-dfs -craig 2 -predH 0` and B2 is `-msvc -nofp -dfs -tproj -cldepth 1 -predH 6 -scope -nolattice`.

of calls to REFINEARG for each program. For BLAST, we show the number of predicates needed to prove or refute the property in question. 'CR' and 'TO' denote a crash and an execution taking longer than 180s, respectively. The programs named `ddd`i`.c` are safe; `ddd`i`err.c` have errors. While all programs are small (~300 LOC), their control structure is relatively complex.

For example, Fig. 4 shows that WHALE created five ARGs while processing `ddd3.c`, called REFINEARG three times and proved the program's correctness in 0.59 seconds. BLAST's configuration B1 tool 5.29 seconds and used 16 predicates, whereas B2 took 2.65 seconds and used 10 predicates. WOLVERINE's performance was comparable to B1, verifying the program in 5.71 seconds.

For most properties and programs, we observe that WHALE outperforms WOLVERINE and BLAST (in both configurations). Note that neither of the used BLAST configurations could handle the entire set of programs without crashing or timing out. `ddd3err.c` contains a deep error, and to find it, WHALE spends a considerable amount of time in SMT solver calls, refining and finding counterexamples to a summary, until the under-approximation leading to the error state is found. For this particular example, we believe WOLVERINE's dominance is an artifact of its search strategy. In the future, we want to experiment with heuristics for picking initial under-approximations and heuristics for refining them, in order to achieve faster convergence.

7 Related Work

The use of interpolants in verification was introduced in [25] in the context of SAT-based bounded model checking (BMC). There, McMillan used interpolation to over-approximate the set of states reachable at depth k in the model, using refutation proofs of length k BMC queries. The process continues until a counterexample is found or a fixed point is reached. At a high level, our summarization technique is similar, as we use interpolants to over-approximate the reachable states of a function by taking finite paths through it. In the context of predicate abstraction, interpolation was used as a method for deriving predicates from spurious counter-examples [18]. Interpolation was also used in [21] to approximate a program's transition relation, leading to more efficient but less precise predicate abstraction queries.

As described earlier, WHALE avoids the expensive step of computing abstractions, necessary in CEGAR-based software model checking tools (e.g., BLAST [17], SLAM [2], and YASM [15]). For inter-procedural verification, approaches like SLAM implement a BDD-based Sharir-Pnueli-style analysis [28] for Boolean programs. It would be interesting to compare it with our SMT-based approach.

McMillan [27] proposes an intra-procedural interpolation-based software model checking algorithm, IMPACT, that computes interpolants from infeasible paths to an error location. WHALE can be viewed as an extension of IMPACT to the inter-procedural case. In fact, our notion of ARG covering is analogous to McMillan's vertex covering lifted to the ARG level. While IMPACT unrolls loops until all vertices are covered or fully expanded (thus, an invariant is found), WHALE unrolls recursive calls until all ARGs are covered or fully expanded (completed). One advantage of WHALE is that it encodes all intra-procedural paths by a single SMT formula. Effectively, this results in delegating intra-procedural covering to the SMT solver.

In [26], interpolants are used as blocking conditions on infeasible symbolic execution paths and as means of computing function summaries. This approach differs from WHALE in that the exploration is not property-driven and thus is more suited for bug finding than verification. Also, handling unbounded loops and recursion requires manual addition of auxiliary variables.

Heizmann et al. [16] propose a procedure that views a program as a nested word automaton. Interpolants or predicate abstraction [12] are used to generalize infeasible paths to error and remove them from the program's automaton until no errors are reachable. In contrast to WHALE, this approach does not produce modular proofs and does not compute function summaries.

SYNERGY [13] and its inter-procedural successor SMASH [11] start with an approximate partitioning of reachable states of a given program. Partition refinement is guided by the weakest precondition computations over infeasible program paths. The main differences between WHALE and [13,11] are: (a) interpolants focus on relevant facts and can force faster convergence than weakest preconditions [18,26]; (b) our use of interpolants does not require an expensive quantifier elimination step employed by SMASH to produce summaries; (c) SMASH [11] does not handle recursion – in fact, our ARG covering technique can be easily adapted to the notion of queries used in [11] to extend it to recursive programs; and finally, (d) SYNERGY and SMASH use concrete test cases to guide their choice of program paths to explore. Compared to WHALE, this makes them better suited for bug finding.

8 Conclusion and Future Work

In this paper, we presented WHALE, an interpolation-based algorithm for inter-procedural verification. WHALE handles (recursive) sequential programs and produces modular safety proofs. Our key insight is the use of Craig interpolants to compute function summaries from under-approximations of functions. We showed that performance of WHALE is comparable, and often better, than state-of-the-art software model checkers from the literature.

This work opens many avenues for future research, both in terms of optimizations and extensions to other program models. For example, due to the range of interpolants that can be generated for a formula, we would like to experiment with different interpolation algorithms to test their effectiveness in this domain. We are also interested in extending WHALE to handle concurrent programs.

References

1. Albarghouthi, A., Gurfinkel, A., Chechik, M.: Whale Homepage, `http://www.cs.toronto.edu/~aws/whale`
2. Ball, T., Podelski, A., Rajamani, S.K.: Boolean and Cartesian Abstraction for Model Checking C Programs. In: Margaria, T., Yi, W. (eds.) TACAS 2001. LNCS, vol. 2031, pp. 268–283. Springer, Heidelberg (2001)

3. Ball, T., Rajamani, S.: The SLAM Toolkit. In: Berry, G., Comon, H., Finkel, A. (eds.) CAV 2001. LNCS, vol. 2102, pp. 260–264. Springer, Heidelberg (2001)
4. Beyer, D., Henzinger, T.A., Jhala, R., Majumdar, R.: The Software Model Checker BLAST. STTT 9(5-6), 505–525 (2007)
5. Bruttomesso, R., Cimatti, A., Franzén, A., Griggio, A., Sebastiani, R.: The MATHSAT 4 SMT Solver. In: Gupta, A., Malik, S. (eds.) CAV 2008. LNCS, vol. 5123, pp. 299–303. Springer, Heidelberg (2008)
6. Cimatti, A., Griggio, A., Sebastiani, R.: Efficient Generation of Craig Interpolants in Satisfiability Modulo Theories. ACM Trans. Comput. Log. 12(1), 7 (2010)
7. Clarke, E., Grumberg, O., Jha, S., Lu, Y., Veith, H.: Counterexample-Guided Abstraction Refinement. In: Emerson, E.A., Sistla, A.P. (eds.) CAV 2000. LNCS, vol. 1855, pp. 154–169. Springer, Heidelberg (2000)
8. Clarke, E., Grumberg, O., Peled, D.: Model Checking. MIT Press (1999)
9. Craig, W.: Three Uses of the Herbrand-Gentzen Theorem in Relating Model Theory and Proof Theory. The Journal of Symbolic Logic 22(3), 269–285 (1957)
10. Cytron, R., Ferrante, J., Rosen, B.K., Wegman, M.N., Zadeck, F.K.: Efficiently Computing Static Single Assignment Form and the Control Dependence Graph. ACM TOPLAS 13(4), 451–490 (1991)
11. Godefroid, P., Nori, A., Rajamani, S., Tetali, S.: Compositional Must Program Analysis: Unleashing the Power of Alternation. In: Proc. of POPL 2010, pp. 43–56 (2010)
12. Graf, S., Saïdi, H.: Construction of Abstract State Graphs with PVS. In: Grumberg, O. (ed.) CAV 1997. LNCS, vol. 1254, pp. 72–83. Springer, Heidelberg (1997)
13. Gulavani, B., Henzinger, T., Kannan, Y., Nori, A., Rajamani, S.: SYNERGY: a New Algorithm for Property Checking. In: Robshaw, M.J.B. (ed.) FSE 2006. LNCS, vol. 4047, pp. 117–127. Springer, Heidelberg (2006)
14. Gurfinkel, A., Chaki, S., Sapra, S.: Efficient Predicate Abstraction of Program Summaries. In: Bobaru, M., Havelund, K., Holzmann, G.J., Joshi, R. (eds.) NFM 2011. LNCS, vol. 6617, pp. 131–145. Springer, Heidelberg (2011)
15. Gurfinkel, A., Wei, O., Chechik, M.: YASM: A Software Model-Checker for Verification and Refutation. In: Ball, T., Jones, R.B. (eds.) CAV 2006. LNCS, vol. 4144, pp. 170–174. Springer, Heidelberg (2006)
16. Heizmann, M., Hoenicke, J., Podelski, A.: Nested Interpolants. In: Proc. of POPL 2010, pp. 471–482 (2010)
17. Henzinger, T., Jhala, R., Majumdar, R., Sutre, G.: Lazy Abstraction. In: Proc. of POPL 2002, pp. 58–70 (2002)
18. Henzinger, T.A., Jhala, R., Majumdar, R., McMillan, K.L.: Abstractions from Proofs. In: Proc. of POPL 2004, pp. 232–244 (2004)
19. Hoare, C.: Procedures and Parameters: An Axiomatic Approach. In: Proc. of Symp. on Semantics of Algorithmic Languages, vol. 188, pp. 102–116 (1971)
20. Hoare, C.: An Axiomatic Basis for Computer Programming. Comm. ACM 12(10), 576–580 (1969)
21. Jhala, R., McMillan, K.L.: Interpolant-Based Transition Relation Approximation. In: Etessami, K., Rajamani, S.K. (eds.) CAV 2005. LNCS, vol. 3576, pp. 39–51. Springer, Heidelberg (2005)
22. Kroening, D., Weissenbacher, G.: Interpolation-Based Software Verification with WOLVERINE. In: Gopalakrishnan, G., Qadeer, S. (eds.) CAV 2011. LNCS, vol. 6806, pp. 573–578. Springer, Heidelberg (2011)
23. Lattner, C., Adve, V.: LLVM: A Compilation Framework for Lifelong Program Analysis & Transformation. In: Proc. of CGP 2004 (March 2004)

24. Manna, Z., McCarthy, J.: Properties of Programs and Partial Function Logic. J. of Machine Intelligence 5 (1970)
25. McMillan, K.L.: Interpolation and SAT-Based Model Checking. In: Hunt Jr., W.A., Somenzi, F. (eds.) CAV 2003. LNCS, vol. 2725, pp. 1–13. Springer, Heidelberg (2003)
26. McMillan, K.L.: Lazy Annotation for Program Testing and Verification. In: Touili, T., Cook, B., Jackson, P. (eds.) CAV 2010. LNCS, vol. 6174, pp. 104–118. Springer, Heidelberg (2010)
27. McMillan, K.L.: Lazy Abstraction with Interpolants. In: Ball, T., Jones, R.B. (eds.) CAV 2006. LNCS, vol. 4144, pp. 123–136. Springer, Heidelberg (2006)
28. Sharir, M., Pnueli, A.: Two Approaches to Interprocedural Data Flow Analysis. In: Program Flow Analysis: Theory and Applications, pp. 189–233. Prentice-Hall (1981)

Synchronizability for Verification of Asynchronously Communicating Systems*

Samik Basu[1], Tevfik Bultan[2], and Meriem Ouederni[3]

[1] Iowa State University
sbasu@iastate.edu
[2] University of California, Santa Barbara
bultan@cs.ucsb.edu
[3] University of Malaga
meriem@lcc.uma.es

Abstract. Message-based communication is an increasingly common interaction mechanism used in concurrent and distributed systems where components interact with each other by sending and receiving messages. It is well-known that verification of systems that use asynchronous message-based communication with unbounded FIFO queues is undecidable even when the component behaviors are expressed using finite state machines. In this paper we show that there is a sub-class of such systems, called synchronizable systems, for which certain reachability properties (over send actions and over states with no pending receives) remain unchanged when asynchronous communication is replaced with synchronous communication. Hence, if a system is synchronizable, then the verification of these reachability properties can be done on the synchronous version of the system and the results hold for the asynchronous case. We present a technique for deciding if a given system is synchronizable. Our results are applicable to a variety of domains including verification and analysis of interactions among processes at the OS level, coordination in service-oriented computing and interactions among distributed programs. In this paper we focus on analysis of channel contracts in the Singularity OS. Our experimental results show that almost all channel contracts in the Singularity OS are synchronizable, and, hence, their properties can be analyzed using synchronous communication semantics.

1 Introduction

The asynchronous message-based communication model has been receiving increasing system support [17,21,2,20] and it is getting increasing attention in a diverse set of areas for handling a variety of issues such as process isolation at the OS level [8], coordination in service-oriented computing [6,27], and interactions in distributed programs [1]. Unfortunately, in general verification problems are

* The authors thank Gwen Salaün for fruitful discussions on the CADP implementation. This work has been partially supported by the US National Science Foundation grants CCF1117708, CCF1116836, CCF0702758, and project TIN2008-05932 funded by the Spanish Ministry of Innovation and Science and FEDER.

V. Kuncak and A. Rybalchenko (Eds.): VMCAI 2012, LNCS 7148, pp. 56–71, 2012.

undecidable for such systems since a set of finite-state machines that communicate with unbounded FIFO message queues can simulate Turing Machines [5]. We present a class of asynchronously communicating systems, called *synchronizable* systems, for which certain reachability properties can be verified automatically, and we show that we can automatically check if an asynchronously communicating system is in this class.

Intuitively, an asynchronously communicating system is synchronizable if executing that system with synchronous communication instead of asynchronous communication preserves its behaviors. We focus on two types of behaviors: 1) the sequences of messages that are sent, and 2) the set of reachable configurations where message queues are empty, i.e., configurations with no pending receives. If a system is synchronizable, then we can check properties about its message sequences or about the reachability of its global configurations with empty message queues, using the synchronous version of the system. Since we are focusing on systems where component behaviors are specified using finite state machines, the synchronous version of the system has a finite state space and its properties can be verified using well-known model checking techniques.

The important question is: *is it possible to check synchronizability automatically*? In this paper we show the following: A system is synchronizable if and only if the behaviors for the synchronous version of the system and the 1-bounded-asynchronous version of the system are equivalent with respect to sent messages and reachable configurations with empty message queues. The 1-bounded-asynchronous version corresponds to the case where all message queues are replaced with queues of size one (hence, if there is an unconsumed message in a message queue any send action to that queue blocks until message is consumed). Since both synchronous and 1-bounded asynchronous versions of a system have finite state space, the equivalence check of their behavior, and therefore, synchronizability check, can be done automatically.

In order to demonstrate the practical value of our results, we have developed a prototype implementation leveraging CADP toolbox [12] and have applied our approach to analyzing channel contracts in Singularity OS [8,16]. A channel contract is a state machine that specifies the allowable ordering of messages exchanged between processes in the Singularity OS. In this paper we show that almost all of the channel contracts in Singularity OS are synchronizable, hence, their reachability properties can be automatically verified.

2 Motivation: Singularity Channel Contracts

Singularity [23] is an experimental operating system developed by Microsoft Research to explore new approaches to OS design in order to improve the dependability of software systems. Process isolation is a chief design principle of the Singularity OS, where processes are not allowed to share memory with each other or the kernel. All inter-process communication occurs via asynchronous message exchange in bidirectional channels. Communication through Singularity channels corresponds to asynchronous communication via FIFO queues. When

```
public contract IoStream {
...
state Start: {
  O? -> {
      OK! -> Open;
      ERR! -> End;
  }
}

state Open: {
  R? -> D! -> Open;
  W? -> Open;
  C? -> End;
}

state End;
...
```

(a)

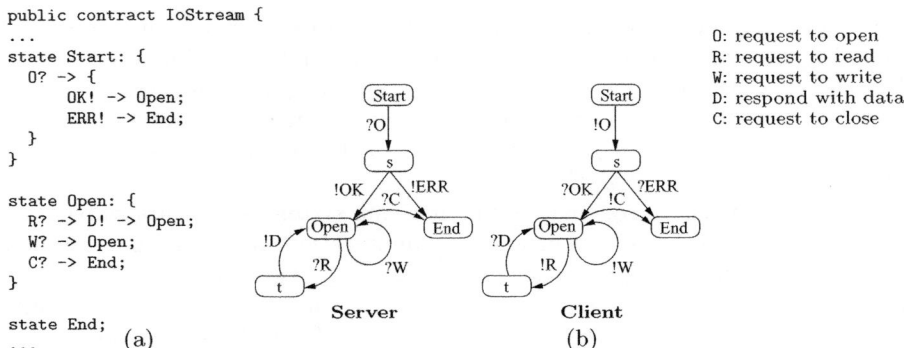

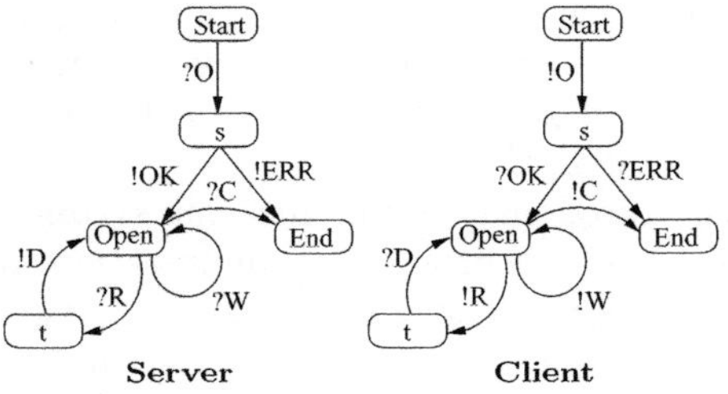

(b)

O: request to open
R: request to read
W: request to write
D: respond with data
C: request to close

Fig. 1. (a) An example channel contract; and (b) corresponding state machines for the Client and the Server

a process sends a message through a channel, the message is appended to a message queue. A message that is at the head of a message queue is removed from the message queue when a receive action is executed by the receiving process at the other end of the channel.

In Singularity, channel contracts (written in an extension of C#, called Sing#) specify the allowable ordering of message exchanges between the processes [8,23]. Figure 1(a) shows a contract governing a channel used by Singularity for communicating between a process (client in this case) and the file server [18]. (The full contract specification also includes the message declarations which are omitted in the figure.) Singularity contracts are written from the perspective of the server, where send actions by the server are appended with `!` to denote communication from the server to the client and receive actions by the server are appended with `?` to denote communication from the client to the server. The contract states that the file server receives a request (`O`) for opening a file and it responds with either `OK` or `ERR`; the destination states are `Open` or `End`. In the `Open` state, the file server can either receive a read request (`R`), a write request (`W`) or a close request (`C`). In the first case, the server responds with the data from the opened file and the destination state of the contract remains `Open`; in the second case, the destination state also remains `Open`; and in the final case, the destination state becomes `End`. The behaviors of the client and the server constructed on the basis of this contract are presented in Figure 1(b). Each local configuration in the client and the server is annotated with the state of the contract; note that there are two temporary/transient states `s` and `t`.

Verification Objectives: Properties of Interest. There are several questions that are of interest in this setting. Does the system obtained from the asynchronously communicating client and server (Figure 1(b)) produces exactly the same behavior (in terms of send actions) as depicted in the channel contract (Figure 1(a))? Does the system conform to some pre-specified desired properties expressed in temporal logic? For instance, a property of interest can be: the `C` (close) send action is eventually followed by a configuration where the client and the server are both at state `End` and their message queues are empty (i.e., there are no pending receives). Another example property can be: every read send action (`R`) is eventually followed by a configuration where the client and the server states are both `Open` and their message queues are empty. These types of properties can be suitably expressed in linear temporal logic.

Verification Challenge. Unfortunately, for finite state processes that communicate asynchronously with unbounded message queues, verification of these types of properties is undecidable in general. Observe that, the system obtained from the asynchronously communicating client and server in Figure 1(b) exhibits behavior with infinite state-space due to existence of potentially unbounded number of `!W` actions from the client before the server consumes via `?W` action.

Our Solution. In this paper, we show that we can automatically check if the asynchronous system under consideration is synchronizable, and, if it is, we can verify the above properties on the synchronized-version of the system using traditional model checking techniques. Verification of properties of asynchronously communicating systems is decidable when the system is synchronizable and we present here the necessary and sufficient condition for synchronizability, which can be efficiently checked using existing equivalence checking techniques that work for systems with finite state-space.

It should be noted that in order to statically determine the amount of memory required for each message buffer, Singularity OS imposes a restriction on channel contracts that bounds the sizes of the message buffers. Such a restriction, therefore, finitizes the behavior of the asynchronous system. Even with such a restriction the results presented in this paper are useful since they allow us to remove the message queues completely during verification. Since the state space of an asynchronously communicating system with bounded queues can be exponential in the size of the queues, our results can be used to avoid state space explosion for such bounded systems. Our experiments show that in fact most of the Singularity channel contracts are synchronizable.

3 Preliminaries

3.1 Behaviors as State Machines

We use finite state machines to describe the behaviors of components or *peers* that asynchronously communicate via messages (sends and receives). The behavior of a system resulting from such communicating peers is described by state machines (with potentially infinite state-space).

Definition 1 (Peer Behavior). *A peer behavior or simply a peer, denoted by* $\mathcal{P}$*, is a state machine* (M, T, s_0, δ) *where* M *is the union of finite input* (M^{in}) *and finite output* (M^{out}) *message sets,* T *is the finite set of states,* $s_0 \in T$ *is the initial state, and* $\delta \subseteq T \times (M \cup \{\epsilon\}) \times T$ *is the transition relation.*

A transition $\tau \in \delta$ *can be one of the following three types: (1) a send-transition of the form* $(t_1, !m_1, t_2)$ *which sends out a message* $m_1 \in M^{out}$*, (2) a receive-transition of the form* $(t_1, ?m_2, t_2)$ *which consumes a message* $m_2 \in M^{in}$*, and (3) an* ϵ*-transition of the form* (t_1, ϵ, t_2)*. We write* $t \xrightarrow{a} t'$ *to denote that* $(t, a, t') \in \delta$*.*

Figures 2(a, b, c) present state machines representing three communicating peers. The start states (s_0, t_0 and r_0) are denoted by arrows with no source state. Each transition is labeled with the action (send or receive) performed when the peer moves from the source state to the destination state of the transition.

We will consider systems that consist of a finite set of peers, $\langle \mathcal{P}_1, \ldots, \mathcal{P}_n \rangle$, where $\mathcal{P}_i = (M_i, T_i, s_{0i}, \delta_i)$ and $M_i = M_i^{\text{in}} \cup M_i^{\text{out}}$, such that $\forall i : M_i^{\text{in}} \cap M_i^{\text{out}} = \emptyset$, $\forall i, j : i \neq j \Rightarrow M_i^{\text{in}} \cap M_j^{\text{in}} = M_i^{\text{out}} \cap M_j^{\text{out}} = \emptyset$.

Definition 2 (System Behavior). *A system behavior or simply a system over a set of peers $\langle \mathcal{P}_1, \ldots, \mathcal{P}_n \rangle$, where $\mathcal{P}_i = (M_i, T_i, s_{0i}, \delta_i)$ and $M_i = M_i^{in} \cup M_i^{out}$, is denoted by a state machine (possibly infinite state) $\mathcal{I} = (M, C, c_0, \Delta)$ where*

1. $M = \cup_i M_i$
2. $C \subseteq \mathcal{Q}_1 \times T_1 \times \mathcal{Q}_2 \times T_2 \ldots \mathcal{Q}_n \times T_n$ *such that* $\forall i \in [1..n] : \mathcal{Q}_i \subseteq (M_i^{in})^*$
3. $c_0 \in C$ *such that* $c_0 = (\epsilon, s_{01}, \epsilon, s_{02} \ldots, \epsilon, s_{0n})$
4. $\Delta \subseteq C \times M \times C$, *and for* $c = (Q_1, t_1, \ldots Q_n, t_n)$ *and* $c' = (Q'_1, t'_1, \ldots Q'_n, t'_n)$
   (a) $c \xrightarrow{!m} c' \in \Delta$ *if* $\exists i, j \in [1..n] : m \in M_i^{out} \cap M_j^{in}$,
   (i) $t_i \xrightarrow{!m} t'_i \in \delta_i$, *(ii)* $Q'_j = Q_j m$, *(iii)* $\forall k \in [1..n] : k \neq j \Rightarrow Q_k = Q'_k$ *and (iv)* $\forall k \in [1..n] : k \neq i \Rightarrow t'_k = t_k$
   (b) $c \xrightarrow{?m} c' \in \Delta$ *if* $\exists i \in [1..n] : m \in M_i^{in}$,
   (i) $t_i \xrightarrow{?m} t'_i \in \delta_i$, *(ii)* $Q_i = mQ'_i$, *(iii)* $\forall k \in [1..n] : k \neq i \Rightarrow Q_k = Q'_k$ *and (iv)* $\forall k \in [1..n] : k \neq i \Rightarrow t'_k = t_k$
   (c) $c \xrightarrow{\epsilon} c' \in \Delta$ *if* $\exists i \in [1..n]$: *(i)* $t_i \xrightarrow{\epsilon} t'_i \in \delta_i$, *(ii)* $\forall k \in [1..n] : Q_k = Q'_k$ *and (iii)* $\forall k \in [1..n] : k \neq i \Rightarrow t'_k = t_k$

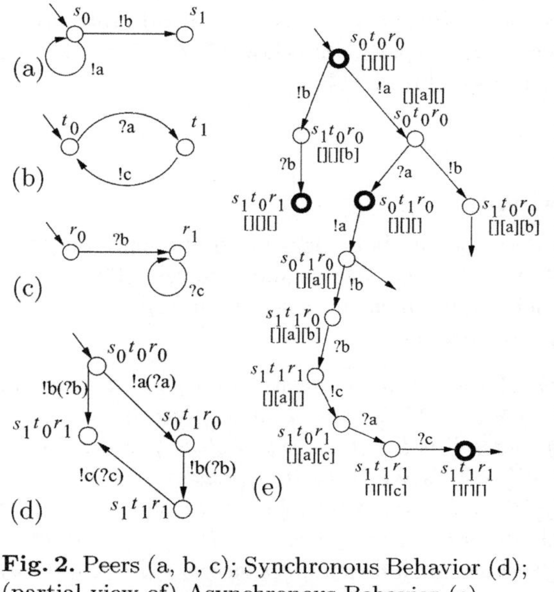

Fig. 2. Peers (a, b, c); Synchronous Behavior (d); (partial view of) Asynchronous Behavior (e)

In the above, Qs describe the message queues associated with each peer in the system. The messages sent to a peer are appended to the tail of its message queue. A peer can perform a receive action if the corresponding message is present at the head of its message queue. After the receive action is performed, the received message is removed from the head of the message queue.

Figure 2(e) presents a snapshot of the behavior of the system realized from the asynchronous composition of the peers shown in Figures 2(a, b, c). Each state is annotated with the local states of the peers and the contents of their message queues. For instance, the state

$s_1t_0r_0$ has the associated message queues $[][][b]$, denoting that the message queue of the third peer has a pending receive b and the message queues of the other peers are empty.

3.2 Verification Objective

We refer to the states where all peers have empty message queues as the *synchronized states* (shown in bold in Figure 2(e)). Note that, start state of the system is a synchronized state (e.g., $s_0t_0r_0$ $[][][]$ in Figure 2(e)). Verification of the above systems may involve checking for properties describing certain desired temporal ordering of send actions and reachability of synchronized states. In this paper, we focus on the following types of global properties:

1. reachability of a synchronized state via a sequence of send actions.
2. existence of a sequence of send actions.

Note that, it is reasonable to ignore the ordering of the receive actions as they are performed *locally* by the peers by consuming messages from their respective message queues. Similarly, it is reasonable to ignore the temporal ordering of states that are not synchronized since these states can be viewed as "transient" states where one or more peers are yet to consume messages and, therefore, have not reacted to the messages sent to them.

4 Synchronizability

We define the notion of send- and synchronized-traces described over the sequence of send actions and synchronized states. Formally,

Definition 3 (Send- & Synchronized-Trace). *A* ***send-trace*** *of a system* $\mathcal{I} = (M, C, c_0, \Delta)$ *is a sequence of send actions starting from* c_0. *This is obtained by projecting a trace of* $\mathcal{I}$ *starting from* c_0 *to the send actions (by ignoring labels of all the other transitions).*

A ***synchronized-trace*** *of a system, on the other hand, corresponds to a send-trace that starts from* c_0 *and ends in a synchronized state. A synchronized-trace also includes the start state and the synchronized state reached at the end of the trace (in addition to the sequence of send actions).*

The union of the set of send-traces and the set of synchronized-traces of $\mathcal{I}$ *is denoted by* $\mathcal{L}(\mathcal{I})$.

$(s_0t_0r_0[][][])aabc(s_1t_1r_1[][][])$ is a synchronized-trace of the system in Figure 2(e). We will denote such a trace as follows: $s_0t_0r_0 \overset{aabc}{\rightsquigarrow} s_1t_1r_1$ (as the message queues of the peers in synchronized states are empty, we omit them). On the other hand, the send-traces of the system include b, a, aa, aab, $aabc$, $aabc\ldots$, etc. We will denote the send-trace as follows $\cdot \overset{a}{\Longrightarrow} \cdot \overset{a}{\Longrightarrow} \cdot \overset{b}{\Longrightarrow} \cdot \overset{c}{\Longrightarrow} \ldots$, where $\overset{m}{\Longrightarrow}$ denotes a transition-sequence containing zero or more receive actions and a single send action $!m$.

Next, we describe synchronizability in terms of a system and its synchronous variant. In the synchronous variant, all peers communicate synchronously, that is, all peers *immediately* consume the messages sent to them.

Definition 4 (Synchronous System Behavior). *The synchronous system behavior containing a set of peers* $\langle \mathcal{P}_1, \ldots, \mathcal{P}_n \rangle$*, where* $\mathcal{P}_i = (M_i, T_i, s_{0i}, \delta_i)$ *and* $M_i = M_i^{in} \cup M_i^{out}$*, is denoted by a state machine* $\mathcal{I}_0 = (M, C, c_0, \Delta)$ *where*

1. $M = \cup_i M_i$ *2.* $C \subseteq T_1 \times T_2 \ldots \times T_n$
3. $c_0 \in C$ *such that* $c_0 = (s_{01}, s_{02} \ldots, s_{0n})$
4. $\Delta \subseteq C \times M \times C$ *and for* $c = (t_1, t_2, \ldots, t_n)$ *and* $c' = (t'_1, t'_2, \ldots, t'_n)$

1. $c \xrightarrow{!m} c' \in \Delta$ *if* $\exists i, j \in [1..n] : m \in M_i^{out} \cap M_j^{in}$,
(i) $t_i \xrightarrow{!m} t'_i \in \delta_i$, *(ii)* $t_j \xrightarrow{?m} t'_j \in \delta_j$, *(iii)* $\forall k \in [1..n] : k \neq i \wedge k \neq j \Rightarrow t'_k = t_k$
2. $c \xrightarrow{\epsilon} c' \in \Delta$ *if* $\exists i \in [1..n]$,
(i) $t_i \xrightarrow{\epsilon} t'_i \in \delta_i$, *(ii)* $\forall k \in [1..n] : k \neq i \Rightarrow t'_k = t_k$

Figure 2(d) presents the behavior of the system realized from synchronous composition of peers in Figure 2(a, b, c). Each transition is annotated with the send action; the corresponding receive action which happens synchronously is shown in parenthesis. Note that, in synchronous behavior, there is no pending receives and system states are represented by the tuples of the participating peers' local states. Finally, synchronizability is formally defined as:

Definition 5 (Trace Synchronizability). *The system* $\mathcal{I}$ *over a set of peers* $\langle \mathcal{P}_1, \ldots, \mathcal{P}_n \rangle$ *is said to be trace synchronizable if and only if* $\mathcal{L}(\mathcal{I}) = \mathcal{L}(\mathcal{I}_0)$*, where* $\mathcal{I}_0$ *is the synchronous system over the same set of peers.*

Verification of properties described in Section 3.2 is decidable for trace synchronizable systems, where such verification can be performed using synchronous version of the system (which does not have message queues and therefore has a finite state-space) using standard model checking techniques. The system in Figure 2(e) is not trace synchronizable as it contains a synchronized trace $s_0 t_0 r_0 \overset{aabc}{\rightsquigarrow} s_1 t_1 r_1$ which is not present in its synchronous variant in Figure 2(d).

5 Deciding Trace Synchronizability

We will show that the necessary and sufficient condition for synchronizability involves the equivalence between the synchronous system behavior and the system behavior using bounded asynchronous communication with message queues of size 1 for each participating peer.

Definition 6 (k-bounded System). *For any* $k \geq 1$*, a k-bounded system (denoted by* $\mathcal{I}_k$*) is a system where the length of message queue for any peer is at most k. The description of k-bounded system behavior is, therefore, realized by augmenting condition 4(a) in Definition 2 to include the condition* $|Q_j| < k$*, where* $|Q_j|$ *denotes the number of pending receives in the queue for peer j.*

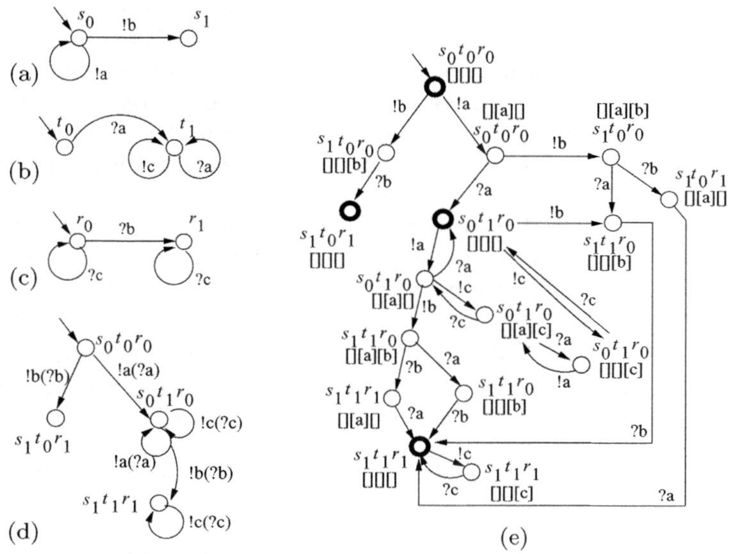

Fig. 3. Peers (a, b, c); Synchronous (d); 1-bounded Asynchronous Behavior (e)

Figure 3(e) shows the 1-bounded system behavior obtained from asynchronously communicating peers in Figures 3(a, b, c). Note that the peer behavior in Figure 3(a) is identical to that in Figure 2(a), while the two peers in Figures 3(b, c) are modified versions of the ones presented in Figures 2(b, c).

Recall that, the synchronous system behavior is denoted by $\mathcal{I}_0$ (Definition 4). In the rest of the section, we will assume that $\mathcal{I}$ and $\mathcal{I}_k$ ($\forall k$) are described over the same set of peers.

Proposition 1. $\forall k \geq 0 : [\mathcal{L}(\mathcal{I}_k) \subseteq \mathcal{L}(\mathcal{I}_{k+1})]$.

Proof. For any $k \geq 0$, every move of $\mathcal{I}_k$ can be matched by $\mathcal{I}_{k+1}$ by avoiding the send actions that make the receiving peers' pending receives to exceed k. □

Theorem 1. $\mathcal{L}(\mathcal{I}_0) = \mathcal{L}(\mathcal{I}_1) \Rightarrow \forall k \geq 0 : \mathcal{L}(\mathcal{I}_k) = \mathcal{L}(\mathcal{I}_{k+1})$.

We prove the theorem by contradiction. We assume that there exists $k > 1$ such that $\mathcal{L}(\mathcal{I}_k) \neq \mathcal{L}(\mathcal{I}_1)$. Therefore, there exists a finite trace (either a send-trace or a synchronized-trace) in $\mathcal{I}_k$ (as $\mathcal{L}(\mathcal{I}_1) \subseteq \mathcal{L}(\mathcal{I}_k)$, by Proposition 1) distinguishing $\mathcal{I}_k$ from $\mathcal{I}_1$. The following Lemmas 1 and 2 contradict the above assumption.

Lemma 1. $\mathcal{L}(\mathcal{I}_0) = \mathcal{L}(\mathcal{I}_1) \Rightarrow$ *all send-traces in* $\mathcal{I}_k$ *for all* $k > 1$ *are present in* $\mathcal{I}_0$ *and* $\mathcal{I}_1$.

Proof. This lemma follows directly from the result in [3], where we have proved that $\mathcal{I}_0$ and $\mathcal{I}_1$ have the same set of send-traces if and only if the sets of send-traces in $\mathcal{I}_0$ and $\mathcal{I}$ are identical. □

Before proceeding with the proof of Lemma 2, we informally describe the concepts that will be used in the proof. A synchronized-trace is realized by a system that consists of a set of peers, if each peer follows a path in its behavioral state machine that is consistent with the synchronized-trace and reaches a state where its messages queue is empty. In such a path, we will consider the sequence of send and receive actions leading to the local state of the peer with empty message queue. We refer to such a sequence when we say that a peer moves along a trace to realize the synchronized-trace. Similarly, we say that a set of peers move along a trace to realize a synchronized-trace to refer to the sequence of send and receive actions performed by the peers to reach their respective local states describing the synchronized-state of the system. For instance, in Figure 3(e), consider the synchronized trace $s_0t_0r_0 \overset{aabc}{\rightsquigarrow} s_1t_1r_1$. We say that the synchronized trace is realized when the first peer (Figure 3(a)) moves along the trace $(!a!a!b)s_1$; while the other peers (Figures 3(b, c)) move along the traces $(?a?a?b)t_1r_1$ or $(?a?b?a)t_1r_1$.

Lemma 2. *$\mathcal{L}(\mathcal{I}_0) = \mathcal{L}(\mathcal{I}_1) \Rightarrow$ all synchronized-traces in $\mathcal{I}_k$ for all $k > 1$ are present in $\mathcal{I}_0$ and $\mathcal{I}_1$.*

Proof. Let $t_0^k \overset{\omega}{\rightsquigarrow} t_1^k \ldots$ be a synchronized-trace belonging to $\mathcal{I}_k$ where t_0^k is the start state, t_1^k is a synchronized state and ω is a sequence of send actions.

$\mathcal{I}_0$ and $\mathcal{I}_1$ contain the send-trace ω as they contain all send-traces present in $\mathcal{I}_k$, for any $k > 1$ (Lemma 1). As $\mathcal{I}_0$ reaches one or more synchronized states via the send-trace ω, $\mathcal{I}_1$ also reaches the same set of synchronized states after ω (as $\mathcal{L}(\mathcal{I}_0) = \mathcal{L}(\mathcal{I}_1)$). We denote this set of states by T^{01}. To prove by contradiction, we assume that t_1^k is different from all the synchronized states in T^{01}. We will contradict this assumption by considering differences between t_1^k and the states in T^{01} in terms of the local states of the peers.

Consider that in $\mathcal{I}_k$, there exists a peer $\mathcal{P}_1$ that moves along a trace A_k and other peers move along a trace B_k to realize the synchronized-trace $t_0^k \overset{\omega}{\rightsquigarrow} t_1^k$. Further, consider that in $\mathcal{I}_1$, the peer $\mathcal{P}_1$ moves along the trace A_1 ($\neq A_k$) and the other peers move along a trace B_1 to realize a synchronized-trace with ω as the sequence of send actions. Let the synchronized state reached in $\mathcal{I}_1$ in this case be $t_1^{01} \in T^{01}$. Let B_1 and B_k eventually lead to identical local states for all peers other than $\mathcal{P}_1$. In short, we are considering the case where t_1^{01} and t_1^k differ only in terms of the states of $\mathcal{P}_1$. Figure 4 illustrates this situation.

We analyze the condition under which, in $\mathcal{I}_1$, the peer $\mathcal{P}_1$ cannot move along A_k when other peers are moving along B_k to realize the send-trace ω. The condition is that in A_k, the peer $\mathcal{P}_1$ has a full message queue (containing a pending receive a) and is trying to send a message m to some other peer; while in B_k, the other peers cannot move without sending a message b to $\mathcal{P}_1$; and $\ldots abm \ldots$ is present in ω. In other words, the peers cannot move without sending each other messages in a specific order and such sending is not possible as the buffer of $\mathcal{P}_1$ in $\mathcal{I}_1$ in the path A_k is full. That is,

- in A_k, $\mathcal{P}_1$ sends $!m$ when it has some pending receive action (say, a);
- in B_k, some peer sends $!b$ to $\mathcal{P}_1$; and
- $\ldots abm \ldots$ is present in ω.

For simplicity, we consider the above scenario with the following assumptions:

Assumption 1: $\mathcal{P}_1$'s message queue contains two pending receives at most once when it moves along the trace A_k in $\mathcal{I}_k$ to realize the given synchronized-trace, and
Assumption 2: t_1^k differs from t_1^{01} in terms of local states of one peer ($\mathcal{P}_1$).

We will prove that the scenario is not possible with the above assumptions and later proceed to prove the same without the assumptions.

As $\mathcal{L}(\mathcal{I}_0) = \mathcal{L}(\mathcal{I}_1)$, the peer $\mathcal{P}_1$ in $\mathcal{I}_0$ moves along a trace A_0 and the other peers move along a trace B_0 to reach t_1^{01} via $\omega = \ldots abm \ldots$. Note that, A_0 and A_1 end in identical local states for the peer $\mathcal{P}_1$, while B_0, B_1 and B_k end in identical local states for peers other than $\mathcal{P}_1$ according to Assumption 2 above (see Figure 4).

Furthermore, the peers moving along B_0 immediately consume any message sent to them (all sends are immediately received in $\mathcal{I}_0$). This implies that B_0 contains the subsequence $!a!b?m$. Therefore, in $\mathcal{I}_1$, the peer $\mathcal{P}_1$ can move along the trace A_k and other peers can move along B_0 to realize a send sequence $\ldots amb \ldots$ and reach the synchronized state t_1^k (see Figure 4). As $\mathcal{L}(\mathcal{I}_1) = \mathcal{L}(\mathcal{I}_0)$, this synchronized-trace is also present in $\mathcal{I}_0$. In other words, in $\mathcal{I}_0$, $\mathcal{P}_1$ can move along a trace A'_0 and other peers can move along a trace B'_0 such that the send sequence $\ldots amb \ldots$ is realized and the synchronized state t_1^k is reached. Therefore, the destination states for $\mathcal{P}_1$ along the traces A'_0 and A_k are identical and the destination states for the peers other than $\mathcal{P}_1$ along the traces B'_0, B_0, B_1 and B_k are identical (see Figure 4). Furthermore, there exists a subsequence $?a!m?b$ in A'_0 as all sends are immediately consumed by $\mathcal{P}_1$ in $\mathcal{I}_0$.

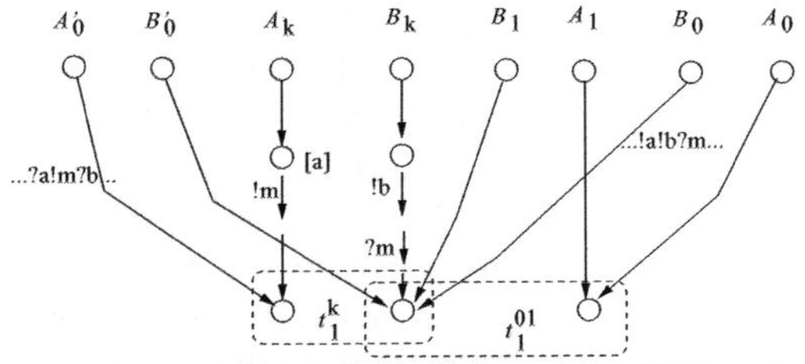

$\mathcal{P}_1$ Path	Others Path	Send-trace	System
A_k	B_k	$\ldots abm \ldots$	$\mathcal{I}_k$
A_1	B_1	$\ldots abm \ldots$	$\mathcal{I}_1$
A_0	B_0	$\ldots abm \ldots$	$\mathcal{I}_0$
A_k	B_0	$\ldots amb \ldots$	$\mathcal{I}_1$
A'_0	B'_0	$\ldots amb \ldots$	$\mathcal{I}_0$
A'_0	B_0	$\ldots abm \ldots$	$\mathcal{I}_1$

Fig. 4. Proof Schema 1 for Lemma 2

Proceeding further, in $\mathcal{I}_1$, the peer $\mathcal{P}_1$ can move along the trace A'_0 and the other peers can move along the trace B_0 to realize the send sequence $\omega = \ldots abm \ldots$ and reach the destination synchronized state t_1^k (see Figure 4). This is because, in $\mathcal{I}_1$, each peer has a message queue of size 1. This contradicts the assumption that $\mathcal{I}_k$ can reach a synchronized state t_1^k via ω that is not reachable by $\mathcal{I}_1$ via the same send sequence.

Addressing Assumption 1. Recall the two assumptions made for simplifying the arguments of the proof. The arguments hold even when the first assumption is not considered. This is because, if $\mathcal{P}_1$ considers $n > 2$ pending receives in A_k, then we can construct a path for $\mathcal{I}_1$ where $\mathcal{P}_1$ consumes $n-1$ pending receives before the send action $!m$ and reaches the same state as in trace A_k.

Similarly, if $\mathcal{P}_1$ considers $n > 2$ pending receives multiple times along the trace A_k before sending m_0, m_1, etc., we can construct a trace for $\mathcal{P}_1$ in $\mathcal{I}_1$, where $\mathcal{P}_1$ consumes $n-1$ pending receives before performing the send actions $!m_0, !m_1$, etc. and reaches the same destination state as in A_k.

Addressing Assumption 2. Next, we discard the second assumption that t_1^k differ from $t_1^{01} (\in T^{01})$ due to only the local states of $\mathcal{P}_1$. Let the difference between t_1^k and t_1^{01} be due to two peers $\mathcal{P}_1$ and $\mathcal{P}_2$. In $\mathcal{I}_k$, $\mathcal{P}_1$ moves along the trace A_{k1}, $\mathcal{P}_2$ moves along the trace A_{k2}, and peers other than $\mathcal{P}_1$ and $\mathcal{P}_2$ move along the trace B_k. On the other hand, in $\mathcal{I}_1$, $\mathcal{P}_1$ moves along A_1 ($\neq A_{k1}$), $\mathcal{P}_2$ moves along A_2 ($\neq A_{k2}$) and other peers move along B_1 (destination states of these peers in B_1 and B_k are identical). Figure 5 illustrates this scenario.

$\mathcal{I}_k$ has a synchronized-trace with send sequence ω where $\mathcal{P}_1$ moves along A_{k1}, $\mathcal{P}_2$ moves along A_2 and the rest of the peers move along B_1. This synchronized-trace is possible because the size of the message queues of peers in $\mathcal{I}_k$ is greater than those in $\mathcal{I}_1$. Therefore, $\mathcal{I}_k$ and $\mathcal{I}_1$ reach two different synchronized states via send sequence ω, where the destination states differ only in terms of local states of $\mathcal{P}_1$ (see Figure 5). We have already proved that this is not possible. Therefore, there exists a path (with send sequence ω) in $\mathcal{I}_1$ such that $\mathcal{P}_1$ moves along A'_1, $\mathcal{P}_2$ moves along A'_2 and other peers move along B'_1, where the destination states in A'_1 and A_{k1} are identical, the destination states in A'_2 and A_2 are identical, and the destination states in B'_1 and B_1 are identical (see Figure 5).

Next, consider this newly constructed synchronized-trace for $\mathcal{I}_1$ and the original synchronized-trace for $\mathcal{I}_k$ ($\mathcal{P}_1$ moves along A_{k1}, $\mathcal{P}_2$ moves along A_{k_2} and other peers move along B_k). The synchronized states reached via the same send sequence (ω) differ only in terms of local states of $\mathcal{P}_2$. We have proved this is not possible. Therefore, there exists a synchronized-trace (with send sequence ω) in $\mathcal{I}_1$ such that $\mathcal{P}_1$ moves along A''_1, $\mathcal{P}_2$ moves along A''_2 and others move along B''_1 where the destination states of A''_1 and A_{k1} are identical, the destination states of A''_2 and A_{k2} are identical, and the destination states of B''_1 and B_1 are identical. This contradicts our assumption.

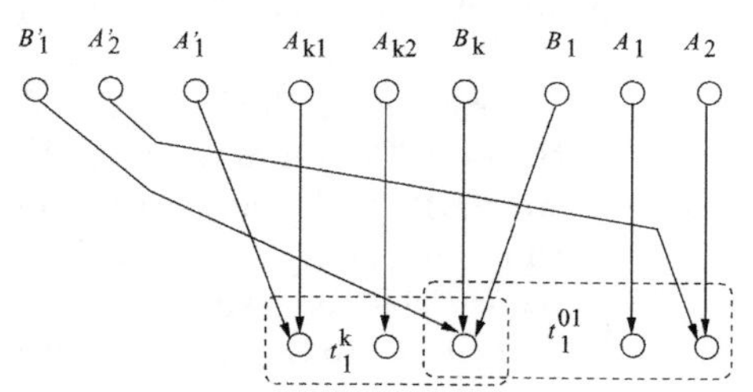

$\mathcal{P}_1$ Path	$\mathcal{P}_2$ Path	Others Path	Send-trace	System
A_{k1}	A_{k2}	B_k	ω	$\mathcal{I}_k$
A_1	A_2	B_1	ω	$\mathcal{I}_1$
A_{k1}	A_2	B_1	ω	$\mathcal{I}_k$
A'_1	A'_2	B'_1	ω	$\mathcal{I}_1$

Fig. 5. Proof Schema 2 for Lemma 2

The above arguments also hold when differences in synchronized states are due to local states of more than two peers participating in the system. □

The proof for Theorem 1 directly follows from Lemmas 1 and 2.

Theorem 2. *$\mathcal{L}(\mathcal{I}_0) = \mathcal{L}(\mathcal{I}_1)$ if and only if $\mathcal{I}$ is trace synchronizable.*

Proof. Follows from Theorem 1, Definition 3 and Proposition 1. □

The system in Figure 2(e) is not synchronizable as its 1-bounded asynchronous version is not trace equivalent to its synchronous counterpart (Figure 2(d)). The 1-bounded asynchronous system contains traces (e.g., send trace $\stackrel{a}{\Longrightarrow}\stackrel{a}{\Longrightarrow}$ and synchronized trace $s_0t_0r_0 \stackrel{aabc}{\rightsquigarrow} s_1t_1r_1$) which are absent in the synchronous version. Figure 3(d) and (e) shows the synchronous and 1-bounded asynchronous system realized from the peers in Figures 3(a, b, c). These two systems are trace equivalent and as such the corresponding asynchronous system is trace synchronizable.

Note that, we have proved that synchronizability can be decided by checking the equivalence between two finite-state systems, $\mathcal{I}_0$ and $\mathcal{I}_1$. This can be performed automatically. Once an asynchronous system (with possibly infinite state-state) has been classified as trace synchronizable, we can verify reachability properties over its send actions and synchronized states using the synchronous variant of the system.

6 Experiments with Singularity Channel Contracts

We automated our approach for analyzing Singularity channel contracts by implementing a translator which takes a Singularity channel contract specification as input and generates two LOTOS specifications that correspond to the synchronous and 1-bounded-asynchronous versions of the input contract. Then we use the CADP toolbox [12] to check the equivalence of the synchronous and 1-bounded-asynchronous versions.

Synchronous Model. Given a Singularity channel contract, the state machine of the participating peers (a client and a server) is obtained as follows. For every transition between a state s to a state t, in the contract with label `m!`, a send transition labeled with `m` is added to the state machine of server peer from its local state corresponding to s to its local state corresponding to t; a receive action `m` is added to the state machine of client peer from its local state corresponding to s to its local state corresponding to t. The dual strategy is used for actions of the form `m?` in the contract (the server peer receives `m` sent by the client peer).

The state machines for the peers are encoded in LOTOS using process constructs which allows sequential (ordering), branching (choice) and loop specifications. The synchronous system is constructed from the peer specifications in LOTOS by using the composition operator in LOTOS, which specifies synchronous communication between processes over pre-specified channels.

Asynchronous Model. The LOTOS language does not support asynchronous communication directly. In order to generate the 1-bounded asynchronous model in

LOTOS we create a bounded FIFO queue process (which can store at most one message) for each message queue. The FIFO queue process representing the message queue of a peer $\mathcal{P}$ synchronously receives messages from peers sending messages to $\mathcal{P}$, and it synchronously sends these messages to $\mathcal{P}$. The messages sent from the FIFO queue process of peer $\mathcal{P}$ are essentially receive actions by $\mathcal{P}$ which are not considered in send- and synchronized-traces. These actions are, therefore, hidden during the composition process and they become internal transitions (τ-transitions in LOTOS).

Equivalence Checking. After generating the LOTOS specifications for the synchronous and 1-bounded asynchronous models, we generate the two corresponding LTSs using the state space generation tools in the CADP toolbox. During the equivalence check the only visible events are the message send events from any peer since the receive events are hidden. To optimize the equivalence check we reduce the resulting LTS modulo the hidden actions (using the τ-confluence relation). This reduces the transition system without modifying the send- and synchronized-traces of the system. Then we check the equivalence of the reduced LTSs for the synchronous and 1-bounded asynchronous systems. If two LTSs are equivalent, the system (i.e, the system obtained from the peers participating in the given Singularity contract) is synchronizable; otherwise it is not.

The construction of LTSs from LOTOS specifications, the reduction of the LTSs and their equivalence checking are performed automatically using SVL scripts [11] and by using the Reductor and the Bisimulator tools that are part of the CADP toolbox [12].

We applied our approach to 86 channel contracts that are available in the Singularity code base. The size of the synchronous systems obtained from the projected peers of these contracts ranges between 2 to 23 states and 1 to 60 transitions. The size of the 1-bounded asynchronous variant, on the other hand, ranges between 3 to 99 states and 2 to 136 transitions. The time taken to reduce the asynchronous model is on an average 10 secs and the equivalence checking time is on an average 3 secs. We have found that all channel contracts in the Singularity code base are synchronizable except two. The two contracts that fail the synchronizability test are faulty (allow deadlocks, as was previously reported and confirmed by the Singularity developers [24]). Hence, if we ignore these two faulty contracts, *all* channel contracts in the Singularity code base are synchronizable, i.e., their properties concerning the sequence of send actions and reachability of synchronized states can be verified automatically.

7 Related Work

The synchronizability problem was first proposed in [9,10] in the context of analyzing interactions among web services. Synchronizability definition in these papers only considered sequence of send actions, i.e., send-traces. The synchronizability conditions given in [9,10] are sufficient but not necessary conditions. One of the synchronizability conditions used in [9,10] is called autonomous condition, and this condition prevents a process from having a send and a receive transition from the same state. This condition sometimes fails for protocols that are synchronizable. In [3] it is argued that synchronizability analysis can be used for checking the conformance of a set of web services to a given global interaction protocol (called a choreography specification in the web services domain). The synchronizability analysis presented in [3] provides a necessary and sufficient condition for synchronizability when only send-traces are considered. Recent results reported in [4] also build on the results from [3] to show the decidability of the choreography realizability problem.

The synchronizability definitions used in these earlier papers do not correspond to the synchronizability definition we use in this paper since they do not take into account synchronized state reachability. In particular, the main result presented in [3] corresponds to the Lemma 1 from this paper. In this paper we present a non-trivial and important extension to this earlier result and introduce the synchronized-state reachability by proving Lemma 2. This extension allows for verification of reachability properties over send actions and configurations where the message queues are empty. Moreover, the synchronizability analysis presented in [3] is not implemented, whereas we implement the proposed synchronizability analysis and apply it to the Singularity channel contracts.

The work on session types [14,15] focuses on conformance of an interaction to a predefined protocol and formulates this as a typing problem. The idea is to first define a global type for interaction behavior and then to check if each local peer implementation is "typable" with respect to the global type. If that is the case then the typing rules ensure that when the peers are executed, they conform to the interaction protocol specification that corresponds to the global type. Interestingly, the type system for session types contains an analogue of the autonomous condition from [9,10] and therefore is more restrictive then the synchronizability condition presented in this paper.

In [7], the authors presented various decidability results for half-duplex asynchronous systems containing two peers, one where at any system state at most one message queue is non-empty. The authors proved that half-duplex systems have a recognizable reachability set which can be computed in polynomial time, and which makes it possible to verify in polynomial time the reachability of system states. The authors proved that determining whether an asynchronous system with two peers is half-duplex is decidable. Finally, the authors showed that systems with more than two peers and participating in pair-wise half-duplex communication can simulate a Turing machines, and therefore, reachability analysis of such systems is undecidable, in general. In this paper, we examined a different subclass of asynchronous systems, namely synchronizable systems. Synchronizability does not require half-duplex communication and is applicable for systems containing more than two peers.

In [25,13], the authors discuss the type of communication topologies (e.g., trees) that leads to decidability of reachability analysis in communicating systems, including communicating push-down systems. Our results hold for any communication topology. We conjecture that our results also hold for well-queuing push-down systems considered in [25]; a well-queuing push-down system is one where communications occur when the execution stack is empty. We plan to investigate synchronizability of such communicating push-down systems.

In the context of parallel programming, where concurrently executing processes communicate via message passing (MPI programs), several papers (e.g., [19,22,26]) discuss the impact of buffering on the behavior in terms of deadlock freedom and conformance to local sequence of actions. Specifically, these works discuss how buffering can lead to deadlock when there are "wildcard" receives (states in the peer behavior where any receive action of that peer is possible), and address the problem of deadlock detection efficiently using partial order reduction [22] or using "happens before" relation [26]. There is one main difference between our work and these earlier results. We are concerned with the global ordering of send actions and reachability of synchronized states as opposed to local ordering of actions. As a result, deadlock-freedom in the synchronous and asynchronous variants does not imply that these variants are trace equivalent (Definition 3). Hence, the premise of the work on MPI programming that deadlock-freedom ensures conformance to desired behavior does not hold in our setting. Additionally, [22] imposes certain MPI domain-specific restrictions regarding dependencies between sends and receives, whereas our approach does not depend on such conditions.

8 Conclusion

In this paper we introduced a notion of synchronizability that identifies a class of asynchronously communicating systems for which the sequences of sent messages and the set of reachable synchronized states (i.e., states with empty-message queues) remain the same when asynchronous communication is replaced with synchronous communication. We showed that synchronizability of a system can be determined by checking the equivalence between its synchronous and 1-bounded asynchronous models. We applied this approach to Singularity channel contracts and our experimental results show that all Singularity channel contracts that are not faulty are synchronizable. Hence, their properties can be verified using the synchronous communication model.

References

1. Armstrong, J.: Getting Erlang to talk to the outside world. In: Proc. ACM SIGPLAN Workshop on Erlang, pp. 64–72 (2002)
2. Banavar, G., Chandra, T., Strom, R.E., Sturman, D.: A Case for Message Oriented Middleware. In: Jayanti, P. (ed.) DISC 1999. LNCS, vol. 1693, pp. 1–17. Springer, Heidelberg (1999)
3. Basu, S., Bultan, T.: Choreography conformance via synchronizability. In: Proc. 20th Int. World Wide Web Conf., WWW (2011)
4. Basu, S., Bultan, T., Ouederni, M.: Deciding choreography realizability. In: Proc. 39th Symp. Principles of Programming Languages, POPL (2012)
5. Brand, D., Zafiropulo, P.: On communicating finite-state machines. J. ACM 30(2), 323–342 (1983)

6. Carbone, M., Honda, K., Yoshida, N., Milner, R., Brown, G., Ross-Talbot, S.: A theoretical basis of communication-centred concurrent programming
7. Cécé, G., Finkel, A.: Verification of programs with half-duplex communication. Information and Computation 202, 166–190 (2005)
8. Fähndrich, M., Aiken, M., Hawblitzel, C., Hodson, O., Hunt, G.C., Larus, J.R., Levi, S.: Language support for fast and reliable message-based communication in singularity os. In: Proc. 2006 EuroSys Conf., pp. 177–190 (2006)
9. Fu, X., Bultan, T., Su, J.: Analysis of interacting BPEL web services. In: Proc. 13th Int. World Wide Web Conf., pp. 621–630 (2004)
10. Fu, X., Bultan, T., Su, J.: Synchronizability of conversations among web services. IEEE Trans. Software Eng. 31(12), 1042–1055 (2005)
11. Garavel, H., Lang, F.: SVL: A Scripting Language for Compositional Verification. In: Proc. of FORTE, pp. 377–394 (2001)
12. Garavel, H., Mateescu, R., Lang, F., Serwe, W.: CADP 2006: A Toolbox for the Construction and Analysis of Distributed Processes. In: Damm, W., Hermanns, H. (eds.) CAV 2007. LNCS, vol. 4590, pp. 158–163. Springer, Heidelberg (2007)
13. Heußner, A., Leroux, J., Muscholl, A., Sutre, G.: Reachability Analysis of Communicating Pushdown Systems. In: Ong, L. (ed.) FOSSACS 2010. LNCS, vol. 6014, pp. 267–281. Springer, Heidelberg (2010)
14. Honda, K., Vasconcelos, V.T., Kubo, M.: Language Primitives and Type Discipline for Structured Communication-Based Programming. In: Hankin, C. (ed.) ESOP 1998. LNCS, vol. 1381, pp. 122–138. Springer, Heidelberg (1998)
15. Honda, K., Yoshida, N., Carbone, M.: Multiparty asynchronous session types. In: Proc. 35th Symp. Prin. Programming Languages (POPL), pp. 273–284 (2008)
16. Hunt, G.C., Larus, J.R.: Singularity: rethinking the software stack. Operating Systems Review 41(2), 37–49 (2007)
17. Java Message Service, `http://java.sun.com/products/jms/`
18. Larus, J., Hunt, G.: Using the singularity research development kit. In: Tutorial, Int. Conf. Arch. Support for Prog. Lang. and OS (2008)
19. Manohar, R., Martin, A.J.: Slack Elasticity in Concurrent Computing. In: Jeuring, J. (ed.) MPC 1998. LNCS, vol. 1422, pp. 272–285. Springer, Heidelberg (1998)
20. Menascé, D.A.: Mom vs. rpc: Communication models for distributed applications. IEEE Internet Computing 9(2), 90–93 (2005)
21. Microsoft Message Queuing Service, `http://www.microsoft.com/windowsserver2003/technologies/msmq/default.mspx`
22. Siegel, S.F.: Efficient Verification of Halting Properties for MPI Programs with Wildcard Receives. In: Cousot, R. (ed.) VMCAI 2005. LNCS, vol. 3385, pp. 413–429. Springer, Heidelberg (2005)
23. Singularity design note 5: Channel contracts. singularity rdk documentation, v1.1 (2004), `http://www.codeplex.com/singularity`
24. Stengel, Z., Bultan, T.: Analyzing singularity channel contracts. In: Proc. 18th Int. Symp. on Software Testing and Analysis (ISSTA), pp. 13–24 (2009)
25. La Torre, S., Madhusudan, P., Parlato, G.: Context-Bounded Analysis of Concurrent Queue Systems. In: Ramakrishnan, C.R., Rehof, J. (eds.) TACAS 2008. LNCS, vol. 4963, pp. 299–314. Springer, Heidelberg (2008)
26. Vakkalanka, S., Vo, A., Gopalakrishnan, G., Kirby, R.M.: Precise dynamic analysis for slack elasticity: adding buffering without adding bugs. In: 17th Euro. MPI Conf. Advances in Message Passing Interface, pp. 152–159 (2010)
27. Web Service Choreography Description Language, WS-CDL (2005), `http://www.w3.org/TR/ws-cdl-10/`

On the Termination of Integer Loops

Amir M. Ben-Amram[1], Samir Genaim[2], and Abu Naser Masud[3]

[1] School of Computer Science, The Tel-Aviv Academic College, Israel
[2] DSIC, Complutense University of Madrid (UCM), Spain
[3] DLSIIS, Technical University of Madrid (UPM), Spain

Abstract. In this paper we study the decidability of termination of several variants of simple integer loops, without branching in the loop body and with affine constraints as the loop guard (and possibly a precondition). We show that termination of such loops is undecidable in some cases, in particular, when the body of the loop is expressed by a set of linear inequalities where the coefficients are from $\mathbb{Z} \cup \{r\}$ with r an arbitrary irrational; or when the loop is a sequence of instructions, that compute either linear expressions or the step function. The undecidability result is proven by a reduction from counter programs, whose termination is known to be undecidable. For the common case of integer constraints loops with rational coefficients only we have not succeeded in proving decidability nor undecidability of termination, however, this attempt led to the result that a Petri net can be simulated with such a loop, which implies some interesting lower bounds. For example, termination for a given input is at least EXPSPACE-hard.

1 Introduction

Termination analysis has received a considerable attention and nowadays several powerful tools for the automatic termination analysis of different programming languages and computational models exist [15,12,1,25]. Two important aspects of termination analysis tools are their scalability and ability to handle a large class of programs, which are directly related to the theoretical limits, regarding complexity and completeness, of the underlying techniques. Since termination of general programs is undecidable, every attempt at solving it in practice will have at its core certain restricted problems, or classes of programs, that the algorithm designer targets. To understand the theoretical limits of an approach, we are looking for the decidability and complexity properties of these restricted problems. Note that understanding the boundaries set by inherent undecidability or intractability of problems yields more profound information than evaluating the performance of one particular algorithm.

Much of the recent development in termination analysis has benefited from techniques that deal with one simple loop at a time, where a simple loop is specified by (optionally) some initial conditions, a loop guard, and a "loop body" of a very restricted form. Very often, the state of the program during the loop is represented by a finite set of scalar variables (this simplification may be the result of an abstraction, such as size abstraction of structured data [25,11]).

V. Kuncak and A. Rybalchenko (Eds.): VMCAI 2012, LNCS 7148, pp. 72–87, 2012.

Regarding the representation of the loop body, the most natural one is, perhaps, a block of straight-line code, namely a sequence of assignment statements, as in the following example:

$$\textit{while } X > 0 \textit{ do } \{ X := X + Y;\ Y := Y - 1; \} \tag{1}$$

To define a restricted problem for theoretical study, one just has to state the types of loop conditions and assignments that are admitted.

By symbolically evaluating the sequence of assignments, a straight-line loop body may be put into the simple form of a simultaneous deterministic update, namely loops of the form

$$\textit{while } C \textit{ do } \langle x_1, \ldots, x_n \rangle := f(\langle x_1, \ldots, x_n \rangle)$$

where f is a function of some restricted class. For function classes that are sufficiently simple to analyze, one can hope that termination of such loops would be decidable; in fact, the main motivation to this paper has been the remarkable results by Tiwari [26] and Braverman [10] on the termination of *linear loops*, a kind of loops where the update function f is linear. The loop conditions in these works are conjunctions of linear inequalities. Specifically, Tiwari proved that the termination problem is decidable for loops of the following form:

$$\textit{while } (B\boldsymbol{x} > \boldsymbol{b}) \textit{ do } \boldsymbol{x} := A\boldsymbol{x} + \boldsymbol{c} \tag{2}$$

where the arithmetic is done over the reals; thus the variable vector $\boldsymbol{x}$ has values in $\mathbb{R}^n$, and the constant matrices in the loop are $B \in \mathbb{R}^{m \times n}$, $A \in \mathbb{R}^{n \times n}$, $\boldsymbol{b} \in \mathbb{R}^m$ and $\boldsymbol{c} \in \mathbb{R}^n$.

Consequently, Braverman proved decidability of termination of loops of the following form:

$$\textit{while } (B_s\boldsymbol{x} > \boldsymbol{b}_s) \land (B_w\boldsymbol{x} \geq \boldsymbol{b}_w) \textit{ do } \boldsymbol{x} := A\boldsymbol{x} + \boldsymbol{c} \tag{3}$$

where the constant matrices and vectors are *rational*, and the variables are of either real or rational type; moreover, in the homogeneous case ($\boldsymbol{b}_s, \boldsymbol{b}_w, \boldsymbol{c} = 0$) he proved decidability when the variables range over $\mathbb{Z}$. This is a significant and non-trivial addition, since algorithmic methods that work for the reals often fail to extend to the integers (a notorious example is finding the roots of polynomials; while decidable over the reals, over the integers, it is the undecidable *Hilbert* 10th *problem*[1]).

Going back to program analysis, we note that it is typical in this field to assume that some degree of approximation is necessary in order to express the effect of the loop body by linear arithmetics alone. Hence, rather than loops with a linear update as above, one defines the representation of a loop body to be a set of *constraints* (again, usually linear). The general form of such a loop is

$$\textit{while } (B\boldsymbol{x} \geq \boldsymbol{b}) \textit{ do } A \begin{pmatrix} \boldsymbol{x} \\ \boldsymbol{x}' \end{pmatrix} \leq \boldsymbol{c} \tag{4}$$

[1] Over the rationals, the problem is still open, according to [18].

where the loop body is interpreted as expressing a relation between the new values $\boldsymbol{x}'$ and the previous values $\boldsymbol{x}$. Thus, in general, this representation is a non-deterministic kind of program and may super-approximate the semantics of the source program analyzed. But this is a form which lends itself naturally to analysis methods based on linear programming techniques, and there has been a series of publications on proving termination of such loops [24,19,22] — all of which rely on the generation of *linear ranking functions.* For example, the termination analysis tools *Terminator* [12], COSTA [1], and Julia [25], are based on proving termination of such loops by means of a linear ranking function.

It is known that the linear-ranking approach cannot completely resolve the problem [22,10], since there are terminating programs having no such ranking function, e.g., the loop (1) above. Moreover, the linear-programming based approaches are not sensitive to the assumption that the data are integers. Thus, the problem of decidability of termination for linear constraint loops (4) stays open, in its different variants. We feel that the most intriguing problem is:

> Is the termination of a single linear constraints loop decidable, when the coefficients are rational (or integer) numbers and the variables range over the integers?

The problem may be considered for a given initial state, for any initial state, or for a (linearly) constrained initial state.

Our contribution. In this research, we focused on hardness proofs. Our basic tool is a new simulation of counter programs (also known as counter machines) by a simple integer loop. The termination of counter programs is a well-known undecidable problem. While we have not been able to fully answer the major problem above, this technique led to some interesting results which improve our understanding of the simple-loop termination problem. We next summarize our main results. All concern integer variables.

1. We prove undecidability of termination, either for all inputs or a given input, for simple loops which iterate a straight-line sequence of simple assignment instructions. The right-hand sides are integer linear expressions except for one instruction type, which computes the step function

   $$f(x) = \begin{cases} 0 & x \leq 0 \\ 1 & x > 0 \end{cases}$$

   At first sight it may seem like the inclusion of such an instruction is tantamount to including a branch on zero, which would immediately allow for implementing a counter program. This is not the case, because the result of the function is put into a variable which can only be combined with other variables in a very limited way. We complement this result by pointing out other natural instructions that can be used to simulate the step function. This include integer division by a constant (with truncation towards zero) and truncated subtraction.

2. Building upon the previous result, we prove undecidability of termination, either for all inputs or for a given input, of linear constraint loops where *one irrational number may appear* (more precisely, the coefficients are from $\mathbb{Z} \cup \{r\}$ for an arbitrary irrational number r).
3. Finally, we observe that while linear constraints with rational coefficients seem to be insufficient for simulating *all* counter programs, it is possible to simulate a subclass, namely Petri nets, leading to the conclusion that termination for a given input is at least EXPSPACE-hard.

We would like to highlight the relation of our results to the discussion at the end of [10]. Braverman notes that constraint loops are non-deterministic and asks:

> How much non-determinism can be introduced in a linear loop with no initial conditions before termination becomes undecidable?

It is interesting that our reduction to constraint loops, when using the irrational coefficient, produces constraints that are *deterministic*. The role of the constraints is not to create non-determinism; it is to express complex relationships among variables. We may also point out that some limited forms of linear constraint loops (that are very non-deterministic since they are weaker constraints) have a *decidable* termination problem (see Section 6). Braverman also discusses the difficulty of deciding termination for a given input, a problem that he left open. Our results apply to this variant, providing a partial answer to this open problem.

The rest of this paper is organized as follows. Section 2 presents some preliminaries; Section 3 study the termination of straight-line while loops with a "built-in" function that represents the step function; Section 4 attempts to apply the technique of Section 3 to the case of integer constraints loops, and discusses extensions of integer constraints loops for which termination is undecidable; Section 5 describes how a Petri net can be simulated with linear constraint loops; Section 6 discusses some related work; and Section 7 concludes.

2 Preliminaries

In this section we define the syntax of integer piecewise linear while loops, integer linear constraints loops, and counter programs.

2.1 Integer Piecewise Linear Loops

An integer piecewise linear loop (*IPL* loop for short) with integer variables $X_1, \ldots, X_n$ is a while loop of the form

$$\textit{while } b_1 \wedge \cdots \wedge b_m \textit{ do } \{c_1; \ldots; c_n\}$$

where each condition b_i is a linear inequality $a_0 + a_1 * X_1 + \cdots + a_n * X_n \geq 0$ with $a_i \in \mathbb{Z}$, and each c_i is one of the following instructions

$$X_i := X_j + X_k \mid X_i := a * X_j \mid X_i := a \mid X_i = \textit{isPositive}(X_j)$$

such that $a \in \mathbb{Z}$ and

$$isPositive(X) = \begin{cases} 0 & X \leq 0 \\ 1 & X > 0 \end{cases}$$

We consider *isPositive* to be a primitive, but in the next section we will consider alternatives. The semantics of an *IPL* loop is the obvious: starting from initial values for the variables $X_1, \ldots, X_n$ (the input), the instructions $c_1, \ldots, c_n$ are executed sequentially as far as the condition $b_1 \wedge \cdots \wedge b_n$ holds. We say that the loop terminates for a given input if the condition $b_1 \wedge \cdots \wedge b_n$ eventually evaluates to *false*. For simplicity, sometime we use a composite expression, e.g, $X_1 := 2 * X_2 + 3 * X_3 + 1$, which should be taken to be a syntactic sugar for a series of assignments, possibly using temporary variables. We will also make use of a "macro" $isZero(X)$ which should be understood as representing the expression $1 - isPositive(X) - isPositive(-X)$.

2.2 Integer Linear Constraints Loops

An integer linear constraints loop (*ILC* loop for short) over n variables $\boldsymbol{x} = \langle X_1, \ldots, X_n \rangle$ has the form

$$while\ (B\boldsymbol{x} \geq \boldsymbol{b})\ do\ A \begin{pmatrix} \boldsymbol{x} \\ \boldsymbol{x}' \end{pmatrix} \leq \boldsymbol{c}$$

where for some $m, p > 0$, $B \in \mathbb{R}^{m \times n}$, $A \in \mathbb{R}^{p \times 2n}$, $\boldsymbol{b} \in \mathbb{R}^m$ and $\boldsymbol{c} \in \mathbb{R}^p$. The case we are most interested in is that in which the constant matrices and vectors are composed of rational numbers; this is equivalent to assuming that they are all integers (just multiply by a common denominator).

Semantically, a state of such a loop is an n-tuple $\langle x_1, \ldots, x_n \rangle$ of integers, and a transition to a new state $\boldsymbol{x}' = \langle x'_1, \ldots, x'_n \rangle$ is possible if $\boldsymbol{x}, \boldsymbol{x}'$ satisfy all the constraints in the loop guard and the loop body. We say that the loop terminates for given initial state if all possible executions from that state are finite, and that it universally terminates if it terminates for every initial state. We say that the loop is *deterministic* if there is at most one successor state to any state.

2.3 Counter Programs

A (deterministic) counter program P_C with n counters $X_1, \cdots, X_n$ is a list of labeled instructions $1{:}I_1, \ldots, m{:}I_m, m{+}1{:}stop$ where each instruction I_k is one of the following:

$$incr(X_j) \mid decr(X_j) \mid if\ X_i > 0\ then\ k_1\ else\ k_2$$

with $1 \leq k_1, k_2 \leq m{+}1$ and $1 \leq j \leq n$. A state is of the form $(i, \langle a_1, \ldots, a_n \rangle)$ which indicates that Instruction i is to be executed next, and the current values of the counters are $X_1 = a_1, \ldots, X_n = a_n$. In a valid state, $1 \leq i \leq m + 1$ and all $a_i \in \mathbb{N}$ (it will sometimes be useful to also consider invalid states, and assume that they cause a halt). Any state in which $i = m + 1$ is a halting state. For any other valid state $(i, \langle a_1, \ldots, a_n \rangle)$, the successor state is defined as follows.

- If I_i is $decr(X_j)$ (resp. $incr(X_j)$), then X_j is increased (resp. decreased) by 1 and the execution moves to label $i + 1$.
- If I_i is "*if* $X_j > 0$ *then* k_1 *else* k_2" then the execution moves to label k_1 if X_j is positive, and to k_2 if it is 0. The values of the counters do not change.

For simplicity, we assume that a counter with value 0 is never decremented, this can be guaranteed by adding a conditional statement before each $decr(X_j)$. The following are known facts about the halting problem for counter programs.

Theorem 1 ([21]). *The halting problem for counter programs with* $n \geq 2$ *counters and the initial state* $(1, \langle 0, \dots, 0 \rangle)$ *is undecidable.*

The *universal halting problem* is the problem of deciding whether a given program halts for any initial state.

Theorem 2 ([7]). *The universal halting problem for counter programs with* $n \geq 2$ *counters is undecidable.*

3 Termination of *IPL* Loops

In this section, we investigate the decidability of the following problems: given an *IPL* loop P

1. Does P terminate for a given input?
2. Does P terminate for all inputs?

We show that both problems are undecidable by reduction from the halting problem for counter programs. To see where the challenge in this reduction lies, note that the loops we iterate a fixed block of straight-line code, while a counter program has a program counter that determines the next instruction to execute. While one can easily keep the value of the PC in a variable (which is what we do), it is not obvious how to make the computation depend on this variable, and how to simulate branching.

3.1 The Reduction

Given a counter program $P_C \equiv 1{:}I_1, \dots, m{:}I_m, m{+}1{:}stop$ with counters $X_1, \dots,$ X_n, we generate a corresponding *IPL* loop $\mathcal{T}(P_C)$ as follows:

while $(PC \geq 1 \wedge PC \leq m \wedge X_1 \geq 0 \wedge \cdots \wedge X_n \geq 0)$ **do** {
  $\mathcal{T}(1{:}I_1)$
  ⋮
  $\mathcal{T}(m{:}I_m)$
  $PC := N_1 + \cdots + N_m;$
}

where $\mathcal{T}(k{:}I_k)$ is defined as follows

- If $I_k \equiv incr(X_j)$, then $\mathcal{T}(k{:}I_k)$ is

  $A_k := isZero(PC - k);$
  $X_j := X_j + A_k;$
  $N_k := (k+1) * A_k;$

- If $I_k \equiv decr(X_j)$, then $\mathcal{T}(k{:}I_k)$ is

  $A_k := isZero(PC - k);$
  $X_j := X_j - A_k;$
  $N_k := (k+1) * A_k;$

- If $I_k \equiv$ *if* $X_j > 0$ *then* k_1 *else* k_2, then $\mathcal{T}(k{:}I_k)$ is

  $A_k := isZero(PC - k);$
  $F_k := isPositive(X_j);$
  $T_k := isPositive(A_k + F_k - 1);$
  $N_k := T_k * (k_1 - k_2) + A_k * k_2;$

In Section 3.2 we prove the following:

Lemma 1. *A counter program P_C with $n \geq 2$ counters terminates for the initial state $(i, \langle a_1, \ldots, a_n \rangle)$ if and only if $\mathcal{T}(P_C)$ terminates for the initial input $PC = i \wedge X_1 = a_1 \wedge \cdots \wedge X_n = a_n$.*

Lemma 1, together with theorems 1 and 2, imply.

Theorem 3. *The halting problem and universal halting problem for IPL loops are undecidable.*

3.2 Proof of Correctness

Let us first state, informally, the main ideas behind the reduction, and then formally prove Lemma 1 which in turn implies Theorem 3.

1. Variable PC represents the program counter, i.e., the label of the instruction to be executed next.
2. Variables $A_1, \ldots, A_m$ are flags: when $PC = i$, then $A_k = 1$ if $k = i$, and $A_k = 0$ if $k \neq i$. Thus, an operation $X_j := X_j + A_k$ (resp. $X_j := X_j - A_k$) will have effect only when $A_k = 1$, and otherwise it is a no-op. This is a way of simulating only one instruction in every iteration.
3. Variables $N_1, \ldots, N_m$ are used to compute the value of PC for the next iteration. The idea is that when $PC = k$, N_k is set to the label of the next instruction; while N_i, for $i \neq k$, is set to 0. Thus, the new PC can be obtained by summing these variables.

Note that point (3) guarantees that $PC := N_1 + \cdots + N_m$ correctly computes the label of the next instruction. Thus, the while loop simulates the execution of the counter program. Now we move to the formal proof.

Lemma 2. *Let $PC = i$; then for all k, A_k is set to* 1 *when $k = i$, and to* 0 *when $k \neq i$.*

Proof. Immediate from the semantics of *isZero* and the code that sets A_k.

Lemma 3. *Let $PC = i$, then (1) for $k \neq i$, it holds that $N_k = 0$; and (2) for $k = i$, it holds that $N_k = k+1$ if I_k is $decr(X_j)$ or $incr(X_j)$, and $N_k = k_1$ (resp. $N_k = k_2$) if I_k is "if $X_j > 0$ then k_1 else k_2" and $X_j > 0$ (resp. $X_j = 0$).*

Proof. We consider the following two cases

1. Assume $k \neq i$, then (a) for $incr(X_j)$ and $decr(X_j)$ it is obvious that $N_k = 0$ since by Lemma 2 we have $A_k = 0$; and (b) for "*if* $X_j > 0$ *then* k_1 *else* k_2", since A_k equals 0 by Lemma 2, then also $T_k = 0$ (regardless of the value of F_k), and thus $N_k = 0 * (k_1 - k_2) + 0 * k_2 = 0$;
2. Assume $k = i$, then (a) for $incr(X_j)$ and $decr(X_j)$ it is obvious that $N_k = k + 1$ since by Lemma 2 we have $A_k = 1$; and (b) for "*if* $X_j > 0$ *then* k_1 *else* k_2", by Lemma 2 we have $A_k = 1$, and by definition of *isPositive* we have $F_k = 0$ when $X_j = 0$ and $F_k = 1$ when $X_j > 0$. Thus

X_j	F_k	T_k	N_k
> 0	1	1	$1 * (k_1 - k_2) + 1 * k_2 = k_1$
$= 0$	0	0	$0 * (k_1 - k_2) + 1 * k_2 = k_2$

In order to prove Lemma 1, it is enough to show that $\mathcal{T}(P_C)$ simulates the corresponding counter program P_C.

Lemma 4. *Let P_C be a counter program, $\mathcal{T}(P_C)$ its corresponding IPL loop, $C \equiv (\ell, \langle a_1, \ldots, a_n \rangle)$ a configuration for P_C, and S a state of $\mathcal{T}(P_C)$ where $PC = \ell, X_1 = a_1, \ldots, X_n = a_n$. Then C is a halting configuration of P_C if and only if S terminates $\mathcal{T}(P_C)$; while if C has a successor state $(\ell', \langle a'_1, \ldots, a'_n \rangle)$ in P_C, then the loop body of $\mathcal{T}(P_C)$ is enabled at S and its execution leads to a state in which $PC = \ell', X_1 = a'_1, \ldots, X_n = a'_n$.*

Proof. For invalid initial states both the counter programs and the corresponding while loop terminate immediately. For valid states the proof follows from Lemmata 2 and 3.

3.3 Examples of Piecewise-Linear Operations

The *isPositive* operation can be easily simulated by other natural instructions, yielding different instruction sets that suffice for undecidability.

Example 1 (Integer division). Consider an instruction that divides an integer by an integer constant and truncates the result towards zero (also if it is negative). Using this kind of division, we have

$$isPositive(X) = X - \frac{2 * X - 1}{2}$$

and thus, termination is undecidable for loops with linear assignments and integer division of this kind.

Example 2 (truncated subtraction). Another common piecewise-linear function is *truncated subtraction*, such that $x \dot{-} y$ is the same as $x - y$ if it is positive, and otherwise 0. This operation allows for implementing *isPositive* thus:

$$isPositive(X) = 1 \dot{-} (1 \dot{-} X)$$

4 Reduction to *ILC* Loops

In this section we turn to Integer Linear Constraint loops. We attempt to apply the reduction described in Section 3, and explain where and why it fails. So we do not obtain undecidability for *ILC* loops, but we show that if there is one irrational number that we are allowed to use in the constraints (any irrational will do) the reduction can be completed and undecidability of termination proved.

In Section 5 we describe another way of handling the failure of the reduction with rational coefficients only: reducing from a weaker model, and thereby proving a lower bound which is weaker than undecidability (but still non-trivial).

Observe that the loop constructed in Section 3 uses non-linear expressions only for setting the flags A_k, F_k and T_k, the rest is clearly linear. Assuming that we can encode these flags with integer linear constraints, then adapting the rest of the reduction to *ILC* loops is straightforward: it can be done by rewriting $\mathcal{T}(P_C)$ to avoid multiple updates of a variable (that is, to *single static assignment form*) and then representing each assignment as an equation instead. Thus, in what follows we concentrate on how to represent those flags using integer linear constraints.

4.1 Encoding T_k with Integer Linear Constraints

In Section 3, we defined T_k as $isPositive(A_k + F_k - 1)$. Since $0 \leq A_k + F_k \leq 2$, it is easy to verify that this is equivalent to imposing the constraint $F_k + A_k - 1 \leq 2 \cdot T_k \leq F_k + A_k$.

4.2 Encoding A_k with Integer Linear Constraints

The role of the flag A_k is to indicate if PC is equal to k. Expressing this relation by linear constraints is possible thanks to the finite range of PC, as shown by the following lemma.

Lemma 5. *Let P_1 and P_2 be the following polyhedra*

$$P_1 = \bigwedge_i (A_i \geq 0) \wedge (A_1 + ... + A_m = 1)$$

$$P_2 = (PC = 1 \cdot A_1 + 2 \cdot A_2 + \cdots + m \cdot A_m)$$

Then $P_1 \wedge P_2 \wedge (PC = k) \rightarrow (A_k = 1)$ and $P_1 \wedge P_2 \wedge PC \neq k \rightarrow (A_k = 0)$.

Proof. It is easy to see that the only integer points in P_1 are such that for a single k, $A_k = 1$, while for all $j \neq k$, $A_j = 0$. Then, P_2 forces PC to equal k.

4.3 Encoding F_k with Integer Linear Constraints

Now we discuss the difficulty of encoding the flag F_k using linear constraints. The following lemma states that such encoding is not possible when using rational coefficients.

Lemma 6. *Given non-negative integer variables X and F, it is not possible to define a system of integer linear constraints Ψ (with rational coefficients) over X, F, and possibly other integer variables, such that $\Psi \wedge (X = 0) \rightarrow (F = 0)$ and $\Psi \wedge (X > 0) \rightarrow (F = 1)$.*

Proof. The proof relies on a theorem in [20] which states that the following piecewise linear function

$$f(x) = \begin{cases} 0 & x = 0 \\ 1 & x > 0, \end{cases}$$

where x is a non-negative *real* variable, cannot be defined as a minimization mixed integer programming (*MIP* for short) problem with rational coefficients only. More precisely, it is not possible to define $f(x)$ as

$$f(x) = \text{minimize } g \text{ w.r.t. } \Psi$$

where Ψ is a system of linear constraints with rational coefficients over x and other integer and real variables, and g is a linear function over $vars(\Psi)$. Now suppose that Lemma 6 is false, i.e., there exists Ψ such that $\Psi \wedge (X = 0) \rightarrow (F = 0)$ and $\Psi \wedge (X > 0) \rightarrow (F = 1)$, then the following *MIP* problem

$$f(x) = \text{minimize } F \text{ w.r.t. } \Psi \wedge (x \leq X)$$

defines the function $f(x)$, which contradicts [20].

4.4 An Undecidable Extension of *ILC* Loops

There are certain extensions of the *ILC* model that allow our reduction to be carried out. Basically, the extension should allow for encoding the flag F_k. The extension which we find most interesting allows the use of a single, arbitrary irrational number r (thus, we do not require the specific value of r to represent any particular information). Thus, the coefficients are now over $\mathbb{Z} \cup \{r\}$. The variables still hold integers.

Lemma 7. *Let r be an arbitrary positive irrational number, and let*

$$\begin{aligned} \Psi_1 &= (0 \leq F_k \leq 1) \wedge (F_k \leq X) \\ \Psi_2 &= (rX \leq B) \wedge (rY \leq A) \wedge (-Y \leq X) \wedge (A + B \leq F_k) \end{aligned}$$

then $(\Psi_1 \wedge \Psi_2 \wedge X = 0) \rightarrow F_k = 0$ and $(\Psi_1 \wedge \Psi_2 \wedge X > 0) \rightarrow F_k = 1$.

Proof. The constraints Ψ_1 force F_k to be 0 when X is 0, and when X is positive F_k can be either 0 or 1. The role of Ψ_2 is to eliminate the non-determinism for the case $X > 0$, namely, for $X > 0$ it forces F_k to be 1. The property that makes Ψ_2 work is that for a given *non-integer* number d, the condition $-A \leq d \leq B$ implies $A + B \geq 1$, whereas for $d = 0$ the sum may be zero. The role of the irrational coefficient is to translate any integer value X, except 0, to a non-integer number: $d = rX$ (similarly also for Y and rY). The variable Y is introduced to avoid using another irrational coefficient $-r$.

Example 3. Let us consider $r = \sqrt{2}$ in lemma 7. When $X = 0$, Ψ_1 forces F_k to be 0, and it is easy to verify that Ψ_2 is satisfiable for $X = Y = A = B = F_k = 0$. Now, for the positive case, let for example $X = 5$, then Ψ_1 limits F_k to the values 0 or 1, and Ψ_2 implies $(\sqrt{2} \cdot 5 \leq B) \wedge (-\sqrt{2} \cdot 5 \leq A)$ since $Y \geq -5$. The minimum values that A and B can take are respectively -7 and 8, thus it is not possible to choose A and B such that $A + B \leq 0$. This eliminates $F_k = 0$ as a solution. However, for these minimum values we have $A + B = 1$ and thus $A + B \leq F_k$ satisfiable for $F_k = 1$.

Theorem 4. *The termination of ILC loops where the coefficients are from* $\mathbb{Z} \cup \{r\}$*, for a single arbitrary irrational constant* r*, is undecidable.*

We have mentioned, above, Meyer's result that *MIP* problems with rational coefficients cannot represent the step function over reals. Interestingly, he also shows that it *is* possible using an irrational constant, in a manner similar to our Lemma 7. Our technique construction differs in that we do not make use of minimization or maximization to define the function.

5 Simulation of Petri Nets

Let us consider a counter machine as defined in Section 2, but with a *weak* conditional statement "*if* $X_j < a$ *then* k_1 *else* k_2" (where a is a positive integer) which is interpreted as: if X_j is smaller than a then the execution *must* continue at label k_1, otherwise it *may* continue to label k_1 or label k_2. This computational model is equivalent to a Petri net. From considerations as those presented in Section 4, we arrived at the conclusion that the weak conditional, and therefore Petri nets, *can* be simulated by an *ILC* loop.

A (place/transition) Petri net [23] is composed of a set of counters $X_1, \ldots, X_n$ (known as *places*) and a set of transitions $t_1, \ldots, t_m$. A transition is essentially a command to increment or decrement some places. This may be represented formally by associating with transition t its set of decremented places $^\bullet t$ and its set of incremented places $t^\bullet$. A transition is said to be enabled if all its decremented places are non-zero, and it can then be *fired*, causing the decrements and increments associated with it to take place. Starting from an initial marking (values for the places), the state of the net evaluates by repeatedly firing one of the enabled transitions.

Lemma 8. *Given a Petri net P with initial marking M, a simulating ILC loop with an initial condition Ψ_M can be constructed in polynomial time. In particular, the termination of the loop from an initial state in Ψ_M is equivalent to the termination of P starting from M.*

How this is done: The *ILC* loop will have variables $X_1, \ldots, X_n$ that represent the counters in a straight-forward way, and flags $A_1, \ldots, A_m$ that represent the choice of the next transition much as we did for counter programs (except that there is no *PC* variable). For each $1 \leq i \leq n$ we create the following constraints in the body of the loop:

$$P_1 = \bigwedge_k (A'_k \geq 0) \wedge (A'_1 + \ldots . + A'_m = 1)$$

$$\Psi_i = \bigwedge_i (X_i \geq \sum_{k:i \in {}^\bullet t_k} A'_k)$$

$$\Phi_i = (X'_i = X_i - \sum_{k:i \in {}^\bullet t_k} A'_k + \sum_{k:i \in t_k{}^\bullet} A'_k)$$

The loop guard is $X_1 \geq 0 \wedge \cdots \wedge X_n \geq 0$. The initial state Ψ_M simply forces each X_i to have the value as stated by the initial marking M. Note that the initial values of A_i are not important since they are not used (we only use A'_k). As before, the constraint P_1 ensures that one and only one of the A'_k will equal 1 at every iteration. The constraints Ψ_i ensure that A'_k may receive the value 1 only if transition k is enabled in the state. The constraints Φ_i (the update) clearly simulate the chosen transition.

The importance of this result is that complexity results for Petri net are lower bounds on the complexity of the corresponding problems in the context of *ILC* loops, and in particular, from a known results about the termination problem [14,17], we obtain the following.

Theorem 5. *The halting problem for ILC loops, for a given input, is at least EXPSPACE-hard.*

Note that the reduction does not provide useful information on universal termination of *ILC* loops, since for Petri net it is PTIME-decidable [13].

6 Related Work

Termination of integer loops has received considerable attention recently, both from theoretical (e.g., decidability, complexity), and practical (e.g, developing tools) perspectives. Research has considered: straight-line while loops, and loops in a constraint setting possibly with multiple-paths.

For straight-line while loops, the most remarkable results are those of Tiwari [26] and Braverman [10]. Tiwari proved that the problem is decidable for linear deterministic updates when the domain of the variables is $\mathbb{R}$. Braverman proved that this holds also for $\mathbb{Q}$, and for the homogeneous case it holds for $\mathbb{Z}$

(see discussion in Section 1). Both have considered universal termination, the termination for a given input left open.

Decidability and complexity of termination of single and multiple-path integer linear constraints loops has been intensively studied for different classes of constraints. Lee et al. [16] proved that termination of a multiple-path *ILC* loop, when the constraints are restricted to size-change constraints (i.e., constraints of the form $X_i > X'_j$ or $X_i \geq X'_j$ over $\mathbb{N}$), is PSPACE-complete [16]. Later, Lee and Ben-Amram [6] identified sub-classes of such loops for which the termination can be decided in polynomial time. Ben-Amram [4] showed how to extend and adapt some theory from the domain of size-change constraints to general monotonicity constraints (i.e., constraints of the form $X_i > Y$, $X_i \geq Y$, where Y can be primed or unprimed variable), he proved that termination for such loops is PSPACE-complete. It is important to note that his results hold for any well-founded domain, not necessarily $\mathbb{N}$. In [5], Ben-Amram considered loops with monotonicity constraints over $\mathbb{Z}$, and prove that the termination problem is PSPACE-complete. Recently, Bozzelli and Pinchinat [8] proved that it is still PSPACE-complete also for gap-constraints, i.e., constraints of the form $X - Y \geq c$ where $c \in \mathbb{N}$. Ben-Amram [3] proved that when extending size-change constraints with integer constants, i.e., allowing difference constraints of the form $X_i - X'_j \geq c$ where $c \in \mathbb{Z}$, the termination problem become undecidable. However for a subclass in which each source (i.e., unprimed) variable might be used only once (in each path) the problem is PSPACE-complete.

All the above work concerns multiple-path loops. Petri nets and various extensions, such as Reset and Transfers nets, can also be seen as multiple-path constraint loops. The termination of Petri net and several extensions is known to be decidable [13,14,17].

Back to single-path loops, a topic that received much attention is the synthesis of ranking functions for such loops, as a means of proving termination. Sohn and Van Gelder [24] proposed a method for the synthesis of linear ranking functions for *ILC* loops over $\mathbb{N}$. Later, their method was extended by Mesnard and Serebrenik [19] to $\mathbb{Z}$ and to multiple-path loops. Both rely on the duality theorem of linear programming. Podelski and Rybalchenko [22] also proposed a method for synthesizing linear ranking function for *ILC* loops. Their method is based on Farkas' lemma. It is important to note that [19,22] are complete when the variables range over $\mathbb{R}$ or $\mathbb{Q}$, but not $\mathbb{Z}$. Recently, Bagnara et al. [2] proved that [19,22] are actually equivalent, in the sense that they compute the same set of ranking functions, and that the method of Podelski and Rybalchenko has better worst-case complexity. Bradley et al. [9] presented an algorithm for computing linear ranking functions for straight-line integer while loops with integer division.

Piecewise affine functions have been long used to describe the step of a discrete time dynamical system. Blondel el al. [7] considered systems of the form $x(t+1) = f(x(t))$ where f is a piecewise affine function over $\mathbb{R}^n$ (defined by rational coefficients). They show that some problems are undecidable for $n \geq 2$, in particular, whether all trajectories go through 0 (the moartality problem). This can be seen as termination of the loop `while` $x \neq 0$ `do x := f(x)`.

7 Conclusion

Motivated by the increasing interest in the termination of integer loops, in this research, we have studied the hardness of terminations proofs for several variants of such loops. In particular, we have considered straight-line while loops, and integer linear constraints loops. The later are very common in the context of program analysis.

For straight-line while loops, we proved that if the underlying instructions set allows the implementation of a simple piecewise linear function, namely the step function, then the termination problem is undecidable. For integer linear constraints loops, we have showed that allowing the constraints to include a single arbitrary irrational number makes the termination problem undecidable. For the case of integer constraints loops with rational coefficients only, which is very common in program analysis, we could simulate a Petri net. This result provide interesting lower bound on the complexity of the termination, and other related problems, of *ILC* loops.

We have recently obtained additional results using techniques similar to those described in this paper. Specifically, we have shown an EXPSPACE lower bound, as in Section 5, that holds for *ILC* loops with a deterministic update. We have also shown undecidability for a while loop having the body of the following form

`if (x > 0) then` (one deterministic update) `else` (another update)

and the guard as in *IPL* loops, where the updates are linear (and do not involve the step function).

We hope that our results shed some light on the termination problem of simple integer loops and perhaps will inspire further progress on the open problems.

Acknowledgments. We thank Pierre Ganty for discussions on Petri nets. Amir Ben-Amram's work was done while visiting DIKU, the department of Computer Science at the University of Copenhagen. This work was funded in part by the Information & Communication Technologies program of the EC, Future and Emerging Technologies (FET), under the ICT-231620 *HATS* project, by the Spanish Ministry of Science and Innovation (MICINN) under the TIN-2008-05624 *DOVES* project, the UCM-BSCH-GR35/10-A-910502 *GPD* Research Group and by the Madrid Regional Government under the S2009TIC-1465 *PROMETIDOS-CM* project.

References

1. Albert, E., Arenas, P., Genaim, S., Puebla, G., Zanardini, D.: COSTA: Design and Implementation of a Cost and Termination Analyzer for Java Bytecode. In: de Boer, F.S., Bonsangue, M.M., Graf, S., de Roever, W.-P. (eds.) FMCO 2007. LNCS, vol. 5382, pp. 113–132. Springer, Heidelberg (2008)

2. Bagnara, R., Mesnard, F., Pescetti, A., Zaffanella, E.: The automatic synthesis of linear ranking functions: The complete unabridged version. Quaderno 498, Dipartimento di Matematica, Università di Parma, Italy, Published as arXiv:cs.PL/1004.0944 (2010)
3. Ben-Amram, A.M.: Size-change termination with difference constraints. ACM Trans. Program. Lang. Syst. 30(3) (2008)
4. Ben-Amram, A.M.: Size-change termination, monotonicity constraints and ranking functions. Logical Methods in Computer Science 6(3) (2010)
5. Ben-Amram, A.M.: Monotonicity constraints for termination in the integer domain. CoRR, abs/1105.6317 (2011)
6. Ben-Amram, A.M., Lee, C.S.: Program termination analysis in polynomial time. ACM Trans. Program. Lang. Syst. 29(1) (2007)
7. Blondel, V.D., Bournez, O., Koiran, P., Papadimitriou, C.H., Tsitsiklis, J.N.: Deciding stability and mortality of piecewise affine dynamical systems. Theor. Comput. Sci. 255(1-2), 687–696 (2001)
8. Bozzelli, L., Pinchinat, S.: Verification of Gap-Order Constraint Abstractions of Counter Systems. In: Kuncak, V., Rybalchenko, A. (eds.) VMCAI 2012. LNCS, vol. 7148, pp. 88–103. Springer, Heidelberg (2012)
9. Bradley, A.R., Manna, Z., Sipma, H.B.: Termination Analysis of Integer Linear Loops. In: Abadi, M., de Alfaro, L. (eds.) CONCUR 2005. LNCS, vol. 3653, pp. 488–502. Springer, Heidelberg (2005)
10. Braverman, M.: Termination of Integer Linear Programs. In: Ball, T., Jones, R.B. (eds.) CAV 2006. LNCS, vol. 4144, pp. 372–385. Springer, Heidelberg (2006)
11. Bruynooghe, M., Codish, M., Gallagher, J.P., Genaim, S., Vanhoof, W.: Termination analysis of logic programs through combination of type-based norms. ACM Trans. Program. Lang. Syst. 29(2) (2007)
12. Cook, B., Podelski, A., Rybalchenko, A.: Termination proofs for systems code. In: Schwartzbach, M.I., Ball, T. (eds.) Proceedings of the ACM SIGPLAN 2006 Conference on Programming Language Design and Implementation (PLDI), Ottawa, Canada, pp. 415–426. ACM (2006); Terminator
13. Dufourd, C., Jančar, P., Schnoebelen, P.: Boundedness of Reset P/T Nets. In: Wiedermann, J., Van Emde Boas, P., Nielsen, M. (eds.) ICALP 1999. LNCS, vol. 1644, pp. 301–310. Springer, Heidelberg (1999)
14. Esparza, J.: Decidability and Complexity of Petri Net Problems—an Introduction. In: Reisig, W., Rozenberg, G. (eds.) APN 1998. LNCS, vol. 1491, pp. 374–428. Springer, Heidelberg (1998)
15. Giesl, J., Thiemann, R., Schneider-Kamp, P., Falke, S.: Automated Termination Proofs with AProVE. In: van Oostrom, V. (ed.) RTA 2004. LNCS, vol. 3091, pp. 210–220. Springer, Heidelberg (2004)
16. Lee, C.S., Jones, N.D., Ben-Amram, A.M.: The size-change principle for program termination. In: POPL, pp. 81–92 (2001)
17. Lipton, R.J.: The reachability problem requires exponential space. Technical Report 63, Yale University (1976), `http://www.cs.yale.edu/publications/techreports/tr63.pdf`
18. Matiyasevich, Y.: Hilbert's tenth problem: What was done and what is to be done. In: Denef, J., Lipshitz, L., Pheidas, T., Van Geel, J. (eds.) Hilbert's Tenth Problem: Relations with Arithmetic and Algebraic Geometry. AMS (2000)
19. Mesnard, F., Serebrenik, A.: Recurrence with affine level mappings is p-time decidable for clp(r). TPLP 8(1), 111–119 (2008)

20. Meyer, R.R.: Integer and mixed-integer programming models: General properties. Journal of Optimization Theory and Applications 16, 191–206 (1975), doi:10.1007/BF01262932
21. Minsky, M.L.: Computation: finite and infinite machines. Prentice-Hall, Inc., Upper Saddle River (1967)
22. Podelski, A., Rybalchenko, A.: A Complete Method for the Synthesis of Linear Ranking Functions. In: Steffen, B., Levi, G. (eds.) VMCAI 2004. LNCS, vol. 2937, pp. 239–251. Springer, Heidelberg (2004)
23. Reisig, W.: Petri Nets: An Introduction. EATCS Monographs on Theoretical Computer Science. Springer, Berlin (1985)
24. Sohn, K., Van Gelder, A.: Termination detection in logic programs using argument sizes. In: PODS, pp. 216–226. ACM Press (1991)
25. Spoto, F., Mesnard, F., Payet, É.: A termination analyzer for java bytecode based on path-length. ACM Trans. Program. Lang. Syst. 32(3) (2010)
26. Tiwari, A.: Termination of Linear Programs. In: Alur, R., Peled, D.A. (eds.) CAV 2004. LNCS, vol. 3114, pp. 70–82. Springer, Heidelberg (2004)

Verification of Gap-Order Constraint Abstractions of Counter Systems

Laura Bozzelli[1] and Sophie Pinchinat[2]

[1] Technical University of Madrid (UPM), 28660 Boadilla del Monte, Madrid, Spain
[2] IRISA, Campus de Beaulieu, 35042 Rennes Cedex, France

Abstract. We investigate verification problems for *gap-order constraint systems* (GCS), an (infinitely-branching) abstract model of counter machines, in which constraints (over $\mathbb{Z}$) between the variables of the source state and the target state of a transition are *gap-order constraints* (GC) [27]. GCS extend monotonicity constraint systems [5], integral relation automata [12], and constraint automata in [15]. First, we show that checking the existence of infinite runs in GCS satisfying acceptance conditions à la Büchi (fairness problem) is decidable and PSPACE-complete. Next, we consider a constrained branching-time logic, GCCTL*, obtained by enriching CTL* with GC, thus enabling expressive properties and subsuming the setting of [12]. We establish that, while model-checking GCS against the universal fragment of GCCTL* is undecidable, model-checking against the existential fragment, and satisfiability of both the universal and existential fragments are instead decidable and PSPACE-complete (note that the two fragments are not dual since GC are not closed under negation). Moreover, our results imply PSPACE-completeness of the verification problems investigated and shown to be decidable in [12], but for which no elementary upper bounds are known.

1 Introduction

Abstractions of Counter systems. Counter systems are a widely investigated complete computational model, used for instance to model broadcast protocols [19] and programs with pointer variables [7]. Though simple problems like reachability are already undecidable for 2-counter Minsky machines [24], interesting abstractions of counter systems have been studied, for which interesting classes of verification problems have been shown to be decidable. Many of these abstractions are in fact restrictions: examples include Petri nets [25], reversal-bounded counter machines [21], and flat counter systems [6,13]. Genuine abstractions are obtained by approximating counting operations by non-functional fragments of Presburger constraints between the variables of the current state and the variables of the next state. Examples include the class of Monotonicity Constraint Systems (MCS) [5] and its variants, like constraint automata in [15], and integral relation automata (IRA) [12], for which the (monotonicity) constraints (MC) are boolean combinations of inequalities of the form $u < v$ or $u \leq v$, where u and v range over variables or integer constants. MCS and their subclasses (namely, *size-change systems*) have found important applications for automated termination proofs of functional programs (see e.g. [5]). Richer classes of non-functional fragments of Presburger constraints have been investigated, e.g. difference bound constraints [14], and their extension, namely octagon relations [9], where it is shown that the transitive closure of a

V. Kuncak and A. Rybalchenko (Eds.): VMCAI 2012, LNCS 7148, pp. 88–103, 2012.

single constraint is Presburger definable (these results are useful for the verification of safety properties of flat counter systems). Note that difference bound constraints over (real-valued or integer-valued) variables (clocks) are also used as guards of transitions in timed automata [3]. Size-change systems extended with difference bound constraints over the natural number domain have been investigated in [4]: there, the atomic difference constraints are of the form $x - y' \geq c$, where c is an integer constant, and y' (resp., x) range over the variables of the target (resp., source) state. Termination for this class of systems is shown to be undecidable. To regain decidability, the authors consider a restriction, where at most one bound per target variable in each transition is allowed.

Temporal logics with Presburger constraints. An important classification of temporal logics is based on the underlying nature of time. In the *linear-time* setting , formulas are interpreted over linear sequences (corresponding to single computations of the system), and temporal operators are provided for describing the ordering of events along a single computation path. In the *branching-time* setting, formulas are instead interpreted over computation trees, which describe all the possible computations of the system from a designated initial state. Branching-time temporal logics are in general more expressive than linear-time temporal logics since they provide both temporal operators for describing properties of a path in the computation tree, and path quantifiers for describing the branching structure in computation trees.

In order to specify behavioral properties of counter systems, standard propositional linear-time temporal logics (like LTL) and propositional branching-time temporal logics (like CTL*) can be extended by replacing atomic propositions with Presburger constraints, which usually refer to the values of the (counter) variables at two consecutive states along a computation path (run). These enriched temporal logics allow to specify properties of counter systems that go beyond simple reachability. Hence, basic decision problems are generally undecidable. However, decidability has been established for various interesting fragments. We focus on fragments where the constraint language includes MC. For the *linear-time setting*, many decidable fragments of full Presburger LTL have been obtained either by restricting the underlying constraint language, see e.g. [15,17], or by restricting the logical language, see e.g. [8,13]. In particular, satisfiability and model checking (w.r.t. constraint automata) of standard LTL extended with MC are decidable and PSPACE-complete [15] (which matches the complexity of LTL). For the *branching-time setting*, to the best of our knowledge, very few decidability results are known. The extension of standard CTL* with MC, here denoted by MCCTL*, has been introduced in [12], where it is shown that model checking IRA against its existential and universal fragments, E–MCCTL* and A–MCCTL*, is decidable (by contrast, model checking for full MCCTL* is undecidable, even for its CTL-like fragment[1]). As done in [17], adding periodicity constraints and the ability for a fixed $k \geq 1$, to compare the variable values at states of a run at distance at most k, decidability of the above problems is preserved [10]. However, no elementary upper bounds for these problems are known [12,10]. Moreover, it is shown in [16] that model checking a subclass of flat counter machines w.r.t. full Presburger CTL* is decidable. In this subclass of systems, counting acceleration over every cycle in the control graph is Presburger definable. Thus, since the relation between the variables at the current and next state

[1] Quantification over variables can be simulated by the path quantifiers of the logic.

is functional and the control graph is flat, Presburger definability can be extended in a natural way to the set of states satisfying a given formula.

Our contribution. We investigate verification problems for an (infinitely-branching) abstract model of counter machines, we call *gap-order constraint systems* (GCS), in which constraints (over $\mathbb{Z}$) between the variables of the source state and the target state of a transition are (transitional) *gap-order constraints* (GC) [27]. These constraints are positive boolean combinations of inequalities of the form $u - v \geq k$, where u, v range over variables and integer constants and k is a natural number. Thus, GC can express simple relations on variables such as lower and upper bounds on the values of individual variables; and equality, and gaps (minimal differences) between values of pairs of variables. GC have been introduced in the field of constraint query languages (constraint Datalog) for deductive databases [27], and also have found applications in the analysis of safety properties for parameterized systems [1,2] and for determining state invariants in counter systems [20]. As pointed out in [2], using GC for expressing the enabling conditions of transitions allow to handle a large class of protocols, where the behavior depends on the relative ordering of values among variables, rather than the actual values of these variables.

GCS strictly extend IRA (and its variants, namely, MCS and the constraint automata in [15]). This because GC extend MC and, differently from MC, are closed under existential quantification (but not under negation).[2] Moreover, the parameterized systems investigated in [1,2] correspond to the parameterized version of GCS, where a system consists of an arbitrary number of processes which are instances of the same GCS (additionally, transitions of a process can specify global conditions which check the current local states and variables of all, or some of, other active processes). This framework is useful to verify correctness regardless of the number of processes. However, basic decision problems like reachability for the parameterized version of GCS are undecidable [1,2]. Decidability of reachability can be regained for a restricted class of parameterized systems in which processes have at most one integer local variable [1,2].

Note that if we extend the constraint language of GCS by allowing either negation, or constraints of the form $u - v \geq -k$, with $k \in \mathbb{N}$, then the resulting class of systems can trivially emulate Minsky counter machines, leading to undecidable basic decision problems. Moreover, note that GC extended with constraints of the form $u - v \geq -k$, with $k \in \mathbb{N}$, correspond to standard diagonal bound constraints [3,14]. As mentioned above, these constraints are used as guards in timed automata [3], where (integer-valued or real-valued) variables (clocks) record the elapsed time among events. However, guards in timed automata express constraints only over the clocks of the source state, and clocks are synchronized, i.e., they always advance at same speed. Hence, timed automata with integer-valued clocks and GCS are incomparable formalisms.

Our results are as follows. First, we investigate the *fairness problem* for GCS (which is crucial for the verification of liveness properties), that is checking the existence of infinite runs satisfying acceptance conditions à la Büchi. We show that this problem is decidable and PSPACE-complete; moreover, for the given GCS, one can compute a GC representation of the set of states from which there is a 'fair' infinite run. Next, we

[2] Hence, GC are closed under composition which captures the reachability relation in GCS for a fixed path in the control graph.

address verification problems of GCS against a *strict* extension, denoted by GCCTL*, of the logic MCCTL* (given in *complete* positive normal form) [12] obtained by adding transitional GC (we also allow existential quantification over variables in the underlying constraint language). Note that while MCCTL* is closed under negation, its strict extension GCCTL* is not (if we allow negation, the resulting logic would be undecidable also for small fragments). We show that while model-checking GCS against the *universal fragment* A–GCCTL* of GCCTL* is undecidable, model checking GCS against the existential fragment E–GCCTL* of GCCTL*, and satisfiability of both A–GCCTL* and E–GCCTL* are instead decidable and PSPACE-complete (which matches the complexity of model checking and satisfiability for the existential and universal fragments of standard CTL* [23]). Note that E–GCCTL* and A–GCCTL* are not dual. Moreover, for a given GCS S and E–GCCTL* formula φ, the set of states in S satisfying φ is *effectively* GC representable.

Since E–GCCTL* subsumes E–MCCTL*, and E–MCCTL* and A–MCCTL* are dual, our results imply PSPACE-completeness for model-checking (w.r.t. IRA or GCS) of both E–MCCTL* and A–MCCTL*. Hence, in particular, we solve complexity issues left open in [12] (see also [10]). Due to space reasons, many proofs are omitted and can be found in [11].

2 Preliminaries

Let $\mathbb{Z}$ (resp., $\mathbb{N}$) be the set of integers (resp., natural numbers). We fix a finite set $Var = \{x_1, \ldots, x_r\}$ of variables, a finite set of constants $Const \subseteq \mathbb{Z}$ such that $0 \in Const$, and a fresh copy of Var, $Var' = \{x'_1, \ldots, x'_r\}$. For an arbitrary finite set of variables V, an (integer) *valuation* over V is a mapping of the form $\nu : V \to \mathbb{Z}$, assigning to each variable in V an integer value. For $V' \subseteq V$, $\nu_{V'}$ denotes the restriction of ν to V'. For a valuation ν, by convention, we define $\nu(c) = c$ for all $c \in \mathbb{Z}$.

Definition 1. *[27]* A *gap-order constraint* (GC) over V and *Const* is a conjunction ξ of inequalities of the form $u - v \geq k$, where $u, v \in V \cup Const$ and $k \in \mathbb{N}$. W.l.o.g. we assume that for all $u, v \in V \cup Const$, there is at most one conjunct in ξ of the form $u - v \geq k$ for some k. A valuation $\nu : V \to \mathbb{Z}$ *satisfies* ξ if for each conjunct $u - v \geq k$ of ξ, $\nu(u) - \nu(v) \geq k$. We denote by $Sat(\xi)$ the set of such valuations.

Definition 2. *[12]* A (*gap-order*) *monotonicity graph* (MG) over V and *Const* is a directed weighted graph G with set of vertices $V \cup Const$ and edges $u \xrightarrow{k} v$ labeled by natural numbers k, and s.t.: if $u \xrightarrow{k} v$ and $u \xrightarrow{k'} v$ are edges of G, then $k = k'$. The set $Sat(G)$ of *solutions* of G is the set of valuations ν over V s.t. for each $u \xrightarrow{k} v$ in G, $\nu(u) - \nu(v) \geq k$. GC and MG are equivalent formalisms since there is a trivial linear-time computable bijection assigning to each GC ξ an MG $G(\xi)$ such that $Sat(G(\xi)) = Sat(\xi)$.[3]

The notation $G \models u < v$ means that there is an edge in G from v to u with weight $k > 0$. Moreover, $G \models u \leq v$ means that there is an edge of G from v to u, and $G \models u = v$

[3] MG are called Positive Graphose Inequality Systems in [12]. A different constraint graph representation of GC can be found in [27].

means $G \models u \leq v$ and $G \models v \leq u$. Also, we write $G \models u_1 \lhd_1 \ldots \lhd_{n-1} u_n$ to mean that $G \models u_i \lhd_i u_{i+1}$ for each $1 \leq i < n$, where $\lhd_i \in \{<, \leq, =\}$. A *transitional* GC (resp., *transitional* MG) is a GC (resp., MG) over $Var \cup Var'$ and *Const*. For valuations $\nu, \nu' : Var \to \mathbb{Z}$, we denote by $\nu \oplus \nu'$ the valuation over $Var \cup Var'$ defined as follows: $(\nu \oplus \nu')(x_i) = \nu(x_i)$ and $(\nu \oplus \nu')(x'_i) = \nu'(x_i)$ for $i = 1, \ldots, r$.

Definition 3. A *gap-order constraint system* (GCS) over *Var* and *Const* is a finite directed labeled graph $\mathcal{S}$ such that each edge is labeled by a *transitional* GC. $Q(\mathcal{S})$ denotes the set of vertices in $\mathcal{S}$, called *control points*, and $E(\mathcal{S})$ the set of edges.

For a finite path $\wp$ of a GCS $\mathcal{S}$, $s(\wp)$ and $t(\wp)$ denote the source and target control points of $\wp$. For a finite path $\wp$ and a path $\wp'$ such that $t(\wp) = s(\wp')$, the composition of $\wp$ and $\wp'$, written $\wp\wp'$, is defined as usual.

The semantics of a GCS $\mathcal{S}$ is given by an infinite directed graph $[\![\mathcal{S}]\!]$ defined as:

- The vertices of $[\![\mathcal{S}]\!]$, called *states* of $\mathcal{S}$, are the pairs of the form (q, ν), where q is a control point of $\mathcal{S}$ and $\nu : Var \to \mathbb{Z}$ is a valuation over *Var*;
- There is an edge in $[\![\mathcal{S}]\!]$ from (q, ν) to (q', ν') iff there is a (labeled) edge in $\mathcal{S}$ of the form $q \xrightarrow{\xi} q'$ such that $\nu \oplus \nu' \in Sat(\xi)$. We say that the edge of $[\![\mathcal{S}]\!]$ from (q, ν) to (q', ν') is an *instance* of the edge $q \xrightarrow{\xi} q'$ of $\mathcal{S}$.

A path of $[\![\mathcal{S}]\!]$ is called a *run* of $\mathcal{S}$. The length $|\wp|$ (resp., $|\pi|$) of a path $\wp$ (resp., run π) of $\mathcal{S}$ is defined in the standard way. A *non-null* path of $\mathcal{S}$ is a path of $\mathcal{S}$ of non-null length. Let $\wp = q_0 \xrightarrow{\xi_0} q_1 \xrightarrow{\xi_1} q_2, \ldots$ be a path of $\mathcal{S}$. A run π of $\mathcal{S}$ is an *instance* of $\wp$ if π is of the form $\pi = (q_0, \nu_0) \to (q_1, \nu_1) \to (q_2, \nu_2), \ldots$ and for each i, $(q_i, \nu_i) \to (q_{i+1}, \nu_{i+1})$ is an instance of $q_i \xrightarrow{\xi_i} q_{i+1}$. Given $F \subseteq Q(\mathcal{S})$, an infinite run $(q_0, \nu_0) \to (q_1, \nu_1) \to \ldots$ of $\mathcal{S}$ is *fair w.r.t* F if for infinitely many $i \geq 0$, $q_i \in F$.

Example 1. The figure depicts a GCS $\mathcal{S}$ consisting of a unique control point q and two self-loops. Note that there is no infinite run since along any run, the pair (x_1, x_2) decreases strictly w.r.t. the lexicographic order (over $\mathbb{N} \times \mathbb{N}$). On the other hand, one can easily check that for each state (q, ν) with $\nu(x_1) > 0$ and $\nu(x_2) \geq 0$, the set of the lengths of the runs from (q, ν) is unbounded.

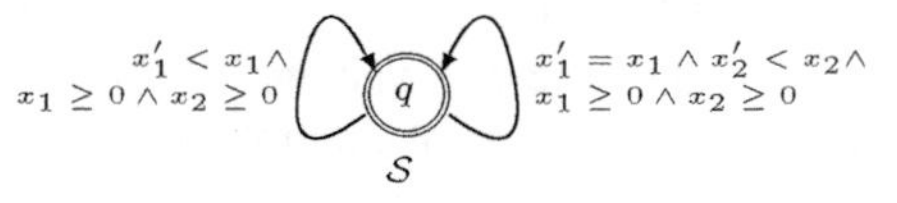

Convention: since we use MG representations to manipulate GC, we assume that the edge-labels in GCS are transitional MG.

2.1 Properties of Monotonicity Graphs

We recall some basic operations on MG [12] which can be computed in polynomial time. Furthermore, we define a sound and complete (w.r.t. satisfiability) approximation scheme of MG and show that the basic operations preserve soundness and completeness of this approximation. A different approximation scheme for GC can be found in [27].

A MG G is *satisfiable* if $Sat(G) \neq \emptyset$. Let G be a MG over V and *Const*. For $V' \subseteq V$, *the restriction of* G *to* V', written $G_{V'}$, is the MG given by the subgraph of G whose set of vertices is $V' \cup Const$. For all vertices u, v of G, we denote by $p_G(u,v)$ the least upper bound (possibly ∞) of the weight sums on all paths in G from u to v (we set $p_G(u,v) = -\infty$ if there is no such a path). The MG G is *normalized* iff: (1) for all vertices u, v of G, if $p_G(u,v) > -\infty$, then $p_G(u,v) \neq \infty$ and $u \stackrel{p_G(u,v)}{\longrightarrow} v$ is an edge of G, and (2) for all constants $c_1, c_2 \in Const$, $p_G(c_1, c_2) \leq c_1 - c_2$.

Proposition 1. [12] *Let G be a* MG *over V and Const. Then:*

1. *If G is* normalized *and $V' \subseteq V$, then G is satisfiable and every solution of $G_{V'}$ can be extended to a whole solution of G.*
2. *G is satisfiable $\Leftrightarrow$ G contains no loop with positive weight sum and for all $c_1, c_2 \in Const$, $p_G(c_1, c_2) \leq c_1 - c_2$ (this can be checked in polynomial time).*
3. *If G is satisfiable, then one can build in polynomial time an equivalent* normalized MG $\overline{G}$ *(i.e., $Sat(\overline{G}) = Sat(G)$), called the* closure *of G.*

According to Proposition 1, for a satisfiable MG G, we denote by $\overline{G}$ the closure of G. Moreover, for all unsatisfiable MG G over V and *Const*, we use a unique closure corresponding to some MG G_{nil} over V and *Const* such that $(G_{nil})_\emptyset$ is unsatisfiable (recall that $(G_{nil})_\emptyset$ denotes the MG given by the subgraph of G_{nil} whose set of vertices is *Const*). Now, we recall some effective operations on MG. Let $Var'' = \{x''_1, \ldots, x''_r\}$ be an additional copy of $Var = \{x_1 \ldots, x_r\}$.

Definition 4. [12] Let G be a MG on V and *Const* and G' be a MG on V' and *Const*.
1. **Projection:** if $V' \subseteq V$, the *projection of G over V'* is the MG given by $(\overline{G})_{V'}$.
2. **Intersection:** the *intersection $G \bigotimes G'$ of G and G'* is the MG over $V \cup V'$ and *Const* defined as: $u \stackrel{k}{\rightarrow} v$ is an edge of $G \bigotimes G'$ iff *either* (1) $u \stackrel{k}{\rightarrow} v$ is an edge of G (resp., G') and there is no edge from u to v in G' (resp., G), *or* (2) $k = \max(\{k', k''\})$, $u \stackrel{k'}{\rightarrow} v$ is an edge of G and $u \stackrel{k''}{\rightarrow} v$ is an edge of G'.
3. **Composition:** assume that G and G' are two transitional MG. Let G'' be obtained from G' by renaming any variable x'_i into x''_i and x_i into x'_i. The *composition $G \bullet G'$* of G and G' is the transitional MG obtained from the *projection* of $G \bigotimes G''$ over $Var \cup Var''$ by renaming any variable x''_i into x'_i.

By Definition 4 and Proposition 1, we easily obtain the following known result [12], which essentially asserts that MG (or, equivalently, GC) are closed under intersection and existential quantification.

Proposition 2. *Let G be a* MG *over V and Const and G' be a* MG *over V' and Const.*
1. ***Projection:** if G' is the projection of G over V', then for $\nu' : V' \to \mathbb{Z}$, $\nu' \in Sat(G')$ iff $\nu' = \nu|_{V'}$ for some $\nu \in Sat(G)$.*
2. ***Intersection:** for $\nu : V \cup V' \to \mathbb{Z}$, $\nu \in Sat(G \bigotimes G')$* iff *$\nu|_V \in Sat(G)$ and $\nu|_{V'} \in Sat(G')$. Hence, for $V = V'$, $Sat(G \bigotimes G') = Sat(G) \cap Sat(G')$.*
3. ***Composition:** assume that G and G' are transitional* MG*. Then, for all $\nu, \nu' : Var \to \mathbb{Z}$. $\nu \oplus \nu' \in Sat(G \bullet G')$ iff $\nu \oplus \nu'' \in Sat(G)$ and $\nu'' \oplus \nu' \in Sat(G')$ for some $\nu'' : Var \to \mathbb{Z}$. Moreover, the composition operator $\bullet$ is associative.*

Approximation scheme: let K stand for $\max(\{|c_1 - c_2| + 1 \mid c_1, c_2 \in Const\})$. Note that $K > 0$. For each $h \in \mathbb{N}$, let $\lfloor h \rfloor_K = h$ if $h \leq K$, and $\lfloor h \rfloor_K = K$ otherwise.

Definition 5 **(K-bounded MG).** A MG is *K-bounded* iff for each of its edges $u \xrightarrow{k} v$, $k \leq K$. For a MG G over V and *Const*, $\lfloor G \rfloor_K$ denotes the K-bounded MG over V and *Const* obtained from G by replacing each edge $u \xrightarrow{k} v$ of G with the edge $u \xrightarrow{\lfloor k \rfloor_K} v$.

The proofs of the following propositions are in [11].

Proposition 3. *Let G be a* MG *over V and Const. Then, G is satisfiable iff $\lfloor G \rfloor_K$ is satisfiable. Moreover, $\lfloor \overline{G} \rfloor_K = \lfloor \overline{\lfloor G \rfloor_K} \rfloor_K$.*

Proposition 4. *For transitional* MG *G_1 and G_2, $\lfloor G_1 \bullet G_2 \rfloor_K = \lfloor \lfloor G_1 \rfloor_K \bullet \lfloor G_2 \rfloor_K \rfloor_K$.*

2.2 Results on the Reachability Relation in GCS

In this subsection, we give constructive results on the reachability relation in GCS.

Definition 6. *A transitional* MG *G is said to be* complete *if:*

- *for all $u, v \in Var \cup Var' \cup Const$, $G \models u \leq v \Rightarrow G \models u \lhd v$ for some $\lhd \in \{<, =\}$;*
- *for all $u, v \in Var \cup Const$, either $G \models u \leq v$ or $G \models v \leq u$;*
- *for all $u, v \in Var' \cup Const$, either $G \models u \leq v$ or $G \models v \leq u$.*

A GCS $\mathcal{S}$ is *complete* iff each MG in $\mathcal{S}$ is complete. Fix a *complete* GCS $\mathcal{S}$. For a finite path $\wp$ of $\mathcal{S}$, the *reachability relation w.r.t.* $\wp$, denoted by $\leadsto_\wp$, is the binary relation on the set of valuations over *Var* defined as: for all $\nu, \nu' : Var \rightarrow \mathbb{Z}$, $\nu \leadsto_\wp \nu'$ iff there is a run of $\mathcal{S}$ from $(s(\wp), \nu)$ to $(t(\wp), \nu')$ which is an instance of the path $\wp$. For a transitional MG G, *G characterizes the reachability relation* $\leadsto_\wp$ iff $Sat(G) = \{\nu \oplus \nu' \mid \nu \leadsto_\wp \nu'\}$. We associate to each non-null finite path $\wp$ of $\mathcal{S}$ a transitional MG $G_\wp$ and a transitional K-bounded MG $G^{bd}_\wp$, defined by induction on $\wp$ as follows:

- $\wp = q \xrightarrow{G} q'$: $G_\wp = \overline{G}$ and $G^{bd}_\wp = \lfloor \overline{G} \rfloor_K$;
- $\wp = \wp'\wp''$, $|\wp'| > 0$, and $\wp'' = q \xrightarrow{G} q'$: $G_\wp = G_{\wp'} \bullet G$ and $G^{bd}_\wp = \lfloor G^{bd}_{\wp'} \bullet \lfloor G \rfloor_K \rfloor_K$.

Note that the composition operator preserves completeness, and for a transitional MG G, G is complete iff $\lfloor G \rfloor_K$ is complete. Thus, by a straightforward induction on the length of the path $\wp$ and by using Propositions 2 and 4, we obtain the following.

Proposition 5. *For a non-null finite path $\wp$ of $\mathcal{S}$, $G_\wp = \overline{G_\wp}$, and $G_\wp$ is complete and characterizes the reachability relation $\leadsto_\wp$. Moreover, $G^{bd}_\wp = \lfloor G_\wp \rfloor_K$ and is complete.*

Let $\mathcal{G}^K_\mathcal{S} = \{(\lfloor G_\wp \rfloor_K, s(\wp), t(\wp)) \mid \wp$ is a non-null finite path and $G_\wp$ is satisfiable$\}$. Note that $\mathcal{G}^K_\mathcal{S}$ is finite since the set of transitional K-bounded MG is finite. By Proposition 5, $\mathcal{G}^K_\mathcal{S}$ is exactly the set $\{(G^{bd}_\wp, s(\wp), t(\wp)) \mid \wp$ is a non-null finite path and $G^{bd}_\wp$ is satisfiable$\}$. It follows that we can compute the set $\mathcal{G}^K_\mathcal{S}$ by a simple transitive closure procedure. In particular, we obtain the following result.

Theorem 1. *For a* complete GCS *$\mathcal{S}$, each $G \in \mathcal{G}^K_\mathcal{S}$ is* complete, *and the size of $\mathcal{G}^K_\mathcal{S}$ is bounded by $O(|Q(\mathcal{S})|^2 \cdot (K+2)^{(2|Var|+|Const|)^2})$. Moreover, the set $\mathcal{G}^K_\mathcal{S}$ can be computed in time $O(|E(\mathcal{S})| \cdot |Q(\mathcal{S})|^2 \cdot (K+2)^{(2|Var|+|Const|)^2})$.*

Proof. An upper bound on the cardinality of the finite set of K-bounded transitional MG is $(K+2)^{(2|Var|+|Const|)^2}$, as each transitional K-bounded MG has at most $(2|Var|+|Const|)$ vertices and for all vertices u and v, there is at most one edge from u to v, and this edge has the form $u \xrightarrow{k} v$, where $k = 0, 1, \ldots, K$. It follows that the cardinality of $\mathcal{G}_S^K$ is bounded by $|Q(\mathcal{S})|^2 \cdot (K+2)^{(2|Var|+|Const|)^2}$. By Proposition 5, $\mathcal{G}_S^K$ is exactly the set $\{(G_\wp^{bd}, s(\wp), t(\wp)) \mid \wp$ is a non-null finite path and $G_\wp^{bd}$ is satisfiable$\}$. It follows that we can compute the set $\mathcal{G}_S^K$ by the following transitive closure procedure: initialize a set B to $\{(\lfloor \overline{G} \rfloor_K, q, q') \mid q \xrightarrow{G} q'$ is an edge of $\mathcal{S}$ and $\lfloor G \rfloor_K$ is satisfiable$\}$ and repeat the following step until no more elements can be added to B (at this point $B = \mathcal{G}_S^K$): for each $(G^{bd}, q, q') \in B$ and edge $q' \xrightarrow{G} q''$ of $\mathcal{S}$ include in B also $\lfloor G^{bd} \bullet \lfloor G \rfloor_K \rfloor_K$, unless it is unsatisfiable. Hence, the result follows. □

By [12] (see also [10]), for a GCS $\mathcal{S}$, the reflexive transitive closure of the transition relation of $[\![\mathcal{S}]\!]$ is effectively GC definable (a similar result can be found in [27], where it is shown that for Datalog queries with GC, there is a closed form evaluation). The GC representation can be computed by a fixpoint iteration whose termination is guaranteed by a suitable decidable well-quasi ordering defined over the set of transitional MG. By an insight in the proof given in [12] (see also [10]), and applying the K-bounded approximation scheme, we easily obtain the following. For details, see [11]. Note that we are not able to give an upper bound on the cardinality of the set $\mathcal{P}_\mathcal{S}$.

Theorem 2. *One can compute a* finite *set $\mathcal{P}_\mathcal{S}$ of non-null finite paths of $\mathcal{S}$ such that: for each non-null finite path $\wp'$ of $\mathcal{S}$ from q to q', there is a path $\wp \in \mathcal{P}_\mathcal{S}$ from q to q' so that $\lfloor G_{\wp'} \rfloor_K = \lfloor G_\wp \rfloor_K$, and $\leadsto_{\wp'}$ implies $\leadsto_\wp$.*

3 Checking Fairness

For a GCS $\mathcal{S}$ and a set F of control points of $\mathcal{S}$, we denote by $Inf_{\mathcal{S},F}$ the set of states of $\mathcal{S}$ from which there is an infinite run that is fair w.r.t. F. In this section, we show that the problem of checking for a given GCS $\mathcal{S}$ and set $F \subseteq Q(\mathcal{S})$, whether $Inf_{\mathcal{S},F} \neq \emptyset$ (*fairness problem*) is decidable and PSPACE-complete.

First, we give additional definitions. Let $\mathcal{S}$ be a GCS. We denote by $\lfloor \mathcal{S} \rfloor_K$ the GCS obtained from $\mathcal{S}$ by replacing each edge $q \xrightarrow{G} q'$ of $\mathcal{S}$ with the edge $q \xrightarrow{\lfloor G \rfloor_K} q'$.

A set U of states of $\mathcal{S}$ is MG *representable* if there is a family $\{\mathcal{G}_q\}_{q \in Q(\mathcal{S})}$ of finite sets of MG over *Var* and *Const* such that $\bigcup_{G \in \mathcal{G}_q} Sat(G) = \{\nu \mid (q, \nu) \in U\}$ for each $q \in Q(\mathcal{S})$. For a set $\mathcal{G}$ of MG, $\lfloor \mathcal{G} \rfloor_K$ denotes the set of K-bounded MG given by $\{\lfloor G \rfloor_K \mid G \in \mathcal{G}\}$. We extend the previous set operation to families of sets of MG in the obvious way. For $F \subseteq Q(\mathcal{S})$ and $q \in Q(\mathcal{S})$, $Inf^q_{\mathcal{S},F}$ denotes the set of states in $Inf_{\mathcal{S},F}$ of the form (q, ν) for some valuation ν. Moreover, $Inf_\mathcal{S}$ stands for $Inf_{\mathcal{S},Q(\mathcal{S})}$.

A MG G is *weakly normalized* if for all vertices u, v, $p_G(u,v) \geq 0$ (resp., $p_G(u,v) > 0$) implies $G \models v \leq u$ (resp., $G \models v < u$). Note that G is weakly normalized iff $\lfloor G \rfloor_K$ is weakly normalized. A transitional MG G is *(weakly) idempotent* iff $\lfloor G \bullet G \rfloor_K = \lfloor G \rfloor_K$.

3.1 Checking Fairness for Simple GCS

In this section, we solve the fairness problem for a restricted class of GCS.

Definition 7 (Simple GCS). *A (satisfiable) simple* GCS *is a* GCS *consisting of just two edges of the form* $q_0 \xrightarrow{G_0} q$ *and* $q \xrightarrow{G} q$ *such that* $q_0 \neq q$*. Moreover, we require that* $G_0 \bullet G$ *is satisfiable, and* G *is complete,* weakly *normalized, and idempotent.*

To present our results on simple GCS, we need additional definitions.

Definition 8 (Lower and upper variables). We denote by *MAX* (resp., *MIN*) the maximum (resp., minimum) of *Const*. For a transitional MG G and $y \in Var \cup Var'$, y is a *lower* (resp., *upper*) *variable* of G if $G \models y < MIN$ (resp., $G \models MAX < y$). Moreover, y is a *bounded variable* of G if $G \models MIN \leq y$ and $G \models y \leq MAX$.

Definition 9. A transitional MG is *balanced* iff for all $u, v \in Var \cup Const$ and $\lhd \in \{<, =\}$, $G \models u \lhd v$ iff $G \models u' \lhd v'$ (where for $u \in Var \cup Const$, we write u' to denote the corresponding variable in Var' if $u \in Var$, and u itself otherwise).

Fix a simple GCS $\mathcal{S}$ with edges $q_0 \xrightarrow{G_0} q$ and $q \xrightarrow{G} q$. Since G is idempotent, by the associativity of composition $\bullet$ and Proposition 4, we obtain that for each $k \geq 1$, $\lfloor G_0 \bullet \underbrace{G \bullet \ldots \bullet G}_{k \text{ times}} \rfloor_K = \lfloor G_0 \bullet G \rfloor_K$. Hence, $G_0 \bullet \underbrace{G \bullet \ldots \bullet G}_{k \text{ times}}$ and $\underbrace{G \bullet \ldots \bullet G}_{k \text{ times}}$ are satisfiable for each $k \geq 1$. Since G is complete, it follows that G is *balanced* as well. Moreover, since G is satisfiable and complete, a variable $y \in Var \cup Var'$ is either a lower variable, or an upper variable, or a bounded variable of G, where the "or" is exclusive. We denote by $\mathrm{L}_1, \ldots, \mathrm{L}_N$ (resp., $\mathrm{U}_1, \ldots, \mathrm{U}_M$) the lower (resp., the upper) variables of G in *Var*, and by $\mathrm{B}_1, \ldots, \mathrm{B}_H$ the bounded variables of G in *Var*. Hence, we can assume that

$$G \models \mathrm{L}_1 \lhd_2 \ldots \lhd_N \mathrm{L}_N < \mathrm{B}_1 \lhd'_2 \ldots \lhd'_H \mathrm{B}_H < \mathrm{U}_1 \lhd''_2 \ldots \lhd''_M \mathrm{U}_M$$

where $\lhd_2 \ldots \lhd_N, \lhd'_2 \ldots \lhd'_H, \lhd''_2 \ldots \lhd''_M \in \{<, =\}$. Since G is balanced it follows that the lower variables (resp., upper variables) of G in Var' are $\mathrm{L}'_1, \ldots, \mathrm{L}'_N$ (resp., $\mathrm{U}'_1, \ldots, \mathrm{U}'_M$), and the bounded variables of G in Var' are $\mathrm{B}'_1, \ldots, \mathrm{B}'_H$. Moreover,

$$G \models \mathrm{L}'_1 \lhd_2 \ldots \lhd_N \mathrm{L}'_N < \mathrm{B}'_1 \lhd'_2 \ldots \lhd'_H \mathrm{B}'_H < \mathrm{U}'_1 \lhd''_2 \ldots \lhd''_M \mathrm{U}'_M$$

Now, we define a polynomial-time checkable condition on simple GCS.

Definition 10 (termination condition). We say that G satisfies the termination condition iff one of the following holds:

lower variables: either $G \models \mathrm{L}_i < \mathrm{L}'_i$ *for some* $1 \leq i \leq N$,
or $G \models \mathrm{L}_i = \mathrm{L}'_i$ *and* $G \models \mathrm{L}'_j < \mathrm{L}_j$ *for some* $1 \leq i < j \leq N$.

upper variables: either $G \models \mathrm{U}'_i < \mathrm{U}_i$ *for some* $1 \leq i \leq M$,
or $G \models \mathrm{U}_j = \mathrm{U}'_j$ *and* $G \models \mathrm{U}_i < \mathrm{U}'_i$ *for some* $1 \leq i < j \leq M$.

Intuitively, the above condition asserts that either there is a lower (resp., upper) variable of G_{Var} whose value strictly increases (resp., decreases) along each run of $\mathcal{S}$, or there are two lower (resp., upper) variables of G_{Var} such that their distance strictly decreases along each run of $\mathcal{S}$. Let $\mathcal{TC}$ be the class of simple GCS satisfying the termination condition. By Definition 10, we easily obtain the following.

Proposition 6. *If $\mathcal{S} \in \mathcal{TC}$, then $Inf_{\mathcal{S}} = \emptyset$.*

It remains to consider the case when $\mathcal{S} \notin \mathcal{TC}$. We define two integers L and U as follows: L is the smallest $1 \leq i \leq N$ such that $G \models \mathtt{L}_i = \mathtt{L}'_i$ (if such an i does not exist, we set $L = N + 1$). Finally, U is the greatest $1 \leq i \leq M$ such that $G \models \mathtt{U}_i = \mathtt{U}'_i$ (if such an i does not exist, we set $U = 0$). Note that $1 \leq L \leq N + 1$ and $0 \leq U \leq M$. The set of *unconstrained variables* in Var, written *Unc*, consists of the lower variables $\mathtt{L}_i$ such that $1 \leq i < L$ and the upper variables $\mathtt{U}_j$ such that $U < j \leq M$. We denote by Unc' the corresponding subset in Var'. Evidently, the following holds.

Lemma 1. *For a valuation $\nu_0 : Var \to \mathbb{Z}$, the set of valuations $\{\nu_{(Var \setminus Unc)} \mid (q, \nu)$ is reachable from (q, ν_0) in $[\![\mathcal{S}]\!]\}$ is finite.*

The proof of the following lemma is in [11]. Essentially, the result follows from Lemma 1 and the following property (which is a consequence of the idempotence of G): if $\mathcal{S} \notin \mathcal{TC}$, then $G \not\models \mathtt{U}'_i \leq \mathtt{U}_j$ and $G \not\models \mathtt{L}_h \leq \mathtt{L}'_k$ for all upper variables $\mathtt{U}'_i, \mathtt{U}_j$ and lower variables $\mathtt{L}_h, \mathtt{L}'_k$ in $Unc \cup Unc'$. In other terms, along a run of $\mathcal{S}$, the unconstrained upper (resp., lower) variables can increase (resp., decrease) arbitrarily.

Lemma 2. *Let $\mathcal{S} \notin \mathcal{TC}$. Then, $(q, \nu_0) \in Inf_{\mathcal{S}}$ iff there is a finite run π of $\mathcal{S}$ from (q, ν_0) of the form $\pi = (q, \nu_0) \ldots (q, \nu) \ldots (q, \nu')(q, \nu'')$ such that $\nu''_{(Var \setminus Unc)} = \nu_{(Var \setminus Unc)}$.*

Now, we can prove the main result of this subsection.

Theorem 3. *Let $\mathcal{S} \notin \mathcal{TC}$. Then, $Inf_{\mathcal{S}}$ is* MG *representable and one can construct a* MG *representation of $Inf_{\mathcal{S}}$, written $\sigma(\mathcal{S})$, such that: (1) $\lfloor \sigma(\mathcal{S}) \rfloor_K$ can be computed in polynomial time, and (2) $\lfloor \sigma(\mathcal{S}) \rfloor_K = \lfloor \sigma(\lfloor \mathcal{S} \rfloor_K) \rfloor_K$ ($\lfloor \mathcal{S} \rfloor_K$ is simple and $\lfloor \mathcal{S} \rfloor_K \notin \mathcal{TC}$).*

Proof. By Theorem 2, one can compute a *finite* set $\mathcal{P}$ of non-null finite paths of $\mathcal{S}$ from q to q such that for each non-null finite path $\wp'$ of $\mathcal{S}$ from q to q, there is a path $\wp \in \mathcal{P}$ so that $\leadsto_{\wp'}$ implies $\leadsto_{\wp}$. Note that given $\wp \in \mathcal{P}$, the transitional MG $G_{\wp}$ (which characterizes the reachability relation $\leadsto_{\wp}$) has the form $\underbrace{G \bullet \ldots \bullet G}_{k \text{ times}}$ for some $k \geq 1$.

Let $G_=$ be the transitional MG corresponding to the GC given by $\bigwedge_{x \in Var \setminus Unc} x' = x$, and $\mathcal{G} = \{G_{\wp} \bullet (G_{\wp'} \bigotimes G_=) \mid \wp, \wp' \in \mathcal{P}\} \cup \{G_{\wp} \bigotimes G_= \mid \wp \in \mathcal{P}\}$. Then, $\sigma(\mathcal{S}) = \{\mathcal{G}^q, \mathcal{G}^{q_0}\}$, where $\mathcal{G}^q$ and $\mathcal{G}^{q_0}$ are defined as follows:

$$\mathcal{G}^q = \{G' \mid G' \text{ is the projection of } G'' \text{ over } Var \text{ for some } G'' \in \mathcal{G}\}$$
$$\mathcal{G}^{q_0} = \{G' \mid G' \text{ is the projection of } G_0 \bullet G'' \text{ over } Var \text{ for some } G'' \in \mathcal{G}\}$$

Correctness of the construction easily follows from Lemma 2. The second part of the theorem follows from Propositions 3–4, and the fact that for each $\wp \in \mathcal{P}$, $\lfloor G_{\wp} \rfloor_K = \lfloor G \rfloor_K$ (G is idempotent) and $\lfloor G_{\wp} \bigotimes G_= \rfloor_K = \lfloor \lfloor G_{\wp} \rfloor_K \bigotimes \lfloor G_= \rfloor_K \rfloor_K$. For details, see [11]. □

3.2 Checking Fairness for Unrestricted GCS

Fix a GCS $\mathcal{S}$. For a non-null finite path $\wp$ of $\mathcal{S}$ such that $s(\wp) = t(\wp)$ (i.e., $\wp$ is cyclic), $(\wp)^\omega$ denotes the infinite path $\wp\wp \ldots$. A infinite path $\wp$ of $\mathcal{S}$ of the form $\wp = \wp'(\wp'')^\omega$ is said to be *ultimately periodic*. By using Theorem 2 and Ramsey's Theorem (in its infinite version) [26], we show the following result.

Theorem 4 (Characterization Theorem). *Let $\mathcal{S}$ be a complete* GCS*, $F \subseteq Q(\mathcal{S})$, and $\mathcal{P}_\mathcal{S}$ be the finite set of non-null finite paths of $\mathcal{S}$ satisfying Theorem 2. Then, for each state s, $s \in Inf_{\mathcal{S},F}$* iff *there is an infinite run of $\mathcal{S}$ starting from s which is an instance of an* ultimately periodic *path $\wp_0 \cdot (\wp)^\omega$ such that $\wp_0, \wp \in \mathcal{P}_\mathcal{S}$, $s(\wp) \in F$, $G_{\wp_0} \bullet G_\wp$ is satisfiable, $G_\wp$ is idempotent, and $G_{\wp_0}$ and $G_\wp$ are complete and normalized.*

Proof. The left implication $\Leftarrow$ is obvious. For the right implication $\Rightarrow$, assume that $s \in Inf_{\mathcal{S},F}$. Then, there is an infinite run π of $\mathcal{S}$ starting from s which visits infinitely often states whose control points are in F. Moreover, there is an infinite path $\wp_\infty$ of $\mathcal{S}$ such that π is an instance of $\wp_\infty$.

Let us consider the finite set $\mathcal{P}_\mathcal{S}$ of non-null finite paths of $\mathcal{S}$ satisfying the statement of Theorem 2. For each $\wp \in \mathcal{P}_\mathcal{S}$ from q to q', we denote by $[\wp]$ the set of non-null finite paths $\wp'$ of $\mathcal{S}$ from q to q' such that $\leadsto_{\wp'}$ implies $\leadsto_\wp$, and $\lfloor G_{\wp'} \rfloor_K = \lfloor G_\wp \rfloor_K$. Let H be the *finite* set given by $H = \{[\wp] \mid \wp \in \mathcal{P}_\mathcal{S}\}$. For each non-null finite path $\wp'$ of $\mathcal{S}$, we associate to $\wp'$ a *color* given by some element $[\wp] \in H$ such that $\wp' \in [\wp]$ (note that such an element of H must exist). Let us consider the infinite path $\wp_\infty$. Then, there is a control point $q \in F$ such that $\wp_\infty$ is of the form $\wp_\infty = \wp_0\wp_1\wp_2\ldots$, where for each $i \geq 1$, $\wp_i$ is a non-null (cyclic) path from q to q. Let us consider the set of positive natural numbers, and label each pair (i,j) of its elements with $i < j$ with the color of the subpath $\wp_i \ldots \wp_j$ of $\wp_\infty$. By Ramsey's Theorem (in its infinite version)[26], there is an infinite set I of positive natural numbers such that all the pairs (i,j) with $i, j \in I$ (and $i < j$) carry the same label in H, say $[\wp]$. It follows that $\wp_\infty$ can be written in the form $\wp_\infty = \wp'_0\wp'_1\wp'_2\ldots$ such that $|\wp'_0| > 0$ and for all $i \geq 1$, $\wp'_i \in [\wp]$ and $\wp'_i\wp'_{i+1} \in [\wp]$. Hence, in particular, $\lfloor G_{\wp'_i} \rfloor_K = \lfloor G_\wp \rfloor_K$ and $\lfloor G_{\wp'_i\wp'_{i+1}} \rfloor_K = \lfloor G_\wp \rfloor_K$. By Proposition 4 and associativity of $\bullet$, we obtain that $\lfloor G_\wp \rfloor_K = \lfloor G_\wp \bullet G_\wp \rfloor_K$. Hence, $G_\wp$ is idempotent.

Let $\wp''_0 \in \mathcal{P}_\mathcal{S}$ such that $\wp'_0 \in [\wp''_0]$. Since π is an instance of $\wp_\infty = \wp'_0\wp'_1\ldots$, and $\wp'_i \in [\wp]$ for each $i \geq 1$, it follows that there is an infinite run π' starting from s which is an instance of the *ultimately periodic* path $\wp''_0(\wp)^\omega$. Moreover, $s(\wp) = q \in F$, $\wp''_0, \wp \in \mathcal{P}_\mathcal{S}$, $G_{\wp''_0} \cdot G_\wp$ is satisfiable, $G_\wp$ is idempotent, and by Proposition 5, $G_{\wp''_0}$ and $G_\wp$ are complete and normalized, which concludes. □

Theorem 5. *Let $\mathcal{S}$ be a* GCS *and $F \subseteq Q(\mathcal{S})$. Then, $Inf_{\mathcal{S},F}$ is* MG *representable and one can construct a* MG *representation of $Inf_{\mathcal{S},F}$, written $\sigma_F(\mathcal{S})$, such that:*

1. *$\lfloor \sigma_F(\mathcal{S}) \rfloor_K$ can be computed in time $O(|E(\mathcal{S})| \cdot |Q(\mathcal{S})|^2 \cdot (K+2)^{(2|Var|+|Const|)^2})$;*
2. *$\lfloor \sigma_F(\mathcal{S}) \rfloor_K = \lfloor \sigma_F(\lfloor \mathcal{S} \rfloor_K) \rfloor_K$;*
3. *given $q \in Q(\mathcal{S})$ and a K-bounded* MG *G over Var, checking whether G is in the q-component of $\lfloor \sigma_F(\mathcal{S}) \rfloor_K$ can be done in polynomial space.*

Sketched proof. (A detailed proof is in [11]). We assume that $\mathcal{S}$ is complete (the general case easily follows). Let $\mathcal{P}_\mathcal{S}$ be the computable finite set of non-null finite paths of $\mathcal{S}$ satisfying the statement of Theorem 2, and let $\mathcal{F}_\mathcal{S}$ be the finite set of *simple* GCS constructed as: $\mathcal{S}' \in \mathcal{F}_\mathcal{S}$ iff $\mathcal{S}' \notin \mathcal{TC}$ and $\mathcal{S}'$ is a simple GCS consisting of two edges of the form $(\natural, s(\wp_0)) \stackrel{G_{\wp_0}}{\rightarrow} t(\wp_0)$ and $s(\wp) \stackrel{G_\wp}{\rightarrow} t(\wp)$ such that $\wp_0, \wp \in \mathcal{P}_\mathcal{S}$ and $s(\wp) = t(\wp) \in F$. By Theorem 3, for each $\mathcal{S}' \in \mathcal{F}_\mathcal{S}$ one can compute a MG representation $\mathcal{G}_{\mathcal{S}',in(\mathcal{S}')}$ (resp., $\mathcal{G}_{\lfloor \mathcal{S}' \rfloor_K,in(\mathcal{S}')}$) of $Inf_{\mathcal{S}'}^{(\natural,in(\mathcal{S}'))}$ (resp., $Inf_{\lfloor \mathcal{S}' \rfloor_K}^{(\natural,in(\mathcal{S}'))}$), where $(\natural, in(\mathcal{S}'))$

is the initial control point of $\mathcal{S}'$. Moreover, $\lfloor \mathcal{G}_{\mathcal{S}',in(\mathcal{S}')} \rfloor_K = \lfloor \mathcal{G}_{\lfloor \mathcal{S}' \rfloor_K, in(\mathcal{S}')} \rfloor_K$. Then, $\sigma_F(\mathcal{S})$ is given by

$$\sigma_F(\mathcal{S}) = \{ \bigcup_{\{\mathcal{S}' \in \mathcal{F}_{\mathcal{S}} \mid in(\mathcal{S}')=q\}} \mathcal{G}_{\mathcal{S}',in(\mathcal{S}')} \}_{q \in Q(\mathcal{S})}.$$

By Theorems 2 and 4, and Proposition 6, $\sigma_F(\mathcal{S})$ is a MG representation of $Inf_{\mathcal{S},F}$. Thus, the first part of the theorem holds. Now, let us consider Properties 1–3. Here, we focus on Property 1. Let $\mathcal{F}_{\mathcal{S},K}$ be the set of simple GCS $\mathcal{S}'$ such that $\mathcal{S}' = \lfloor \mathcal{S}'' \rfloor_K$ for some $\mathcal{S}'' \in \mathcal{F}_{\mathcal{S}}$. Since $\lfloor \mathcal{G}_{\mathcal{S}',in(\mathcal{S}')} \rfloor_K = \lfloor \mathcal{G}_{\lfloor \mathcal{S}' \rfloor_K, in(\mathcal{S}')} \rfloor_K$ for each $\mathcal{S}' \in \mathcal{F}_{\mathcal{S}}$, we obtain

$$\lfloor \sigma_F(\mathcal{S}) \rfloor_K = \{ \bigcup_{\{\mathcal{S}' \in \mathcal{F}_{\mathcal{S},K} \mid in(\mathcal{S}')=q\}} \lfloor \mathcal{G}_{\mathcal{S}',in(\mathcal{S}')} \rfloor_K \}_{q \in Q(\mathcal{S})}$$

Since for each $\mathcal{S}' \in \mathcal{F}_{\mathcal{S},K}$, $\lfloor \mathcal{G}_{\mathcal{S}',in(\mathcal{S}')} \rfloor_K$ can be computed in polynomial time in the size of $\mathcal{S}'$ (Theorem 3), it suffices to show that $\mathcal{F}_{\mathcal{S},K}$ can be computed in time $O(|E(\mathcal{S})| \cdot |Q(\mathcal{S})|^2 \cdot (K+2)^{(2|Var|+|Const|)^2})$. This last condition holds since: (i) for a GCS $\mathcal{S}'$, $\mathcal{S}'$ is simple iff $\lfloor \mathcal{S}' \rfloor_K$ is simple, (ii) for a simple GCS $\mathcal{S}''$, $\mathcal{S}'' \notin \mathcal{TC}$ iff $\lfloor \mathcal{S}'' \rfloor_K \notin \mathcal{TC}$, (iii) by Theorem 2, the set $\{(\lfloor G_\wp \rfloor_K, s(\wp), t(\wp)) \mid \wp \in \mathcal{P}_{\mathcal{S}}$ and $\lfloor G_\wp \rfloor_K$ is satisfiable$\}$ coincides with the set $\mathcal{G}_{\mathcal{S}}^K = \{(\lfloor G_\wp \rfloor_K, s(\wp), t(\wp)) \mid \wp$ is a non-null finite path of $\mathcal{S}$ and $\lfloor G_\wp \rfloor_K$ is satisfiable$\}$, and (iv) by Theorem 1, the set $\mathcal{G}_{\mathcal{S}}^K$ is computable in time $O(|E(\mathcal{S})| \cdot |Q(\mathcal{S})|^2 \cdot (K+2)^{(2|Var|+|Const|)^2})$. Thus, Property 1 holds. □

Corollary 1. *The fairness problem is* PSPACE*-complete.*

Proof. The upper bound easily follows from Property 3 in Theorem 5, and the fact that for each set $\mathcal{G}$ of MG, $\mathcal{G}$ contains a satisfiable MG iff $\lfloor \mathcal{G} \rfloor_K$ contains a satisfiable MG. Moreover, PSPACE-hardness follows from PSPACE-hardness of non-termination for Boolean Programs [22] and the fact that GCS subsume Boolean Programs. □

4 The Constrained Branching–Time Temporal Logic (GCCTL*)

We introduce the *constrained branching–time temporal logic* (GCCTL*) and investigate the related satisfiability and model checking problems. The logic GCCTL* is an extension of standard logic CTL* [18], where the set of atomic propositions is replaced with a subclass of Presburger constraints whose atomic formulas correspond to transitional GC. Formally, for a set of variables V and a set of constants *Const*, the *language of constraints* η, denoted by $\exists$GC, over V and *Const* is defined as follows:

$$\eta := u - v \geq k \mid \eta \vee \eta \mid \eta \wedge \eta \mid \exists x.\, \eta$$

where $u, v \in V \cup Const$, $k \in \mathbb{N}$, and $x \in V$. For a $\exists$GC constraint η and a valuation $\nu : V \to \mathbb{Z}$ over V, the satisfaction relation $v \models \eta$ is defined as follows (we omit the standard clauses for conjunction and disjunction):

- $\nu \models u - v \geq k \overset{\text{def}}{\Leftrightarrow} \nu(u) - \nu(v) \geq k$;
- $\nu \models \exists x.\, \eta \overset{\text{def}}{\Leftrightarrow}$ there is $c \in \mathbb{Z}$ such that $\nu[x \leftarrow c] \models \eta$.

where $\nu[x \leftarrow c](y) = \nu(y)$ if $y \neq x$, and $\nu[x \leftarrow c](y) = c$ otherwise. Note that $\exists$GC constraints are not closed under negation. Moreover, by Proposition 1(3) and Proposition 2(1) (see also [27]), GC are closed under existential quantification and quantification elimination can be done in polynomial time.

Syntax and semantics of GCCTL*: for the fixed set of variables *Var* and set of constants *Const*, the *state formulas* φ and *path formulas* ψ of GCCTL* are defined as:

$$\varphi := \top \mid \varphi \vee \varphi \mid \varphi \wedge \varphi \mid A\,\varphi \mid E\,\varphi$$
$$\psi := \varphi \mid \eta \mid \psi \vee \psi \mid \psi \wedge \psi \mid \mathsf{O}\psi \mid \Box\psi \mid \psi \mathsf{U} \psi$$

where $\top$ denotes "true", E ("for some path") and A ("for all paths") are path quantifiers, η is a $\exists$GC constraint over *Var* $\cup$ *Var'* and *Const*, and O ("next"), U ("until"), and $\Box$ ("always") are the usual linear temporal operators. Since $\exists$GC constraints are not closed under negation, the logic is not closed under negation as well.[4] The set of state formulas φ forms the language GCCTL*. We also consider the existential and universal fragments E–GCCTL* and A–GCCTL* of GCCTL*, obtained by disallowing the universal and existential path quantifiers, respectively. GCCTL* formulas are interpreted over directed graphs $\mathcal{G} = \langle S, \rightarrow, \mu \rangle$ augmented with a mapping μ assigning to each vertex (or state) a valuation over *Var*. For an infinite path $\pi = s_0, s_1, \ldots$ of $\mathcal{G}$, we denote the suffix $s_i, s_{i+1}, \ldots$ of π by π^i, and the i-th state of π by $\pi(i)$. Let $s \in S$ and π be a infinite path of $\mathcal{G}$. For a state (resp., path) formula φ (resp. ψ), the satisfaction relation $(\mathcal{G}, s) \models \varphi$ (resp., $(\mathcal{G}, \pi) \models \psi$), meaning that φ (resp., ψ) holds at state s (resp., holds along π) in $\mathcal{G}$, is defined as (we omit the clauses for conjunction and disjunction):

- $(\mathcal{G}, s) \models A\,\psi \overset{\text{def}}{\Leftrightarrow}$ for each infinite path π from s, $(\mathcal{G}, \pi) \models \psi$;
- $(\mathcal{G}, s) \models E\,\psi \overset{\text{def}}{\Leftrightarrow}$ there exists an infinite path π from s such that $(\mathcal{G}, \pi) \models \psi$;
- $(\mathcal{G}, \pi) \models \varphi \overset{\text{def}}{\Leftrightarrow} (\mathcal{G}, \pi(0)) \models \varphi$;
- $(\mathcal{G}, \pi) \models \eta \overset{\text{def}}{\Leftrightarrow} \mu(\pi(0)) \oplus \mu(\pi(1)) \models \eta$;
- $(\mathcal{G}, \pi) \models \mathsf{O}\psi \overset{\text{def}}{\Leftrightarrow} (\mathcal{G}, \pi^1) \models \psi$;
- $(\mathcal{G}, \pi) \models \Box\psi \overset{\text{def}}{\Leftrightarrow}$ for all $i \geq 0$, $(\mathcal{G}, \pi^i) \models \psi$;
- $(\mathcal{G}, \pi) \models \psi_1 \mathsf{U} \psi_2 \overset{\text{def}}{\Leftrightarrow}$ there is $i \geq 0$. $(\mathcal{G}, \pi^i) \models \psi_2$ and for all $j < i$. $(\mathcal{G}, \pi^j) \models \psi_1$.

Note that the *dual* until operator $\widetilde{\mathsf{U}}$ can be expressed in the logic since: $\psi_1 \widetilde{\mathsf{U}} \psi_2 \equiv \Box\psi_2 \vee (\psi_2 \mathsf{U}(\psi_1 \wedge \psi_2))$. A GCCTL* formula ξ is *satisfiable* if $(\mathcal{G}, s) \models \varphi$ for some labeled graph $\mathcal{G}$ and $\mathcal{G}$-state s. The *model checking problem of* GCS *against* GCCTL* is checking for a given GCS $\mathcal{S}$, state s of $\mathcal{S}$, and GCCTL* formula φ, whether $(\mathcal{G}(\mathcal{S}), s) \models \varphi$, where $\mathcal{G}(\mathcal{S})$ is obtained from $[\![\mathcal{S}]\!]$ by adding the mapping which assigns to each state of $\mathcal{S}$ the associated valuation over *Var*. We denote by $[\![\varphi]\!]_{\mathcal{S}}$ the set of states s of $\mathcal{S}$ such that $(\mathcal{G}(\mathcal{S}), s) \models \varphi$.

Example 2. Let us consider the requirement: "there is an infinite run from the given state such that variables x and y behave like clocks with rates at least k and k', respectively". This can be expressed by the E–GCCTL* formula

$$E\Box[((x' = 0) \vee (x' - x) \geq k) \wedge ((y' = 0) \vee (y' - y) \geq k')$$

[4] If we allow negation, then the successor relation is definable and by [17], basic decision problems become undecidable.

We can also use our framework to solve verification of non-local constraints (between variables at states arbitrarily far away from each other), which are not directly expressible in GCCTL*. As a relevant example, we consider *unboundedness requirements* on the values of a given variable along an infinite run. For each $x \in \mathit{Var}$, let us denote by ξ_x a special atomic formula (*unboundedness constraint*) that hold along an infinite run π iff the set of x-values along π is unbounded. Let E–GCCTL$^*_{Unb}$ be the extension of E–GCCTL* with these constraints. By the following result (whose proof is in [11]), it follows that model checking GCS against E–GCCTL$^*_{Unb}$ can be reduced in polynomial time to model checking GCS against E–GCCTL*.

Theorem 6. *Let $\mathcal{S}$ be a* GCS *over Var and φ be a* E–GCCTL$^*_{Unb}$ *formula over Var. Then, one can construct in polynomial-time an extension Var_{ext} of Var, a* GCS *$\mathcal{S}_{ext}$ over Var_{ext}, and a* E–GCCTL* *formula $f(\varphi)$ over Var_{ext} such that: for each state s of $\mathcal{S}$, one can compute in linear-time a state s_{ext} of $\mathcal{S}_{ext}$ so that*

$$(\mathcal{G}(\mathcal{S}), s) \models \varphi \text{ if and only if } (\mathcal{G}(\mathcal{S}_{ext}), s_{ext}) \models f(\varphi)$$

Decision procedures. By [12], model checking GCS against GCCTL* is undecidable. It is straightforward to extend this negative result to model checking GCS against A–GCCTL* (see [11]). In the following, we show that model checking GCS against E–GCCTL*, and satisfiability for E–GCCTL* and A–GCCTL* are instead decidable and PSPACE-complete.

Theorem 7. *Given a* GCS *$\mathcal{S}$ and a* E–GCCTL* *formula φ, $[\![\varphi]\!]_{\mathcal{S}}$ is* MG *representable and one can construct a* MG *representation of $[\![\varphi]\!]_{\mathcal{S}}$, written $\pi(\mathcal{S}, \varphi)$, such that: (1) $\lfloor \pi(\mathcal{S}, \varphi) \rfloor_K$ can be built in time $O(|E(\mathcal{S})| \cdot |Q(\mathcal{S})|^2 \cdot 2^{O(|\varphi|)} \cdot (K+2)^{O((2|\mathit{Var}|+|\mathit{Const}|)^2)})$, and (2) for a K-bounded* MG *G on Var and $q \in Q(\mathcal{S})$, checking whether G is in the q-component of $\lfloor \pi(\mathcal{S}, \varphi) \rfloor_K$ can be done in space polynomial in the sizes of $\mathcal{S}$ and φ.*

Sketched proof. (A detailed proof is in [11]). Fix a GCS $\mathcal{S}$. For a (state) E–GCCTL* formula φ, we construct $\pi(\mathcal{S}, \varphi)$ and prove Properties 1–2 by induction on the structure of φ. Note that we can assume that each $\exists$GC constraint occurring in φ is a disjunction of transitional GC. The non-trivial case is when $\varphi = E\,\psi$ for some path formula ψ. Let X be the set of state formulas θ such that there is an occurrence of θ in ψ which is not in the scope of E. By induction hypothesis, we can assume that the result holds for each formula in X. By a generalization of the standard construction for LTL model-checking, we show the following: one can build two GCS $\mathcal{S}_\varphi$ and $\mathcal{S}^{bd}_\varphi$ with set of control points $Q(\mathcal{S}) \times Q_\varphi$, where $Q_\varphi = O(2^{|\varphi|})$, and two subsets $Q^0_\varphi \subseteq Q_\varphi$ and $F \subseteq Q(\mathcal{S}_\varphi)$ such that the following holds:

Claim 1: $(q, \nu) \in [\![\varphi]\!]_{\mathcal{S}}$ *iff* $((q, q_0), \nu) \in \mathit{Inf}_{\mathcal{S}_\varphi, F}$ for some $q_0 \in Q^0_\varphi$.

Claim 2: $\mathcal{S}^{bd}_\varphi$ can be built in time $O(|E(\mathcal{S})| \cdot |Q(\mathcal{S})|^2 \cdot 2^{O(|\varphi|)} \cdot (K+2)^{O((2|\mathit{Var}|+|\mathit{Const}|)^2)})$ starting from $\mathcal{S}$ and $\{\lfloor \pi(\mathcal{S}, \theta) \rfloor_K \mid \theta \in X\}$. Moreover, $E(\mathcal{S}^{bd}_\varphi)$ has cardinality bounded by $|E(\mathcal{S})| \cdot 2^{O(|\varphi|)} \cdot (K+2)^{(2|\mathit{Var}|+|\mathit{Const}|)^2}$, and $\mathcal{S}^{bd}_\varphi = \lfloor \mathcal{S}_\varphi \rfloor_K$.

Let $\sigma_F(\mathcal{S}_\varphi)$ be the *computable* MG representation of $\mathit{Inf}_{\mathcal{S}_\varphi, F}$ satisfying the statement of Theorem 5. Then, for each $q \in Q(\mathcal{S})$, the q-component of $\pi(\mathcal{S}, \varphi)$ is the union of the (q, q_0)-components of $\sigma_F(\mathcal{S}_\varphi)$ such that $q_0 \in Q^0_\varphi$. By Claim 1, it follows that $\pi(\mathcal{S}, \varphi)$

is a *computable* MG representation of $[\![\varphi]\!]_{\mathcal{S}}$. For the remaining part of the theorem, here, we focus on Property 1. By Claim 2, $\mathcal{S}_{\varphi}^{bd} = \lfloor \mathcal{S}_{\varphi} \rfloor_K$, hence, by Property 2 of Theorem 5, $\lfloor \sigma_F(\mathcal{S}_{\varphi}) \rfloor_K = \lfloor \sigma_F(\mathcal{S}_{\varphi}^{bd}) \rfloor_K$. Thus, since $Q(\mathcal{S}_{\varphi}^{bd})$ has cardinality bounded by $|Q(\mathcal{S})| \cdot 2^{O(|\varphi|)}$, by Property 1 of Theorem 5, and Claim 2, Property 1 follows. □

Theorem 8. *The model checking problem of* GCS *against* E–GCCTL* *and satisfiability of* E–GCCTL* *and* A–GCCTL* *are* PSPACE-*complete.*

Sketched proof. By Theorem 7, checking for a GCS $\mathcal{S}$, control point q, and E–GCCTL* formula φ, whether $(\mathcal{G}(\mathcal{S}), (q, \nu)) \models \varphi$ for some valuation ν, is in PSPACE. By an easy linear-time reduction to this last problem, the upper bound for model checking GCS against E–GCCTL* follows. The upper bounds for satisfiability of E–GCCTL* and A–GCCTL* easily follow by a linear-time reduction to the considered model checking problem. For details, see [11]. Finally, the lower bounds directly follow from PSPACE-hardness of model checking and satisfiability for the existential and universal fragments of standard CTL* (see, e.g., [23]). □

5 Concluding Remarks

We focus on the logic GCCTL*. An intriguing question left open is the decidability status for satisfiability of full GCCTL*. Moreover, it would be interesting to investigate extensions of GCCTL* which allow to compare variables at states arbitrarily far away from each other. A possibility would be to permit atomic formulas of the form $x - \Diamond y \geq k$, or $\Diamond y - x \geq k$, or $x - \Box y \geq k$, or $\Box y - x \geq k$ ($k \in \mathbb{N}$), where $\Diamond y$ means "for some future value of y" and $\Box y$ means "for each future value of y". Thus, for example, $x - \Box y \geq 1$ asserts that the future values of y remain below the current value of x. We conjecture that with this extension, Theorem 8 still holds.

References

1. Abdulla, P.A., Delzanno, G.: On the coverability problem for constrained multiset rewriting. In: Proc. 5th AVIS (2006)
2. Abdulla, P.A., Delzanno, G., Rezine, A.: Approximated parameterized verification of infinite-state processes with global conditions. Formal Methods in System Design 34(2), 126–156 (2009)
3. Alur, R., Dill, D.L.: Automata For Modeling Real-Time Systems. In: Paterson, M. (ed.) ICALP 1990. LNCS, vol. 443, pp. 322–335. Springer, Heidelberg (1990)
4. Ben-Amram, A.M.: Size-change termination with difference constraints. ACM Transactions on Programming Languages and Systems 30(3) (2008)
5. Ben-Amram, A.M.: Size-change termination, monotonicity constraints and ranking functions. Logical Methods in Computer Science 6(3) (2010)
6. Boigelot, B.: Symbolic methods for exploring infinite state spaces. PhD thesis, Université de Liège (1998)
7. Bouajjani, A., Bozga, M., Habermehl, P., Iosif, R., Moro, P., Vojnar, T.: Programs with Lists Are Counter Automata. In: Ball, T., Jones, R.B. (eds.) CAV 2006. LNCS, vol. 4144, pp. 517–531. Springer, Heidelberg (2006)

8. Bouajjani, A., Echahed, R., Habermehl, P.: On the verification problem of nonregular properties for nonregular processes. In: LICS 1995, pp. 123–133. IEEE Computer Society Press (1995)
9. Bozga, M., Gîrlea, C., Iosif, R.: Iterating Octagons. In: Kowalewski, S., Philippou, A. (eds.) TACAS 2009. LNCS, vol. 5505, pp. 337–351. Springer, Heidelberg (2009)
10. Bozzelli, L., Gascon, R.: Branching-Time Temporal Logic Extended with Qualitative Presburger Constraints. In: Hermann, M., Voronkov, A. (eds.) LPAR 2006. LNCS (LNAI), vol. 4246, pp. 197–211. Springer, Heidelberg (2006)
11. Bozzelli, L., Pinchinat, S.: Verification of gap-order constraint abstractions of counter systems. Technical report (2011), `http://clip.dia.fi.upm.es/~lbozzelli`
12. Cerans, K.: Deciding Properties of Integral Relational Automata (Extended Abstract). In: Shamir, E., Abiteboul, S. (eds.) ICALP 1994. LNCS, vol. 820, pp. 35–46. Springer, Heidelberg (1994)
13. Comon, H., Cortier, V.: Flatness Is Not a Weakness. In: Clote, P.G., Schwichtenberg, H. (eds.) CSL 2000. LNCS, vol. 1862, pp. 262–276. Springer, Heidelberg (2000)
14. Comon, H., Jurski, Y.: Multiple Counters Automata, Safety Analysis and Presburger Arithmetic. In: Vardi, M.Y. (ed.) CAV 1998. LNCS, vol. 1427, pp. 268–279. Springer, Heidelberg (1998)
15. Demri, S., D'Souza, D.: An automata-theoretic approach to constraint LTL. Information and Computation 205(3), 380–415 (2007)
16. Demri, S., Finkel, A., Goranko, V., van Drimmelen, G.: Towards a Model-Checker for Counter Systems. In: Graf, S., Zhang, W. (eds.) ATVA 2006. LNCS, vol. 4218, pp. 493–507. Springer, Heidelberg (2006)
17. Demri, S., Gascon, R.: Verification of qualitative Z constraints. Theoretical Computer Science 409(1), 24–40 (2008)
18. Emerson, E.A., Halpern, J.Y.: Sometimes and not never revisited: On branching versus linear time. Journal of the ACM 33(1), 151–178 (1986)
19. Finkel, A., Leroux, J.: How to Compose Presburger-Accelerations: Applications to Broadcast Protocols. In: Agrawal, M., Seth, A.K. (eds.) FSTTCS 2002. LNCS, vol. 2556, pp. 145–156. Springer, Heidelberg (2002)
20. Fribourg, L., Richardson, J.: Symbolic Verification with Gap-Order Constraints. In: Gallagher, J.P. (ed.) LOPSTR 1996. LNCS, vol. 1207, pp. 20–37. Springer, Heidelberg (1997)
21. Ibarra, O.: Reversal-bounded multicounter machines and their decision problems. Journal of ACM 25(1), 116–133 (1978)
22. Jonson, N.D.: Computability and Complexity from a Programming Perspective. Foundations of Computing Series. MIT Press (1997)
23. Kupferman, O., Vardi, M.Y.: An automata-theoretic approach to modular model checking. ACM Trans. Program. Lang. Syst. 22(1), 87–128 (2000)
24. Minsky, M.: Computation: Finite and Infinite Machines. Prentice Hall (1967)
25. Peterson, J.L.: Petri Net Theory and the Modelling of Systems. Prentice-Hall (1981)
26. Ramsey, F.: On a problem of formal logic. Proceedings of the London Mathematical Society 30, 264–286 (1930)
27. Revesz, P.Z.: A Closed-Form Evaluation for Datalog Queries with Integer (Gap)-Order Constraints. Theoretical Computer Science 116(1-2), 117–149 (1993)

On Application of Multi-Rooted Binary Decision Diagrams to Probabilistic Model Checking

Dmitry Bugaychenko

Saint-Petersburg State University,
DmitryBugaychenko@gmail.com

Abstract. In this paper we consider the applicability of multi-rooted binary decision diagrams for the probabilistic model checking. The symbolic probabilistic model checking involves manipulation of functions and matrices with the values in $[0, 1]$, and multi-terminal binary decision diagrams, sparse matrices, and combinations thereof are used to represent these objects. We propose algorithms for representing these objects by means of multi-rooted binary decision diagrams when a function with the values in $[0, 1]$ is approximated by a set of Boolean functions. Each Boolean function is represented by a binary decision diagram and being combined together these diagrams form a mutli-rooted binary decision diagram. Presented experimental results show that this approach allows for the model checking for large problems with a smaller memory footprint, compared to the use of the multi-terminal binary decision diagrams.

Keywords: probabilistic model checking, binary decision diagrams

Introduction[1]

Re-invention of the *binary decision diagrams* (BDD) by Bryant [2] created a breakthrough in the area of model checking. Using these data structures many researchers had presented algorithms and tools for *symbolic model checking* [7]. By allowing compact representation of the model in memory (by exploiting its implicit regularity) and by offering efficient algorithms for operations with sets BDDs have solved the state space explosion problem for many kinds of tasks. Multiple open-source libraries — *decision diagrams packages* — were implemented [11,6], which allowed researchers to utilize the power of the decision diagrams in many areas, including the symbolic model checking.

Being an efficient tool for the representation of Boolean functions classical BDDs do not handle arbitrary finite valued functions. In order to address that *multi-terminal binary decision diagrams* (MTBDD) [5] are used. This modification extends the set of terminal vertices for decision diagram from $\{0, 1\}$ to any finite set (e.g. a subset of integers or rationals). The main benefit of that extension is that all operations in the target domain can be applied to the MTBDD using a uniform straightforward APPLY algorithm. However, MTBDD representation remains compact only while the set of terminals is small (function takes

[1] Supported by the Russian Foundation for Basic Research project 09-01-00525-a.

V. Kuncak and A. Rybalchenko (Eds.): VMCAI 2012, LNCS 7148, pp. 104–118, 2012.

only limited amount of values) and even for simplest functions with the full range of values (e.g. identity function $f(x) = x$) the size of the MTBDD grows exponentially with the number of BDD variables. A larger set of terminals increases variability in the structure of the diagram and decreases probability of a node being reused in a different context (while reuse of the nodes is the key aspect of the decision diagrams allowing them to keep reasonable size). Furthermore, the extension of the set of terminals introduces inconsistency — the arguments of the decision diagram remain Booleans, but their values become more complex. This inconsistency prevents efficient implementation of the composition of functions.

Despite all the shortcomings MTBDD became popular, they were supported by the decision diagrams packages [11] and were employed as the foundation for symbolic probabilistic model checking [10], although in this area they compete with other data structures (e.g. sparse matrices) and algorithms (e.g. simulation). In [9] authors present a comparison of tools for probabilistic model checking showing where MTBDD-based algorithms work well and where they don't.

An alternative to the extension of the set of terminals vertices is the usage of multiple classical BDD to represent a single finite valued function. Similarly as we *encode* function arguments into bits, we can represent function result as a bit vector which can be *decoded* into a value from an arbitrary finite set. This way of modeling was mentioned in the early works on BDD, but then it lost researchers' attention[2]. The main challenge with this representation is that implementation of an operation in the target domain requires a mapping to a set of bit operations and this mapping can not be constructed automatically. Furthermore, the computational complexity of the bitwise algorithms is in most cases higher then the complexity of MTBDD `APPLY` procedure. However, the size of the set of BDD can be significantly smaller comparing to the size of the equivalent MTBDD (e.g. the size of representation of identity function and additive functions grows linearly with the number of variables).

In this paper we name a set of BDD representing a single finite valued function — *multi-rooted binary decision diagram.* Below in the paper (section 1) we propose a binary encoding for functions on the segment $[0, 1]$ and a set of algorithms for basic operations with these functions. Section 2 introduces MRBDD-based model checking algorithms using the proposed encoding and operations. Section 3 presents experimental results, comparing the performance of model checking based on MTBDD (using PRISM model checker [10]) and on MRBDD. And the final section concludes the paper and discusses possible further steps.

1 Multi-Rooted Binary Decision Diagrams Package

Formally, an ordered binary decision diagram is an oriented rooted acyclic graph with vertex set $V = N \cup T$, where $N \cap T = \emptyset$. The vertices from the set N are *nonterminals*; for every such vertex $v \in N$, an *order index*$(v) \in \{1, \ldots, n\}$

[2] Recently similar approach has been mentioned again with respect to the modeling and analysis of analog circuits [12].

and precisely two child vertices $low(v), high(v) \in V$ are defined. The vertices from the set T are *terminals* and have no child vertices. For such vertices $v \in T$, value $value(v) \in \{0, 1\}$ is defined. The following *ordering condition* holds: for any nonterminal $v \in N$ and its child vertex v', either $v' \in T$ or $index(v) < index(v')$. Each vertex $v \in V$ represents the function $f_v : \{0,1\}^n \to \{0,1\}$ of n variables as follows:

- If $v \in T$, then $f_v(x_1, \dots, x_n) \doteq value(v)$;
- If $v \in N$, and $index(v) = i$ then

$$f_v(x_1, \dots, x_n) \doteq \begin{cases} f_{high(v)}(x_1, \dots, x_n), \text{iff } x_i = 1 \\ f_{low(v)}(x_1, \dots, x_n), \text{iff } x_i = 0 \end{cases} .$$

In practice *reduced* decision diagrams are used. In a reduced decision diagram there can be no different vertices each representing the same function. Therefore, reduced decision diagram reuses equivalent fragments keeping the overall size reasonable. It is known that decision diagrams are very sensitive to the variables ordering. The task of identifying the best ordering is NP-complete, but a good heuristic can be proposed in many cases [1]. Further down we refer to ordered reduced binary decision diagrams as decision diagrams.

As seen from the definition, decision diagrams are used for modeling Boolean functions of multiple Boolean variables. In order to model a function taking arguments from a finite set S *binary encoding* $bin : S \to \{0,1\}^n$ is required. Similarly, in order to model a function returning values from a finite set S *binary decoding* $bin^{-1} : \{0,1\}^n \to S$ is required. With both encoding and decoding in place function $f : S \to S$ can be modeled with a set of Boolean functions $\{f_i : \{0,1\}^n \to \{0,1\}\}_1^n$ as follows: $f(x) = bin^{-1}(f_1(bin(x)), \dots, f_n(bin(x)))$. Each of the functions f_i can be represented with a decision diagram v_i. The set of decision diagrams $\{v_i\}_1^n$ can be seen as a single graph with multiple entry points[3] which we call *multi-rooted binary decision diagram* (MRBDD).

However, it is not enough to construct a representation of a function. For two functions $f, g : S \to S$ and an operation $\oplus$ in the set S there is a task of computing function $(f \oplus g)$ such that $\forall x \in S : (f \oplus g)(x) = f(x) \oplus g(x)$.[4]. This task can be re-formulated as follows: having multi-rooted decision diagrams for the functions f and g construct multi-rooted decision diagram representing the function $f \oplus g$. It is not possible to construct a practical generic algorithm which is capable of handling any operation in the target domain. However, for each particular operation it is possible to construct an algorithm applying it.

In probabilistic model checking there is a need to operate with probability distributions and stochastic matrices, which are functions with values from the segment $[0, 1]$. Thus, further in this section we consider this set and operations in it.

[3] In practice all decision diagrams packages use the concept of *shared* decision diagrams reusing nodes across diagrams constructed for different functions [8].

[4] Assuming, for simplicity, that f, g and $\oplus$ are defined for all elements in S.

1.1 Encoding

The segment $[0,1]$ is an infinite set, thus a finite approximation of this set is required. There are two commonly used methods of approximation for real numbers: floating point and fixed point methods. In the floating point method a real number x is approximated with two bounded integers m and e as follows: $x \approx m \cdot 2^e$. This method is the most commonly used. However, this kind of encoding is not well suited for MRBDD: bitwise algorithms in this model are rather complex. Furthermore, certain commonly used operations (e.g. conditional bit shift) reduce regularity of the result and cause fast growth of the MRBDD.

Therefore, for our purpose the fixed point approach is preferable. In this approach real number x is approximated with a single integer $m \in \{0, \dots, 2^n - 1\}$ as follows: $x \approx \frac{m}{2^n}$. This gives an approximation of $[0,1]$ with precision up to 2^{-n}. It is important to note that this approximation has an element exactly equal to 0, but has no elements exactly equal to 1. This asymmetry introduces systematic error when performing multiple operations with rounding. In order to remove the asymmetry an extra $n+1$ signaling bit is used to indicate the value which is exactly equal 1. As a result, $[0,1]$ can be approximated with precision up to 2^{-n} by $\{0,1\}^{n+1}$ using encoding $bin : [0,1] \to \{0,1\}^{n+1}$ such that:

$$bin_i(x) \doteq \begin{cases} 1, \text{iff } x - \sum_{j=1}^{i-1} \left(bin_j(x) \cdot 2^{-j}\right) >= 2^{-min(i,n)} \\ 0, otherwise \end{cases} . \quad (1)$$

This encoding calculates i-th bit using previously calculated bits. It subtracts already processed part of the number from x and compares result with the current component 2^{-i}. If the remainder is greater or equal to the current component, the bit is set to 1. The component for the last $n+1$-th bit is 2^n, therefore the bit is set to 1 only if x exactly equals 1. The decoding for this representation can be constructed as follows:

$$bin^{-1}(x_1, \dots, x_{n+1}) \doteq \sum_{i=1}^{n} \frac{x_i}{2^i} + \frac{x_{n+1}}{2^n}. \quad (2)$$

An important benefit of this encoding is that most common operations (sum, product and matrix product) can be implemented using algorithms for integer functions presented in [4] with minor adjustments. Thus, here we consider only algorithms specific to the interval $[0,1]$.

1.2 Rounding

Whenever the result of computation requires more bits of representation then available (e.g. product of two functions requires twice as many bits), rounding is required. Depending on the context, different rounding strategies can be used: *ceiling*, *flooring* or *rounding*. The task of rounding can be formulated as follows: having a function $f : \{0,1\}^m \to \{0,1\}^{n+k}$, construct a function $f' : \{0,1\}^m \to \{0,1\}^n$ which is the closest match to f for rounding, the closest lower bound for flooring and the closest upper bound for ceiling. All rounding operations should keep the signaling bit unchanged, thus it is not considered explicitly.

The function $f : \{0,1\}^m \to \{0,1\}^{n+k}$ can be seen as a sum of two functions $f = f_{base} + f_{ex} \cdot 2^{-n}$, where $f_{base} : \{0,1\}^m \to \{0,1\}^n$ represents first n bits and $f_{ex} : \{0,1\}^m \to \{0,1\}^k$ represents the rest k bits. In this case flooring can be done by omitting extra bits:

$$floor(f) = f_{base}. \tag{3}$$

For ceiling extra bits are combined by "OR" and the base is increased by 2^{-n}:

$$ceil(f) = f_{base} + 2^{-n} \cdot \bigvee_{i=1}^{k} f_{ex,i}. \tag{4}$$

Rounding is implemented by adding only the most significant extra bit:

$$round(f) = f_{base} + 2^{-n} \cdot f_{ex,1}. \tag{5}$$

However, this algorithm always rounds boundary values up (e.g. 0.5 is always rounded to 1). This introduces systematic error when applying rounding multiple times. In order to compensate the error *banker's rounding* is used: floor boundary case if the last bit of base is 1 and ceil if it is 0. This could be calculated as follows:

$$round_b(f) = f_{base} + 2^{-n} \cdot f_{ex,1} \wedge \left(\neg f_{base,n} \vee \bigvee_{i=2}^{k} f_{ex,i} \right). \tag{6}$$

1.3 Non-negative Integer Exponent

Having function $f : S \to [0,1]$ and function $k : S \to \mathbb{Z}^{+,0}$ there is a task of calculating $f^k : S \to [0,1]$ such that $f^k(x) = f(x)^{k(x)}$. MRBDD representation of the exponentiation can be calculated using exponentiation by squaring:

$$f^k = \prod_{i=1}^{m} (ITE(k_i, f^{2^{i-1}}, 1)), \tag{7}$$

where $\{k_i\}_1^m$ is the binary encoding for integer functions taken from [4] ($k(x) = \sum_{i=1}^{n} k_i(x) \cdot 2^{i-1}$) and ITE stands for *if-then-else*. In this schema f^{2^i} can be computed recursively as follows: $f^{2^0} = f, f^{2^i} = f^{2^{i-1}} \cdot f^{2^{i-1}}$.

Each f^{2^i} requires twice as many bits as $f^{2^{i-1}}$, thus calculating with the full precision would require $n * 2^m$ bits. On the over hand, applying rounding to n bits for each intermediate result causes significant error, especially when ceiling or flooring is used. In order to reduce the error, we use $4 \cdot n$ bits for calculation and round each intermediate result to $2 \cdot n$ bits and only final result to n bits.

Signaling bit f_{n+1} is considered at the latest using the fact that 1 is 1 in any power and any number in power 0 is 1:

$$(f^k)_{n+1} = ITE\left(f_{n+1} \vee \bigwedge_{j=1}^{m} \neg k_j, 1, 0 \right). \tag{8}$$

1.4 Multiplicative Inverse of Positive Integer

Having a function $k : S \to \mathbb{Z}^+$ there is a task of computing function $\frac{1}{k} : S \to [0,1]$ such that $\frac{1}{k}(x) = \frac{1}{k(x)}$. In order to compute the inverse we use the Newton's iterations with following schema:

$$\left(\frac{1}{k}\right)_{n+1} = 2 \cdot \left(\frac{1}{k}\right)_n - k \cdot \left(\frac{1}{k}\right)_n^2 . \tag{9}$$

For the first approximation $\left(\frac{1}{k}\right)_0$ we use following heuristic:

$$\left(\frac{1}{k}\right)_{0,i} = \begin{cases} 1, \text{iff } k_i = 1 \land \forall j \in \{1, \ldots, i-1\} : k_j = 0 \\ 0, otherwise \end{cases} . \tag{10}$$

The heuristic sets 2^{-i} bit in the approximation to 1 if 2^i bit in the original number is the highest non-zero bit. The signaling bit is set to 1 only where k equals 1. Note that the amount of bits in the representation of $\frac{1}{k}$ does not have to be the same as the numbers of bits in k.

1.5 Composition

Having two functions $f, g : S \to S$ there is a task of computing function $f(g) : S \to S$ such that $f(g)(x) = f(g(x))$. If the same encoding of size n is used for the arguments and for the result, composition can be calculated using n BDD compositions as follows:

$$f(g)_i = f_i(g_1, \ldots, g_n). \tag{11}$$

2 Model Checking with MRBDD

Having MRBDD support for the segment $[0,1]$ in order to implement probabilistic model checking we define modeling approach and model checking algorithms.

2.1 Modeling Approach

Using the same approach as in [10] we define model $\mathcal{M}$ as a triple $\langle P, M, L\rangle$ where P is a set of *parameters*, M is a set of *modules* and L is a set of *labels*. Each parameter $p \in P$ has a *type* S_p and the set of model's states is defined as a combination of all parameters ($S = \times_{p \in P} S_p$). Each module $m \in M$ is defined as a pair $\langle P_m, R_m\rangle$ where $P_m \subseteq P$ is a set of *module's parameters* and R_m is a set of *rules*. Each parameter p might belong to at most one module ($\forall m_1, m_2 \in M : m_1 \neq m_2 \Rightarrow P_{m_1} \cap P_{m_2} = \emptyset$). Parameters which do not belong to any module are called *global parameters* ($P_G = \{p \in P \mid \nexists m \in M : p \in P_m\}$). Each rule $r \in R_m$ is defined as a triple $\langle l_r, pre_r, E_r\rangle$ where $l_r \in L \cup \{\emptyset\}$ is an optional label, $pre_r \subseteq S$ is a precondition and E_r is a set of effects. Each effect $e \in E_r$ is defined as a pair $\langle prob_e, A_e\rangle$ where $prob_e \in (0,1]$ is the *probability* of the effect and A_e is a set of *assignments*. The sum of effects' probabilities for each rule must be equal 1 ($\forall m \in M, r \in R_m : \sum_{e \in E_r} prob_e = 1$). Each assignment $a \in A_e$ is defined as a pair $\langle p_a, f_a \rangle$ where $p_a \in P$ is a *target* and $f_a : S \to S_{p_a}$ is a *new value function*. Assignments can not change values of other modules' parameters ($\forall m \in M, r \in R_m, e \in E_r, a \in A_e : p_a \in P_m \cup P_G$). If an effect does not include explicit assignments for any of the module's or global parameters, then those parameters remain unchanged (identity function is used as f_a). If rule has a non-empty label, then it can not modify global parameters. For each label $l \in L$ a set of *participants* $M_l \subseteq M$ can be defined as $M_l = \{m \in M \mid \exists r \in R_m : l_r = l\}$.

In other words, the system is divided into modules each of those has its own set of parameters and its own behavior. Module can read all parameters in the model, but it can modify only its own parameters or global parameters. Behavior is described as a set of rules with a precondition and a set of effects with their probabilities. By default at most one module can make a transition at a time, but labels can be used to define *synchronous transitions* when multiple modules make transition simultaneously (and in this case non of those can modify global variables). The model can be interpreted as a discrete time Markov chain (DTMC).

An algorithm for constructing MTBDD representation of the transition probability matrix for the model is given in [10], but it can not be used "as is" to construct MRBDD representation since it produces intermediate results with the range wider then $[0, 1]$. This happens due to existence of multiple non-deterministic choices. Model has two kind of the non-determinism: *external* (in each state multiple modules or synchronous transitions might be executed) and *internal* (module or synchronous transition can have multiple rules with matching preconditions to execute). For each module $m \in M$ amount of its choices $c_m : S \to \mathbb{Z}^{0,+}$ is calculated as follows:

$$c_m(s) = \sum_{r \in R_m, l_r = \emptyset} ITE(s \in pre, 1, 0). \tag{12}$$

Similarly, for label $l \in L$ and its participant $m \in M_l$ we can count labeled rules:

$$c_{l,m}(s) = \sum_{r \in R_m, l_r = l} ITE(s \in pre, 1, 0). \tag{13}$$

These functions describes internal non-determinism of the model. External non-determinism $c : S \to \mathbb{Z}^{0,+}$ is then calculated as follows:

$$c(s) = \sum_{m \in M} ITE(c_m(s) > 0, 1, 0) + \sum_{l \in L} \prod_{m \in M_l} ITE(c_{l,m}(s) > 0, 1, 0). \tag{14}$$

After that we can compute transition matrix in parts. For an effect e we calculate transition matrix $\Pi_e : S \times S \to [0, 1]$ as:

$$\Pi_e(s, s') = ITE(\forall a \in A_e : s'(p_a) = f_a(s), prob_e, 0), \tag{15}$$

where $s'(p_a)$ represents the value of p_a in s'. The value $\Pi_e(s, s')$ represents probability of transiting from s to s' when the effect is applied. For a rule r we calculate transition matrix Π_r as follows:

$$\Pi_r(s, s') = ITE\left(s \in pre_r, \sum_{e \in E_r} \Pi_e(s, s'), 0\right). \tag{16}$$

For a module m transition matrix Π_m is calculated as follows:

$$\Pi_m = \sum_{r \in R_m, l_r = \emptyset} \left(\frac{1}{c_m} \cdot \Pi_r\right). \tag{17}$$

Note that before summing transition matrices for individual rules their values are reduced in order to compensate the internal non-determinism. In the same way for a label l transition matrix Π_l is calculated as follows:

$$\Pi_l = \prod_{m \in M_l} \left[\sum_{r \in R_m, l_r = l} \left(\frac{1}{c_{m,l}} \cdot \Pi_r\right)\right]. \tag{18}$$

For the entire model the representation of the transition probability matrix is constructed as follows:

$$\Pi_{\mathcal{M}} = \sum_{m \in M} \left(\frac{1}{c} \cdot \Pi_m \cdot I_{M \setminus \{m\}}\right) + \sum_{l \in L} \left(\frac{1}{c} \cdot \Pi_l \cdot I_{M \setminus M_l}\right), \tag{19}$$

where $I_{M'} : S \times S \to [0, 1]$ is the identity matrix calculated as follows:

$$I_{M'}(s, s') = ITE(\forall m \in M', p \in P_m : s'(p) = s(p), 1, 0). \tag{20}$$

This matrix represents the fact that the state of all modules not involved in the transition remains unchanged.

2.2 Model Checking Algorithms

We chose Probabilistic Computation Tree Logic (PCTL) as a tool for the specification of the model properties. The syntax of the logic is defined as follows:

$$\begin{aligned} \psi &::= \bigcirc\phi \mid \phi\,\mathcal{U}\,\phi \mid \phi\,\mathcal{U}^k\phi; \\ \phi &::= \chi \mid \neg\phi \mid \phi \wedge \phi \mid P^{[<=,>=]p}\psi. \end{aligned} \tag{21}$$

Formulas of type ϕ are called *state* formulas. Model checking of the state formulas calculates set $[\phi] \subseteq S$ such that $\forall s \in [\phi] : \mathcal{M}, s \models \phi$. State formulas are constructed from *atomic formulas* χ using standard logical junctions. The atomic formulas are defined using functions and predicates in the target domain. Model checking of the state formulas is mainly the same for MTBDD and MRBDD.

Formulas of type ψ are *path* formulas which are interpreted for a sequence of states $(s_1, s_2, \ldots) \in S^*$. Path formulas are constructed using temporal operators "next time", "until" and "bounded until". Model checking for the path formulas calculates a function $[\psi] : S \to [0,1]$ such that:

$$[\psi](s) = \sum_{(s_1,s_2,\ldots)\in S^*} ITE(\mathcal{M},(s,s_1,s_2,\ldots) \models \psi, prob_{\mathcal{M}}(s,s_1,s_2,\ldots),0), \quad (22)$$

where $prob_{\mathcal{M}} : S^* \to [0,1]$ is the probability of the path in the model calculated as follows: $prob_{\mathcal{M}}(s_1,s_2,\ldots) = \prod_{i=1}^{\infty} \Pi_{\mathcal{M}}(s_i,s_{i+1})$. $[\psi](s)$ denotes the probability that the model execution started from the state s satisfies ψ. The path formulas can be grounded to the state formulas using probability constraint quantifier $P^{[<=,>=]p}$ ($[P^{[<=,>=]p}\psi] = \{s \in S \mid [\psi](s)[<=,>=]p\}$).

Model checking "next time" and "bounded until". Temporal operator $\bigcirc\phi$ is interpreted as "next state satisfies ϕ" and $\phi_1 \,\mathcal{U}^k \phi_2$ is interpreted as "in k steps system reaches state satisfying ϕ_2 passing only through states satisfying ϕ_1". Function $[\bigcirc\phi]$ can be calculates as follows:

$$[\bigcirc\phi](s) = \sum_{s'\in S} \Pi_{\mathcal{M}}(s,s') \cdot ITE(s' \in [\phi],1,0). \quad (23)$$

For each state s the probabilities of transitions leading to any state from $[\phi]$ is summed. This calculation can also be done as a matrix-vector multiplication of the matrix $\Pi_{\mathcal{M}}$ and the vector $ITE(s \in [\phi],1,0)$.

In order to calculate $\phi_1 \,\mathcal{U}^k \phi_2$ following recursive schema is used:

$$[\phi_1 \,\mathcal{U}^k \phi_2] = \begin{cases} 1 & s \in [\phi_2] \\ \sum_{s'\in S} \Pi_{\mathcal{M}}(s,s') \cdot [\phi_1 \,\mathcal{U}^{k-1} \phi_2](s') & k > 0, s \in [\phi_1] \\ 0 & otherwise \end{cases}. \quad (24)$$

This schema can be calculated using k matrix-vector multiplications of the matrix $ITE(s \in [\phi_2],1,ITE(s \in [\phi_1],\Pi_{\mathcal{M}},0))$ and the vector $ITE(s \in [\phi_2],1,0)$.

Model checking "until". Temporal operator $\phi_1 \,\mathcal{U}\, \phi_2$ is interpreted as "eventually system reaches state satisfying ϕ_2 passing only through states satisfying ϕ_1" and its model checking requires analysis of unbounded paths (although for each path satisfying $\phi_1 \,\mathcal{U}\, \phi_2$ there is a finite prefix satisfying it).

As the first step we calculate sets of states $[\phi_1 \,\mathcal{U}\, \phi_2]_0$ from which it is not possible to reach a state from $[\phi_2]$ passing only states from $[\phi_1]$ (at these points $[\phi_1 \,\mathcal{U}\, \phi_2]$ equals 0) and $[\phi_1 \,\mathcal{U}\, \phi_2]_1$ from which it is not possible to reach any of the states from $[\phi_1 \,\mathcal{U}\, \phi_2]_0$ without passing a state from ϕ_2 (the value of $[\phi_1 \,\mathcal{U}\, \phi_2]$ equals 1). The algorithms for calculation of these sets are given in [10]. After that in order to calculate $[\phi_1 \,\mathcal{U}\, \phi_2]$ the following schema is used:

$$[\phi_1 \,\mathcal{U}\, \phi_2] = \begin{cases} 1 & s \in [\phi_1 \,\mathcal{U}\, \phi_2]_1 \\ \sum_{s'\in S} \Pi_{\mathcal{M}}(s,s') \cdot [\phi_1 \,\mathcal{U}\, \phi_2](s') & s \notin [\phi_1 \,\mathcal{U}\, \phi_2]_1 \cup [\phi_1 \,\mathcal{U}\, \phi_2]_0 \\ 0 & s \in [\phi_1 \,\mathcal{U}\, \phi_2]_0 \end{cases}. \quad (25)$$

This means that $[\phi_1 \,\mathcal{U}\, \phi_2]$ can be calculated as a solution of a linear equations system $x = A \cdot x$ where matrix $A = ITE(s \in [\phi_1 \,\mathcal{U}\, \phi_2]_1, 1, ITE(s \notin [\phi_1 \,\mathcal{U}\, \phi_2]_0, \Pi_{\mathcal{M}}, 0))$. [10] proposes multiple iterative methods which can be used to solve the equations system, however for the MRBDD only *power iteration* can be used (other approaches create intermediate result out of the range of $[0, 1]$ and use arithmetic operation which are not currently supported). The main idea of the power iteration is to having an initial guess x_0 calculate $x_i = A \cdot x_{i-1}$ while difference between x_i and x_{i-1} is significant.

The first guess x_0 can be calculated differently depending on the kind of probability constraint. If constraint is of type $P^{<=p}$, then the model checking must calculate an upper-bound for the $[\phi_1 \,\mathcal{U}\, \phi_2]$, and in case if $P^{>=p}$ is used, then a lower-bound needs to be calculated. For the first case the roughest upper-bound $x_0 = ITE(x \notin [\phi_1 \,\mathcal{U}\, \phi_2]_0, 1, 0)$ is used and for the second case the roughest lower-bound $x_0 = ITE(x \in [\phi_1 \,\mathcal{U}\, \phi_2]_1, 1, 0)$ is used.

For faster convergence, a modified version of the iteration can be used: $x_i = A_i \cdot x_{i-1}, A_i = A_{i-1}^2$, where $A_0 = A$. This requires significantly less iterations, however the cost of a single iteration increases. Furthermore, it causes a more significant precision loss when used with ceiling or flooring. Memory demand of this schema is also higher. However, this approach still can be used in combination with the original schema to reduce the amount of iterations.

Compositional approach. The model checking algorithms described above are based on matrix-vector multiplication. The essential meaning of this multiplication is to calculate *probabilistic predecessor*. Having a set of states $x \subseteq S$ this operation calculates for each state in S the probability of getting into x in one step. If x is not a plain set, but a vector of probabilities $x : S \to [0, 1]$, then it can be seen as fuzzy set with the same meaning of the operation.

Probabilistic predecessor can also be calculated using functions composition. For an effect e we can construct function $f_e : S \to S$ such that for each state it returns the next state in case if the effect is applied. Then, having a fuzzy set $x : S \to [0, 1]$ we can calculate its predecessor in case if effect is applied as:

$$pred_e(x) = x(f_e) \cdot prob_e. \tag{26}$$

For a rule r the predecessor of x is calculated as a sum of effects, with the respect to the rule's precondition:

$$pred_r(x) = ITE\left(s \in pre_r, \sum_{e \in E_r} pred_e(x), 0\right). \tag{27}$$

For a module m it is calculated as sum of the rules' predecessors, with the respect to the internal non-determinism:

$$pred_m(x) = \sum_{r \in R_m, l_r = \emptyset} \left(\frac{1}{c_m} \cdot pred_r(x)\right). \tag{28}$$

For synchronous transitions involving multiple modules this calculation is more complicated. Modules can apply their rules and effects in different combinations.

Having two rules r_1 and r_2 for modules m_1 and m_2 combined rule (r_1, r_2) is constructed as follows:

$$(r_1, r_2) =< pre_{r_1} \cap pre_{r_2}, \bigcup_{e_1 \in E_{r_1}, e_2 \in E_{r_2}} \{< prob_{e_1} \cdot prob_{e_2}, A_{e_1} \cup A_{e_2} >\} > . \quad (29)$$

Then for a label l with participants $\{m_1, \ldots, m_n\} = M_l$ predecessor $pred_l$ is calculated as follows:

$$pred_l(x) = \sum_{(r_1,\ldots,r_n) \in R_{m_1} \times \ldots \times R_{m_n}, l_r = l} \left(\frac{1}{c_l} \cdot pred_{(r_1,\ldots,r_2)}(x) \right), \quad (30)$$

where $\frac{1}{c_l} = \prod_{m \in M_l} \frac{1}{c_m}$. Having that calculated predecessor for the entire model can be calculated as follows:

$$pred_{\mathcal{M}}(x) = \sum_{m \in M} \left(\frac{1}{c} \cdot pred_m(x) \right) + \sum_{l \in L} \left(\frac{1}{c} \cdot pred_l(x) \right). \quad (31)$$

Model checking $\bigcirc \phi$ can then be done by calculating $pred_{\mathcal{M}}([\phi])$. Model checking $\phi_1 \,\mathcal{U}^k \phi_2$ can be done iteratively using the following schema:

$$[\phi_1 \,\mathcal{U}^k \phi_2] = \begin{cases} 1 & s \in [\phi_2] \\ pred_{\mathcal{M}}([\phi_1 \,\mathcal{U}^{k-1} \phi_2]) & k > 0, s \in [\phi_1] \\ 0 & otherwise \end{cases} . \quad (32)$$

Having calculated $[\phi_1 \,\mathcal{U}\, \phi_2]_0$ and $[\phi_1 \,\mathcal{U}\, \phi_2]_1$ in the same way as described above, model checking of $\phi_1 \,\mathcal{U}\, \phi_2$ can be done by applying the following schema until stabilization:

$$[\phi_1 \,\mathcal{U}\, \phi_2]^k = \begin{cases} 1 & s \in [\phi_1 \,\mathcal{U}\, \phi_2]_1 \\ pred_{\mathcal{M}}([\phi_1 \,\mathcal{U}\, \phi_2]^{k-1}) & k > 0, s \notin [\phi_1 \,\mathcal{U}\, \phi_2]_0 \\ 0 & otherwise \end{cases} . \quad (33)$$

Compositional approach consumes significantly less memory comparing with the matrix multiplication approach. On the other hand, amount of computations made in a single iteration of the compositional approach is higher. This is especially noticeable in synchronous transitions — amount of combinatorial effects grows exponentially with amount of individual effects from each participant.

3 Experimental Results

In order to evaluate performance characteristics of the proposed approach we chosen two well known examples of probabilistic model checking tasks: synchronous leader election in a ring of processors and a birth-death process. As an implementation of MRBDD operations we used package BddFunctions [3] and as an example of MTBDD-based model checking — PRISM model checker [10].

3.1 Synchronous Leader Election

In order to select a leader in a ring of N processors each processor selects a random number from $\{1, \ldots, K\}$ and passes it through the ring so that all processors can see it. When all the processors know the numbers of each other, the one with the highest unique number is elected as the leader. If the leader can not be elected, then the processors repeat the elections. With this task following properties are a matter of interest: "the leader is eventually elected" and "the leader is elected in L iterations".

Table 1. Synchronous leader election (memory in megabytes, time in seconds)

N	K	PRISM		MRBDD		N	K	PRISM		MRBDD	
		Memory	Time	Memory	Time			Memory	Time	Memory	Time
3	2	62,08	1	7,77	1	5	2	62,39	2	8,03	1
	3	62,29	2	7,86	1		3	64,66	3	10,10	4
	4	62,54	2	7,91	1		4	68,04	8	14,03	13
	5	62,72	2	8,31	2		5	79,67	30	33,02	33
	6	63,12	2	8,46	2		6	103,69	69	63,72	95
	8	63,43	2	9,05	2		8	215,13	285	167,68	581
4	2	62,28	2	7,83	1	6	2	62,96	2	8,38	3
	3	62,76	2	8,33	1		3	68,72	8	14,48	18
	4	63,79	3	9,15	4		4	87,82	44	44,82	77
	5	62,72	6	12,00	7		5	170,82	230	149,75	346
	6	68,73	8	14,28	7		6	375,41	1065	300,80	1083
	8	79,18	24	26,38	21		8	1193,38	25118	985,23	5785

Table 1 shows the computation time and the peak memory usage for the model checking of these properties for different values of N and K with $L = 7$. As the table shows, for small problems ($N <= 4$) MRBDD and MTBDD model checking show similar performance. Larger memory consumption of PRISM is due to the fact that the process runs in a Java virtual machine which requires a constant extra amount of memory. For the average problems ($(5, 6)$, $(5, 8)$ and $(6, 5)$) PRISM shows better running time up to 50% for $N = 5$ and $K = 8$. However, for the largest considered problem ($N = 6$ and $K = 8$) PRISM's running time 5 times exceeded the time taken by the MRBDD approach: 7,5 hours against 1,5.

3.2 Birth-Death Process

The birth-death processes are used to describe a large number of physical, biological, informational, economic and social stochastic processes. The mathematical essence of the process is that for some *population* of objects the rules of *birth* (inclusion of a set of new objects) and *death* (exclusion of a set of existing objects) are defined. These rules depend on the current population size. Acting simultaneously birth and death can affect the population in a hardly predictable way. Of particular interest in this process are *points of no return*, such as 0 (complete exhausting). From these points the population can never recover.

For the experiment we chosen the following law of births: for $i \in \{1, \ldots, 10\}$ with probability $\frac{1}{2^i}$ the number of births is equal to $\frac{1}{2^{11-i}}$ fraction of the current population and with probability $\frac{1}{2^{10}}$ the number of births is 0. Accordingly, the most probable are small relative increase in the population. For the deaths the law is the same. The birth and death are acting together at every turn. The main parameter of the model in this case is the number N which limits the maximum size of the population ($population < 2^N$).

For the model checking an interesting property is "eventually threshold x of the population size is reached" ($P^{>=p} true\ \mathcal{U}\ population >= x$). Performance results for the model checking of this property are listed in the table 2. For small problems MRBDD approach shows better time, but with the growth of N execution time for both tools "explodes". As a result, model checking for $N = 9$ (about 500 individuals in the population) takes ten hours. The reason for that is a too slow convergence of the iterative methods (more then 100000 iterations), which makes model checking for a realistic problem size not feasible. In this example for MRBDD approach the "fast" version of the iteration is used (calculating A^2 at each iteration), which caused a higher memory consumption.

Table 2. Birth-death process

N	PRISM		MRBDD	
	Memory	**Time**	**Memory**	**Time**
3	62,00	3	7,84	1
4	66,05	6	9,89	3,8
5	62,75	65	17,71	28
6	68,03	392	46,84	130
7	65,52	1967	151,16	1275
8	97,41	9330	532,04	9360
9	197,45	37560	783,70	45936

While model checking of the unbounded version of the property is not feasible, a bounded version is worth considering: "threshold x of the population size is reached in L iterations" ($P^{>=p} true\ \mathcal{U}^L population >= x$). The performance results for the model checking of this property are listed in table 3. PRISM results are almost unchanged — with $N = 11$ (population of about 2,000 individuals) calculation takes more than 10 hours using more than 1 gigabyte of memory. MRBDD approach shows much more attractive results: verification with $N = 16$ (population of 65,000 individuals) can be carried out in 5 hours using about 260 megabytes of memory.

Table 3. Birth-death process (bounded property)

N	PRISM		MRBDD		MRBDD (comp.)	
	Memory	Time	Memory	Time	Memory	Time
3	61,72	1	7,74	1	7,49	1
4	61,63	1	7,93	1	7,5	2
5	61,95	2	11,56	2	7,97	4
6	63,24	3	11,62	12	8,19	7
7	65,22	11	18,36	22	8,59	18
8	92,98	75	30,70	30	8,71	31
9	197,17	628	46,29	114	9,58	64
10	357,88	3633	66,04	256	10,69	164
11	1222,36	39555	104,18	494	13,57	448
12			108,22	805	26,71	1158
13			112,64	1677	57,06	2739
14			124,13	3630	64	6404
15			180,22	6549	71,57	14239
16			261,55	19278	72,13	21115

Table 3 also shows performance characteristics for the compositional model checking approach. Running time in this case is comparable to the traditional matrix multiplication approach, but memory consumption is significantly less. After $N = 15$ peak memory usage stabilizes around 73 megabytes and does not exceed this limit even for $N = 17$ and $N = 18$. These results are very promising since with a stable and small memory demand there is a potential for efficient distributed calculations.

4 Conclusions and Further Work

We have shown that the multi-rooted binary decision diagrams can efficiently be used as a foundation for probabilistic symbolic model checking. Compared with multi-terminal binary decision diagrams multi-rooted diagrams use memory more efficiently, which allows model checking for problems of larger size. Of particular interest is the possibility of replacing the matrix multiplication by the composition of functions during the model checking. This approach allows further reduce of memory consumption.

A comparison with PRISM model checker shows that MRBDD-based model checking has similar performance, but for large problems MRBDD-based approach can perform several times faster. In particular, model checking of the birth and death process with MRBDD can handle much larger problems.

Although the idea of multi-rooted binary decision diagrams was formulated long ago, invention of the multi-terminal binary decision diagrams shifted researchers' focus away from it. Results presented in the paper show that despite of implementation complexity MRBDD are a promising tool for probabilistic model checking. Combinations of MRBDD with other data structures and combination of compositional model checking with matrix multiplication are worth considering. Techniques and tool for parallel and distributed calculations using MRBDD can significantly reduce model checking time.

References

1. Bollig, B., Wegener, I.: Improving the variable ordering of OBDDs is NP-complete. IEEE Transactions on Computers 45(9), 993–1002 (1996)
2. Bryant, R.E.: Symbolic boolean manipulation with ordered binary-decision diagrams. ACM Computing Surveys 24(3), 293–318 (1992)
3. Bugaychenko, D.: BddFunctions: Multi-rooted binary decision diagrams package, `http://code.google.com/p/bddfunctions/`
4. Bugaychenko, D., Soloviev, I.: Application of multiroot decision diagrams for integer functions. Vestnik St. Petersburg University: Mathematics 43(2), 92–97 (2010)
5. Fujita, M., McGeer, P.C., Yang, J.C.Y.: Multi-terminal binary decision diagrams: An efficient datastructure for matrix representation. Form. Methods Syst. Des. 10(2-3), 149–169 (1997)
6. Lind-Nielsen, J.: BDD Package BuDDy, `http://buddy.sourceforge.net`
7. McMillan, K.L.: Symbolic model checking. Kluwer Academic Publishers, Dordrecht (1993)
8. Minato, S., Ishiura, N., Yajima, S.: Shared binary decision diagram with attributed edges for efficient boolean function manipulation. In: Proceedings of the 27th ACM/IEEE Design Automation Conference, pp. 52–57. ACM (1991)
9. Oldenkamp, H.: Probabilistic model checking. A comparison of tools. Master's thesis, University of Twente, Niederlande (2007)
10. Parker, D.: Implementation of symbolic model checking for probabilistic system. Ph.D. thesis, University of Birmingham (2002)
11. Somenzi, F.: CUDD: Colorado University Decision Diagram package, `http://vlsi.colorado.edu/~fabio/CUDD`
12. Xie, B.: Symbolic moment computation with application to statistical timing analysis. In: Asia Pacific Conference on Postgraduate Research in Microelectronics & Electronics, PrimeAsia 2009, pp. 460–463. IEEE (2009)

Regression Verification for Multi-threaded Programs

Sagar Chaki[1], Arie Gurfinkel[1], and Ofer Strichman[1,2]

[1] SEI/CMU, Pittsburgh, USA
[2] Technion, Haifa, Israel
chaki@sei.cmu.edu, arie@cmu.edu, ofers@ie.technion.ac.il

Abstract. Regression verification is the problem of deciding whether two similar programs are equivalent under an arbitrary yet equal context, given some definition of equivalence. So far this problem has only been studied for the case of single-threaded deterministic programs. We present a method for regression verification to establish partial equivalence (i.e., input/output equivalence of terminating executions) of multi-threaded programs. Specifically, we develop two proof-rules that decompose the regression verification between *concurrent* programs to that of regression verification between *sequential* functions, a more tractable problem. This ability to avoid composing threads altogether when discharging premises, in a fully automatic way and for general programs, uniquely distinguishes our proof rules from others used for classical verification of concurrent programs.

1 Introduction

Regression verification [4,5] is the problem of deciding whether two similar programs are equivalent under an arbitrary yet equal context. The problem is parameterized by a notion of equivalence. In this paper, we focus on *partial equivalence* [4], i.e., input/output equivalence of terminating executions. Regression verification under partial equivalence – which we refer to simply as regression verification – is undecidable in general. However, in practice it can be solved in many cases fully automatically for *deterministic single-threaded programs*, even in the presence of loops, recursion and dynamic memory allocation. For example, the algorithm suggested in [5] progresses bottom-up on the call graphs of the two programs, and attempts to prove equivalence of pairs of functions while abstracting descendants that were already proved equivalent with uninterpreted functions. This algorithm is implemented in two tools – RVT [5] and Microsoft's SymDiff [9] – both of which output a list of provably equivalent function pairs.

The ability to perform regression verification adds several elements to the developer's toolbox: checking that no change has propagated to the interface after refactoring or performance optimization; checking backward compatibility; performing impact analysis (checking which functions may possibly be affected by a change, in order to know which tests should be repeated), and more.

Multithreaded (MT) programs are widely deployed, which makes the extension of regression verification to such programs an important problem. This task

V. Kuncak and A. Rybalchenko (Eds.): VMCAI 2012, LNCS 7148, pp. 119–135, 2012.

is challenging for at least two reasons. First — since MT programs are inherently nondeterministic due to the scheduler, we need an appropriate notion of equivalence for nondeterministic programs. The standard definition of partial equivalence mentioned above is inadequate, since it implies that a nondeterministic program is not even equivalent to itself: given the same input, the program may produce different outputs.[1]

Second — while regression verification of sequential programs is broken down to proofs of I/O equivalence of pairs of functions, in the case of MT programs the behavior of functions is affected by other threads, which makes a similar decomposition to the level of functions much harder. Compositional verification methodologies [11,7] and tools [6,2] for MT programs target reachability properties of a *single* program, and decompose only to the level of individual *threads*. They are therefore not directly applicable to our problem.

In this paper we propose theoretical foundations for regression verification of multi-threaded recursive programs and address the above two challenges. First, we extend the definition of partial equivalence to non-deterministic programs. Second, assuming a bijective correspondence mapping between the functions and global variables of the two programs, we present two proof rules whose premises only require verification of sequential programs, at the granularity of individual functions. We prove that these rules are sound under our extended notion of partial equivalence. For the first rule, each premise verifies that a pair of corresponding functions generate the same observable behavior under an arbitrary yet equal environment. The second rule has premises that are weaker, but also computationally harder to discharge. Specifically, each premise verifies that a pair of corresponding functions generate the same observable behavior under an arbitrary yet equal environment that is consistent with some overapproximation of the other threads in the program. For both rules, each premise is discharged by verifying a sequential program. A key feature of our proof rules therefore is that they enable decomposition to the level of both threads and functions.

The rest of the article is structured as follows. In the next section we present our extended notion of partial equivalence. In Sec. 3 we list our assumptions about the input programs, and describe how they should be preprocessed for our procedure to work. In Sec. 4 we describe our first rule and prove its soundness. In Sec. 5 we present the second rule and prove its soundness. Finally, in Sec. 6, we conclude and describe some directions for future work.

2 Equivalence of Multi-threaded Programs

Let P be a multi-threaded program. P defines a relation between inputs and outputs, which we denote by $R(P)$. Let $\Pi(P)$ denote the set of terminating computations of P. Then:

$$R(P) = \{(\boldsymbol{in}, \boldsymbol{out}) \mid \exists \pi \in \Pi(P) \boldsymbol{.} \ \ \pi \text{ begins in } \boldsymbol{in} \text{ and ends in } \boldsymbol{out}\} \ .$$

[1] An indication of the difficulty of this problem is given by Lee's statement in [10], that "with threads, there is no useful theory of equivalence".

Definition 1 (Partial equivalence of nondeterministic programs). *Two nondeterministic programs P, P' are partially equivalent if $R(P) = R(P')$.*

We denote by $p.e.(P, P')$ the fact that P and P' are partially equivalent. Note that the definition refers to whole programs, and that by this definition every program is equivalent to itself. If loops and recursion are bounded this problem is decidable, as we show in the full version of this article [1]. Recall, however, that here we are concerned with the unbounded case, and with the question of how to decompose the verification problem to the granularity of threads and functions. This is the subject of this article.

3 Assumptions, Preprocessing and Mapping

We assume C as the input languages, with few restrictions that will be mentioned throughout this section. We generally refrain in this paper from discussing in detail issues that are also relevant to regression verification of sequential programs (e.g., issues concerning the heap, aliasing etc), because these are covered in earlier publications [4,9].

The input program P is assumed to consist of a finite and fixed set of threads, i.e., no dynamic thread creation and deletion. A k-threaded program P is written as $f_1 \parallel \ldots \parallel f_k$ where, for $i \in [1..k]$, the i-th thread is rooted at f_i. The call graph of P is written as $\textsc{cg}(P)$. The call graph of a function f in P, denoted $\textsc{cg}(f)$, is the subgraph of P that can be reached from f. We assume that threads have disjoint call graphs.

We denote by *ReadParam*(f) and *WriteParam*(f) the set of parameters and global variables that are read and written-to, respectively, by functions in $\textsc{cg}(f)$. In general computing this information precisely is impossible, but over-approximations are easy to compute, while sacrificing completeness. For simplicity we will assume that these sets are given to us. Note that the intersection of these sets is not necessarily empty. A global variable is called *shared* if it is accessed by more than one thread. For simplicity, but without losing generality, *we consider all outputs of each function as if they were shared*, even if in practice they are local to a thread.

By convention x, x_1, x_2 etc. denote variables that are (really) shared (i.e., not outputs), t, t_1, t_2 etc. denote local variables, and *exp* denotes an expression over local variables. Primed symbols indicate that they refer to P'. Function names prefixed by `UF` denote uninterpreted functions. The signature and return type of these functions are declared implicitly, by the actual parameters and the variable at the left-hand side of the assignment, respectively. For example, if we use a statement of the form `t = UF_x(t1, t2)`, where `t,t1,t2` are integers, it means that we also declare an uninterpreted function `int UF_x(int, int)`.

3.1 Global Preprocessing

We assume that all programs are preprocessed as follows:

- Loops are outlined [3] to recursive functions.
- Mutually recursive functions are converted [8] to simple recursion.
- Non-recursive functions are inlined.
- Auxiliary local variables are introduced to load and store shared variables explicitly such that: (i) a shared variable x only appears in statements of the form $t = x$ or $x = exp$, and (ii) every auxiliary variable is read once.
- If a function has a formal return value, it is replaced with an additional parameter sent to it by reference.

3.2 Mapping

We assume that after preprocessing, the target programs P and P' have the same number of threads and overall number of functions. Specifically, let $P = f_1 \parallel \ldots \parallel f_k$ and $P' = f'_1 \parallel \ldots \parallel f'_k$, and let the set of overall functions of P and P' be $\{g_1, \ldots, g_n\}$ and $\{g'_1, \ldots, g'_n\}$, respectively. We assume the following two mappings:

- A bijection $\phi_F : \{g_1, \ldots, g_n\} \mapsto \{g'_1, \ldots, g'_n\}$, such that $\forall i \in [1..k].\ \phi_F(f_i) = f'_i$ and furthermore, if $(g, g') \in \phi_F$, then
  - $\forall i \in [1..k].\ g \in \text{CG}(f_i) \iff g' \in \text{CG}(f'_i)$.
  - g and g' have the same prototype (list of formal parameter types).
  - Let p_i and p'_i denote the i-th parameter of g and g' respectively. Then $p_i \in ReadParam(g) \iff p'_i \in ReadParam(g')$ and $p_i \in WriteParam(f) \iff p'_i \in WriteParam(g')$.

  For convenience, we assume that $\forall i \in [1..n].\ \phi_F(g_i) = g'_i$.
- A bijection ϕ_G between the global variables of P and P', such that if $(v, v') \in \phi_G$, then
  - v and v' are of the same type,
  - v is a shared variable iff v' is a shared variable,
  - $\forall (g, g') \in \phi_F.\ v \in ReadParam(g) \iff v' \in ReadParam(g')$ and $v \in WriteParam(g) \iff v' \in WriteParam(g')$.

Failure in finding the above two mappings dooms the proof. Note that the existence of ϕ_G implies that after preprocessing, P and P' also have the same number of global variables.

4 First Proof Rule

We now present our first proof rule for regression verification of P and P'. We begin with a specific transformation of a function f to a new function $\widehat{f}$, which we use subsequently in the premise of our proof rule.

4.1 Function Transformation: From f to $\widehat{f}$.

Let $ActualReadParam(f)$ be the actual parameters and global variables sent respectively to the elements in $ReadParam(f)$. We construct $\widehat{f}$ from f via the transformation described in Fig. 1. In the figure, $\Rightarrow$ indicates a specific transformation,

- Introduce a global counter `c` initialized to 0, and a list `out` of tuples $\langle Action, identifier, values \ldots \rangle$.
- *Read*: `t := x;` $\Rightarrow$ `t := UF_x(c); out += (R, "x"); c++;`
- *Write*: `x := exp;` $\Rightarrow$ `x := exp; out += (W, "x", exp); c++;`
- *Function call*: `foo`$(a_1, \ldots, a_m)$; $\Rightarrow$
  $\forall$`w` $\in$ *WriteParam*(`foo`). `w = UF`$_{foo\_w}$(*ActualReadParam*(`foo`));
  `out += (C, "foo",` *ActualReadParam*`(foo));`

Fig. 1. Constructing $\widehat{f}$ from f, for a function f in P. The operator "+=" appends an element to the end of `out`. Functions in P' are translated slightly differently (see text).

```
f(int t1) {
  int t2, t3 = 1;
  x = t1 + 1;
  t2 = x;
  foo(t3, &t1, &t2);
}
```

```
g(int i1,int *o1) {
  int t;
  if (i1 ≤ 0) {
    *o1 = 1;
  } else {
    g(i1 - 1, &t);
    *o1 = (*t) * i1;
} }
```

```
f̂(int t1) {
  int t2, t3 = 1, c = 0;
  x = t1 + 1;
  out+=(W,"x", t1 + 1); c++;
  t2 = UF_x(c);
  out+=(R, "x"); c++;
  t1 = UF_foo_t1(t3);
  t2 = UF_foo_t2(t3);
  out+=(C, foo, t3);
}
```

```
ĝ(int t1,int *o1) {
  int t, c = 0;
  if (i1 ≤ 0) {
    out+=(W, "o1", 1); c++;
  } else {
    t = UF_g_t(i1 - 1);
    out+=(C, g, i1 - 1);
    out+=(W, "o1", (*t) * i1); c++;
} }
```

Fig. 2. Example conversions of functions `f` and `g` to $\widehat{\texttt{f}}$ and $\widehat{\texttt{g}}$

with the left being the original code (in f) and the right being the new code (in $\widehat{f}$). The transformation of a function f' in P' is the same except that the elements in $WriteParam(f')$ are renamed to their counterparts in f according to the map ϕ_G, ensuring that f and $\phi_F(f)$ invoke the same uninterpreted function.

Example 1. Fig. 2 shows functions `f` and `g` and their translations to $\widehat{\texttt{f}}$ and $\widehat{\texttt{g}}$. Function `foo` called in `f` has three parameters, the first of which is only in *ReadParam*(`foo`) and the other two only in *WriteParam*(`foo`). The update of `x` in $\widehat{\texttt{f}}$ is not necessary in this case because it is not used, but it would have been used had `x` was an element of *ReadParam*(`foo`). Shifting our attention to `g`, this function computes the factorial of its input. It has two parameters, which are in *ReadParam*(`g`) and *WriteParam*(`g`), respectively. □

Intuition. Intuitively, the environment in which each thread operates is a stream of read and write (RW) instructions to shared variables. Let f and f' be two functions and let E and E' be environments generated by the *other* threads in their respective programs (P and P'). To prove the equivalence of f, f', we assume that E and E' are identical *but only if f and f''s interaction with them so far* has been equivalent. This assumption is checked as part of the premise of our rule as follows. Consider two shared variables x, x' in f, f', respectively. To emulate a possible preemption of f just before it reads x, it is sound to let it read a nondeterministic value. But since we want to assume that f and f' operate in the same environment, we want to ensure that if they are read at equal locations in their own RW stream, then they are assigned the *same* nondeterministic value. To this end, we replace each read of x and x' with the uninterpreted function call $UF_x(c)$. Since c is the current location in the RW stream and we use the same uninterpreted function $UF_x()$ for both x and x', we achieve the desired effect.

We prove that f and f' are observationally equivalent via the list `out`. For simplicity, we refer to the list `out` introduced during the construction of $\widehat{f}$ as $\widehat{f}.out$. In essence, the equality of $\widehat{f}.out$ and $\widehat{f}'.out$ implies that f and f' read (and write) the same values from (and to) the shared variables, and call the same functions with the same actual parameters, and in the same order. We now present our first proof rule formally.

4.2 The Proof Rule

We define the predicate $\delta(f)$ to be true if and only if the sequential program $VC_\delta(f)$, given below in pseudo-code, is valid (i.e., the assertion in $VC_\delta(f)$ is not violated) for all input vectors $\boldsymbol{in}$:

$$VC_\delta(f): \quad \widehat{f}(\boldsymbol{in}); \widehat{f}'(\boldsymbol{in}); rename(\widehat{f}'.out); assert(\widehat{f}.out = \widehat{f}'.out);$$

The function *rename* renames identifiers of functions and shared variables to their counterparts according to ϕ_F and ϕ_G, respectively. We omit some details on the construction (e.g., how $\boldsymbol{in}$ is generated when the signatures of f, f' include pointers), and verification of $VC_\delta(f)$. These details are available elsewhere [3], where similar programs are constructed for single-threaded programs. It should be clear, though, that validity of $VC_\delta(f)$ is decidable because there are no loops and (interpreted) function calls in $\widehat{f}$ and $\widehat{f}'$. Our first proof rule for partial equivalence of two MT programs P, P' is:

$$\frac{\forall i \in [1..n].\ \delta(f_i)}{p.e.(P, P')} \ . \qquad (1)$$

Example 2. Consider the programs P in Fig. 3. For a fixed positive value of the shared variable `x`, `f1` computes recursively the GCD of `x` and the input argument `t`, if `t` > 0. The second thread `f2` changes the value of `x` to a nondeterministic value. `f1()` is assumed to be called from another function that first sets x

```
void f1(int td, int *o) {
  int t1, t2, t3;
  if (td <= 0) t2 = x;
  else {
    t1 = x;
    t3 = t1 % td;
    x  = td;
    f1(t3, &t2);
  }
  *o = t2;
}

void f2() {
  int t;
  x = t;
}
```

P

```
void f1'(int td, int *o') {
  int t1, t2;
  t2 = x';
  if (td > 0) {
    t1 = x';
    x' = td;
    f1'(t1 % td, &t2);
  }

  *o' = t2;
}

f2'() {
  int t;
  x' = t;
}
```

P′

Fig. 3. Two MT-programs for Example 2

to some initial value (not shown here for simplicity). The program P' on the right does the same in a different way. We wish to check whether these two programs are partially equivalent. We assume that $\phi_F = \{(\texttt{f1,f1'}), (\texttt{f2,f2'})\}$, $\phi_G = \{\texttt{(x,x'), (o,o')}\}$. Note that in the construction we refer to `o,o'` as shared, although they are not, because of our convention that output variables are considered as shared. Also, we have $\mathit{ActualReadParam}(\texttt{f1}) = \{\texttt{t3, x}\}$, $\mathit{WriteParam}(\texttt{f1}) = \{\texttt{o, x}\}$, $\mathit{ActualReadParam}(\texttt{f1'}) = \{\texttt{t1 \% td, x'}\}$ and $\mathit{WriteParam}(\texttt{f1'}) = \{\texttt{o, x'}\}$. Fig. 4 presents pseudo-code for $\delta(\texttt{f1})$. Note that the input `in` sent to $\widehat{\texttt{f1}}$ and $\widehat{\texttt{f1'}}$ is nondeterministic. $\delta(\texttt{f2})$ is trivial and not shown here. Both programs are valid, and hence by (1), $p.e.(P, P')$ holds. □

Note that when constructing $\widehat{f}$, we record both reads and writes in $\widehat{f}.out$. The following example shows that ignoring the order of reads makes (1) unsound.

Example 3. Consider the 2-threaded programs P (left) and P' (right) shown in Fig. 5. Assume that all variables are initialized to 0, and `x3,x4` are the outputs. P' is identical to P other than the fact that the first two lines in `f1()` are swapped. Thus, if reads are not recorded in $\widehat{f}.out$, then $VC_\delta(f_1)$ and $VC_\delta(f_2)$ are both valid. Hence, our proof rule would imply that P and P' are partially equivalent. But this is in fact wrong, as we now demonstrate.

If `x4 = 1` at the end of P's execution, then the instruction `t2 = x1` in `f2()` must have happened after the instruction `x1 = 1` in `f1()`. Therefore `t1` reads the value of `x2` before it is updated by `f2()`, which means that `t1`, and hence `x3`, are equal to 0. Hence, at the end of any execution of P, `x4 = 1` $\Rightarrow$ `x3 = 0`.

On the other hand, in P', after the computation `x1 = 1; t2 = x1; x2 = 2; t1 = x2; x3 = t1; x4 = t2;` we have (`x4 = 1, x3 = 2`). Since this output is impossible in P, then $\neg p.e.(P, P')$. Hence, our proof rule would be unsound. □

```
void f̂1 (int td, int *o) {
  int t1, t2, t3, c = 0;
  if (td <= 0) {
    //2 ▷ t2 = x;
    t2 = UF_x(c);
    out1 += (R, "x"); c++;
  } else {
    //2 ▷ t1 = x;
    t1 = UF_x(c);
    out1 += (R, "x"); c++;
    //3 ▷ x  = td;
    t3 = t1 % td;
    x  = td;
    out1 += (W, "x", td); c++;
    //3 ▷ t2 = f1(t3, &t2);
    t2 = UF_f1_o(t3, x);
    x  = UF_f1_x(t3, x);
    out1 += (C, f1, t3, x);
  }
  //1 ▷ *o = t2;
  out1 += (W, "*o", t2); c++;
}
```

```
void f̂1'(int td, int *o') {
  int t1, t2, c = 0;
  //2 ▷ t2 = x';
  t2 = UF_x(c);
  out2 += (R, "x'"); c++;
  if (td > 0) {
    //2 ▷ t1 = x';
    t1 = UF_x(c);
    out2 += (R, "x'"); c++;
    //2 ▷ x' = td;
    x' = td;
    out2 += (W, "x'", td); c++;
    //3 ▷ f1'(t1 % td, &t2);
    t2 = UF_f1_o(t1 % td, x');
    x' = UF_f1_x(t1 % td, x');
    out2 += (C, f1, t1 % td, x');
  }
  //1 ▷ *o' = t2;
  out2 += (W, "*o'", t2); c++;
}

main() {
  int in;
  f̂1(in);  f̂1'(in);
  rename(out2);
  assert(out1 == out2);
}
```

Fig. 4. For Example 2: Pseudo-code for $\delta(\mathtt{f1})$, where $n \triangleright X$ denotes that the next n lines encode X

The above example also demonstrates that even minor alterations in the order of reads and writes in a thread – alterations that do have any effect in a sequential program – lead to loss of partial equivalence. This leads us to believe that there is little hope for a rule with a significantly weaker premise than (1).

4.3   Definitions

In this section we present definitions used later to prove the soundness of (1).

Definition 2 (Finite Read-Write trace). *A finite Read-Write trace (or RW-trace for short) is a sequence $(A, var, val)^*$, where $A \in \{R, W\}$, var is a shared variable identifier and val is the value corresponding to the action A on var.*

By 'trace' we mean a finite RW trace, and RW is the set of all RW traces.

Definition 3 (Function semantics). *The semantics of a function f under input **in** is the set of traces possible in $f(\mathbf{in})$ under an arbitrary program environment and input.*

We denote by $[f(\mathbf{in})]$ the semantics of f under input **in**.

```
f1() {                f2() {                    f1'() {              f2'() {
  t1 = x2;              t2 = x1;                  x1 = 1;              t2 = x1;
  x1 = 1;               x2 = 2;                   t1 = x2;             x2 = 2;
  x3 = t1;              x4 = t2;                  x3 = t1;             x4 = t2;
}                     }                         }                    }
```

Fig. 5. Example programs P (left) and P' (right). All variables are of integer type.

Definition 4 (Sequential consistency). *An interleaving* t *of traces* $t_1, \dots, t_n$ *is* sequentially consistent *if when* (W, var, v_1) *is the last write action to var before a read action* (R, var, v_2) *in* t*, then* $v_1 = v_2$.

Let $\bowtie (t_1, \dots, t_n)$ denote the set of sequentially consistent interleavings of $t_1, \dots, t_n$. The extension to sets of traces $S_1, \dots, S_n$ is given by:

$$\bowtie (S_1, \dots, S_n) = \bigcup_{t \in S_1 \times \dots \times S_n} \bowtie (t) \; .$$

Definition 5 (Program semantics). *Let* $P = f_1 \parallel \dots \parallel f_k$ *be a program. The semantics of* P*, denoted by* $[P]$*, is the set of terminating traces defined by:*

$$[P] = \bigcup_{\boldsymbol{in}} \bowtie ([f_1(\boldsymbol{in})], \dots, [f_k(\boldsymbol{in})]) \; .$$

Example 4. Consider the functions `f1()` and `f2()` from Fig. 5. Let $\mathbb{Z}$ be the set of all integers. We have:

$$[\texttt{f1}] = \bigcup_{z \in \mathbb{Z}} \{\langle (R, \texttt{x2}, z), (W, \texttt{x1}, 1), (W, \texttt{x3}, z) \rangle\}$$

$$[\texttt{f2}] = \bigcup_{z \in \mathbb{Z}} \{\langle (R, \texttt{x1}, z), (W, \texttt{x2}, 2), (W, \texttt{x4}, z) \rangle\}$$

Now consider the program $P = \texttt{f1} \parallel \texttt{f2}$. Assume that all global variables are initialized to 0 Then, we have:

$$\begin{aligned}[P] = \{ & \langle (R, \texttt{x2}, 0), (W, \texttt{x1}, 1), (W, \texttt{x3}, 0), (R, \texttt{x1}, 1), (W, \texttt{x2}, 2), (W, \texttt{x4}, 1) \rangle, \\ & \langle (R, \texttt{x1}, 0), (W, \texttt{x2}, 2), (W, \texttt{x4}, 0), (R, \texttt{x2}, 2), (W, \texttt{x1}, 1), (W, \texttt{x3}, 2) \rangle, \\ & \langle (R, \texttt{x2}, 0), (R, \texttt{x1}, 0), (W, \texttt{x1}, 1), (W, \texttt{x3}, 0), (W, \texttt{x2}, 2), (W, \texttt{x4}, 0) \rangle, \dots \} \; \square \end{aligned}$$

Let $[\widehat{f}(\boldsymbol{in})]$ denote the possible values of $\widehat{f}.out$ under input $\boldsymbol{in}$. We now show how $[f(\boldsymbol{in})]$ is obtained from $[\widehat{f}(\boldsymbol{in})]$, by recursively expanding all function calls. For conciseness from hereon we frequently omit $\boldsymbol{in}$ from the notations $[\widehat{f}(\boldsymbol{in})]$ and $[f(\boldsymbol{in})]$, i.e., we write $[\widehat{f}]$ and $[f]$ instead.

Definition 6 (Finite Read-Write-Call trace). *A finite Read-Write-Call trace (or RWC trace for short) is a sequence* $\{(A, var, val) \cup (C, f, a_1, \dots, a_k)\}^*$*, where* A*, var and val are the same as RW traces,* f *is a function, and* $a_1, \dots, a_k$ *are values passed as arguments to* f.

For an RWC trace t, we write $CS(t)$ to mean the set of functions appearing in t, i.e.,:

$$CS(t) = \{f \mid (C, f, \ldots) \in t\} .$$

Expanding a function call requires to map it to the traces of the called function. For this purpose we define a function $\mu : CS(t) \mapsto 2^{RW}$ (recall that RW is the set of all traces). Then, $\mathbf{inline}(t, \mu) \subseteq RW$ is defined as follows: a trace t' belongs to $\mathbf{inline}(t, \mu)$ iff t' is obtained by replacing each element $(C, f, \ldots)$ in t with an element of $\mu(f)$.

Definition 7 (Bounded semantics of a function). *The* bounded semantics *of a function f is its RW traces up to a given recursion depth. Formally:*

$$[f]^0 = [\widehat{f}] \cap RW$$

and for $i > 0$,

$$[f]^i = \bigcup_{w \in [\widehat{f}]} \mathbf{inline}(w, \mu^i_f) \cap [f], \textit{ where}$$

$$\mu^i_f(f) = [f]^{i-1} \textit{ and } \forall g \neq f \textit{ called by } f\textbf{.}\ \mu^i_f(g) = [g] .$$

Less formally, at a recursive call (i.e., when $g = f$), μ^i_f inlines a trace of f that involves fewer than i recursive calls of f, and at a nonrecursive function call (i.e., when $g \neq f$) it inlines an arbitrary trace of g. Observe that the semantics of a function can be defined as a union of its bounded semantics:

$$[f] = \bigcup_{i \geq 0} [f]^i . \quad (2)$$

Example 5. Recall the factorial function g from Fig. 2. Then we have:

$$[\widehat{\mathrm{g}}] = \{\langle (W, \mathtt{o1}, 0!) \rangle\} \cup \bigcup_{z \in \mathbb{Z} \wedge z > 0} \langle (C, \mathrm{g}, z-1), (W, \mathtt{o1}, z!) \rangle$$

$$\forall i \geq 0\textbf{.}\ [\mathrm{g}]^i = \bigcup_{0 \leq z \leq i} \{\langle (W, \mathtt{o1}, 0!), (W, \mathtt{o1}, 1!), \ldots, (W, \mathtt{o1}, z!) \rangle\}$$

$$[\mathrm{g}] = \bigcup_{z \geq 0} \{\langle (W, \mathtt{o1}, 0!), (W, \mathtt{o1}, 1!), \ldots, (W, \mathtt{o1}, z!) \rangle\}$$

□

4.4 Soundness

We now prove the soundness of (1) in three stages:

1. In Theorem 1 we prove that for any function f, the following inference is sound:

   $$\frac{\forall g \in \mathrm{CG}(f)\textbf{.}\ \delta(g)}{\forall \boldsymbol{in}\textbf{.}\ [f(\boldsymbol{in})] = [f'(\boldsymbol{in})]} .$$

   This establishes the connection between the premise of (1) and the equal semantics of mapped threads.

2. Then, in Theorem 2 we prove that the following inference is sound:

$$\frac{\forall i \in [1..k]\ \forall \boldsymbol{in}.\ [f_i(\boldsymbol{in})] = [f'_i(\boldsymbol{in})]}{[P] = [P']}.$$

   This establishes the connection between the equivalence of semantics of individual threads, and the equal semantics of their composition.
3. Finally, in Theorem 3 we prove that $[P] = [P'] \Rightarrow p.e.(P, P')$, which is the desired conclusion.

Theorem 1. *For any function f, the following inference is sound:*

$$\frac{\forall g \in \textsc{cg}(f).\ \delta(g)}{(\forall i \geq 0\ \forall \boldsymbol{in}.\ [f(\boldsymbol{in})]^i = [f'(\boldsymbol{in})]^i) \ \wedge\ \forall \boldsymbol{in}.\ [f(\boldsymbol{in})] = [f'(\boldsymbol{in})]}.$$

Proof. Note that, owing to (2), the left conjunct in the consequent implies the right one. Hence it suffices to prove the former.

Let $L(f)$ be the number of nodes in $\textsc{cg}(f)$. The proof is by simultaneous induction on i and $L(f)$, for an arbitrary input $\boldsymbol{in}$.

Base Case: Suppose $i = 0$ and $L(f) = 1$, which means that f and f' do not have function calls. In this case the inference holds by construction of $\delta(f)$, because the RW traces in $\widehat{f}(\boldsymbol{in})$ are exactly those in $[f(\boldsymbol{in})]^0$, and $\delta(f)$ implies that $\widehat{f}$ and $\widehat{f'}$ generate the same RW trace given the same input.

Inductive step: Suppose $i = n$ and $L(f) = l$ and suppose that the theorem holds for all $i < n$ and for all $L(f) < l$. Consider any $t \in [f(\boldsymbol{in})]^i$ and let $\widehat{t} \in [\widehat{f}(\boldsymbol{in})]$ such that $t \in \textbf{inline}(\widehat{t}, \mu^i_f)$. Now define:

$$\mu^i_{f'}(f'(\boldsymbol{in})) = [f'(\boldsymbol{in})]^{i-1} \text{ and } \forall g' \neq f' \text{called by } f'.\ \mu^i_{f'}(g'(\boldsymbol{in})) = [g'(\boldsymbol{in})]\ .$$

By the inductive hypothesis, we know that $\forall g \in \textsc{cg}(f).\ \mu^i_f(g(\boldsymbol{in})) = \mu^i_{f'}(g'(\boldsymbol{in}))$. Therefore, $t \in \textbf{inline}(\widehat{t}, \mu^i_{f'})$. Using the same argument as in the base case, we know that $\widehat{t} \in [\widehat{f'}(\boldsymbol{in})]$. Therefore, from the definition of $[f'(\boldsymbol{in})]^i$, we know that $t \in [f'(\boldsymbol{in})]^i$. Since t is an arbitrary element of $[f(\boldsymbol{in})]^i$, we conclude that $[f(\boldsymbol{in})]^i \subseteq [f'(\boldsymbol{in})]^i$. The same argument applies if we swap f and f'. Thus, $[f'(\boldsymbol{in})]^i \subseteq [f(\boldsymbol{in})]^i$ and, therefore, $[f(\boldsymbol{in})]^i = [f'(\boldsymbol{in})]^i$. This result holds for all inputs, since we did not rely on any particular value of $\boldsymbol{in}$. □

Theorem 2. *The following inference is sound:*

$$\frac{\forall i \in [1..k]\ \forall \boldsymbol{in}.\ [f_i(\boldsymbol{in})] = [f'_i(\boldsymbol{in})]}{[P] = [P']}.$$

Proof. By definitions 3, 4, and 5, we know that:

$$[P] = \bigcup_{\boldsymbol{in}} \bowtie ([f_1(\boldsymbol{in})], \ldots, [f_k(\boldsymbol{in})]) = \bigcup_{\boldsymbol{in}} \quad \bigcup_{t \in [f_1(\boldsymbol{in})] \times \cdots \times [f_k(\boldsymbol{in})]} \bowtie (\boldsymbol{t}) \text{ and,}$$

$$[P'] = \bigcup_{\boldsymbol{in}} \bowtie ([f_1'(\boldsymbol{in})], \ldots, [f_k'(\boldsymbol{in})]) = \bigcup_{\boldsymbol{in}} \bigcup_{\boldsymbol{t'} \in [f_1'(\boldsymbol{in})] \times \cdots \times [f_k'(\boldsymbol{in})]} \bowtie (\boldsymbol{t'}) .$$

But since for $i \in [1..k]$ and for all input $\boldsymbol{in}$ $[f_i(\boldsymbol{in})] = [f_i'(\boldsymbol{in})]$, t and t' range over the same sets of trace vectors. Hence $[P] = [P']$. □

We now prove the soundness of the first rule.

Theorem 3. *Proof rule (1) is sound.*

Proof. Let $P = f_1 \parallel \ldots \parallel f_k$ and $P' = f_1' \parallel \ldots \parallel f_k'$. From the premise of the proof rule, and Theorem 1, we know that:

$$\forall i \in [1..k]\ \forall \boldsymbol{in}.\ [f_i(\boldsymbol{in})] = [f_i'(\boldsymbol{in})] .$$

Therefore, by Theorem 2, we know that $[P] = [P']$. Observe that for any input $\boldsymbol{in}$ and output $\boldsymbol{out}$, $(\boldsymbol{in}, \boldsymbol{out}) \in R(P)$ iff $\exists t \in [P]$ starting from $\boldsymbol{in}$ and ending with $\boldsymbol{out}$. Recall that all the outputs of P, P' are assumed to be through shared variables. It is clear then, that if $[P] = [P']$ then for a given input they have the same set of outputs. Hence, we reach the desired conclusion. □

4.5 The Value of Partial Success

Since (1) requires $\delta(f)$ to hold for all functions, it is interesting to see if anything is gained by proving that it holds for only some of the functions. Recall that Definition 1 referred to whole programs. We now define a similar notion for a function f with respect to the program P to which it belongs. By $R(f)$ we denote the I/O relation of f with respect to P. Formally, $R(f)$ is the set of all pairs $(\boldsymbol{in}, \boldsymbol{out})$ such that there exists a computation of P (including infinite ones) in which there is a call to f that begins with $ReadParam(f) = \boldsymbol{in}$ and ends with $WriteParam(f) = \boldsymbol{out}$.

Definition 8 (Partial equivalence of functions in MT programs). *Two functions f and f' are partially equivalent in their respective nondeterministic programs if $R(f) = R(f')$.*

Denote by $p.e.(f, f')$ the fact that f and f' are partially equivalent according to Definition 8. Now, suppose that for some function f, $\forall g \in \text{CG}(f).\ \delta(g)$. Then, Theorem 1 implies that $\forall \boldsymbol{in}.\ [f(\boldsymbol{in})] = [f'(\boldsymbol{in})]$. Considering the main goal of regression verification – providing feedback about the impact of changes to a program – this is valuable information. It implies that the observable behavior of f, f' can only be distinguished by running them in different environments. Note that this does not imply that f, f' are partially equivalent according to Definition 8, since they may have different I/O relation under the environments provided by P and P' respectively. On the other hand it is stronger than I/O equivalence of f, f' under arbitrary but equivalent environments, because it makes a statement about the entire observable behavior and not just the outputs.

While partial results are useful, our first rule prevents us from proving $p.e.(P, P')$ if even for one function g, $\delta(g)$ is false. Our second rule is aimed at improving this situation.

```
void f1(int *o)     void f2(int i)     void f1'(int *o')     void f2'(int i)
{                   {                  {                     {
  int t = x;          int t = i;         int t = x';           int t = i;
  if (t < 0)          if (t < 0)                               if (t < 0)
    t = -t;             t = -t;                                  t = -t;
  *o = t;             x = t;             *o' = t;              x' = t;
}                   }                  }                     }
```

Fig. 6. The programs `f1` || `f2` and `f1'` || `f2'` are partially equivalent, but since the equivalence of `f1` and `f1'` depend on the *values* generated by `f2` and `f2'` (specifically, it depends on the fact that these functions update the shared variable with a positive value), $\delta($`f1`$)$ is false, which falsifies the premise of (1). On the other hand rule (4) proves their equivalence.

5 Second Proof Rule

The premise of our second rule, like the first one, is observable equivalence of pairs of functions under equal environments. However, unlike the first rule, the environments are not arbitrary, but rather consistent with the other threads in the program. This enables us to prove equivalence of programs like the ones in Fig. 6. Note that the functions `f1` and `f1'` are equivalent only if their respective environments always write non-negative values to `x` and `x'`.

5.1 Recursion-Bounded Abstraction

As mentioned, for our second rule, when checking the equivalence of f and f', we want to restrict their inputs from the environment to those that are actually produced by the other threads. In general this is of course impossible, but we now suggest an abstraction based on the observation that a bound on the number of reads of shared variables in any execution of $\widehat{f}$ can be computed, since it does not contain loops and interpreted function calls. Let $B(\widehat{f})$ denote this bound.

Given a thread rooted at f_q, and a bound b, we construct its *recursion-bounded abstraction* f_q^b, which overapproximates that thread, by transforming each recursive function $g \in \textsc{cg}(f_q)$ according to the scheme shown in Fig. 7. The key idea is to bound the number of recursive calls, and make each of them start from a nondeterministic state (this is achieved with `havoc_vars`) . This emulates b calls to g that are not necessarily consecutive in the call stack.

To understand what this construction guarantees, we define the following: let W denote the set of all possible sequences of writes to shared variables that can be observed in an execution of f_q. A b-sequence is a sequence of b or less elements from $s \in W$ that is consistent with the order of s. For example, if $W = \langle (x, 1), (x1, 2), (x, 2), (x1, 1)\rangle$ and $b = 2$, then some b-sequences are $\langle (x, 1), (x1, 1)\rangle$, $\langle (x1, 2), (x, 2)\rangle$, $\langle (x, 1)\rangle$ etc. We now claim without proof that:

Claim 1. *Every b-sequence of f_q can also be observed in some execution of f_q^b.*

```
bool rec_flag_g = 0; int rec_count_g = 0;
g^b() {
    assume(rec_count_g < b); ++rec_count_g;
    if (rec_flag_g) havoc_vars();
    The rest is the same as ĝ , except that:
    1. the RWC trace is recorded in a list out_q common to all g ∈ CG(f_q).
    2. a recursive call to g() is replaced by: rec_flag_g = 1; g^b(); rec_flag_g = 0;
}
```

Fig. 7. To derive the recursion-bounded abstraction f_q^b of a thread root-function f_q, we replace each $g \in \text{CG}(f_q)$ with g^b as described here. Although g^b is still recursive, the `assume` statement in the beginning guarantees that only b calls are made, which makes reachability decidable.

This fact guarantees that the recursion-based abstraction allows a function $\widehat{f}$ to interact with f_q^b in any way it can interact with f_q, if $b \geq B(\widehat{f})$.

5.2 The Proof Rule

Let $f \in \text{CG}(f_i)$ and $b = B(\widehat{f})$. Define the predicate $\Delta(f)$ as being true iff the following sequential program, $VC_\Delta(f)$, is valid for all input vectors $\boldsymbol{in}$:

$$\begin{aligned} VC_\Delta(f): \quad & f_1^b(\boldsymbol{in}); \ldots; f_{i-1}^b(\boldsymbol{in}); \widehat{f}(\boldsymbol{in}); f_{i+1}^b(\boldsymbol{in}); \ldots; f_k^b(\boldsymbol{in}); \\ & check\_assumption(\widehat{f}.out, i); \\ & \widehat{f'}(\boldsymbol{in}); assert(f.out == f'.out); \end{aligned} \tag{3}$$

Here $\widehat{f}$ is constructed from f as before (see Sec. 4.1). The implementation of *check_assumption* is shown in Fig. 8. The goal of this function is to constrain the values of shared variables read by $\widehat{f}$ to the last value written by either $\widehat{f}$ or some other thread. We assume that the array `w` used in lines 6 and 11 is initialized to 0, emulating a case that the variable read in line 11 is the initial value (in C global variables are initialized to 0 by default). Furthermore, it guarantees (through lines 13–15) that the values are read in the same order that they are produced by the environment, while allowing skips. The function $last(var, tid, loc)$ that is invoked in line 16 returns the index of the last write to var in thread tid at or before location loc. More information is given in the comments and caption.

Our second proof rule for partial equivalence of two MT programs P, P' is:

$$\frac{\forall i \in [1..n].\ \Delta(f_i)}{p.e.(P, P')} \; . \tag{4}$$

Example 6. Rule (4) proves the equivalence of the programs in Fig. 6, whereas rule (1) fails because $\delta(\texttt{f1})$ is false. □

```
check_assumption(list out, thread-id i) {
  int cf[k] = {0,..,0};          // location in 'out_j' for j ≠ i
  for(; q < |out|; ++q) {        // recall that out is f.out
    if(out[q] == (C,...)) continue;       // skipping function calls
    if(out[q] == (W,...)) {        // suppose out[q] == (W, "x", v))
6:      w['x'] = v;        // storing the written value
    } else {       // suppose out[q] = (R, "x")
        j = *;       // j is the thread from which we will read x
        assume (j ∈ {i | 1 <= i <= k, thread i already wrote to x});
        if (j == i)       // reading x from f itself
11:       assume(UF_f_x(q) == w['x']);       // enforcing x = last written value
        else {       // reading x from another thread
13:       oldcf = cf[j];
14:       cf[j] = *;       // nondet jump
15:       assume(oldcf <= cf[j] < |out_j|);
16:       ll = last("x", j, cf[j]);       // last location ≤ cf[j] in out_j
                                          // in which x was written to
17:       assume(UF_f_x(q) == out_j[ll]);       // enforcing x to a value
                                                // written-to by thread j
} } } }
```

Fig. 8. Pseudocode of *check_assumption*(). This function enforces the value that was read into a shared variable (through a call to an uninterpreted function) be equal to the last value it wrote or to a value written to this variable by some other thread. Lines 13–15 guarantee that the values are read in the same order that they are produced while allowing skips. The lists `out_1`...`out_k` correspond to the lists mentioned in Fig. 7.

5.3 Soundness of the Proof Rule

Let f and g be functions such that $g \in \textsc{cg}(f)$ and let $t \in [f]$ be a RW trace. Consider all computations of f that run through g and whose observable behavior is t. Their subcomputations in g have corresponding subcomputations in $[\widehat{g}]$. Let $[\widehat{g}]_t$ denote this set of subcomputations. The following claim, which follows from Claim 1, will be useful to prove the soundness of our proof rule.

Claim 2. *Let $f_1, \ldots, f_k$ be functions and let $t_1, \ldots, t_k$ be traces such that $\forall i \in [1..k]$. $t_i \in [f_i]$ and $\bowtie (t_1, \ldots, t_k) \neq \emptyset$. Then, $\forall i \in [1..k]$. $\forall g \in \textsc{cg}(f_i)$. $\forall \widehat{t} \in [\widehat{g}]_{t_i}$, there exists an execution of the program:*

$$f_1^b(\boldsymbol{in}); \ldots; f_{i-1}^b(\boldsymbol{in}); \widehat{g}(\boldsymbol{in}); f_{i+1}^b(\boldsymbol{in}); \ldots; f_k^b(\boldsymbol{in});$$
$$check\_assumption(i);$$

such that at the end of the execution $\widehat{g}.out = \widehat{t}$.

Theorem 4. *Inference rule (4) is sound.*

Proof. Falsely assume that P and P' are not partially equivalent despite the validity of the premise. This means that $\exists t \in [P] \setminus [P']$, which in itself implies

$\exists t \in\bowtie ([f_1], \ldots, [f_k]) \setminus \bowtie ([f'_1], \ldots, [f'_k])$. Since $t \in\bowtie ([f_1], \ldots, [f_k])$, we know that $\exists t_1, \ldots, t_k$ such that $\forall i \in [1..k].\ t_i \in [f_i]$ and $t \in\bowtie (t_1, \ldots, t_k)$.

Since $t \not\in\bowtie ([f'_1], \ldots, [f'_k])$, there exists at least one index $i \in [1..k]$ such that $t_i \not\in [f'_i]$. This implies that there must be at least one function $g \in \text{CG}(f_i)$ for which $\exists \widehat{t} \in [\widehat{g}]_{t_i}.\ \widehat{t} \not\in [\widehat{g'}]$. By Claim 2 there exists an execution e of the program:

$$f_1^b(\boldsymbol{in}); \ldots ; f_{i-1}^b(\boldsymbol{in}); \widehat{g}(\boldsymbol{in}); f_{i+1}^b(\boldsymbol{in}); \ldots ; f_k^b(\boldsymbol{in});$$
$$check\_assumption(i);$$

such that at the end of the execution $\widehat{g}.out = \widehat{t}$. But since $\Delta(g)$ is valid, then $\widehat{g}.out = \widehat{g'}.out$, and hence $\widehat{t} \in [\widehat{g'}]$ — a contradiction. □

6 Conclusion and Future Work

We proposed theoretical foundations for extending regression verification to multi-threaded programs. We defined a notion of equivalence of nondeterministic programs, and presented two proof rules for regression verification of general multi-threaded programs against this notion of equivalence. The premises of the rules are defined by a set of sequential programs (one for each function), whose validity is decidable and expected to be relatively easy to check.

One of the main areas for further investigation is to improve completeness. One direction is to use reachability invariants to strengthen the inference rules, similar to those found by THREADER [6] for the case of property verification. Also, note that we did not consider locks at all, and indeed without locks it is very hard to change a program and keep it equivalent. We therefore expect that integrating synchronization primitives into our framework will also assist in making the rules more complete. Finally, adding support for reactive programs and dynamic thread creation are also important avenues for further work.

References

1. Full version at `ie.technion.ac.il/~ofers/publications/vmcai12_full.pdf`
2. Cobleigh, J.M., Giannakopoulou, D., Păsăreanu, C.S.: Learning Assumptions for Compositional Verification. In: Garavel, H., Hatcliff, J. (eds.) TACAS 2003. LNCS, vol. 2619, pp. 331–346. Springer, Heidelberg (2003)
3. Godlin, B.: Regression verification: Theoretical and implementation aspects. Master's thesis, Technion, Israel Institute of Technology (2008)
4. Godlin, B., Strichman, O.: Inference rules for proving the equivalence of recursive procedures. Acta Informatica 45(6), 403–439 (2008)
5. Godlin, B., Strichman, O.: Regression verification. In: 46th Design Automation Conference, DAC (2009)
6. Gupta, A., Popeea, C., Rybalchenko, A.: Threader: A Constraint-Based Verifier for Multi-threaded Programs. In: Gopalakrishnan, G., Qadeer, S. (eds.) CAV 2011. LNCS, vol. 6806, pp. 412–417. Springer, Heidelberg (2011)
7. Jones, C.B.: Tentative steps toward a development method for interfering programs. ACM Trans. Program. Lang. Syst. 5(4), 596–619 (1983)

8. Kaser, O., Ramakrishnan, C.R., Pawagi, S.: On the conversion of indirect to direct recursion. LOPLAS 2(1-4), 151–164 (1993)
9. Kawaguchi, M., Lahiri, S.K., Rebelo, H.: Conditional equivalence. Technical Report MSR-TR-2010-119, Microsoft Research (2010)
10. Lee, E.A.: The problem with threads. IEEE Computer 39(5), 33–42 (2006)
11. Owicki, S.S., Gries, D.: An Axiomatic Proof Technique for Parallel Programs I. Acta Inf. 6, 319–340 (1976)

Crowfoot: A Verifier for Higher-Order Store Programs*

Nathaniel Charlton, Ben Horsfall, and Bernhard Reus

Department of Informatics, University of Sussex
{n.a.charlton,b.g.horsfall,bernhard}@sussex.ac.uk

Abstract. We present Crowfoot, an automatic verification tool for imperative programs that manipulate procedures dynamically at runtime; these programs use a heap that can store not only data but also code (commands or procedures). Such heaps are often called *higher-order store*, and allow for instance the creation of new recursions on the fly. One can use higher-order store to model phenomena such as runtime loading and unloading of code, runtime update of code and runtime code generation. Crowfoot's assertion language, based on separation logic, features *nested Hoare triples* which describe the behaviour of procedures stored on the heap. The tool addresses complex issues like deep frame rules and recursion through the store, and is the first verification tool based on recent developments in the mathematical foundations of Hoare logics with nested triples.

1 Introduction

Dynamic memory that can store not only data but also code is often called *higher-order store*. Such memory allows program code to change during execution with the manipulation performed by the program itself. For instance, one may be able to write code onto a mutable heap, invoke it, manipulate it, and then invoke it again later when needed. With higher-order store one can model phenomena such as runtime loading and unloading of code — as performed in plugin systems, operating system kernels and dynamic software update systems — and runtime code generation.

Logics with *nested triples* [17,11], where assertions can contain Hoare triples which describe the behaviour of code stored on the program's heap, have been proposed as a way to reason modularly about higher-order store programs. Recent developments [17,18] have provided solid theoretical foundations for separation logics with nested triples. In this paper we present Crowfoot, the first automatic verification system to apply these developments in practice. Crowfoot has been inspired by previous tools for automated verification using (conventional) separation logic, such as Smallfoot [3].

* We acknowledge the support of EPSRC grant *"From Reasoning Principles for Function Pointers To Logics for Self-Configuring Programs"* (EP/G003173/1).

V. Kuncak and A. Rybalchenko (Eds.): VMCAI 2012, LNCS 7148, pp. 136–151, 2012.

The Crowfoot tool provides (semi-)automatic verification for imperative programs which make use of higher-order store. Crowfoot uses an extension of separation logic for higher-order store, and performs its proofs by symbolic execution [4]. The main distinctive features of the Crowfoot verifier are:

- availability of nested triples for reasoning about stored procedures
- built-in support for recursive specifications for recursion through the store
- built-in support of the "deep frame rule", allowing correct and powerful framing of invariants in the presence of stored procedures
- built-in support of partial application of stored procedures
- an automatic prover for entailments between triples (as well as the usual entailments between assertions), supporting modular verification
- a sound theoretical underpinning of the implementation.

Running example. We demonstrate Crowfoot using the program in Fig. 1. Note that grey shaded parts are annotations for the verifier and are *not* part of the program code. They will be explained in Section 2.3. Our example concerns a recursive implementation *fib* of the Fibonacci function, which makes its recursive calls through the store. Since the "internal" recursive calls are made through the store, we can "hook into" the recursion and provide a memoisation routine *mem* which also caches these internal calls. This kind of memoisation cannot be implemented for a conventional recursive implementation of the Fibonacci function. This is more challenging than the factorial function which is typically used [11,2,9] to illustrate recursion through the store.

We will use Crowfoot to prove that the *fib* code, with or without the memoiser, is memory safe and correctly computes the Fibonacci function. In the process we will demonstrate the features of Crowfoot which make this possible.

2 Programming and Assertion Languages

2.1 Programming Language Featuring Higher-Order Store

Crowfoot works with an imperative heap-manipulating language with recursive procedures and, crucially, higher-order store operations. Fig. 2 includes a grammar for program statements. Square brackets are used for dereferencing addresses, so $x := [a]$ *reads* the content at address a into the variable x, whereas $[a] := x$ *stores* the value of x at address a in the heap[1].

There are two statements for using the higher-order store. Statements like $[a] := \mathsf{proc}\ \mathcal{F}(x, \_)$ write the code of fixed procedure $\mathcal{F}$ to the heap at address a. Each argument is either a variable or the _ symbol; where variables are given these are used to perform *partial application* of the procedure. Allowing procedures to be partially applied at the time they are stored on the heap is the simplest way to enable programs to write non-constant procedures onto the heap.

[1] In Fig. 2, where there is a danger of confusion, we write [] for square brackets that are part of the programming language, and [] for "meta-brackets" that are used in grammar definitions. We write | for choice and ? for optional elements.

```
const res;

proc fib(a,n) {
  locals p, q, k;
  if n ≤ 0 then {
    [res] := 0;
    ghost fold $Rel(n,0)
  } else {
    if n = 1 then {
      [res] := 1;
      ghost fold $Rel(?,?)
    } else {
      k := n − 2;
      eval [a](a,k); p := [res];
      k := n − 1;
      eval [a](a,k); q := [res];
      [res] := p + q;
      ghost fold $Rel(n,p+q)
}}}

proc mem(lookupL, addL, createL,
    disposeL, al, f, a, n) {
  locals found, b, v;
  ghost unfold $S(?,?,?,?,?,?,?);
  found := new 0;
  eval [lookupL](al, n, found, res);
  b := [found]; dispose found;
  if b = 0 then {
    ghost fold $S(?,?,?,?,?,?,?);
    eval [f](a,n);
    ghost unfold $S(?,?,?,?,?,?,?);
    v := [res]; eval [addL](al, n, v)
  } else { skip };
  ghost fold $S(?,?,?,?,?,?,?) }

proc useFib(lookupL, addL, createL,
    disposeL) {
  locals al, a, f, n;
  f := new 0;
  al := new 0;
  eval [createL](al);
  [f] := proc fib(_,_) deepframe DeepInv ;
  a := new 0;
  [a] := proc mem(lookupL, addL, createL,
    disposeL, al, f, _, _);
  ghost fold $S(?,?,?,?,?,?,?);
  n := 31337;
  eval[a](a,n);
  ghost unfold $S(?,?,?,?,?,?,?);
  ghost unfold $ListLibWeak(?,?,?,?);
  eval [disposeL](al);
  dispose a; dispose f; dispose lookupL;
  dispose addL; dispose createL;
  dispose disposeL; dispose res
}

proc main() {
  locals lookupL, addL, createL, disposeL;
  lookupL := new 0; addL := new 0;
  createL := new 0; disposeL := new 0;
  call load_list_lib(lookupL, addL,
    createL, disposeL);
  ghost unfold $ListLibStrong(?,?,?,?);
  ghost fold $ListLibWeak(?,?,?,?);
  call useFib(lookupL, addL, createL, disposeL)
}

proc load_list_lib(lookupL,
  addL, createL, disposeL) {...}
```

Fig. 1. Our running example program. (*DeepInv* is defined in Fig. 4.)

integer variables x, fixed procedure names $\mathcal{F}$, integer literals n, declared constants c

$$
\begin{array}{rcl}
\text{address expr } e_A & ::= & x \mid c \mid x+n \mid x+c \\
\text{value expr } e_V & ::= & n \mid x \mid c \mid e_V + e_V \mid e_V - e_V \mid e_V \times e_V \\
\text{statement } C & ::= & \mathsf{skip} \mid At \mid C; C \mid \mathsf{if}\ e_V = e_V\ \mathsf{then}\ C\ \mathsf{else}\ C \\
 & & \mid \mathsf{while}\ e_V = e_V\ \mathsf{do}\ C \mid \mathsf{while}\ e_V \neq e_V\ \mathsf{do}\ C \\
\text{argument } t & ::= & x \mid c \\
\text{atomic statement } At & ::= & x := e_V \mid x := [e_A] \mid [e_A] := e_V \mid [e_A] := [e_A] \\
 & & \mid x := \mathsf{new}\ {e_V}^{+} \mid \mathsf{dispose}\ e_A \mid \mathsf{call}\ \mathcal{F}(t^*) \\
 & & \mid \mathsf{eval}\ [e_A](t^*) \mid [e_A] := \mathsf{proc}\ \mathcal{F}([t|\_]^*)
\end{array}
$$

Fig. 2. Abstract syntax for program statements

As our syntax uses _ to represent arguments not yet "filled in", we can supply any subset of the arguments, not just initial segments. The statement $\mathsf{eval}[a](\boldsymbol{t})$ runs the procedure stored on the heap at address a, with value parameters $\boldsymbol{t}$, faulting if address a does not contain a procedure of the appropriate arity.

2.2 Assertion Language

Fig. 3 gives the syntax for the assertion language. Based on [17], the language allows *nested triples* to appear in assertions, such that we can reason about stored procedures. The assertion $x \mapsto \forall a.\, \{a \mapsto \_\} \cdot (a)\, \{a \mapsto \_\}$, for example, states that the content at address x is a procedure which satisfies the given Hoare triple.[2] Additions to the logic of [17] are the set and element expressions. In the formula $\mathrm{P}({e_V}^*; {e_S}^*)$, the ; separates integer arguments from set arguments. An assertion is called *pure* if it is made up only of (in)equalities, set constraints and predicates whose definitions are pure; pure formulae do not depend on the heap[3].

When building formal verification tools there is a trade-off between expressiveness of the specifications that one considers, and the degree of automation one can achieve. Rather than using the full assertion language, we restrict ourselves to the fragment given in Fig. 3; in return for this sacrifice we are able to program an effective automatic entailment prover in a fairly natural way.

2.3 Crowfoot Input Language

Crowfoot accepts annotated programs written using the programming and assertion languages given in the previous subsections. Specifically, a Crowfoot input program is a sequence of declarations, which can be of the following kinds:

[2] During the proof process, constants may be substituted into the arguments of the nested triple, which explains why the definition of B in Fig. 3 uses t.

[3] Here for convenience we follow Smallfoot's implementation and have only one kind of conjunction $\star$ in our logic; we do not include $\wedge$. The pure formulae such as $x = y$ are then given a non-standard interpretation, also requiring that the heap be empty.

set variables α, predicate names P

element expressions	e_E	$::=$	$e_V \mid (e_E{}^+)$
set expressions	e_S	$::=$	$\alpha \mid e_S \cup e_S \mid \{e_E\} \mid \emptyset$
behavioural spec.	B	$::=$	$\forall[x\|\alpha]^*. \ \{P\} \cdot (t^*)\{Q\}$
content spec.	$\mathscr{C}$	$::=$	$e_V \mid \_ \mid B$
atomic formula	A	$::=$	$e_A \mapsto \mathscr{C}^+ \mid \mathrm{P}(e_V{}^*; e_S{}^*) \mid e_V = e_V \mid e_V \neq e_V$
			$\mid e_E \in e_S \mid e_E \notin e_S \mid e_S \subseteq e_S \mid e_S = e_S$
spatial conjunction	Φ, Θ, Υ	$::=$	$\mathsf{emp} \mid A \star \Theta$
assertion disjunct	Ψ	$::=$	$\exists[x\|\alpha]^*.\Theta$
assertion	P, Q	$::=$	$\mathit{false} \mid \Psi \vee P$

Fig. 3. Abstract syntax for Crowfoot's assertion language

$$
\begin{aligned}
\text{decl} ::= \ & \mathsf{const}\ c \mid \mathsf{const}\ c = n \mid \mathsf{forall}\ \mathrm{P} \\
& \mid \mathsf{recdef}\ \mathrm{P}(x^*; \alpha^*) := P \mid \mathsf{recdef}\ \mathrm{P}(x^*) := \mathrm{P}(x^*) \circ \Psi \\
& \mid \mathsf{proc}\ \mathcal{F}(x^*)\ \mathsf{forall}\ [x|\alpha]^*.\ \mathsf{pre} : P\ \mathsf{post} : Q\ \{\ \mathsf{locals}\ x^*;\ C\ \} \\
& \mid \mathsf{proc\ abstract}\ \mathcal{F}(x^*)\ \mathsf{forall}\ [x|\alpha]^*.\ \mathsf{pre} : P\ \mathsf{post} : Q
\end{aligned}
$$

The keyword const is used to declare named constants, optionally with a particular value. The keyword recdef is used to declare user-defined inductive or recursive predicates, such as for linked data structures and for recursion through the store. Examples, in Fig. 4, will be discussed in the next section. Declaration forall P declares P to be an "abstract" or universally quantified predicate, i.e. one that may be used in specifications but has no definition (and thus cannot be folded or unfolded).

Finally, the keyword proc is used to declare procedures. Procedures have a name, a formal parameter list, a pre- and post-condition, and a body. The forall keyword is used to universally quantify variables over both the pre- and post-condition. Procedures declared as abstract do not have a body, just a specification; abstract procedures are typically used when we want to describe the behaviour of some library routine without giving an implementation.

Statement annotations. In programs checked by Crowfoot, some of the statements need to be annotated with extra information to help the verifier. These annotations consist of the following changes to the statement grammar of Fig. 2:

$$
\begin{aligned}
\text{statement } C \quad & ::= \quad \ldots \mid \mathsf{while}\ e_V\ [=|\neq]\ e_V\ \ P\ \ \mathsf{do}\ C \\
\text{atomicst } At \quad & ::= \quad \ldots \mid \mathsf{ghost}\ \text{ghoststmt} \ \mid \mathsf{call}\ \mathcal{F}(t^*)\ \ \text{deepfr-annot?} \\
& \qquad \mid [e_A] := \mathsf{proc}\ \mathcal{F}([t|\_]^*)\ \ \text{deepfr-annot?} \\
\text{ghoststmt} \quad & ::= \quad \mathsf{fold}\ \mathrm{P}([e_V|?]^*; [e_S|?]^*) \ \mid \ \mathsf{unfold}\ \mathrm{P}([e_V|?]^*; [e_S|?]^*) \\
\text{deepfr-annot} \quad & ::= \quad \mathsf{deepframe}\ \Psi
\end{aligned}
$$

Loops are annotated with invariants (as in Smallfoot and VeriFast). Like VeriFast, Crowfoot needs annotations to indicate at which locations it is necessary to fold or unfold user-defined predicates[4]. These annotations take the form of ghost fold and ghost unfold statements. For example, in order to reason about code which disposes the head of a linked list, one needs to unfold the inductively defined list predicate to expose the head node. Arguments to predicates being folded and unfolded can be given, or they can be left blank using '?' in which case Crowfoot attempts to find appropriate instantiations. Crowfoot is able to recognise predicate definitions which fit a general pattern for being "list-segment-like", and two further ghost statements split and join are available for these; as they are not needed in our running example we will not describe them.

2.4 Deep Framing

The *deep frame rule* [5,17] allows one to infer $\{P\}\,C\,\{Q\} \otimes I$ from $\{P\}\,C\,\{Q\}$, where $\otimes$ is a deep framing operator. Intuitively this operator adds the invariant I not just to the pre- and post-conditions of the triple $\{P\}\,C\,\{Q\}$, but also to all triples nested *inside* P and Q, at all levels. For example,

$$\begin{aligned} & \forall a.\, \{a \mapsto \{\mathsf{emp}\} \cdot ()\, \{\mathsf{emp}\}\} \cdot (a)\, \{\mathsf{emp}\} \otimes y \mapsto \_ \\ \Leftrightarrow\quad & \forall a.\, \{a \mapsto \{y \mapsto \_\} \cdot ()\, \{y \mapsto \_\} \star y \mapsto \_\} \cdot (a)\, \{y \mapsto \_\} \end{aligned}$$

as can be proved using the distribution laws for $\otimes$ found in [17]. This is useful for modular reasoning as explained in [5] and as will be demonstrated by our running example. The operator $\circ$ from [17], used in recdef definitions, is a convenient shorthand: $A \circ I := (A \otimes I) \star I$.

The annotation deepframe I tells Crowfoot to add the invariant I deeply onto the triple for a procedure; this can be done when a procedure is invoked with call (but not with eval [8]), or when a procedure is first written to the heap.

Crowfoot implements deep framing using the $\otimes$ distribution laws from [17]. However there is no simple law for distributing $\otimes$ through recursively defined predicates; instead, Crowfoot uses the following lemma.

Lemma 1. *Given the following predicate definition*

$$\mathrm{R}(\boldsymbol{x}) \quad := \quad \mathop{\bigstar}_{i=1}^{n} v_i \mapsto \forall \boldsymbol{a}_i.\, \{\mathrm{R}(\boldsymbol{e}) \,\star\, F_i\} \cdot (\boldsymbol{p}_i)\, \{\mathrm{R}(\boldsymbol{e}) \,\star\, G_i\} \;\star\; H$$

where: $\boldsymbol{e}$ *may contain variables* $\boldsymbol{a}_i$ *as well as* $\boldsymbol{x}$*, each* F_i*, each* G_i *and* H *are all left zeroes of* $\otimes$ *(i.e. informally they do not contain any nested triples), let us define* $\mathrm{S}(\boldsymbol{x},\boldsymbol{y}) := \mathrm{R}(\boldsymbol{x}) \circ T(\boldsymbol{y})$ *where* $fv(T(\boldsymbol{y})) = \boldsymbol{y}$ *and* $\boldsymbol{y} \cap \boldsymbol{a}_i = \emptyset$ *(implicitly also* $\boldsymbol{x} \cap \boldsymbol{y} = \emptyset$*). Note that* T *may contain occurrences of* S *again. Then the following equivalence holds:*

$$\mathrm{S}(\boldsymbol{x},\boldsymbol{y}) \;\Leftrightarrow\; \left(\mathop{\bigstar}_{i=1}^{n} v_i \mapsto \forall \boldsymbol{a}_i.\, \{\mathrm{S}(\boldsymbol{e},\boldsymbol{y}) \,\star\, F_i\} \cdot (\boldsymbol{p}_i)\, \{\mathrm{S}(\boldsymbol{e},\boldsymbol{y}) \,\star\, G_i\}\right) \star\; H \;\star\; T(\boldsymbol{y})$$

[4] Smallfoot [3] did not need fold/unfold ghost statements because only particular built-in list and tree predicates were available. Crowfoot allows users to write their own inductive definitions and thus, like VeriFast [13], requires extra annotations.

$$\textsf{recdef } \$Rel(n,m) := \; n \leq 0 \star m = 0 \;\vee\; n = 1 \star m = 1 \;\vee\; \exists a, b.\, 2 \leq n \star \$Rel(n-2,a) \star \$Rel(n-1,b) \star m = a + b$$

$$\textsf{recdef } \$RecFn(f) := f \mapsto \forall n, a.\; \{\$RecFn(a) \star res \mapsto \_\} \cdot (a,n) \, \{\exists v.\, \$RecFn(a) \star res \mapsto v * \$Rel(n,v)\}$$

$$\begin{array}{l} \textsf{recdef } \$ListLibStrong(lookupL, addL, createL, disposeL) := \\ \quad lookupL \mapsto \ldots \star createL \mapsto \ldots \star disposeL \mapsto \ldots \\ \quad \star\, addL \mapsto \forall al, key, value, \kappa. \\ \quad \left\{ \begin{array}{l} \$AssocListH(al;\kappa) \\ \star\, \$Rel(key, value) \end{array} \right\} \cdot (al, key, value) \; \{\$AssocListH(al; \{key\} \cup \kappa)\} \end{array}$$

$$\begin{array}{l} \textsf{recdef } \$ListLibWeak(lookupL, addL, createL, disposeL) := \\ \quad lookupL \mapsto \ldots \star createL \mapsto \ldots \star disposeL \mapsto \ldots \\ \quad \star\, addL \mapsto \forall al, key, value. \\ \quad \left\{ \begin{array}{l} \exists \kappa.\, \$AssocListH(al;\kappa) \\ \star\, \$Rel(key, value) \end{array} \right\} \cdot (al, key, value) \; \left\{ \begin{array}{l} \exists \kappa. \\ \$AssocListH(al;\kappa) \end{array} \right\} \end{array}$$

$$\textsf{recdef } \$S(a, f, al, lookupL, addL, createL, disposeL) := \$RecFn(a) \circ DeepInv$$

where *DeepInv* abbreviates

$$\exists \kappa. \left(\begin{array}{l} f \mapsto \forall n, a. \\ \qquad \{\$S(a, f, al, lookupL, addL, createL, disposeL) \star res \mapsto \_\} \\ \qquad\qquad \cdot (a,n) \\ \quad \{\exists v.\, \$S(a, f, al, lookupL, addL, createL, disposeL) \star res \mapsto v \star \$Rel(n,v)\} \\ \star\, \$AssocListH(al;\kappa) \star \$ListLibWeak(lookupL, addL, createL, disposeL) \end{array} \right)$$

$$\begin{array}{l} \textsf{recdef } \$AssocList(x;\tau) := x = 0 \star \tau = \emptyset \\ \quad \vee\; \exists next, k, v, \tau'.\, x \mapsto k, v, next \star \$Rel(k,v) \star \$AssocList(next;\tau') \star \tau = \{k\} \cup \tau' \end{array}$$

$$\textsf{recdef } \$AssocListH(x;\tau) := \exists y.\, x \mapsto y \star \$AssocList(y;\tau)$$

Fig. 4. User-defined predicates used to specify and verify our running example

3 Specification of the Running Example

The specifications of the procedures in Fig. 1 can be found in Fig. 5. The auxiliary predicate definitions are given in Fig. 4.

The *fib* implementation. Let us first examine how to specify the *fib* code. Predicate $\$Rel(n,m)$ says that n and m are appropriately related for the function

proc $main()$
  pre : $res \mapsto \_$;
  post : emp;

proc $fib(a, n)$
  pre : $\$RecFn(a) \star res \mapsto \_$;
  post : $\exists v.\ \$RecFn(a) \star res \mapsto v \star \$Rel(n, v)$;

proc $mem(lookupL, addL, createL, disposeL, al, f, a, n)$
  pre : $\$S(a, f, al, lookupL, addL, createL, disposeL) \star res \mapsto \_$;
  post : $\exists m.\ \$S(a, f, al, lookupL, addL, createL, disposeL) \star res \mapsto m \star \$Rel(n, m)$;

proc $useFib(lookupL, addL, createL, disposeL)$
  pre : $res \mapsto \_ \star \$ListLibWeak(lookupL, addL, createL, disposeL)$; post : emp;

proc $load\_list\_lib(lookupL, addL, createL, disposeL)$
  pre : $lookupL \mapsto \_ \star addL \mapsto \_ \star createL \mapsto \_ \star disposeL \mapsto \_$;
  post : $\$ListLibStrong(lookupL, addL, createL, disposeL)$;

Fig. 5. Procedure specifications for the memoiser example

being computed; in this case we define $\$Rel(n, m)$ to mean that m is the nth Fibonacci number. But this definition is only used inside the proof of *fib*, and not when proving the generic components such as *mem*.

Suppose we try to write a precondition for the *fib* code. This precondition must mention all the heap resources needed by *fib*. Firstly a cell $res \mapsto \_$ is needed into which we write the result. Secondly, since *fib* makes its recursive call through the heap at the address given by parameter a, the precondition must include $a \mapsto B$ where B is a nested triple. In particular, B must state that the code stored at a has the same kind of behaviour as we specify for the *fib* procedure. But we don't have *fib*'s specification yet, because we are still trying to formulate its precondition! It appears that we need a specification which depends on itself. Using the recdef keyword we can declare such a recursively defined specification, namely the $\$RecFn$ predicate, which appears nested inside its own definition.

The memoiser. The memoiser implementation uses an association list data structure, at address al, to cache the input-output pairs for the function being memoised. An association list with a header cell, starting at address al and containing values for a set κ of keys, is described by $\$AssocListH(al; \kappa)$. Such lists are manipulated via four library routines, pointers to which are passed in the arguments *lookupL*, *addL*, *createL*, *disposeL*. Argument f to procedure *mem* is a pointer to the code of the function being memoised; the memoiser must call this code when the required data is not found in the cache. The arguments *lookupL*, *addL*, *createL*, *disposeL*, al, f are fixed by partial application when the memoiser is first loaded onto the heap. This leaves a two-argument procedure: the first argument a is passed straight through to the function being memoised, and the second argument n is the input at which to apply the function.

The memoiser is designed to be placed into mutual recursion with *fib*, or similar code for computing other functions. During computations the *fib* code and the memoiser then invoke each other in a "zig-zag" mutual recursion. The "ensemble" of these two functions stored on the heap and able to invoke each other can be described by $\$S(a, f, al, \mathit{lookupL}, \mathit{addL}, \mathit{createL}, \mathit{disposeL})$ which, by Lemma 1, is equivalent to:

$$\begin{aligned}\exists\kappa.\quad & a \mapsto \mathit{RecFnMem}(\cdot) \star f \mapsto \mathit{RecFnMem}(\cdot)\\ & \star\ \$\mathit{AssocListH}(al;\kappa)\ \star\ \$\mathit{ListLibWeak}(\mathit{lookupL}, \mathit{addL}, \mathit{createL}, \mathit{disposeL})\end{aligned}$$

where $\mathit{RecFnMem}(\cdot)$ is shorthand for

$$\begin{aligned}&\{\,\$S(a, f, al, \mathit{lookupL}, \mathit{addL}, \mathit{createL}, \mathit{disposeL}) \star \mathit{res} \mapsto \_\,\}\\ \forall a, n.\quad & \cdot(a, n)\\ &\{\,\exists v.\ \$S(a, f, al, \mathit{lookupL}, \mathit{addL}, \mathit{createL}, \mathit{disposeL}) \star \mathit{res} \mapsto v \star \$\mathit{Rel}(n, v)\,\}\end{aligned}$$

Intuitively *RecFnMem* describes code which computes a function as specified by $\$\mathit{Rel}$, provided the heap contains the "ensemble" of function and memoiser code as described above.

The main program. The *main* procedure first calls *load_list_lib* to load the association list library routines onto the heap. Then, *main* invokes *useFib* which loads the *fib* code and the memoiser, places them into mutual recursion, and finally uses this to compute the 31337th Fibonacci number.

In *useFib* we see the crucial role of the deep frame rule. We have specified (and Crowfoot will prove) *fib* for the case where it is placed in recursion *only with itself*, using $\$\mathit{RecFn}$. Hence, if the deepframe annotation were not used in *useFib*, the symbolic heap after the statement $[f] :=$ proc $\mathit{fib}(\_,\_)$ would contain

$$f \mapsto \forall a, n.\,\{\$\mathit{RecFn}(a) \star \mathit{res} \mapsto \_\}\cdot(a, n)\,\{\exists v.\ \$\mathit{RecFn}(a) \star \mathit{res} \mapsto v \star \$\mathit{Rel}(n, v)\}$$

However the annotation deepframe *DeepInv* tells Crowfoot to apply $-\otimes \mathit{DeepInv}$ to the above triple, resulting in $\mathit{RecFnMem}(\cdot)$. In this way, we have used the deep frame rule to *derive* another specification for the *fib* code, which describes how that code works in mutual recursion with a memoiser. We did not need to respecify or reprove *fib*.

The list library. The memoiser depends only on relatively weak properties of the association list library; a library with these properties is specified by $\$\mathit{ListLibWeak}$. But the list library is specified with a stronger specification $\$\mathit{ListLibStrong}$ so that it can also be used with other clients which need additional guarantees. Specifications for three of the routines are omitted in Fig. 4, but with the remaining "add" routine one can see a difference. In order to compute the correct function, the memoiser does not care whether the $(\mathit{key}, \mathit{value})$ pair is actually added to the list or not, as long as whatever pairs are in the list afterwards are suitably related by $\$\mathit{Rel}$. But other clients of the list library will certainly care about this.

Our verification will go through because Crowfoot can prove the entailment

$$\begin{aligned}&\$\mathit{ListLibStrong}(\mathit{lookupL}, \mathit{addL}, \mathit{createL}, \mathit{disposeL})\\ \Rightarrow\ &\$\mathit{ListLibWeak}(\mathit{lookupL}, \mathit{addL}, \mathit{createL}, \mathit{disposeL})\end{aligned}\tag{1}$$

as we shall discuss in Section 5. Having such entailments proved automatically facilitates reasoning when one is "plugging together" different pieces of code.

4 Automation of Program Verification

4.1 Overview

The introduction of nested triples into the logic increases considerably the difficulty of proving entailments automatically: because assertions can contain triples and vice versa, we need provers for entailments between both assertions and triples, and these provers need to invoke each other. In fact, at the heart of Crowfoot are automated provers for five interrelated judgements:

- Symbolic execution: $\Pi, \Gamma \rhd \{P\}C\{\ Q\ \}$
- Entailment between assertion disjuncts: $\Phi \vdash^{I} \exists \boldsymbol{v}.\, \Upsilon \star \Theta$
- Entailment between behavioural specifications (triples): $B_1 \vdash B_2$
- Computing the postcondition for a call or eval: $B \vdash_{\textsf{find-post}} \{\Phi\} \cdot (\boldsymbol{t})\{\ Q\ \}$
- Finding specifications inside a symbolic state: $\Upsilon \vdash_{\textsf{find-tr}} e \mapsto B$.

Here, Π is a *predicate context* mapping predicate names to their definitions (given by recdef) and Γ is a *procedure context* mapping fixed procedure names to their specifications (given by pre and post). C is a program statement. (As in Fig. 3) P, Q are assertions, Ψ is used for assertion disjuncts, and Φ, Θ, Υ for spatial conjunctions. Behavioural specifications are named B, and I is an *instantiation map* mapping the existentially quantified variables $\boldsymbol{v}$ to appropriate witnesses.

Shaded variables (such as the frame Θ) are those whose value is not given as an input to the prover, but rather is inferred by the proof rules. The meanings of these judgements can be seen in the following soundness theorem, which for now we simply state; we will discuss it later in Section 4.4.

Theorem 1. Soundness theorem. *Our five proof systems are sound, that is:*

- *If* $\Phi \vdash^I \exists \boldsymbol{v}.\Upsilon \star \Theta$ *(where* $fv(\Phi) \cap \boldsymbol{v} = \emptyset$*) then* $\Phi \Rightarrow \Upsilon[\boldsymbol{v}\backslash I(\boldsymbol{v})] \star \Theta$ *where:* $fv(\Theta) \subseteq fv(\Phi)$, $dom(I) = \boldsymbol{v}$ *and* $fv(Im(I)) \subseteq fv(\Phi)$.
- *If* $B_1 \vdash B_2$ *then* $B_1 \Rightarrow B_2$.
- *If* $B \vdash_{\textit{find-post}} \{\Phi\} \cdot (\boldsymbol{t})\, \{Q\}$ *then* $B \Rightarrow \{\Phi\} \cdot (\boldsymbol{t})\, \{Q\}$.
- *If* $\Upsilon \vdash_{\textit{find-tr}} e \mapsto B$ *then* $\Upsilon \Leftrightarrow e \mapsto B \star \Upsilon'$ *for some* Υ'.
- *Our symbolic execution rules are sound.* □

Verification of a program by Crowfoot proceeds as follows. First, Crowfoot's verification condition (VC) generator reads in the annotated program and produces a set of VCs, each of the form $\Pi; \Gamma \rhd \{P\}\, C\, \{Q\}$, such that if all the VCs hold then the input program meets its specifications. There is one such VC for each concrete procedure of the input program, with C being its body and P, Q the pre- and post-conditions. Then the generated VCs are passed to the symbolic execution engine which attempts to prove them. During symbolic execution, entailment problems of various kinds arise: for instance when the end of a procedure (resp. loop body) is reached, one must check an entailment between the current symbolic state and the postcondition (resp. loop invariant). These entailments (between assertions) may give rise to entailments between triples because triples can appear nested. When an eval statement is reached, $\vdash_{\text{find-tr}}$ is employed to find a triple to use for the invocation, and then $\vdash_{\text{find-post}}$ is used to compute a symbolic state holding after the invoked code returns.

4.2 Symbolic Execution Engine

Crowfoot's symbolic execution engine is based on ideas put forward in [4] and now well established. The symbolic execution rules, a few of which can be seen in Fig. 7, depend on all four of the other judgements. One such rule is:

LOOKUP

$$\frac{\begin{array}{c} purify(\Upsilon) \vdash_{SMT} E = G + o \\ \Pi; \Gamma \rhd \{x = (e[x\backslash x']) \star (\Upsilon \star G \mapsto \mathscr{C}_0, \ldots, \mathscr{C}_{o-1}, e, \mathscr{C}_{o+1}, \ldots, \mathscr{C}_n)[x\backslash x']\}\, C\, \{Q\} \end{array}}{\Pi; \Gamma \rhd \{\Upsilon \star G \mapsto \mathscr{C}_0, \ldots, \mathscr{C}_{o-1}, e, \mathscr{C}_{o+1}, \ldots, \mathscr{C}_n\}\, x := [E];\ C\, \{Q\}}\ x' \text{ fresh}$$

where $purify(\Upsilon)$ extracts the pure parts of Υ, and $\vdash_{SMT}$ represents sending a pure goal to an SMT solver to be checked. The rules which are intrinsically new in our work are those for the statements which make use of higher-order store, namely eval $[E](\boldsymbol{t})$ and $[E] :=$ proc $\mathcal{F}([t|\_]^*)$. The rule for eval (where $\boldsymbol{a} \in [x|\alpha]^*$) is:

EVAL

$$\frac{\begin{array}{c} \Upsilon \vdash_{\text{find-tr}} E \mapsto \forall \boldsymbol{a}.\{P\} \cdot (\boldsymbol{t})\{Q\} \\ \forall \boldsymbol{a}.\{P\} \cdot (\boldsymbol{t})\{Q\} \vdash_{\text{find-post}} \{\Upsilon\} \cdot (\boldsymbol{t}') \left\{ \bigvee_{i=1}^{m} \exists \boldsymbol{v}_i.\Phi_i \right\} \\ \Pi; \Gamma \rhd \left\{ \bigvee_{i=1}^{m} \Phi_i[\boldsymbol{v}_i \backslash \boldsymbol{v}_i'] \right\} C\, \{Q'\} \end{array}}{\Pi; \Gamma \rhd \{\Upsilon\}\, \text{eval } [E](\boldsymbol{t}')\ ;\ C\, \{Q'\}}\ \boldsymbol{v}_i' \text{ fresh}$$

This uses the $\vdash_{\text{find-tr}}$ prover to find the specification $\forall \boldsymbol{a}.\{P\} \cdot (\boldsymbol{t})\{Q\}$ of the code being invoked from the heap. Then the $\vdash_{\text{find-post}}$ prover is used to compute all the possible symbolic states $\exists \boldsymbol{v}_i.\Phi_i$ that may result from running that code. Finally, symbolic execution is performed on the "continuation" statement C.

4.3 Entailment Provers

We sketch how our different entailment provers work. The selected rules we refer to are listed in Fig. 6.

Entailments between assertion disjuncts. The main part of these proofs involves successively cancelling spatial formulae from the left and right sides of $\vdash$. Sometimes these steps involve computing witnesses for existentially quantified variables, which are added to the instantiation map I. For instance, the goal

$$\Phi \star x \mapsto 3 \vdash^{I} \exists u, \boldsymbol{v}.\, \Upsilon \star x \mapsto u \star \Theta \quad \text{reduces to} \quad \Phi \vdash^{I'} \exists \boldsymbol{v}.\, \Upsilon[u\backslash 3] \star \Theta$$

by CANCELPTINSTCONTENTS, where we will take $I := I'[u := 3]$. Note how the rule CANCELPTTRIPLE for cancelling cells containing code invokes the prover for entailments between triples (specifications). The cancellation rules are designed to reduce the goal to the form $\Upsilon \vdash^I \Phi \star \Theta$ where Φ is pure. We finish by sending the pure entailment problem $purify(\Upsilon) \vdash_{SMT} \Phi$ to an SMT solver, and we take Υ as the inferred frame Θ.

Entailments between specifications. Most of the work of proving judgements $B_1 \vdash B_2$ is done by the TRIPLEENT rule, which breaks down the checking of an entailment $B \vdash \{\Phi\} \cdot (\boldsymbol{t}) \{Q'\}$ between specifications into two tasks. Intuitively, we first use $\vdash_{\textbf{find-post}}$ to try to compute a state Q we will end up in if we run some code with specification B in a state satisfying Φ. We then check whether Q implies the postcondition Q'.

Inferring postconditions for invocations. The main rule for $\vdash_{\textbf{find-post}}$ is INFERSPECFORCALL. Underlying it is a combination of $\forall$-instantiation, the shallow frame axiom $\{P\}C\{Q\} \Rightarrow \{P \star R\}C\{Q \star R\}$ and the consequence axiom.

Finding specifications inside a symbolic state. To be able to symbolically execute an eval $[e](\boldsymbol{t})$ statement, we need to first find in our symbolic heap a cell $e \mapsto B$; we can then use the specification B to reason about the invocation. We use $\vdash_{\textbf{find-tr}}$ for finding such specifications. The most commonly used proof rule for $\vdash_{\textbf{find-tr}}$ is FIND which covers the case when the required cell $e \mapsto B$ is available in the symbolic heap without performing any unfolding. Other proof rules, omitted for space reasons, look inside occurrences of user-defined predicates to find the appropriate specification.

4.4 Theoretical Basis

One distinctive feature of our tool is that we can prove its soundness, embodied by Theorem 1. Due to lack of space we cannot go into detail, but we briefly explain our soundness argument. Soundness is proved with respect to another logic with nested triples, an extension of the logic of [17][5] which in turn has been proved sound in *loc. cit.* via a model construction. It is relatively straightforward to construct a step-indexed analogue which encompasses Crowfoot's extra features. It should be pointed out that soundness only holds for recursive predicates that *exist*. For a predicate R such as $\$RecFn$ (Fig. 4), existence is guaranteed because in its definition, R itself always occurs inside pre- and postconditions of some triple. The corresponding semantic functional is contractive and thus the predicate does exist via Banach's fixpoint theorem. In general however, reasons for existence may not be immediately clear, particularly for definitions that combine the recursive uses of R (as in $\$RecFn$) with inductive uses of R, as found in definitions of linked list predicates. Our tool does not check for existence.

5 Excerpt from the Verification of the Running Example

During the symbolic execution of *main*, we see how the entailment prover for assertions and the prover for specifications are mutually recursive. Before calling

[5] Enriched by inductive and abstract predicates as well as recursively defined procedures with explicit calls.

InferSpecForCall

$$\frac{\Phi \ \vdash^{I} \ \exists \boldsymbol{u}_k, \boldsymbol{a}.\, \Upsilon_k \star \Theta}{\forall \boldsymbol{a}. \left\{ \bigvee_{i=1}^{n} \exists \boldsymbol{u}_i.\Upsilon_i \right\} \cdot (\boldsymbol{t}) \left\{ \bigvee_{i=1}^{m} \exists \boldsymbol{v}_i.\Upsilon'_i \right\} \ \vdash_{\text{find-post}} \ \{\Phi\} \cdot (\boldsymbol{t}) \left\{ \bigvee_{i=1}^{m} (\exists \boldsymbol{v}_i.\Upsilon'_i[\boldsymbol{a}\backslash I(\boldsymbol{a})] \star \Theta) \right\}}$$

1. $\boldsymbol{t} \cap \boldsymbol{a} = \emptyset$ 2. $fv(\Phi) \cap \boldsymbol{u}_k = \emptyset$ and $fv(\Phi) \cap \boldsymbol{a} = \emptyset$
3. for each $i \in \{1, \ldots, m\}$ we have $\boldsymbol{v}_i \cap \boldsymbol{a} = \emptyset$
4. for each $i \in \{1, \ldots, m\}$, no formula in $I(\boldsymbol{a})$ contains a variable from $\boldsymbol{v}_i$
5. $k \in \{1, \ldots, n\}$ 6. $\boldsymbol{u}_k \cap \boldsymbol{a} = \emptyset$

TripleEnt

$$\frac{B \ \vdash_{\text{find-post}} \ \{\Phi\} \cdot (\boldsymbol{t}) \left\{ \bigvee_{i=1}^{m} \exists \boldsymbol{v}_i.\Upsilon_i \right\} \qquad \bigwedge_{i=1}^{m} \left(\Upsilon_i[\boldsymbol{v}_i \backslash \boldsymbol{a}_i] \ \vdash^{I_i} \ \exists \boldsymbol{b}_{j_i}.(\Upsilon'_{j_i}[\boldsymbol{w}_{j_i} \backslash \boldsymbol{b}_{j_i}]) \star \Theta_i \right)}{B \ \vdash \ \{\Phi\} \cdot (\boldsymbol{t}) \left\{ \bigvee_{i=1}^{m'} \exists \boldsymbol{w}_i.\Upsilon'_i \right\}}$$

1. $j_1, \ldots, j_m \in \{1, \ldots, m'\}$
2. $\boldsymbol{a}_1, \ldots, \boldsymbol{a}_m$ all chosen fresh
3. $\boldsymbol{b}_{j_1}, \ldots, \boldsymbol{b}_{j_{m'}}$ all chosen fresh
4. $\Theta_1, \ldots, \Theta_m$ pure

CancelPtInstContents

$$\frac{\Phi \ \vdash^{I} \ \exists \boldsymbol{v} \,.\, \Upsilon[v \backslash E] \star \Theta}{\Phi \star e \mapsto E \ \vdash^{I[v:=E]} \ \exists \boldsymbol{v}, v \,.\, \Upsilon \star e' \mapsto v \star \Theta}$$

1. $fv(e') \cap \boldsymbol{v} = \emptyset$ 2. $v \notin fv(e')$
3. $purify(\Phi) \vdash_{SMT} e = e'$

CancelPtTriple

$$\frac{\Phi \ \vdash^{I} \ \exists \boldsymbol{v} \,.\, \Upsilon \star \Theta \qquad B_1 \vdash B_2}{\Phi \star e \mapsto B_1 \ \vdash^{I} \ \exists \boldsymbol{v} \,.\, \Upsilon \star e' \mapsto B_2 \star \Theta}$$

1. $fv(e', B_2) \cap \boldsymbol{v} = \emptyset$
2. $purify(\Phi) \vdash_{SMT} e = e'$

Find

$$\frac{}{\Phi \star E \mapsto \mathscr{C}_0, \ldots, \mathscr{C}_{o-1}, B, \mathscr{C}_{o+1}, \ldots \mathscr{C}_n \vdash_{\text{find-tr}} e \mapsto B} \quad purify(\Phi) \vdash_{SMT} e = E + o$$

Fig. 6. Notable rules used in our automatic entailment provers

the *useFib* procedure, the *\$ListLibStrong* predicate is unfolded, and folded up into *\$ListLibWeak*. This essentially means proving (1) on page 144, which is an entailment between assertion disjuncts.

The proof proceeds by cancelling out the atomic formulae, which in this case means using CancelPtTriple for each of the four library procedures. This is where the entailment prover for specifications is needed: the premise of this rule requires that each strong specification entails the respective weak variation.

This entailment is checked by the TripleEnt rule, which has two premises. The first uses the judgement $\vdash_{\text{find-post}}$ (with InferSpecForCall) which will check that the weak pre-condition entails the strong pre-condition, with some inferred frame left over (in this case the frame is trivial). For the second premise it is required to prove that the strong postcondition (together with the frame) entails the weak one. Using again the entailment prover for assertion disjuncts, Crowfoot proves: $\$AssocListH(al, \{key\} \cup \kappa) \vdash^{[\kappa' \mapsto \{key\} \cup \kappa]} \exists \kappa'.\ \$AssocListH(al, \kappa')$.

6 Related and Future Work

Crowfoot can be considered as extending Smallfoot [4] (though Crowfoot was written from scratch) by allowing (partially applicable) procedures to be stored on the heap. Our assertion language uses nested triples to specify stored procedures and recursively defined assertions to deal with recursion through the store. Crowfoot uses an SMT solver to deal with pure assertions and therefore can be used to prove more than just memory safety (see our example).

The system most closely related to Crowfoot is the VeriFast [13,12] tool, also based on symbolic execution with separation logic. VeriFast supports a C-like language (and also Java) and supports C-style function pointers. Functions in the C-like language live in an immutable memory and can be pointed to but not updated, whereas Crowfoot's programming language stores procedures in dynamic, mutable memory. However these setups seem to have a similar character.

A key difference is that while Crowfoot uses nested triples to express requirements for procedure pointers, VeriFast expresses such requirements via *function types* with which the C type system is extended. A function type declaration associates a pre- and post-condition with the function type; the declared type can have extra arguments to simulate nested triples which can contain free variables. These can be recursive since for every function type F there is a predicate 'is_F(_)' which states that (the function pointed to by) its first argument satisfies the "contract" for function type F (possibly with additional arguments).

Crowfoot offers some features which VeriFast does not, such as partial application of which our example makes essential use in *useFib* when loading the memoiser *mem*. Another important feature to support stored procedures is entailment between Hoare triples which is automated in our verifier and needed in our example, as explained in Section 5. VeriFast does not support such proofs (which in that system would be proofs of entailments of shape is_F(_) $\Rightarrow$ is_G(_)), even manual ones, whereas Crowfoot finds them automatically. Crowfoot supports annotations for deep frame rule application (thus implementing the $\otimes$ operator) and allows extensions of predicates via $\circ$, thus allowing elegant use of deep framing on recursively defined specifications (cf. definition of $\$S$ in our example in Fig. 4). In VeriFast one can simulate the effect of the deep frame rule by using (second order) function types which take as argument a predicate representing the deeply framed invariant. However, this means one must write all specifications that can appear for stored procedures *a priori* in that style.

On the other hand, VeriFast offers features that Crowfoot does not, such as concurrency, termination checking and the use of more types (such as mathematical lists and functions on them) in the assertions. VeriFast's support for second order logic is useful for specifying and reasoning about higher-order and polymorphic functions.

Other related work includes four systems developed in Coq: XCAP [16], Bedrock [10], GCAP [6] and Ynot [14]. XCAP allows reasoning about programs

$$\textsc{New}\quad \frac{\Pi; \Gamma \rhd \{\Phi[x \backslash x'] \star x \mapsto (e_0, \ldots, e_n)[x \backslash x']\}\, C\, \{Q\}}{\Pi; \Gamma \rhd \{\Phi\}\, x := \mathsf{new}\ e_0, \ldots, e_n;\ C\, \{Q\}}\ x' \text{ fresh}$$

$$\textsc{Call}\quad \frac{\begin{array}{c} \forall \boldsymbol{a}.\, \{P\} \cdot (\boldsymbol{t})\, \{Q\} \ \otimes \Psi \vdash_{\text{find-post}} \{\Phi\} \cdot (\boldsymbol{t}') \left\{ \bigvee_{i=1}^{m} \exists \boldsymbol{v}_i . \Upsilon_i \right\} \\ \Pi; \forall \boldsymbol{a}.\, \{P\}\, \mathcal{F}(\boldsymbol{t})\, \{Q\}, \Gamma \rhd \left\{ \bigvee_{i=1}^{m} \Upsilon_i[\boldsymbol{v}_i \backslash \boldsymbol{v}_i'] \right\} C\, \{Q'\} \end{array}}{\Pi; \forall \boldsymbol{a}.\, \{P\}\, \mathcal{F}(\boldsymbol{t})\, \{Q\}, \Gamma \rhd \{\Phi\}\, \mathsf{call}\ \mathcal{F}(\boldsymbol{t}')\ \mathsf{deepframe}\ \Psi;\ C\, \{Q'\}}\ \boldsymbol{v}_i' \text{ fresh}$$

$$\textsc{StoreCode}\quad \frac{\begin{array}{c} \Gamma = \Gamma', \forall \boldsymbol{t}, \boldsymbol{a}.\, \{P\}\, \mathcal{F}(\boldsymbol{t})\, \{Q\} \\ B = (\forall \boldsymbol{t}|_U, \boldsymbol{a}.\ \{P\} \cdot (\boldsymbol{t}|_U)\, \{Q\})\, [\boldsymbol{t}|_{I \backslash U} \backslash \boldsymbol{r}|_{I \backslash U}] \\ \Pi; \Gamma \rhd \{\Phi \star G \mapsto \mathscr{C}_0, \ldots, \mathscr{C}_{o-1}, B \otimes \Psi, \mathscr{C}_{o+1}, \ldots, \mathscr{C}_n\}\, C\, \{Q'\} \end{array}}{\Pi; \Gamma \rhd \{\Phi \star G \mapsto \mathscr{C}_0, \ldots, \mathscr{C}_n\}\, [E] := \mathsf{proc}\ \mathcal{F}(\boldsymbol{r})\ \mathsf{deepframe}\ \Psi;\ C\, \{Q'\}}$$

1. $\boldsymbol{r} \in [x \vert c \vert \_]^*$	2. $\boldsymbol{a} = fv(P, Q) - \boldsymbol{t}$	3. $purify(\Phi) \vdash_{SMT} E = G + o$
4. $\boldsymbol{t} = (t_i)_{i \in I}$	5. $U = \{i \in I \mid r_i = \_\}$	6. $\boldsymbol{t}\vert_X = (t_i)_{i \in I \cap X}$

Fig. 7. Some of our symbolic execution rules

which use pointers to (immutable) functions, by introducing a special cptr predicate which in proofs behaves much like nested triples, though its underlying semantics is very different. GCAP is a related system supporting reasoning about low-level runtime code modification. Ynot builds a type theory in which Hoare triples ("Hoare types") can be used as the types for side-effecting commands; these Hoare types can be nested. To our knowledge, Ynot does not support recursion through the store.

Previous work [7] briefly described one application of Crowfoot, namely the verification of runtime code updates, but did not go into detail about Crowfoot, its implementation or its theoretical basis. An interactive version of Crowfoot, which includes the example of this paper and others, can be used online [1].

Future work. The following extensions would permit the verification of more examples. As the *antiframe rule* is consistent with the logic used in Crowfoot (as proved in [18]), annotations similar to those for the deep frame rule could be implemented to allow hiding of invariants in "antiframe style". Though we do not need it for deep framing like VeriFast does, second order logic would support the specification of parametric procedures. A minor but useful extension is to allow proper functions with result values. We believe that Lemma 1 can be generalised to support mutually recursive definitions and to allow deep framing onto abstract (universally quantified) predicates. We plan to investigate extensions required to support reasoning about reflective programs and, finally, it is likely that many fold/unfold annotations can be discovered automatically, as done in [15].

References

1. The Crowfoot website (2011), `http://www.sussex.ac.uk/informatics/crowfoot`
2. Benton, N., Kennedy, A., Beringer, L., Hofmann, M.: Relational semantics for effect-based program transformations: higher-order store. In: PPDP, pp. 301–312 (2009)
3. Berdine, J., Calcagno, C., O'Hearn, P.W.: Smallfoot: Modular Automatic Assertion Checking with Separation Logic. In: de Boer, F.S., Bonsangue, M.M., Graf, S., de Roever, W.-P. (eds.) FMCO 2005. LNCS, vol. 4111, pp. 115–137. Springer, Heidelberg (2006)
4. Berdine, J., Calcagno, C., O'Hearn, P.W.: Symbolic Execution with Separation Logic. In: Yi, K. (ed.) APLAS 2005. LNCS, vol. 3780, pp. 52–68. Springer, Heidelberg (2005)
5. Birkedal, L., Torp-Smith, N., Yang, H.: Semantics of separation-logic typing and higher-order frame rules for Algol-like languages. LMCS 2(5) (2006)
6. Cai, H., Shao, Z., Vaynberg, A.: Certified self-modifying code. In: PLDI, pp. 66–77 (2007)
7. Charlton, N., Horsfall, B., Reus, B.: Formal reasoning about runtime code update. In: Abiteboul, S., Böhm, K., Koch, C., Tan, K.-L. (eds.) ICDE Workshops, pp. 134–138. IEEE (2011)
8. Charlton, N., Reus, B.: A deeper understanding of the deep frame axiom. Extended abstract, presented at LOLA (Syntax and Semantics of Low Level Languages) (2010)
9. Charlton, N., Reus, B.: Specification Patterns and Proofs for Recursion through the Store. In: Owe, O., Steffen, M., Telle, J.A. (eds.) FCT 2011. LNCS, vol. 6914, pp. 310–321. Springer, Heidelberg (2011)
10. Chlipala, A.: Mostly-automated verification of low-level programs in computational separation logic. In: Hall, M.W., Padua, D.A. (eds.) PLDI, pp. 234–245. ACM (2011)
11. Honda, K., Yoshida, N., Berger, M.: An observationally complete program logic for imperative higher-order functions. In: LICS, pp. 270–279 (2005)
12. Jacobs, B., Smans, J., Philippaerts, P., Vogels, F., Penninckx, W., Piessens, F.: VeriFast: A powerful, sound, predictable, fast verifier for C and Java. In: NASA Formal Methods, pp. 41–55 (2011)
13. Jacobs, B., Smans, J., Piessens, F.: A Quick Tour of the VeriFast Program Verifier. In: Ueda, K. (ed.) APLAS 2010. LNCS, vol. 6461, pp. 304–311. Springer, Heidelberg (2010)
14. Nanevski, A., Morrisett, J.G., Birkedal, L.: Hoare type theory, polymorphism and separation. J. Funct. Program. 18(5-6), 865–911 (2008)
15. Nguyen, H.H., David, C., Qin, S.C., Chin, W.-N.: Automated Verification of Shape and Size Properties Via Separation Logic. In: Cook, B., Podelski, A. (eds.) VMCAI 2007. LNCS, vol. 4349, pp. 251–266. Springer, Heidelberg (2007)
16. Ni, Z., Shao, Z.: Certified assembly programming with embedded code pointers. In: POPL, pp. 320–333 (2006)
17. Schwinghammer, J., Birkedal, L., Reus, B., Yang, H.: Nested Hoare Triples and Frame Rules for Higher-Order Store. In: Grädel, E., Kahle, R. (eds.) CSL 2009. LNCS, vol. 5771, pp. 440–454. Springer, Heidelberg (2009)
18. Schwinghammer, J., Yang, H., Birkedal, L., Pottier, F., Reus, B.: A Semantic Foundation for Hidden State. In: Ong, L. (ed.) FOSSACS 2010. LNCS, vol. 6014, pp. 2–17. Springer, Heidelberg (2010)

Synthesizing Protocols for Digital Contract Signing

Krishnendu Chatterjee[1] and Vishwanath Raman[2]

[1] IST Austria (Institute of Science and Technology Austria)
[2] Carnegie Mellon Silicon Valley, Moffett Field, USA
krishnendu.chatterjee@ist.ac.at, vishwa.raman@west.cmu.edu

Abstract. We study the automatic synthesis of fair non-repudiation protocols, a class of fair exchange protocols, used for digital contract signing. First, we show how to specify the objectives of the participating agents, the trusted third party (TTP) and the protocols as path formulas in Linear Temporal Logic (LTL) and prove that the satisfaction of the objectives of the agents and the TTP imply satisfaction of the protocol objectives. We then show that *weak (co-operative) co-synthesis* and *classical (strictly competitive) co-synthesis* fail in synthesizing these protocols, whereas *assume-guarantee synthesis (AGS)* succeeds. We demonstrate the success of assume-guarantee synthesis as follows: (a) any solution of assume-guarantee synthesis is *attack-free*; no subset of participants can violate the objectives of the other participants without violating their own objectives; (b) the Asokan-Shoup-Waidner (ASW) certified mail protocol that has known vulnerabilities is not a solution of AGS; and (c) the Kremer-Markowitch (KM) non-repudiation protocol is a solution of AGS. To our knowledge this is the first application of synthesis to fair non-repudiation protocols, and our results show how synthesis can generate correct protocols and automatically discover vulnerabilities. The solution to assume-guarantee synthesis can be computed efficiently as the secure equilibrium solution of three-player graph games.

1 Introduction

Digital contract signing. The traditional two party paper-based contract signing mechanism involves two participants with an intent to sign a piece of contractual text that is in front of them. In this case, either they agree and sign the contract or they do not. The mechanism is "fair" to both participants in that it does not afford either participant an unfair "advantage" over the other. In digital contract signing an *originator* sends her intent to sign a contractual text to a *recipient*. Over the course of a set of messages they then proceed to exchange their actual signatures on the contract. In this case, it is in general difficult to ensure fairness as one of the participants gains an advantage over the other during the course of the exchange. If the participants do not trust each other, then neither wants to sign the contract first as doing so does not guarantee a reciprocal signature from the other participant. Moreover, as these contracts are typically signed over asynchronous networks, the communication channels may provide no guarantees on message delivery. The same situation arises in other related areas such as fair exchange and certified email.

Protocols for digital contract signing. Many protocols have been designed to facilitate the exchange of digital signatures. Even and Yacobi [9] first showed that no

V. Kuncak and A. Rybalchenko (Eds.): VMCAI 2012, LNCS 7148, pp. 152–168, 2012.

deterministic contract signing protocol can be realized without the involvement of a third party arbitrator who is trusted by all participants. This was formalized as an impossibility result in [16], where the authors show that fair exchange is impossible without a *trusted third party (TTP)* for non-repudiation protocols. A simple protocol with a TTP has a TTP collect all signatures and then distribute them to the participants. But this is very inefficient as it involves an online TTP to facilitate every exchange, easily creating a bottleneck at the site of the TTP. This has lead to the development of *optimistic protocols*, where participants exchange signatures without involving a TTP, requesting the TTP to adjudicate only when one of the participants is dishonest. These protocols are called *fair non-repudiation protocols* with *offline* TTP.

Fair non-repudiation protocols. A *fair non-repudiation* protocol falls under the category of fair exchange protocols and ensures that at the end of the exchange of signatures over a network, neither participant can deny having participated in the protocol. A non-repudiation protocol, upon successful termination, provides each participant evidence of commitment to a contract that cannot be repudiated by the other participant. A *non-repudiation of origin (NRO)* provides the recipient in an exchange, the ability to present to an adjudicator, evidence of the senders commitment to a contract. Similarly, a *non-repudiation of receipt (NRR)* provides the sender in an exchange, the ability to present to an adjudicator, evidence of the recipient's commitment to a contract.

Sources of attacks. There are two sources of attacks in fair exchange protocols. The first is based on the content of the messages being exchanged. The second is based on the interaction between various participants, producing a multitude of interleavings of the messages that can be composed and sent, over the course of an exchange. The former are typically fixed by including more information in vulnerable messages and by the use of appropriate cryptographic primitives. This paper focusses on the latter. We assume that the contents of the messages are invulnerable but their interleavings are vulnerable. We address automatically deriving correct fair non-repudiation protocols that prevent malicious participants from gaining an unfair advantage by modeling the problem as an automated synthesis problem.

Existing protocols. Some of the existing fair non-repudiation protocols are the Zhou-Gollmann (ZG) protocol [25], the Asokan-Shoup-Waidner (ASW) protocol [2], the Garay-Jakobsson-MacKenzie (GJM) protocol [10] and the Kremer-Markowitch (KM) protocol [15]. Non-repudiation protocols are difficult to design in general [22,14,12] and much literature covers the design and verification of these protocols. While some of the literature covers the discovery of vulnerabilities in these protocols based on the content of the exchanged messages, others have tried to find attacks based on the sequences of messages that can be exchanged, as dictated by the rules of the protocols. However, there is no work that focuses on automatically obtaining correct solutions of these subtle and hard to design protocols.

Our contributions. We show that the classical synthesis formulations that are strictly competitive are inadequate for synthesizing these protocols and that *conditionally competitive* formulations are more appropriate. To our knowledge this is the first application of game-theoretic controller synthesis to security protocols. Synthesis has many advantages over model checking. While model checking finds specific vulnerabilities for a designed protocol, the counter-examples in synthesis are strategies (or refinements) that exhibit vulnerabilities against a set of protocol realizations. Moreover, impossibility results such as failure to realize non-repudiation protocols without a TTP cannot be deduced with model checking, whereas such results can be deduced in a synthesis framework as we show in this paper. Our main contributions are as follows:

1. We formalize the objectives of the participants, the TTP and the protocols as path formulas in Linear Temporal Logic (LTL) and prove that satisfaction of the objectives of the participants, and the TTP, imply satisfaction of the protocol objectives.
2. We show that classical (strictly competitive) and weak (co-operative) co-synthesis fail, whereas assume-guarantee (conditionally competitive) co-synthesis succeeds.
3. We show that all solutions in the set P_{AGS} of assume-guarantee solutions are *attack-free*; any solution in P_{AGS} prevents malicious participants from gaining an unfair advantage.
4. We show that the ASW certified mail protocol is not in P_{AGS}, due to known vulnerabilities that could have been automatically discovered. The GJM protocol, while fair to the agents, is not in P_{AGS} as it compromises our objective for the TTP. The KM protocol is in P_{AGS} and it follows that it could have been automatically generated by formalizing the problem of protocol design as a synthesis problem.

It was shown in [5] that the solutions of assume-guarantee synthesis can be obtained through the solution of secure equilibria [6] in graph games. Applying the results of [5], given our objectives, we show that for fair non-repudiation protocols the solutions can be obtained in quadratic time.

Related works. The formal verification of fair exchange protocols uses model checking to verify a set of protocol objectives specified in a suitable temporal logic. The work of Shmatikov and Mitchell [22] uses the finite state tool Murφ to model the participants in a protocol together with an intruder model, to check a set of safety properties by state space exploration. They expose a number of vulnerabilities that may lead to replay attacks in both the ASW protocol and the GJM protocol. The works [11,12,3] use game theoretic models and the logic ATL to formally specify fairness, abuse-freeness and timeliness, that they verify using the tool MOCHA [1]. Independently, in [3] the authors use a game-based approach, with a set-rewriting technique, to verify fair exchange protocols. However, these works focus on verification and not on synthesis.

The notion of weak or *co-operative* co-synthesis was introduced in [8], classical or *strictly competitive* co-synthesis was studied in [19,20] and assume-guarantee or *conditionally competitive* co-synthesis was introduced in [5]. But none of these works consider security protocols. The first effort at synthesizing security protocols is [17,23] and is related to the automatic generation of mutual authentication protocols, where the authors use iterative deepening with a cost function to generate correct protocols that minimize cost; they do not address digital contract signing. In [21], the authors describe a prototype synthesis tool that uses the BAN logic to describe protocol goals with extensions to describe protocol rules that, when combined with a proof system, can be used to generate protocols satisfying those goals. None of the above works use a conditionally competitive synthesis formulation, which we show is necessary for fair non-repudiation protocols. Our technique is very different from these and all previous works, as we use the rich body of research in controller synthesis to construct fair exchange protocols efficiently; in time that is quadratic in the size of the model. The finite state models are typically small, so that the application of synthesis techniques as we propose in this paper is both appealing and realizable in practice. Our emphasis in this paper is in a synthesis technique that enables the automatic discovery of subtle errors in these protocols and that holds promise for security protocol synthesis in general.

2 Fair Non-repudiation Protocols

In this section we introduce fair non-repudiation protocols. We first define a participant model, a protocol model and an attack model. We then introduce the agents and the trusted third party that participate in fair exchange protocols, the messages that they may send and receive, and the channels over which they communicate. Finally, we introduce a set of predicates that are set based on messages that are sent and received and that form the basis for our protocol and participant objectives in the subsequent section.

A participant model. Our protocol model is different from the Strand Space model and is closer to the model required for the synthesis of protocols as participant refinements. We define our model as follows: Let V be a finite set of variables that take values in some domain D_v. A *valuation* f over the variables V is a function $f : V \mapsto D_v$ that assigns to each variable $v \in V$, a value $f(v) \in D_v$; we take $\mathcal{F}[V]$ as the set of all valuations over the variables in V. Let $\mathcal{M}$ be a finite set of messages (*terms* in the Strand Space model) that are exchanged between a set $A = \{A_i \mid 0 \leq i \leq n\}$ (*roles* in the Strand Space model) of participants. We define each participant as the tuple $A_i = (L_i, V_i, \Lambda_i, \delta_i)$, where L_i is a finite set of control points or values taken by a program counter, $V_i \subseteq V$ is a set of variables, $\Lambda_i : \mathcal{F}[V_i] \mapsto 2^{\mathcal{M}}$ is a message assignment, that given a valuation $f \in \mathcal{F}[V_i]$, returns the set of messages that can be sent by A_i at f; this set includes all messages that can be composed by A_i based on what she knows in the valuation f. Valuations over variables represent what a participant knows at a given control point. We take $V = \bigcup_{i=0}^{n} V_i$ and assume that the sets V_i form a partition of V. An A_i transition function is $\delta_i : L_i \times \mathcal{F}[V_i] \times \mathcal{M} \mapsto L_i \times \mathcal{F}[V_i]$, that given a control point, a valuation over V_i and a message either sent or received by A_i, returns the next control point of A_i and an updated valuation. The participants may send messages simultaneously and independently, and can either receive a message or send a message at every control point.

The most general participants. We interpret the elements of A as the *most general participants* in an exchange; the participants in A can send any message that can be composed at each control point, based on messages they have received up to that control point and on their respective transition functions. We take the interaction between the elements of A as the *most general exchange program.* Every participant in an exchange has her own objective to satisfy. We take the objective of a participant as a set of desired sequences of valuations of the protocol variables.

A protocol model. A realization of an exchange protocol is a restriction of the most general exchange program that consists of the set $A' = \{A'_i \mid 0 \leq i \leq n\}$ of participants, with behaviors restricted by the rules of the protocol. We take $A'_i = (L'_i, V_i, \Lambda'_i, \delta'_i)$, where $L'_i \subseteq L_i$; V_i is the same set of variables as in A_i; for every valuation $f \in \mathcal{F}[V_i]$ we have $\Lambda'_i(f) \subseteq \Lambda_i(f)$; and $\delta'_i : L'_i \times \mathcal{F}[V_i] \times \mathcal{M} \mapsto L'_i \times \mathcal{F}[V_i]$ is the transition function, that given a control point in L'_i, a valuation over V_i and a message either sent or received by A'_i returns the next control point of A'_i and an updated valuation. For $l \in L'_i$, $v \in \mathcal{F}[V_i]$ and $m \in \mathcal{M}$, we have $\delta'_i(l, v, m) = \delta_i(l, v, m)$. We define a *protocol instance* (or a *protocol run*) as any sequence of valuations generated by the participants in A' and take the set of all possible protocol runs as *Runs*(A'). We refer to a message that can be sent by a participant as a *move* of that participant.

An attack model. We define an *attack* on a protocol as the behavior of a subset of protocol participants such that the resulting sequence of messages is in their objective but not in the objective of at least one of the other participants. Formally, let $Y \subseteq A$ be a subset of the most general participants with $(A \setminus Y)' = \{A'_i | A_i \in (A \setminus Y)\}$ being the remaining participants that follow the rules of the protocol. A protocol has a Y-attack if the most general participants in Y can generate a message sequence, given $(A \setminus Y)'$ follow the protocol, that is not in the objective of at least one participant in $(A \setminus Y)'$ but is in the objectives of all participants in Y. A protocol is *attack-free*, if there exists no Y-attack for all $Y \in 2^A$.

Agents. An *agent* in a two-party exchange protocol is one of the two participating entities signing an online contract. Based on whether an agent proposes a contract or accepts a contract originating from another agent, we get two roles that an agent can play; that of an *originator* of a contract, designated by O or the *recipient* of a contract, designated by R. Agents communicate with each other over channels.

Trusted third party (TTP). The *trusted third party* or TTP is a participant who is trusted by the agents and adjudicates and resolves disputes. It is known that a fair exchange protocol cannot be realized without the TTP [9,16]. We model the TTP explicitly as a participant, define her objective and using our formulation give a game-theoretic justification that the TTP is necessary. Agents and the TTP communicate with each other over channels.

Messages. A *message* is an encrypted stream of bytes; we treat each message as an atomic unit. We assume each message contains a *nonce* that uniquely identifies a protocol instance; participants can simultaneously participate in multiple protocol instances. We are not concerned with the exact contents of each message, but in what each message conveys; this is in keeping with our objective of synthesizing protocols that are attack-free with respect to message interleavings. From the definition of messages in fair exchange protocols in [11,12,22] and other works, we define the set $\mathcal{M}$ of messages as follows:

- m_1 is a message that may be sent by O to R. The intent of this message is to convey O's desire to sign a contract with a recipient R.

- m_2 is a message that may be sent by R to O and conveys R's intent to sign the contract from O.
- m_3 is a message that may be sent by O to R and contains the actual signature of O.
- m_4 is a message that contains the actual signature of R and may be sent by R to O.
- a_1^{O} is a message that may be sent by O to the TTP and conveys O's desire to *abort* the protocol.
- a_2^{O} (resp. a_2^{R}) is a message that may be sent by the TTP to O (resp. R) that confirms the abort by including an abort token for O (resp. R).
- r_1^{O} (resp. r_1^{R}) is a message that may be sent by O (resp. R) to the TTP and conveys O's (resp. R's) desire to get the TTP to *resolve* a protocol instance by explicitly requesting the TTP to adjudicate. We do not specify the content of r_1^{O} or r_1^{R} but make the assumption that the TTP needs m_1 to resolve the protocol for R and similarly needs m_2 to resolve the protocol for O.
- r_2^{O} (resp. r_2^{R}) is a message that may be sent by the TTP to O (resp. R) and contains a universally verifiable signature in lieu of the signature of R (resp. O).

We impose an order on the messages m_1, m_2, m_3 and m_4 as it can be shown trivially in our synthesis formulation that O sending m_3 before receiving m_2 and R sending m_4 before receiving m_3 violates their respective objectives. In our formulations, we consider a *reasonable TTP* that satisfies the following restrictions on behavior:

1. The TTP sends messages only in response to an abort or a resolve request and processes messages in a first-in-first-out fashion.
2. If the first message received by the TTP is an abort request from O, then the TTP will eventually send an abort token.
3. If the first message received by the TTP is a resolve request, then the TTP will eventually send an agent signature.

Channels. A channel is used to deliver a *message*. There are three types of channels that are typically modeled in the literature. We present them here in decreasing order of reliability: (1) An *operational* channel delivers all messages within a known, finite amount of time, (2) a *resilient* channel eventually delivers all messages, but there is no fixed finite bound on the time to deliver a message, and (3) an *unreliable* channel may not deliver messages. We model the channels between the agents as unreliable and those between the agents and the TTP as resilient as in prevailing models; messages sent to the TTP and by the TTP will be eventually delivered. Further, we assume that channels cannot corrupt messages but can re-order them.

Scheduler. A scheduler is not explicitly part of any fair exchange protocol. The protocols need to provide all agents the ability to send messages asynchronously, which implies agents can choose their actions simultaneously and independently. We model this behavior by using a *fair scheduler* that assigns each participant a turn, infinitely often, and we synthesize refinements against *all possible behaviors* of a fair scheduler.

Predicates. We introduce the following set of predicates.
- M_1 is set by O, when she sends message m_1 to R.
- EOO, referred to as the *Evidence Of Origin*, is set by R when either m_1 or r_2^{R} is received.

- EOR, referred to as the *Evidence of Receipt*, is set by O when either m_2 or r_2^{O} is received.
- $\mathrm{EOO}_k^{\mathrm{O}}$ and $\mathrm{EOO}_k^{\mathrm{TTP}}$ are referred to as *O's signature*. $\mathrm{EOO}_k^{\mathrm{O}}$ is set by R when R receives m_3 and $\mathrm{EOO}_k^{\mathrm{TTP}}$ is set by R when he receives r_2^{R}.
- $\mathrm{EOR}_k^{\mathrm{R}}$ and $\mathrm{EOR}_k^{\mathrm{TTP}}$ are referred to as *R's signature*. $\mathrm{EOR}_k^{\mathrm{R}}$ is set by O when O receives m_4 and $\mathrm{EOR}_k^{\mathrm{TTP}}$ is set by O when she receives r_2^{O}.
- AO is set by O and indicates that a_2^{O} has been received.
- AR is set by R and indicates that a_2^{R} has been received.
- ABR is set by the TTP when an abort request, a_1^{O} is received.
- RES is set by the TTP when a resolve request, r_1^{O} or r_1^{R}, is received.

All predicates are *monotonic* in that once they are set, they remain set for the duration of a protocol instance [22]. We distinguish between a signature sent by an agent and the signature sent by the TTP as a replacement for an agent's signature. Distinguishing these signatures enables modeling TTP accountability [22]. The non-repudiation of origin for R, denoted by NRO, means that R has received both O's intent to sign a contract and O's signature on the contract so that O cannot deny having signed the contract to a third party. Formally, NRO is defined as: $\mathrm{NRO} = \mathrm{EOO} \wedge (\mathrm{EOO}_k^{\mathrm{O}} \vee \mathrm{EOO}_k^{\mathrm{TTP}})$. The non-repudiation of receipt for O, denoted by NRR, means that O has received both the intent and signature of R on a contract so that R cannot deny having signed the contract to a third party. Formally, NRR is defined as: $\mathrm{NRR} = \mathrm{EOR} \wedge (\mathrm{EOR}_k^{\mathrm{R}} \vee \mathrm{EOR}_k^{\mathrm{TTP}})$.

3 LTL Objectives for the Protocols

The synthesis of programs requires a formal objective of their requirements. One of our contributions in this paper is to present a precise and formal description of the protocol requirement as a path formula in Linear Temporal Logic (LTL [18,13]), which then becomes our synthesis objective. In this section, we define the objective for fair non-repudiation protocols, objectives for the agents and the TTP and show that satisfaction of the objectives of the agents and the TTP imply satisfaction of the objective of the protocols. We use LTL, a logic that is used to specify properties of infinite paths in finite-state transition systems.

Fairness. Informally, fairness for O can be stated as *"For all protocol instances, if the non-repudiation of origin (NRO) is ever true, then eventually the non-repudiation of receipt (NRR) is also true"* [12]. The fairness property for O is expressed by the LTL formula $\varphi_f^{\mathrm{O}} = \square(\mathrm{NRO} \Rightarrow \diamond\mathrm{NRR})$. Similarly, the fairness property for R is expressed by the LTL formula $\varphi_f^{\mathrm{R}} = \square(\mathrm{NRR} \Rightarrow \diamond\mathrm{NRO})$. We say that a protocol is fair, if in all instances of the protocol, fairness for both O and R holds. Hence the fairness requirement for the protocol is expressed by the formula $\varphi_f = \varphi_f^{\mathrm{O}} \wedge \varphi_f^{\mathrm{R}}$.

Abuse-freeness. In [4], the authors prove that in any fair optimistic protocol, an optimistic participant yields an advantage to the other participant. In a given protocol instance, once an agent has the other agent's intent to sign a contract, he can use this intent to negotiate a different contract with a third party, while ensuring that the original protocol instance is aborted. The term aborted is used here to mean that neither agent can get a non-repudiation evidence in a given protocol instance, once that instance is aborted. As noted by the authors of [4], the best that one can hope for is to prevent either participant from proving to a third party that he has an advantage, or in other words, that he has the other participant's intent to sign the contract. This is defined as *abuse-freeness*. As noted by the authors of [10,11], using PCS or *Private Contract Signatures*, introduced by Garay et al., in [10], which provides the designated verifier property, neither agent can prove the other agent's intent to sign the contract to anyone other than the TTP. Therefore, ensuring abuse-freeness requires the use of PCS. Since PCS are requisite to ensure abuse-freeness, we do not model abuse-freeness, or the stronger property balance [3], in our formalism.

Signature exchange. A protocol is an exchange protocol if it enables the exchange of signatures. This is also referred to as *Viability* in the literature. For an exchange protocol to be a non-repudiation protocol, at the end of every run of the protocol, either the agents have their respective non-repudiation evidences, or, if they do not have their non-repudiation evidences, they have the abort token. The property that evidences once obtained are not repudiable is referred to as *Non-repudiability*. A fair non-repudiation protocol must satisfy fairness, abuse-freeness, non-repudiability and viability.

We now present intuitive objectives for the agents and the TTP and show that satisfaction of these objectives implies that the protocols we synthesize are fair.

Specification for O. The objective of the originator O is expressed as follows:

- In all protocol instances, she eventually sends the evidence of origin. This is expressed by the LTL formula $\varphi_{\mathrm{O}}^1 = \Diamond M_1$.
- In all protocol instances, one of the following statements should be true:
  1. (a) The originator eventually gets the recipient's signature $\mathrm{EOR}_k^{\mathrm{R}}$ or, (b) she eventually gets the recipient's signature $\mathrm{EOR}_k^{\mathrm{TTP}}$ and never gets the abort token AO. This is expressed by the LTL formula $\varphi_{\mathrm{O}}^2 = (\Diamond \mathrm{EOR}_k^{\mathrm{R}} \vee (\Diamond \mathrm{EOR}_k^{\mathrm{TTP}} \wedge \Box \neg \mathrm{AO}))$.
  2. (a) The originator eventually gets the abort token and (b) the recipient never gets her signature $\mathrm{EOO}_k^{\mathrm{O}}$ and never gets her signature $\mathrm{EOO}_k^{\mathrm{TTP}}$ from the TTP. This is expressed by the LTL formula $\varphi_{\mathrm{O}}^3 = \Diamond \mathrm{AO} \wedge (\Box \neg \mathrm{EOO}_k^{\mathrm{O}} \wedge \Box \neg \mathrm{EOO}_k^{\mathrm{TTP}}) = \Diamond \mathrm{AO} \wedge \Box(\neg \mathrm{EOO}_k^{\mathrm{O}} \wedge \neg \mathrm{EOO}_k^{\mathrm{TTP}})$.

The objective φ_{O} of O can therefore be expressed by the LTL formula $\varphi_{\mathrm{O}} = \varphi_{\mathrm{O}}^1 \wedge \Box(\varphi_{\mathrm{O}}^2 \vee \varphi_{\mathrm{O}}^3)$. There are two interpretations of the abort token in the literature. On the one hand the abort token was never intended to serve as a proof that a protocol instance was not successfully completed; it was to guarantee that the TTP would never resolve a protocol after it has been aborted. On the other hand, there is mention of the abort token being used by the recipient to prove that the protocol was aborted. We take the position that the abort token may be used to ensure TTP accountability as noted in [22] and hence include it in the objective of O. If the TTP misbehaves and issues both $\mathrm{EOR}_k^{\mathrm{TTP}}$ and AO, we claim that the objective φ_{O} of the originator should be violated, but in this case, she has the power to prove that the TTP misbehaved by presenting both $\mathrm{EOR}_k^{\mathrm{TTP}}$ and AO to demonstrate inconsistent behavior. While having both $\mathrm{EOR}_k^{\mathrm{R}}$ and $\mathrm{EOR}_k^{\mathrm{TTP}}$ may be interpreted as O having inconsistent signatures, we do not consider this to be a violation of O's objective; given the nature of asynchronous networks it may well be the case that both these evidences arrive eventually, one from the TTP and the other from R, as O did not wait long enough before sending r_1^{O}.

Specification for R. The objective of the recipient R can be expressed as follows:

- In all protocol instances, if he gets the evidence of origin EOO, then one of the following statements should be true:
  1. (a) The recipient eventually gets the originator's signature $\mathrm{EOO}_k^{\mathrm{O}}$ or, (b) he eventually gets the originator's signature $\mathrm{EOO}_k^{\mathrm{TTP}}$ and never gets the abort token AR. This is expressed by the LTL formula $\varphi_{\mathrm{R}}^1 = (\Diamond \mathrm{EOO}_k^{\mathrm{O}} \vee (\Diamond \mathrm{EOO}_k^{\mathrm{TTP}} \wedge \Box\neg \mathrm{AR}))$.
  2. (a) The recipient eventually gets the abort token and (b) the originator never gets his signature $\mathrm{EOR}_k^{\mathrm{R}}$ and never gets his signature $\mathrm{EOR}_k^{\mathrm{TTP}}$ from the TTP. This is expressed by the LTL formula $\varphi_{\mathrm{R}}^2 = \Diamond \mathrm{AR} \wedge (\Box\neg \mathrm{EOR}_k^{\mathrm{R}} \wedge \Box\neg \mathrm{EOR}_k^{\mathrm{TTP}}) = \Diamond \mathrm{AR} \wedge \Box(\neg \mathrm{EOR}_k^{\mathrm{R}} \wedge \neg \mathrm{EOR}_k^{\mathrm{TTP}})$.

The objective φ_{R} can therefore be expressed by the LTL formula $\varphi_{\mathrm{R}} = \Box(\mathrm{EOO} \Rightarrow (\varphi_R^1 \vee \varphi_R^2))$. If the TTP misbehaves and issues both $\mathrm{EOO}_k^{\mathrm{TTP}}$ and AR, we claim that the objective φ_{R} of the recipient should be violated, but in this case he has the power to prove that the TTP misbehaved by presenting both $\mathrm{EOO}_k^{\mathrm{TTP}}$ and AR.

Specification for the TTP. Our objective for the TTP is expressed as follows:

- In all protocol instances, if the abort request a_1^{O} or a resolve request r_1^{O} or r_1^{R} is received, then eventually the TTP sends the abort token AO or the abort token AR or the originator's signature $\mathrm{EOO}_k^{\mathrm{TTP}}$ or the recipient's signature $\mathrm{EOR}_k^{\mathrm{TTP}}$. This can be expressed by the LTL formula $\varphi_{\mathrm{TTP}}^1 = \Box((\mathrm{ABR} \vee \mathrm{RES}) \Rightarrow (\Diamond \mathrm{AO} \vee \Diamond \mathrm{AR} \vee \Diamond \mathrm{EOO}_k^{\mathrm{TTP}} \vee \Diamond \mathrm{EOR}_k^{\mathrm{TTP}}))$.
- In all protocol instances, if the originator's signature $\mathrm{EOO}_k^{\mathrm{TTP}}$ has been sent to the recipient, then the originator should eventually get the recipient's signature $\mathrm{EOR}_k^{\mathrm{TTP}}$ and the agents should never get the abort token. This can be expressed by the LTL formula $\varphi_{\mathrm{TTP}}^2 = \Box(\mathrm{EOO}_k^{\mathrm{TTP}} \Rightarrow (\Diamond \mathrm{EOR}_k^{\mathrm{TTP}} \wedge \Box(\neg \mathrm{AO} \wedge \neg \mathrm{AR})))$.
- Symmetrically, in all protocol instances, if the recipient's signature $\mathrm{EOR}_k^{\mathrm{TTP}}$ has been sent to the originator, then the recipient should eventually get the originator's signature $\mathrm{EOO}_k^{\mathrm{TTP}}$ and the agents should never get the abort token. This can be expressed by the LTL formula $\varphi_{\mathrm{TTP}}^3 = \Box(\mathrm{EOR}_k^{\mathrm{TTP}} \Rightarrow (\Diamond \mathrm{EOO}_k^{\mathrm{TTP}} \wedge \Box(\neg \mathrm{AO} \wedge \neg \mathrm{AR})))$.
- In all protocol instances, if the originator gets the abort token AO, then the recipient should eventually get the abort token AR and the originator should never get the recipient's signature $\mathrm{EOR}_k^{\mathrm{TTP}}$ and the recipient should never get the originator's signature $\mathrm{EOO}_k^{\mathrm{TTP}}$. This can be expressed by the LTL formula $\varphi_{\mathrm{TTP}}^4 = \Box(\mathrm{AO} \Rightarrow (\Diamond \mathrm{AR} \wedge \Box(\neg \mathrm{EOO}_k^{\mathrm{TTP}} \wedge \neg \mathrm{EOR}_k^{\mathrm{TTP}})))$.
- Symmetrically, in all protocol instances, if the recipient gets the abort token AR, then the originator should eventually get the abort token AO and the originator should never get the recipient's signature $\mathrm{EOR}_k^{\mathrm{TTP}}$ and the recipient should never get the originator's signature $\mathrm{EOO}_k^{\mathrm{TTP}}$. This can be expressed by the LTL formula $\varphi_{\mathrm{TTP}}^5 = \Box(\mathrm{AR} \Rightarrow (\Diamond \mathrm{AO} \wedge \Box(\neg \mathrm{EOO}_k^{\mathrm{TTP}} \wedge \neg \mathrm{EOR}_k^{\mathrm{TTP}})))$.

The objective φ_{TTP} of the TTP is then defined as, $\varphi_{\text{TTP}} = \varphi_{\text{TTP}}^1 \wedge \varphi_{\text{TTP}}^2 \wedge \varphi_{\text{TTP}}^3 \wedge \varphi_{\text{TTP}}^4 \wedge \varphi_{\text{TTP}}^5$. Note that our objective for the TTP treats both agents symmetrically. In this paper we present assume-guarantee synthesis for the above objective of the TTP. But in general, the objective of the TTP can be weakened if desired, by treating the agents asymmetrically, and the assume-guarantee synthesis technique can be applied with this weakened objective.

We remark that the objectives of the participants in our protocol model are sequences of messages. Using predicates that are set when messages are sent or received by the agents or the TTP, we formalize those objectives using the predicates and LTL. The following theorem shows that satisfaction of the objectives of the participants implies fairness, the protocol objective. We use the fact that the predicates are monotonic and show that when fairness is violated it must be the case that the objective of either O or the TTP must also be violated.

Theorem 1 (Objectives imply fairness). *We have,* $\varphi_O \wedge \varphi_R \wedge \varphi_{TTP} \Rightarrow \varphi_f$.

4 Co-synthesis

In this section we first define processes, schedulers and objectives for synthesis along the lines of [5]. Next we define traditional co-operative [8] and strictly competitive [19,20] versions of the co-synthesis problem; we refer to them as *weak co-synthesis* and *classical co-synthesis*, respectively. We then define a formulation of co-synthesis introduced in [5] called *assume-guarantee synthesis*. We show later in the paper that the protocol model of Section 2 reduces to the process model for synthesis that we present in this section.

Variables, valuations, and traces. Let X be a finite set of variables such that each variable $x \in X$ has a finite domain D_x. A *valuation* f on X is a function $f : X \to \bigcup_{x \in X} D_x$ that assigns to each variable $x \in X$ a value $f(x) \in D_x$. We write $\mathcal{F}[X]$ for the set of valuations on X. A *trace* on X is an infinite sequence $(v_0, v_1, v_2, \ldots) \in \mathcal{F}[X]^\omega$ of valuations on X. Given a valuation $f[X] \in \mathcal{F}[X]$ and a subset $Y \subseteq X$ of the variables, we denote by $f[X] \downarrow Y$ the restriction of the valuation $f[X]$ to the variables in Y. Similarly, for a trace $\tau(X) = (v_0, v_1, v_2, \ldots)$ on X, we write $\tau(X) \downarrow Y = (v_0 \downarrow Y, v_1 \downarrow Y, v_2 \downarrow Y, \ldots)$ for the restriction of $\tau(X)$ to the variables in Y. The restriction operator is lifted to sets of valuations, and to sets of traces.

Processes and refinement. Let *Moves* be a finite set of elements which are called moves. For $i \in \{1, 2, 3\}$, a *process* is defined by the tuple $P_i = (X_i, \Gamma_i, \delta_i)$ where,

1. X_i is a finite set of variables of process P_i and $X = \bigcup_{i=1}^3 X_i$ is the set of all variables,
2. $\Gamma_i : \mathcal{F}[X_i] \to 2^{\mathit{Moves}} \setminus \emptyset$ is a move assignment that given a valuation in $\mathcal{F}[X_i]$, returns a non-empty set of moves, where $\mathcal{F}[X_i]$ is the set of valuations on X_i, and
3. $\delta_i : \mathcal{F}[X_i] \times \mathit{Moves} \to 2^{\mathcal{F}[X_i]} \setminus \emptyset$ is a non-deterministic transition function.

The set of process variables X may be shared between processes. The processes only choose amongst available moves at every valuation of their variables as determined by their move assignment. The transition function maps a present valuation and a process move to a nonempty set of possible successor valuations such that each successor valuation has a unique pre-image. The uniqueness of the pre-image is a property of exchange protocols; unique messages convey unique content and generate unique valuations.

A *refinement* of process $P_i = (X_i, \Gamma_i, \delta_i)$ is a process $P'_i = (X'_i, \Gamma'_i, \delta'_i)$ such that: (1) $X_i \subseteq X'_i$, (2) for all valuations $f[X'_i]$ on X'_i, we have $\Gamma'_i(f[X'_i]) \subseteq \Gamma_i(f[X'_i] \downarrow X_i)$, and (3) for all valuations $f[X'_i]$ on X'_i and for all moves $a \in \Gamma'_i(f[X'_i])$, we have $\delta'_i(f[X'_i], a) \downarrow X_i \subseteq \delta_i(f[X'_i] \downarrow X_i, a)$. In other words, the refined process P'_i has possibly more variables than the original process P_i, at most the same moves as the moves of P_i at every valuation, and every possible update of the variables in X_i given Γ'_i by P'_i is a possible update by P_i. We write $P'_i \preceq P_i$ to denote that P'_i is a refinement of P_i. Given refinements $P'_i \preceq P_i$, we write $X' = \bigcup_{i=1}^{3} X'_i$ for the set of variables of all refinements, and we denote the set of valuations on X' by $\mathcal{F}[X']$.

Schedulers. Given processes P_i, where $i \in \{1, 2, 3\}$, a *scheduler* Sc for P_i chooses at each computation step whether it is process P_1's turn, process P_2's turn or process P_3's turn to update her variables. The scheduler Sc is *fair* if it assigns turns to P_1, P_2 and P_3 infinitely often; Given three processes $P_1 = (X_1, \Gamma_1, \delta_1)$, $P_2 = (X_2, \Gamma_2, \delta_2)$ and $P_3 = (X_3, \Gamma_3, \delta_3)$, a scheduler Sc for P_1, P_2 and P_3, and a start valuation $v_0 \in \mathcal{F}[X]$, the set of possible traces is denoted by $[\![(P_1 \parallel P_2 \parallel P_3 \parallel \mathrm{Sc})(v_0)]\!]$. The projection of traces to moves is denoted by $(v_0, v_1, v_2, \ldots) \downarrow \mathit{Moves}$; formal descriptions are in [7].

Objectives. An *objective* φ_i for process P_i is a set of traces on X; that is, $\varphi_i \subseteq \mathcal{F}[X]^\omega$. We consider only ω-regular objectives [24]. We define boolean operations on objectives using logical operators such as $\wedge$ (conjunction) and $\Rightarrow$ (implication).

The input to the co-synthesis problem is given as follows: for $i \in \{1, 2, 3\}$, processes $P_i = (X_i, \Gamma_i, \delta_i)$, objectives φ_i for process i, and a start valuation $v_0 \in \mathcal{F}[X]$.

Weak co-synthesis. The *weak co-synthesis* problem is defined as follows: do there exist refinements $P'_i = (X'_i, \Gamma'_i, \delta'_i)$ and a valuation $v'_0 \in \mathcal{F}[X']$, such that, $P'_i \preceq P_i$ and $v'_0 \downarrow X = v_0$, and for all fair schedulers Sc for P'_i we have, $[\![(P'_1 \parallel P'_2 \parallel P'_3 \parallel \mathrm{Sc})(v'_0)]\!] \downarrow X \subseteq (\varphi_1 \wedge \varphi_2 \wedge \varphi_3)$. Intuitively, weak co-synthesis or co-operative co-synthesis is a synthesis formulation that seeks refinements P'_1, P'_2 and P'_3 where the processes co-operate to satisfy their respective objectives.

Classical co-synthesis. The *classical co-synthesis* problem is defined as follows: do there exist refinements $P'_i = (X'_i, \Gamma'_i, \delta'_i)$ and a valuation $v'_0 \in \mathcal{F}[X']$, such that, $P'_i \preceq P_i$ and $v'_0 \downarrow X = v_0$, and for all fair schedulers Sc for P'_i we have, (a) $[\![(P'_1 \parallel P_2 \parallel P_3 \parallel \mathrm{Sc})(v'_0)]\!] \downarrow X \subseteq \varphi_1$; (b) $[\![(P_1 \parallel P'_2 \parallel P_3 \parallel \mathrm{Sc})(v'_0)]\!] \downarrow X \subseteq \varphi_2$; (c) $[\![(P_1 \parallel P_2 \parallel P'_3 \parallel \mathrm{Sc})(v'_0)]\!] \downarrow X \subseteq \varphi_3$. Classical or strictly competitive co-synthesis is a formulation that seeks refinements P'_1, P'_2 and P'_3 such that P'_1 can satisfy φ_1 against all possible, and hence adversarial, behaviors of the other processes; similarly for P'_2 and P'_3.

Assume-guarantee synthesis [5]. The *assume-guarantee synthesis* problem is defined as follows: do there exist refinements $P'_i = (X'_i, \Gamma'_i, \delta'_i)$ and a valuation $v'_0 \in \mathcal{F}[X']$, such that, $P'_i \preceq P_i$ and $v'_0 \downarrow X = v_0$, and for all fair schedulers Sc for P'_i we have, (a) $[\![(P'_1 \parallel P_2 \parallel P_3 \parallel \mathrm{Sc})(v'_0)]\!] \downarrow X \subseteq (\varphi_2 \wedge \varphi_3) \Rightarrow \varphi_1$; (b) $[\![(P_1 \parallel P'_2 \parallel P_3 \parallel \mathrm{Sc})(v'_0)]\!] \downarrow X \subseteq (\varphi_1 \wedge \varphi_3) \Rightarrow \varphi_2$; (c) $[\![(P_1 \parallel P_2 \parallel P'_3 \parallel \mathrm{Sc})(v'_0)]\!] \downarrow X \subseteq (\varphi_1 \wedge \varphi_2) \Rightarrow \varphi_3$; (d) $[\![(P'_1 \parallel P'_2 \parallel P'_3 \parallel \mathrm{Sc})(v'_0)]\!] \downarrow X \subseteq (\varphi_1 \wedge \varphi_2 \wedge \varphi_3)$. Assume-guarantee synthesis or conditionally competitive co-synthesis is a formulation that seeks refinements P'_1,

P'_2 and P'_3 such that P'_1 can satisfy φ_1 as long as processes P_2 and P_3 satisfy their objectives; similarly for P'_2 and P'_3. This synthesis formulation is well suited for those cases where processes are primarily concerned with satisfying their own objectives and only secondarily concerned with violating the objectives of the other processes. We want protocols to be correct under *arbitrary* behaviors of the participants, and the arbitrary or worst case behavior of a participant without sabotaging her own objective, is to first satisfy her own objective, and only then to falsify the objectives of the other participants. We show that this synthesis formulation is the only one that works for fair non-repudiation protocols. While classical co-synthesis can be solved as zero-sum games, assume-guarantee synthesis can be solved using non zero-sum games with lexicographic objectives [5]. For brevity, we drop the initial valuation v_0 in the set of traces.

5 Protocol Co-synthesis

We now present our results on synthesizing fair non-repudiation protocols. We use the process model in Section 4 to define agent and TTP processes, with objectives as defined in Section 3. We show that, given these agent and TTP processes and their objectives, (a) classical co-synthesis fails, (b) weak co-synthesis generates unacceptable solutions and (c) neither classical nor assume-guarantee synthesis can be used to synthesize fair non-repudiation protocols without the TTP. We then define the set P_{AGS} of assume-guarantee refinements and prove that the refinements are attack-free. It is straight forward to show the equivalence of the protocol model and the process model. The details, including precise process models for O, R and the TTP, are in [7].

Theorem 2 (Trace equivalence of models). *For all participant restrictions A'_i and refinements $O' \preceq O$, $R' \preceq R$ and $TTP' \preceq TTP$, such that $i \in \{0, 1, 2\}$ with $j = O$ when $i = 0$, $j = R$ when $i = 1$ and $j = TTP$ when $i = 2$, for all valuations $v \in \mathcal{F}[V_i]$, if $A'_i(v) = \Gamma_{j'}(v)$, then we have,* $\text{Runs}(\{A'_0, A'_1, A'_2\}) = [\![O' \parallel R' \parallel TTP' \parallel Sc]\!]$.

5.1 Failure of Classical and Weak Co-synthesis, and the Need for a TTP

In this subsection we show that classical co-synthesis fails while weak co-synthesis generates solutions that are not attack-free and are hence unacceptable. We first tackle classical co-synthesis. In order to show failure of classical co-synthesis we need to show that one of the following conditions: (1) $[\![(\mathrm{O}' \parallel \mathrm{R} \parallel \mathrm{TTP} \parallel \mathrm{Sc})]\!] \subseteq \varphi_{\mathrm{O}}$; (2) $[\![(\mathrm{O} \parallel \mathrm{R}' \parallel \mathrm{TTP} \parallel \mathrm{Sc})]\!] \subseteq \varphi_{\mathrm{R}}$; (3) $[\![(\mathrm{O} \parallel \mathrm{R} \parallel \mathrm{TTP}' \parallel \mathrm{Sc})]\!] \subseteq \varphi_{\mathrm{TTP}}$, can be violated. The following theorem states that for all refinements R' of the recipient R, there exist behaviors of the processes O, TTP and Sc such that φ_{R} is violated. The proof of Theorem 3 is in [7].

Theorem 3 (Classical co-synthesis fails for R). *For all refinements $R' \preceq R$, we have $[\![O \parallel R' \parallel TTP \parallel Sc]\!] \not\subseteq \varphi_R$.*

In [7], we provide an example to illustrate that given our objectives, given a reasonable TTP as defined in Section 2, weak co-synthesis yields solutions that are not attack-free. The following theorem states that without the TTP, neither classical nor assume-guarantee synthesis generate refinements that satisfy all participant objectives.

Theorem 4 (Classical and assume-guarantee synthesis fail without the TTP). *For all refinements $O' \preceq O$, the following assertions hold:*

1. Classical co-synthesis fails*:* $[\![O' \parallel R \parallel Sc]\!] \not\subseteq \varphi_O$.
2. Assume-guarantee synthesis fails*:* $[\![O' \parallel R \parallel Sc]\!] \not\subseteq (\varphi_R \Rightarrow \varphi_O)$ *or, (1)* $[\![O' \parallel R \parallel Sc]\!] \subseteq (\varphi_R \Rightarrow \varphi_O)$*; (2)* $[\![R' \parallel O \parallel Sc]\!] \subseteq (\varphi_O \Rightarrow \varphi_R)$*; and (3)* $[\![O' \parallel R' \parallel Sc]\!] \not\subseteq (\varphi_O \wedge \varphi_R)$.

5.2 Assume-Guarantee Solutions Are Attack-Free

In this subsection we show that assume-guarantee solutions are attack free; no coalition of participants can violate the objective of at least one of the other participants while satisfying their own objectives. Let $P' = (\mathrm{O}', \mathrm{R}', \mathrm{TTP}')$ be a tuple of refinements of the agents and the TTP. For two refinements $P' = (\mathrm{O}', \mathrm{R}', \mathrm{TTP}')$ and $P'' = (\mathrm{O}'', \mathrm{R}'', \mathrm{TTP}'')$, we write $P' \preceq P''$ if $\mathrm{O}' \preceq \mathrm{O}''$, $\mathrm{R}' \preceq \mathrm{R}''$ and $\mathrm{TTP}' \preceq \mathrm{TTP}''$. Given $P = (\mathrm{O}, \mathrm{R}, \mathrm{TTP})$, the most general behaviors of the agents and the TTP, let P_{AGS} be the set of all possible refinements $P' \preceq P$ that satisfy the conditions of assume-guarantee synthesis. For a refinement $P' = (\mathrm{O}', \mathrm{R}', \mathrm{TTP}')$ to be in P_{AGS}, we require that $\mathrm{O}' \preceq \mathrm{O}$, $\mathrm{R}' \preceq \mathrm{R}$ and $\mathrm{TTP}' \preceq \mathrm{TTP}$ satisfy the following conditions:

For all fair schedulers Sc, for all possible behaviors of the channels, (1) $[\![(\mathrm{O}' \parallel \mathrm{R} \parallel \mathrm{TTP} \parallel \mathrm{Sc})]\!] \subseteq (\varphi_{\mathrm{R}} \wedge \varphi_{\mathrm{TTP}}) \Rightarrow \varphi_{\mathrm{O}}$; (2) $[\![(\mathrm{O} \parallel \mathrm{R}' \parallel \mathrm{TTP} \parallel \mathrm{Sc})]\!] \subseteq (\varphi_{\mathrm{O}} \wedge \varphi_{\mathrm{TTP}}) \Rightarrow \varphi_{\mathrm{R}}$; (3) $[\![(\mathrm{O} \parallel \mathrm{R} \parallel \mathrm{TTP}' \parallel \mathrm{Sc})]\!] \subseteq (\varphi_{\mathrm{O}} \wedge \varphi_{\mathrm{R}}) \Rightarrow \varphi_{\mathrm{TTP}}$; (4) $[\![(\mathrm{O}' \parallel \mathrm{R}' \parallel \mathrm{TTP}' \parallel \mathrm{Sc})]\!] \subseteq (\varphi_{\mathrm{O}} \wedge \varphi_{\mathrm{R}} \wedge \varphi_{\mathrm{TTP}})$. We now characterize the smallest restriction on the refinements $\mathrm{TTP}' \preceq \mathrm{TTP}$ that satisfy the condition,

$$[\![(\mathrm{O} \parallel \mathrm{R} \parallel \mathrm{TTP}' \parallel \mathrm{Sc})]\!] \subseteq (\varphi_{\mathrm{O}} \wedge \varphi_{\mathrm{R}}) \Rightarrow \varphi_{\mathrm{TTP}} \,. \tag{1}$$

In order to characterize the smallest restriction on TTP′ we first define the following constraints on the TTP and prove that they are both necessary and sufficient to satisfy (1) in [7].

AGS constraints on the TTP. We say that a refinement $\mathrm{TTP}' \preceq \mathrm{TTP}$ satisfies the *AGS constraints on the TTP*, if TTP′ satisfies the the following constraints:

1. *Abort constraint.* If the first request received by the TTP is an abort request, then her response to that request should be $[a_2^{\mathrm{O}}, a_2^{\mathrm{R}}]$;
2. *Resolve constraint.* If the first request received by the TTP is a resolve request, then her response to that request should be $[r_2^{\mathrm{O}}, r_2^{\mathrm{R}}]$;
3. *Accountability constraint.* If the first response from the TTP is $[x, y]$, then for all subsequent abort or resolve requests her response should be in the set $\{\iota, x, y, [x, y]\}$.

We assume a reasonable TTP, as defined in Section 2; in particular she only responds to abort or resolve requests. In the following lemma, assertion 1 states that for all refinements $\mathrm{TTP}' \preceq \mathrm{TTP}$ that satisfy the AGS constraints on the TTP, we have TTP′ is inviolable, i.e., neither agent can violate the objective φ_{TTP}, and hence satisfies the implication condition (1); assertion (2) states that if TTP′ does not satisfy the AGS constraints on the TTP, the implication condition (1) is not satisfied. We prove Lemma 1, and Theorem 5 that follows, in [7].

Lemma 1 (TTP inviolability). *For all refinements $TTP' \preceq TTP$, the following assertions hold: (1) if TTP' satisfies the AGS constraints on the TTP, then $[\![O \parallel R \parallel TTP' \parallel Sc]\!] \subseteq \varphi_{TTP} \subseteq (\varphi_O \wedge \varphi_R) \Rightarrow \varphi_{TTP}$ and (2) if TTP' does not satisfy the AGS constraints on the TTP, then $[\![O \parallel R \parallel TTP' \parallel Sc]\!] \not\subseteq (\varphi_O \wedge \varphi_R) \Rightarrow \varphi_{TTP}$.*

Theorem 5 (AGS is attack-free). *All refinements $P' \in P_{AGS}$ are attack-free.*

Corollary 1 establishes conditions for any refinement in P_{AGS} to be an attack-free fair non-repudiation protocol. Corollary 1 follows easily from Theorem 5.

Corollary 1 (Attack-free fair non-repudiation protocols). *For all refinements $P' \in P_{AGS}$, if $[\![O' \parallel R' \parallel TTP' \parallel Sc]\!] \cap (\Diamond NRO \wedge \Diamond NRR) \neq \emptyset$, then P' is an attack-free fair non-repudiation protocol.*

6 Analysis of Existing Protocols

We now analyze existing fair non-repudiation protocols and check if they are solutions to assume-guarantee synthesis. To facilitate the analysis, we first present an alternate characterization of the set P_{AGS} of assume-guarantee refinements. Towards an alternate characterization of P_{AGS}, we begin by defining constraints on O, similar to the AGS constraints on the TTP, that ensure satisfaction of the implication condition for O. We then present the most flexible refinements $O' \preceq O$ and $R' \preceq R$ and define maximal and minimal refinements that satisfy all the implication conditions of assume-guarantee synthesis. Finally, we introduce a *bounded idle time* requirement to ensure satisfaction of weak co-synthesis. Our alternate characterization is then the space of refinements between the minimal and maximal refinements, subject to the satisfaction of the AGS constraints on the TTP, the AGS constraints on O and the bounded idle time requirement. Using this alternate characterization, we show that the KM non-repudiation protocol is in P_{AGS} whereas the ASW protocol is not. We analyze the GJM protocol in [7].

AGS constraints on O. Given $P = (\mathrm{O}, \mathrm{R}, \mathrm{TTP})$, the most general behaviors of the agents and the TTP, we say a refinement $P' \preceq P$ satisfies the *AGS constraints on O*, if the following conditions hold: (1) $a_1^{\mathrm{O}} \notin \Gamma_{\mathrm{O'}}(v_{\mathrm{O}})$; (2) $\mathrm{EOO}_k^{\mathrm{O}} \notin \Gamma_{\mathrm{O'}}(\{M_1, \mathrm{EOR}, \mathrm{ABR}^{\mathrm{O}}\})$; and (3) $a_1^{\mathrm{O}} \notin \Gamma_{\mathrm{O'}}(\{M_1, \mathrm{EOR}, M_3\})$.

We show that satisfaction of the AGS constraints on O ensure satisfaction of the implication condition $[\![(\mathrm{O'} \parallel \mathrm{R} \parallel \mathrm{TTP} \parallel \mathrm{Sc})]\!] \subseteq (\varphi_{\mathrm{R}} \wedge \varphi_{\mathrm{TTP}}) \Rightarrow \varphi_{\mathrm{O}}$ in [7].

The maximal refinement P^*. We define the maximal refinement $\mathrm{P}^* = (\mathrm{O}^*, \mathrm{R}^*, \mathrm{TTP}^*)$ as follows: (1) $\mathrm{O}^* \preceq \mathrm{O}$ satisfies the AGS constraints on O and for all $\mathrm{O'}$ that satisfy the constraints, we have $O' \preceq \mathrm{O}^*$; (2) $\mathrm{R}^* = \mathrm{R}$; and (3) $\mathrm{TTP}^* \preceq \mathrm{TTP}$ satisfies the AGS constraints on the TTP and for all $\mathrm{TTP'}$ that satisfy the constraints, we have $\mathrm{TTP'} \preceq \mathrm{TTP}^*$. P^* corresponds to the smallest restriction on the moves of O and the TTP to be a witness to P_{AGS}.

The minimal refinement P_*. We present the smallest refinement $\mathrm{P}_* = (\mathrm{O}_*, \mathrm{R}_*, \mathrm{TTP}_*)$ in P_{AGS}, as the largest restriction on the moves of O, R and the TTP as follows: (1)

$\mathrm{P}_* \preceq \mathrm{P}^*$; (2) $Moves_{\mathrm{O}_*} = \{m_1, a_1^{\mathrm{O}}\}$; (3) $Moves_{\mathrm{R}_*} = \{\iota\}$; (4) O_* satisfies the AGS constraints on O; and (5) TTP_* satisfies the AGS constraints on the TTP.

The bounded idle time requirement. We say that a refinement P' satisfies *bounded idle time* if O and the TTP in P' choose the idle move ι, when scheduled by Sc, at most b times for a finite $b \in \mathbb{N}$. We show that satisfaction of the bounded idle time requirement ensures satisfaction of the weak co-synthesis requirement of assume-guarantee synthesis in [7].

Alternate characterization. We now use P_* and P^* to provide an alternate characterization of the set P_{AGS}. We first define the following set of refinements $\overline{\mathrm{P}}$:

$$\overline{\mathrm{P}} = \{P' = (\mathrm{O}', \mathrm{R}', \mathrm{TTP}') \mid P' \text{ satisfies bounded idle time}; \\ \mathrm{P}_* \preceq P' \preceq \mathrm{P}^*; \mathrm{TTP}' \text{ satisfies AGS constraints on the TTP}\} .$$

The following lemma states that the set $\overline{\mathrm{P}}$ and the set P_{AGS} coincide.

Lemma 2 (Alternate characterization). *We have* $\overline{P} = P_{AGS}$.

Using the above alternate characterization, we now analyze the KM and the ASW protocols. The analysis of the GJM protocol together with a systematic method to search through refinements in P_{AGS} leading to P_{KM} is in [7].

The KM non-repudiation protocol. The KM protocol, like the ASW and GJM protocols consists of a main protocol, an abort subprotocol and a resolve subprotocol. Let $P_{KM} = (\mathrm{O}_{KM}, \mathrm{R}_{KM}, \mathrm{TTP}_{KM})$ correspond to the agent and TTP refinements in the KM protocol. Since O does not abort the protocol in state v_0 and in state $\{M_1, \mathrm{EOR}, M_3\}$ in O_{KM}, it follows that $\mathrm{O}_* \preceq \mathrm{O}_{KM} \preceq \mathrm{O}^*$. It is easy to verify that $\mathrm{R}_* \preceq \mathrm{R}_{KM} \preceq \mathrm{R}^*$ and $\mathrm{TTP}_* \preceq \mathrm{TTP}_{KM} \preceq \mathrm{TTP}^*$. Moreover, TTP_{KM} satisfies the AGS constraints on the TTP and P_{KM} satisfies bounded idle time. Therefore $P_{KM} \in \overline{\mathrm{P}}$ and hence by Lemma 2, $P_{KM} \in P_{AGS}$.

The ASW certified mail protocol. The ASW certified mail protocol differs from the KM protocol in its abort and resolve sequences. To define the abort protocol, the TTP needs a move req^O that can be used to request O to resolve a protocol instance if R has already resolved it. Let $P_{ASW} = (\mathrm{O}_{ASW}, \mathrm{R}_{ASW}, \mathrm{TTP}_{ASW})$ correspond to the agent and TTP refinements in the ASW certified mail protocol. Since TTP_{ASW} neither has move $[a_2^{\mathrm{O}}, a_2^{\mathrm{R}}]$ nor $[r_2^{\mathrm{O}}, r_2^{\mathrm{R}}]$, TTP_{ASW} does not satisfy the AGS constraints on the TTP and hence by Lemma 1 (assertion 2), we have $P_{ASW} \notin P_{AGS}$. Moreover, the ASW certified mail protocol is not attack-free as shown by the following attacks [12]: Consider a behavior of the channels that deliver all messages and the sequence of messages $\langle m_1, r_1^{\mathrm{R}}, r_2^{\mathrm{R}}, a_1^{\mathrm{O}}, req^O \rangle$ in the ASW protocol. In this sequence a malicious R decides to resolve the protocol after receiving m_1 and thus succeeds in getting $\mathrm{EOO}_k^{\mathrm{TTP}}$. When O_{ASW} attempts to abort the protocol, TTP_{ASW} expects her to resolve the protocol as R has already resolved it, but O_{ASW} cannot do so as she does not have m_2. Therefore, φ_{O} is violated; O_{ASW} cannot abort or resolve the protocol and cannot get R's signature. Consider the sequence of messages $\langle m_1, m_2, r_1^{\mathrm{O}}, r_2^{\mathrm{O}}, a_1^{\mathrm{O}}, a_2^{\mathrm{O}} \rangle$. This is an attack that compromises fairness for R; in the words of [12] the protocol designers did not foresee that O could resolve the protocol and then abort it. This violates φ_{R} and TTP accountability, violating φ_{TTP}, while satisfying φ_{O}.

Theorem 6 (AGS results on existing protocols). *The refinement corresponding to the KM non-repudiation protocol is in P_{AGS} and the refinements corresponding to the ASW certified mail protocol and the GJM protocol are not in P_{AGS}.*

7 Conclusion

In this work we introduce and demonstrate the effectiveness of assume-guarantee synthesis in synthesizing fair exchange protocols. Our main goal is to introduce a general assume-guarantee synthesis framework that can be used with a variety of objectives; we considered a TTP objective that treats the agents symmetrically, but the framework can be used with possibly weaker TTP objectives that treat agents asymmetrically. Using assume-guarantee analysis we have obtained a new symmetric protocol that is attack-free, given the channels to the TTP are operational. The details of the symmetric protocol are in the full version of the paper in [7]. For future work we will study the application of assume-guarantee synthesis to other security protocols.

Acknowledgment. The authors would like to thank Avik Chaudhuri for his invaluable help and feedback. The research was supported by Austrian Science Fund (FWF) Grant No P 23499-N23 (Modern Graph Algorithmic Techniques in Formal Verification), FWF NFN Grant No S11407-N23 (RiSE), ERC Start grant (279307: Graph Games), and Microsoft faculty fellows award.

References

1. Alur, R., Henzinger, T.A., Mang, F.Y.C., Qadeer, S., Rajamani, S.K., Tasiran, S.: Mocha: Modularity in Model Checking. In: Vardi, M.Y. (ed.) CAV 1998. LNCS, vol. 1427, pp. 521–525. Springer, Heidelberg (1998)
2. Asokan, N., Shoup, V., Waidner, M.: Asynchronous protocols for optimistic fair exchange. In: IEEE S&P, pp. 86–99 (1998)
3. Chadha, R., Kanovich, M.I., Scedrov, A.: Inductive methods and contract-signing protocols. In: CCS, pp. 176–185. ACM (2001)
4. Chadha, R., Mitchell, J.C., Scedrov, A., Shmatikov, V.: Contract Signing, Optimism, and Advantage. In: Amadio, R.M., Lugiez, D. (eds.) CONCUR 2003. LNCS, vol. 2761, pp. 366–382. Springer, Heidelberg (2003)
5. Chatterjee, K., Henzinger, T.A.: Assume-Guarantee Synthesis. In: Grumberg, O., Huth, M. (eds.) TACAS 2007. LNCS, vol. 4424, pp. 261–275. Springer, Heidelberg (2007)
6. Chatterjee, K., Henzinger, T.A., Jurdzinski, M.: Games with secure equilibria. Theor. Comput. Sci. 365(1-2), 67–82 (2006)
7. Chatterjee, K., Raman, V.: Assume-guarantee synthesis for digital contract signing. CoRR, abs/1004.2697 (2010)
8. Clarke, E.M., Emerson, E.A.: Design and Synthesis of Synchronization Skeletons using Branching-Time Temporal Logic. In: Engeler, E. (ed.) Logic of Programs 1979. LNCS, vol. 125, pp. 52–71. Springer, Heidelberg (1981)
9. Even, S., Yacobi, Y.: Relations among public key signature systems, technical report 175. Technical report, Technion, Haifa, Israel (1980)
10. Garay, J.A., Jakobsson, M., MacKenzie, P.D.: Abuse-Free Optimistic Contract Signing. In: Wiener, M. (ed.) CRYPTO 1999. LNCS, vol. 1666, pp. 449–466. Springer, Heidelberg (1999)

11. Kremer, S., Raskin, J.-F.: Game analysis of abuse-free contract signing. In: CSFW, pp. 206–220. IEEE (2002)
12. Kremer, S., Raskin, J.-F.: A game-based verification of non-repudiation and fair exchange protocols. JCS 11(3), 399–430 (2003)
13. Manna, Z., Pnueli, A.: The Temporal Logic of Reactive and Concurrent Systems: Specification. Springer, New York (1991)
14. Markowitch, O., Gollmann, D., Kremer, S.: On Fairness in Exchange Protocols. In: Lee, P.J., Lim, C.H. (eds.) ICISC 2002. LNCS, vol. 2587, pp. 451–464. Springer, Heidelberg (2003)
15. Markowitch, O., Kremer, S.: An Optimistic Non-repudiation Protocol with Transparent Trusted Third Party. In: Davida, G.I., Frankel, Y. (eds.) ISC 2001. LNCS, vol. 2200, pp. 363–378. Springer, Heidelberg (2001)
16. Pagnia, H., Gärtner, F.C.: On the impossibility of fair exchange without a trusted third party. Technical report, Darmstadt (1999)
17. Perrig, A., Song, D.X.: A first step towards the automatic generation of security protocols. In: NDSS (2000)
18. Pnueli, A.: The temporal logic of programs. In: Proc. 18th IEEE Symp. Found. of Comp. Sci., pp. 46–57. IEEE Computer Society Press (1977)
19. Pnueli, A., Rosner, R.: On the synthesis of a reactive module. In: POPL, pp. 179–190. ACM Press (1989)
20. Ramadge, P., Wonham, W.: Supervisory control of a class of discrete event processes. Siam J. Control and Optimization 25(1) (1987)
21. Saïdi, H.: Toward automatic synthesis of security protocols. AAAI Technical Report, SS-02-05 (2002)
22. Shmatikov, V., Mitchell, J.C.: Finite-state analysis of two contract signing protocols. Theor. Comput. Sci. 283(2), 419–450 (2002)
23. Song, D., Berezin, S., Perrig, A.: Athena: a novel approach to efficient automatic security protocol analysis. JCS 9 (2001)
24. Thomas, W.: Languages, automata, and logic, pp. 389–455 (1997)
25. Zhou, J., Gollmann, D.: An efficient non-repudiation protocol. In: PCSFW, pp. 126–132. IEEE Computer Society Press (1997)

Model Checking Information Flow in Reactive Systems*

Rayna Dimitrova[1], Bernd Finkbeiner[1], Máté Kovács[2], Markus N. Rabe[1], and Helmut Seidl[2]

[1] Universität des Saarlandes, Germany
[2] Technische Universität München, Germany

Abstract. Most analysis methods for information flow properties do not consider temporal restrictions. In practice, however, such properties rarely occur statically, but have to consider constraints such as *when and under which conditions* a variable has to be kept secret. In this paper, we propose a natural integration of information flow properties into linear-time temporal logics (LTL). We add a new modal operator, the hide operator, expressing that the observable behavior of a system is independent of the valuations of a secret variable. We provide a complexity analysis for the model checking problem of the resulting logic SecLTL and we identify an expressive fragment for which this question is efficiently decidable. We also show that the path based nature of the hide operator allows for seamless integration into branching time logics.

1 Introduction

Temporal logics are well-suited for specifying classical requirements on the behavior of reactive systems. The key to the success of automated verification methods for temporal logics is the rich set of automata-theoretic techniques [1,2,3]. Based on these theoretical foundations, efficient model-checkers that are capable of verifying intricate properties have emerged over the last two decades. Reactive systems, however, often are not only safety-critical but also *security-critical.* Examples of reactive systems handling confidential information include communication protocols, cell phone apps, and document servers.

Information flow properties are of great importance in the realm of security-critical systems. Information flow summarizes properties that argue about the transfer of information from a secret source towards an observer or attacker. Notable examples of such properties are non-interference [4] and observational determinism [5], which require that no information is leaked in a strict sense. For many practical applications, however, requiring that information is kept secret forever is too strong: often secrets may (or even must) be released under certain conditions. The controlled release of information is called *declassification* [6,7].

* This work was partially supported by the German Research Foundation (DFG) under the project SpAGAT (grant no. FI 936/2-1) in the priority program "Reliably Secure Software Systems – RS3".

V. Kuncak and A. Rybalchenko (Eds.): VMCAI 2012, LNCS 7148, pp. 169–185, 2012.

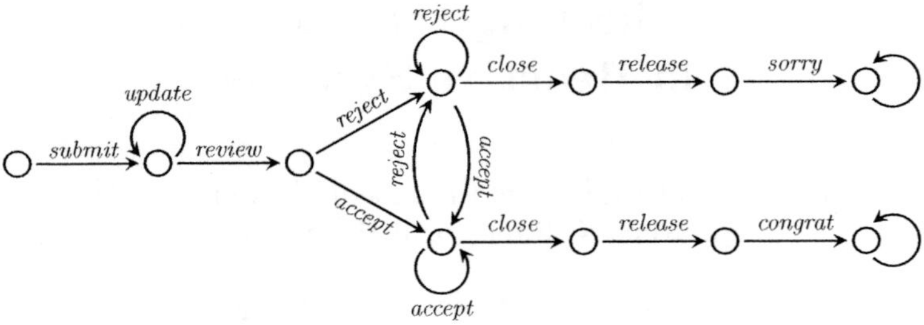

Fig. 1. Model of a conference management system. The variables *submit*, *update*, *review*, *accept*, *reject*, *close* and *release* are input variables. An author can submit a paper and later receive a notification of whether the paper was accepted or rejected via the output variables *congrat* and *sorry*, which he or she can observe.

For reactive systems it is typical that secrecy requirements vary over time, depending on the interaction of the system with its environment. For example access rights are seldom static, and secret data may be released under certain conditions. Therefore, it is imperative to consider information flow properties in their temporal context and integrate them in the theory of temporal logics.

A typical example for a security-critical reactive system is a conference management system. A minimalistic model of such a system is given in Fig. 1. Two properties of interest for this system are: (1) *"The final decision of the program committee remains secret until the notification"* and (2) *"All intermediate decisions of the program committee are never revealed to the author"*. These two information flow properties can be informally specified as follows:

(1) **last** *accept/reject* **before** *close* **remains secret until** *release* and
(2) **all** *accept/reject* **except the last before** *close* **remain secret forever**.

The above properties illustrate the two temporal aspects of information flow properties. Firstly, they specify *at which points in time a variable is considered secret*, e.g., "last before" or "all except last before". Secondly, they specify *for how long certain information should remain secret*, e.g., "forever" or "until release". Despite their obvious temporal nature, these properties cannot be expressed in classical temporal logics like LTL (Linear-time Temporal Logic), CTL (Computation Tree Logic), or even the μ-calculus [8].

The reason is that most information flow properties have structural differences to classical temporal properties. While the latter are interpreted on a single execution (in the linear-time case) or on the execution tree of a system (in the branching-time case), information flow properties require the comparison of multiple executions.

Contribution. In this paper we introduce a new modal operator $\mathcal{H}$ (*hide*), that expresses the requirement that the observable behavior of a system is independent of the choice of a secret. The novelty is the integration into the temporal context—the operator itself is evaluated over a single path, but tracks the alternative paths the system could take for different valuations of the secret.

Extending LTL with the operator $\mathcal{H}$ (Section 3) yields a powerful—yet decidable—logic called *SecLTL*. We provide an automata-theoretic verification technique for SecLTL that extends the standard approach for LTL. We establish PSPACE-completeness of the model checking problem for SecLTL both in the size of the specification and in the size of the system under scrutiny.

We identify a fragment, *Restricted SecLTL*, for which the model checking problem is efficiently solvable: it is in NLOGSPACE with respect to the size of the system (Section 4). What makes Restricted SecLTL of practical relevance is the combination of efficiency and expressiveness. It is able to capture properties like non-interference and observational determinism.

The path-based semantics of the hide operator enables seamless integration in branching time logics (Section 5). We define the logics SecCTL and SecCTL* and determine the complexity of the corresponding model checking problems. Surprisingly, even for SecCTL the model checking problem is PSPACE-complete.

2 Preliminaries

In this section we introduce the system model we consider throughout the paper: transition systems whose edges are labeled with valuations of their input and output variables. The external behavior of such a system consists of the infinite sequences of labels during the possible executions. The temporal properties we specify are over such behavior paths and are consequently translated to automata over infinite words over the same alphabet.

For a finite set $\mathcal{V}$ of binary variables, we denote with $\mathsf{vals}(\mathcal{V})$ the set of all possible valuations of the variables in $\mathcal{V}$, i.e., all total functions from $\mathcal{V}$ to $\mathbb{B}$. For $a \in \mathsf{vals}(\mathcal{V})$ and $V \subseteq \mathcal{V}$ we use $a|_V$ to note the projection of a on the set V.

For a set A, A^* is the set of all finite sequences of elements of A and A^ω is the set of all infinite sequences of elements of A. For a finite or infinite sequence π of elements of A and $i \in \mathbb{N}$, $\pi[i]$ is the $(i+1)$-th element of π, $\pi[0, i)$ is the prefix of π of up to (excluding) position i, $\pi[0, i]$ is the prefix of π up to (including) position i and, if π is infinite, $\pi[i, \infty)$ is its infinite suffix starting at position i. For a finite sequence $\pi \in A^*$, we denote its length with $|\pi|$.

Definition 1 (Transition system). *A* transition system *(Mealy machine)* $M = (\mathcal{V}_\mathcal{I}, \mathcal{V}_\mathcal{O}, S, s_0, \delta)$ *consists of a finite set of states* S*, an initial state* s_0*, two disjoint finite sets of binary variables, the input variables* $\mathcal{V}_\mathcal{I}$ *and the output variables* $\mathcal{V}_\mathcal{O}$*, and a transition function that is a partial function* $\delta : S \times \Sigma \to S$*, where the alphabet* $\Sigma = \mathsf{vals}(\mathcal{V}_\mathcal{I} \cup \mathcal{V}_\mathcal{O})$ *is the set of valuations of the input and output variables. We define the size of a transitions system as* $|M| = |S| + |\Sigma|$*.*

We consider input enabled systems, *that is, we require for every* $s \in S$ *and* $i \in \mathsf{vals}(\mathcal{V}_\mathcal{I})$ *that there exists an* $a \in \Sigma$ *with* $a|_{\mathcal{V}_\mathcal{I}} = i$ *such that* $\delta(s, a)$ *is defined.*

Definition 2 (Transition function δ^*_M). *We extend the transition function of a transition system* M *to partial labels:* $\delta^*_M : S \times \mathsf{vals}(V) \to 2^{\Sigma \times S}$*, where* $V \subseteq \mathcal{V}_\mathcal{I} \cup \mathcal{V}_\mathcal{O}$*,* $\delta^*_M(s, v) = \{(a, s') \in \Sigma \times S \mid a|_V = v \text{ and } \delta(s, a) = s'\}$*.*

Definition 3 (Path, execution). Paths *of a transition system* M *are infinite sequences of labels:* $\pi = a_0, a_1, \ldots$, *with* $a_i \in \Sigma$. *Given a state* $s \in S$, *each path* π *is associated with a unique finite or infinite sequence of states,* $s_0, \ldots, s_n$ *or* $s_0, s_1, \ldots$, *called* execution of M from s on π *and denoted* $\mathsf{Exec}_M(s, \pi)$, *such that* $s_0 = s$ *and* $s_{i+1} = \delta(s_i, a_i)$ *for all* $i \geq 0$. *The execution is unique, since the transition function is a function and might be finite since this function is partial.*

Given a state s, *we denote the set of possible infinite paths in* M *by* $\mathsf{Paths}_{s,M}$. *Note that for every* $\pi \in \mathsf{Paths}_{s,M}$, *the execution* $\mathsf{Exec}_M(s, \pi)$ *is infinite.*

Definition 4 (Observational equivalence). *Given a set of variables* $V \subseteq \mathcal{V}_\mathcal{I} \cup \mathcal{V}_\mathcal{O}$, *we define two valuations* $a, a' \in \Sigma$, *to be* observationally equivalent w.r.t. V, *noted* $a =_V a'$, *if the valuations' projections to the variables in* V *is the same:* $a|_V = a'|_V$. *Pairwise comparison immediately provides us with a notion of observational equivalence on paths.*

For a finite set Q, $\mathcal{B}^+(Q)$ is the set of positive boolean formulas over Q. These are formulas built from the formulas true, false and the elements of Q using $\wedge$ and $\vee$. For $\theta \in \mathcal{B}^+(Q)$ and a set $K \subseteq Q$ we write $K \models \theta$ if K satisfies θ.

A *tree* T is a subset of $\mathbb{N}^*_{>0}$ such that for every *node* $\tau \in \mathbb{N}^*_{>0}$ and every positive integer $n \in \mathbb{N}_{>0}$, if $\tau \cdot n \in T$ then the following hold:

- $\tau \in T$ (i.e., T is prefix-closed) and there is an edge from τ to $\tau \cdot n$, and
- for every $m \in \mathbb{N}^*_{>0}$ with $m < n$ it holds that $\tau \cdot m \in T$.

The root of T is the empty sequence ε and for a node $\tau \in T$, $|\tau|$ is the distance of τ from the root. A *Q-labeled tree* is a tuple (T, r), where T is a tree and the function $r : T \to Q$ labels every node with an element of Q.

Definition 5 (Alternating Büchi automaton). *An* alternating Büchi automaton *is a tuple* $\mathcal{A} = (Q, q_0, \Sigma, \rho, F)$, *where* Q *is a finite set of states,* $q_0 \in Q$ *is the initial state,* Σ *is a finite alphabet,* $\rho : Q \times \Sigma \to \mathcal{B}^+(Q)$ *is a transition function that maps a state and a letter to a positive boolean combination of states, and* $F \subseteq Q$ *is a set of accepting states.*

A run *of* $\mathcal{A}$ *on an infinite word* $\pi \in \Sigma^\omega$ *is a Q-labeled tree* (T, r) *such that* $r(\varepsilon) = q_0$ *and for every node* τ *in* T *with children* $\tau_1, \ldots, \tau_k$ *it holds that* $k \leq |Q|$ *and* $\{r(\tau_1), \ldots, r(\tau_k)\} \models \rho(q, \pi[i])$, *where* $q = r(\tau)$ *and* $i = |\tau|$.

A run r *of* $\mathcal{A}$ *on* $\pi \in \Sigma^\omega$ *is* accepting *iff for every infinite path* $\tau_0\tau_1\ldots$ *in* T, $r(\tau_i) \in F$ *for infinitely many* $i \in \mathbb{N}$. *We denote with* $L_\omega(\mathcal{A})$ *the set of infinite words in* Σ^ω accepted *by* $\mathcal{A}$, *i.e., for which there exists an accepting run of* $\mathcal{A}$. *For a state* $q \in Q$, *we note* $L_\omega(\mathcal{A}, q) = L_\omega(\mathcal{A}_q)$, *where* $\mathcal{A}_q = (Q, q, \Sigma, \rho, F)$.

Definition 6 (Nondeterministic Büchi automaton). *A* nondeterministic Büchi automaton *is an alternating Büchi automaton* $\mathcal{N} = (Q, q_0, \Sigma, \rho, F)$ *for which the transition formula* $\rho(q, a)$ *for each* $q \in Q$ *and* $a \in \Sigma$ *does not contain* $\wedge$. *Thus, for a nondeterministic Büchi automaton we can represent the transition function* ρ *as a function* $\rho : Q \times \Sigma \to 2^Q$.

A run of $\mathcal{N}$ *on an infinite word* $\pi \in \Sigma^\omega$ *is an infinite sequence* $\tau \in Q^\omega$ *such that* $\tau[0] = q_0$ *and for every* $i \in \mathbb{N}$, $\tau[i+1] \in \rho(\tau[i], \pi[i])$.

3 The Temporal Logic SecLTL

The logic SecLTL extends LTL with the *hide operator* $\mathcal{H}$. The SecLTL formulas over a set of variables $\mathcal{V} = \mathcal{V}_\mathcal{I} \dot\cup \mathcal{V}_\mathcal{O}$ are defined according to the following grammar, where $v \in \mathcal{V}$, φ and ψ are SecLTL formulas, $H \subseteq \mathcal{V}_\mathcal{I}$ and $O \subseteq \mathcal{V}_\mathcal{O}$,

$$\varphi \quad ::= \quad v \quad | \quad \neg\varphi \quad | \quad \varphi \vee \psi \quad | \quad \bigcirc\varphi \quad | \quad \varphi\,\mathcal{U}\,\psi \quad | \quad \mathcal{H}_{H,O}\varphi.$$

Additionally, we introduce the common abbreviations $\mathsf{true} = v \vee \neg v$, $\mathsf{false} = \neg\mathsf{true}$, $\Diamond\varphi = \mathsf{true}\,\mathcal{U}\,\varphi$, $\Box\varphi = \neg\Diamond\neg\varphi$, and $\varphi\mathcal{W}\psi = \varphi\,\mathcal{U}\,\psi \vee \Box\varphi$.

Intuitively, the operator $\mathcal{H}_{H,O}\varphi$ requires that the observable behavior of the system does not depend on the initial values of the *secret variables* H before the formula φ is satisfied. The operator also allows to specify the power of the observer, by choosing an appropriate set O of *observable variables* or *outputs*. That is, the hide operator specifies what is to be considered the secret, what we consider to be observable, and when the secret may be released.

What may seem a little odd initially, that we only consider the *first valuation* of the H-variables to be secret, is actually one of the strengths of SecLTL. It allows us, to precisely characterize the secret by using the hide operator within an appropriate temporal context. For example, we can express the temporal information flow properties from our motivating example in the introduction, as we demonstrate in Section 3.1.

Although SecLTL specifications are path properties, their semantics, more precisely the semantics of the hide operator, is defined using a *set of alternative paths* and involves comparison of each of these paths to the *main path*, i.e., the path over which the SecLTL formula is interpreted.

Definition 7 (Alternative paths). *The* set of alternative paths *for a given path $\pi \in \Sigma^\omega$ and a given state $s \in S$ with respect to a set of variables $H \subseteq \mathcal{V}$ is the set of paths starting in state s with a possibly different valuation of the secret variables H in the first position but otherwise adhering to the same input values.*

$$\mathsf{AltPaths}_M(s,\pi,H) = \{\, \pi' \in \mathsf{Paths}_{s,M} \mid \pi[0] =_{\mathcal{V}_\mathcal{I}\setminus H} \pi'[0], \; \textit{and} \; \pi[1,\infty) =_{\mathcal{V}_\mathcal{I}} \pi'[1,\infty) \,\}.$$

Definition 8 (Semantics of SecLTL). *Let $M = (\mathcal{V}_\mathcal{I}, \mathcal{V}_\mathcal{O}, S, s_0, \delta)$ be a transition system and $\Sigma = \mathsf{vals}(\mathcal{V}_\mathcal{I} \cup \mathcal{V}_\mathcal{O})$. An infinite path $\pi \in \mathsf{Paths}_{s,M}$ for some state $s \in S$ and the state s satisfy a SecLTL formula φ, denoted $M, s, \pi \models \varphi$ when the following conditions are satisfied:*

- *if $\varphi = v$ for some $v \in \mathcal{V}$, then $M, s, \pi \models \varphi$ iff $\pi[0]|_v$ is true;*
- *if $\varphi = \neg\varphi'$, then $M, s, \pi \models \varphi$ iff $M, s, \pi \not\models \varphi'$;*
- *if $\varphi = \varphi_1 \vee \varphi_2$, then $M, s, \pi \models \varphi$ iff $M, s, \pi \models \varphi_1$ or $M, s, \pi \models \varphi_2$,*
- *if $\varphi = \bigcirc\varphi'$, then $M, s, \pi \models \varphi$ iff $M, s', \pi[1,\infty) \models \varphi'$ where $s' = \delta(s, \pi[0])$,*
- *if $\varphi = \varphi_1\mathcal{U}\varphi_2$, then $M, s, \pi \models \varphi$ iff for some $i \geq 0$, we have $M, \sigma[i], \pi[i,\infty) \models \varphi_2$ and for all j with $0 \leq j < i$ we have $M, \sigma[j], \pi[j,\infty) \models \varphi_1$, where $\sigma = \mathsf{Exec}_M(s,\pi)$.*

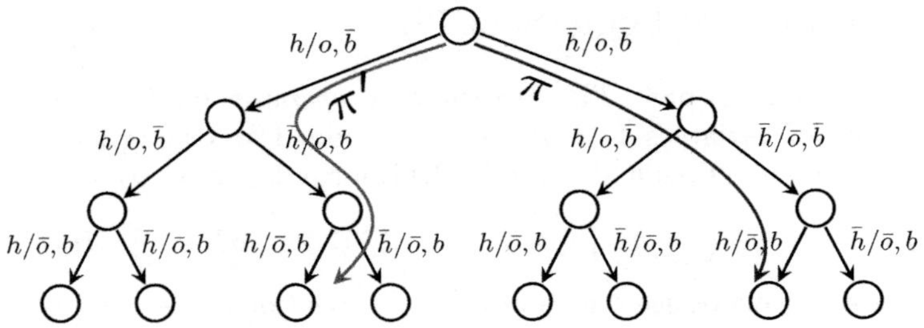

Fig. 2. Consider the formula $\varphi = \mathcal{H}_{\{h\},\{o\}}b$. This figure displays a computation tree of a system and a path π with its (in this case single) alternative path π'. The formula φ holds on π if π is observably equivalent (here, that is, equivalent with respect to variable o) to π' until b holds on π. Note that the occurrence of b in step 2 of path π' does not affect the evaluation of φ on path π—thus π violates property φ. The other path π', however, satisfies the property, as the comparison stops after the first step.

– *if* $\varphi = \mathcal{H}_{H,O}\psi$, *then* $M, s, \pi \models \varphi$ *iff for every* $\pi' \in \mathsf{AltPaths}_M(s, \pi, H)$ *it holds that* $\pi =_O \pi'$ *or there exists* $i \in \mathbb{N}$ *such that* $M, \sigma[i], \pi[i, \infty) \models \psi$ *and* $\pi[0, i) =_O \pi'[0, i)$, *where* $\sigma = \mathsf{Exec}_M(s, \pi)$.

We say that a transition system M satisfies a SecLTL formula φ, *denoted* $M \models \varphi$, *iff* $M, s_o, \pi \models \varphi$ *for every* $\pi \in \mathsf{Paths}_{s_0,M}$.

Using the operator $\mathcal{H}$ we can specify secrecy requirements within a temporal context. It *generates a secret at a single point* partitioning the input variables into *public* and *secret* variables. Thus we can use the standard LTL operators to capture the temporal aspect in that respect, i.e., *when are secrets introduced.* The hide operator is a temporal operator with a "weak until flavor" that captures requirements about for *how long the secret should be kept.*

The examples below demonstrate that these features enable the specification of a rich set of temporal information flow properties for reactive systems.

3.1 Examples

Example 1 (Non-interference and Observational determinism). Classical non-interference and related notions are fundamental security properties that any logic designed as a specification language for information flow requirements should be able to express. Classical non-interference as defined for (output) deterministic systems by Gougen and Meseguer [4] requires that the system's observable behavior may not change if the high user's actions would not have been issued. Modeling the high actions h_i and low actions l_i as input variables that are true iff the action is performed and defining O as the set of observable variables, we can translate [9] non-interference to our setting as follows:

$$NI(M) = \{\pi \in \mathsf{Paths}_{s_0,M} \mid \forall \pi' \in \mathsf{Paths}_{s_0,M} :\ \pi' =_H \vec{0} \wedge \pi =_L \pi' \Rightarrow \pi =_O \pi'\}$$

where $H = \bigcup_i h_i$ and $L = \bigcup_i l_i$. That is, we compare all paths with non-zero high inputs to their counterpart having only zero high inputs. By symmetry and transitivity this compares all paths having the same low inputs to each other.

This property can be expressed in SecLTL with the following formula:

$$\varphi_{NI(M)} = \Box\, \mathcal{H}_{H,O}\, \mathsf{false}.$$

While a single hide operator only hides the first valuation of the secret variable, using it in combination with the globally operator ($\Box$) has the effect that for all steps the valuations of the variables H are considered secret. In this case, the subformula of the hide operator is false, which means that the comparison will never stop—the secrets must be kept forever.

Zdancewic and Myers [5] generalize non-interference to systems that are *not* output deterministic. The resulting property, *observational determinism*, states that for all possible computations (paths) π and π' the observations must be indistinguishable: $\pi =_O \pi'$. Note that the model in [5] does not allow for low input, but we can easily extend it by such:

$$OD(M) = \{\pi \in \mathsf{Paths}_{s_0,M} \mid \forall \pi' \in \mathsf{Paths}_{s_0,M} : \; \pi =_L \pi' \implies \pi =_O \pi'\}$$

As it is easy to see, this property is also captured by the formula $\varphi_{NI(M)}$ above.

There are several other approaches, all with different semantics, that generalize non-interference to not output deterministic systems. We decided to follow the approach of Zdancewic and Myers as we consider it to be conservative.

Example 2 (Conference management system). Consider the model of a conference management system depicted on Fig. 1. The information flow properties informally specified there can be specified as follows:

$$(1) \quad \Box\big((\bigcirc close) \Rightarrow \mathcal{H}_{H,O}\, release\big)$$

$$(2) \quad \Box\big((\neg \bigcirc\, close) \Rightarrow \mathcal{H}_{H,O}\, \mathsf{false}\big).$$

where $H = \{accept, reject\}$ and $O = \{congrat, sorry\}$.

Here, the set H in the $\mathcal{H}$ subformulas specifies that the variables whose values in the corresponding point of time constitute the secret are *accept* and *reject*, and the set $O = \{congrat, sorry\}$ means that the observer, in this case the author, can observe all output variables of this system.

The subformula *release* of the $\mathcal{H}$ subformula in (1) specifies that the secret may be released as soon as *release* is satisfied, while in (2) the false in the $\mathcal{H}$ subformula requires that the secret is never released (as false is never satisfied).

Example 3 (Combination of path properties). Using combinations of path properties, we can rule out certain leaks in the analysis, which allows to analyze different sources of secrets in separation. To rule out security violations other than the obvious copy-operation from high to low variables, we can require that the hide operator is only evaluated on paths that do not show such behavior:

$$(\neg \mathsf{readhigh}\ \mathcal{W}\ \mathsf{writelow}) \Rightarrow \mathcal{H}_{H,O}\mathsf{false}.$$

As side conditions we need to require that readhigh and writelow are not part of the set of variables H, as in this case the hide operator would explore alternatives with different valuations for these variables.

Example 4 (Auction). We consider the bounded creation of secrets as one of the strengths of SecLTL. For example, we can express that all bids submitted before closing an auction are kept secret until the winner is announced:

$$(\mathcal{H}_{\mathsf{bids},O}\ \mathsf{winnerAnnounced})\ \mathcal{U}\ \mathsf{closingAuction}.$$

Example 5 (Key retrieval). SecLTL also enables specifications that argue about more than one different secrets. The following property specifies that on every path at most one of the two secrets can be compromised:

$$(\mathcal{H}_{\{k_1\},O}\ \mathsf{false})\ \vee\ (\mathcal{H}_{\{k_2\},O}\ \mathsf{false}).$$

This does not prevent the leakage of either secret for all paths but only prevents per path that both secrets are leaked.

Example 6 (Nesting). Nesting can be used to express that a secret (e.g. a key) may not be leaked until the generation of a second secret that is secure:

$$\mathcal{H}_{\{k_1\},O}(\mathcal{H}_{\{k_2\},O}\mathsf{false}).$$

3.2 Model Checking SecLTL

The *model checking problem* for SecLTL is, given a SecLTL formula φ and a transition system M to determine whether $M \models \varphi$.

We now describe an automata-theoretic technique for model checking SecLTL. To this end we show that given a SecLTL formula φ and a transition system M, we can construct a nondeterministic Büchi word automaton that accepts exactly those paths in $\mathsf{Paths}_{s_0,M}$ that satisfy φ. As an intermediate step of this translation we construct an alternating Büchi word automaton from M and φ with this property. This construction extends the standard translation for LTL and thus inherits its intuitiveness. An important advantage of the use of alternation is that it allows us to naturally follow the semantics of the operator $\mathcal{H}$ employing the universal branching in the automaton transitions.

One of the differences between the automaton we construct for a SecLTL formula and the one for an LTL formula obtained by the standard construction is that each state of the automaton for SecLTL carries a state of M as a component. This allows the automaton to keep track of the executions of M on the alternative paths for a given input word when necessary. Note that this construction could be slightly adapted in order to eliminate the need for a subsequent product construction of the resulting automaton with M. We decided, however, not to do that, in order to give a better intuition about the construction here and its relation to the corresponding construction for Restricted SecLTL in Section 4.

Definition 9. *The* closure operator $cl(\varphi)$ *maps a SecLTL formula* φ *to a set of SecLTL formulas that consists of all subformulas of* φ *and their negations. For LTL operators we use the standard definition of subformulas and the subformulas of a formula* $\mathcal{H}_{H,O}\varphi$ *contain the formula itself and the subformulas of* φ.

Proposition 1. *For a transition system $M = (\mathcal{V}_\mathcal{I}, \mathcal{V}_\mathcal{O}, S, s_0, \delta)$ and a SecLTL formula φ we can construct an alternating Büchi word automaton $\mathcal{A}_{M,\varphi} = (Q, q_0, \Sigma, \rho, F)$ with $\Sigma = \mathsf{vals}(\mathcal{V}_\mathcal{I} \cup \mathcal{V}_\mathcal{O})$ such that $|Q|$ is in $\mathcal{O}(|\varphi| \cdot |S|^2)$ and for every path $\pi \in \mathsf{Paths}_{s_0,M}$ it holds that $\pi \in L_\omega(\mathcal{A}_{M,\varphi})$ iff $M, s_0, \pi \models \varphi$.*

Proof. We define the set of states $Q = Q_\varphi \times S_\perp$, where $S_\perp = S \cup \{\perp\}$ and

$$Q_\varphi = cl(\varphi) \cup \{(O, \psi, m, s) \in 2^{\mathcal{V}_\mathcal{O}} \times \{\psi\} \times \{\forall, \exists\} \times S \mid \exists H \subseteq \mathcal{V}_\mathcal{I}.\mathcal{H}_{H,O}\psi \in cl(\varphi)\}.$$

The initial state of $\mathcal{A}_{M,\varphi}$ is $q_0 = (\varphi, s_0)$ and the set F of accepting states is defined as $F = \{(\neg(\psi\,\mathcal{U}\,\psi'), s) \in Q\} \cup \{((O, \psi, \forall, s'), s) \in Q\}$.

To define the transition function $\rho : Q \times \Sigma \to \mathcal{B}^+(Q)$, we extend the transition function δ of M to a total function $\delta_\perp : S_\perp \times \Sigma \to S_\perp$: for $s \in S$, $\delta_\perp(s, a) = \delta(s, a)$ if $\delta(s, a)$ is defined and $\delta_\perp(s, a) = \perp$ otherwise, and $\delta_\perp(\perp, a) = \perp$.

For convenience, we define the dual $\overline{q}$ of states in $q \in Q$: $\overline{(\psi, s)} = (\neg\psi, s)$, $\overline{((O, \psi, \forall, s'), s)} = ((O, \neg\psi, \exists, s'), s)$, and $\overline{((O, \psi, \exists, s'), s)} = ((O, \neg\psi, \forall, s'), s)$.

For $(\psi, \perp) \in Q$ where ψ is not an LTL formula and $a \in \Sigma$ we define $\rho((\psi, \perp), a) = \mathsf{false}$. For $((O, \psi, m, s'), \perp) \in Q$ where ψ is not an LTL formula and $a \in \Sigma$, $\rho(((O, \psi, m, s'), \perp), a) = \mathsf{false}$. For the remaining cases we define:

$$\begin{aligned}
\rho((v, s), a) &= \mathsf{true}\text{ if } a|_v = 1 \text{ and } \mathsf{false} \text{ if } a|_v = 0,\\
\rho((\neg\psi, s), a) &= \overline{\rho((\psi, s), a)},\\
\rho((\psi \vee \psi', s), a) &= \rho((\psi, s), a) \vee \rho((\psi', s), a),\\
\rho((\bigcirc\psi, s), a) &= (\psi, \delta_\perp(s, a)),\\
\rho((\psi\,\mathcal{U}\,\psi', s), a) &= \rho((\psi', s), a) \vee \rho((\psi, s), a) \wedge (\psi\,\mathcal{U}\,\psi', \delta_\perp(s, a)),\\
\rho((\mathcal{H}_{H,O}\psi, s), a) &= \rho((\psi, s), a) \vee \mathsf{check}(O, a, \delta^*_M(s, a|_{\mathcal{V}_\mathcal{I}\setminus H})) \wedge\\
&\quad \textstyle\bigwedge_{(a', s') \in \delta^*_M(s, a|_{\mathcal{V}_\mathcal{I}\setminus H})} ((O, \psi, \forall, s'), \delta_\perp(s, a)),\\
\rho(((O, \psi, \forall, s'), s), a) &= \rho((\psi, s), a) \vee \mathsf{check}(O, a, \delta^*_M(s', a|_{\mathcal{V}_\mathcal{I}})) \wedge\\
&\quad \textstyle\bigwedge_{(a', s'') \in \delta^*_M(s', a|_{\mathcal{V}_\mathcal{I}})} ((O, \psi, \forall, s''), \delta_\perp(s, a)),\\
\rho(((O, \psi, \exists, s'), s), a) &= \overline{\rho(((O, \neg\psi, \forall, s'), s), a)}\\
&= \rho((\psi, s), a) \wedge \big(\overline{\mathsf{check}(O, a, \delta^*_M(s', a|_{\mathcal{V}_\mathcal{I}}))} \vee\\
&\quad \textstyle\bigvee_{(a', s'') \in \delta^*_M(s', a|_{\mathcal{V}_\mathcal{I}})} ((O, \psi, \exists, s''), \delta_\perp(s, a))\big).
\end{aligned}$$

where check is defined as $\mathsf{check}(O, a, A) = \big(\forall (a', s') \in A : a' =_O a\big)$. Note that this function can be evaluated during the construction of $\mathcal{A}_{M,\varphi}$ in time $|M|$.

Applied to a state of the form $(\mathcal{H}_{H,O}\psi, s)$, the transition function follows the semantics of $\mathcal{H}$, which involves universal branching w.r.t. the alternative paths that start at state s. For states of the form $((O, \psi, \forall, s'), s)$, the transition relation is again defined according to the semantics of $\mathcal{H}$, which in its temporal aspect is similar to the LTL *weak until* operator. Here the transition relation verifies ψ on the main path or branches universally according to the alternative paths starting from s'. The function check has a similar effect to that of evaluating a variable but it instead compares for O-equivalence.

States of the form $((O, \psi, \forall, s'), s)$ are accepting, as branches for alternative paths that are forever equivalent to the main path should be accepting.

Let $\pi \in \Sigma^\omega$ and let τ be a path in some run tree of $\mathcal{A}_{M,\varphi}$ on π. Let us consider a state $\tau[i] \in Q$ for some $i \geq 0$. The set Q of states of $\mathcal{A}_{M,\varphi}$ contains two types of states. If $\tau[i]$ is of the form $(\psi, s) \in cl(\varphi) \times S_\bot$ and $s \neq \bot$, then $s = \sigma[i]$, where $\sigma = \mathsf{Exec}_M(s_0, \pi)$. That is, s is a state on the execution of M on π starting from s_0 that corresponds to the prefix of π read so far. Similarly, if $\tau[i]$ is of the form $((O, \psi, m, s'), s) \in (2^{\mathcal{V}_O} \times cl(\varphi) \times \{\forall, \exists\} \times S) \times S_\bot$ and $s \neq \bot$, we have $s = \sigma[i]$. The state $s' \in S$ is a state on the execution $\mathsf{Exec}_M(\sigma[j], \pi')$, where $0 \leq j < i$ and $\pi' \in \mathsf{AltPaths}_M(\sigma[j], \pi[j,\infty), H)$ for some $H \subseteq \mathcal{V}_\mathcal{I}$. That is, the state s' is a state on the execution of M on some alternative path π' that branches off form π at some position prior to position i. We point out that:

Remark 1. For every $(\psi, s) \in Q$ where ψ is an LTL formula, it holds that $L_\omega(\mathcal{A}_{M,\varphi}, (\psi, s)) = L_\omega(\mathcal{A}_{M,\varphi}, (\psi, \bot))$. If the formula φ does not contain nested $\mathcal{H}$ operators, then for every $((O, \psi, m, s'), s)$ it holds that ψ is an LTL formula and, as a consequence of the above and the definition of ρ, we have that $L_\omega(\mathcal{A}_{M,\varphi}, ((O, \psi, m, s'), s)) = L_\omega(\mathcal{A}_{M,\varphi}, ((O, \psi, m, s'), \bot))$. □

Proposition 2. *[10] For every alternating Büchi word automaton $\mathcal{A}$ with n states there exists a nondeterministic Büchi word automaton $\mathcal{N}$ with $2^{\mathcal{O}(n)}$ states such that $L_\omega(\mathcal{N}) = L_\omega(\mathcal{A})$.*

Proof. Let $\mathcal{A} = (Q, q_0, \Sigma, \rho, F)$ be an alternating Büchi word automaton. We construct a nondeterministic Büchi word automaton $\mathcal{N} = (Q^{\mathsf{nd}}, q_0^{\mathsf{nd}}, \Sigma, \rho^{\mathsf{nd}}, F^{\mathsf{nd}})$ as follows: $Q^{\mathsf{nd}} = 2^Q \times 2^Q$, $q_0^{\mathsf{nd}} = (\{q_0\}, \emptyset)$, $F^{\mathsf{nd}} = \{(R, \emptyset) \mid R \subseteq Q\}$ and

$$\rho^{\mathsf{nd}}((R_1, R_2), a) = \begin{cases} \{(R_1', R_1' \setminus F) \mid R_1' \models \bigwedge_{q \in R_1} \rho(q, a)\} & \text{if } R_2 = \emptyset, \\ \{(R_1', R_2' \setminus F) \mid R_2' \subseteq R_1', R_1' \models \bigwedge_{q \in R_1} \rho(q, a), & \text{if } R_2 \neq \emptyset. \\ \qquad R_2' \models \bigwedge_{q \in R_2} \rho(q, a)\} & \end{cases}$$

Theorem 1. *For a transition system $M = (\mathcal{V}_\mathcal{I}, \mathcal{V}_\mathcal{O}, S, s_0, \delta)$ and a SecLTL formula φ we can check in time $\mathcal{O}(|M| \cdot 2^{\mathcal{O}(|\varphi| \cdot |S|^2)})$ or in space $\mathcal{O}((\log |M| + |\varphi| \cdot |S|^2)^2)$ whether $M \models \varphi$ holds.*

Proof. We can view M as a nondeterministic Büchi word automaton and construct the product $\mathcal{B}_{M,\neg\varphi}$ of M and the nondeterministic automaton $\mathcal{N}_{M,\neg\varphi}$ for the negation of φ. Then $M \models \varphi$ iff $L_\omega(\mathcal{B}_{M,\neg\varphi}) = \emptyset$ and the claim of the theorem follows from the fact that the nonemptiness problem for nondeterministic Büchi automata of size n is decidable in time $\mathcal{O}(n)$ or in space $\mathcal{O}(\log^2 n)$ [1]. □

3.3 Complexity of the Model Checking Problem for SecLTL

A *concurrent program* is a parallel composition of a number of components using the interleaving semantics and synchronizing over shared actions. We reduce the model checking problem for concurrent programs (as defined in [2]) to the SecLTL model checking problem for a monolithic transition system.

Theorem 2. *[2] Model Checking CTL and CTL* for concurrent programs is* PSPACE*-complete both in the size of the formula [2, Thm. 6.1] and in the size of the transition systems [2, Thm. 6.2].*

Theorems 6.1 and 6.2 in [2] make use of a single CTL formula: $EF(a_1 \vee \cdots \vee a_n)$, for some atomic propositions a_i and a number of processes n. As the negation of that property can be expressed in LTL ($\Box(\neg a_1 \wedge \cdots \wedge \neg a_n)$), we can immediately extend their result to LTL.

Lemma 1. *Model Checking LTL for concurrent programs is* PSPACE*-complete both in the size of the formula and in the size of the transition systems.*

Theorem 3. *The model checking problem for SecLTL is* PSPACE*-complete.*

Proof sketch. We reduce the LTL model checking problem for concurrent programs to model checking a SecLTL formula on a single transition system, which is the union of all individual programs together with a new initial state. For the initial state the transition function allows to select a program whose transition function is used subsequently. The program is then executed independently from the others. We give a SecLTL formula that ensures that the original specification is checked only on valid interleavings.

4 Restricted SecLTL

For some cases the nondeterministic automaton for a SecLTL formula does not have to track a set of executions on alternative paths, but it suffices to track one such execution. This raises hopes for more efficient fragments of SecLTL. In this section, we identify one such fragment, which we call *Restricted SecLTL*, that is characterized by a simple set of syntactic restrictions. We show that, indeed, the model checking problem for Restricted SecLTL has a lower computational complexity in terms of the size of the transition system.

Negation normal form (NNF). In order to elegantly state the restrictions, we introduce negation normal form for (not necessarily restricted) SecLTL formulas. As usual, the LTL operator $\mathcal{R}$ is the dual of $\mathcal{U}$, i.e., $\neg(\varphi\,\mathcal{U}\,\psi) \equiv \neg\varphi\,\mathcal{R}\,\neg\psi$. We define the SecLTL operator $\mathcal{L}$, the *leak* operator, as the dual of the SecLTL operator $\mathcal{H}$: For a given transition system $M = (\mathcal{V}_\mathcal{I}, \mathcal{V}_\mathcal{O}, S, s_0, \delta)$, infinite word $\pi \in \Sigma^\omega$, where $\Sigma = \mathsf{vals}(\mathcal{V}_\mathcal{I} \cup \mathcal{V}_\mathcal{O})$, and state $s \in S$, it holds that

$$M, s, \pi \models \mathcal{L}_{H,O}\varphi \text{ iff } M, s, \pi \models \neg(\mathcal{H}_{H,O}\neg\varphi).$$

For every SecLTL formula φ, we denote with $\mathsf{NNF}(\varphi)$ the NNF of φ. SecLTL formulas in NNF are defined according to the following grammar, where $v \in \mathcal{V}$, φ, ψ are SecLTL formulas in NNF, $H \subseteq \mathcal{V}_\mathcal{I}$ and $O \subseteq \mathcal{V}_\mathcal{O}$,

$$\begin{array}{rccccc} \varphi ::= & v & \mid \neg v & \mid \varphi \vee \psi & \mid \varphi \wedge \psi & \mid \bigcirc \varphi \\ & \varphi\,\mathcal{U}\,\psi & \mid \varphi\,\mathcal{R}\,\psi & \mid \mathcal{H}_{H,O}\,\varphi & \mid \mathcal{L}_{H,O}\,\varphi. & \end{array}$$

Restricted SecLTL. A *Restricted SecLTL formula* is a SecLTL formula φ in NNF that does not contain the operator$\mathcal{L}$, does not contain nested $\mathcal{H}$ operators, and:

($\mathcal{U}$) for every subformula $\varphi_1\,\mathcal{U}\,\varphi_2$ of φ, the formula φ_2 is an LTL formula,
($\mathcal{R}$) for every subformula $\varphi_1\,\mathcal{R}\,\varphi_2$ of φ, the formula φ_1 is an LTL formula.

Since we will build an alternating automaton for the negated formula, we also formulate the restrictions on the negated version for reference: For a Restricted SecLTL formula, the formula $\mathsf{NNF}(\neg\varphi)$ does not contain the operator $\mathcal{H}$, does not contain nested $\mathcal{L}$ operators, and satisfies the dual versions of ($\mathcal{U}$) and ($\mathcal{R}$):

($\mathcal{U}\neg$) for every subformula $\varphi_1 \,\mathcal{U}\, \varphi_2$ of $\mathsf{NNF}(\neg\varphi)$, φ_1 is an LTL formula,
($\mathcal{R}\neg$) for every subformula $\varphi_1 \,\mathcal{R}\, \varphi_2$ of $\mathsf{NNF}(\neg\varphi)$, φ_2 is an LTL formula.

Expressive power. The above restrictions do not have a significant effect on the expressive power. Examples 1 to 4 are still expressible in Restricted SecLTL. Thus, the main assets of SecLTL, that is the bounded secret generation and the use of hide operators in temporal contexts, are preserved.

Proposition 3. *The system complexity of the model checking problem for Restricted SecLTL is in* NLOGSPACE.

Proof. We adapt the construction from Proposition 1 to the special case of formulas of the form $\neg\varphi$ where φ is a Restricted SecLTL formula. As in the formula $\mathsf{NNF}(\neg\varphi)$ negation occurs only in front of variables, instead of $cl(\neg\varphi)$ we can use the set $sf(\mathsf{NNF}(\neg\varphi))$ that consists of all subformulas of $\mathsf{NNF}(\neg\varphi)$. Furthermore, since $\mathsf{NNF}(\neg\varphi)$ does not contain $\mathcal{H}$ operators, states of the form $((O,\psi,\forall,s'),s)$ are no longer needed. We define $Q = Q'_{\neg\varphi} \times S_\perp$, where $S_\perp = S\dot\cup\{\perp\}$ and

$$Q'_{\neg\varphi} = sf(\mathsf{NNF}(\neg\varphi)) \cup \{(O,\psi,\exists,s) \mid \exists H : \mathcal{L}_{H,O}\psi \in sf(\mathsf{NNF}(\neg\varphi))\}.$$

In the alternating Büchi word automaton $\mathcal{A}_{M,\neg\varphi} = (Q, q_0, \Sigma, \rho, F)$ the initial state is $q_0 = (\mathsf{NNF}(\neg\varphi), s_0)$ if φ is not an LTL formula and $q_0 = (\mathsf{NNF}(\neg\varphi), \perp)$ otherwise, and the set of accepting states is $F = \{(\psi \,\mathcal{R}\, \psi', s) \in Q\}$.

According to Remark 1 we can replace in the definition of the function ρ the function $\delta_\perp$ by the function $\delta'_\perp : sf(\mathsf{NNF}(\neg\varphi)) \times S_\perp \times \Sigma \to S_\perp$ where $\delta'_\perp(\psi,s,a) = \perp$ if ψ is an LTL formula and $\delta'_\perp(\psi,s,a) = \delta_\perp(s,a)$ otherwise.

As $\mathsf{NNF}(\neg\varphi)$ does not contain nested $\mathcal{L}$ operators we ensure by the definition of $\delta'_\perp$ that states of the form $((O,\psi,\exists,s'),s)$ where $s \neq \perp$ are not reachable.

The transition relation ρ is defined as follows:

$$\begin{aligned}
\rho((v,s),a) &= \mathsf{true} \text{ if } a|_v = 1 \text{ and } \mathsf{false} \text{ if } a|_v = 0,\\
\rho((\neg v,s),a) &= \mathsf{true} \text{ if } a|_v = 0 \text{ and } \mathsf{false} \text{ if } a|_v = 1,\\
\rho((\psi \vee \psi',s),a) &= \rho((\psi,s),a) \vee \rho((\psi',s),a),\\
\rho((\psi \wedge \psi',s),a) &= \rho((\psi,s),a) \wedge \rho((\psi',s),a),\\
\rho((\bigcirc\psi,s),a) &= (\psi, \delta'_\perp(\psi,s,a)),\\
\rho((\psi \,\mathcal{U}\, \psi',s),a) &= \rho((\psi',s),a) \vee \rho((\psi,s),a) \wedge (\psi \,\mathcal{U}\, \psi', \delta'_\perp(\psi \,\mathcal{U}\, \psi',s,a)),\\
\rho((\psi \mathcal{R} \psi',s),a) &= \rho((\psi',s),a) \wedge (\rho((\psi,s),a) \vee (\psi\mathcal{R}\psi', \delta'_\perp(\psi\mathcal{R}\psi',s,a))),\\
\rho((\mathcal{L}_{H,O}\psi,s),a) &= \rho((\psi,s),a) \wedge \big(\overline{\mathsf{check}(O,a,\delta^*_M(s,a|_{\mathcal{V}_\mathcal{I}\setminus H}))} \vee\\
&\quad \textstyle\bigvee_{(a',s')\in\delta^*_M(s,a|_{\mathcal{V}_\mathcal{I}\setminus H})} ((O,\psi,\exists,s'), \delta'_\perp(\psi,s,a))\big),\\
\rho(((O,\psi,\exists,s'),s),a) &= \rho((\psi,s),a) \wedge \big(\overline{\mathsf{check}(O,a,\delta^*_M(s',a|_{\mathcal{V}_\mathcal{I}}))} \vee\\
&\quad \textstyle\bigvee_{(a',s'')\in\delta^*_M(s',a|_{\mathcal{V}_\mathcal{I}})} ((O,\psi,\exists,s''), \delta'_\perp(\psi,s,a))\big).
\end{aligned}$$

We see already that the restrictions eliminated universal branching over successors. Disjunctive branching over successors does not lead to an exponential blow up in the size of the system during the construction of the nondeterministic Büchi automaton. In the following, we show that the number of executions that we have to track is bounded by the number of leak operators in the formula.

Let k be the number of leak operators in $\mathsf{NNF}(\neg\varphi)$. We construct a nondeterministic Büchi word automaton $\mathcal{N}'_{M,\neg\varphi} = (Q', q'_0, \Sigma, \rho', F')$ with $|Q'|$ in $\mathcal{O}(2^{\mathcal{O}(|\varphi|)} \cdot |S|^k)$ and such that $L_\omega(\mathcal{N}'_{M,\neg\varphi}) = L_\omega(\mathcal{N}_{M,\neg\varphi})$, where $\mathcal{N}_{M,\neg\varphi} = (Q^{\mathsf{nd}}, q_0^{\mathsf{nd}}, \Sigma, \rho^{\mathsf{nd}}, F^{\mathsf{nd}})$ is the nondeterministic Büchi automaton for $\mathcal{A}_{M,\neg\varphi}$ constructed using the construction from Proposition 2.

For a set $R \subseteq Q$, we denote with $\mathsf{ns}(R)$ the sum of the number of states in R of the form (ψ, s) with $s \neq \bot$ and the number of states in R of the form $((O, \psi, \exists, s'), s)$. We denote with $\mathsf{nl}(R)$ the sum of the number of occurrences of $\mathcal{L}$ in formulas in R and the number of states in R of the form $((O, \psi, \exists, s'), s)$. We define $Q' = \{(R_1, R_2) \in Q^{\mathsf{nd}} \mid \mathsf{ns}(R_1) \leq k, \mathsf{nl}(R_1) \leq k \text{ and } R_2 \subseteq R_1\}$.

Each state in $(R_1, R_2) \in Q'$ can be represented as a tuple $(A_1, A_2, \overline{s})$, where A_i is obtained from R_i by replacing each state of the form (ψ, s) where $s \neq \bot$ by $(\psi, ?)$ and each state of the form $((O, \psi, \exists, s'), s)$ by $(O, \psi, \exists, ?)$ and $\overline{s}$ is a vector of states in S of size k that assigns states to the ?-elements in A_1 and A_2 according to some fixed order on the formulas in $sf(\mathsf{NNF}(\neg\varphi))$. This is possible as the definition of Q' guarantees that A_1 contains at most k ?-elements and $A_2 \subseteq A_1$. Thus, the number of states of $\mathcal{N}'_{M,\neg\varphi}$ is in $\mathcal{O}(2^{\mathcal{O}(|\varphi|)} \cdot |S|^k)$.

The initial state of $\mathcal{N}'_{M,\neg\varphi}$ is $q'_0 = q_0^{\mathsf{nd}}$ and the accepting states and the transition relation are defined as in $\mathcal{N}_{M,\neg\varphi}$: $F' = \{(R_1, R_2) \in Q' \mid R_2 = \emptyset\}$ and

$$\rho'((R_1, R_2), a) = \begin{cases} \{(R'_1, R'_1 \setminus F) \in Q' \mid R'_1 \models \bigwedge_{q \in R_1} \rho(q, a)\} & \text{if } R_2 = \emptyset, \\ \{(R'_1, R'_2 \setminus F) \in Q' \mid R'_2 \subseteq R'_1, R'_1 \models \bigwedge_{q \in R_1} \rho(q, a), & \text{if } R_2 \neq \emptyset. \\ \qquad R'_2 \models \bigwedge_{q \in R_2} \rho(q, a)\} & \end{cases}$$

For every $(R_1, R_2) \in Q'$ and $a \in \Sigma$, $\rho'((R_1, R_2), a) \subseteq \rho^{\mathsf{nd}}((R_1, R_2), a)$. Therefore, since $q'_0 = q_0^{\mathsf{nd}}$, it holds that $L_\omega(\mathcal{N}'_{M,\neg\varphi}) \subseteq L_\omega(\mathcal{N}_{M,\neg\varphi})$.

For $R_1, R_2, S_1, S_2 \in 2^Q$, $(R_1, R_2) \subseteq (S_1, S_2)$ iff $R_1 \subseteq S_1$ and $R_2 \subseteq S_2$.

We now show that for every $(S_1, S_2) \in Q^{\mathsf{nd}}$, $(S'_1, S'_2) \in \rho^{\mathsf{nd}}((S_1, S_2), a)$ and $(R_1, R_2) \subseteq (S_1, S_2)$ there exists $(R'_1, R'_2) \in Q'$ such that $(R'_1, R'_2) \in \rho'((R_1, R_2), a)$ and $(R'_1, R'_2) \subseteq (S'_1, S'_2)$. To this end, we prove by induction on the structure of Restricted SecLTL formulas and the definition of ρ that for every $i \in \{1, 2\}$, $q \in R_i$ there exists a set $R'_{i,q} \subseteq S'_i$ such that $R'_{i,q} \models \rho(q, a)$ and $\mathsf{nl}(R'_{i,q}) \leq \mathsf{nl}(\{q\})$. If $q = (\psi, s)$ where ψ is an LTL formula, we can clearly choose $R'_{i,q}$ such that $\mathsf{nl}(R'_{i,q}) = 0$. For $q = (\mathcal{L}_{H,O}\psi, s)$ or $q = ((O, \psi, \exists, s'), s)$ we have $\mathsf{nl}(\{q\}) = 1$ and, since ψ is an LTL formula, we can choose $R'_{i,q}$ with $\mathsf{nl}(R'_{i,q}) = 1$. For the other cases the property follows from the induction hypothesis and the fact that if $q = (\psi \; \mathcal{U} \; \psi')$ then ψ is an LTL formula and if $q = (\psi \; \mathcal{R} \; \psi')$ then ψ' is an LTL formula. Thus, we can choose $(R'_1, R'_2) \in Q^{\mathsf{nd}}$ such that $(R'_1, R'_2) \in \rho^{\mathsf{nd}}((R_1, R_2), a)$, $(R'_1, R'_2) \subseteq (S'_1, S'_2)$ and $\mathsf{nl}(R'_i) \leq k$ and hence also $\mathsf{ns}(R'_i) \leq k$ for $i \in \{1, 2\}$. Thus, $(R'_1, R'_2) \in \rho'((R_1, R_2), a)$.

The property above implies that for every run τ of $\mathcal{N}_{M,\neg\varphi}$ on a word $\pi \in \Sigma^\omega$ there exists a run τ' of $\mathcal{N}'_{M,\neg\varphi}$ on π such that $\tau'[i] \subseteq \tau[i]$ for every $i \geq 0$. If τ is accepting, then τ' is also accepting. This implies that $L_\omega(\mathcal{N}_{M,\neg\varphi}) \subseteq L_\omega(\mathcal{N}'_{M,\neg\varphi})$, which concludes the proof that $L_\omega(\mathcal{N}_{M,\neg\varphi}) = L_\omega(\mathcal{N}'_{M,\neg\varphi})$. □

Theorem 4. *Model Checking Restricted SecLTL is* PSPACE*-complete, and its system complexity is* NLOGSPACE*-complete.*

Proof. PSPACE-completeness follows from the fact that the model checking problem for LTL is PSPACE-hard and that we already showed that model checking full SecLTL is in PSPACE. By Proposition 3, model checking SecLTL can be done in space NLOGSPACE in the size of the system. Since the system complexity of LTL model checking is NLOGSPACE-hard, the theorem follows. □

5 Extension to Branching Time

To demonstrate that the hide operator allows for smooth extension of other temporal logics, we integrate it in the well known branching time logics CTL and CTL*. While for *SecCTL** the complexity is straight-forward to determine, the result for the extension of CTL might be surprising: it is PSPACE-complete.

We define the logic SecCTL* as a standard *branching-time extension of SecLTL.* SecCTL* state formulas are defined as follows, where $v \in V$, φ and φ' are SecCTL* state formulas and ψ and ψ' are SecCTL* path formulas:

$$\varphi \ ::= \ v \mid \neg\varphi \mid \varphi \vee \varphi' \mid A\psi \mid E\psi.$$

SecCTL* path formulas, defined below, can contain the temporal operator $\mathcal{H}$:

$$\psi \ ::= \ \varphi \mid \neg\psi \mid \psi \vee \psi' \mid \bigcirc\psi \mid \psi\,\mathcal{U}\,\psi' \mid \mathcal{H}_{H,O}\,\psi.$$

The path-based definition provides a simple and unique semantics for the hide operator in SecCTL*.

Since SecCTL* is a standard branching-time extension of SecLTL, we can employ the dynamic programming approach used for CTL* but use a SecLTL model checker instead of an LTL model checker. Formulas are, as usual, evaluated in a bottom-up manner. For a formula ψ, we evaluate all maximal proper state subformulas of ψ and label the edges of the transition system accordingly with values for fresh output variables. Then replace each maximal proper state subformula in ψ by the corresponding fresh output variable and proceed. For formulas of the form $E\psi$ after the substitution in ψ we have that ψ is a SecLTL formula and thus, we can compute the set of states that satisfy $E\psi$ using a SecLTL model checker.

Thus, for a SecCTL* formula φ and a transition system $M = (\mathcal{V}_\mathcal{I}, \mathcal{V}_\mathcal{O}, S, s_0, \delta)$ we can check $M \models \varphi$ by using $\mathcal{O}(|S| \cdot |\varphi|)$ calls of a SecLTL model checker.

Theorem 5. *The model checking problem for SecCTL* is* PSPACE*-complete.*

Proof. Membership in $\mathsf{P}^{\mathsf{PSPACE}}$, that is, in PSPACE, is implied by the algorithm described above. PSPACE-hardness follows from Theorem 3. □

SecCTL. The subset SecCTL of SecCTL* is defined in the standard way by restricting the path formulas to be of the form $\bigcirc\varphi$, $\varphi\,\mathcal{U}\,\varphi'$ or $\mathcal{H}_{H,O}\,\varphi$, where φ and φ' are SecCTL *state* formulas.

Theorem 6. *The model checking problem for SecCTL is* PSPACE*-complete.*

Proof sketch. Similarly to the hardness proof for SecLTL, we provide a reduction from the CTL model checking problem for concurrent systems to model checking a SecCTL formula on a monolithic system of polynomial size.

6 Related Work

Recent works [9] provide a uniform framework for classification of properties that refer to multiple paths at once, called *hyperproperties.* These works, however, do not provide means to specify and verify hyperproperties. Such a formalism is, of course, not even possible for the set of hyperproperties in its full generality. Of particular interest is the class of k-safety hyperproperties which consists of those hyperproperties that can be refuted by considering at most k finite paths. The verification problem for such properties can be reduced to checking a safety property on a system obtained by k-fold *self-composition.* Huisman et al. [11] specify observational determinism in CTL* and in the polyadic modal μ-calculus interpreted over the 2-fold self-composition of the system.

SecLTL, in contrast, can express properties that go beyond k-safety hyperproperties; a counterexample for a SecLTL specification (e.g. for $\mathcal{L}_{H,O}$ true) might require an infinite number of paths, and are therefore out of the scope of self-composition based approaches.

A different approach to analyze information flow properties in combination with temporal properties, is that of *epistemic logics* [12,13,14]. Epistemic logics introduce *knowledge operators* to temporal logics and allow for properties that refer to the knowledge of an agent at a certain point in the system run—thus they are able to express information flow properties like non-interference [15,16].

The fundamental difference between epistemic logics and SecLTL is, that a knowledge operator expresses the knowledge of an agent, whereas the hide operator specifies the secret. This allows us to argue in a forward-manner, starting at the point at which the secret is introduced.

Alur et al. [17] extended CTL and μ-calculus by two modal operators, the first of which, similarly to the knowledge operator in epistemic logics, allows for quantifying over a set of equivalent states, and the second allows for referring to non-equivalent states. The formulas in the resulting logics are interpreted over computation trees augmented with edges representing observational equivalences between path prefixes. The main advantage of SecLTL over these logics is the path-based integration of observational determinism into the temporal context that results into more intuitive specifications while still being able to express many information flow properties of interest. Furthermore, we identified an expressive fragment of our logic for which the model checking problem has lower complexity in terms of the system's size than the logics proposed in [17].

7 Conclusion

We proposed a new modal operator that allows for natural path-based integration of information flow properties in temporal logics. The rich set of examples we considered demonstrates that the resulting linear time logic is expressive enough to precisely specify many interesting information flow and secrecy properties. The operator allows for simple characterizations of sufficiently expressive fragments with better computational complexity, like Restricted SecLTL, and seamless integration into branching time logics like the presented SecCTL and SecCTL*. Future work includes identifying fragments of the branching time logics with reduced complexity and extensions to the alternating-time setting.

References

1. Vardi, M.Y., Wolper, P.: Reasoning about infinite computations. Inf. Comput. 115, 1–37 (1994)
2. Kupferman, O., Vardi, M.Y., Wolper, P.: An automata-theoretic approach to branching-time model checking. J. ACM 47, 312–360 (2000)
3. Vardi, M.Y.: Alternating Automata and Program Verification. In: van Leeuwen, J. (ed.) Computer Science Today. LNCS, vol. 1000, pp. 471–485. Springer, Heidelberg (1995)
4. Goguen, J.A., Meseguer, J.: Security policies and security models. In: IEEE Symposium on Security and Privacy, pp. 11–20 (1982)
5. Zdancewic, S., Myers, A.C.: Observational determinism for concurrent program security. In: Proc. 16th IEEE Computer Security Foundations Workshop (2003)
6. Broberg, N., Sands, D.: Paralocks – role-based information flow control and beyond. In: Proc. of POPL 2010 (2010)
7. Askarov, A., Myers, A.: A Semantic Framework for Declassification and Endorsement. In: Gordon, A.D. (ed.) ESOP 2010. LNCS, vol. 6012, pp. 64–84. Springer, Heidelberg (2010)
8. Alur, R., Černý, P., Zdancewic, S.: Preserving Secrecy Under Refinement. In: Bugliesi, M., Preneel, B., Sassone, V., Wegener, I. (eds.) ICALP 2006. LNCS, vol. 4052, pp. 107–118. Springer, Heidelberg (2006)
9. Clarkson, M.R., Schneider, F.B.: Hyperproperties. Journal of Computer Security 18, 1157–1210 (2010)
10. Miyano, S., Hayashi, T.: Alternating finite automata on omega-words. Theor. Comput. Sci. 32, 321–330 (1984)
11. Huisman, M., Worah, P., Sunesen, K.: A temporal logic characterisation of observational determinism. In: CSFW, p. 3. IEEE Computer Society (2006)
12. Fagin, R., Halpern, J.Y., Moses, Y., Vardi, M.Y.: Reasoning About Knowledge. MIT Press (1995)
13. van der Meyden, R., Shilov, N.V.: Model Checking Knowledge and Time in Systems with Perfect Recall. In: Pandu Rangan, C., Raman, V., Sarukkai, S. (eds.) FST TCS 1999. LNCS, vol. 1738, pp. 432–445. Springer, Heidelberg (1999)
14. Shilov, N.V., Garanina, N.O.: Model checking knowledge and fixpoints. In: FICS, pp. 25–39 (2002)

15. Engelhardt, K., Gammie, P., van der Meyden, R.: Model Checking Knowledge and Linear Time: PSPACE Cases. In: Artemov, S., Nerode, A. (eds.) LFCS 2007. LNCS, vol. 4514, pp. 195–211. Springer, Heidelberg (2007)
16. Balliu, M., Dam, M., Guernic, G.L.: Epistemic temporal logic for information flow security. In: Proc. PLAS 2011 (2011)
17. Alur, R., Černý, P., Chaudhuri, S.: Model Checking on Trees with Path Equivalences. In: Grumberg, O., Huth, M. (eds.) TACAS 2007. LNCS, vol. 4424, pp. 664–678. Springer, Heidelberg (2007)

Splitting via Interpolants*

Evren Ermis, Jochen Hoenicke, and Andreas Podelski

University of Freiburg
{ermis,hoenicke,podelski}@informatik.uni-freiburg.de

Abstract. A common problem in software model checking is the automatic computation of accurate loop invariants. Loop invariants can be derived from interpolants for every path leading through the corresponding loop header. However, in practice, the consideration of single paths often leads to very path specific interpolants. Inductive invariants can only be derived after several iterations by also taking previous interpolants into account.

In this paper, we introduce a software model checking approach that uses the concept of *path insensitive* interpolation to compute loop invariants. In contrast to current approaches, path insensitive interpolation summarizes *several* paths through a program location instead of one. As a consequence, it takes the abstraction refinement considerably less effort to obtain an adequate interpolant. First experiments show the potential of our approach.

1 Introduction

In software model checking, abstraction refinement is used to prove properties of a system on an abstract model without actually expanding this model to the state level. The challenge when refining is to modify the abstract model in a way that the desired property can be shown before the model becomes prohibitively large. This can be achieved by extending the model with computed invariants. The use of Craig interpolants is one promising approach for this purpose [15]. However, interpolation on single paths computes path specific interpolants. In order to find an accurate invariant the desired interpolant must be inductive. Current interpolation-based approaches find an interpolant for each infeasible error path separately. These interpolants can be combined into a single inductive invariant for all paths.

We introduce the concept of *path insensitive interpolation* as a technique to derive inductive interpolants more directly. The idea is to put more information into the interpolation process by considering several paths through the observed location. Thus, we are more likely to obtain an inductive invariant for this location. We present a novel software model checking approach that combines *path insensitive interpolation* with splitting as abstraction refinement.

Splitting separates the states along an infeasible path to those reachable from the initial location and those leading to the erroneous location. The refined model

* UNU-IIST, Macau, Technical Report 449, June 2011.

V. Kuncak and A. Rybalchenko (Eds.): VMCAI 2012, LNCS 7148, pp. 186–201, 2012.

can contain several nodes representing the same location of the original program. Each node carries an invariant that characterizes a set of states. Using splitting as refinement step has the benefit, that the loop invariant does not have to be derived as a single inductive interpolant. It can be constructed as a union of all interpolants. The main task is to find useful interpolants.

Path insensitive interpolation returns an interpolant for a location ℓ considering several paths through ℓ. If in the extreme case all possible paths through ℓ are considered, the interpolant is guaranteed to be the right inductive invariant for ℓ. If loops are present this is not possible, but one can still merge loop-free paths through ℓ to get an interpolant that holds for all the considered paths. This interpolant will be an inductive invariant for this location ℓ for the loop-free subprogram considered. In a first approach our algorithm collapses non-looping subprograms into single transitions using *large-block encoding* (LBE) [4]. In the resulting graph, each path corresponds to a set of original program paths. On this compressed model we can compute path interpolants [16]. Thus, we can derive interpolants from the refutation of sets of paths rather than single paths. This approach allows to compute interpolants that are path insensitive modulo the loop iterations of the program. E.g. programs with multiple outer loops cannot be compressed by LBE to achieve path insensitive interpolation but our results show that *partial path insensitivity* still works efficiently. It helps to reduce the number of splits needed to an extent that our algorithm can efficiently handle programs of a realistic size.

In the following, we illustrate our model checking approach using an example in Section 2. In Section 3 we introduce the basic definitions for technical Section 4. In Section 4 we present our interpolation-based model checking approach. An experimental evaluation of the approach is given in Section 5.

2 Example

We will illustrate the approach by applying it to program `main` (Fig. 1). The program has non-deterministic branches. The sum of x, y, and z is equal to the initial value n in each iteration of the loop. Consequently, the assertion $n = y + z$ holds when the loop exits with $x = 0$. The program has the corresponding program graph $\mathcal{P}$ (Fig. 2).

Our approach uses splitting as refinement step. The path interpolants [16] derived from infeasible error paths are used as splitting criteria. An error path is encoded as a FOL formula and passed to the interpolating SMT solver. Our approach compresses paths in the model by applying large block encoding (LBE). LBE compresses loop-free subgraphs to single edges. Hence, checking one path in the compressed model covers multiple paths in the original program graph. The effect is that the obtained interpolants are at least partially path insensitive. LBE iteratively (1) compresses *sequential nodes* to single edges by using conjunctions and (2) merges *multiple edges* by using disjunctions. Via the introduced disjunctions the decision of the branching is shifted to the interpolating SMT solver. The edges of the compressed model represent contiguous loop-free code segments.

```
1  procedure main() {
2          var x,y,z,n: int;
3          assume(n == x && y == 0 && z == 0);
4          while(x != 0) {
5                  if (*) {
6                          x := x + 1;
7                          y := y - 1;
8                  }
9                  if (*) {
10                         y := y + 1;
11                         z := z - 1;
12                 }
13                 if (*) {
14                         x := x - 1;
15                         z := z + 1;
16                 }
17         }
18         assert(n == y + z);
19 }
```

Fig. 1. Code of program `main`. Non-deterministically increments one variable whilst decrementing a second variable. The program is safe if the assertion (Line 18) holds on every execution.

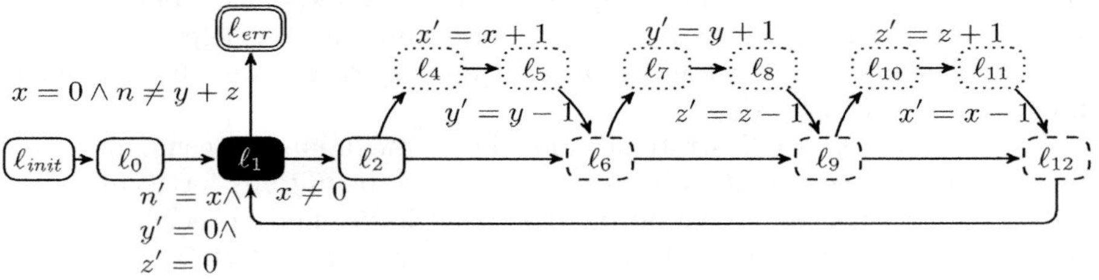

Fig. 2. Program graph P of `main` (Fig. 1). Edges without labeling carry the formula $\top$. ℓ_{err}'s guard is the negated assertion (Fig. 1, Line 18). ℓ_1 represents the loop head (Fig. 1, Line 4). ℓ_6, ℓ_9 and ℓ_{12} are nodes that will have entering multiple edges because of the preceding branches.

Sequential nodes. ℓ_i and ℓ_{i+1} are compressed, if ℓ_i is the only predecessor of ℓ_{i+1} and they're connected by a single transition (Dotted nodes (Fig. 2)). E. g., $x' = x + 1 \wedge y' = y - 1$ encodes the `then`-branch of the conditional branching in line 5 (Fig. 1). If a variable is changed in both transition, we introduce new auxiliary variable (e. g., y'') for the intermediate value. An alternative would be to use single static assignment (SSA).

Multiple edges. occur if the original program has conditional branchings. The branchings are merged by joining the formulas with a disjunction. If the branches disagree on the changed variable they have to be adapted to each other by inserting frame conditions, e. g., the first `else`-branch from ℓ_2 to ℓ_6 is changed to $x' = x \wedge y' = y$. In our example (Fig. 3) the disjunctions encode the three conditional branchings at Line 5, 9, and 13 (Fig. 1). LBE provides a partially

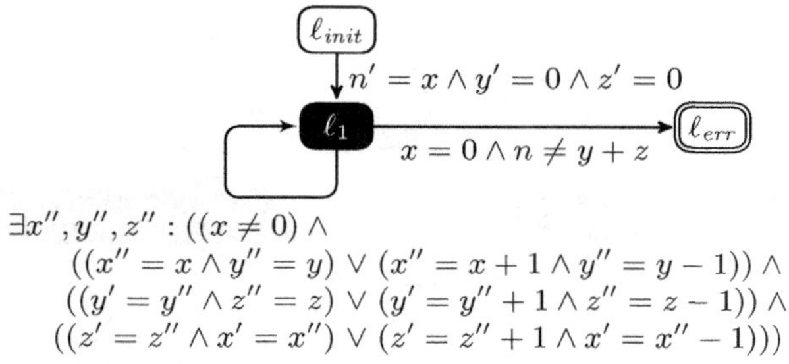

Fig. 3. The resulting model after compressing P (Fig. 2). The entire body of the loop is encoded in a single edge. Only the loop header (Fig. 1, Line 4) cannot be reduced any further.

path insensitive observation of locations and their interpolants. In Figure 3 the shortest error path through ℓ_1 has the corresponding FOL formula

$$\begin{array}{ll}
\ell_{init} \rightarrow \ell_1 & \exists x, y''', z''', n' : ((n' = x \wedge y''' = 0 \wedge z''' = 0) \wedge \\
\ell_1 \rightarrow \ell_1 & \left(\begin{array}{l} \exists x'', y'', z'' : ((x \neq 0) \wedge \\ \quad ((x'' = x \wedge y'' = y''') \vee (x'' = x + 1 \wedge y'' = y''' - 1)) \wedge \\ \quad ((y' = y'' \wedge z'' = z''') \vee (y' = y'' + 1 \wedge z'' = z''' - 1)) \wedge \\ \quad ((z' = z'' \wedge x' = x'') \vee (z' = z'' + 1 \wedge x' = x'' - 1))) \end{array} \right) \wedge \\
\ell_1 \rightarrow \ell_{err} & (x' = 0 \wedge n' \neq y' + z'))
\end{array}$$

The solver returns either a configuration that proves the feasibility of the error path or an array of interpolants [16]. Each interpolant corresponds to a location but is not bound to a single execution path. It rather summarizes a set of execution paths through this location. This way we get partial path insensitivity. It is partial because it summarizes all paths through ℓ_1 modulo the loop iterations. If the path is feasible, the program is unsafe. If it is not feasible, the interpolants are used to split the path (Fig. 4). The returned interpolant I_i (e.g. $(n = x) \wedge (y = 0) \wedge (z = 0)$, Fig. 4) is appended to the corresponding node $\ell_{i+1}(\ell_1$, Fig. 4). Its negation is appended to the split node ℓ'_{i+1}. ℓ'_{i+1} inherits all incoming and outgoing edges of ℓ_{i+1}. Infeasible edges of ℓ_{i+1} and ℓ'_{i+1} are removed from the model (dotted edges, Fig. 4).

In the next iteration we take the error path $\ell_{init}, \ell_1, \ell_1^1, \ell_{err}$. The edge from ℓ_1 to ℓ_1^1 is annotated with the disjunction from the edge ℓ_1 to ℓ_1 in the previous graph. Due to this disjunction the interpolant generator has to find an interpolant that works for all branches through the if statements. This will most probably result in the interpolant $n = x + y + z$, which is then used to split ℓ_1^1 (Fig. 5). Node ℓ_1 is not split, since its interpolants is **true**. The subsequent feasibility check of the edges renders the subgraph, consisting of ℓ_1^2 and ℓ_{err}, unreachable from ℓ_{init}. Hence after removing the infeasible edges, our model does not contain any error paths. The algorithm stops and has proven the safety of the program `main` by deriving the loop invariant.

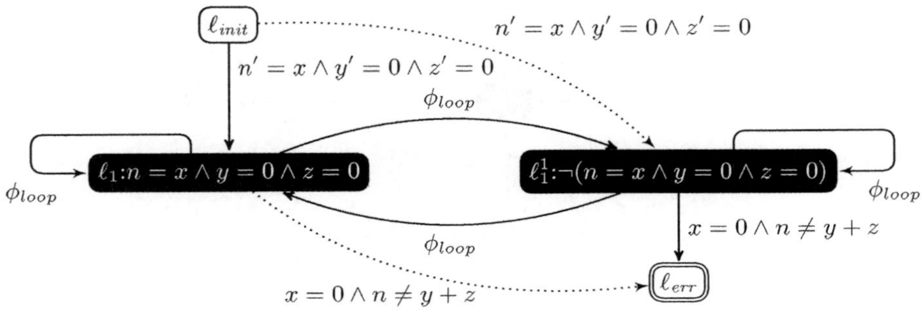

Fig. 4. Model after splitting the error path. The control flow is partitioned by appending the interpolant $n = x \wedge y = 0 \wedge z = 0$ to ℓ_1 and its negation to ℓ_1^1. The label ϕ_{loop} denotes the formula on the loop edge of Figure 3. Dotted edges are infeasible and will be removed.

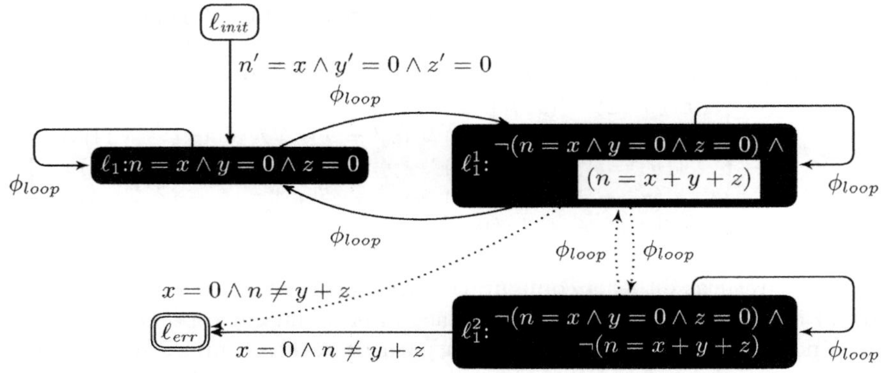

Fig. 5. Final model that proves the safety of program `main`. The highlighted interpolant is a loop invariant. The edges leading to subgraph (ℓ_1^2, ℓ_{err}) are infeasible.

3 Preliminaries

A program is represented by a *program graph* $\mathcal{P} := (Loc, \ell_{init}, \ell_{err}, \delta)$ where Loc is a finite set of control locations, $\ell_{init} \in Loc$ is the initial location, $\ell_{err} \in Loc$ is the error location. The relation δ describes how control passes from one location to another and forms a directed graph. An edge $(\ell, \varphi, \ell') \in \delta$ is labeled with a *transition formula* φ. A transition formula is a formula over unprimed and primed program variables V and V' (see e.g., [15]). We think of a transition formula as representing a set of pairs of states (s, s'), s.t. $(s, s') \models \varphi$. For brevity of exposure, we assume that transition formulas are formulas over *all* unprimed and primed program variables. This assumption is lifted in practice by introducing a frame condition like $x = x'$ only when necessary, i. e., when computing the disjunction with a formula that changes x. A path in a program graph $\mathcal{P}$ from a location ℓ_0 to a location ℓ_{n+1} is an alternating sequence of locations and transition formulas $\pi = \ell_0\varphi_0\ell_1\varphi_1 \ldots \ell_n\varphi_n\ell_{n+1}$ where $(\ell_i, \varphi_i, \ell_{i+1}) \in \delta$ for $0 \leq i \leq n$. A path from the initial location ℓ_{init} to the error location ℓ_{err} is called *error path*. We extend the concept of transition formulas from edges to paths as follows: given a path $\pi = \ell_1\varphi_1\ell_2\varphi_2\ell_3$, where both φ_1 and φ_2 are formulas over the unprimed and primed variables $V = \{v_0, \ldots, v_n\}$ and $V' = \{v'_0, \ldots, v'_n\}$. The path formula $\varphi(\pi)$ is the *sequential composition* $\varphi_1 \circ \varphi_2$, such that

$$\exists v''_1, \ldots, v''_n : \varphi_1[v''_0/v'_0 \ldots v''_n/v'_n] \wedge \varphi_2[v''_0/v_0 \ldots v''_n/v_n]$$

and $\varphi(\pi)$ is a formula over the unprimed and primed program variables.

Infeasibility and Interpolants. An error path in the program graph must not necessarily correspond to a real error. There may be no valuations for the program variables for which the transition formula is satisfied. We call paths that have an unsatisfiable transition formula infeasible.

Definition 1. *A path $\pi = \ell_0\varphi_0\ell_1 \ldots \ell_n\varphi_n\ell_{n+1}$ in a program $\mathcal{P}$ is* infeasible *if and only if its path formula $\varphi(\pi) := \varphi_0 \circ \ldots \circ \varphi_n$ is unsatisfiable.*

That is, the path π is infeasible if, for any valuation of the unprimed variables V, there is no valuation of V', s.t. $\varphi(\pi)$ is satisfied. In particular, a location is unreachable if any path from ℓ_{init} to this location is infeasible. The program graph is safe if the error location ℓ_{err} is unreachable:

Definition 2. *A program graph $\mathcal{P}$ is* safe *if and only if every error path is infeasible.*

For an infeasible error path we can compute Craig interpolants that separate the states reachable from the initial location from the states that can reach the error location on this path. We compute one interpolant for every location on the error path, using the following definition of interpolants for a path formula.

Definition 3. *Given an unsatisfiable formula $\varphi_0 \circ \cdots \circ \varphi_n$ where φ_i is a transition formula over V and V', the sequence $I_1, \ldots, I_n$ of formulas over V is an* inductive sequence of interpolants *if the formulas*

$$\varphi_0 \circ \neg I_1, \qquad I_i \wedge \varphi_i \circ \neg I_{i+1} \text{ for } 1 \leq i < n, \qquad I_n \wedge \varphi_n$$

are all unsatisfiable.

The I_i can be computed step by step as the Craig interpolant of the formulas $(\exists v_1 \ldots v_n. I_{i-1} \wedge \varphi_{i-1})[v_1/v'_1 \ldots v_n/v'_n]$ and $\varphi_i \circ \cdots \circ \varphi_n$ (using $I_0 = true$). Note that the formulas contain only existential quantifiers provided that φ_i is quantifier free. Hence, the quantifiers can be removed by skolemization and we can use interpolation algorithms for quantifier-free logics.

4 Splitting via Path Insensitive Interpolants

4.1 Underlying Splitting Algorithm

Our model checking algorithm given by Algorithm 1 takes a program graph $\mathcal{P}$ as input and returns *safe*, if no error location can be reached, *unsafe*, if a feasible error path is found.

Our algorithm is based on abstraction refinement. An abstract state of the program is a tuple (ℓ, Inv) where ℓ is a program location and Inv a formula over the program variables. It represents the concrete states of the program where the program counter is in location ℓ and program variables fulfill the formula Inv. The initial abstraction is given by the program graph where each node is additionally labeled with the invariant **true** represents the initial abstraction. I. e., all program states that have the same location are combined into one abstract state. A refinement step splits an abstract state by a formula into those states that satisfy the formula and those that do not. The formulas are interpolants computed from an infeasible error path. After each split, there is a slicing step that removes all edges from the program graph that are no longer feasible.

Due to the splitting step, we will have several abstract states (we call them nodes) representing the same location, each associated with a different formula (invariant). In the abstract transition system, a path is feasible if there is a sequence of program variable valuations that satisfies the transition constraints and the invariants labeled to each state. Thus the path formula for a path $\pi = (\ell_0, Inv_0)\varphi_0(\ell_1, Inv_1)\ldots\varphi_n(\ell_{n+1}, Inv_{n+1})$ is augmented by the node invariants:

$$\varphi(\pi) := Inv_0 \wedge \varphi_0 \circ Inv_1 \wedge \varphi_1 \circ \ldots \circ \varphi_n \circ Inv_{n+1} .$$

We define correctness for a abstract transition systems exactly as for program graphs, i. e., the labeled program graph is safe if for all error paths π the path formula $\varphi(\pi)$ is unsatisfiable. It is obvious that the program graph is safe if and only if the initial abstract transition system is safe where each location ℓ is replaced with the node $(\ell, \mathbf{true})$.

The outer loop of the algorithm repeatedly checks if there exists an error path π in $\mathcal{P}$. If not, the algorithm terminates and returns that $\mathcal{P}$ is safe. Otherwise we check whether π is feasible using the procedure `satisfiable`. This procedure checks the satisfiability of the path formula $\varphi(\pi)$. The procedure is implemented by an interpolating theorem prover. If the prover determines that the formula is satisfiable, i. e., the error path π is feasible, our algorithm returns *unsafe* because π is a counterexample that witnesses the reachability of the error location in $\mathcal{P}$. Otherwise the error path is infeasible and our algorithm computes a sequence of interpolants $I_1, \ldots, I_n$ for π using the procedure `Interpolants` (e.g.,[16]). The procedure `Interpolants` returns one interpolant for each location ℓ_i on the path π. We use $I_1, \ldots, I_n$ to *split* the nodes into states that cannot reach the error location following the path π and states that cannot be reached from the initial location on π. The next step is called *slicing* and removes all edges $((\ell, Inv), \varphi, (\ell', Inv'))$ that are not feasible *in every path* π because their transition constraint φ is incompatible with Inv and Inv'.

Algorithm 1. Model checker algorithm

Data: $\mathcal{P} = (Loc, \ell_{init}, \ell_{err}, \delta)$;
Map Inv from Loc to formulas;
Result: *Safe*, *Unsafe*, or *Unknown*.

1 **begin**
2   **foreach** ℓ_i *in* $\mathcal{P}$ **do**
3   `Replace` ℓ_i `with` $(\ell_i, \mathbf{true})$
4   **while** *exists an error path* π *in* $\mathcal{P}$ **do**
5   **switch** `satisfiable`$(\varphi(\pi))$ **do**
6   **case** *sat:* **return** *unsafe*;
7   **case** *unsat:*
8         $I_1, \ldots, I_n :=$ `Interpolants`(π);
9   **foreach** (ℓ_i, Inv_i) *in* π **do**
10   `Split` (ℓ_i, Inv_i) `into` $(\ell_i, Inv_i \wedge I_i), (\ell_i, Inv_i \wedge \neg I_i)$;
11   `Slice` $(\mathcal{P})$;
12   **otherwise return** *unknown*;
13   **return** *safe*;

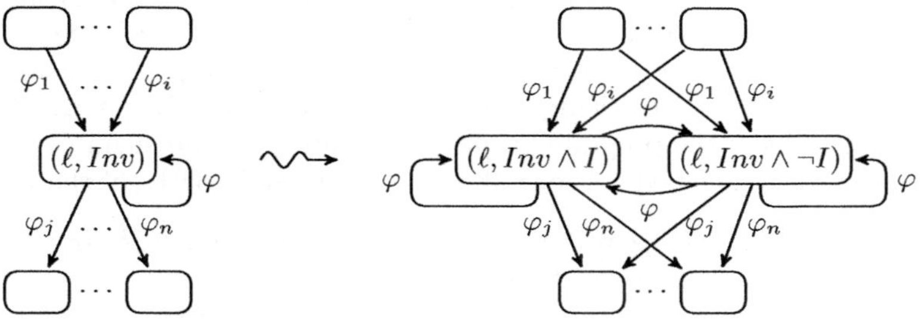

Fig. 6. Splitting the node ℓ on the formula I in a labeled program graph. The node and its incoming and outgoing edges are duplicated and one copy of the node is labeled with I and the other with $\neg I$.

Splitting. The function `Split` in line 10 duplicates the node (ℓ, Inv) and augments the labeling of one copy with I and the labeling of the other copy with $\neg I$, see Fig. 6. When the node is duplicated, all incoming and all outgoing edges are duplicated as well. For the loop edge that is both incoming and outgoing we create four new edges.

Lemma 1. *Splitting a location does not change the set of feasible paths (except for annotating a different invariant). The resulting abstract transition system is correct if and only if the input system is correct and it has the same feasible error paths.*

Proof. The second statement is a direct consequence of the first statement. To prove the first statement, consider a feasible path of the original program graph visiting location ℓ once:

$$\pi = (\ell_0, Inv_0)\varphi_0(\ell_1, Inv_1)\dots(\ell, Inv)\dots\varphi_n(\ell_{n+1}, Inv_{n+1}).$$

Since π is feasible its path formula

$$\pi(\phi) = Inv_0 \wedge \varphi_0 \circ \dots Inv \wedge \phi_i \circ \dots \varphi_n \circ Inv_{n+1}$$

is satisfiable. By definition of $\circ$, there exists a valuation of variables for location ℓ satisfying Inv. Obviously this valuation must satisfy either I or $\neg I$. Hence either $F = I$ or $F = \neg I$ is satisfied and the path

$$\pi = (\ell_0, Inv_0)\varphi_0(\ell_1, Inv_1)\dots(\ell, Inv \wedge F)\dots\varphi_n(\ell_{n+1}, Inv_{n+1})$$

is feasible (with the same valuation). The argument can be inductively extended to paths visiting the location more than once (each time a different $(\ell, Inv \wedge F)$ may be visited). □

Slicing. In the slicing step the labeled program graph is simplified by removing infeasible edges. An edge $((\ell, Inv), \varphi, (\ell', Inv'))$ is infeasible if the formula $Inv \wedge \varphi \circ Inv'$ is unsatisfiable. Since this formula is a part of every path formula containing the edge, every path containing an infeasible edge is infeasible. Thus, removing the edge does not change the set of feasible paths. Removing edges may render subgraphs of the program graph unreachable. All unreachable edges and locations are also removed without affecting the feasible paths of the program.

Lemma 2. *The slicing operation preserves all feasible error paths in the abstract transition system and its correctness.*

Proof. As sketched above, slicing does not change the feasible paths and hence the feasible error paths.

Soundness and Progress. Using the above lemmas, we can immediately prove soundness of our algorithm:

Theorem 1 (Soundness). *The application of splitting and slicing on a program graph $\mathcal{P}$ as performed by Algorithm 1 preserves all feasible error paths in $\mathcal{P}$. Hence, if the algorithm returns safe the original program graph has no feasible error path and if the algorithm returns unsafe the feasible error path found by the algorithm is also present in the original program graph.*

Proof. By Lemma 1 and Lemma 2.

Provided that the transition formulas φ in the program graph are from a decidable theory and that the interpolants are given in the same theory, the SMT solver will always terminate and return either *sat* or *unsat*. There are several decidable theories for which interpolation is possible, e. g., quantifier free formulas over linear arithmetic and uninterpreted functions. For the theory of arrays there exist decidable fragments, e. g., [7]. Recently there has also been work on a decidable fragment closed under interpolation [9].

If we use a decidable and interpolating theory, our algorithm will never terminate with *unknown*. Since the software model checking problem is undecidable (even for simple integer programs using only linear arithmetic), it is clear that our algorithm does not always terminate. However, we can show a progress property:

Theorem 2 (Progress). *In each loop iteration our algorithm will exclude one infeasible error path from the program.*

Proof. Let $I_1, \ldots, I_n$ be the interpolants for the infeasible error path

$$\pi = (\ell_{init}, Inv_{init})\varphi_0(\ell_1, Inv_1)\ldots\varphi_n(\ell_{err}, Inv_{err}).$$

By the definition of interpolants we know that the formulas

$$Inv_{init} \wedge \varphi_0 \circ \neg I_1, \;\; I_i \wedge Inv_i \wedge \varphi_i \circ \neg I_{i+1}, \;\; I_n \wedge Inv_n \wedge \varphi_n \circ Inv_{err}$$

are unsatisfiable. After splitting, the edge φ_0 from $(\ell_{init}, Inv_{init})$ to $(\ell_1, Inv_1 \wedge \neg I_1)$, the edges φ_i from $(\ell_i, Inv_i \wedge I_i)$ to $(\ell_{i+1}, Inv_{i+1} \wedge \neg I_{i+1})$ $(1 \leq i < n)$, and the edge φ_n from $(\ell_n Inv_n \wedge I_n)$ to (ℓ_{err}, Inv_{err}) are infeasible and thus removed in the slicing step. Thus after slicing, the nodes $(\ell_i, Inv_i \wedge \neg I_i)$ and (ℓ_{err}, Inv_{err}) are not reachable *on the path* π. This shows that error path π is not present in the resulting program graph any more. □

4.2 Path Insensitive Interpolation

In this section, we will present a first approach to apply path insensitive interpolation. Path insensitive interpolation finds an interpolant I for a location ℓ that holds for any infeasible error path $\pi = (\ell_{init}, Inv_{init})\ldots(\ell, Inv)\ldots(\ell_{err}, Inv_{err})$. Therefore the interpolant I is not just a summary in the context of a single path but *insensitively* of any path.

Definition 4. *Given a program graph* $\mathcal{P} = (Loc, \ell_{init}, \ell_{err}, \delta)$. *For any location* $\ell \in Loc \setminus \{\ell_{init}, \ell_{err},\}$, *there exists a set* Π_ℓ *of all error paths*

$$\pi_i = (\ell_{init}, Inv_{init})\ldots(\ell^i_{n-1}, Inv^i_{n-1}), (\ell, Inv), (\ell^i_{n+1}, Inv^i_{n+1})\ldots(\ell_{err}, Inv_{err}).$$

If there exists an interpolant I, *s.t.*

$$\varphi((\ell_{init}, Inv_{init})\ldots(\ell^i_{n-1}, Inv^i_{n-1})) \Rightarrow I$$

holds and

$$\varphi((\ell^i_{n+1}, Inv^i_{n+1})\ldots(\ell_{err}, Inv_{err})) \wedge I$$

is unsatisfiable for every $\pi_i \in \Pi_\ell$ *then* I *is a path insensitive interpolant of* ℓ *in* $\mathcal{P}$.

To enforce path insensitive interpolants we use a method to simplify the program graph without changing its correctness and without loosing information about its structure. We will first sketch the method for loop free program graphs and then generalize it. Given a program graph without loops, there are only finitely many error paths whose infeasibility can be checked by a theorem prover call for every path. However, the number of paths may be exponential in the number of program transitions. A better way to check correctness is to encode the branching structure in the formula by using disjunction. Given a location ℓ with outgoing edges $((\ell, Inv), \varphi_1, (\ell_1, Inv_1)), \dots, ((\ell, Inv), \varphi_n, (\ell_n, Inv_n))$ we can define its error transition formula describing all paths from ℓ to ℓ_{err} by

$$err \leftrightarrow (\varphi_1 \circ err_1) \vee \dots \vee (\varphi_n \circ err_n).$$

The symbols err_i for the other locations are similarly defined. This is only well defined for loop-free code; otherwise the definition would be cyclic. We can then check the satisfiability of err_{init} in conjunction using the above definition (the symbols err_i are boolean variables). This trick will move the burden of enumerating the error paths to the theorem prover. Moreover, the theorem prover can use its advanced techniques to avoid the exponential blow-up. Modern static checkers are based on this method [3]. For program graphs containing loops, one cannot encode the disjunction of the path formulas of all error path by a single (quantifier-free) transition formula. However, at least the loop-free fragments of the program graph can be transformed into a single transition formula. One way to achieve this is by large-block encoding [4]. The resulting program graph is much smaller and contains basically one location for every loop-header. But LBE does not give us the desired full path insensitivity. It is rather a *partial path insensitivity.* Partial path insensitivity does not consider all execution

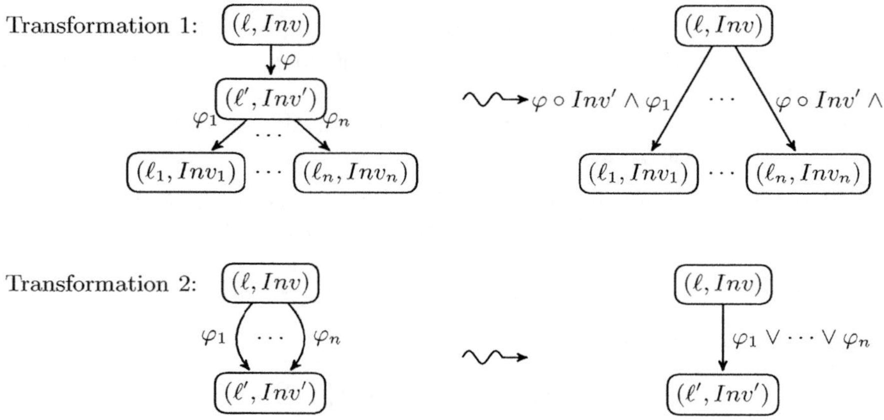

Fig. 7. The reduction rules for simplifying the program graph. Our implementation of large-block encoding follows closely [4]. Transformation 1 uses sequential composition to remove intermediate locations and Transformation 2 uses disjunction to remove multiple edges resulting from branches in the original program graph.

paths through a location but a sub set. Especially for loops, it is intuitively clear that it is not possible to consider all execution paths through the loop header since we cannot encode all iteration of the loop. Besides being smaller, another advantage of large block encoding is that only the program states at the beginning of a loop need to be considered in the model checking process. Thus we concentrate on finding loop invariants instead of looking at every single computation step of the program. Moreover, the interpolating theorem prover looks at several parallel paths in the program at once. Thus it can output more informed interpolants that are more likely to capture the inductive invariant of the program, than if every path is considered separately. We fold each loop-free subgraph in a program $\mathcal{P}$ to a single edge using the fix-point application of sequential and disjunctive composition of edges. We express this using the two transformation rules given in Figure 7. The first rule compresses sequential code into a single edge by sequentially composing the edge labels. It is applicable if there is a location ℓ' with a single incoming edge. The transition formula of the incoming edge is composed with every transition formula on all outgoing edges to create new outgoing edges from the predecessor. The location ℓ' and all its incoming and outgoing edges are then removed.

Transformation 1. *Given a program graph $\mathcal{P} = (Loc, \ell_{init}, \ell_{err}, \delta)$. For any location $\ell' \in Loc\backslash\{\ell_{init}, \ell_{err}\}$, s.t. the edge $((\ell, Inv), \varphi, (\ell', Inv'))$ exists uniquely, we reduce the program graph $\mathcal{P}$ as follows: 1) remove the location ℓ' from Loc, and 2) replace all pairs of edges $((\ell, Inv), \varphi, (\ell', Inv'))$, $((\ell', Inv'), \varphi', (\ell'', Inv''))$ by a new edge $((\ell, Inv), \varphi \circ Inv' \wedge \varphi', (\ell'', Inv''))$.*

Note that the rule duplicates the formulas φ and Inv' for every outgoing edge of location ℓ'. We can avoid exponential blow-up by replacing them by a boolean variable which are defined as φ resp. Inv', the same way we defined the variables err above.

After applying Transformation 1, each location in the program graph $\mathcal{P}$ is either a sink or has more than one outgoing edge. The compression of sequential code by Transformation 1 can create multiple edges with the same source and destination location. We can fold such a sequence of edges into one by using the disjunctive composition.

Transformation 2. *Given a program graph $\mathcal{P} = (Loc, \ell_{init}, \ell_{err}, \delta)$ and two nodes $\ell, \ell' \in Loc$. For any two edges $((\ell, Inv), \varphi, (\ell', Inv'))$, $((\ell, Inv), \varphi', (\ell', Inv'))$ $\in \delta$, we reduce the graph by replacing these edges by a new edge $((\ell, Inv), \varphi \vee \varphi', (\ell', Inv'))$.*

In a graph $\mathcal{P}$ for which neither Transformation 1 nor Transformation 2 can be applied, we know, that each location is either sink node or a loop header. Hence, the application of Transformation 1 and Transformation 2 on a program $\mathcal{P}$ does not change the satisfiability of the formula $\varphi(\mathcal{P})$.

Theorem 3. *The fix-point application of Transformation 1 and Transformation 2 on a program graph $\mathcal{P} = (Loc, \ell_{init}, \ell_{err}, \delta)$ results in a program graph $\mathcal{P} = (Loc', \ell'_{init}, \ell'_{err}, \delta')$, where $Loc' \subseteq Loc$ and any location $\ell \in Loc'$ is* *reachable in $\mathcal{P}$ if and only if ℓ is reachable in $\mathcal{P}$. We say that $\mathcal{P}$ is the reduced graph of $\mathcal{P}$.*

A proof for Theorem 3 is given in [4].

5 Experimental Evaluation

Our implementation is called ULTIMATE. It is based on the Eclipse RCP Framework. It allows to build tools as chains of plugins. For the purpose of experimental comparison we have also reimplemented the IMPACT [1] software model checker as a plugin in our framework. IMPACT is also an interpolation-based software model checker. But IMPACT builds an unwinding instead of manipulating the model itself. The framework allows us to compare the two approaches without changing the peripherals, i.e. input file, parser, SMT solver etc. In both cases we use Boogie PL [13] as input format and use SMTInterpol[1] as SMT solver. Subsequently, we denote our reimplementation of IMPACT as REIMPACT. As base for the comparison we use a set of simple examples (Table 1). The programs are all written in Boogie PL and have less than 100 lines of code. Their purpose is to emphasis the differences between our approach and the underlying approach

Table 1. The table shows the results of both model checking approaches on our example Boogie files. *Splits* shows how often nodes have been copied. *TPC* is number of theorem prover calls. Time is measured in millisec. *LBE* shows the results for path insensitive interpolation turned on(Yes) and off(No). Whereas, the symbols stand for ✔correct, ✗incorrect, – time out. The values in column *Splits*, *TPC* and *Time* relate to the runs with path insensitive interpolation turned on.

			ULTIMATE					REIMPACT				
No.	Nodes	Loops	Splits	TPC	Time	LBE Yes	LBE No	Splits	TPC	Time	LBE Yes	LBE No
01	14	1	0	3	34	✔	✔	3	1	35	✔	✔
02	5	1	3	33	288	✔	✔	4	8	108	✔	✔
03	7	2	13	156	2040	✔	–	–	–	–	–	–
04	36	1	42	766	13827	✔	–	6	52	1246	✔	–
05	31	1	1	16	462	✗	–	5	10	133	✗	–
06	11	1	6	85	9611	✔	–	–	–	–	–	–
07	26	1	0	3	66	✔	–	6	19	539	✔	–
08	50	1	0	3	79	✔	–	6	25	5447	✔	✔
19	98	1	0	3	116	✔	–	–	–	–	–	–
10	194	1	0	3	165	✔	–	–	–	–	–	–

[1] `http://swt.informatik.uni-freiburg.de/research/tools/smtinterpol`

of IMPACT. They also show the effect of path insensitive interpolation on both approaches. The tests were run on an AMD Athlon 64x2 Dual Core Processor with 2.50 Ghz and 4.00 GB of RAM. The operating system is an 64-bit Windows Server 2008 R2 Standard. Both approaches profit from the path insensitive interpolation. Without path insensitive interpolation, REIMPACT performs better than ULTIMATE since it returns results for more of the example programs. But with path insensitive interpolation, ULTIMATE returns more often a result than REIMPACT. Example 01 is an 4-bit counter with nested conditional branchings. And the final assertion states only about the highest bit. Therefore there are less paths to be checked and the assertion is a direct effect of the loop condition. As expected, both approaches perform similarly on this example. Example 02 has a single loop and no nested branching. The ART is a simple unrolling of the loop. But the splitting causes more nodes in the model and therefore also more theorem prover calls. Therefore, REIMPACT performs slightly better than ULTIMATE. Examples 04 is a standard planning example, gripper. The single loop can be considered as an event handler. Its nested conditional branchings are actions that can be performed. In each iteration only one of the branches can be taken. As in example 02, this reduces the number of paths. Due to the splitting, ULTIMATE produces more edges as the unwinding of REIMPACT does. Hence, we have more theorem prover calls. Example 05 is the same program as example 04 but with a bug insertion. REIMPACT is still faster but this time ULTIMATE shows comparable performance. Example 03 and 06(Example Sec. 2) have more complex branching structures. Additionally the necessary invariants are less obvious. It takes REIMPACT considerably more time to derive an invariant to proof the correctness of the programs. Examples 07 - 10 show the major advantage of our approach. The examples are 4-, 8-, 16-, 32-bit counters with a single loop that contain 4, 8, 16 and 32 `If-Then-Else` branchings, respectively. In contrast to examples 01-06, in examples 07-10 the control flow is not restricted by the semantics but depends on the current state of the variables. In these kind of programs our approach is much fast than REIMPACT. The manipulation of the model itself, as done by our splitting refinement, has the effect that obtained information of previous iterations is taken into account in the current iteration. This avoids the examination of paths that can't be taken by the branching anyway. REIMPACT iterates through all permutations of the branching. In our approach the number of iterations remains the same and the additional time is only spend in the SMT solver. This also shows that the shifting of the branching into the formula is handled by the solver very well. Overall, the examples show that the combination of splitting with path insensitive interpolation has potential. On our experimental set of examples it terminates more often than the IMPACT approach. The slower performance on some examples, results from creation of unnecessary edges in the splitting. This can be optimized further.

6 Related Work

We compare our tool to modern software model checking tools like Blast [5], CPACHECKER [6], and IMPACT [16]. The most common approaches, e.g. Blast,

SLAM [2], SATABS [10], use CEGAR algorithms with predicate abstraction. In predicate abstraction the model is refined by newly obtained predicates e.g. derived from interplants. In our approach we use the interpolants themselves in order to refine the model. This technique has been introduced by Ken McMillan [14]. In [16] he showed that his implementation of an interpolation-based model checker, IMPACT, has a serious performance gain compared to tools using predicate abstraction by avoiding the abstract image computation. As abstraction process IMPACT uses lazy abstraction as known from BLAST. The software model checking procedure of IMPACT has also been implemented in other tools e.g. Wolverine [12]. The main difference to our approach is the abstraction technique. In contrast to our approach, IMPACT uses an abstract reachability tree. Our approach modifies the model itself. In this model the gathered information is reused on every path examination. This approach is based on slicing abstraction [8]. Slicing abstraction was implemented in a tool called SLAB [11]. But in contrast to our approach, SLAB uses predicate abstraction. In order to adapt interpolation to slicing abstraction we use a technique called large block encoding [4] which is implemented in CPAchecker. CPAchecker uses the same software model checker procedure as Blast but compresses the model by joining sequential code segments to single transitions.

7 Conclusion

We have introduced the concept of path insensitive interpolation. We also presented a first approach to use path insensitive interpolation in combination with splitting refinement to derive loop invariants. We demonstrated with an experimental implementation that it is in fact efficient to burden the SMT solver the task to find useful interpolants by providing it more information about the program. We did this by using large block encoding as a compression technique and computing path interpolants on the compressed model. We showed that, although just partially path insensitive, we obtain promising results with this approach.

Applying LBE on the entire model allows us a partial path insensitivity. But the future work will be to find techniques to improve the path insensitivity. This can be done by computing interpolants not over the paths of the compressed model but by focusing on single locations. If considering a single location, one can summarize the entire prefixes of the paths leading from the initial location to the observed location and also summarize all suffixes leading from the oberserved location to the error location. But even this approach would not be fully path insensitive since we can still not take all loop iteration into consideration. Additionally this appraoch might cause a lot of redundant computations in the SMT solver. Instead of one SMT solver call per path, we would cause one per each location. This would get too costly. For this purpose, the communication between the SMT solver and the software model checker must be improved. A steering by the software model checker could also effect the quality of the interpolants. Further, an optimization of the splitting refinement would reduce the number of theorem prover calls and increase the performance of the approach.

References

[1] Amla, N., McMillan, K.L.: Combining Abstraction Refinement and SAT-Based Model Checking. In: Grumberg, O., Huth, M. (eds.) TACAS 2007. LNCS, vol. 4424, pp. 405–419. Springer, Heidelberg (2007)
[2] Ball, T., Rajamani, S.K.: The slam project: debugging system software via static analysis. In: POPL, pp. 1–3. ACM, New York (2002)
[3] Barnett, M., Leino, K.R.M.: Weakest-precondition of unstructured programs. SIGSOFT Softw. Eng. Notes 31, 82–87 (2005)
[4] Beyer, D., Cimatti, A., Griggio, A., Keremoglu, M.E., Sebastiani, R.: Software model checking via large-block encoding. In: FMCAD, pp. 25–32 (2009)
[5] Beyer, D., Henzinger, T.A., Jhala, R., Majumdar, R.: The software model checker blast: Applications to software engineering. Int. J. Softw. Tools Technol. Transf. 9, 505–525 (2007)
[6] Beyer, D., Keremoglu, M.E.: CPAchecker: A Tool for Configurable Software Verification. In: Gopalakrishnan, G., Qadeer, S. (eds.) CAV 2011. LNCS, vol. 6806, pp. 184–190. Springer, Heidelberg (2011)
[7] Bradley, A., Manna, Z., Sipma, H.: What's Decidable About Arrays? In: Emerson, E.A., Namjoshi, K.S. (eds.) VMCAI 2006. LNCS, vol. 3855, pp. 427–442. Springer, Heidelberg (2005)
[8] Brückner, I., Dräger, K., Finkbeiner, B., Wehrheim, H.: Slicing Abstractions. In: Arbab, F., Sirjani, M. (eds.) FSEN 2007. LNCS, vol. 4767, pp. 17–32. Springer, Heidelberg (2007)
[9] Bruttomesso, R., Ghilardi, S., Ranise, S.: Rewriting-based quantifier-free interpolation for a theory of arrays. In: RTA, pp. 171–186 (2011)
[10] Clarke, E., Kroning, D., Sharygina, N., Yorav, K.: SATABS: SAT-Based Predicate Abstraction for ANSI-C. In: Halbwachs, N., Zuck, L.D. (eds.) TACAS 2005. LNCS, vol. 3440, pp. 570–574. Springer, Heidelberg (2005)
[11] Dräger, K., Kupriyanov, A., Finkbeiner, B., Wehrheim, H.: SLAB: A Certifying Model Checker for Infinite-State Concurrent Systems. In: Esparza, J., Majumdar, R. (eds.) TACAS 2010. LNCS, vol. 6015, pp. 271–274. Springer, Heidelberg (2010)
[12] Kroening, D., Weissenbacher, G.: Interpolation-Based Software Verification with Wolverine. In: Gopalakrishnan, G., Qadeer, S. (eds.) CAV 2011. LNCS, vol. 6806, pp. 573–578. Springer, Heidelberg (2011)
[13] Leino, K.R.M.: This is Boogie 2. Manuscript KRML 178 (2008), `http://research.microsoft.com/~leino/papers.html`
[14] McMillan, K.L.: Interpolation and SAT-Based Model Checking. In: Hunt Jr., W.A., Somenzi, F. (eds.) CAV 2003. LNCS, vol. 2725, pp. 1–13. Springer, Heidelberg (2003)
[15] McMillan, K.L.: Applications of Craig Interpolants in Model Checking. In: Halbwachs, N., Zuck, L.D. (eds.) TACAS 2005. LNCS, vol. 3440, pp. 1–12. Springer, Heidelberg (2005)
[16] McMillan, K.L.: Lazy Abstraction with Interpolants. In: Ball, T., Jones, R.B. (eds.) CAV 2006. LNCS, vol. 4144, pp. 123–136. Springer, Heidelberg (2006)

Automatic Inference of Access Permissions

Pietro Ferrara and Peter Müller

ETH Zurich, Switzerland
{pietro.ferrara,peter.mueller}@inf.ethz.ch

Abstract. Access permissions are used in several program verification approaches such as those based on separation logic or implicit dynamic frames to simplify framing and to provide a basis for reasoning about concurrent code. However, access permissions increase the annotation overhead because programmers need to specify for each program component which permissions it requires or provides. We present a new static analysis based on abstract interpretation to infer access permissions automatically. Our analysis computes a symbolic approximation of the permissions owned for each heap location at each program point and infers a constraint system over these symbolic permissions that reflects the permission requirements of each heap access in the program. The constraint system is solved using linear programming. Our analysis is parametric in the permission system and supports, for instance, fractional and counting permissions. Experimental results demonstrate that our analysis is fast and is able to infer almost all access permissions for our case studies.

1 Introduction

Verification techniques based on access permissions associate a permission with each heap location. A thread may access a location if and only if it has the access permission for that location. This rule enables the verification of concurrent programs since it guarantees the absence of data races (two threads cannot both have the access permission for a memory location) and allows one to reason about thread interleavings (if a thread has the permission for a location, no other thread can modify it). Permissions can be transferred between threads when a thread is forked or joined, or via synchronization primitives such as monitors. To support procedure-modular verification, permissions are often associated with procedure (or method) incarnations; permissions are then transferred not only between different threads but also between callers and callees of the same thread. In this case, permissions simplify framing because a method may modify at most those locations for which it has permission; all other locations are guaranteed to remain unchanged. Permissions are used for instance in separation logic [22] and implicit dynamic frames [25].

Fractional permissions [2] and counting permissions [1] refine the permission model by allowing a full permission to be split (repeatedly) into fractions or into any number of units, which can be re-composed into a full permission. Both fractional and counting permissions allow one to distinguish between read access

V. Kuncak and A. Rybalchenko (Eds.): VMCAI 2012, LNCS 7148, pp. 202–218, 2012.

```
class Coord {
  var x: int;
  var y: int;

  invariant acc(x) && acc(y)
```

```
method client() {
  acquire this;
  var oldX := x; var oldY := y;
  this.FlipH();
  assert x == -oldX;
  assert y == oldY;
  release this;
}
```

```
method FlipH()
  requires acc(x)
  ensures acc(x)
  ensures x == -old(x)
  { x := -x; }
}
```

Fig. 1. An example illustrating access permissions

(requiring any non-zero permission) and write access (requiring full permission) and, thus, support parallel reads while still enforcing exclusive writes.

Fig. 1 illustrates the use of permissions in Chalice [14,15]. A full permission to a location e.f is denoted by acc(e.f), which corresponds to e.f $\mapsto$ _ in separation logic. Chalice associates permissions with method incarnations and with monitors. The precondition and postcondition of a method specify the permissions a method expects from its caller and provides to its caller, respectively. A monitor invariant specifies the permissions associated with a monitor. When a method acquires a monitor, these permissions are transferred from the monitor to the method, and returned to the monitor when it is released.

In Fig. 1, the monitor invariant of class Coord expresses that the monitor holds the permission to this.x and this.y when the monitor is not currently held by any thread. Method client obtains permissions to this.x and this.y by acquiring the monitor of this. Method FlipH requires permission to location this.x via its preconditions, and returns it via its postcondition. When client calls FlipH, the permission to this.x is passed to FlipH; the permission is returned when FlipH terminates. Method client can call FlipH passing and receiving back access permission to this.x. Both assertions in client verify. The first assertion is established by the call to FlipH; since the current thread holds the permission to x, no other thread could invalidate the property between the call and the assertion. The second assertion illustrates framing: since client does not pass its permission for y to FlipH, we can conclude that FlipH cannot modify y. Both assertions would not verify if they were placed after the release statement because then other threads could obtain permissions to x and y and invalidate the asserted properties.

A drawback of all permission systems is that they require programmers to annotate their programs with access permissions, which increases the annotation overhead significantly. To address this issue, we present a new static analysis based on abstract interpretation to infer access permissions automatically. In this paper, we focus on the inference of access annotations for pre- and postconditions as well as monitor invariants, but our analysis also supports loop invariants and abstract predicates with fold and unfold statements [20]. Our paper makes four technical contributions: (1) a representation of permissions with symbolic values, (2) an inference of constraints over these symbolic values, (3) an inference of annotations, which supports fractional and counting permissions, as well as the combination of both, and (4) an implementation and experimental evaluation of the analysis in Sample (Static Analyzer for Multiple Programming LanguagEs).

The experimental results show that our analysis is practical and effective. It infers permission annotations for all examples in the Chalice test suite in under three seconds, and the necessary annotations in all examples except for four that use recursive data structures, for which our heap abstraction is too coarse. We expect that more precise heap analyses like TVLA [23] will solve this issue.

Approach. Our approach is based on abstract interpretation [6], a theory for defining and soundly approximating the semantics of a program. The main components of our analysis are: (1) an *abstract domain* that is a complete lattice, (2) a *widening* operator to make the analysis convergent, and (3) an *abstract semantics* defined as a transfer function that, given a statement and an initial abstract state, defines the abstract state obtained after the statement.

We introduce a *symbolic value* for each location and each possible occurrence of an access permission in a pre- or postcondition, or monitor invariant. For instance, $Pre(\mathsf{C}, \mathsf{m}, \mathsf{x.f})$ represents the permission specified in the precondition of method m of class C for the location denoted by the path x.f. Using these symbolic values, the analysis infers a sound approximation of the access permissions that the current method incarnation has for any given heap location at any given program point. These *symbolic permissions* have the form $\sum a_i * \mathsf{v}_i + c$ where a_i is an integer number, c is a real, and v_i is a symbolic value. For instance, if method m's first statement acquires the monitor of this then its symbolic permission for a location x.f is $1 * Pre(\mathsf{C}, \mathsf{m}, \mathsf{x.f}) + 1 * MI(\mathsf{C}, \mathsf{x.f}) + 0$.

We then extract a set of *constraints* over the symbolic values, which reflect the permission rules of the verification technique. For instance, for an assignment to x.f, we introduce a constraint that the symbolic permission at this program point is equal to the full (write) permission. Our constraints are parametric in the permission system being used. We solve the constraints using linear programming and obtain a numerical access permission for each symbolic value. For simplicity, we assume here that the inference is run on un-annotated programs, but partial annotations could be easily represented as additional constraints.

Outline. Sec. 2 introduces the language supported by our analysis and the running example. Sec. 3 sketches our heap analysis. Sec. 4 defines the abstract domain and semantics to approximate access permissions. Sec. 5 explains how we infer permission annotations. Sec. 6 reports the experimental results. Sec. 7 discusses related work, and Sec. 8 concludes.

2 Language

We present our analysis for a class-based language with threads and monitors.

Programs. A program consists of a sequence of class declarations. Each class declares fields, a monitor invariant, and methods. A method declaration contains the method signature, pre- and postconditions, and a method body, which is given as a control flow graph of basic blocks. Each basic block consists of a sequence of statements. Different blocks are connected through edges that optionally contain a boolean condition to represent conditional jumps.

Table 1. Expressions and statements. We denote thread identifiers by t.

		E ::= x | x.f		
St ::= x := E	| x := new T	| acquire x	| t := fork x.m()	| share x
| x.f := E	| x.m()	| release x	| join t	

The expressions and statements of our language are summarized in Table 1. We omit uninteresting expressions such as boolean and arithmetic operators here. We adopt the share statement from Chalice; it associates a (non-reentrant) monitor with a previously thread-local object to make it available for locking. We omit Chalice's unshare statement since it does not affect permissions.

Specifications and Permissions. Specifications are expressed using the expressions of the programming language, an old-expression to let postconditions refer to prestate-values, and permission predicates. A *permission predicate* has the form **acc**(x.f,p), where p denotes a permission. With fractional permissions, p is a fraction between 0 and 1, with counting permissions, p is an integer (negative numbers are interpreted as a full permission plus p counting permissions), and in Chalice, p is an expression of the form $q\% + n \cdot \epsilon$, where q is a natural number between 0 and 100, n is an integer, and ϵ is a constant that denotes an infinitesimal permission, that is, an arbitrarily small, positive number. The percentage encodes fractional permissions, whereas the infinitesimal permission is used as a unit of counting permissions. Independently of the permission system, we abbreviate a full permission as **acc**(x.f). For sound verification, it is important that specifications are *self-framing*, that is, a specification may refer to x.f only if it has the permission to access x.f. So **acc**(x.f) && x.f > 0 is a valid specification, but x.f > 0 is not. We enforce this requirement by generating constraints not only for heap accesses in code but also in specifications.

Permission Transfer. Permissions can be transferred between two method incarnations and between a method incarnation and a monitor. For modular verification, we can describe these transfers from the perspective of the method incarnation that is currently executing. We say that a method *exhales* a permission if it transfers the permission to another method or a monitor, that is, gives up the permission. It *inhales* a permission if the transfer happens in the other direction, that is, when the method obtains the permission. For instance, when a monitor is released, its invariant is exhaled, while the invariant is inhaled when the monitor is acquired. Exhaling a permission entails a proof obligation that the method actually has the permission to be transferred. We say that a method exhales or inhales a specification, if it exhales or inhales all permissions mentioned in the specification. The statements of our language transfer permissions as follows. Assignments involve no permission transfer. When creating an object, we inhale full permissions for all locations of the fresh object. When we call a method, we first exhale the precondition of the callee and then inhale its postcondition. When a method acquires a monitor, we inhale the monitor

```
class W1 {
  var c : Cell;
  method Inc()
  ensures c.c1==old(c.c1)+1
  {
    acquire c;
    c.x := c.x+1;
    c.c1 := c.c1+1;
    release c;
  }
}

class Cell {
  var x, c1, c2: int;
  invariant x==c1+c2;
}
```

```
class W2 {
  var c : Cell;
  method Inc()
  ensures c.c2==old(c.c2)+1
  {
    acquire c;
    c.x := c.x+1;
    c.c2 := c.c2+1;
    release c;
  }
}
```

```
class OwickiGries {
  method main() {
    var c := new Cell;
    share c;
    var w1 := new W1;
    w1.c := c;
    var w2 := new W2;
    w2.c = c;
    t1 := fork w1.Inc();
    t2 := fork w2.Inc();
    join t1;
    join t2;
    acquire c;
    assert c.x==2;
  }
}
```

Fig. 2. The Owicki-Gries example without permission annotations

invariant, and we exhale the invariant when the monitor is released and when we first share the object. When forking a thread, we exhale the precondition of the forked method, while we inhale the postcondition when joining.

Running Example. We illustrate our inference using Owicki and Gries's classical example [19], see Fig. 2. Two worker threads, implemented in classes W1 and W2 each increment a shared variable x (of class Cell) by 1. The client (method main) asserts that the effect of running both workers is to increment x by 2. The standard solution to proving this assertion requires ghost (that is, specification-only) variables; the ghost fields c1 and c2 store the contribution of each worker to the overall effect. These ghost variables are related to x in Cell's monitor invariant and also mentioned in the workers' postconditions. Therefore, to enforce self-framing specifications, the postconditions and the monitor invariant need some access permission to the ghost variables. This can be achieved by using fractional or counting permissions to split the permissions over the postconditions and the monitor invariant. The example then verifies: From the postconditions, we know that after the two join operations in main, c1 and c2 have each been increased by 1. From Cell's monitor invariant, which we assume after the acquire statement, we know that then x has been increased by 2; so since fields of new objects are initialized to zero-equivalent values, the assertion verifies. We will show how our analysis infers the permission annotation to enable this verification.

3 Heap Analysis

Since access permissions guard accesses to heap locations, our inference requires information about the heap, for instance, to decide whether two expressions may refer to the same heap location. The analysis that approximates properties of the heap is crucial for the effectiveness of the permission inference. However, since the heap analysis is not the main focus of this paper, we only sketch the main ideas and notations of the implemented heap analysis here, which is an extension of our earlier work [10]. We expect that more sophisticated heap analyses such as shape analysis [23] could be combined with our inference.

Our heap analysis abstracts objects in the concrete heap to *abstract nodes* (set $\overline{\mathsf{L}}$) in an abstract heap. The abstraction identifies each object with the program point where it is created. That is, it abstracts all concrete objects created at the same program point (for instance, inside a loop) by the same abstract *summary node*. The heap analysis works modularly, that is, analyzes each method separately. The initial heap for a method contains one abstract node for each method argument and abstract object reachable from an argument. If some of these objects may be aliases (that is, their types do not exclude that they refer to the same object), they are instead represented by one summary node. The function $\overline{isSummary} : \overline{\mathsf{L}} \rightarrow \{\mathsf{true}, \mathsf{false}\}$ yields whether a node is a summary node, that is, whether it may represent more than one object.

Our permission inference uses type information for abstract nodes to determine which monitor invariant to inhale and exhale. The function $class : \overline{\mathsf{L}} \rightarrow \mathsf{C}$ yields the class of an abstract node (C is the set of class identifiers); for summary nodes, it returns the smallest superclass of the classes of each concrete object represented by the summary node.

The function $fields : \overline{\mathsf{L}} \rightarrow \wp(\mathsf{F})$ yields the set of fields of an abstract node, and the union of these sets for a summary node; F is the set of field identifiers. A path in Path is a sequence starting with a variable and followed by field identifiers. As usual, we denote by $\mathsf{x.f}$ the concatenation of variable x with field identifier f.

The heap analysis needs to define the semantics of expressions and statements in order to describe their effects on the abstract heap. The function $\overline{\mathbb{E}} : (\overline{\mathsf{H}}, \mathsf{E}) \rightarrow \overline{\mathsf{L}}$ evaluates an expression in an abstract heap and yields the resulting abstract node ($\overline{\mathsf{H}}$ is the set of abstract heaps). We assume a semantics of statements that tracks how each statement modifies the abstract heap. We do not present the heap semantics here, and we leave the heap modifications implicit in the abstract semantics for the permission inference.

4 Symbolic Permissions

In this section we present the symbolic values, which represent permission predicates in specifications, the abstract domain, the abstract semantics, and an unsound approximation that can improve the results of the inference.

4.1 Symbolic Values

Programs may contain permission predicates in pre- and postconditions and monitor invariants (we ignore loop invariants here, but our analysis supports them). We represent the permissions in these specifications by symbolic values (set $\overline{\mathsf{SV}}$). The access permission for a path $\mathsf{p.f}$ specified (1) by the precondition or postcondition of a method m in class C is represented by $Pre(\mathsf{C}, \mathsf{m}, \mathsf{p.f})$ or $Post(\mathsf{C}, \mathsf{m}, \mathsf{p.f})$, respectively, and (2) by the monitor invariant of class C is represented by $MI(\mathsf{C}, \mathsf{p.f})$. Since there could be many (possibly infinite) paths to a location, our semantics always considers a shortest path.

4.2 Abstract Domain

The *symbolic access permission* for a single abstract location, that is, field of an abstract node, could combine several symbolic values, since it could be the result of inhaling and exhaling different method specifications and monitor invariants. Therefore we represent the symbolic permission as the *summation* of symbolic values s_i multiplied by integer coefficients a_i (to represent how many times we have inhaled or exhaled a permission) and an integer constant c (to represent the full permission that is inhaled when an object is created). Formally, $\overline{\mathsf{AV}} = \{\sum_\mathsf{i} \mathsf{a}_\mathsf{i} * \mathsf{s}_i + \mathsf{c} \text{ where } \mathsf{a}_\mathsf{i}, \mathsf{c} \in \mathbb{R}, \mathsf{s}_i \in \overline{\mathsf{SV}}\}$.

On these summations we define a lattice structure. Fig. 3 formalizes the lattice operators. To be sound, we compute at each program point the access permissions the current method *surely* has, that is, it has in all possible executions. For this reason, the upper bound—which is used in the abstract semantics for joins in the control flow—of two symbolic permissions $\bar{\mathsf{l}}_1$ and $\bar{\mathsf{l}}_2$ is the *minimum* of $\bar{\mathsf{l}}_1$ and $\bar{\mathsf{l}}_2$. Since symbolic values represent non-negative values, a safe approximation of the minimum of two symbolic permissions is computed using the minimum of the corresponding coefficients a_i and of the integer constant c. Conversely, the lower bound is the *maximum* of $\bar{\mathsf{l}}_1$ and $\bar{\mathsf{l}}_2$, which is computed analogously. In the lattice order, symbolic permission $\bar{\mathsf{l}}_1$ is less or equal $\bar{\mathsf{l}}_2$ iff $\bar{\mathsf{l}}_1$ represents *greater* or equal permissions than $\bar{\mathsf{l}}_2$, that is, each coefficient and the constant in $\bar{\mathsf{l}}_1$ is greater or equal than the corresponding coefficient and the constant in $\bar{\mathsf{l}}_2$; this definition is in line with defining the upper bound as the minimum. We assume that each concrete permission system defines two constants, zero and full, to denote the zero-permission and full permission, respectively. The bottom element is any value greater than full or less than zero, that is, any invalid value for a permission. The top element is zero. Then the lattice can be defined by $\langle \overline{\mathsf{AV}}, \leq_{\overline{\mathsf{AV}}}, \mathsf{zero} - 1, \mathsf{zero}, \sqcup_{\overline{\mathsf{AV}}}, \sqcap_{\overline{\mathsf{AV}}} \rangle$. Note that this domain does not track disjunctive information like $\mathsf{b} \Rightarrow \mathsf{acc(x.f)}$, but it can be used inside other generic domains to obtain precise disjunctive information [18].

In the above domain, we have a finite number of symbolic values, but the integer coefficients could decrease indefinitely. Therefore, we need a widening operator to ensure the termination of the analysis. Our widening abstracts the symbolic access permission to zero if it is decreasing. This definition reflects that if a loop exhales permissions in each iteration, we approximate it assuming that no permission is left when the loop terminates because we do not know statically how many times the loop body will be executed. However, none of the examples we analyzed required widening because such loops are not common.

The abstract domain $\overline{\mathsf{PL}}$ tracks the symbolic access permissions at a given program point for each field of each abstract node. Therefore, its state is repre-

$$(\textstyle\sum_j a_j^1 * \bar{\mathsf{s}}_j + c_1) \sqcup_{\overline{\mathsf{AV}}} (\sum_j a_j^2 * \bar{\mathsf{s}}_j + c_2) = (\sum_j \min(a_j^1, a_j^2) * \bar{\mathsf{s}}_j + \min(c_1, c_2))$$
$$(\textstyle\sum_j a_j^1 * \bar{\mathsf{s}}_j + c_1) \sqcap_{\overline{\mathsf{AV}}} (\sum_j a_j^2 * \bar{\mathsf{s}}_j + c_2) = (\sum_j \max(a_j^1, a_j^2) * \bar{\mathsf{s}}_j + \max(c_1, c_2))$$
$$(\textstyle\sum_j a_j^1 * \bar{\mathsf{s}}_j + c_1) \leq_{\overline{\mathsf{AV}}} (\sum_j a_j^2 * \bar{\mathsf{s}}_j + c_2) = \mathsf{true} \Leftrightarrow c_1 \geq c_2 \wedge \forall j : a_j^1 \geq a_j^2$$

Fig. 3. Lattice operators on $\overline{\mathsf{AV}}$

sented by a function that maps abstract locations to symbolic access permissions: $\overline{\mathsf{PL}} : (\overline{\mathsf{L}} \times \mathsf{F}) \rightarrow \overline{\mathsf{AV}}$. The lattice operators are defined as the functional extensions of the lattice operators of $\overline{\mathsf{AV}}$.

4.3 Abstract Semantics

The abstract semantics formalizes the effects of statements on symbolic permissions. It uses the helper functions in Fig. 4. $\overline{reach}(\bar{\mathsf{r}}, \bar{\mathsf{h}}, \overline{\mathsf{R}}, \mathsf{p})$ yields the set of abstract locations that can be reached from an abstract node $\bar{\mathsf{r}}$ in a heap $\bar{\mathsf{h}}$, without traversing the abstract nodes in $\overline{\mathsf{R}}$, and for each reachable abstract location a path through which it can be reached; this path is an extension of path p, through which node $\bar{\mathsf{r}}$ is reachable from some starting point. The set $\overline{\mathsf{R}}$ is used to discard alternative paths to the same abstract location. Note that the definition of $\overline{reach}$ is recursive. For each recursive application, we use function $\overline{reach1}$ to add all abstract locations that are reachable in one step, that is, by accessing a field of $\bar{\mathsf{r}}$. The recursion is well-founded since the heap domain contains a finite number of abstract nodes, and the set $\overline{\mathsf{R}}$ grows in each recursive application.

Function $\overline{reach}$ is used to extract all the abstract locations for which we *potentially* inhale or exhale permissions, together with a shortest path through which these permissions could be inhaled or exhaled. Function $\overline{rep}$ uses these abstract locations and paths to construct a symbolic value for each of them. Its last argument determines what kind of symbolic value we want to obtain.

$$\overline{reach} : (\overline{\mathsf{L}} \times \overline{\mathsf{H}} \times \wp(\overline{\mathsf{L}}) \times \mathsf{Path}) \rightarrow \wp(\overline{\mathsf{L}} \times \mathsf{F} \times \mathsf{Path})$$
$$\overline{reach}(\bar{\mathsf{r}}, \bar{\mathsf{h}}, \overline{\mathsf{R}}, \mathsf{p}) = \{(\bar{\mathsf{r}}_1, \mathsf{f}, \mathsf{p}) : (\bar{\mathsf{r}}_1, \mathsf{f}) \in \overline{reach1}(\bar{\mathsf{h}}, \mathsf{p}) \wedge \bar{\mathsf{r}}_1 \notin \overline{\mathsf{R}}\} \cup$$
$$\cup \{(\bar{\mathsf{r}}_2, \mathsf{f}_1, \mathsf{p}_1) \in \overline{reach}(\bar{\mathsf{r}}_1, \bar{\mathsf{h}}, \overline{\mathsf{R}} \cup \downarrow_1 (\overline{reach1}(\bar{\mathsf{h}}, \mathsf{p})), \mathsf{p.f}) : (\bar{\mathsf{r}}_1, \mathsf{f}) \in \overline{reach1}(\bar{\mathsf{h}}, \mathsf{p})\}$$

$$\overline{reach1} : (\overline{\mathsf{H}} \times \mathsf{Path}) \rightarrow \wp(\overline{\mathsf{L}} \times \mathsf{F})$$
$$\overline{reach1}(\bar{\mathsf{h}}, \mathsf{p}) = \{(\bar{\mathsf{r}}, \mathsf{f}) : \overline{\mathbb{E}}(\bar{\mathsf{h}}, \mathsf{p}) = \bar{\mathsf{r}} \wedge \mathsf{f} \in \mathit{fields}(\bar{\mathsf{r}})\}$$

$$\overline{rep} : (\wp(\overline{\mathsf{L}} \times \mathsf{F} \times \mathsf{Path}) \times \overline{\mathsf{SV}}) \rightarrow \wp(\overline{\mathsf{L}} \times \mathsf{F} \times \overline{\mathsf{SV}})$$
$$\overline{rep}(\{(\bar{\mathsf{r}}_1, \mathsf{f}_1, \mathsf{p}_1), \cdots, (\bar{\mathsf{r}}_i, \mathsf{f}_i, \mathsf{p}_i)\}, \bar{\mathsf{s}}) = \{(\bar{\mathsf{r}}_1, \mathsf{f}_1, \bar{\mathsf{s}}_1), \cdots, (\bar{\mathsf{r}}_i, \mathsf{f}_i, \bar{\mathsf{s}}_i)\} : \forall \mathsf{j} \in [1..\mathsf{i}] :$$
$$\bar{\mathsf{s}}_j = \begin{cases} MI(\mathsf{c}, \mathsf{p_j.f_j}) & \text{if } \bar{\mathsf{s}} = MI(\mathsf{c}, \mathsf{p}) \\ Pre(\mathsf{c}, \mathsf{m}, \mathsf{p_j.f_j}) & \text{if } \bar{\mathsf{s}} = Pre(\mathsf{c}, \mathsf{m}, \mathsf{p}) \\ Post(\mathsf{c}, \mathsf{m}, \mathsf{p_j.f_j}) & \text{if } \bar{\mathsf{s}} = Post(\mathsf{c}, \mathsf{m}, \mathsf{p}) \end{cases} \}$$

$$\overline{inhS} : (\overline{\mathsf{PL}} \times \overline{\mathsf{L}} \times \mathsf{F} \times \overline{\mathsf{SV}}) \rightarrow \overline{\mathsf{PL}}$$
$$\overline{inhS}(\bar{\sigma}, \bar{\mathsf{r}}, \mathsf{f}, \bar{\mathsf{s}}) = \begin{cases} \bar{\sigma}[(\bar{\mathsf{r}}, \mathsf{f}) \mapsto \bar{\sigma}(\bar{\mathsf{r}}, \mathsf{f}) + 1 * \bar{\mathsf{s}}] & \text{if } \overline{isSummary}(\bar{\mathsf{r}}) = \mathsf{false} \\ \bar{\sigma} & \text{otherwise} \end{cases}$$
$$\overline{inh} : (\overline{\mathsf{PL}} \times \wp(\overline{\mathsf{L}} \times \mathsf{F} \times \overline{\mathsf{SV}})) \rightarrow \overline{\mathsf{PL}}$$
$$\overline{inh}(\bar{\sigma}, \{(\bar{\mathsf{r}}_1, \mathsf{f}_1, \bar{\mathsf{s}}_1), \cdots, (\bar{\mathsf{r}}_i, \mathsf{f_i}, \bar{\mathsf{s}}_i)\}) = \bar{\sigma}_i :$$
$$\exists \bar{\sigma}_0, \cdots, \bar{\sigma}_i \in \overline{\mathsf{PL}} : \bar{\sigma}_0 = \bar{\sigma} \wedge \forall \mathsf{j} \in [1..\mathsf{i}] : \bar{\sigma}_j = \overline{inhS}(\bar{\sigma}_{j-1}, \bar{\mathsf{r}}_j, \mathsf{f_j}, \bar{\mathsf{s}}_j)$$

$$\overline{exhS} : (\overline{\mathsf{PL}} \times \overline{\mathsf{L}} \times \mathsf{F} \times \overline{\mathsf{SV}}) \rightarrow \overline{\mathsf{PL}}$$
$$\overline{exhS}(\bar{\sigma}, \bar{\mathsf{r}}, \mathsf{f}, \bar{\mathsf{s}}) = \bar{\sigma}[(\bar{\mathsf{r}}, \mathsf{f}) \mapsto \bar{\sigma}(\bar{\mathsf{r}}, \mathsf{f}) - 1 * \bar{\mathsf{s}}]$$

$$\overline{exh} : (\overline{\mathsf{PL}} \times \wp(\overline{\mathsf{L}} \times \mathsf{F} \times \overline{\mathsf{SV}})) \rightarrow \overline{\mathsf{PL}}$$
$$\overline{exh}(\bar{\sigma}, \{(\bar{\mathsf{r}}_1, \mathsf{f}_1, \bar{\mathsf{s}}_1), \cdots, (\bar{\mathsf{r}}_i, \mathsf{f_i}, \bar{\mathsf{s}}_i)\}) = \bar{\sigma}_i :$$
$$\exists \bar{\sigma}_0, \cdots, \bar{\sigma}_i \in \overline{\mathsf{PL}} : \bar{\sigma}_0 = \bar{\sigma} \wedge \forall \mathsf{j} \in [1..\mathsf{i}] : \bar{\sigma}_j = \overline{exhS}(\bar{\sigma}_{j-1}, \bar{\mathsf{r}}_j, \mathsf{f_j}, \bar{\mathsf{s}}_j)$$

Fig. 4. Helper functions for the abstract semantics. The prefix operator $\downarrow_1$ denotes the projection of a pair on its first component; it is lifted to sets of pairs.

Finally, we define two functions $\overline{inhS}$ and $\overline{exhS}$ to inhale and exhale permissions, respectively. They map a state of the abstract domain to another state. The permissions are determined by pairs of abstract locations and symbolic values. The functions $\overline{inh}$ and $\overline{exh}$ lift $\overline{inhS}$ and $\overline{exhS}$ to sets of pairs. In order to be sound, we inhale a permission iff the abstract node is not summary. The abstract semantics of statements (Fig. 5) maps a statement, a state of the abstract domain, and a heap to another state. It reflects the permission transfer described in Sec. 2. For instance, acquiring a monitor inhales all the symbolic permissions that its invariant could potentially specify. These are permissions for all abstract locations reachable from the object whose monitor is being acquired. To determine these abstract locations, we apply $\overline{rep}$ to the result of $\overline{reach}$.

Running Example. In method Inc of class W1, we obtain that between the acquire and the release statements (lines 7 and 8), the current thread has the symbolic access permission $1{*}Pre(\mathsf{W1}, \mathsf{Inc}, \mathsf{this.c.f}){+}1{*}MI(\mathsf{Cell}, \mathsf{this.f})$ for each field f of Cell (that is, x, c1, and c2). At the end of the method, it has only $1{*}Pre(\mathsf{W1}, \mathsf{Inc}, \mathsf{this.c.f})$ since we released the monitor of c. The permissions for class W2 are analogous. Before the fork in method main of class OwickiGries, the current thread has $-1{*}MI(\mathsf{Cell}, \mathsf{c.f}){+}\mathsf{full}$ for all fields f of class Cell. The negated permissions from the monitor invariant stem from exhaling the monitor invariant when sharing c; the constant full is inhaled when c is created. When forking the two threads (lines 35 and 36), we exhale the preconditions of the forked methods, obtaining $-1{*}MI(\mathsf{Cell}, \mathsf{c.f}){-}1{*}Pre(\mathsf{W1}, \mathsf{Inc}, \mathsf{c.f}){-}1{*}Pre(\mathsf{W2}, \mathsf{Inc}, \mathsf{c.f}){+}\mathsf{full}$. When joining the forked threads, we inhale the postconditions of the forked methods, and when acquiring c's monitor (line 39), we inhale the monitor invariant of class Cell. Then at line 41, the current thread has $-1{*}Pre(\mathsf{W1}, \mathsf{Inc}, \mathsf{c.f}){+}1{*}Post(\mathsf{W1}, \mathsf{Inc}, \mathsf{c.f}){-}1{*}Pre(\mathsf{W2}, \mathsf{Inc}, \mathsf{c.f}){+}1{*}Post(\mathsf{W2}, \mathsf{Inc}, \mathsf{c.f}){+}\mathsf{full}$ for each field f of Cell.

4.4 Unsound Approximations

The analysis we described so far is sound, but sometimes too coarse in its treatment of summary nodes. Even with a more precise heap analysis, the inference becomes more practical when it uses two unsound approximations.

$$
\begin{array}{l}
\overline{\mathbb{S}} : (\mathsf{St}, \overline{\mathsf{PL}}, \overline{\mathsf{H}}) \rightarrow \overline{\mathsf{PL}} \\
\overline{\mathbb{S}}(\mathsf{x} := \mathsf{E}, \overline{\sigma}, \overline{\mathsf{h}}) = \overline{\sigma} \\
\overline{\mathbb{S}}(\mathsf{x.f} := \mathsf{E}, \overline{\sigma}, \overline{\mathsf{h}}) = \overline{\sigma} \\
\overline{\mathbb{S}}(\mathsf{x} := \mathsf{new}\ \mathsf{T}, \overline{\sigma}, \overline{\mathsf{h}}) = \overline{\sigma}[\overline{\mathsf{r}} \mapsto \mathsf{full} : (\overline{\mathsf{r}}, \mathsf{p}) \in \overline{reach1}(\overline{\mathsf{h}'}, \mathsf{x})] \\
\qquad\qquad\qquad\qquad\qquad \text{where } \overline{\mathsf{h}'} \text{ is the abstract heap obtained after } \mathsf{x} := \mathsf{new}\ \mathsf{T} \\
\overline{\mathbb{S}}(\mathsf{x.m}(), \overline{\sigma}, \overline{\mathsf{h}}) = \overline{\sigma}_2 : \overline{\sigma}_1 = \overline{exh}(\sigma, \overline{rep}(\overline{reach}(\overline{\mathbb{E}}(\overline{\mathsf{h}}, \mathsf{x}), \overline{\mathsf{h}}, \emptyset, \mathsf{this}), Pre(class(\overline{\mathbb{E}}(\overline{\mathsf{h}}, \mathsf{x})), \mathsf{m}, \emptyset))) \wedge \\
\qquad\qquad\qquad\qquad\qquad \overline{\sigma}_2 = \overline{inh}(\overline{\sigma}_1, \overline{rep}(\overline{reach}(\overline{\mathbb{E}}(\overline{\mathsf{h}}, \mathsf{x}), \overline{\mathsf{h}}, \emptyset, \mathsf{this}), Post(class(\overline{\mathbb{E}}(\overline{\mathsf{h}}, \mathsf{x})), \mathsf{m}, \emptyset))) \\
\overline{\mathbb{S}}(\mathsf{acquire}\ \mathsf{x}, \overline{\sigma}, \overline{\mathsf{h}}) = \overline{inh}(\sigma, \overline{rep}(\overline{reach}(\overline{\mathbb{E}}(\overline{\mathsf{h}}, \mathsf{x}), \overline{\mathsf{h}}, \emptyset, \mathsf{this}), MI(class(\overline{\mathbb{E}}(\overline{\mathsf{h}}, \mathsf{x})), \emptyset))) \\
\overline{\mathbb{S}}(\mathsf{release}\ \mathsf{x}, \overline{\sigma}, \overline{\mathsf{h}}) = \overline{exh}(\sigma, \overline{rep}(\overline{reach}(\overline{\mathbb{E}}(\overline{\mathsf{h}}, \mathsf{x}), \overline{\mathsf{h}}, \emptyset, \mathsf{this}), MI(class(\overline{\mathbb{E}}(\overline{\mathsf{h}}, \mathsf{x})), \emptyset))) \\
\overline{\mathbb{S}}(\mathsf{t} := \mathsf{fork}\ \mathsf{x.m}(), \overline{\sigma}, \overline{\mathsf{h}}) = \overline{exh}(\sigma, \overline{rep}(\overline{reach}(\overline{\mathbb{E}}(\overline{\mathsf{h}}, \mathsf{x}), \overline{\mathsf{h}}, \emptyset, \mathsf{this}), Pre(class(\overline{\mathbb{E}}(\overline{\mathsf{h}}, \mathsf{x})), \mathsf{m}, \emptyset))) \\
\overline{\mathbb{S}}(\mathsf{join}\ \mathsf{t}, \overline{\sigma}, \overline{\mathsf{h}}) = \overline{inh}(\sigma, \overline{rep}(\overline{reach}(\overline{\mathbb{E}}(\overline{\mathsf{h}}, \mathsf{x}), \overline{\mathsf{h}}, \emptyset, \mathsf{this}), Post(\mathsf{C}, \mathsf{m}, \emptyset))) : TM(\mathsf{t}) = \mathsf{C.m} \\
\overline{\mathbb{S}}(\mathsf{share}\ \mathsf{x}, \overline{\sigma}, \overline{\mathsf{h}}) = \overline{exh}(\sigma, \overline{rep}(\overline{reach}(\overline{\mathbb{E}}(\overline{\mathsf{h}}, \mathsf{x}), \overline{\mathsf{h}}, \emptyset, \mathsf{this}), MI(class(\overline{\mathsf{h}}(\mathsf{x})), \emptyset)))
\end{array}
$$

Fig. 5. The definition of the abstract semantics. The function TM yields the method with which a given thread was forked.

Table 2. Instances of permission systems

System	zero	full	fractional	infinitesimal	ensureRead(p)
Fractional	0	1	true	false	$p > 0$
Counting	0	Integer.MAX_VALUE	false	false	$p \geq 1$
Chalice	0	100	true	true	$p \geq \epsilon$

First, as we explained earlier, a sound analysis must not inhale permissions on summary nodes because this might forge permissions. Removing this restriction improves especially the treatment of recursive data structures, which are usually abstracted to summary nodes. Second, our analysis conservatively assumes maximum aliasing in the input state of a method, that is, arguments or fields whose types do not rule out aliasing are represented by summary nodes. Following Clousot [17], we suggest to assume that aliasing does not occur in the input state. This unsound assumption is useful when methods take several parameters of the same type and when a parameter is a recursive data structure.

These unsound approximations may lead to permission annotations that cause a subsequent verification attempt to fail. For instance, unsoundly inhaling on a summary node representing x and y might provide permission to access x.f even if in the concrete execution, there is only permission for y.f. However, in our experiments (see Sec. 6), the unsound approximations helped inferring complete annotations, without compromising their precision.

5 Annotation Inference

In this section, we explain how we infer permission annotations by generating constraints on symbolic permissions and how we solve the constraint system.

5.1 Permission Systems

To support various permission systems, our analysis is parametric in the following aspects: (1) the numerical values that represent permissions, (2) the value that represents the absence of a permission, (3) the value that represents a full permission, and (4) the condition that permits read access. Aspect (1) is expressed via two boolean flags fractional and infinitesimal, which express whether fractional and infinitesimal (ϵ) permissions are supported. Aspects (2) and (3) are expressed via the constants zero and full as presented in the previous section. Aspect (4) is expressed by a function ensureRead : $\overline{\mathsf{PL}} \rightarrow \mathsf{Constr}$ (where Constr is the set of linear constraints over permissions in $\overline{\mathsf{AV}}$). These parameters are aimed at soundly overapproximating different permission systems in a finite way. Therefore they do not define the semantics of concrete systems, but they propose a way of abstracting them. Table 2 presents the parameters for fractional, counting, and Chalice permissions.

Fractional permissions are represented by fractions between 0 and 1, infinitesimal values are not supported, and reading is permitted by any non-zero permission. Counting permissions are represented by integers between 0 and the maximum integer value; again, infinitesimal values are not supported, and reading is permitted by any non-zero permission. We interpret a value i between 0 and Integer.MAX_VALUE/2 as i counting permissions and a value between Integer.MAX_VALUE/2 and Integer.MAX_VALUE as a full permission minus i counting permissions. Chalice permissions are represented by integers between 0 and 100, infinitesimal values are supported, and reading is permitted by permissions that are at least one infinitesimal permission (symbolic value ϵ).

5.2 Inferring Constraints

A permission-based verification technique prescribes rules that guard the access of heap locations, for instance, that a full permission is required to update the location. We reflect these rules in the analysis through the following constraints on the symbolic permission $\bar{\mathsf{l}}$ for an abstract location at a given program point: (1) $\mathsf{ensureRead}(\bar{\mathsf{l}})$ when the location is read, (2) $\bar{\mathsf{l}} == \mathsf{full}$ when the location is written, (3) $\bar{\mathsf{l}} \leq \mathsf{full}$ after a permission gets inhaled to encode that a method cannot obtain more than a full permission, and (4) $\mathsf{zero} \leq \bar{\mathsf{l}}$ after a permission is exhaled to encode the check that a method must possess the permissions it exhales. To ensure that specifications are self-framing (see Sec. 1), we generate constraint (1) also for field accesses within preconditions, postconditions, and monitor invariants. An additional constraint ensures that all symbolic values represent valid permissions: $\forall \bar{\mathsf{s}} \in \overline{\mathsf{SV}} : \mathsf{zero} \leq \bar{\mathsf{s}} \leq \mathsf{full}$.

In systems that support infinitesimal permissions, we introduce the following constraint on the concrete value of ϵ: $0 < n * \epsilon < 0.5$, where n is the maximal coefficient multiplied by infinitesimal permissions in all symbolic permissions. We interpret permission values in the open interval $(0; 0.5)$ as a positive number of ϵ's and values in $(0.5; 1)$ as 1 plus a negative number of ϵ's.

To infer strong postconditions, we introduce additional constraints for the exit states of the analysis that ensure that each method returns as many permissions to its caller as possible. For each field of a non-summary node reachable through a path p, we determine the upper bound $\bar{\mathsf{l}}$ of the symbolic permissions for all possible exit states of a method m of class C and require $Post(\mathsf{C}, \mathsf{m}, \mathsf{p}) = \bar{\mathsf{l}}$.

Running Example. Fig. 6 reports some of the constraints for the example from Fig. 2. We have already discussed the results of its abstract semantics in Sec. 4.3. For each constraint, we report the code line that induced the constraint. As before, f stands for any field of class Cell (x, c1, or c2).

The first four constraints are introduced for method Inc of class W1. The constraints for class W2 are analogous (with c2 instead of c1). The constraint for line 4 is introduced because Inc's postcondition reads c.c1; in the exit state of the method, the only permission for c.c1 is the one specified in the precondition since we already released the monitor of c. The identical constraint is introduced for the field read **old**(c.c1), which reads c.c1's pre-state value. The field writes

Constraint	Line
ensureRead(1*$Post$(W1, Inc, c.c1))	4
1*Pre(W1, Inc, c.x) + 1*MI(Cell, x) = full	7
1*Pre(W1, Inc, c.c1) + 1*MI(Cell, c1) = full	8
1*$Post$(W1, Inc, c.f) = 1*Pre(W1, Inc, c.f)	10
ensureRead(1*MI(Cell, f))	14
zero ≤ full − 1 ∗ MI(Cell, f) − 1 ∗ Pre(W1, Inc, c.f) − 1 ∗ Pre(W2, Inc, c.f)	36

Fig. 6. Some constraints for the running example

to c.x and c.c1 (lines 7 and 8) require that the method has write permission for the corresponding abstract locations. Therefore, we introduce a constraint that for these locations, the sum of the permissions in Inc's precondition and in Cell's monitor invariant must be a full permission. By the abstract semantics the permissions in the exit state of Inc are exactly those specified in the precondition. So we enforce that the precondition and the postcondition specify the same permissions for each field f of c. The monitor invariant of class Cell (line 14) reads all fields of the class and, thus, requires read permission for them.

Several constraints are produced for the main method of class OwickiGries. We discuss the one for the second fork (line 36). By the heap analysis, we know that c is fresh in method main. So the permission held after the second fork for any field c.f is the full permission (from the creation of c) minus what is specified in Cell's monitor invariant (from sharing c) minus what is specified in W1.Inc's precondition (from the first fork) minus what is specified in W2.Inc's precondition (from the second fork). The constraint ensures that main has sufficient permissions for the second fork, that is, that exhaling the precondition does not lead to permissions smaller than zero.

5.3 Resolution of the Constraints

We solve the inferred constraint system using linear programming [8]. We define an objective function that lets us infer the *minimal* permissions that satisfy the constraints. Maximizing the permissions would often result in full permissions for each reachable location, even if the location is never accessed. Such a solution complicates subsequent verification, for instance, by providing weaker framing.

Through the objective function we also express *priorities* defining where to put annotations when several solutions are possible, for instance, in the method specification or in the monitor invariant. To do that, we multiply each symbolic value in the objective function by a factor. A bigger factor expresses a lower priority for that symbolic value, since we minimize the objective function.

Solving the linear programming system determines whether the system is feasible, that is, whether there are numerical values (real numbers) for all symbolic values that satisfy the constraints. An infeasible system may occur because of approximation, for instance, if we soundly abstain from inhaling on summary nodes, the constraint for a subsequent field access might not be satisfiable. If the system is feasible, we use the solution to compute the permission predicates for pre- and postconditions as well as monitor invariants.

The constraints resolution provides a numerical value that has to be translated to a permission predicate. This step is straightforward for fractional permissions. For counting permissions, we translate a value differently, depending on whether it is less or greater than Integer.MAX_VALUE/2 (see Sec. 5.1). For Chalice permissions, the integer part of each numerical value is turned into a percentage, whereas the mantissa is turned into a (positive or negative) number of counting permissions by dividing it by the solution for the symbolic value ϵ.

Running Example. In the following, we present the annotations obtained by solving the constraints in Fig. 6 for Chalice's permission model. Fractional and counting permissions lead to similar results. The constraint system is feasible, and we obtain different solutions, depending on the priorities encoded in the objective function. Here, we give priority to monitor invariants. Assume that the numerical value for ϵ is 0.1. Then for W1's Inc method we obtain 0.1 for c.c1 and 0 for all other fields, which are the smallest possible values that satisfy the constraints (especially the first) in Fig. 6. This solution results in acc(c.c1, ϵ) for the pre- and postcondition, and analogous results for W2.Inc.

By the second and third constraint, and by the analogous constraints for W2.Inc, we obtain for Cell's monitor invariant 99.9 (that is, $100-\epsilon$) permission for c.c1 and c.c2, and 100 for c.x. This solution cannot be expressed in Chalice, which does not have syntax for a negative number of ϵ's. However, we could easily add a constraint that for each symbolic value, the mantissa of the numerical value in the solution must be in $[0; 0.5)$ and, thus, translate into a non-negative number of ϵ's. With this additional constraint, we obtain the pre- and postcondition **acc**(c.c1,1), and the monitor invariant **acc**(x) && **acc**(c1,99) && **acc**(c2,99). This solution reflects the need to split the permissions as discussed in Sec. 2, and allows one to verify the example in Chalice.

6 Experimental Results

We implemented our inference system in Sample, a generic compositional static analyzer. We executed the analysis on an Intel Code 2 Quad CPU 2.83 GHz with 4 GB of RAM, running Windows 7, and the Java SE Runtime Environment 1.6.0_16-b01. Table 3 summarizes the experimental results when we apply the analysis to case studies taken from (i) the Chalice tutorial [15] and the Chalice distribution, (ii) VeriCool [24], and (iii) VeriFast [12] libraries. Sample analyzes Scala programs. Therefore all the examples have been written in Scala using a custom library to represent statements that are not natively supported.

We performed the experiments applying the heap analysis with the unsound entry state and unsound inhaling, giving higher priorities to monitor invariants. Column Program reports the program we analyzed and LOC the lines of code; columns `Fractional`, `Counting`, and `Chalice` report the time of the analysis (in msec) when using fractional, counting, and Chalice permissions, respectively. `% Inferred Contracts` reports the percentage of inferred contracts including

Table 3. Experimental results

Program	LOC	Fractional	Counting	Chalice	% Inferred Contracts	Heap Analysis
Fig1	20	45	50	55	100%	22
Fig2	12	12	9	8	100%	11
Fig3	13	9	6	7	100%	8
Fig4	25	3	3	5	100%	8
Fig5	24	143	142	163	100%	80
Fig6	27	53	50	61	100%	20
Fig11	32	15	9	17	100%	20
Fig12	31	15	13	23	100%	25
Fig13	35	706	726	760	100%	223
OwickiGries	59	164	129	131	100%	39
cell – defaults	164	115	97	120	100%	55
linkedlist	77	78	82	86	100%	61
swap	15	10	9	10	100%	5
AssociationList	113	668	753	741	36%	305
HandOverHand	128	564	532	611	36%	478
Master	65	76	81	89	100%	57
CellLib	116	148	154	160	100%	79
CompositePattern	67	1217	1282	1279	71%	1009
Spouse	58	221	135	164	100%	33
Account	52	12	9	9	100%	16
Stack	54	76	74	78	67%	35
Iterator	57	46	55	53	100%	28

loop invariants w.r.t. the contracts that were in the original annotated program. Column `Heap Analysis` contains the time of the heap analysis (in msec).

The analysis takes less than a second in all cases except CompositePattern, and the times of execution are similar using different permission systems. We were able to infer all contracts for most of the examples, obtaining the same precision using different permission systems. On the other hand, we infer only one third of the annotation for AssociationList and HandOverHand and two thirds for Stack since these examples deal with recursive data structures, which are roughly approximated by our heap analysis. Similarly, CompositePattern contains a set of nodes that is roughly abstracted by the heap analysis, and so our approach is able to infer annotations for the fields of the class but not for the elements contained in such a set. The verification of programs with partial annotations would fail, but the user could manually add the missing contracts.

7 Related Work

There is a large body of work on the inference of program annotations. Ernst et al.'s Daikon system [9] uses a dynamic analysis to infer object invariants. Flanagan and Leino's Houdini tool [11] generates a large number of candidate annotations and uses ESC/Java to verify or refute each of them. Leino and Logozzo [13] integrate abstract interpretation and program verification to infer loop invariants. However, none of these inferences supports access permissions.

The Chalice language [14] provides an option `-autoMagic` to infer certain permission predicates. However, the inference does not find non-trivial splittings of permissions as required by our running example, and it cannot be applied to other permission models.

Calcagno et al. [3] propose an inference system based on bi-abduction. Their approach uses a compositional shape analysis to infer annotations over separation logic formulas. The approach has been extended to infer resource invariants for concurrent programs [4], that is, the (full) access permissions that are associated with a lock.

Yasuoka and Terauchi [27] propose a calculus to infer fractional permissions. Like our approach, they represent constraints with linear inequalities, and they solve them using linear programming. Their approach is focused on a simple region language, and it does not support object-oriented features and concurrency.

A major application of access permissions is to simplify framing, that is, determining what is definitely not changed by a method execution. There are several static analyses for frame information. Rakamarić and Hu [21] propose a technique to infer frame information for functions and loops on C programs. Spoto and Poll [26] introduce a static analysis based on abstract interpretation for JML's assignable clauses. However, their analysis only checks existing annotations, rather than inferring annotations. Cataño and Huisman's Chase tool [5] performs similar checks. The practical effectiveness of their approach has been demonstrated both in terms of precision and efficiency on industrial code. However, the approach is not sound, since it does not consider aliasing. In contrast to these approaches, we infer access permissions, which can then be used to infer framing information [25], and for other purposes like verifying concurrent code.

8 Conclusion

We presented an analysis to infer access permissions for various permission systems. Our approach infers pre- and postconditions and monitor invariants. It also handles loop invariants and abstract predicates, but we omitted them in the paper for brevity. The experimental results indicate that our analysis is efficient and precise. As future work, we plan to increase the precision of our approach adopting shape analysis [16] to obtain more precise heap abstractions, and to mutually refine the heap abstraction and the permission inference through a reduced product [7]. We also plan to extend the analysis to permission predicates where the permission is expressed by a program variable.

Acknowledgments. We are grateful to the anonymous referees, Agostino Cortesi, and Alexander J. Summers for their helpful feedback. This work was partially supported by the SNF project "Verification-Driven Inference of Contracts".

References

1. Bornat, R., Calcagno, C., O'Hearn, P.W., Parkinson, M.J.: Permission accounting in separation logic. In: POPL 2005. ACM (2005)
2. Boyland, J.: Checking Interference with Fractional Permissions. In: Cousot, R. (ed.) SAS 2003. LNCS, vol. 2694, pp. 55–72. Springer, Heidelberg (2003)

3. Calcagno, C., Distefano, D., O'Hearn, P., Yang, H.: Compositional shape analysis by means of bi-abduction. In: POPL 2009. ACM (2009)
4. Calcagno, C., Distefano, D., Vafeiadis, V.: Bi-abductive Resource Invariant Synthesis. In: Hu, Z. (ed.) APLAS 2009. LNCS, vol. 5904, pp. 259–274. Springer, Heidelberg (2009)
5. Cataño, N., Huisman, M.: CHASE: A Static Checker for JML's *Assignable* Clause. In: Zuck, L.D., Attie, P.C., Cortesi, A., Mukhopadhyay, S. (eds.) VMCAI 2003. LNCS, vol. 2575, pp. 26–40. Springer, Heidelberg (2002)
6. Cousot, P., Cousot, R.: Abstract interpretation: a unified lattice model for static analysis of programs by construction or approximation of fixpoints. In: POPL 1977. ACM (1977)
7. Cousot, P., Cousot, R.: Systematic design of program analysis frameworks. In: POPL 1979. ACM (1979)
8. Dantzig, G.B.: Linear programming and extensions. Rand Corporation Research Study. Princeton Univ. Press (1963)
9. Ernst, M.D., Perkins, J.H., Guo, P.J., Mccamant, S., Pacheco, C., Tschantz, M.S., Xiao, C.: The Daikon system for dynamic detection of likely invariants. Science of Computer Programming 69, 35–45 (2007)
10. Ferrara, P.: A fast and precise analysis for data race detection. In: Bytecode (2008)
11. Flanagan, C., Leino, K.R.M.: Houdini, an Annotation Assistant for ESC/Java. In: Oliveira, J.N., Zave, P. (eds.) FME 2001. LNCS, vol. 2021, pp. 500–517. Springer, Heidelberg (2001)
12. Jacobs, B., Smans, J., Philippaerts, P., Vogels, F., Penninckx, W., Piessens, F.: VeriFast: A Powerful, Sound, Predictable, Fast Verifier for C and Java. In: Bobaru, M., Havelund, K., Holzmann, G.J., Joshi, R. (eds.) NFM 2011. LNCS, vol. 6617, pp. 41–55. Springer, Heidelberg (2011)
13. Leino, K.R.M., Logozzo, F.: Loop Invariants on Demand. In: Yi, K. (ed.) APLAS 2005. LNCS, vol. 3780, pp. 119–134. Springer, Heidelberg (2005)
14. Leino, K.R.M., Müller, P.: A Basis for Verifying Multi-threaded Programs. In: Castagna, G. (ed.) ESOP 2009. LNCS, vol. 5502, pp. 378–393. Springer, Heidelberg (2009)
15. Leino, K.R.M., Müller, P., Smans, J.: Verification of Concurrent Programs with Chalice. In: FOSAD 2009. LNCS, vol. 5705, pp. 195–222. Springer, Heidelberg (2009)
16. Lev-Ami, T., Sagiv, M.: TVLA: A System for Implementing Static Analyses. In: SAS 2000. LNCS, vol. 1824, pp. 280–302. Springer, Heidelberg (2000)
17. Fähndrich, M., Logozzo, F.: Static Contract Checking with Abstract Interpretation. In: Beckert, B., Marché, C. (eds.) FoVeOOS 2010. LNCS, vol. 6528, pp. 10–30. Springer, Heidelberg (2011)
18. Mauborgne, L., Rival, X.: Trace Partitioning in Abstract Interpretation Based Static Analyzers. In: Sagiv, M. (ed.) ESOP 2005. LNCS, vol. 3444, pp. 5–20. Springer, Heidelberg (2005)
19. Owicki, S., Gries, D.: Verifying properties of parallel programs: an axiomatic approach. Commun. ACM 19, 279–285 (1976)
20. Parkinson, M., Bierman, G.: Separation logic and abstraction. In: POPL 2005. ACM (2005)
21. Rakamaric, Z., Hu, A.J.: Automatic inference of frame axioms using static analysis. In: ASE 2008. IEEE (2008)
22. Reynolds, J.C.: Separation logic: A logic for shared mutable data structures. In: Proceedings 17th Annual IEEE Symposium on Logic in Computer Science, pp. 55–74. IEEE Computer Society (2002)

23. Sagiv, M., Reps, T., Wilhelm, R.: Parametric shape analysis via 3-valued logic. ACM ToPLaS 24(3), 217–298 (2002)
24. Smans, J., Jacobs, B., Piessens, F.: VeriCool: An Automatic Verifier for a Concurrent Object-Oriented Language. In: Barthe, G., de Boer, F.S. (eds.) FMOODS 2008. LNCS, vol. 5051, pp. 220–239. Springer, Heidelberg (2008)
25. Smans, J., Jacobs, B., Piessens, F.: Implicit Dynamic Frames: Combining Dynamic Frames and Separation Logic. In: Drossopoulou, S. (ed.) ECOOP 2009. LNCS, vol. 5653, pp. 148–172. Springer, Heidelberg (2009)
26. Spoto, F., Poll, E.: Static analysis for JML's assignable clauses. In: FOOL 2003 (2003)
27. Yasuoka, H., Terauchi, T.: Polymorphic Fractional Capabilities. In: Palsberg, J., Su, Z. (eds.) SAS 2009. LNCS, vol. 5673, pp. 36–51. Springer, Heidelberg (2009)

Lazy Synthesis*

Bernd Finkbeiner[1] and Swen Jacobs[2]

[1] Universität des Saarlandes
finkbeiner@cs.uni-saarland.de
[2] École Polytechnique Fédérale de Lausanne
swen.jacobs@epfl.ch

Abstract. We present an automatic method for the synthesis of processes in a reactive system from specifications in linear-time temporal logic (LTL). The synthesis algorithm executes a loop consisting of three phases: Solve, Check, and Refine. In the Solve phase, a candidate solution is obtained as a model of a Boolean constraint system; in the Check phase, the candidate solution is checked for reachable error states; in the Refine phase, the constraint system is refined to eliminate any errors found in the Check phase. The algorithm terminates when an implementation without errors is found. We call our approach "lazy," because constraints on possible process implementations are only considered incrementally, as needed to rule out incorrect candidate solutions. This contrasts with the standard "eager" approach, where the full specification is considered right away. We report on experience in the arbiter synthesis for the AMBA bus protocol, where lazy synthesis leads to significantly smaller implementations than the previous eager approach.

1 Introduction

A major advantage of synthesis over verification is that manual programming is no longer required: synthesis automatically derives an implementation that is correct by construction. A major disadvantage is that synthesis requires a much more detailed specification. While the specifications used for verification typically focus on a small set of *safety-critical* properties, specifications for synthesis must describe *all* relevant properties of the process one wishes to synthesize as well as of the cooperating processes in the remainder of the system. This results in a *state explosion* problem similar to the infamous problem in verification, because the state space of the synthesized implementation is based on the product of all these properties.

An interesting example for this phenomenon is the synthesis of the AMBA bus protocol, which is currently the largest published case study carried out with automatic synthesis methods. Bloem *et al.* [1,2] report that the automatically

* This work was partly supported by the German Research Foundation (DFG) as part of the Transregional Collaborative Research Center "Automatic Verification and Analysis of Complex Systems" (SFB/TR 14 AVACS) and by the Swiss NSF Grant #200021_132176.

V. Kuncak and A. Rybalchenko (Eds.): VMCAI 2012, LNCS 7148, pp. 219–234, 2012.

generated implementation is about 100 times larger than the manually written code and, furthermore, grows exponentially with the number of bus masters, even though the manually written code almost remains constant. The approach used by Bloem *et al.* may in fact not even show the full scale of the problem, because the simplifying assumption is made that the synthesized process has access to the full system state. Under incomplete information, i.e., when some state variables are hidden from the synthesized process, an additional subset construction is required that causes a further exponential blowup [3].

In this paper, we address the explosion of the state space during synthesis with a novel combination of synthesis and verification. Rather than running a synthesis procedure based on a full specification, we use verification to *lazily* identify and add constraints on the synthesized process that are actually needed to rule out incorrect implementations. Our starting point is a *partial design*, which includes an implementation for the already implemented part of the system, which we call the *white-box* process, and the interface to the part of the system that is to be synthesized, which we call the *black-box* process. The implementation of the white-box process is given as a labeled transition system; for the black-box process, an implementation is to be synthesized such that the composition of white-box and black-box implementation satisfies the specification, which is given as a formula of linear-time temporal logic (LTL). Nondeterminism in the white-box process is interpreted as hostile: the black-box process must ensure the satisfaction of the specification for all possible behaviors. Disjunctions in the LTL specification, by contrast, represent friendly nondeterminism, leaving design choices open to the synthesis of the black-box process.

Starting with an initial (trivial) constraint on the black-box process, we use an SMT-solver to generate a sequence of candidate implementations. Each candidate is combined with the white-box processes and checked for reachable errors. As long as such errors exist, we extract new constraints on the black-box process that exclude the error in future iterations. The algorithm terminates when an implementation without errors is found.

The new synthesis technique, which we call *lazy synthesis*, thus alternates between constraint solving, which produces new candidates, and model checking, which identifies errors in the candidates that lead to a refinement of the constraints. We refer to the individual phases of this process as SOLVE, CHECK, and REFINE. The SOLVE-CHECK-REFINE loop of lazy synthesis can be understood as an extension of the CEGAR (Counter-Example Guided Abstraction Refinement) loop [4] commonly used in verification, with the difference that the counterexamples that drive the refinement process are not found in abstractions of the given implementation, but rather in the continuously changing candidate solutions produced by the SMT-solver.

As described so far, lazy synthesis tends to find implementations that are significantly smaller than those found by eager methods, because we avoid the full construction of the product state space, but the implementations are not necessarily minimal. To further reduce the size of the synthesized implementations, we have integrated the *bounded synthesis* technique [5] into lazy synthesis.

Bounded synthesis searches for implementations up to a given bound on the number of states. To ensure the minimality of the synthesized implementation, we maintain a constraint that limits the number of states of the implementation. Starting with an initial low value (such as a single state), we increase the bound whenever the constraint system becomes unsatisfiable. In our experience, the number of states that is actually needed for a correct implementation is usually very small compared to the product state space constructed by eager methods.

To evaluate this observation experimentally, we have repeated the AMBA case study with lazy synthesis. It turns out that a large part of the protocol specification [6] is already deterministic. We modeled this part as the white-box process and thus focused the synthesis effort on the arbitration policy, which is left open in the protocol specification. Unlike Bloem *et al.*, we do not assume complete information, and were therefore able to minimize the number of signals the arbitration policy depends on. For typical fairness properties such as "every bus master that requests a grant, will eventually get one," expressed in LTL, lazy synthesis finds implementations with a linear number of states in the number of bus masters. This is in contrast with the exponential growth of the size of the implementations reported by Bloem *et al.* [1,2] using eager synthesis.

The remainder of the paper is structured as follows. Section 2 introduces the AMBA protocol case study as a motivating example. In Section 3, we introduce the basic notions needed to discuss the synthesis problem; these notions allow us, in Section 4, to formalize the synthesis problem of the AMBA protocol case study. In Section 5, we describe the lazy synthesis algorithm. Section 6 gives some details on our current implementation of the approach, and in Section 7 we demonstrate how we used the approach and its implementation to synthesize arbiters for the AMBA specification. We conclude in Section 8 with a summary and some ideas for future research directions.

2 The AMBA Case Study

We will use the *Advanced Microcontroller Bus Architecture* (AMBA) specification [6] as a motivating example. This specification describes a communication bus for a number of masters and clients on a microchip. The bus controller keeps track of requests, and assigns the bus to one master at a time. Additionally, masters can ask for different kinds of *locked bursts*, i.e., sequences of transfers during which only this master is allowed to use the bus. We introduce briefly the signals that are used to realize the controller of this bus.

Requests and grants. To request the bus, master i will raise a signal HBUSREQi. The controller decides who will be granted the bus by raising signal HGRANTi. HMASTER[n:0] is an $n+1$-bit signal, where n is chosen such that the number of masters fits into $n+1$ bits. It always contains the identifier of the master which is currently active. Whenever the client raises HREADY, it is updated by letting HMASTER[n:0] = i, where HGRANTi is currently active.

Locks and bursts. A master can request a locked access by raising HLOCKi (in addition to HBUSREQi). If the locked access is granted, the master can set HBURST[1:0] to either SINGLE (single cycle access), BURST4 (four cycle burst) or INCR (unspecified length burst). For a BURST4 access, the bus will remain locked until the client has accepted 4 inputs from the master (signaled by raising HREADY 4 times). In case of an INCR access, the bus will remain locked until HBUSREQi is lowered. The arbiter raises signal HMASTLOCK if the bus is currently locked.

3 The Synthesis Problem

In this section we formalize the setting of our synthesis approach.

Partial designs. A *partial design* is a tuple $\mathcal{D} = (V, I, O, \mathcal{T}_W)$, where V is a set of boolean system variables, which also serve as the *atomic propositions*, the disjoint subsets $I, O \subseteq V$, $I \cap O = \emptyset$, are the *input* and *output* variables, respectively, of the black-box process. Input variables of the white-box are all variables from V, and outputs all variables from $V \setminus O$. $\mathcal{T}_W$ is the implementation of the white-box process, given as a labeled transition system, which is defined in the following.

Implementations. We represent implementations as labeled transition systems. For a given finite set Υ of directions and a finite set Σ of labels, a Σ-labeled Υ-*transition system* is a tuple $\mathcal{T} = (T, t_0, \tau, o)$, consisting of a finite set of states T, an initial state $t_0 \in T$, a (nondeterministic) transition function $\tau : T \times \Upsilon \to 2^T$, and a labeling function $o : T \to \Sigma$.

A *path* in a labeled transition system is a sequence $\mu : \omega \to T \times \Upsilon$ of states and directions that follows the successor relation, i.e., for all $i \in \omega$ if $\mu(i) = (t_i, e_i)$ then $\mu(i+1) = (t_{i+1}, e_{i+1})$ where $t_{i+1} \in \tau(t_i, e_{i+1})$. We call the path *initial* if it starts with the initial state and initial environment input: $\mu(0) = (t_0, e_0)$.

A process with input variables I and output variables O is implemented as a 2^O-labeled 2^I-transition system. Let $\mathcal{T}_1 = (T_1, t_{0,1}, \tau_1, o_1)$ be a 2^{O_1}-labeled 2^{I_1}-transition system, representing a process with inputs I_1 and outputs O_2, and let, likewise, $\mathcal{T}_2 = (T_2, t_{0,2}, \tau_2, o_2)$ be a 2^{O_2}-labeled 2^{I_2}-transition system, representing a second process with inputs I_2 and outputs O_2. The *parallel composition* of $\mathcal{T}_1$ and $\mathcal{T}_2$, denoted by $\mathcal{T}_1 \| \mathcal{T}_2$, is the $2^{O_1 \cup O_2}$-labeled $2^{(I_1 \cup I_2) \setminus (O_1 \cup O_2)}$-transition system $\mathcal{T} = (T, t, \tau, o)$, where the states consist of the product $T = T_1 \times T_2$, $t_0 = (t_{0,1}, t_{0,2})$, the transition function matches inputs with outputs generated in the previous step: $\tau((s_1, s_2), l) = \tau_1(s_1, (l \cup o_2(s_2)) \cap I_1) \times \tau_2(s_2, (l \cup o_1(s_1)) \cap I_2)$, and the labeling function is the union $o(s_1, s_2) = o_1(s_1) \cup o_2(s_2)$. We call the parallel composition of the white-box implementation and the black-box implementation the *system implementation.*

Specifications. We use linear-time temporal logic (LTL) [7], with the usual modalities Next $\bigcirc$, Until $\mathcal{U}$, Eventually $\diamondsuit$, and Globally $\square$, as the specification logic. If a sequence $\pi \in \omega \to 2^V$ satisfies an LTL formula φ, we say that π is a *model* of φ, denoted by $\pi \models \varphi$. A $2^{V \setminus O_{env}}$-labeled $2^{O_{env}}$-transition system (T, t_0, τ, o) *satisfies* an LTL formula φ if, for all initial paths $\mu : \omega \to T \times 2^{O_{env}}$ of the transition system, the sequence $\sigma_\mu : i \mapsto \tilde{o}(\mu(i))$ is a model of φ, where $\tilde{o}(t, e) = o(t) \cup e$.

Realizability and synthesis. An LTL specification φ is (finite-state) *realizable* in a partial design $\mathcal{D} = (V, I, O, \mathcal{T}_W)$ iff there exists an implementation $\mathcal{T}_B$ for the black-box process, such that the system implementation $\mathcal{T}_W \| \mathcal{T}_B$ satisfies φ. In this case, we say that the black-box implementation is *correct*.

Following the *bounded synthesis* approach [5], we introduce a bound $n \in \mathbb{N}$ on the size of the black-box implementation. Given an architecture $D = (V, I, O, \mathcal{T})$, a specification φ, and a bound n, we say that φ is n-realizable in D if there exists a correct implementation $\mathcal{T}_B$ of the black-box process, such that T_B has no more than n states.

The *synthesis problem* is to compute a correct black-box implementation if the given LTL specification is realizable in the given partial design.

4 The Partial Design of the AMBA Protocol

The starting point of the AMBA case study is the informal specification [6] available from the ARM website. In order to apply lazy synthesis, the informal specification needs to be formalized into a partial design and an LTL specification. In this section, we discuss these modeling decisions.

The white-box process. Upon inspection of the AMBA specification, one can easily see that at any given time, the valuations of variables HMASTER[n:0] and HMASTLOCK are completely determined by the history of the other variables of the system: whenever HREADY holds, the specification requires that in the next state HMASTER[n:0] will be equal to i, for every i such that HGRANTi holds in the current state. In addition to determining HMASTER[n:0] wrt. HREADY and the HGRANTi, this indirectly imposes a mutual exclusion property on the HGRANTi, since the property cannot be satisfied for multiple HGRANTi at the same time. In a similar fashion, HMASTLOCK is determined: whenever a master i is granted an access, variable HLOCKi determines whether it will be a locked access. If this is the case, and HBURST[1:0] is either BURST4 or INCR, then HMASTLOCK has to be set until the desired burst access is over, i.e. either until the client accepted 4 transmissions from the master (each signaled by HREADY being high), or until the master lowers HBUSREQi. Using this deterministic specification, we can easily build a white-box process that governs variables HMASTER[n:0] and HMASTLOCK and satisfies this part of the specification.

The black-box process. The remaining variables controlled by the system are the HGRANTi variables. Except for their valuation in the initial state, these are only indirectly specified by their influence on the other variables, and the global requirements on the overall system. These variables are controlled by the black-box process.

The interface of the white-box process. To keep the interface of the black-box small, we add an auxiliary variable DECIDE to the white-box process, which is set whenever the access of a master is finished. We will see that the right definition of DECIDE allows the lazy synthesis algorithm to find a correct black box process without knowing about the valuations of any other variables.

Figure 1 gives a slice of the resulting white-box process. In all of the depicted states, HMASTER[n:0] has the same value. The overall white-box consists of such a slice for every master, and transitions to states with a different valuation of HMASTER[n:0] are only possible from state 0, or the corresponding state in the given slice. HMASTLOCK is true in all states except 0 and 1, and DECIDE is true in the states depicted as dashed circles. Transitions that do not contain any conditions are taken unconditionally, and whenever none of the outgoing transitions is possible, we remain in the state. From 0, transitions into several different states of the other slices of the system are possible.

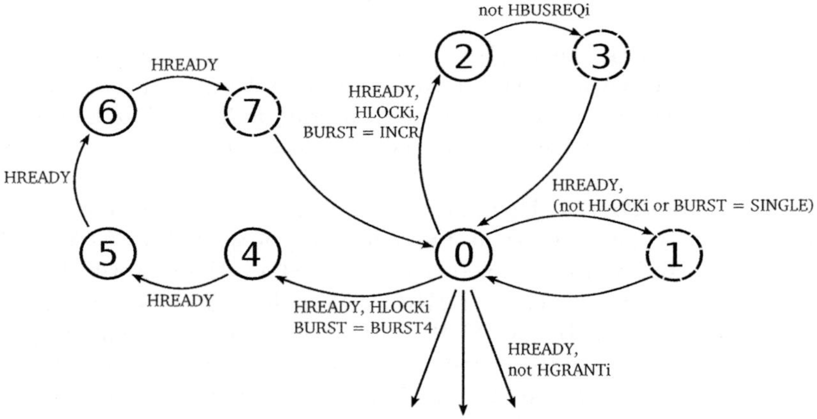

Fig. 1. Slice for one master of the AMBA white-box process

LTL specification. The LTL specification consists of the formula $A1 \wedge A2 \Rightarrow G1 \wedge G2 \wedge G3 \wedge G4$ with the assumptions and guarantees shown in Figure 2. Formula (A1) and (A2) are assumptions on the environment: neither are the clients busy forever, nor is the bus locked forever. The second formula is an indirect assumption on the environment, as the only way HMASTLOCK can be true forever in our white-box process is if HBUSREQi holds forever after master i acquires a lock on an INCR burst. ($G1$) and ($G2$) are guarantees that follow from the requirement that whenever HREADY is high, the white-box process must update HMASTER with any i s.t. HGRANTi is true. As HMASTER

Assumptions :

$$\Box\Diamond\ \text{HREADY} \qquad (A1)$$

$$\Box\Diamond\ \neg\text{HMASTLOCK} \qquad (A2)$$

Guarantees :

$$\Box\ (\text{HREADY} \rightarrow \bigvee_{\text{i}} \text{HGRANTi}) \qquad (G1)$$

$$\forall \text{i} \neq \text{j} : \Box\ (\text{HREADY} \rightarrow \neg(\text{HGRANTi} \wedge \text{HGRANTj})) \qquad (G2)$$

$$\forall \text{i} : \Box\ (\text{HBUSREQi} \rightarrow \Diamond(\neg\text{HBUSREQi} \vee \text{HMASTER} = \text{i})) \qquad (G3)$$

$$\forall i : \Box\ (\neg\text{DECIDE} \rightarrow (\text{HGRANTi} \leftrightarrow \bigcirc\text{HGRANTi})) \qquad (G4)$$

Fig. 2. The LTL specification of the AMBA specification

can only hold exactly one value, this implies that always exactly one grant must be true. ($G3$) is the fairness guarantee of the system: a HBUSREQi that is not lowered again will eventually be answered by setting HMASTER[n:0] = i. Finally, ($G4$) is an optional constraint on the auxiliary DECIDE variable. Similar to the definition of auxiliary variables for verification, this property of DECIDE will help guide the lazy synthesis algorithm.

5 Lazy Synthesis

We now describe the lazy synthesis algorithm, which solves the synthesis problem for a given partial design and LTL specification. The first subsection gives an overview of the Solve-Check-Refine loop, the individual building blocks of the loop are described in more detail in the following subsections.

5.1 The Solve-Check-Refine Loop

Figure 3 shows the main loop of the lazy synthesis algorithm. Given a partial design $\mathcal{D}$ and a specification φ, Procedure LazySynthesis($\mathcal{D}, \varphi$) computes the least bound $n \in \mathbb{N}$ such that φ is n-realizable in $\mathcal{D}$ and returns a black-box implementation with n states.

The algorithm incrementally increases the bound n on the number of states of the black-box implementation until an implementation is found. For each bound, we incrementally strengthen the constraint C, starting with *init_constraint*, until either the constraint becomes unsatisfiable and we try with higher bound n, or a correct implementation is found, at which point the algorithm terminates.

The algorithm builds on the following subroutines, which will be explained in the following subsections.

– Solve. The constraint C is a ground formula over booleans (representing inputs) and integers (representing states), with function symbols that represent transitions and outputs of the black-box component. It is used to forbid certain input/output patterns of the black-box process. Given such a constraint

```
LazySynthesis(D, φ)
n ← 1
correct ← false
C ← init_constraint
while correct = false
      do
          (model-found, T_B) = Solve(C, n)
          if model-found = true
             then
                  (correct, error-sequence) = Check(D, φ, model)
                  if correct = false
                     then C ← Refine(C, error-sequence)
             else n ← n + 1
                  C ← init_constraint
return T_B
```

Fig. 3. Algorithm for lazy synthesis. Given a partial design $\mathcal{D}$ and a specification φ, procedure LazySynthesis($\mathcal{D}, \varphi$) computes the least bound n such that φ is n-realizable in $\mathcal{D}$ and returns a black-box implementation with n states.

C and a bound n, procedure Solve(C, n) checks if there exists a black-box implementation with at most n states that satisfies the constraint C. The result is a pair (*model-found*, $\mathcal{T}_B$), where the first component *model-found* is a boolean flag indicating whether a solution has been found, and if this flag is true, then the second component is a candidate implementation for the black-box process.

- Check. Given a partial design $\mathcal{D}$, a specification φ, and a black-box implementation $\mathcal{T}_B$ constructed by Solve, Check($\mathcal{D}, \varphi, \mathcal{T}_B$) verifies whether the composition of white-box and black-box implementation satisfies φ. The procedure returns a pair (*correct*, *error-sequence*), where the first component is a boolean flag indicating whether the implementation is correct, and the second component is a representation of the error paths found if the implementation is not correct.
- Refine. Procedure Refine(C, *error-sequence*) organizes the error paths found by procedure Check into a tree representation that starts with the initial state. This error tree is then translated into a new conjunct in the constraint that forbids all error paths collected by procedure Check.

5.2 Solve

The goal of procedure Solve is to find an implementation for the black-box process that satisfies the constraints collected so far. For a black-box process with at most n states, we assume, without loss of generality, that the states are the natural numbers from 0 to $n - 1$ and that the initial state is 0. We can also assume that the black-box implementation is deterministic, because any given nondeterministic implementation, for which the system implementation satisfies the specification, can obviously safely be replaced by any of its deterministic restrictions. We represent the unknown transition function using an uninterpreted function symbol *trans* of type $\mathbb{B}^{|I|} \times \{0, \ldots n-1\} \to \{0, \ldots n-1\}$. The unknown labeling function is represented by an uninterpreted function symbol *label* of type $\{0, \ldots, n-1\} \to 2^O$.

We denote with $\mathbb{T}(X)$ the set of terms over a set X of function symbols and constants, and with $\mathbb{C}(X)$ the set of constraints over X. We use terms in $\mathbb{T}(\{trans, label, 0\})$ to symbolically identify the states that are reached after a certain sequence of inputs and outputs, and constraints in $\mathbb{C}(\{trans, label, 0\})$ to describe conditions on such states. Any interpretation τ, o of the symbols *trans* and *label* defines an implementation of the black-box process, the 2^O-labeled 2^I-transition system $\mathcal{T}_B = (\{0, \ldots n-1\}, 0, \tau, o)$. To improve readability, we will also use, for a given interpretation o of *label*, directly the variable names to denote functions from states to Boolean values. I.e., HGRANT0(1)= true iff HGRANT0 $\in o(1)$. In the synthesis loop, procedure SOLVE(C, n) uses an SMT-solver to find such interpretations. To enforce the limit on the size of the implementation, we extend the constraint system that is passed to the solver with an appropriate type constraint (i.e, $\forall\, \bar{b} \in \mathbb{B}^{|I|}, t \in \{0, \ldots, n-1\}.\ 0 \leq trans(\bar{b}, t) \leq n-1$).

Example 1. In the AMBA specification, the black-box process initially is only constrained by an upper bound on the size of the implementation we are currently looking for and the valuations of its output variables in the initial state 0. Suppose we want to synthesize an implementation for 2 masters, we are looking for models of size up to 3, the only input to the black-box process is DECIDE, and initially HGRANT0 should be high, and HGRANT1 low. Thus, we assert

$$\text{HGRANT0}(0) \wedge \neg\text{HGRANT1}(0) \wedge \forall\, b \in \mathbb{B},\ n \in \{0, \ldots, n-1\}.\ 0 \leq trans(b, n) \leq 2$$

in the SMT solver. We may get the model

$$\begin{array}{rlrl}
\text{HGRANT0}: & 0 \mapsto true & trans: & (false, 0) \mapsto 1 \\
 & 1 \mapsto false & & (true, 0) \mapsto 1 \\
 & 2 \mapsto true & & (false, 1) \mapsto 2 \\
\text{HGRANT1}: & 0 \mapsto false & & (true, 1) \mapsto 0 \\
 & 1 \mapsto false & & (false, 2) \mapsto 0 \\
 & 2 \mapsto true & & (true, 2) \mapsto 0,
\end{array}$$

representing a candidate implementation of the black box.

5.3 CHECK

Procedure CHECK verifies whether the composition of the candidate black-box implementation constructed by SOLVE with the white-box implementation satisfies the specification φ. If φ is violated, we extract a set of counterexamples. We are interested in *finite* counterexamples, because they can easily be eliminated in the subsequent REFINE phase. Since counterexamples to LTL specifications are in general infinite, we first translate the LTL formula φ to a safety property, for which all counterexamples are finite. As pointed out in [5], a reduction to safety is possible whenever the size of the implementation is bounded. To construct a monitor process for an LTL specification, we adapt a reduction given in [5], Theorem 4 (there stated in terms of a translation from universal co-Büchi tree automata to deterministic safety tree automata) to our setting.

Recall that a Büchi word automaton over alphabet Σ is a tuple $\mathcal{A} = (Q, Q_0, \Delta, F)$, where Q is a finite set of states, $Q_0 \subseteq Q$ a subset of initial states, $\Delta \subseteq Q \times \Sigma \times Q$ a set of transitions, and $F \subseteq Q$ a subset of accepting states. A Büchi automaton accepts an infinite word $w = w_0 w_1 w_2 \ldots \in \Sigma^\omega$ iff there exists a run r of $\mathcal{A}$ on w, i.e., an infinite sequence $r_0 r_1 r_2 \ldots \in Q^\omega$ of states such that $r_0 \in Q_0$ and $(r_i, w_i, r_{i+1}) \in \Delta$ for all $i \in \mathbb{N}$, such that $r_j \in F$ for infinitely many $j \in \mathbb{N}$. The set of sequences accepted by $\mathcal{A}$ is called the *language* $\mathcal{L}(\mathcal{A})$ of $\mathcal{A}$. Let $\mathcal{A}_{\neg\varphi} = (Q_{\neg\varphi}, Q_{0,\neg\varphi}, \Delta_{\neg\varphi}, F_{\neg\varphi})$ be a Büchi automaton that accepts all sequences in $(2^V)^\omega$ that satisfy $\neg\varphi$, and therefore violate φ.

Proposition 1. *For every LTL formula φ and every bound $m \in \mathbb{N}$ on the number of states of the system implementation, there exists a family of monitor processes $\{\mathcal{T}_{\neg\varphi,m'} \mid m' \in \mathbb{N}\}$ with error state err, such that*

1. *any system implementation $\mathcal{T}$ satisfies φ* if *err is unreachable in $\mathcal{T} \| \mathcal{T}_{\neg\varphi,m'}$, and*
2. *for $m' \geq m \cdot |Q_{\neg\varphi}| + 1$, any system implementation $\mathcal{T}$ with at most m states satisfies φ* if and only if *err is unreachable in $\mathcal{T} \| \mathcal{T}_{\neg\varphi,m'}$.*

Proof. We construct a monitoring process $\mathcal{T}_{\neg\varphi,m'} = (T, t_0, \tau, o)$ with designated error state *err*:

- $T = (Q \to \{0, \ldots m', \_\}) \cup \{err\}$;
- t_0 is the function $t_0 : Q \to \{0, \ldots, m', \_\}$ with $t_0(q) = 0$ if $q \in Q_0$ and $t_0(q) = \_$ otherwise;
- $\tau(err, \sigma) = \{err\}$, $\tau(f, \sigma) = \{err\}$ if there are two states $q \in F, q' \in Q$ such that $f(q) = m'$ and the transition (q, σ, q') is in Δ, and $\tau(f, \sigma) = \{f'\}$, otherwise, with $f'(q') = \max\{f(q) + g(q) \mid f(q) \neq \_, (q, \sigma, q') \in \Delta\}$, where $g(q) = 1$ if $q \in F$ and $g(q) = 0$ if $q \notin F$, and $\max \emptyset = \_$;
- $o(t) = \emptyset$ for all $t \in T$.

Each state of the monitoring process thus maintains, for each state q of $\mathcal{A}_{\neg\varphi}$, two pieces of information: (1) whether or not q is, in the current position, visited on some run (if not, q is assigned a blank $\_$ symbol), and (2) the maximum number of visits to accepting states on any run prefix of $\mathcal{A}_{\neg\varphi}$ ending in state q. If the number of visits to accepting states is bounded by m', the monitor does not reach *err* and the system implementation satisfies φ. For system implementations with up to m states, it suffices to use $m' = m \cdot |Q_{\neg\varphi}| + 1$. Consider the product $\mathcal{A}' = (Q \times T, Q_0 \times \{t_0\}, \{(q,t), \sigma, (q',t')) \mid (q, \sigma, q') \in \Delta, o(t') = \sigma\}, F_{\neg\varphi} \times T)$ of the system implementation and $\mathcal{A}_{\neg\varphi}$. If, on some run of the product automaton, the accepting states of $\mathcal{A}_{\neg\varphi}$ have been visited more than $m \cdot |Q_{\neg\varphi}|$ times, some product state consisting of some state of the implementation and some accepting state of $\mathcal{A}_{\neg\varphi}$ must have been visited twice, and we can hence construct a path in the implementation and an accepting run of $\mathcal{A}_{\neg\varphi}$ by repeating the cycle infinitely often. $\square$

Let $\mathcal{D} = (V, I, O, \mathcal{T}_W)$ be a partial design, φ an LTL specification, $m' \in \mathbb{N}$ a natural number, and T_W the states of $\mathcal{T}_W$. We call the pair $\mathcal{E} = ((V, I, O, \mathcal{T}_W \| \mathcal{T}_{\neg\varphi,m'}), T_W \times \{err\})$, consisting of a partial design and a set of error states, the *extended* partial design. The white-box process of $\mathcal{E}$ additionally keeps track of the state of the monitor process $\mathcal{T}_{\neg\varphi,m'}$.

An *error path* of a system implementation $\mathcal{T}$ of an extended partial design is a finite prefix $\mu(0)\mu(1)\ldots\mu(k)$ of a path μ such that $\mu(k)$ is an error state. A *counterexample* is an initial error path. If no counterexamples have been found, the algorithm terminates and returns $\mathcal{T}_B$. Otherwise, the set of counterexamples for $m' = m \cdot |Q_{\neg\varphi}|$ is collected in the form of an *error sequence* $E_0, E_1, \ldots E_k \in (2^T)^*$, such that for each $0 \leq i \leq k$, the states in E_i have a minimal error path of length i.

Procedure CHECK assumes a fixed bound m'. While $m' = m \cdot |Q_{\neg\varphi}| + 1$ is a safe choice, in practice it is more efficient to start with small bounds and incrementally increase m' if no implementation is found.

Example 2. The properties from Figure 2 are translated into a monitoring process. For simplicity, assume we only have a monitor for $(G2)$, with i=0 and j=1. The monitor moves from its initial state 0 into the error state *err* whenever HREADY, HGRANT0 and HGRANT1 are simultaneously true.

In the system implementation of the extended partial design, with the white-box implementation from Fig. 1 and the black-box implementation from Example 1, error states E_0 are all tuples (a, b, err), where a is any state of the black-box process and b is any state of the white-box process. We will denote this set of states as $(*, *, err)$. The backwards reachable states from $(*, *, err)$ are all states in which the black-box is in state 2, since this triggers the monitor to move into *err*. The black-box process only moves into 2 when it is in 1 and DECIDE is false, so in all pre-states the white-box needs to be in one of the states in $S_1 = \{0, 2, 3, 4, 5, 6\}$, or the corresponding states with HMASTER $= 1$. Denoting these states by S_1', the backwards reachable states from $E_1 = (2, *, *)$ are $E_2 = (1, S_1 \cup S_1', *)$. Finally, the black-box process can only reach state 1 from state 0, and does so without further conditions. Pre-states of $S_1 \cup S_1'$ in the white-box are $S_2 = \{0, 1, 2, 4, 5, 7\}$ and the corresponding S_2', so backwards reachable states from $(1, S_1 \cup S_1', *)$ are $E_3 = (0, S_2 \cup S_2', *)$. Since E_3 contains the initial state $(0, 0, 0)$, the sequence $E_0, \ldots, E_3$ is an error sequence.

5.4 REFINE

REFINE uses the error sequence found by CHECK to refine the constraint on the black-box process. For this purpose, we first organize the error sequence into a tree that starts with the initial state and branches according to the values of the variables visible to the black-box process. We denote a Σ-labeled finite tree over a set Υ of directions as a pair (N, l), where $N \subseteq \Upsilon^*$ is a prefix-closed set of finite words over Υ, identifying the nodes of the tree, and $l : N \rightarrow \Sigma$ is the labeling function. The root of the tree is the empty word ϵ. A node $w \in N$ is a leaf if it has no children, i.e., $\{w \cdot \upsilon \mid \upsilon \in \Upsilon\} \cap N = \emptyset$. Let $V_B = I \cup O$ be the set of variables visible to the black-box process.

A *counterexample tree* for a system implementation $\mathcal{T} = (T, t_0, \tau, o)$, an extended partial design $\mathcal{E} = \big((V, I, O, \mathcal{T}_W \| \mathcal{T}_{\neg\varphi,m'}), T_W \times \{err\}\big)$ and an error sequence $E_0, E_1, \ldots E_k \in (2^T)^*$ is a finite 2^T-labeled tree (N, l) with directions $\Upsilon = 2^I$ such that the following conditions hold:

- The root of the tree is labeled with the singleton set $\{t_0\}$ consisting of the initial state.
- For each node $w \in N$ and each direction $\upsilon \in \Upsilon$ there is a child $w \cdot \upsilon \in N$ iff (1) the label of w does not contain an error state, i.e., $l(w) \cap E_0 = \emptyset$, and (2) the set of states in $E_{k-|w|-1}$ that are υ-successors of states in the label of the parent is non-empty. In this case, the child is labeled with this set:

  $w \cdot \upsilon \in N$ iff $l(w) \cap E_0 = \emptyset$ and $\{\tau(q, \upsilon) \mid q \in l(w)\} \cap E_{k-|w|-1} \neq \emptyset$, and
  $l(w \cdot \upsilon) = \{\tau(q, \upsilon) \mid q \in l(w)\} \cap E_{k-|w|-1}$.

To refine the constraint on the black-box process, we translate the counterexample tree (N, l) into a constraint that ensures that, in future iterations, each counterexample is prevented by the black-box process.

Proposition 2. *Let (N, l) be a counterexample tree. There exists a constraint $C_{(N,l)}$ that eliminates exactly those black-box implementations for which the system implementation has one of the counterexamples in (N, l).*

Proof. We set $C_{(N,l)} := constr(\epsilon, 0)$, where the function $constr : (N \times \mathbb{T}(\{trans, label, 0\})) \rightarrow \mathbb{C}(\{trans, label, 0\})$ is defined inductively as follows:

- for a leaf node $w \in N, l(w) \cap E_0 \neq \emptyset$,
  $constr(w, t) = false$;
- for a non-leaf node $w \in N, l(w) \cap E_0 = \emptyset$,

$$constr(w, t) = \bigwedge_{w \cdot \upsilon \in N, \upsilon \in 2^I} \begin{pmatrix} label(t) \neq (\upsilon \cap O) \\ \vee\ constr(w \cdot \upsilon, trans(t, \upsilon)) \end{pmatrix}.$$

□

Example 3. We inspect the error sequence obtained during the CHECK phase in Example 2. Forward reachable states from $(0, 0, 0)$ are $(1, S_3 \cup S_3', 0)$, where $S_3 = \{0, 1, 2, 4\}$.

Construction of the counterexample tree can be seen as a branching model checking procedure, which first partitions S_3 into states $S_4 = \{1\}$ where DECIDE holds, and $S_5 = \{0, 2, 4\}$ where it does not hold. Then, state sets $(1, S_4 \cup S_4', 0)$ and $(1, S_5 \cup S_5', 0)$ are intersected with E_2 from Example 2, resulting in the empty set and $(1, S_5 \cup S_5', 0)$, respectively. Forward reachable from $(1, S_5 \cup S_5', 0)$ are $(2, S_6 \cup S_6', 0)$, where $S_6 = \{0, 1, 2, 3, 4, 5\}$.

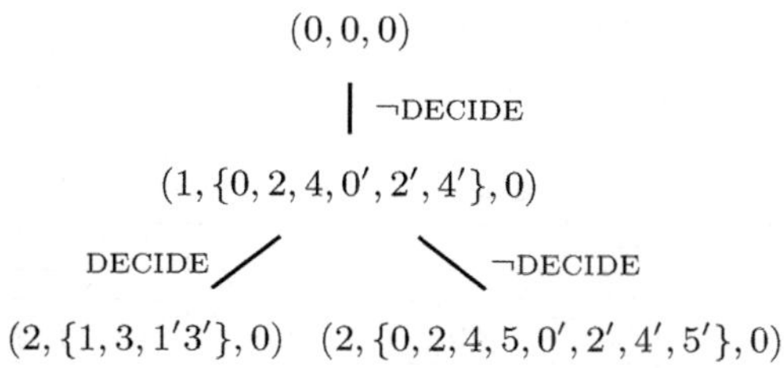

Fig. 4. Counterexample Tree

Partitioning states again wrt. DECIDE gives us $(2, \{1, 3, 1'3'\}, 0)$, and $(2, \{0, 2, 4, 5, 0', 2', 4', 5'\}, 0)$. Since we have reached state 2 of the black-box process (which triggers the monitor to move into *err*), all successor states of these will be error states. Figure 4 depicts the resulting counterexample tree (leaving out the leaves labeled with *false*). The corresponding counterexample constraint is

$$\begin{aligned}
&\neg \text{HGRANT0}(0) \vee \text{HGRANT1}(0)\\
\vee\ &\text{HGRANT0}(trans(false, 0)) \vee \text{HGRANT1}(trans(false, 0))\\
\vee\ &((\neg \text{HGRANT0}(trans(true, trans(false, 0)))\\
&\quad \vee\ \neg \text{HGRANT1}(trans(true, trans(false, 0))))\\
&\ \wedge (\neg \text{HGRANT0}(trans(false, trans(false, 0)))\\
&\quad \vee\ \neg \text{HGRANT1}(trans(false, trans(false, 0)))))).
\end{aligned}$$

6 Symbolic Implementation

We have implemented the algorithm described in Section 5 in OCaml, tightly integrating the SMT solver Z3 [8] and the BDD package CUDD [9].

Initialization. The input to our tool contains the partial design $\mathcal{D}$ and specification φ of the desired system in one file. White box and monitor automata are translated into a BDD representation of their initial and error states, as well as their respective transition relations. These will not change during the main loop of the algorithm.[1]

Main Loop: SOLVE, CHECK, REFINE

- SOLVE. The solve phase is handled by the SMT solver, which receives the current set C of constraints on the black-box process, and either returns a model or the result *unsatisfiable*. In the latter case, we increase the bound and try again.
- CHECK. The model obtained from the SMT solver is translated into a BDD representation, and we construct a BDD representation of the complete system, including the candidate black box. We apply backward model checking, storing BDD representations of the error sequence $E_0, \ldots, E_k$.

[1] This means that monitor automata currently do not grow with the size bound, but their size m' must be chosen large enough from start.

Table 1. Experimental Results

	DEC					w/o DEC				
	m'=10			m'=14	m'=18	m'=10			m'=14	m'=18
	$\|I\| = 1$	$\|I\| = 2$	$\|I\| = 3$	$\|I\| = 1$	$\|I\| = 1$	$\|I\| = 1$	$\|I\| = 2$	$\|I\| = 3$	$\|I\| = 1$	$\|I\| = 1$
2 Masters	0.6	0.6	0.6	0.4	0.7	0.3	0.3	0.5	0.4	0.5
4 Masters	14.6	18.4	61.0	39.1	242.9	47.6	162.6	TO	332.6	923.9
6 Masters	unsat	unsat	unsat	9952.0	TO	unsat	unsat	unsat	TO	TO

– REFINE. To obtain the *counterexample tree*, we start another model checking run, this time going forward from the backwards reachable initial states identified in the CHECK phase. In every iteration, we partition the reachable states according to the valuations of input variables of the black-box process, resulting in a branching model checking process. To allow efficient partitioning, we enforce an ordering on the BDD which always keeps input variables on top. Furthermore, every element of this partition is intersected with E_{k-j}, where j is the number of steps we have taken in the forward model checking process. As a consequence, state sets that will not lead to an error in the minimal number of steps become empty, and these branches of the process are pruned.

  During the branching model checking process, we store constraints on input variables that correspond to the partitioning of the reachable states in the counterexample tree. By construction, every branch of the process will have reached the error states after k steps, and we obtain an error tree of depth k. The constraints in this tree are combined as described in Section 5, such that they exclude all minimal error paths from this model in the future candidate models produced by SOLVE.

7 Experiments

Table 1 gives experimental results on the AMBA case study obtained with our prototype implementation of the lazy synthesis approach. We synthesized arbiters for architectures with 2, 4 or 6 masters, using lazy synthesis with monitors with a fixed valuation of m' of 10, 14, or 18. For the interface of the black-box, we tested the cases $I = \{\text{DECIDE}\}$, $I = \{\text{DECIDE}, \text{HMASTLOCK}\}$, and $I = \{\text{DECIDE}, \text{HMASTLOCK}, \text{HREADY}\}$. DEC indicates that we used the optional constraint $(G4)$ from Figure 2 to guide the search.

Times are given in seconds, on an Intel Core i7 CPU @ 2.67GHz. TO marks cases where a timeout of 5 hours has been reached, “unsat” cases where the specification is unsatisfiable for the given monitor. The size of the synthesized black-box is equal to the number of masters in the system. For 8 masters, the tool timed out for all options mentioned above.

Comparison to Bloem *et al.* The AMBA case study has been carried out with an eager synthesis method by Bloem *et al.* [1,2]. Similar to our auxiliary variable DECIDE, they defined several auxiliary variables and constraints that help guide the synthesis process. However, in contrast to our approach, Bloem *et al.* synthesized the complete controller, including the deterministic parts we have included in our white box. The advantage of synthesizing the complete controller is that it justifies the assumption of complete information, which results in a simpler synthesis problem. However, focusing the synthesis on the black-box process, which does not have access to the full state, allows us to obtain smaller implementations. Using lazy synthesis, we can minimize both the interface between black and white box (and thus, find the signals on which the arbitration policy depends) and minimize the number of states of the the black-box implementation. The size of the implementation synthesized using the lazy approach is linear in the number of masters, while Bloem *et al.* report exponential growth.

8 Conclusions

We have presented *lazy synthesis*, a novel combination of synthesis and verification. Lazy synthesis focuses the synthesis effort on the relevant part of the design, the *black-box* process and ensures that only constraints that are needed to rule out incorrect implementations are considered. The main practical advantage of lazy synthesis is that it produces dramatically smaller implementations than eager methods. This has three main reasons. First, unnecessary constraints are avoided. Second, the incomplete information of the black-box process is treated accurately, and, hence, irrelevant dependencies are avoided. Third, lazy synthesis integrates bounded synthesis, and thus ensures that the number of states in the implementation is minimal.

A related method, called *counter-example guided inductive synthesis* (CEGIS), has been proposed for functional synthesis of sequential and concurrent programs [10,11]. Like lazy synthesis, the approach is based on generating candidate solutions to the synthesis problem, and refining them based on error traces, but there are several differences. One of the main differences to lazy synthesis is that program executions in CEGIS are finite, while we consider properties of reactive systems on possibly infinite traces. Furthermore, synthesis in CEGIS is restricted to specific constructs, like finding values for constants and regular expressions, or reordering program statements given in the partial implementation. Finally, in case the candidate implementation does not satisfy the specification, we produce a constraint that excludes all minimal error paths from subsequent models, while the CEGIS approach only excludes one particular error per iteration.

Future Work. There are two major issues that deserve further investigation. The first issue concerns the limitation of the presented approach to finite-state white-box processes. This limitation could be avoided by integrating lazy synthesis with automatic abstraction refinement (cf. [12]). The second issue is the limitation to single black-box processes. In distributed systems, there are typically multiple processes that each have an incomplete view of the global state. Even though the synthesis problem for distributed architectures is, in general, undecidable, lazy synthesis should, in principle, be applicable to distributed architectures, because both the verification problem and the bounded synthesis problem are decidable.

Acknowledgments. We thank Bertrand Jeannet for help with the OCaml interface of CUDD.

References

1. Bloem, R., Galler, S., Jobstmann, B., Piterman, N., Pnueli, A., Weiglhofer, M.: Automatic hardware synthesis from specifications: A case study. In: Proc. DATE, pp. 1188–1193 (2007)
2. Bloem, R., Galler, S., Jobstmann, B., Piterman, N., Pnueli, A., Weiglhofer, M.: Specify, compile, run: Hardware from PSL. In: Proc. COCV, pp. 3–16 (2007)
3. Reif, J.H.: The complexity of two-player games of incomplete information. J. Comput. Syst. Sci. 29(2), 274–301 (1984)
4. Clarke, E.M., Grumberg, O., Jha, S., Lu, Y., Veith, H.: Counterexample-guided Abstraction Refinement. In: Emerson, E.A., Sistla, A.P. (eds.) CAV 2000. LNCS, vol. 1855, pp. 154–169. Springer, Heidelberg (2000)
5. Schewe, S., Finkbeiner, B.: Bounded Synthesis. In: Namjoshi, K.S., Yoneda, T., Higashino, T., Okamura, Y. (eds.) ATVA 2007. LNCS, vol. 4762, pp. 474–488. Springer, Heidelberg (2007)
6. ARM Ltd.: AMBA specification (rev.2) (1999), `www.arm.com`
7. Pnueli, A.: The temporal logic of programs. In: Proc. FOCS, pp. 46–57. IEEE Computer Society Press (1977)
8. de Moura, L., Bjørner, N.: Z3: An Efficient SMT Solver. In: Ramakrishnan, C.R., Rehof, J. (eds.) TACAS 2008. LNCS, vol. 4963, pp. 337–340. Springer, Heidelberg (2008)
9. Somenzi, F.: CUDD: CU Decision Diagram Package, Release 2.4.2. University of Colorado at Boulder (2009)
10. Solar-Lezama, A., Tancau, L., Bodík, R., Seshia, S.A., Saraswat, V.A.: Combinatorial sketching for finite programs. In: ASPLOS, pp. 404–415 (2006)
11. Solar-Lezama, A., Jones, C.G., Bodík, R.: Sketching concurrent data structures. In: PLDI, pp. 136–148 (2008)
12. Dimitrova, R., Finkbeiner, B.: Abstraction refinement for games with incomplete information. In: Hariharan, R., Mukund, M., Vinay, V. (eds.) FSTTCS (2008)

Donut Domains: Efficient Non-convex Domains for Abstract Interpretation

Khalil Ghorbal[1], Franjo Ivančić[1], Gogul Balakrishnan[1], Naoto Maeda[2], and Aarti Gupta[1]

[1] NEC Laboratories America, Inc.
[2] NEC Corporation, Kanagawa 211-8666, Japan

Abstract. Program analysis using abstract interpretation has been successfully applied in practice to find runtime bugs or prove software correct. Most abstract domains that are used widely rely on convexity for their scalability. However, the ability to express non-convex properties is sometimes required in order to achieve a precise analysis of some numerical properties. This work combines already known abstract domains in a novel way in order to design new abstract domains that tackle some non-convex invariants. The abstract objects of interest are encoded as a pair of two convex abstract objects: the first abstract object defines an over-approximation of the possible reached values, as is done customarily. The second abstract object under-approximates the set of impossible values within the state-space of the first abstract object. Therefore, the geometrical concretization of our objects is defined by a convex set minus another convex set (or hole). We thus call these domains *donut domains.*

1 Introduction

Efficient program analysis using abstract interpretation [12] typically uses convex domains such as intervals, octagons, zonotopes or polyhedra [11,13,15,18,27]. However, certain properties of interest require reasoning about non-convex structures. One approach to non-convex reasoning is to utilize powerset domains of elementary convex domains [3,5,21,22]. In general, it has proved to be difficult to provide satisfactory improvements over elementary convex domains with powerset domains while maintaining small enough performance degradation. Furthermore, it would be difficult to maintain enough disjunctions in the powerset depending on the particular non-convex shape being approximated. Note, however, that the recently proposed Boxes domain by Gurfinkel and Chaki [21] can potentially represent exponentially many interval constraints compactly. It utilizes a BDD-like extension to elementary range constraints called LDD [9]. However, we are interested in relational domains such as octagons, zonotopes or polyhedra as well.

Additional non-convex domains based on congruence analysis (either linear [20] or trapezoid [26]) have been developed. Such domains capture a congruence relation that variables satisfy and are suitable for the analysis of indexes of arrays for instance. Recent work by Chen et al. considered a polyhedral abstract

V. Kuncak and A. Rybalchenko (Eds.): VMCAI 2012, LNCS 7148, pp. 235–250, 2012.

domain with interval coefficients [10]. This abstract domain has the ability to express certain non-convex invariants. For example, in this domain some multiplications can be evaluated precisely. Other interesting non-convex abstract domains were introduced to capture specific invariants such as min-max invariants [2] and quadratic templates [1].

We address a different type of non-convexity commonly occurring in software, which relates to small sub-regions of instability within a normal operating (convex) region of interest. The non-convex region of values that may cause the bug is (under-)approximated using a convex inner region (or hole) that is subtracted from a convex outer region. We call this representation *donut domains*. Our approach relies on the usual operations defined on (convex) sub-domains, except for the need to compute under-approximations in the inner domain. The donut domains give a convenient framework to reason about disequality constraints in abstract domains such as in [29]. It can be considered as a generalization of the work on signed types domain introduced in [28]. There, we start with a finite set of types, and allow a set-minus operation only from the universal set.

Under-approximations of polyhedra. Under-approximations have been utilized for applications such as test vector generation and counterexample generation, by providing *must-reach sets*. Bemporad et al. introduced the notion of inner-approximations of polyhedra using intervals in [7]. In [24], polyhedra are under-approximated for test vector generation of Simulink/Stateflow models using a *bounded vertex representation* (BVR). Goubault and Putot describe a method to compute an under-approximating zonotope [19] using modal intervals [17] for non-linear operations.

In this work, we propose a novel technique to find under-approximations of polyhedra based on a fixed template. We first re-formulate the problem by introducing an auxiliary matrix. This matrix represents the fact that we are looking for an inner polyhedral object of a particular shape. Using this auxiliary matrix re-formulation, we can then use standard convex analysis techniques to characterize an under-approximations of polyhedra.

Motivating example. Figure 1 highlights a code snippet taken from XTIDE [1]. The XTIDE package provides accurate tide and current predictions in a number of formats based on algorithms. Similar patterns may exist in controller-related software to avoid regions of controller or numerical instability.

After the step marked `initializations`, (dx, dy) could be any point in $\mathbb{R}^2$ except the origin $(0, 0)$. In our analysis, this particular point is kept and propagated forward as a "hole". After the `if`-statement, the set of reachable values is: $(dy > dx \wedge dy > -dx) \vee (-dy > dx \wedge -dy > -dx)$. The above region is non-convex; therefore, a classical abstract domain will end up at this control point with $\top$ for both variables. Moreover, here, the interpretation of the strict inequality of the test is required to prove that $dx \neq 0$. The `else` case is even harder: in addition to the non-convexity of the set of possible values, one needs

[1] See `www.flaterco.com/xtide`

```
static void p_line16_primary (...) {
  double dx, dy, x, y, slope;
  ...                                /* initializations */
  if (dx == 0.0 && dy == 0.0)        /* full-zero-test  */
    return ;
  if (fabs(dy) > fabs(dx)) {         /* fabs-based test */
    slope = dx / dy;                 /* division-by-dy  */
    ...
  } else {
    slope = dy / dx;                 /* division-by-dx  */
    ...
  }}
```

Fig. 1. Motivating example from XTIDE

to consider the `full-zero-test` together with the negation of $|dy| > |dx|$, to prove that the division by dy is safe.

Contents. The rest of this paper is organized as follows. In section 2, we define a new set of domains called donut domains. Section 3 proposes a novel method to compute polyhedral under-approximations for arbitrary linear templates. Finally, in Section 4, first experiments and promising results are discussed.

2 Donut Abstract Domains

In this section we introduce donut domains, and define the operation on donut domains based on operations in the component domains.

2.1 Lattice Structure

Let $(\mathcal{A}_1, \leq_1, \sqcup_1, \sqcap_1, \perp_1, \top_1, \gamma_1)$ and $(\mathcal{A}_2, \leq_2, \sqcup_2, \sqcap_2, \perp_2, \top_2, \gamma_2)$ denote two classical numerical abstract domains, where $\leq_\star$, $\sqcup_\star$,$\sqcap_\star$,$\perp_\star$,$\top_\star$,$\gamma_\star$ denote the partial order, the join and meet operations, the bottom and top elements and the concretization function of the classical abstract domain for $\star \in \{1, 2\}$, respectively.

In this work, we extend a given abstract domain with an under-approximation operator $\breve{\alpha}$, such that for any concrete object X, we have $\gamma \circ \breve{\alpha}(X) \subseteq X$. An abstract object $X^\sharp_{1\setminus 2}$ of the domain $\mathcal{A}_1 \setminus \mathcal{A}_2$ is defined by a pair of objects $(X^\sharp_1, X^\sharp_2)$, such that $X^\sharp_1 \in \mathcal{A}_1$ and $X^\sharp_2 \in \mathcal{A}_2$. The object $X^\sharp_{1\setminus 2}$ abstracts the set of possible values reached by the variables as follows:

- The object $X^\sharp_1 \in \mathcal{A}_1$ represents an over-approximation of the set of reachable values.
- The object $X^\sharp_2 \in \mathcal{A}_2$ represents an under-approximation of the set of unreachable values (usually within $\gamma_1(X^\sharp_1)$).

The concretization function is defined as follows.

$$\gamma_{1\backslash 2}(X_1^\sharp, X_2^\sharp) \stackrel{\text{def}}{=} \gamma_1(X_1^\sharp) \setminus \gamma_2(X_2^\sharp) \ .$$

Figure 2 depicts a concretization of a typical donut object where the domain $\mathcal{A}_1$ is the affine sets domain [16] and $\mathcal{A}_2$ is the octagons domain.

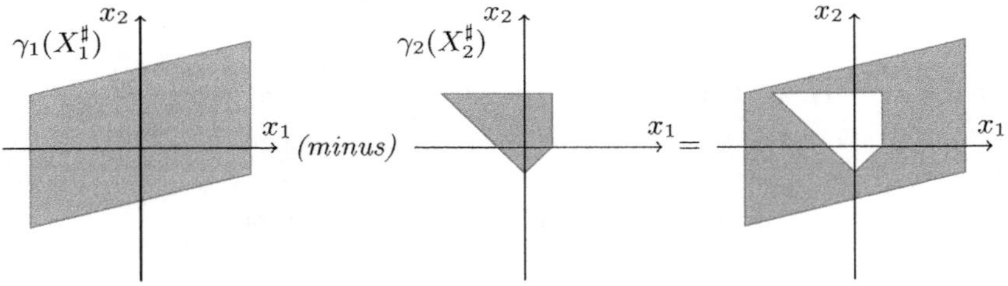

Fig. 2. The concretization of a typical non-convex abstract object

One should keep in mind the implicit set of unreachable values implied by $\gamma_1(X_1^\sharp)$ – namely $\mathbb{R}^p \setminus \gamma_1(X_1^\sharp)$ denoted in the sequel by $\bar{\gamma}_1(X_1^\sharp)$. Indeed, the set of unreachable values is actually $\bar{\gamma}_1(X_1^\sharp) \cup \gamma_2(X_2^\sharp)$. As said earlier, $\gamma_2(X_2^\sharp)$ is a (convex) under-approximation of the set of unreachable values. The fact that the intersection $\gamma_1(X_1^\sharp) \cap \gamma_2(X_2^\sharp)$ is not empty permits to encode a hole inside $\gamma_1(X_1^\sharp)$ (see Figure 2).

Interval Concretization. The interval concretization of the variable x_k, $1 \leq k \leq p$, denoted by $[x_k]$, is defined by $\pi_k(\gamma_1(X_1^\sharp) \setminus \gamma_2(X_2^\sharp))$, where π_k denotes the orthogonal projection of a given set onto dimension k. Note that $[x_k] \supseteq \pi_k(\gamma_1(X_1^\sharp)) \setminus \pi_k(\gamma_2(X_2^\sharp))$. For instance in $([-2,2] \times [-2,2], [-1,1] \times [-\infty,+\infty])$, we have $[x_2] = [-2,2]$, whereas $[-2,2] \setminus [-\infty,+\infty] = \emptyset$.

We embed $\mathcal{A}_1 \setminus \mathcal{A}_2$ with a binary relation and prove that it is a pre-order.

Definition 1. *Given $X_1^\sharp, Y_1^\sharp \in \mathcal{A}_1$ and $X_2^\sharp, Y_2^\sharp \in \mathcal{A}_2$, we say that $(X_1^\sharp, X_2^\sharp)$ is less than or equal to $(Y_1^\sharp, Y_2^\sharp)$ denoted by $(X_1^\sharp, X_2^\sharp) \leq_{1\backslash 2} (Y_1^\sharp, Y_2^\sharp)$ if and only if $X_1^\sharp \leq_1 Y_1^\sharp$ and*

$$\bar{\gamma}_1(X_1^\sharp) \cup \gamma_2(X_2^\sharp) \supseteq \bar{\gamma}_1(Y_1^\sharp) \cup \gamma_2(Y_2^\sharp) \ . \tag{1}$$

Proposition 1. *The binary relation $\leq_{1\backslash 2}$ is a pre-order over $\mathcal{A}_1 \setminus \mathcal{A}_2$. It defines an equivalence relation $\sim$ defined by $(X_1^\sharp, X_2^\sharp) \leq_{1\backslash 2} (Y_1^\sharp, Y_2^\sharp)$ and $(Y_1^\sharp, Y_2^\sharp) \leq_{1\backslash 2} (X_1^\sharp, X_2^\sharp)$ and characterized by $X_1^\sharp = Y_1^\sharp$ ($X_1^\sharp \leq_1 Y_1^\sharp$ and $Y_1^\sharp \leq_1 X_1^\sharp$), $\gamma_2(X_2^\sharp) \subseteq \gamma_2(Y_2^\sharp) \cup \bar{\gamma}_1(Y_1^\sharp)$ and $\gamma_2(Y_2^\sharp) \subseteq \gamma_2(X_2^\sharp) \cup \bar{\gamma}_1(X_1^\sharp)$. We reuse the symbol $\leq_{1\backslash 2}$ to also denote the partial order quotiented by the equivalence relation $\sim$.*

With respect to $\leq_{1\backslash 2}$, we have

$$(\bot_1, \bot_2) \sim (\bot_1, \top_2) \leq_{1\backslash 2} (\top_1, \top_2) \leq_{1\backslash 2} (\top_1, \bot_2);$$

therefore, we define the bottom and top elements of $\mathcal{A}_1 \setminus \mathcal{A}_2$ by

$$\bot_{1\backslash 2} \stackrel{\text{def}}{=} (\bot_1, -) \qquad\qquad \top_{1\backslash 2} \stackrel{\text{def}}{=} (\top_1, \bot_2) \ .$$

2.2 Decidability of the Order

Despite the non-convexity of $\bar{\gamma}$, the equivalence class introduced in Proposition 1 suggests particular representatives of objects $(X_1^\sharp, X_2^\sharp)$ which are easily comparable. Indeed, $\bar{\gamma}$ is no longer involved when the concretization of the hole $X_2^\sharp$ is included in the concretization of $X_1^\sharp$. Moreover, observe that the definition of the order relation $\leq_{1\backslash 2}$ allows comparing two abstract objects having their holes in two different abstract domains, since only the concretization functions are involved in (1).

Proposition 2. *Let $(X_1^\sharp, X_2^\sharp)$ and $(Y_1^\sharp, Y_2^\sharp)$ be two elements of $\mathcal{A}_1 \setminus \mathcal{A}_2$ such that $\gamma_2(X_2^\sharp) \subseteq \gamma_1(X_1^\sharp)$, and $\gamma_2(Y_2^\sharp) \subseteq \gamma_1(Y_1^\sharp)$. Therefore, $(X_1^\sharp, X_2^\sharp) \leq_{1\backslash 2} (Y_1^\sharp, Y_2^\sharp)$ if and only if $X_1^\sharp \leq_1 Y_1^\sharp$ and $\gamma_1(X_1^\sharp) \cap \gamma_2(Y_2^\sharp) \subseteq \gamma_2(X_2^\sharp)$.*

The condition $\gamma_1(X_1^\sharp) \cap \gamma_2(Y_2^\sharp) \subseteq \gamma_2(X_2^\sharp)$, can be checked in the abstract world rather than in the concrete domain up to the use of an expressive enough domain for both $\mathcal{A}_2$ and $\mathcal{A}_1$: for instance a box and an octagon can be seen as special polyhedra and the meet operation of the Polyhedra abstract domain can be used.

Let $X_1^{\mathcal{P}}$ denote the abstract representation in the Polyhedra domain of the abstract object $X_1^\sharp$, that is $\alpha_{\mathcal{P}}(\gamma_1(X_1^\sharp))$. To decide whether $(X_1^\sharp, X_2^\sharp)$ is less than or equal to $(Y_1^\sharp, Y_2^\sharp)$, we proceed as follows:

1. First, we "upgrade" $X_2^\sharp$ and $Y_2^\sharp$ to the Polyhedra domain. We denote by $(X_1^\sharp, X_2^{\mathcal{P}})$ and $(Y_1^\sharp, Y_2^{\mathcal{P}})$ the newly obtained abstract objects.
2. Then, we derive our particular representatives, namely $(X_1^\sharp, X_1^{\mathcal{P}} \cap_{\mathcal{P}} X_2^{\mathcal{P}})$ for $(X_1^\sharp, X_2^{\mathcal{P}})$ and $(Y_1^\sharp, Y_1^{\mathcal{P}} \cap_{\mathcal{P}} Y_2^{\mathcal{P}})$ for $(Y_1^\sharp, Y_2^{\mathcal{P}})$ ($\cap_{\mathcal{P}}$ being the meet operation in the Polyhedra domain).
3. Finally, we use Proposition 2 by checking for the inequalities $X_1^\sharp \leq_1 Y_1^\sharp$ and

$$X_1^{\mathcal{P}} \cap_{\mathcal{P}} Y_1^{\mathcal{P}} \cap_{\mathcal{P}} Y_2^{\mathcal{P}} \leq_{\mathcal{P}} X_1^{\mathcal{P}} \cap_{\mathcal{P}} X_2^{\mathcal{P}} \ .$$

2.3 Meet and Join Operations

We start with a simple example to clarify the intuition behind the formal definition given later.

Example 1. Consider a one-dimensional donut domain where $\mathcal{A}_1$ and $\mathcal{A}_2$ are Intervals domains. Assume we are interested in computing

$$([0,3],[1,2]) \cup ([1,6],[2,5]) \ .$$

The above join yields the following union of four intervals: $[0,1) \cup (2,3] \cup [1,2) \cup (5,6]$, which can be combined without loss of precision into $[0,2) \cup (2,3] \cup (5,6]$, or equivalently

$$[0,6] \setminus ([2] \cup (3,5]) \ .$$

What the example suggests is that when computing a join of two elements $(X_1^\sharp, X_2^\sharp)$ and $(Y_1^\sharp, Y_2^\sharp)$, we often end up with multiple (not necessarily convex nor connex) holes defined by $(\gamma_2(X_2^\sharp) \cup \bar{\gamma}_1(X_1^\sharp)) \cap (\gamma_2(Y_2^\sharp) \cup \bar{\gamma}_1(Y_1^\sharp))$. By distributing the meet over the join, we obtain:

$$(\gamma_2(X_2^\sharp) \cap \gamma_2(Y_2^\sharp)) \cup (\gamma_2(X_2^\sharp) \cap \bar{\gamma}_1(Y_1^\sharp)) \cup (\gamma_2(Y_2^\sharp) \cap \bar{\gamma}_1(X_1^\sharp)) \cup (\bar{\gamma}_1(X_1^\sharp) \cap \bar{\gamma}_1(Y_1^\sharp)) \ .$$

An under-approximation of the final element $\bar{\gamma}_1(X_1^\sharp) \cap \bar{\gamma}_1(Y_1^\sharp)$ is implicit since the over-approximation of reachable values is given by $X_1^\sharp \cup_1 Y_1^\sharp$. Thus, only the intersection of the first three sets will be considered (which is sound). In our example, $\bar{\gamma}([1,6]) = [-\infty, 1) \cup (6, +\infty]$, and $\bar{\gamma}([0,3]) = [-\infty, 0) \cup (3, +\infty]$, this gives $[1,2] \cap [2,5] = [2,2]$ and

$$[1,2] \cap ([-\infty,1) \cup (6,+\infty]) = \emptyset$$
$$[2,5] \cap ([-\infty,0) \cup (3,+\infty]) = (3,5] \ .$$

As said earlier, the intersection $([-\infty,1) \cup (6,+\infty]) \cap ([-\infty,0) \cup (3,+\infty])$ is implicit since it is covered by $\bar{\gamma}_1([0,3] \cup [1,6])$.

We now formalize the join operator:

$$(X_1^\sharp, X_2^\sharp) \cup_{1\backslash 2} (Y_1^\sharp, Y_2^\sharp) \stackrel{\text{def}}{=} (X_1^\sharp \cup_1 Y_1^\sharp, (X_1^\sharp, X_2^\sharp) \breve{\cap} (Y_1^\sharp, Y_2^\sharp)),$$

where $\breve{\cap}$ is defined by:

$$(X_1^\sharp, X_2^\sharp) \breve{\cap} (Y_1^\sharp, Y_2^\sharp) \stackrel{\text{def}}{=}$$
$$\breve{\alpha}((\gamma_2(X_2^\sharp) \cap \gamma_2(Y_2^\sharp)) \cup (\gamma_2(X_2^\sharp) \cap \bar{\gamma}_1(Y_1^\sharp)) \cup (\gamma_2(Y_2^\sharp) \cap \bar{\gamma}_1(X_1^\sharp))) \ .$$

We may perform heuristic checks to prioritize which hole (if many) to keep, which may also depend on the under-approximation abstraction function $\breve{\alpha}$. For instance we may choose an inner approximation (if working with closed domains) of the hole $(3,5]$ instead of choosing the hole $[2,2]$.

Notice also that we have a straightforward fallback operator $\breve{\cap}_{\text{fb}}$, that involves only $X_2^\sharp$ and $Y_2^\sharp$:

$$X_2^\sharp \breve{\cap}_{\text{fb}} Y_2^\sharp \stackrel{\text{def}}{=} \breve{\alpha}(\gamma_2(X_2^\sharp) \cap \gamma_2(Y_2^\sharp)) \ .$$

The operator is sound with respect to under-approximation. It focuses only on a particular hole, namely $\gamma_2(X_2^\sharp) \cap \gamma_2(Y_2^\sharp)$, instead of considering all possibilities. In our current implementation, we use this fallback operator in a smart manner: before computing the meet of both holes, we relax, whenever possible, in a convex way, these holes. This relaxation is performed by removing all constraints that

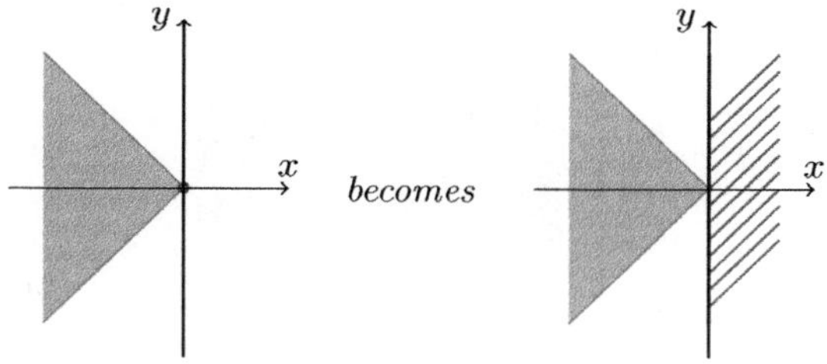

Fig. 3. Relaxing the hole $(0, 0)$ (red circle in the left hand side figure) to $x \geq 0$

could be removed while preserving $\gamma_1(X_1^\sharp)$. For instance, if the hole is the point $(0, 0)$, and the abstraction of $X_1^\sharp$ is given by the conjunction $y \geq x \wedge -y \geq x$, then the hole $(0, 0)$ is relaxed to $x \geq 0$ (see Figure 3).

For the meet operation, we proceed in a similar manner. If the domain $\mathcal{A}_2$ is closed under the meet operation (almost all polyhedra-like abstract domains), it is possible to replace $\breve{\alpha}$ by α, and $\breve{\cap}_{\text{fb}}$ by $\cap_2$. In our example, the fallback operator gives the box $[2, 2]$.

The meet operator $\cap_{1\backslash 2}$ is defined in a similar manner:

$$(X_1^\sharp, X_2^\sharp) \cap_{1\backslash 2} (Y_1^\sharp, Y_2^\sharp) \stackrel{\text{def}}{=} (X_1^\sharp \cap_1 Y_1^\sharp, X_2^\sharp \breve{\cup} Y_2^\sharp)$$
$$\text{where } X_2^\sharp \breve{\cup} Y_2^\sharp \stackrel{\text{def}}{=} \breve{\alpha}_2(\gamma_2(X_2^\sharp) \cup \gamma_2(Y_2^\sharp)) \ .$$

We deliberately omit $\bar{\gamma}_1(X_1^\sharp) \cup \bar{\gamma}_1(Y_1^\sharp)$ in the above definition of $\breve{\cup}$ because it is implicit from $X_1^\sharp \cap_1 Y_1^\sharp$. If the domain $\mathcal{A}_2$ is closed under the join operation, then $\breve{\cup}$ is exactly equal to $\cup_2$. Very often, however, the join operation leads to an over-approximation. Therefore the detection of an exact join as in [8,6] is of particular interest. In our current implementation, if $X_2^\sharp$ and $Y_2^\sharp$ overlap, we soundly extend, in a convex way, the non-empty intersection. For instance, if $X_2^\sharp = [-2, 1] \times [-1, 1]$ and $Y_2^\sharp = [-1, 2] \times [-2, 0]$, the intersection gives the box $[-1, 1] \times [-1, 0]$, and the extension we compute gives the box $[-2, 2] \times [-1, 0]$. If, however, the holes are disjoint, we randomly pick up one of them.

Example 2. Consider 2-dim simple abstract objects. Figure 4 shows a graphical representation of two overlapping objects. The remaining sub-figures highlight some of the pertinent steps with respect to the computation of $\cup_{1\backslash 2}$ and $\cap_{1\backslash 2}$ for such overlapping objects.

2.4 Loop Widening

When processing loop elements in abstract interpretation, we may require widening to guarantee termination of the analysis. For donut domains, we extend the widening operations defined on the component abstract domains. We use the pair-wise definition of widening operators ∇. We thus define widening of donut domains as:

$$(X_1^\sharp, X_2^\sharp) \nabla_{1\backslash 2} (Y_1^\sharp, Y_2^\sharp) = (X_1^\sharp \nabla_1 Y_1^\sharp, X_2^\sharp \cap_2 Y_2^\sharp) \ .$$

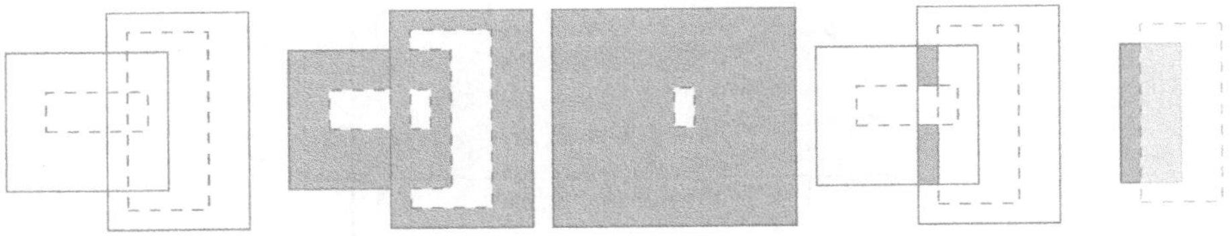

Fig. 4. Illustrating the join and meet operators using interval component domains. The donut holes are highlighted using dashed lines. (a) Two initial abstract objects. (b) The concrete union of the objects. (c) The abstract object representing $\sqcup_{1\setminus 2}$. (d) The concrete intersection of the objects. (e) The abstract object representing $\sqcap_{1\setminus 2}$.

We use the standard widening operator ∇_1 for abstract domain $\mathcal{A}_1$. Similarly, we use the standard meet operator $\sqcap_2$ of abstract domain $\mathcal{A}_2$ for the inner region, which ensures the soundness of $\nabla_{1\setminus 2}$. The convergence of the first component is guaranteed by the widening operator ∇_1. The convergence of the second component needs however more attention. Note that the simple use of narrowing operator of $\mathcal{A}_2$ is unsound as it may give a donut object which is not an upper bound. To ensure the termination we add a parameter k which will encode the maximal number of allowed iterations. If the donut object does not converge within those k iterations, the hole component is reduced to $\perp_2$. Note that the use of the narrowing operator of $\mathcal{A}_2$ instead of $\sqcap_2$ does not give in general an upper bound of $(X_1^\sharp, X_2^\sharp)$ and $(Y_1^\sharp, Y_2^\sharp)$.

2.5 Interpretation of Tests

The ability to express holes allows us to better handle a wide range of non-convex tests such as the $\neq$ test or the strict inequality test. We start with classical tests. For $\diamond \in \{=, \leq\}$:

$$[\![x_k \diamond 0]\!]^\sharp(X_1^\sharp, X_2^\sharp) \stackrel{\text{def}}{=} ([\![x_k \diamond 0]\!]_1^\sharp(X_1^\sharp), [\![x_k \diamond 0]\!]_1^\natural(X_2^\sharp)),$$

where $[\![\cdot]\!]_2^\natural \stackrel{\text{def}}{=} \breve{\alpha}_2 \circ [\![\cdot]\!]_2$. Such under-approximation is required so that the newly computed (exact) hole can be encoded in $\mathcal{A}_2$. Therefore, if the exact hole fits naturally in $\mathcal{A}_2$ (say we have a linear constraint and $\mathcal{A}_2$ is the Polyhedra domain), there is no need to under-approximate ($[\![\cdot]\!]_2^\natural = [\![\cdot]\!]_2^\sharp$). In Section 3, we detail how we compute such an under-approximation, whenever needed. If no algorithm is available for the under-approximation, we keep the object $X_2^\sharp$ unchanged, which is sound.

The non-equality test $\neq$ is defined as follows:

$$[\![x_k \neq 0]\!]^\sharp(X_1^\sharp, X_2^\sharp) \stackrel{\text{def}}{=} ([\![x_k \neq 0]\!]^\sharp(X_1^\sharp), \breve{\alpha}(\gamma_2(X_2^\sharp) \cup [\![x_k = 0]\!]\top_2)) \ .$$

Although $[\![x_k \neq 0]\!]^\sharp(X_1^\sharp)$ is interpreted as the identity function in standard implementations, nothing prevents the use of any available enhancement proposed by the used analyzer. For the hole, we compute the join of the new hole implied by the constraint $x_k \neq 0$ together with the already existing hole $X_2^\sharp$. If holes $\gamma_2(X_2^\sharp)$ and $[\![x_k = 0]\!]\top_2$ do not overlap, we discard $X_2^\sharp$. In fact, very often (as will be seen in experiments), the hole induced by the constraint $x_k \neq 0$ is mandatory in order to prove the safety of subsequent computations.

Finally, our approach offers, for free, an interesting abstraction of the strict inequality tests. A comparison with Not Necessarily Closed domains [4] is planned as future work.

$$[\![x_k < 0]\!]^\sharp(X_1^\sharp, X_2^\sharp) \stackrel{\text{def}}{=} [\![x_k \neq 0]\!]^\sharp \circ [\![x_k \leq 0]\!]^\sharp(X_1^\sharp, X_2^\sharp) \ .$$

2.6 Abstract Assignment

We define in this section the abstraction of the assignment transfer function in $\mathcal{A}_1 \setminus \mathcal{A}_2$. We first give an abstraction of the forget transfer function (non-deterministic assignment) :

$$\begin{aligned}
&[\![x_k \leftarrow ?]\!]_{1\backslash 2}^\sharp(X_1^\sharp, X_2^\sharp) \stackrel{\text{def}}{=} (Y_1^\sharp, Y_2^\sharp), \\
&\quad \text{where } Y_1^\sharp \stackrel{\text{def}}{=} [\![x_k \leftarrow ?]\!]_1^\sharp(X_1^\sharp) \\
&\quad Y_2^\sharp \stackrel{\text{def}}{=} \begin{cases} [\![x_k \leftarrow ?]\!]_2^\sharp(X_2^\sharp) \ \textbf{if}\ \gamma_1(X_1^\sharp) \cap \gamma_2([\![x_k \leftarrow ?]\!]_2^\sharp(X_2^\sharp)) \subseteq \gamma_2(X_2^\sharp) \\ \bot_2 \quad \textbf{otherwise} \ . \end{cases}
\end{aligned}$$

For $Y_2^\sharp$, we basically check whether applying the forget operator to $X_2^\sharp$ intersects $\gamma_{1\backslash 2}(X_1^\sharp, X_2^\sharp)$, by checking if this newly computed hole is included in the original hole, that is $\gamma_2(X_2^\sharp)$. If yes, $Y_2^\sharp$ is set to $\bot_2$. For instance, forgetting x_2 in $(X_1^\sharp, X_2^\sharp) \stackrel{\text{def}}{=} ([-2,2] \times [-2,2], [-1,1] \times [-\infty,+\infty])$ gives $([-2,2] \times [-\infty,+\infty], [-1,1] \times [-\infty,+\infty])$: since $[\![x_2 \leftarrow ?]\!]_2^\sharp(X_2^\sharp) = [-1,1] \times [-\infty,+\infty]$, $\gamma_1(X_1^\sharp) \cap \gamma_2([\![x_2 \leftarrow ?]\!]_2^\sharp(X_2^\sharp)) = [-1,1] \times [-2,2]$ which is included in $\gamma_2(X_2^\sharp)$. Forgetting x_1, however, makes $Y_2^\sharp = \bot_2$.

The assignment could be seen as a sequence of multiple basic, already defined, operations. We distinguish two kind of assignments $x \leftarrow e$, where e is an arithmetic expression: ($\imath$) non-invertible assignments, where the old values of x are lost, such as $x \leftarrow c$, $c \in \mathbb{R}$, and ($\imath\imath$) invertible assignments, such as $x \leftarrow x + y$. For non-invertible assignment, we have:

$$[\![x_k \leftarrow e]\!]_{1\backslash 2}^\sharp \stackrel{\text{def}}{=} [\![x_k = e]\!]_{1\backslash 2}^\sharp \circ [\![x_k \leftarrow ?]\!]_{1\backslash 2}^\sharp \ .$$

Invertible assignments are defined in a similar manner. It augments first the set of variables by a new fresh variable, say v, then enforces the test $v = e$, and finally forgets x and (syntactically) renames v to x. Notice that augmenting the set of variables in $\mathcal{A}_1 \setminus \mathcal{A}_2$ makes the newly added variable, v, unconstrained in both components, $X_1^\sharp$ and $X_2^\sharp$. We can suppose that such a variable v already exists, and used whenever we have an invertible assignment; hence, we obtain:

$$[\![x_k \leftarrow e]\!]_{1\backslash 2}^\sharp \stackrel{\text{def}}{=} \textbf{swap}(x_k, v) \ \textbf{in} \ [\![x_k \leftarrow ?]\!]_{1\backslash 2}^\sharp \circ [\![v = e]\!]_{1\backslash 2}^\sharp \ .$$

3 Template-Based under-Approximations of Polyhedra

In this section we develop a new technique to under-approximate holes obtained after linear tests. Holes obtained after non-linear tests are so far reduced to $\bot_2$, which is sound. We plan to improve this as a future work. Consider for instance the object $([-2,3]\times[-2,2],[-1,1]\times[0,1])$. Figure 5 depicts the exact evaluation of a linear assignment. If we use boxes to encode holes, we need to compute a box inside the white polytope. In Figure 6, an under-approximation is needed for all convex domains, whereas a non-convex domain such as Interval Polyhedra [10] can express exactly this kind of pattern.

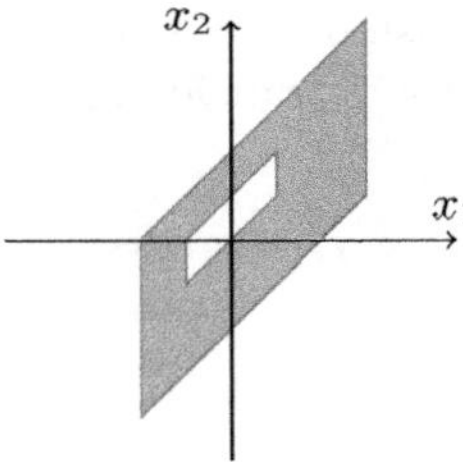

Fig. 5. Evaluation of a linear expression $[\![x_2 \leftarrow x_1 + x_2]\!]^\sharp_{1\backslash 2}$

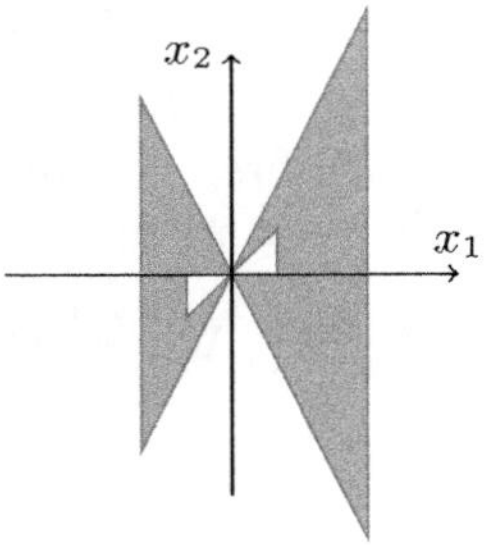

Fig. 6. Evaluation of a non-linear expression $[\![x_2 \leftarrow x_1 \times x_2]\!]^\sharp_{1\backslash 2}$

The problem can be seen as follows: given a polyhedron $\mathcal{P}$, we seek to compute a maximal (in a sense to define) inner polyhedron $\mathcal{T}$ (could be boxes, zones, octagons, linear-templates, etc. depending on $\mathcal{A}_2$), which obeys the template pattern matrix T.

Let $\mathcal{P} = \{x \in \mathbb{R}^p | Ax \leq b\}$ be a non-empty polyhedron, where A is a known $m\times p$ matrix, b a known vector of $\mathbb{R}^m$, and x a vector of $\mathbb{R}^p$. The inner polyhedron $\mathcal{T}$ is expressed in a similar manner: $\mathcal{T} = \{x \in \mathbb{R}^p | Tx \leq c\}$, where T is a known $n \times p$ matrix, and c and x are unknown vectors within $\mathbb{R}^n$ and $\mathbb{R}^p$, respectively. The inclusion $\mathcal{T} \subseteq \mathcal{P}$ holds if and only if

$$\exists c \in \mathbb{R}^n, \text{ such that } \mathcal{T} \text{ is consistent, and } \forall x \in \mathbb{R}^p : Tx \leq c \implies Ax \leq b \ .$$

The consistency of $\mathcal{T}$ (that is the system admits a solution in $\mathbb{R}^p$) discards the trivial (and unwanted) cases where the polyhedron $\mathcal{T}$ is empty. For the non-trivial cases, the existence of the vector c and the characterization of the set of its possible values are given by Proposition 3.

Proposition 3. *Let C be the set of c such that $\mathcal{T}$ is consistent. There exists a vector $c \in C$ such that $\mathcal{T} \subseteq \mathcal{P}$ if and only if there exists an $n \times m$ matrix Λ, such that $\lambda_{i,j}$, the elements of the matrix Λ, are non-negative and $\Lambda T = A$. For a given possible Λ, the set $c_\Lambda \subseteq C$ is characterized by*

$$\{c \in \mathbb{R}^n \mid \Lambda c \leq b\} \ .$$

Proof. Let x denote a vector of $\mathbb{R}^p$, and b denote a known vector of $\mathbb{R}^m$. Let A and T be two known matrices with p columns and m and n rows, respectively. Suppose that c is such that $\mathcal{T}$ is consistent. Therefore, we can assume that

$$\langle t_i, x\rangle \leq c_i, 1 \leq i \leq n,$$

where t_i denotes the ith row of the matrix T, is consistent. For a fixed j, $1 \leq j \leq m$, the inequality $\langle a_j, x\rangle \leq b_j$, is then a consequence of the system $Tx \leq c$ if and only if there exist non-negative real numbers $\lambda_{i,j}$, $1 \leq i \leq n$, such that

$$\sum_{i=1}^{n} \lambda_{i,j} t_i = a_j \text{ and } \sum_{i=1}^{n} \lambda_{i,j} c_i \leq b_j \ .$$

The previous claim of the existence of the non-negative $\lambda_{i,j}$ is a generalization of the classical Farkas' Lemma (see for instance [30, Section 22, Theorem 22.3] for a detailed proof). The matrix Λ is then constructed column by column using the elements $\lambda_{i,j}$, $1 \leq i \leq n$ for the jth column. Of course, by construction, such a Λ has non-negative elements, and satisfies $\Lambda T = A$, and $\Lambda c \leq b$.

On the other hand, if such a matrix exists, and the set $\{c \in \mathbb{R}^n \mid \Lambda c \leq b\}$ is not empty, we have by the fact that Λ has non-negative elements

$$Tx \leq c \implies \Lambda Tx \leq \Lambda c \ .$$

Therefore, $\Lambda T = A$ and $\Lambda c \leq b$, gives $Ax \leq b$. □

On the Consistency of $Tx \leq c$. It not obvious in general, given a matrix T, to characterize the set of c such that $\mathcal{T}$ is consistent. However, given a vector c, we can efficiently check whether the system is consistent or not using its dual form and a LP solver. Indeed, the system $Tx \leq c$ is inconsistent if and only if there exists a non-negative vector $\lambda \in \mathbb{R}^n$ such that $T^t\lambda = 0$ and $\langle \lambda, c\rangle < 0$, where T^t denotes the transpose of T. Therefore, given a vector c, if the objective value of the following problem:

$$\begin{array}{ll} \min & \langle \lambda, c\rangle \\ \text{s.t.} & T^t\lambda = 0 \ . \end{array} \qquad (2)$$

is non-negative, the system is consistent. Observe that, for simple patterns such as boxes, the characterization of the set of c that makes the system consistent is immediate.

Computing Λ. The matrix Λ is built column by column. Let us denote by $\lambda_{-,j} \in \mathbb{R}^n$ the jth column of Λ, by $a_j \in \mathbb{R}^p$, $1 \leq j \leq m$, the jth row of A, by $b_j \in \mathbb{R}$ the jth component of b, and by $t_i \in \mathbb{R}^p$, $1 \leq i \leq m$, the ith row of T. The vector $\lambda_{-,j}$ satisfies $\sum_{i=1}^{n} \lambda_{i,j} t_i = a_j$. To each feasible $\lambda_{-,j}$ corresponds a pattern

$$\mathcal{P}_{\lambda_{-,j}} \stackrel{\text{def}}{=} \{x \in \mathbb{R}^p \mid \bigwedge_{\lambda_{i,j}>0} \langle t_i, x\rangle \leq 0\},$$

which is included in the affine subspace $\mathcal{P}_j \stackrel{\text{def}}{=} \{x \in \mathbb{R}^p \mid \langle a_j, x\rangle \leq 0\}$. The maximal pattern (with respect to set inclusion) corresponds to $\bar{\lambda}$ defined as the solution of the following linear program.

$$\begin{array}{ll} \min & \sum_{i=1}^{n} \lambda_{i,j} \|t_i\| \\ \text{s.t.} & \begin{array}{l} \sum_{i=1}^{n} \lambda_{i,j} t_i = a_j \\ \forall 0 \leq i \leq n, \lambda_{i,j} \geq 0 \end{array} . \end{array} \tag{3}$$

Therefore, computing Λ needs solving p instances of the LP (3).

Computing c. We have already established (Proposition 3) that the vector c verifies $\Lambda c \leq b$. Since Λ is known, any feasible c (that is such that $\Lambda c \leq b$) that makes the system $Tx \leq c$ consistent (the objective value of the LP (2) is non-negative) gives an under-approximation of $\mathcal{P}$ that respects our initial template T. Of course, it is immediate to see that the set of c that lies on the boundaries of the feasible region (that is by making $\Lambda c = b$) gives, in general, a "better" under-approximation than the strict feasible solutions since the saturation makes some of the facets of the inner pattern ($\mathcal{T}$) included in those of the under-approximated polyhedron $\mathcal{P}$. Moreover, in some cases, the saturation gives a unique consistent solution for c. For instance, when we under-approximate a shape $\mathcal{P}$ which respects already the pattern $\mathcal{T}$, c is uniquely determined and gives actually b using our technique. In other words, under-approximating an octagon (for instance) with an octagonal pattern gives exactly the first octagon.

4 Implementation

We have implemented donut domains on top of APRON library [23]. The domains $\mathcal{A}_1$ and $\mathcal{A}_2$ are parameters of the analysis and can be specified by the user among already existing APRON domains. The current version uses an enhanced implementation of the set-theoretic operators, mainly based on already existing routines of the underlying abstract domains, as described earlier, and relies on $\breve{\cup}_{fb}$ and $\breve{\cap}_{fb}$ as fallback operators. This very simple approach allows to build the donut domain without additional effort on top of already existing domains. The analyzed examples[2] (see Table 4) use mainly the absolute value function to avoid the division by zero (widely used technique). The `motiv` example is the motivating example with its two branches. The `gpc` code is extracted from the Generic Polygon Clipper project. The examples `xcor`, `goc` and `x2` are extracted from a geometric object contact detection library. The WCfS column indicates the weakest condition that we need to infer to prove the safety of the program.

[2] `www.nec-labs.com/research/system/systems_SAV-website/benchmarks.php`. The C files are the real source code, while the SPL files extracts the hard piece of code that leads to false alarms, and with which we feed our proof of concept implementation.

Table 1. Division-by-zero analysis results

	WCfS	boxes (hole)	false alarms
`motiv`(if)	$dy \neq 0$	$dy = 0$	0
`motiv`(else)	$dx \neq 0$	$dx = 0$	0
`gpc`	$den \neq 0$	$den \in [-0.1, 0.1]$	0
`goc`	$d \neq 0$	$d \in [-0.09, 0.09]$	0
`x2`	$Dx \neq 0$	$Dx = 0$	0
`xcor`	$usemax \neq 0$	$usemax \in [1, 10]$	1

Whenever the negation of this condition is verified by (included in) the donut hole, the program is proved to be safe. The third column shows the inferred donut holes when using a non-relational domain (boxes) to encode holes. As Table 4 shows, our approach permits to catch almost all division-by-zero false positives that classical domains (even non-convex) fail to prove. Here, the use of boxes is sufficient to eliminate almost all false alarms here. In the last example, among the two possible holes, namely $usemax \in [1, 10]$ and $usemax \in \{0\}$, we choose by default the one created immediately after the test ($usemax > 10$ or $usemax < 1$). Here the safety property can not be proved with this hole and relies on an earlier (disjoint) hole created by a former test, namely $usemax \in \{0\}$. We could also choose systematically (as a heuristic) the hole that contains "zero", which is sufficient here to discard the remaining false alarm. Such a property-driven hole behavior would be an interesting direction for future research.

The proof of the motivating example is really challenging as it requires to handle both the hole that comes from the full-zero-test, together with strict inequality tests and the over-approximation that comes from the join operation. Our technique that consists of relaxing the hole in a convex way before using the fallback operator works here and is able to prove that in both branches the division is safe. In `goc` example, we can see one interesting ability of donuts domain: when we compute a convex join of two non-overlapping objects, the hole in between is directly captured which permits a better precision. Finally, example `x2` needs a precise interpretation of strict inequalities.

Under-approximation. We have implemented our technique of Section 3 using the GLPK [25] solver. Some experiments, obtained for randomly generated polyhedra with octagonal template, are shown in Figure 7. Although all shown polyhedra are bounded, our technique works perfectly well for unbounded shapes. The rate of volume, $\frac{vol\mathcal{T}}{vol\mathcal{P}}$, is used as a metric for the quality of the under-approximation (shown near each pattern in Figure 7). All obtained octagons are maximal with respect to set inclusion. It is not clear which choice among many (see the left graph), is the best. Indeed, such a choice depends on the future computations and the properties one would like to prove.

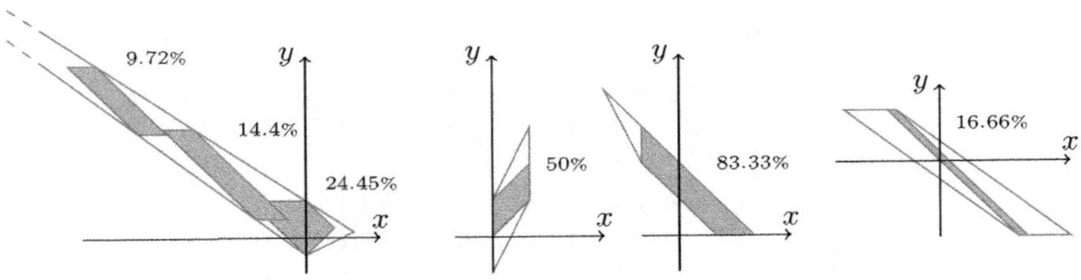

Fig. 7. Under-approximation of randomly generated polyhedra with octagons

5 Conclusions and Future Work

The donut domains can be viewed as an effort to make some Boolean structure in the underlying concrete space visible at the level of abstract domains as a "set-minus" operator. This allows optimization of the related abstract operators (such as meet and join) to take full advantage of its semantics in terms of excluded states. While powerset domains allow handling non-convex sets, this comes at significant cost. In practice, the full expressiveness may not be needed. We exploit the set-minus operator, which is quite versatile in capturing many problems of interest - division by zero, instability regions in numeric computations, sets excluded by contracts in a modular setting, etc. In the future, we wish to expand the experiments performed using donut domains. Furthermore, other non-convexity issues may be addressed by trying to combine the work on LDDs with insights gained here to allow handling many holes in an efficient manner.

Acknowledgments. The authors would like to thank Enea Zaffanella, Sriram Sankaranarayanan, and anonymous reviewers for their valuable comments on an earlier draft of this work.

References

1. Adjé, A., Gaubert, S., Goubault, E.: Coupling Policy Iteration with Semi-definite Relaxation to Compute Accurate Numerical Invariants in Static Analysis. In: Gordon, A.D. (ed.) ESOP 2010. LNCS, vol. 6012, pp. 23–42. Springer, Heidelberg (2010)
2. Allamigeon, X., Gaubert, S., Goubault, É.: Inferring Min and Max Invariants Using Max-Plus Polyhedra. In: Alpuente, M., Vidal, G. (eds.) SAS 2008. LNCS, vol. 5079, pp. 189–204. Springer, Heidelberg (2008)
3. Bagnara, R.: A hierarchy of constraint systems for data-flow analysis of constraint logic-based languages. In: Science of Computer Programming, pp. 2–119 (1999)
4. Bagnara, R., Hill, P.M., Zaffanella, E.: Not necessarily closed convex polyhedra and the double description method. Form. Asp. Comput., 222–257 (2005)

5. Bagnara, R., Hill, P.M., Zaffanella, E.: Widening operators for powerset domains. STTT 8(4-5), 449–466 (2006)
6. Bagnara, R., Hill, P.M., Zaffanella, E.: Exact join detection for convex polyhedra and other numerical abstractions. Comput. Geom. 43(5), 453–473 (2010)
7. Bemporad, A., Filippi, C., Torrisi, F.D.: Inner and outer approximations of polytopes using boxes. Comput. Geom. 27(2), 151–178 (2004)
8. Bemporad, A., Fukuda, K., Torrisi, F.D.: Convexity recognition of the union of polyhedra. Comput. Geom. 18(3), 141–154 (2001)
9. Chaki, S., Gurfinkel, A., Strichman, O.: Decision diagrams for linear arithmetic. In: FMCAD, pp. 53–60. IEEE (2009)
10. Chen, L., Miné, A., Wang, J., Cousot, P.: Interval Polyhedra: An Abstract Domain to Infer Interval Linear Relationships. In: Palsberg, J., Su, Z. (eds.) SAS 2009. LNCS, vol. 5673, pp. 309–325. Springer, Heidelberg (2009)
11. Cousot, P., Cousot, R.: Static determination of dynamic properties of programs. In: 2nd Intl. Symp. on Programming, Dunod, France, pp. 106–130 (1976)
12. Cousot, P., Cousot, R.: Abstract Interpretation: A unified lattice model for static analysis of programs by construction or approximation of fixpoints. In: POPL, pp. 238–252. ACM (1977)
13. Cousot, P., Halbwachs, N.: Automatic discovery of linear restraints among the variables of a program. In: POPL, pp. 84–97. ACM (January 1978)
14. Dams, D., Namjoshi, K.S.: Automata as Abstractions. In: Cousot, R. (ed.) VMCAI 2005. LNCS, vol. 3385, pp. 216–232. Springer, Heidelberg (2005)
15. Ghorbal, K., Goubault, E., Putot, S.: The Zonotope Abstract Domain Taylor1+. In: Bouajjani, A., Maler, O. (eds.) CAV 2009. LNCS, vol. 5643, pp. 627–633. Springer, Heidelberg (2009)
16. Ghorbal, K., Goubault, E., Putot, S.: A Logical Product Approach to Zonotope Intersection. In: Touili, T., Cook, B., Jackson, P. (eds.) CAV 2010. LNCS, vol. 6174, pp. 212–226. Springer, Heidelberg (2010)
17. Goldsztejn, A., Daney, D., Rueher, M., Taillibert, P.: Modal intervals revisited: a mean-value extension to generalized intervals. In: QCP (2005)
18. Goubault, É., Putot, S.: Static Analysis of Numerical Algorithms. In: Yi, K. (ed.) SAS 2006. LNCS, vol. 4134, pp. 18–34. Springer, Heidelberg (2006)
19. Goubault, É., Putot, S.: Under-Approximations of Computations in Real Numbers Based on Generalized Affine Arithmetic. In: Riis Nielson, H., Filé, G. (eds.) SAS 2007. LNCS, vol. 4634, pp. 137–152. Springer, Heidelberg (2007)
20. Granger, P.: Static Analysis of Linear Congruence Equalities Among Variables of a Program. In: Abramsky, S. (ed.) CAAP 1991 and TAPSOFT 1991. LNCS, vol. 493, pp. 169–192. Springer, Heidelberg (1991)
21. Gurfinkel, A., Chaki, S.: Boxes: A Symbolic Abstract Domain of Boxes. In: Cousot, R., Martel, M. (eds.) SAS 2010. LNCS, vol. 6337, pp. 287–303. Springer, Heidelberg (2010)
22. Halbwachs, N., Proy, Y.-E., Raymond, P.: Verification of Linear Hybrid Systems by Means of Convex Approximations. In: LeCharlier, B. (ed.) SAS 1994. LNCS, vol. 864, pp. 223–237. Springer, Heidelberg (1994)
23. Jeannet, B., Miné, A.: Apron: A Library of Numerical Abstract Domains for Static Analysis. In: Bouajjani, A., Maler, O. (eds.) CAV 2009. LNCS, vol. 5643, pp. 661–667. Springer, Heidelberg (2009)
24. Kanade, A., Alur, R., Ivančić, F., Ramesh, S., Sankaranarayanan, S., Shashidhar, K.C.: Generating and Analyzing Symbolic Traces of Simulink/Stateflow Models. In: Bouajjani, A., Maler, O. (eds.) CAV 2009. LNCS, vol. 5643, pp. 430–445. Springer, Heidelberg (2009)

25. Makhorin, A.: The GNU Linear Programming Kit, GLPK (2000), `http://www.gnu.org/software/glpk/glpk.html`
26. Masdupuy, F.: Array abstractions using semantic analysis of trapezoid congruences. In: ICS, pp. 226–235 (1992)
27. Miné, A.: The octagon abstract domain. In: WCRE, pp. 310–319 (October 2001)
28. Prabhu, P., Maeda, N., Balakrishnan, G., Ivančić, F., Gupta, A.: Interprocedural Exception Analysis for C++. In: Mezini, M. (ed.) ECOOP 2011. LNCS, vol. 6813, pp. 583–608. Springer, Heidelberg (2011)
29. Péron, M., Halbwachs, N.: An Abstract Domain Extending Difference-Bound Matrices with Disequality Constraints. In: Cook, B., Podelski, A. (eds.) VMCAI 2007. LNCS, vol. 4349, pp. 268–282. Springer, Heidelberg (2007)
30. Rockafellar, R.T.: Convex Analysis. Princeton University Press (1970)

Inferring Canonical Register Automata*

Falk Howar[1], Bernhard Steffen[1], Bengt Jonsson[2], and Sofia Cassel[2]

[1] Technical University Dortmund, Chair for Programming Systems, Dortmund, D-44227, Germany
{falk.howar,bernhard.steffen}@cs.tu-dortmund.de
[2] Dept. of Information Technology, Uppsala University, Sweden
{bengt.jonsson,sofia.cassel}@it.uu.se

Abstract. In this paper, we present an extension of active automata learning to *register automata*, an automaton model which is capable of expressing the influence of data on control flow. Register automata operate on an infinite data domain, whose values can be assigned to registers and compared for equality. Our active learning algorithm is unique in that it directly infers the effect of data values on control flow as part of the learning process. This effect is expressed by means of registers and guarded transitions in the resulting register automata models. The application of our algorithm to a small example indicates the impact of learning register automata models: Not only are the inferred models much more expressive than finite state machines, but the prototype implementation also drastically outperforms the classic L^* algorithm, even when exploiting optimal data abstraction and symmetry reduction.

1 Introduction

The model-based approach to development, verification, and testing of software systems (e.g., [7,5,11]) is a key path towards efficient development of reliable software systems. However, its application is hampered by the current lack of adequate specifications for most actual systems. The use of component libraries with very partial specifications, and the problem of maintaining specifications of evolving systems aggravate the situation. Automata learning techniques [9] have been proposed to overcome this, by allowing to construct and later update behavioral models automatically. This has been illustrated in a number of case studies like, e.g., the concrete setting of Computer Telephony Integrated (CTI) systems [9], and in protocol specification [18], analysis [22], and testing [24].

Black-box techniques for learning component models broadly fall into two classes. One class generates finite-state models of control skeletons, modeling the sequences of interactions of a component [9,12,2,22], or automata learning techniques (e.g., [3,19]). Another class generates invariants over state variables [8] or exchanged data values by generalizing from concrete observations. For many applications in testing and verification, and also in commercial model-based testing tools (e.g., ConformiQ Qtronic [11]), it is, however, important to generate

* This work is supported by the European FP 7 project CONNECT (IST 231167).

V. Kuncak and A. Rybalchenko (Eds.): VMCAI 2012, LNCS 7148, pp. 251–266, 2012.

models that capture combined behavior of control and data. Parameters such as sequence numbers, identifiers, etc. have a significant impact on control flow in typical protocols. For instance, a valid sequence number or session identifier has a very different influence on continued behavior than an invalid one.

In this paper, we present an extension of active automata learning to *register automata*, an automaton model which is capable of expressing the influence of data on control flow. Register automata operate on an infinite data domain, whose values can be assigned to registers and compared for equality by very natural mechanisms. This suffices to handle parameters like user names, passwords, identifiers of connections, sessions, etc., in a fashion similar to, and slightly more expressive than, the class of "data-independent" systems, which was the subject of some of the first works on model checking of infinite-state systems [25,13]. Thus RA learning is particularly suited for the validation of protocols, connectors or mediators, as we will discuss based on a small fragment of the XMPP protocol (cf. Figure 1).

Our active learning algorithm is unique in that it directly infers the effect of data values on control flow as part of the learning process. Conceptually, our new learning algorithm is based on a generalized Myhill-Nerode theorem for register automata, which, like in the classical regular case, identifies the required control locations [6]. Algorithmically, the L^*-typical partition refinement process [3] needs to be elaborated to a three-dimensional maximum fixpoint computation for simultaneously determining locations, register assignments, and guards of transitions. Technically, working on sequences of interactions with data requires additional care. It involves a "data-aware" way of composing prefixes and suffixes, as well as an adequate way of analyzing counterexamples with data values. We will show the impact of our approach by applying it to a small fragment of the XMPP protocol. The prototype implementation of our new technology drastically outperforms alternative approaches, even when they exploit optimizations like data abstraction and symmetry reduction.

Related Work. We do not know of any other fully automatic learning algorithm that seamlessly integrates the inference and exploitation of data dependencies.

One approach [16,17,15] first generates control skeletons with data-agnostic control actions, which are then extended with data constraints in a post-process using a tool like Daikon [8]. This allows one to infer constraints on data parameters that are exchanged after specific sequences of method invocations, but not to analyze the influence of data parameter on subsequent control behavior. The method presented in [1] achieves a deeper integration of control and data at the price of user-supplied abstraction scheme (mapper), whereas [4] requires a predefined fixed finite data domain. [21] constructs memory automata [14] from sequences of learned deterministic finite automata for increasing finite data domains. This approach could probably be generalized to infer register automata. However, such a generalization would be some exponentials more complex than our algorithm and yield automata of undetermined quality.

Technically, our involved three-dimensional treatment of counterexamples can be regarded as an elaboration of an algorithmic pattern which was originally

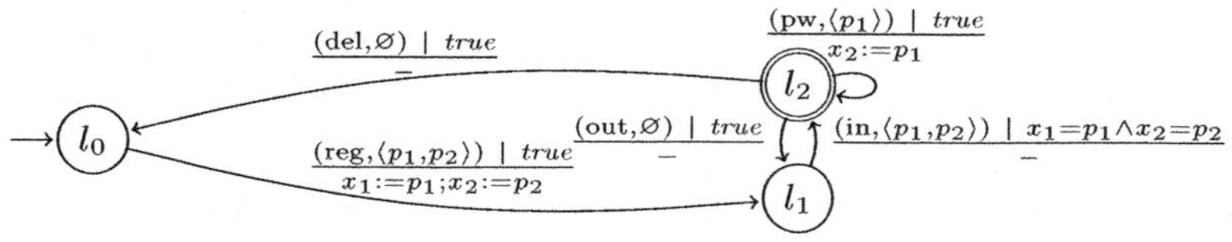

Fig. 1. Partial model for a fragment of XMPP

presented in [19] for learning regular languages. We elaborated this pattern earlier to cover Mealy machine learning [23], and to support automated alphabet abstraction refinement [10].

Organization. After introducing register automata in the next section, we develop our main result in Section 3. This comprises in particular the setup for the generalized Nerode congruence, the corresponding observation table (algorithmic data structure), and the enhanced treatment of counterexamples. Subsequently, we discuss an application example in Section 4 and conclude with Section 5.

2 Register Automata and Data Languages

We assume an unbounded domain D of data values and a set A of *actions*. Each action has a certain *arity* which determines how many parameters it takes from the domain D. A *data action* is a term of form $(\alpha, \bar{d})$, where α is an action with arity n, and $\bar{d} = \langle d_1, \ldots, d_n \rangle$ are data values in D. A *data word* is a sequence of data actions. A *data language* is a set of data words, which is closed under permutations on D. We have presented an automaton model that recognizes data languages in [6].

Let a *parameterized action* be a term of form $(\alpha, \bar{p})$, consisting of an action α and formal parameters $\bar{p} = \langle p_1, \ldots, p_n \rangle$ respecting the arity of α. Let $X = \langle x_1, \ldots, x_m \rangle$ be a finite set of *registers*. A *guard* is a conjunction of equalities and negated equalities, e.g., $p_i \neq x_j$, over formal parameters and registers. An *assignment* is a partial mapping $\rho : X \to X \cup P$ for a set P of formal parameters.

Definition 1. A *Register Automaton* (RA) is a tuple $\mathcal{A} = (A, L, l_0, X, \Gamma, \lambda)$, where

- A is a finite set of *actions*.
- L is a finite set of *locations*.
- $l_0 \in L$ is the *initial location*.
- X is a finite set of *registers*.
- Γ is a finite set of *transitions*, each of which is of form $\langle l, (\alpha, \bar{p}), g, \rho, l' \rangle$, where l is the *source location*, l' is the *target location*, $(\alpha, \bar{p})$ is a parameterized action, g is a guard, and ρ is an assignment.
- $\lambda : L \mapsto \{+, -\}$ maps each location to either $+$ (accept) or $-$ (reject). □

Let us define the semantics of an RA $\mathcal{A} = (A, L, l_0, X, \Gamma, \lambda)$. A *valuation*, denoted by ν, is a (partial) mapping from X to D. A *state* of $\mathcal{A}$ is a pair $\langle l, \nu \rangle$ where $l \in L$ and ν is a valuation. The *initial state* is the pair of initial location and empty valuation $\langle l_0, \nu_0 \rangle$.

A *step* of $\mathcal{A}$, denoted by $\langle l, \nu \rangle \xrightarrow{(\alpha, \bar{d})} \langle l', \nu' \rangle$, transfers $\mathcal{A}$ from $\langle l, \nu \rangle$ to $\langle l', \nu' \rangle$ on input $(\alpha, \bar{d})$ if there is a transition $\langle l, (\alpha, \bar{p}), g, \rho, l' \rangle \in \Gamma$ such that (1) g is modeled by $\bar{d}$ and ν, i.e., if it becomes true when replacing all p_i by d_i and all x_i by $\nu(x_i)$, and such that (2) ν' is the updated valuation, where $\nu'(x_i) = \nu(x_j)$ wherever $\rho(x_i) = x_j$, and $\nu'(x_i) = d_j$ wherever $\rho(x_i) = p_j$.

A *run* of $\mathcal{A}$ over a data word $(\alpha_1, \bar{d_1}) \dots (\alpha_k, \bar{d_k})$ is a sequence of steps

$$\langle l_0, \nu_0 \rangle \xrightarrow{(\alpha_1, \bar{d_1})} \langle l_1, \nu_1 \rangle \quad \dots \quad \langle l_{k-1}, \nu_{k-1} \rangle \xrightarrow{(\alpha_k, \bar{d_k})} \langle l_k, \nu_k \rangle.$$

A run is *accepting* if $\lambda(l_k) = +$, otherwise it is *rejecting*. The data language recognized by $\mathcal{A}$, denoted $L(\mathcal{A})$ is the set of data words that it accepts.

For the remainder of this paper, we will work with RAs that are *completely specified*, meaning for any reachable state $\langle l, \nu \rangle$ and input $(\alpha, \bar{d})$, there is a transition with a guard modeled by $\bar{d}$ and ν, and *determinate*, i.e., no data word has both accepting and rejecting runs. We refer to such automata as DRAs. Data languages that are accepted by a DRA are called *regular*. We will restrict our attention to regular data languages.

Example 1. We model the behavior of a fragment of the XMPP protocol [20] as an example (shown in Figure 1). XMPP is widely used in instant messaging. In our fragment of XMPP, a user can register an account (providing a username and a password), log in using this account, change the password, and delete the account. For example, the user Bob could register his account with the action **reg**(`Bob`, `secret`) (providing his username and password), and then log in with the action **in**(`Bob`, `secret`). Once logged in, he could change his password to `boblovesalice` with the action **pw**(`boblovesalice`). In the figure, accepting locations are denoted by two concentric circles. Note that several transitions are omitted for brevity. We will use the XMPP example in Section 4 to demonstrate our learning algorithm. □

As shown in [6], data languages can be represented concisely using a symbolic representation of data words. Here, we provide a summary using different but isomorphic representations of the concepts in [6] that allow a more amenable presentation.

Let $\mathcal{W}_D$ be the set of all data words over some set A of actions. For some data word $w = (\alpha_1, \bar{d_1}) \dots (\alpha_n, \bar{d_n})$ from $\mathcal{W}_D$ let $Acts(w)$ be the ordered sequence of actions in w, and $Vals(w) = d_1 \dots d_m$ the (ordered) sequence of data values in w. Let $ValSet(w)$ be the set of distinct data values in $Vals(w)$.

Let $w \sqsubseteq w'$ denote that w' can be obtained from w by a not necessarily injective mapping on D, i.e., for two data words w, w' with $Vals(w) = d_1 \dots d_m$, and $Vals(w') = d'_1 \dots d'_m$,

$$w \sqsubseteq w' \Leftrightarrow Acts(w) = Acts(w') \wedge \forall 1 \le i < j \le m \,.\, d_i = d_j \Rightarrow d'_i = d'_j.$$

For example, $\mathbf{reg}(\texttt{Bob}, \texttt{test}) \sqsubseteq \mathbf{reg}(\texttt{Alice}, \texttt{Alice})$. Note that $\sqsubseteq$ is a preorder on $\mathcal{W}_D$. The smallest elements wrt. $\sqsubseteq$ are data words where all data values are pairwisely different. The greatest ones are data words where all data values are equal. For data words w, w', let $w \simeq w'$ denote that $w \sqsubseteq w'$ and $w \sqsupseteq w'$. The equivalence relation $\simeq$ induces a partitioning of data words into equivalence classes.

Let $Vals(w)|_k$ the prefix of length k of $Vals(w)$. For data words w, w' with $Acts(w) = Acts(w')$ let $w < w'$ denote that for some $k > 0$, (1) $Vals(w)|_{k-1} = Vals(w')|_{k-1}$ and (2) the kth data value of $Vals(w)$ is different from any of the $k-1$ first data values, but (3) the kth data value of $Vals(w')$ is equal to some of the $k-1$ first data values. For example, $\mathbf{reg}(\texttt{Bob}, \texttt{test})\mathbf{in}(\texttt{Bob}, \texttt{oth})$ is smaller (wrt. $<$) than $\mathbf{reg}(\texttt{Alice}, \texttt{test})\mathbf{in}(\texttt{Alice}, \texttt{test})$.

We assume an infinite ordered set $D_V = \{\mathbf{1}, \mathbf{2}, \mathbf{3}, \ldots\}$, which is disjoint from D. Let a *suffix* be a data word whose data values are in $D \cup D_V$. To allow for comparing suffixes by equality, we require that data values from D_V appear in canonical order in a suffix v, i.e., such that for every prefix p of $Vals(v)$ the set $ValSet(p) \setminus D$ is of form $\{\mathbf{1}, \mathbf{2}, \ldots, \mathbf{k}\}$ for some $\mathbf{k}$. For a data word u, let an u-suffix be a suffix v where all data values from D in v are also in $ValSet(u)$. We concatenate u and an u-suffix v, denoted by $u;v$ to the word $u\pi(v)$, where $\pi : D_V \to (D \setminus ValSet(u))$ is an injective mapping, and $\pi(v)$ denotes the application of π to all data values from D_V in v. For example, $\mathbf{in}(\texttt{Bob}, \mathbf{1})$ is a $\mathbf{reg}(\texttt{Bob}, \texttt{secret})$-suffix. Concatenation will result in the unique (up to equivalence wrt. $\simeq$) word $\mathbf{reg}(\texttt{Bob}, \texttt{secret})\mathbf{in}(\texttt{Bob}, \texttt{new})$.

3 Active Learning of Canonical RAs

We present a novel active learning algorithm, which infers a canonical DRA for an unknown data language $\mathcal{L}$, of which it initially knows only the set of actions. Active learning proceeds by asking two kinds of queries.

- A *membership query* consists in asking if a data word w is in $\mathcal{L}$.
- An *equivalence query* consists in asking whether a hypothesized DRA $\mathcal{H}$ is correct, i.e., whether $\mathcal{L}(\mathcal{H}) = \mathcal{L}$. The query is answered by *yes* if $\mathcal{H}$ is correct, otherwise by a *counterexample*, which is a data word from the symmetric difference of $\mathcal{L}$ and $\mathcal{L}(\mathcal{H})$.

Key to (classic) L^*-like learning [3] is the well known Nerode congruence, which allows to identify words that lead to the same location in a canonical acceptor for some language $\mathcal{L}$. The Nerode congruence is formulated in terms of residual languages, i.e., languages after some prefix. Words with identical residuals will lead to the same location in a canonical acceptor. Active learning algorithms exploit this by means of two sets of words: (1) a finite prefix-closed set of *prefixes*, which is successively extended until it covers every transition of the canonical acceptor for $\mathcal{L}$, and (2) a finite set of *suffixes*, i.e., selected words from residuals, that allows to approximate the Nerode congruence on the set of prefixes. The necessary information is usually stored in an observation table. The rows and columns of this table are labeled with prefixes and suffixes, respectively. The table cell for a row labeled by u, and a column labeled by v, contains the information whether $uv \in \mathcal{L}$, i.e., whether v is in the $\mathcal{L}$-residual of u.

Active learning iterates two phases: hypothesis construction and hypothesis validation. During hypothesis construction the two sets of prefixes and suffixes are successively extended, using a sequence of membership queries, until the table satisfies satisfies certain "closure conditions", under which a hypothesis automaton can be constructed in a consistent way. Hypothesis validation is performed using equivalence queries, to check if the current hypothesis is correct. From the returned counterexamples, new suffixes can be generated, that will drive a new round of hypothesis construction [19,23]. During learning, hypothesis automata will grow monotonically in size, until they have the size of the canonical acceptor for $\mathcal{L}$. Then, by definition an equivalence query will confirm that the hypothesis is correct.

Our learning algorithm for regular data languages will strictly follow this pattern, and construct the canonical DRA for some data language $\mathcal{L}$. Theoretical backbone will be the new succinct Nerode congruence for data languages that we have presented in [6]. We will use sets of so-called $\mathcal{L}$-essential data words (cf. Section 3.1) and abstract suffixes (cf. Section 3.2) as prefixes and suffixes, from which membership queries for data words can be immediately derived. Due to the potentially complex patterns of relationship between data values in data languages, however, residuals will be more complicated in our algorithm than in the classic regular case, reflected in the more complex cells of our observation table. In the remainder of this section we will show

1. how abstract suffixes can be used to approximate the Nerode congruence (Section 3.1 and Section 3.2),
2. how an observation table can be realized and how at certain points well-defined hypothesis automata can be constructed from the observation table (Section 3.2), and
3. how counterexamples can be exploited to guarantee strictly monotone progress as in the classic regular case [23] (Section 3.3).

Strictly monotone progress together with an invariant on the size of hypothesis automata will deliver a correctness argument resembling the one from the classic case (Section 3.4). The invariant, however, is more complicated than in the classic case: We will show that for all hypothesis automata, the *number of transitions*, the *number of locations*, and the *sum of the number of register assignments* at some location will never exceed the corresponding numbers of the canonical DRA for $\mathcal{L}$. In essence, the overall pattern of learning DRA is a three-dimensional maximum fix-point computation, determining (a) the locations, (b) the required register assignments, and (c) the guarded transitions in a partition-refinement fashion.

3.1 Residual Data Languages

In this section we will define residual data languages and present our Nerode congruence for data languages from [6] in terms of these. The development of this section is relative to canonical DRAs for regular data languages, whose existence has been proved in [6]. This allows us to avoid reciting the technically involved constructions presented in [6] without sacrificing the precision required to establish the correctness of our learning algorithm. The learning algorithm itself, however, does not depend on any a priori knowledge about the canonical DRA for an inferred data language.

Let $\mathcal{A}$ be the canonical DRA of some data language $\mathcal{L}$. For a run of $\mathcal{A}$ on some data word w of length n, i.e., with $|Acts(w)| = n$, let the *trace* of this run be the sequence of transitions $\tau = t_1, \ldots, t_n$ of the run in the order they are traversed, and $Traces_{\mathcal{A}}(w)$ the set of all traces of runs of $\mathcal{A}$ on w (due to determinacy there may be more than one). For a trace τ, let $[\tau]$ be the set of smallest data words triggering this trace. These smallest words are important for the construction of canonical DRAs. Let $Traces_{\mathcal{A}}$ be the set of traces of $\mathcal{A}$.

Definition 2 ($\mathcal{L}$-essential words). Given a data language $\mathcal{L}$ and its canonical DRA $\mathcal{A}$, we define $E_{\mathcal{L}} = \bigcup_{\tau \in Traces_{\mathcal{A}}} [\tau]$ to be the set of $\mathcal{L}$-*essential* words. □

Intuitively, the set of $\mathcal{L}$-essential words is an infinite prefix-closed set of smallest data words that trigger runs in the canonical DRA for $\mathcal{L}$, i.e., which have just enough equal data values to satisfy the guards of all traversed transitions.

When learning an unknown data language $\mathcal{L}$, the canonical DRA for $\mathcal{L}$ is, of course, unknown and cannot be used for the construction of $E_{\mathcal{L}}$. Our algorithm will find a representation system of $\mathcal{L}$-essential words by means of membership queries (cf. Section 3.3). In the XMPP example in Figure 1, ε (the empty word), **reg**(`Bob`, `secret`), and **reg**(`Bob`, `secret`)**in**(`Alice`, `other`) are examples of $\mathcal{L}$-essential words. They are smallest words triggering corresponding traces. Also, **reg**(`Bob`, `oth`)**in**(`Bob`, `oth`) is $\mathcal{L}$-essential, triggering the **reg**-transition from l_0 and the "correct login" from l_1 to l_2 The word **reg**(`Bob`, `Bob`)**in**(`Bob`, `Bob`), on the other hand, is not $\mathcal{L}$-essential. It, too, triggers the **reg**-transition and the "correct login" but it is not the unique (up to $\simeq$) smallest word for its trace.

In [6] we showed how from $E_{\mathcal{L}}$ the canonical DRA for $\mathcal{L}$ can be constructed. To determine the locations of this canonical automaton, we compare $\mathcal{L}$-essential words by their residual languages. Let therefore $\lambda_{\mathcal{L}} : \mathcal{W}_D \to \{+, -\}$ such that $\lambda_{\mathcal{L}}(w) = +$ if $w \in \mathcal{L}$ and $\lambda_{\mathcal{L}}(v) = -$ otherwise. For an $\mathcal{L}$-essential data word u and a set S of u-suffixes, we want to characterize the set of words $\{u; v \mid v \in S\}$ wrt. $\mathcal{L}$ in a concise and canonical way. For a subset $\lfloor S \rfloor$ of S, let $rep_{\lfloor S \rfloor} : S \to 2^{\lfloor S \rfloor}$ be a mapping that maps every suffix in S to a set of suffixes in $\lfloor S \rfloor$. We fix the definition of $rep_{\lfloor S \rfloor}$ independent of u and S. Let

$$rep_{\lfloor S \rfloor}(v) = max_{<}\{v' \in \lfloor S \rfloor \mid v' \sqsubseteq v\}.$$

We say that $\lfloor S \rfloor$ characterizes S faithfully after u if $\lambda_{\mathcal{L}}(u; v) = \lambda_{\mathcal{L}}(u; v')$ for $v' \in rep_{\lfloor S \rfloor}(v)$ and $v \in S$.

Definition 3 (Closures). For an $\mathcal{L}$-essential word u and a set S of u-suffixes, the u-closure $C_u^S : \lfloor S \rfloor \to \{+, -\}$ is a mapping with unique minimal domain $\lfloor S \rfloor \subseteq S$ faithfully characterizing S after u, and $C_u^S(v) = \lambda_{\mathcal{L}}(u; v)$. □

We denote the u-closure for the set of all u-suffixes by C_u. In [6], we have shown that the unique minimal domain of C_u is the set of suffixes that extend u to $\mathcal{L}$-essential words.

For the $\mathcal{L}$-essential word **reg**(`Bob`, `oth`), e.g., the **reg**(`Bob`, `oth`)-suffixes **in**(**1**, **2**) and **in**(`Bob`, `oth`) are in the domain of C_u, extending **reg**(`Bob`, `oth`) to a word equivalent to **reg**(`Bob`, `oth`)**in**(`Alice`, `secret`) and to **reg**(`Bob`, `oth`)**in**(`Bob`, `oth`). These two words suffice to characterize faithfully the behavior of **reg**(`Bob`, `oth`) for all suffixes v with only **in** as action: C_u(**in**(**1**, **2**)) maps to $-$, corresponding to an unsuccessful login from l_1 in the DRA in Figure 1. C_u(**in**(`Bob`, `oth`)) maps to $+$, characterizing correct logins.

Since the suffixes in $Dom(C_u)$ extend u to $\mathcal{L}$-essential words, the data values from D occurring in these suffixes are exactly the ones that are needed to satisfy the guards in the canonical DRA for $\mathcal{L}$. We refer to these data values as the *memorable* data values of u, and denote them by $mem_{\mathcal{L}}(u)$. In the above example, `Bob` and `oth` are in $mem_{\mathcal{L}}$(**reg**(`Bob`, `oth`)). Note, however, that in general $mem_{\mathcal{L}}(u)$ will only be a subset of $ValSet(u)$.

Let π be a permutation on D. We apply π to closures, denoted by πC_u^S, by applying π to all data values from D in suffixes of $Dom(C_u^S)$ simultaneously, thereby exchanging values from D in the suffixes.

Definition 4 (Nerode congruence for essential words). Two $\mathcal{L}$-essential words u and u' are equivalent w.r.t. $\mathcal{L}$, denoted by $u \equiv_{\mathcal{L}} u'$ if there exists a permutation π on D such that $\pi C_u = C_{u'}$. □

Note that $\equiv_{\mathcal{L}}$ is an equivalence relation. The bijection π used in Definition 4 need only relate memorable data values, i.e., it is enough to define it as a bijection $\pi : mem_{\mathcal{L}}(u) \to mem_{\mathcal{L}}(u')$. We say that two closures are incompatible, denoted by $C_u \not\simeq C_{u'}$ if there is no permutation on D under which the closures become equal.

In our example, **reg**(`Alice`, `secret`) and **reg**(`Bob`, `oth`)**in**(`Bob`, `oth`)**out**() are equivalent wrt. $\equiv_{\mathcal{L}}$ since their closures become equal under a permutation π on D, mapping `Alice` to `Bob` and `secret` to `oth`. In the canonical DRA in Figure 1 both words lead to l_1. Intuitively, π exchanges the data values stored in registers after processing the one word by data values stored in registers after processing the other word.

3.2 Hypothesis Construction

Our learning algorithm will use an observation table as underlying data structure. In this section we will define this data structure and explain how hypothesis automata can be generated from observation tables.

So far, we have defined suffixes only relative to fixed prefixes. We assume an infinite set Z of *placeholders*, ranged over by $z_1, z_2, \ldots$, which is disjoint from D and D_V. An *abstract suffix* is a data word with parameters in $Z \cup D_V$. One abstract suffix yields a number of (concrete) u-suffixes for a particular prefix u. For a set of abstract suffixes V, let $V(u)$ be the set of u-suffixes that can be generated from V via injective partial mappings $\sigma : Z \to ValSet(u)$. The abstract suffix **in**(z_1, z_2) for example will yield the **reg**(`bob`, `oth`)-suffixes **in**(**1**, **2**),

$\mathbf{in}(\texttt{bob},\mathbf{1})$, $\mathbf{in}(\texttt{oth},\mathbf{1})$, $\mathbf{in}(\mathbf{1},\texttt{bob})$, $\mathbf{in}(\mathbf{1},\texttt{oth})$, $\mathbf{in}(\texttt{oth},\texttt{bob})$, and $\mathbf{in}(\texttt{bob},\texttt{oth})$. The abstract suffix $\mathbf{in}(z_1,\mathbf{1})$, on the other hand, will result in $\mathbf{in}(\mathbf{1},\mathbf{2})$, $\mathbf{in}(\texttt{bob},\mathbf{1})$, and $\mathbf{in}(\texttt{oth},\mathbf{1})$, only.

During learning, we will use membership queries for all words $u;v$ with $v \in V(u)$ to find the optimal, i.e., minimal, domain of $C_u^{V(u)}$ (along the lines of finding $\mathcal{L}$-essential words [6]). For the u-closure $C_u^{V(u)}$ let $mem_V(u)$ denote the set of data values from $ValSet(u)$ that occur in suffixes in the domain of $C_u^{V(u)}$. Even though the u-closure of an $\mathcal{L}$-essential word u for a set of abstract suffixes V will in general not contain suffixes that extend u to $\mathcal{L}$-essential words, the following propositions hold.

1. For all sets V of abstract suffixes $mem_V(u) \subseteq mem_{\mathcal{L}}(u)$, i.e., we will never wrongly identify data values as memorable. Intuitively, a data value that is not memorable in u cannot influence behavior in any suffix.
2. If $u \equiv_{\mathcal{L}} u'$ then $C_u^{V(u)} \simeq C_{u'}^{V(u')}$ for all sets of abstract suffixes V. This can be shown by proving mutual inclusion of the domains.
3. If $u \not\equiv_{\mathcal{L}} u'$ then there exists a finite set V of abstract suffixes such that $C_u^{V(u)} \not\simeq C_{u'}^{V(u')}$. Since $\equiv_{\mathcal{L}}$ has finite index k, in the worst case V has to generate all suffixes up to length k (We will do better, actually).

We can thus use closures as basis for our observation table.

Definition 5 (Observation table). An observation table is a tuple (U, V, T), of a prefix-closed set of $\mathcal{L}$-essential words U, a set of abstract suffixes V, and a function T, mapping each prefix $u \in U$ to the u-closure $C_u^{V(u)}$. □

The set U consists of a prefixed-closed subset $Sp(U)$ of *short prefixes*, and contains for every prefix $u \in Sp(U)$ at least the one-action extension ua where data values in a do not equal one another or data values in u. The u-closure $T(u)$ is constructed by asking membership queries for all suffixes in $V(u)$, following the approach from [6]. Our algorithm will initialize $Sp(U) = V = \{\varepsilon\}$, and maintain the invariants that $u \not\simeq u'$ for $u, u' \in U$ and $T(u) \not\simeq T(u')$ for $u, u' \in Sp(U)$.

In order to construct hypothesis automata from an observation table, we need two conditions to hold on the table.

Definition 6 (Closedness). An observation table (U, V, T) is *closed* if for every prefix $u \in U \setminus Sp(U)$ there is a prefix $u' \in Sp(U)$ and a permutation π on D such that $\pi T(u) = T(u')$. □

Please note that in general there can be multiple effective permutations. This can be due to true symmetry of parameters, but also to the approximative nature of intermediate results in learning. Since the existence of effective permutations is transitive, there can never be two permutations proving the same word from $U \setminus Sp(U)$ equivalent to different words from $Sp(U)$. The prefixes in $Sp(U)$ will become the locations of a hypothesis automaton. Closedness ensures that all transitions of the hypothesis, defined by prefixes in U, have a defined destination.

Definition 7 (Register-consistency). An observation table (U, V, T) is *register-consistent* if for every prefix $ua \in U$, where a is of length one,

$$mem_V(ua) \cap ValSet(u) \subseteq mem_V(u). \qquad \square$$

When constructing a hypothesis from the table, we will store the parameters from $mem_V(u)$ in registers at the location corresponding to u. Register-consistency ensures that $mem_V(u)$ contains all parameters of u that are assumed to be stored in registers in continuations of u. This will guarantee that the assignments along transitions in the hypothesis are well-defined.

From a closed and register-consistent observation table we can construct a hypothesis automaton $\mathcal{H}$ along the lines of the approach presented in [6]. We will omit a detailed account of the automaton construction here, but simply give the key idea. The automaton is obtained from the observation table, using the set of prefixes and the permutations on D to determine locations and transitions. Registers are determined using the sets $mem_V(u)$ of closures $T(u)$. Guards and assignments can then be generated from the $\mathcal{L}$-essential words in U directly, and λ will be defined using values from the closures. We thus have:

Proposition 1. From a closed and register-consistent observation table (U, V, T) a well-defined hypothesis automaton $\mathcal{H}$ can be constructed, for which $\lambda_{\mathcal{H}}(u) = T(u)(\varepsilon)$ for $u \in U$. $\square$

3.3 Hypothesis Validation

Once we have generated a hypothesis automaton $\mathcal{H}$, an equivalence query will either signal success or return a counterexample, i.e., a data word w^c from the symmetric difference of $\mathcal{L}$ and $\mathcal{L}(\mathcal{H})$. We will process w^c from left to right in order to localize where precisely hypothesis and target system behave differently.

Starting with w^c, we will iteratively generate derived counterexamples, towards the word from $Sp(U)$ that leads to the same location in $\mathcal{H}$ as w^c. We refer to this word as the *access sequence* of w^c and denote it by $\lfloor w^c \rfloor_{\mathcal{H}}$. Key idea is that, since $w^c \in \mathcal{L} \Leftrightarrow \lfloor w^c \rfloor_{\mathcal{H}} \notin \mathcal{L}$, words generated in the process will at some point stop being counterexamples (cf. [19,23]).

Technically, we will construct "triplet constrained words" uav, where $u \in Sp(U)$. We start with the triplet where u is the empty word ε, and av is w^c. We define the following three refinement steps, which will be iterated until we find a concrete discrepancy between $\mathcal{H}$ and the (unknown) canonical acceptor for $\mathcal{L}$. An example illustrating all steps will be given in Section 4.

A: Finding new transitions. For ua of our triplet, let $u\bar{a}$ be a maximal (wrt. $<$) word from U.[1] Intuitively, $u\bar{a}$ corresponds to the trace of ua in $\mathcal{H}$. As shown (schematically) in Figure 2 a), we will try to transform the word $ua; v$ into a word $u\bar{a}; v'$ still being a counterexample. The problem here is deriving a suitable v' from v. If we cannot find such a word, we will find an

[1] Due to determinacy, there may be multiple such words of which we will pick one.

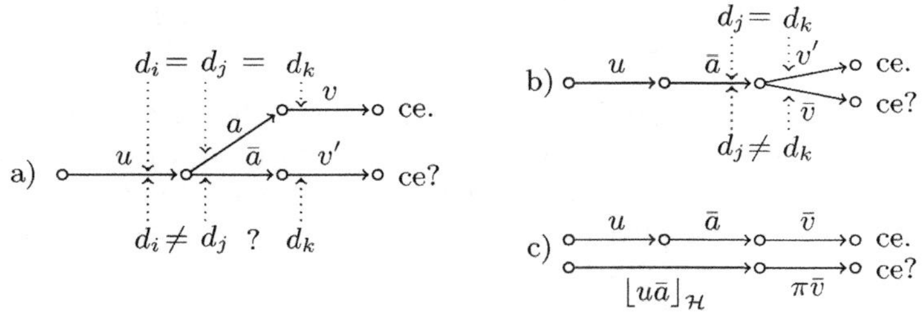

Fig. 2. Counterexamples: a) new transition, b) new register, c) new permutation

$\mathcal{L}$-essential word $u\bar{a} \sqsubseteq ua' \sqsubseteq ua$ that we can use as a new prefix in U. In this case we can continue with *hypothesis construction.* Otherwise, we continue with $u\bar{a}; v'$ and step B.

Technically, we will generate a sequence of counterexamples $ua; v = ua_1; v_1 > ua_2; v_2 > \ldots > ua_k; v_k$, by removing equalities between data values from ua_i that are not present in $u\bar{a}$. Removing equalities in ua_i may require refining the suffix v_i, too. For d_i, d_j, and d_k as shown in the Figure 2, we can try to make d_k equal to d_i, equal to d_j, or un-equal to both. For the at most $d = |Vals(a; v)|$ equal data values in the suffix there are $O(3^d)$ resulting candidate words $ua_{i+1}; v_{i+1}$ in each of the $k < |Vals(a)|$ steps. We continue until $ua_i \simeq u\bar{a}$ or no word $ua_{i+1}; v_{i+1}$ is a counterexample.

B: Finding new registers. As shown in Figure 2 b), it may be that v' in $u\bar{a}; v'$ uses data values of $u\bar{a}$ not in $mem_V(u\bar{a})$, and thus are not stored in registers in $\mathcal{H}$ after processing $u\bar{a}$. Either the word $u\bar{a}; \bar{v}$ that is supported by the assignments in the hypothesis still is a counterexample and we continue with step C, or we will find a suffix v'' indicating a new register and continue with *hypothesis construction.*

The smallest sensible v'' results from a sequence of suffixes $v' = v'_1 > v'_2 > \ldots > v'_k = v''$ still yielding counterexamples, where $(ValSet(v'_{i+1}) \cap ValSet(a)) \subset (ValSet(v'_i) \cap ValSet(a))$. In each of the $k < |Vals(a)|$ steps we have to consider at most $|Vals(a)|$ candidate suffixes. A register will then be introduced by adding the abstract suffix $\langle v'' \rangle$ to V, which we generate from v'' by replacing all data values from D by placeholders.

C: Finding new locations. Finally, let $\lfloor u\bar{a} \rfloor_{\mathcal{H}}$ be the access sequence of $u\bar{a}$, i.e., the word from $Sp(U)$ for which $\pi T(u\bar{a}) \simeq T(\lfloor u\bar{a} \rfloor_{\mathcal{H}})$ for some permutation π on D (used during hypothesis construction). In this step we will replace $u\bar{a}$ by its access sequence using π to replace data values in $\bar{v}$.

If $\lfloor u\bar{a} \rfloor_{\mathcal{H}}; \pi(\bar{v})$ is not a counterexample, as shown in Figure 2 c), either π is the wrong permutation from a set of potential ones, or both words are not equivalent wrt. $\equiv_{\mathcal{L}}$. In both cases, adding the abstract suffix $\langle \bar{v} \rangle$ to the table will make this explicit, and lead to a new permutation or, in case no effective permutation is left, to unclosedness, i.e., a new location. If $\lfloor u\bar{a} \rfloor_{\mathcal{H}}; \pi(\bar{v})$ still is a counterexample, we will start over with step A, using $\lfloor u\bar{a} \rfloor_{\mathcal{H}}$ as u and (misusing notation) $\pi(\bar{v})$ as $a; v$.

Since w^c is a counterexample, at some point one of the three steps will deliver a new prefix or suffix. Denoting the maximal length (i.e., $|Acts(w^c)|$) of a counterexample by m and the arity of the action with most parameters by p, we can estimate the number of membership queries we need to process a counterexample by $O(pm3^{pm})$. We thus have:

Proposition 2. Every counterexample delivers either *a new transition*, or an abstract suffix leading to *an increased number of locations* or *an increased sum of the number of register assignments*, or it leads to a reduced number of *symmetries between assigned registers* at a particular location. □

3.4 Correctness and Complexity

Inferring an unknown data language over the set of actions A, the learning algorithm proceeds in rounds. In each round a well-defined hypothesis automaton can be constructed from the closed and consistent observations (Proposition 1). For initialization $Sp(U) = \{\varepsilon\}$, i.e., it contains the access sequence of the initial location, while $U \setminus Sp(U)$ contains a word with no equal data values for every $\alpha \in A$. The set of abstract suffixes is initialized as $V = \{\varepsilon\}$, distinguishing accepting and rejecting locations.

As usual, we will estimate the number of necessary membership and equivalence queries in terms of the size of the canonical DRA for the considered regular data language. Let the number of registers be denoted by r, the number of locations by n, the number of transitions by t, the arity of the action with most parameters by p, and the length of the longest counterexample by m.

Then, by construction, the number of prefixes in the final observation table is $t + 1$, i.e., in $O(t)$, and the number of suffixes lies in $O(nr)$: less than n to distinguish locations, less than nr to realize *register-consistency*, and less than nr to reduce the number of possible permutations.[2]

Each processing of a counterexample, which may require $O(pm3^{pm})$ membership queries, will lead to a refined observation table from which a new hypothesis automaton can be constructed. This automaton will either have more transitions, more locations, or more registers than the previous one, or it uses a different permutation between prefixes reaching a location, where the number of possible permutations decreases strictly monotonically (Proposition 2). Due to the monotonicity of the refinement steps, chaotic fixpoint iteration is guaranteed to terminate after finitely many rounds with the greatest fixpoint, which resembles the canonical DRA for $\mathcal{L}$.

The number of membership queries needed to fill the observation table depends on the number of membership queries needed to produce all closures. An

[2] Reducing the number of permutations follows the same partition-refinement-pattern as automata learning does in general: With every new suffix a group of symmetric data values / registers is split (at a particular location).

Table 1. Observation Table (only showing a subset of all prefixes)

	ε	$\mathbf{in}(z_1, z_2)$		$\mathbf{out}()\mathbf{in}(z_1, z_2)$	
ε (l_0)	$-$	$\mathbf{in}(\mathbf{1},\mathbf{2})$	$-$	$\mathbf{out}()\mathbf{in}(\mathbf{1},\mathbf{2})$	$-$
$\mathbf{reg}(a, b)$ (l_1)	$-$	$\mathbf{in}(\mathbf{1},\mathbf{2})$ $\mathbf{in}(a, b)$	$-$ $+$	$\mathbf{out}()\mathbf{in}(\mathbf{1},\mathbf{2})$ $\mathbf{out}()\mathbf{in}(a, b)$	$-$ $+$
$\mathbf{reg}(a, b)\mathbf{in}(a, b)$ (l_2)	$+$	$\mathbf{in}(\mathbf{1},\mathbf{2})$	$+$	$\mathbf{out}()\mathbf{in}(\mathbf{1},\mathbf{2})$ $\mathbf{out}()\mathbf{in}(a, b)$	$-$ $+$
$\mathbf{reg}(a, b)\mathbf{in}(c, d)$	$-$	$\mathbf{in}(\mathbf{1},\mathbf{2})$ $\mathbf{in}(a, b)$	$-$ $+$	$\mathbf{out}()\mathbf{in}(\mathbf{1},\mathbf{2})$ $\mathbf{out}()\mathbf{in}(a, b)$	$-$ $+$
$\mathbf{reg}(a, b)\mathbf{in}(a, b)\mathbf{pw}(c)$	$+$	$\mathbf{in}(\mathbf{1},\mathbf{2})$	$+$	$\mathbf{out}()\mathbf{in}(\mathbf{1},\mathbf{2})$ $\mathbf{out}()\mathbf{in}(a, c)$	$-$ $+$
$\mathbf{reg}(a, b)\mathbf{in}(a, b)\mathbf{out}()$	$-$	$\mathbf{in}(\mathbf{1},\mathbf{2})$ $\mathbf{in}(a, b)$	$-$ $+$	$\mathbf{out}()\mathbf{in}(\mathbf{1},\mathbf{2})$ $\mathbf{out}()\mathbf{in}(a, b)$	$-$ $+$

abstract suffix can have at most r abstract parameters, which can be instantiated by less than np parameters in the potential of a word in less than $(np)^r$ combinations. The number of membership queries needed to construct all closures lies therefore in $O(tnr \cdot (np)^r)$.

Theorem 1. Regular data languages can be learned with $O(t+nr)$ equivalence queries and $O(tnr \cdot (np)^r + (t + nr) \cdot pm3^{pm}))$ membership queries. □

Two factors for the number of membership queries look critical. (1) the "concatenation" of prefixes and abstract suffixes, which is responsible for the exponential term of the first summand, and (2) the transformation of arbitrary prefixes of counterexamples into corresponding $\mathcal{L}$-essential words, leading to the exponential term of the second summand. It should be noted, however, that both exponents are typically quite small in practice. In fact, p may well be considered a constant in many contexts, and pm estimates the worst case in which all data values of a counterexample are equal, which usually can be avoided when searching for counterexamples. Finally, the number of required registers r will typically grow much slower than the model size. This observation was also supported by our experiments.

4 Example Application

In this section we give an example of a complete run of our algorithm, using the XMPP example from Figure 1, and present some performance data for our implementation of the algorithm.

The resulting (final) observation table for the example is shown (partly) in Table 1. The left column contains prefixes. Prefixes from $Sp(U)$ are shown in the upper part of the table. The three other columns are labeled with abstract suffixes. Table cells of a row labeled u contain suffixes from the domain of the u-closure $C_u^{V(u)}$ grouped per abstract suffix. The table was initialized as described in Section 3.4. The algorithm starts by constructing closures for all prefixes in U and the empty suffix. Since all prefixes are not in $\mathcal{L}$, the table is immediately

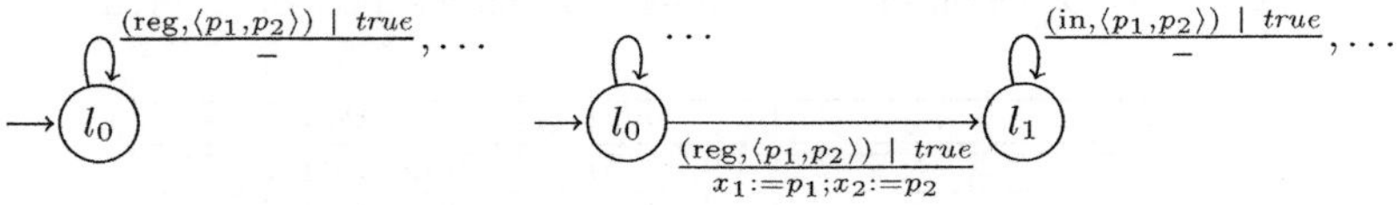

Fig. 3. First and second hypothesis

closed and consistent. In the constructed hypothesis, shown in the left of Figure 3, all prefixes lead to one non-accepting state.

An equivalence query returns the counterexample $\mathbf{reg}(a, a)\mathbf{in}(a, a)$ which is in $\mathcal{L}$ but rejected by the hypothesis. Performing step A of handling counterexamples results in a word $\mathbf{reg}(a, b)\mathbf{in}(a, b)$, which still is a counterexample. When refining the word to be supported by the (empty) assignment along the **reg**-transition in the hypothesis (step B), the words $\mathbf{reg}(a, b)\mathbf{in}(a, d)$ and $\mathbf{reg}(a, b)\mathbf{in}(c, b)$ are no longer counterexamples. In order to subsequently correct the yet empty assignment, we add the abstract suffix $\mathbf{in}(z_1, z_2)$ to the table.

When completing the table, the closure for the prefix $\mathbf{reg}(a, b)$ will be incompatible with the other closures, which can be seen in Table 1. In order to get a *closed* observation table, $\mathbf{reg}(a, b)$ will be added to $Sp(U)$, and $U \setminus Sp(U)$ will be extended accordingly. From the closed table we construct the hypothesis that is shown in the right of Figure 3.

We will get the same counterexample as in the first round. Analyzing it, we perform the refinement steps described in Section 3.3. We first perform the refinement steps for the empty prefix. First we transform $\mathbf{reg}(a, a)\mathbf{in}(a, a)$ to $\mathbf{reg}(a, b)\mathbf{in}(a, b)$ (step A). Steps B and C will not modify this counterexample since the equalities are supported already by the hypothesis and since $\mathbf{reg}(a, b)$ is its own access sequence. The second round starts with $\mathbf{reg}(a, b)$ as u, $\mathbf{in}(a, b)$ as a, and an empty suffix v. When refining $\mathbf{in}(a, b)$ to be supported by the corresponding guard of the **in**-transition from l_1 (step A), we discover that $\mathbf{reg}(a, b)\mathbf{in}(a, d)$ and $\mathbf{reg}(a, b)\mathbf{in}(c, b)$ are no counterexamples. Hence, $\mathbf{reg}(a, b)\mathbf{in}(a, b)$ must be $\mathcal{L}$-essential. We add it to $U \setminus Sp(U)$ in order to represent the guarded **in**-transition in the table.

To *close* the table, we have to move the new prefix to $Sp(U)$ as its closure is incompatible with the other closures. We extend $U \setminus Sp(U)$ accordingly. Now the resulting table is not *register-consistent*: It does not support any (re-)assignment along the new prefix as its closure does not have memorable data values. The closure of its continuation $\mathbf{reg}(a, b)\mathbf{in}(a, b)\mathbf{out}()$, however, has two memorable data values, namely a and b. We add $\mathbf{out}()\mathbf{in}(z_1, z_2)$ to the set of suffixes. From the closed and consistent observation table, shown in Table 1, we construct the final model: the canonical DRA from Figure 1.

We have implemented the outlined algorithm on top of LearnLib [18], and applied it to the discussed example. Counterexamples were found automatically by comparing DFAs, generated from hypothesis and target model for a small, concrete data domain. We compared our new learning algorithm for RAs with algorithms for learning DFAs utilizing abstraction, which to our knowledge would

Table 2. Experimental Results

Setup	# Loc.	# Trans.	MQs	EQs
RA learning algorithm	3	16	403	3
L^*, symmetry reduction, $\|D\| = 6$)	73	5,913	2,776	2
L^*, no optimization, $\|D\| = 6$)	73	5,913	415,333	72

be the state-of-the-art approach to learning a system like the XMPP protocol. We have generated a DFA from the DRA in Figure 1 for the smallest sensible data domain of size 6 (the longest membership query has 6 distinct data values). This can be considered an optimal data abstraction. We have learned the model twice: once with no optimization, and once with a symmetry filter. The key figures of all experiments are shown in Table 2. The experiments show that learning register automata not only delivers much more expressive models, but (in this particular case) also is much more efficient than classic L^*-based learning.

5 Conclusions

In this paper, we have presented an active learning algorithm for register automata, which allows capturing the flow of parameter values taken from arbitrary domains. The application of our algorithm to a small example indicates the impact of learning register automata models: Not only are the inferred models much more expressive than finite state machines, but the prototype implementation also drastically outperforms the classic L^* algorithm, even when exploiting optimal data abstraction and symmetry reduction. Currently, we are investigating the limits of our technology by considering generalizations, in particular concerning the transition structure, and by exploring scalability and potential optimizations.

References

1. Aarts, F., Jonsson, B., Uijen, J.: Generating Models of Infinite-State Communication Protocols Using Regular Inference with Abstraction. In: Petrenko, A., Simão, A., Maldonado, J.C. (eds.) ICTSS 2010. LNCS, vol. 6435, pp. 188–204. Springer, Heidelberg (2010)
2. Ammons, G., Bodik, R., Larus, J.: Mining specifications. In: Proc. 29th ACM Symp. on Principles of Programming Languages, pp. 4–16 (2002)
3. Angluin, D.: Learning regular sets from queries and counterexamples. Information and Computation 75(2), 87–106 (1987)
4. Berg, T., Jonsson, B., Raffelt, H.: Regular Inference for State Machines Using Domains with Equality Tests. In: Fiadeiro, J.L., Inverardi, P. (eds.) FASE 2008. LNCS, vol. 4961, pp. 317–331. Springer, Heidelberg (2008)
5. Broy, M., Jonsson, B., Katoen, J.-P., Leucker, M., Pretschner, A. (eds.): Model-Based Testing of Reactive Systems. LNCS, vol. 3472. Springer, Heidelberg (2005)
6. Cassel, S., Howar, F., Jonsson, B., Merten, M., Steffen, B.: A Succinct Canonical Register Automaton Model. In: Bultan, T., Hsiung, P.-A. (eds.) ATVA 2011. LNCS, vol. 6996, pp. 366–380. Springer, Heidelberg (2011)

7. Clarke, E.M., Grumberg, O., Peled, D.: Model Checking. MIT Press (1999)
8. Ernst, M.D., Perkins, J.H., Guo, P.J., McCamant, S., Pacheco, C., Tschantz, M.S., Xiao, C.: The Daikon system for dynamic detection of likely invariants. Science of Computer Programming 69(1-3), 35–45 (2007)
9. Hagerer, A., Hungar, H., Niese, O., Steffen, B.: Model Generation by Moderated Regular Extrapolation. In: Kutsche, R.-D., Weber, H. (eds.) FASE 2002. LNCS, vol. 2306, pp. 80–95. Springer, Heidelberg (2002)
10. Howar, F., Steffen, B., Merten, M.: Automata Learning with Automated Alphabet Abstraction Refinement. In: Jhala, R., Schmidt, D. (eds.) VMCAI 2011. LNCS, vol. 6538, pp. 263–277. Springer, Heidelberg (2011)
11. Huima, A.: Implementing Conformiq Qtronic. In: Petrenko, A., Veanes, M., Tretmans, J., Grieskamp, W. (eds.) TestCom/FATES 2007. LNCS, vol. 4581, pp. 1–12. Springer, Heidelberg (2007)
12. Hungar, H., Niese, O., Steffen, B.: Domain-Specific Optimization in Automata Learning. In: Hunt Jr., W.A., Somenzi, F. (eds.) CAV 2003. LNCS, vol. 2725, pp. 315–327. Springer, Heidelberg (2003)
13. Jonsson, B., Parrow, J.: Deciding bisimulation equivalences for a class of non-finite-state programs. Information and Computation 107(2), 272–302 (1993)
14. Kaminski, M., Francez, N.: Finite-memory automata. Theoretical Computer Science 134(2), 329–363 (1994)
15. Lo, D., Maoz, S.: Scenario-based and value-based specification mining: better together. In: 25th IEEE/ACM Int. Conf. on Automated Software Engineering, ASE 2010, Antwerp, Belgium, pp. 387–396. ACM (2010)
16. Lorenzoli, D., Mariani, L., Pezzè, M.: Automatic generation of software behavioral models. In: Proc. ICSE 2008: 30th Int. Conf. on Software Enginering, pp. 501–510 (2008)
17. Mariani, L., Pezzé, M.: Dynamic detection of COTS components incompatibility. IEEE Software 24(5), 76–85 (2007)
18. Merten, M., Steffen, B., Howar, F., Margaria, T.: Next Generation LearnLib. In: Abdulla, P.A., Leino, K.R.M. (eds.) TACAS 2011. LNCS, vol. 6605, pp. 220–223. Springer, Heidelberg (2011)
19. Rivest, R.L., Schapire, R.E.: Inference of finite automata using homing sequences. Information and Computation 103(2), 299–347 (1993)
20. Saint-Andre, P.: Extensible Messaging and Presence Protocol (XMPP): Instant Messaging and Presence. RFC 6121 (Proposed Standard) (March 2011)
21. Sakamoto, H.: Learning Simple Deterministic Finite-Memory Automata. In: Li, M. (ed.) ALT 1997. LNCS, vol. 1316, pp. 416–431. Springer, Heidelberg (1997)
22. Shu, G., Lee, D.: Testing security properties of protocol implementations - a machine learning based approach. In: Proc. ICDCS 2007, 27th IEEE Int. Conf. on Distributed Computing Systems, Toronto, Ontario. IEEE Computer Society (2007)
23. Steffen, B., Howar, F., Merten, M.: Introduction to Active Automata Learning from a Practical Perspective. In: Bernardo, M., Issarny, V. (eds.) SFM 2011. LNCS, vol. 6659, pp. 256–296. Springer, Heidelberg (2011)
24. Tretmans, J.: Model-Based Testing and Some Steps towards Test-Based Modelling. In: Bernardo, M., Issarny, V. (eds.) SFM 2011. LNCS, vol. 6659, pp. 297–326. Springer, Heidelberg (2011)
25. Wolper, P.: Expressing interesting properties of programs in propositional temporal logic (extended abstract). In: Proc. 13th ACM Symp. on Principles of Programming Languages, pp. 184–193 (January 1986)

Alternating Control Flow Reconstruction

Johannes Kinder[1] and Dmitry Kravchenko[2]

[1] École Polytechnique Fédérale de Lausanne, CH-1015 Lausanne, Switzerland
johannes.kinder@epfl.ch
[2] Technische Universität Darmstadt, D-64277 Darmstadt, Germany
dmitry.kravchenko@cased.de

Abstract. Unresolved indirect branch instructions are a major obstacle for statically reconstructing a control flow graph (CFG) from machine code. If static analysis cannot compute a precise set of possible targets for a branch, the necessary conservative over-approximation introduces a large amount of spurious edges, leading to even more imprecision and a degenerate CFG.

In this paper, we propose to leverage under-approximation to handle this problem. We provide an abstract interpretation framework for control flow reconstruction that alternates between over- and under-approximation. Effectively, the framework imposes additional preconditions on the program on demand, allowing to avoid conservative over-approximation of indirect branches.

We give an example instantiation of our framework using dynamically observed execution traces and constant propagation. We report preliminary experimental results confirming that our alternating analysis yields CFGs closer to the concrete CFG than pure over- or under-approximation.

1 Introduction

Binary machine code is an attractive analysis target for several reasons: when working with a fully compiled and linked binary, no interfacing with the build process is required and all program parts are available. Inline assembly and differences between programming languages or dialects are all eliminated by the translation to machine code. Moreover, there is often no source code available for a program of interest, e.g., when analyzing proprietary code such as third party device drivers, plugins, or potentially malicious software.

An important first step for applying static analysis to binaries is to recover an accessible program representation in the form of a control flow graph (CFG). The major problem in computing a CFG for low-level machine code lies in the treatment of indirect branches, i.e., instructions such as `jmp eax`, whose targets are computed at runtime. In earlier work [15,14], we showed how abstract interpretation [7] of machine code coupled with on the fly disassembly can compute an over-approximation of the concrete CFG: starting with an empty CFG, data flow information is propagated one instruction at a time. On encountering an indirect branch instruction, possible targets are computed from the partial data flow information and added to the CFG as new edges.

In a purely static approach, the over-approximate analysis has to be precise enough to compute accurate sets of target address values for each indirect branch. Because of

V. Kuncak and A. Rybalchenko (Eds.): VMCAI 2012, LNCS 7148, pp. 267–282, 2012.

imprecise reasoning or because parts of the runtime environment (libraries, operating system behavior) have been abstracted away, however, the static analysis may have to conservatively over-approximate the possible target addresses. In that case, the CFG has to be extended with edges from the branch instruction to the entire program address space (including the branch instruction itself). These mostly spurious edges introduce additional imprecision into the analysis as abstract states propagate across them, in the end yielding a degenerate CFG that is unusable for analysis. In practice, existing tools [13] therefore either immediately report an error whenever they cannot resolve an indirect branch or simply turn the indirect jump into a leaf without any successors.

In the context of dynamic instrumentation, Nanda et al. proposed to resolve indirect branches at runtime, when the concrete jump target has already been computed [16]. In this paper, we generalize this idea to combining over-approximate static analysis with under-approximation and alternating between the two for resolving jump targets. We provide a formalization of our approach in terms of abstract interpretation, which allows us to be precise about the nature of the combined analysis and its results. The resulting framework is parameterized by an over-approximate analysis, an under-approximate analysis, and a predicate for influencing alternation between the two. We make the following contributions:

- We give a new formalization of low-level control flow reconstruction as abstract interpretation of a parameterized semantics (Section 3). In Section 4, we show how this semantics can be instantiated to obtain (i) the concrete semantics of a low-level language, (ii) our existing over-approximate control flow reconstruction [15], and (iii) a purely under-approximate control flow reconstruction.
- Based on these definitions, we present a combined over- and under-approximation as an instance of our framework (Section 5). We split the rule for branch instructions to implement alternation between the two approximations. This yields a well-understood blueprint for using dynamic information in control flow reconstruction, whereas previous approaches relied on ad-hoc solutions.
- We prove that the algorithm for alternating control flow reconstruction terminates (i.e, the alternation semantics has a fixpoint) and computes an over-approximation of the original program restricted by additional preconditions. Subsequent static analysis on the reconstructed CFG is sound with respect to these preconditions.
- We present preliminary experimental results (Section 6) confirming that alternating control flow reconstruction yields a clear quality improvement compared to pure under- or over-approximation (in terms of false positives and negatives) and is essential for obtaining CFGs of realistically-sized programs.

2 Overview

Let us first informally illustrate our approach using an example. Consider the program fragment in Figure 1a. It starts at location 0 and contains two indirect branches at locations 6 and 22. For this example, we will use an over-approximating static analysis that collects for each location and variable a set of explicit values up to size, say, five. At the first indirect branch from location 6, control is transferred to the address stored in a variable x. Assume that x can take the values 10, 15, or 20 at runtime, but that this

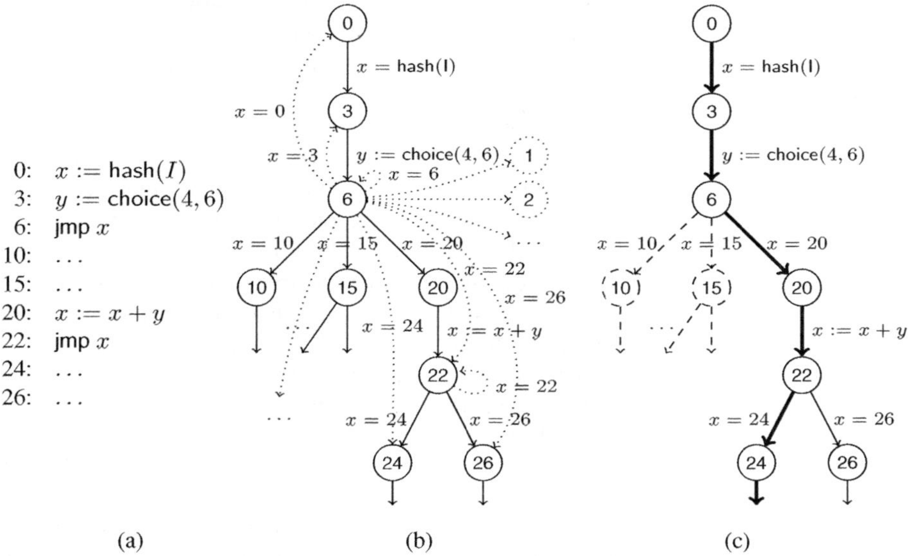

Fig. 1. Indirect jump example. (a) IL code, (b) CFG reconstructed by pure over-approximation, with spurious edges and nodes dotted, (c) CFG reconstructed by alternation using a single trace, with under-approximate edges in bold, over-approximate edges as regular lines, and missed edges dashed (assume edges are shown without an explicit "assume" keyword).

cannot be determined by our static analysis because x depends on the output of a hash function over some input value I. Assume further, that static analysis *can* determine the possible values of 4 and 6 for y, which are selected by some function choice. Note that our intermediate language used in the remainder of the paper does not contain an explicit function call but instead uses jumps. Here we use two calls for ease of exposition. Over-approximate control flow reconstruction by abstract interpretation proceeds on the program as follows. Starting from an empty CFG, the two edges $(0, x := \mathsf{hash}(I), 3)$ and $(3, y := \mathsf{choice}(4,6), 6)$ are created (as simple syntactic fall-through edges) and interpreted, leading to the abstract state $(x = \top, y = \{4, 6\})$.

Upon reaching the indirect jump at location 6, the static analysis computes the set of concrete addresses corresponding to the current abstract value of x. This "downward" concretization yields a superset of the actual, concrete target addresses. For each possible concrete value V, an edge $(6, \mathsf{assume}\ x = V, V)$ is then added to the partial CFG. In general, this algorithm always produces a correct over-approximation of the concrete CFG, but its precision depends critically on whether the abstract value for x concretizes to an accurate set of concrete target addresses.

In our example, however, x is unknown and its concretization ranges over all values in the set $\mathbf{L}$ of program addresses. Thus, the control flow reconstruction algorithm has to add $|\mathbf{L}|$ edges from 6, which renders the resulting CFG useless for all practical purposes. Taking only the locations within the depicted program fragment into account, the CFG already degenerates to the form shown in Figure 1b. In this CFG, control flow can even reach addresses such as 1 and 2, which lie between existing instructions.[1] Moreover, the imprecision of over-approximating the jump edges propagates: through the spurious edge $(6, \textsf{assume}\ (x = 22), 22)$, the second indirect jump can be reached, leading to a self-loop at location 22.

To avoid such loss of precision, we propose *alternating control flow reconstruction*. As soon as a predefined condition χ is met, e.g., that the set of possible targets is unconstrained, the abstract interpreter switches to an under-approximate semantics. To this end, an under-approximation is maintained alongside the over-approximation. Under-approximate states concretize "upward" to a subset of the concrete values.

We can under-approximate the program semantics by simply executing the program with random input. Assume that, in our execution, we have in location 6 that $x = 20$ and $y = 6$. Then x concretizes upward to the singleton set $\{20\}$, and a corresponding edge $(6, \textsf{assume}\ x = 20, 20)$ is created. The simultaneously over- and under-approximate analysis then continues along this edge, which under-approximates the set of concrete edges going out from location 6. From interpreting the edge, the over-approximation can deduce that $x = 20$, leading to the abstract state $(x = \{20\}, y = \{4, 6\})$. The next fall-through edge updates the state to $(x = \{24, 26\}, y = \{4, 6\})$, which allows the over-approximation to precisely resolve all edges from the indirect jump at location 22. The analysis thus explores the CFG by alternation, returning to over-approximation after passing over the unresolved first indirect jump using under-approximation. It missed two outgoing edges from location 6, but reconstructed a CFG (Figure 1c) that differs less from the concrete CFG than the over-approximation. The final CFG represents an over-approximation of the program restricted to $x = 20$ at location 2. Subsequent analyses on the CFG are then performed modulo the additional precondition $\textsf{hash}(I) = 20$.

To obtain a fully over-approximate CFG without additional preconditions, the missing two indirect branches could be covered using dynamic test generation [9,10,17]. Note that complete control flow reconstruction by dynamic test generation alone requires full branch coverage, therefore it would need to create at least 5 tests. Together with alternating control flow reconstruction, both branches of the indirect jump at location 22 can be covered using just a single trace, requiring only 3 test cases for complete reconstruction.

3 Parameterized Semantics for Low-Level Control Flow

Computing the control flow graph in the presence of indirect jumps reduces to a reachability problem, since we want to find for each indirect jump all possible values that its target expression can evaluate to. Defining an analysis that is able to deal with indirect jumps is non-obvious, though, so in earlier work [15] we proposed a generic framework for control flow reconstruction that is parameterized by an over-approximate data flow analysis for a simplified language without indirect jumps. In the following, we provide a new and more flexible formalization of low-level control flow as a parameterized

[1] Such spurious inter-instruction locations cannot be simply ruled out, as "overlapping instructions" are actually legal. They lead to an alternative decoding of the same code bytes and are a popular anti-disassembly measure in hand-crafted assembly code.

semantics that allows to define concrete, under-, and over-approximating semantics in common terms.

3.1 Intermediate Language

To abstract from the details of assembly language while still capturing its nature, in particular the relevant low-level branching behavior, we define the intermediate language IL. The set of statements is denoted by $\mathbf{Stmt}$ and consists of assignments $m[e_1] := e_2$, conditional indirect jumps if e_1 jmp e_2, assume statements assume e_1, and the halt statement, where $e_1, e_2 \in \mathbf{Exp}$ denote expressions from a set $\mathbf{Exp}$ containing constants, memory dereferences $m[e]$, and the usual arithmetic, Boolean, and bitwise operators. For simplicity, we do not explicitly introduce variables; when we use identifiers such as x, these refer to fixed memory locations. The only IL data type are integers; Boolean true and false are represented by 1 and 0, respectively. The finite set of program *locations* $\mathbf{L} \subseteq \mathbb{N}$ denotes all addresses that are part of the program. Note that we could also use bit-vectors as data type (and indeed do so in our implementation); we choose to use integers in the exposition for greater generality. An IL program $\langle \ell_0, P \rangle$ consists of a unique start location ℓ_0 and a finite mapping $P :: \mathbf{L} \to (\mathbf{Stmt} \times \mathbf{L})$ from program locations to statements and successor locations. Successor locations identify the address of the syntactically next instruction and are used here to reflect variable length instruction sets. We will use the notation $[stmt]^{\ell}_{\ell'}$ to refer to the statement *stmt* in P at location ℓ with successor location ℓ'.

Furthermore, we define a reduced language IL$^-$ and its set of statements $\mathbf{Stmt}^-$, which consists only of assignments and assume statements.

3.2 Parameter Semantics Template

Our approach to control flow reconstruction is a parameterized framework in the form of an adapter semantics that lifts an existing semantics $\mathcal{S}$ for the simpler language IL$^-$. In a state that is about to execute an indirect jump next, the adapter semantics converts the jump into a set of assume edges pointing out to the targets that are feasible given the current state. Therefore $\mathcal{S}$ has to be defined only for assignments and assume statements, and a CFG is automatically created by collecting all the edges created by the adapter semantics. The parameter semantics $\mathcal{S} = (\mathcal{A}, \iota, f, \gamma[\![\cdot]\!], \cup^A)$ contains:

- A complete lattice $\mathcal{A} = (A, \sqcup, \sqcap, \sqsubseteq, \bot, \top)$.
- An initial lattice element ι.
- A transfer function $f[\![C]\!](S) :: (\mathbf{Stmt}^-, A) \to A$ for the statements in IL$^-$, i.e., for assignments and assume statements.
- A concretizing evaluation function $\gamma[\![e_1, \ldots, e_n]\!]S :: \mathbf{Exp}^n \times A \to \mathcal{P}(\mathbb{Z}^n)$ that abstractly evaluates and concretizes vectors of expressions $e_1, \ldots, e_n$ to a set of vectors of concrete values ($\mathcal{P}$ denotes the powerset). In principle, the concretizing evaluation function could be synthesized from a regular concretization function γ as $\gamma[\![e_1, \ldots, e_n]\!]S := \{\mathbf{eval}[\![e_1]\!](S^\natural), \ldots, \mathbf{eval}[\![e_n]\!](S^\natural) \mid S^\natural \in \gamma(S)\}$, where $\mathbf{eval}$ denotes concrete expression evaluation, but is usually implemented directly.
- An operator $\cup^A :: A \times A \to A$ that is used by the adapter semantics to combine elements of the domain A reaching the same location. $\cup^A$ may be identical to $\sqcup$ but does not have to be.

$$\frac{[m[A] := E]^{\ell}_{\ell'} \quad f[\![m[A] := E]\!](S) = S'}{\langle \ell, S, G\rangle \longrightarrow \langle \ell', S', G \uplus (\ell, \ell')\rangle} \text{ ASSIGNMENT}$$

$$\frac{[\text{if } B \text{ jmp } E]^{\ell}_{\ell'} \quad (1, V) \in \gamma[\![B, E]\!]S \quad f[\![\text{assume } (B \wedge E = V)]\!](S) = S'}{\langle \ell, S, G\rangle \longrightarrow \langle V, S', G \uplus (\ell, V)\rangle} \text{ JUMP-TRUE}$$

$$\frac{[\text{if } B \text{ jmp } E]^{\ell}_{\ell'} \quad 0 \in \gamma[\![B]\!]S \quad f[\![\text{assume } (\neg B)]\!](S) = S'}{\langle \ell, S, G\rangle \longrightarrow \langle \ell', S', G \uplus (\ell, \ell')\rangle} \text{ JUMP-FALSE}$$

$$\frac{[\text{assume } E]^{\ell}_{\ell'} \quad f[\![\text{assume } E]\!](S) = S'}{\langle \ell, S, G\rangle \longrightarrow \langle \ell', S', G \uplus (\ell, \ell')\rangle} \text{ ASSUME}$$

$$\frac{[\text{halt}]^{\ell}_{\ell'}}{\langle \ell, S, G\rangle \longrightarrow \langle \ell, S, G\rangle} \text{ HALT}$$

Fig. 2. Control flow resolving transition system for an IL program $\langle \ell_0, P\rangle$, parameterized by a forward transfer function f for IL^-

3.3 Control Flow Semantics

Using these parameters, we can define the full IL transition relation $\longrightarrow$ shown in Figure 2. It relates states from the set $\mathbf{L} \times A \times \mathcal{P}(\mathbf{L} \times \mathbf{L})$ consisting of the value of the program counter $\ell \in \mathbf{L}$, the memory state $S \in A$, and the partial CFG $G \subseteq \mathbf{L} \times \mathbf{L}$.

Depending on the statement pointed to by the current program counter value, the rules invoke the transfer function f, update the program counter, and add the current edge to the partial CFG. Assignments and assume statements simply fall through to the syntactically next statement, and halt statements terminate execution. The rule JUMP-TRUE fires if the jump condition is possibly true in the current state and determines the next program counter value from the concretization of the target expression. The rule invokes the transfer function to assume the evaluations of the condition and target expressions, updates the program counter to the jump target, and adds the new edge. The rule JUMP-FALSE fires if the condition of a jump is possibly false, and transfers control to the fall-through successor, assuming the negative evaluation of the condition. The reachability semantics for IL then is the least fixpoint of a function F defined as

$$F(D) := \{\langle \ell_0, \iota, \varnothing\rangle\} \cup \dot{\bigsqcup} \{\langle \ell', S', G'\rangle \mid \exists \langle \ell, S, G\rangle \in D : \langle \ell, S, G\rangle \longrightarrow \langle \ell', S', G'\rangle\}$$

with

$$\langle \ell, S, G\rangle \,\dot{\cup}\, \langle \ell', S', G'\rangle = \begin{cases} \{\langle \ell, S \cup^{A} S', G \cup G'\rangle\} & \text{if } \ell = \ell' \\ \{\langle \ell, S, G\rangle, \langle \ell', S', G'\rangle\} & \text{otherwise} \end{cases}$$

as the pointwise merge function that combines states reaching the same location. The reconstructed CFG then results from

$$CFG = \bigcup \{G \mid \langle \ell, S, G\rangle \in \text{lfp } F\}.$$

4 Instantiating the Parameterized Semantics

Using the template from Section 3.2, we instantiate our semantics framework with semantics for IL^- to obtain concrete, over-approximate, and under-approximate control flow semantics for IL.

4.1 Concrete Semantics

We can now instantiate our framework with a concrete reachability semantics for IL^- to define the concrete semantics of IL. The semantics of IL^- is defined in terms of sets of concrete memory states from $\mathcal{P}(\mathbb{N} \to \mathbb{Z})$, where each memory state maps positive integers (representing memory addresses) to integers. The parameters required by our adapter semantics are given by

- the powerset lattice of concrete memory states $(\mathcal{P}(\mathbb{N} \to \mathbb{Z}), \cup, \cap, \subseteq, \varnothing, \mathbb{N} \to \mathbb{Z})$,
- the initial state set $\iota = \mathbb{N} \to \mathbb{Z}$,
- the concrete transfer function over sets of memory states

$$f^\natural[\![m[A] := E]\!](S) = \{s' \mid \exists s \in S : s' = s[\mathbf{eval}[\![A]\!](s) \mapsto \mathbf{eval}[\![E]\!](s)]\}$$
$$f^\natural[\![\mathsf{assume}\ E]\!](S) = \{s \in S \mid \mathbf{eval}[\![E]\!](s) = 1\},$$

- the concrete evaluation function $\gamma^\natural[\![e_1, \ldots, e_n]\!]S := \{v_1, \ldots, v_n \mid \exists s \in S : v_1 = \mathbf{eval}[\![e]\!](s), \ldots, v_n = \mathbf{eval}[\![e_n]\!](s)\}$ ($\gamma^\natural$ is the identity function),
- and the merging operator $\cup$ for taking the union of two sets of memory states.

This fully instantiated concrete semantics for IL is the reference point for the following over- and under-approximations. Defining the concrete semantics in terms of our framework allows to simplify the correctness proofs for abstract semantics. If the framework is shared by both semantics, it suffices to only establish a correctness relation between the concrete and abstract transfer functions for IL^-.

We define the *concrete control flow graph* of a program as the CFG constructed by the concrete semantics. This definition is equivalent to the one in [15].

4.2 Over-Approximate Semantics

If instantiated with over-approximate IL^- semantics, our adapter semantics computes an over-approximation of the concrete CFG. The over-approximation $f^\sharp$ of the concrete transfer function $f^\natural$ has to satisfy $\gamma^\sharp \circ f^\sharp(S^\sharp) \supseteq f^\natural \circ \gamma^\sharp(S^\sharp)$ for a concretization function $\gamma^\sharp$ from abstract states to concrete sets of states. Any over-approximate forward analysis is suitable here; for useful results in control flow reconstruction, however, the concretizing evaluation function should be able to produce reasonably precise address values for jump targets, however.

The fixpoint of the fully instantiated over-approximate semantics can be computed using chaotic iteration over the locations in the partial CFG, which yields the algorithm for static control flow reconstruction [15]. The resulting CFG over-approximates the concrete CFG, i.e., is a superset of its edges. In the present formalization of the framework, the over-approximate domain must not contain infinite ascending chains to ensure termination. It is straightforward to remove this requirement by including widening (and possibly narrowing), but we omit this extension for simplicity.

4.3 Under-Approximate Semantics

An under-approximate semantics is given using exactly the same parameters as an over-approximate one is, but has dual requirements for correctness. The under-approximation $f^\flat$ of the concrete transfer function $f^\natural$ has to satisfy $\gamma^\flat \circ f^\flat(S^\flat) \subseteq f^\natural \circ \gamma^\flat(S^\flat)$ for the concretization function $\gamma^\flat$ from under-approximate states to sets of concrete states.

We now define an under-approximate semantics $(\mathcal{T}, \iota, f^\flat, \gamma^\flat[\![\cdot]\!], \sqcup^T)$ that replays a set of concrete execution traces. It is essentially equivalent to the concrete semantics but also maintains a total instruction counter for timing out after executing a predefined number N of instructions. The parameters instantiating our framework are

- the product lattice of (i) the chain of integer counters and (ii) the powerset lattice of memory states, $\mathcal{T} = ([0; N] \times \mathcal{P}(\mathbb{N} \to \mathbb{Z}), \sqcup^T, \sqcap^T, \sqsubseteq^T, (0, \varnothing), (N, \mathbb{N} \to \mathbb{Z}))$,
- the initial state $\iota = (0, S)$, which contains the zero counter and a finite set of memory configurations (e.g., command line parameters, file contents, ...) to initialize the executions.
- the under-approximate transfer function $f^\flat(S^\flat) = \begin{cases} (n+1, f^\natural(S^\natural)) & n < N \\ (N, \varnothing) & \text{otherwise} \end{cases}$
  with $S^\flat = (n, S^\natural)$, which satisfies $\gamma^\flat \circ f^\flat(S^\flat) \subseteq f^\natural \circ \gamma^\flat(S^\flat)$.
- the concretizing evaluation function $\gamma^\flat[\![e_1, \ldots, e_n]\!](n, S^\natural) := \{v_1, \ldots, v_n \mid \exists s \in S^\natural : v_1 = \mathbf{eval}[\![e]\!](s), \ldots, v_n = \mathbf{eval}[\![e_n]\!](s)\}$.
- and the merging operator $\sqcup^T$ with $(n_1, S_1^\natural) \sqcup^T (n_2, S_2^\natural) = (\mathsf{max}(n_1, n_2), S_1^\natural \cup S_2^\natural)$ for taking the union of two sets of memory states and setting the counter to the maximum of both individual counters.

Fixpoint computation for the under-approximate semantics is an algorithm for purely dynamic control flow reconstruction. The resulting CFG under-approximates the concrete CFG, i.e., is a subset of its edges. Termination of the fixpoint computation is ensured by the instruction counter.

5 Alternation in Control Flow Reconstruction

To leverage alternation in control flow reconstruction, we perform a simultaneous over- and under-approximation that can be plugged into our parameterized framework in the same way as the concrete and over-approximate semantics before.

5.1 Combined Semantics

We now define an intermediate semantics that allows to plug an over- and an under-approximation into our framework simultaneously. It is itself parameterized by an over-approximation $(\mathcal{A}, \iota^\sharp, f^\sharp, \gamma^\sharp[\![\cdot]\!], \sqcup^\sharp)$ and an under-approximation $(\mathcal{U}, \iota^\flat, f^\flat, \gamma^\flat[\![\cdot]\!], \sqcup^\flat)$, with $\mathcal{A} = (A, \sqcup^\sharp, \sqcap^\sharp, \sqsubseteq^\sharp, \bot^\sharp, \top^\sharp)$ and $\mathcal{U} = (U, \sqcup^\flat, \sqcap^\flat, \sqsubseteq^\flat, \bot^\flat, \top^\flat)$. The combined intermediate semantics is defined as $(\mathcal{C}, \iota^\diamond, f^\diamond, \gamma^\diamond[\![\cdot]\!], \sqcup^\diamond)$ with:

- The complete lattice $\mathcal{C} = (A \times U, \sqcup^\diamond, \sqcap^\diamond, \sqsubseteq^\diamond, (\bot^\sharp, \bot^\flat), (\top^\sharp, \top^\flat))$ with pairwise definitions of $\sqcup^\diamond$, $\sqcap^\diamond$, and $\sqsubseteq^\diamond$, e.g., $(a, u) \sqsubseteq^\diamond (a', u') \Leftrightarrow a \sqsubseteq^\sharp a' \wedge u \sqsubseteq^\flat u'$.

$$\frac{[\text{if } B \text{ jmp } E]_{\ell'}^{\ell} \quad \chi(S,E) \quad (1,V) \in \gamma^{\sharp}[\![B,E]\!]S^{\sharp} \quad f^{\diamond}[\![\text{assume } B \wedge E = V]\!](S) = S'}{\langle \ell, S, G\rangle \longrightarrow \langle V, S', G \uplus (\ell, V)\rangle}\ \text{JT}^{\sharp}$$

$$\frac{[\text{if } B \text{ jmp } E]_{\ell'}^{\ell} \quad \neg\chi(S,E) \quad (1,V) \in \gamma^{\flat}[\![B,E]\!]S^{\flat} \quad f^{\diamond}[\![\text{assume } B \wedge E = V]\!](S) = S'}{\langle \ell, S, G\rangle \longrightarrow \langle V, S', G \uplus (\ell, V)\rangle}\ \text{JT}^{\flat}$$

Fig. 3. Split rules for alternating jump target resolution. $\chi(S, E)$ controls which rule is enabled, with $S = (S^{\sharp}, S^{\flat})$.

- The initial lattice element $\iota^{\diamond} = (\iota^{\sharp}, \iota^{\flat})$.
- A combined transfer function $f^{\diamond}[\![C]\!](S^{\sharp}, S^{\flat}) := (f^{\sharp}[\![C]\!](S^{\sharp}), f^{\flat}[\![C]\!](S^{\flat}))$. The combined transfer function maps over- and under-approximate states to their respective successors. If the under-approximate state has no successor for a particular state (i.e., the condition of an assume statement is false), the under-approximate component is set to $\bot^{\flat}$.
- The concretizing evaluation function $\gamma^{\diamond}[\![\cdot]\!](S^{\sharp}, S^{\flat}) := \gamma^{\sharp}[\![\cdot]\!](S^{\sharp})$, which ignores the under-approximate part of the state.
- The merging operator $\cup^{\diamond}$ such that $(S_1^{\sharp}, S_1^{\flat}) \cup^{\diamond} (S_2^{\sharp}, S_2^{\flat}) := (S_1^{\sharp} \cup^{\sharp} S_2^{\sharp}, S_1^{\flat} \cup^{\flat} S_2^{\flat})$.

This combined semantics can instantiate our control flow reconstruction framework, but will yield the same CFG as the over-approximation alone, as the concretizing evaluation function will yield the same over-approximate branch targets when applying the JUMP-TRUE rule. We need to adapt our framework to make use of the additional under-approximate information.

5.2 Alternation Framework

To allow switching between over- and under-approximate information when resolving indirect jumps, we split the JMP-TRUE rule of our framework into the two rules shown in Figure 3. A definable predicate $\chi(S, E)$ for a state S and an expression E controls which of the two rules is enabled. When $\chi(S, E)$ is true, the rule $\text{JT}^{\sharp}$ resolves jumps exactly as the original JMP-TRUE rule before. Otherwise, $\text{JT}^{\flat}$ is enabled and uses the under-approximate portion of the state to evaluate the jump condition and the target expression.

The definition of χ allows to fine-tune the alternation. For instance, it can be defined as $\chi((S^{\sharp}, S^{\flat}), E) := \gamma^{\sharp}[\![E]\!]S^{\sharp} \subset \mathbb{N}$, such that the over-approximation is used as long as the concretizing evaluation function returns a finite set. We will use this definition of χ for the experiments in Section 6. Another possibility is to use $\chi'((S^{\sharp}, S^{\flat}), E) := S^{\flat} \sqsupset^{\flat} \bot^{\flat} \vee \gamma^{\sharp}[\![E]\!]S^{\sharp} \subset \mathbb{N}$, which only falls back to under-approximation if the under-approximation contains information at the location of the jump. By setting χ to always true or false, the alternation framework falls back to pure over- or under-approximation, respectively.

Note that the under-approximation can often default to the bottom element $\bot^{\flat}$. In the trace replay semantics defined in Section 4.3, this happens when the executions do not cover a statically feasible control flow edge (e.g., the second branch of a conditional jump). Then $f^\flat$ yields the empty set (the $\bot^\flat$ element for the trace replay semantics), which is paired with the over-approximate state for that location. During fixpoint computation, this empty set propagates until it merges with under-approximate states from a covered path.

5.3 Algorithm

As for the other semantics, the combined analysis is performed by computing the least fixpoint by chaotic iteration. Even though our alternating semantics is a considerable detour from regular abstract interpretation, the transfer relation is monotonic, and a fixpoint exists for the full framework instance.

Theorem 1 (Termination). *The alternating control flow reconstruction algorithm terminates in finite time if the over- and under-approximate domains do not contain infinite ascending chains.*

Proof. As $f^\flat$ and $f^\sharp$ are required to be monotonic, $f^\diamond$ is monotonic, i.e., $S_1 \sqsubseteq^\diamond S_2 \Leftrightarrow f^\diamond(S_1) \sqsubseteq^\diamond f^\diamond(S_2)$. The transfer relation $\longrightarrow$ of the parameterized semantics is monotonic in its original form [15], i.e., $\forall S_1, S_1', S_2, S_2' : S_1 \sqsubseteq S_2 \wedge S_1 \longrightarrow S_1' \wedge S_2 \longrightarrow S_2' \Rightarrow S_1' \sqsubseteq S_2'$. It remains to prove that it stays monotonic when JUMP-TRUE is replaced by the two new rules. The critical part is the situation when $\chi(S_1, E) \wedge \neg\chi(S_2, E)$ or $\neg\chi(S_1, E) \wedge \chi(S_2, E)$ holds and $\longrightarrow$ switches between the two rules.

The only difference between the rules, however, is the more restricted concretization of jump targets in $\mathrm{JT}^\flat$, since $|\gamma^\flat[\![B, E]\!]S^\flat| \leq |\gamma^\sharp[\![B, E]\!]S^\sharp|$. Therefore, $\mathrm{JT}^\flat$ may fire fewer times than $\mathrm{JT}^\sharp$, but the individual applications remain monotonic. Obviously, firing strictly more times does not affect the monotonicity of the semantic function F (see Section 3.3). Neither does firing fewer times, because (i) all remaining state updates are still guaranteed to be monotonic by virtue of $f^\diamond$'s monotonicity and (ii) no edges already created are removed from the partial control flow graph G. □

Again, the restriction to finite ascending chains in the over-approximate lattice can be lifted by introducing widening. In under-approximations, infinite ascending chains are easily avoided using counters (see Section 4.3).

5.4 Characterizing the Reconstructed CFG

Soundness. The transfer function of our alternating semantics neither over- nor under-approximates the concrete semantics, i.e., it is not a sound abstraction. After chaotic iteration reaches a fixpoint, the "over-approximate" part $S^\sharp$ of the combined state $S^\diamond = (S^\sharp, S^\flat)$ may not fully over-approximate the concrete reachability semantics. Consequently, the final CFG is neither an over- nor an under-approximation of the concrete CFG for the full program.

However, we can still characterize the kind of approximation that is performed: Alternating control flow reconstruction computes an over-approximation of the concrete CFG of a restricted version of its input program. The restriction asserts that at each indirect jump where the under-approximation was used, control flow follows only the under-approximate set of branches. We define the restricted program as $\langle \ell'_0, P' \rangle$ with $P' = P[\ell'_0 \mapsto [\mathsf{assume}\ \phi]^{\ell'_0}_{\ell_0}]$ enforcing a precondition ϕ. Here, ϕ is the condition under which $\neg\chi((S^\sharp, S^\flat), E) \implies \gamma^\flat[\![B, E]\!]S^\flat = \gamma^\natural[\![B, E]\!]S^\natural$ at each state $\langle \ell, (S^\sharp, S^\flat), G \rangle$ with $[\mathsf{if}\ B\ \mathsf{jmp}\ E]^\ell_{\ell'}$. Then, we can state the following theorem:

Theorem 2 (Relative Soundness). *The CFG computed from the alternating semantics for a program $\langle \ell_0, P \rangle$ soundly over-approximates the concrete CFG of the restricted program version $\langle \ell'_0, P' \rangle$.*

Proof. All rules except $\mathrm{JT}^\flat$ over-approximate G. For all applications of $\mathrm{JT}^\flat$, ϕ enforces that $\gamma^\flat[\![B, E]\!]S^\flat = \gamma^\natural[\![B, E]\!]S^\natural$, which is a (trivial) over-approximation. □

If needed, the precondition ϕ could in principle be determined by backward symbolic execution along the paths leading to the jumps. When using directed test generation, ϕ is the disjunction of the input assignments of the test cases leading to each indirect jump. Note that when an indirect jump is not covered by a test case, ϕ asserts that the jump cannot be reached. A static analysis performed using the reconstructed CFG as program representation will in fact be performed on $\langle \ell'_0, P' \rangle$, thus proofs obtained this way hold for $\langle \ell, P \rangle$ only under the assumption ϕ.

Precision. Note that the fixpoint of the alternating semantics computed by chaotic iteration can depend on the iteration order. Even though the transfer relation "$\longrightarrow$" is monotonic, it does not distribute over the merge operator. That is, merging two states $\langle \ell, S_1, G_1 \rangle \dot\cup \langle \ell, S_2, G_2 \rangle = \langle \ell, S_{1,2}, G_{1,2} \rangle$ and computing the set of successors $\mathbf{T}'_{1,2} = \{\langle \ell', S'_{1,2}, G'_{1,2} \rangle \mid \langle \ell, S_{1,2}, G_{1,2} \rangle \longrightarrow \langle \ell', S'_{1,2}, G'_{1,2} \rangle\}$ can lead to a different result than first computing only, say, the successors $\mathbf{T}'_1$ of $\langle \ell_1, S_1, G_1 \rangle$ and then merging them with $\mathbf{T}'_{1,2}$. This happens if $\chi(S_1, E)$ but $\neg\chi(S_{1,2}, E)$ holds for a jump at ℓ, i.e., rule $\mathrm{JT}^\sharp$ is applied for S_1 but rule $\mathrm{JT}^\flat$ for $S_{1,2}$.

The *least* fixpoint of the alternating semantics can yield a CFG containing more edges than the one obtainable by applying the $\mathrm{JT}^\flat$ rule from the beginning wherever it eventually becomes enabled, because this could avoid some over-approximate edges that are added while still using $\mathrm{JT}^\sharp$. In principle, this "optimal" CFG could be computed by maintaining a list of locations at which to apply $\mathrm{JT}^\flat$ and, each time a location is added to the list, resetting the analysis to the point where that location was reached first. In practice, however, precise target addresses initially resolved using $\mathrm{JT}^\sharp$ are likely to be concrete. For instance, these addresses can be constants that were propagated along a particular path before a $\top$ element from another path overwrote them. Such addresses add concrete edges that could be missed by the under-approximation and can therefore *improve* the precision with respect to the original program.

6 Evaluation

We now report some preliminary results for reconstructing the control flow graphs of microbenchmarks and medium-sized compiled applications.

6.1 Implementation and Setup

We evaluated the proposed approach on our static analysis platform for x86 binaries, JAKSTAB [13].[2] We extended JAKSTAB with a combined adapter analysis modeled after the semantics described in Section 5.1 and implemented a new analysis module that replays pre-recorded execution traces. With the combined analysis, JAKSTAB resorts to under-approximation whenever the static analysis cannot produce a finite concretization for the set of target addresses of an indirect jump.

As analysis targets we used our own microbenchmarks and several C and C++ programs from the SPEC CPU 2006 benchmark, compiled using Visual C++. The benchmarks are single-threaded, so we only had to record and replay the main thread. Our microbenchmarks are hand-written assembly language programs, so we were able to manually construct the concrete CFG as the ground truth. For establishing a ground truth for the C/C++ programs, we enabled debug symbols and disassembled them using IDA PRO [11]. IDA PRO uses the debug symbols and several compiler-specific heuristics to create an accurate assembly language representation. Note that this does not necessarily reflect the concrete CFG, however. Due to its heuristic approach, IDA PRO disassembles *all* identifiable code in an executable and not only that which is actually reachable. This includes a large amount of library and error handling code. Therefore, the number of instructions explored by a non-heuristic approach is expected to be significantly lower.

We recorded concrete execution traces on a single-processor 32-bit Windows XP guest system running in the BitBlaze [17] version of QEMU. As soon as the target process is started, all user-mode instructions (including libraries) are recorded to a file. The SPEC benchmark is designed for long running CPU time evaluations and can yield instruction traces of hundreds of gigabytes. To obtain traces of tractable length while still exercising the same code, we had to remove redundancy from the benchmarking setup. We decreased the size of explicit input data, and if necessary, also reduced bounds of loops that repeatedly invoke the same program functionality. We recorded a single trace per executable.

6.2 Experimental Results

For determining the effectiveness of our approach, we measured the instruction coverage achieved by JAKSTAB using under-approximate, over-approximate, and alternating control flow reconstruction. In this setting, false positives refer to unreachable instructions that are wrongly classified as reachable, and false negatives refer to reachable instructions that have not been covered. We replayed a single trace for the under-approximation and used simple constant propagation for the over-approximation, as it scales to large binaries. The preliminary results of our experiments are shown in Table 1. For each program, we list its implementation language, the number of instructions we accepted as ground truth, and the length of the trace we recorded.

The $\flat$ column contains the results from enabling only trace replay, i.e., the reached instructions as an absolute number and as percentage of the ground truth, and the required execution time of the analysis. Since the analysis is under-approximate, there

[2] Source code available at `http://www.jakstab.org`.

Table 1. Experimental results for control flow reconstruction. $\flat$ denotes under-approximation, $\sharp$ over-approximation, and $\diamond$ alternating control flow reconstruction. * denotes an out of memory error. Under-approximations follow a single trace.

				$\flat$ only			$\sharp$ only			$\diamond$			
Program	Src	Inst	Trace	Inst	Cvrg	Time	Inst	FP	Time	Inst	Cvrg	FP	Time
demo1	asm	9	49K	7	78%	<1s	512	98%	1.5s	9	100%	0%	<1s
demo2	asm	38	87K	29	76%	<1s	512	93%	1.4s	35	92%	0%	<1s
demo3	asm	35	87K	17	49%	<1s	512	93%	2.2s	35	100%	0%	<1s
astar	C++	29645	1.0M	10738	36%	7.2s	*		*	15377	52%	0%	18.3s
bzip	C	29257	531K	9660	33%	5.3s	*		*	20453	70%	0.4%	33.2s
lbm	C	5057	840K	2943	58%	2.2s	*		*	4603	91%	0%	3.5s
omnetpp	C++	171592	4.6M	30627	18%	27.1s	*		*	61461	36%	0.05%	153.9s
milc	C	47382	12.0M	14085	30%	13.4s	*		*	24546	52%	0.3%	54.2s
specrand	C	16937	413K	4720	28%	2.9s	*		*	9166	54%	0%	8.1s

are no false positives, only false negatives (i.e., uncovered instructions). The $\sharp$ column contains the number of instructions reported by constant propagation when unresolved indirect jumps are truly over-approximated. For all programs but the microbenchmarks, the large number of spurious edges caused the analysis to run out of memory after using 2 GB of heap space. In the microbenchmarks, the number of 512 instructions results from padding in the code section. Since the analysis is over-approximate, there are no false negatives. The "FP" column shows the fraction of false positives in the total instructions discovered (i.e., unreachable instructions included in the CFG). The $\diamond$ column shows the number of instructions reported by alternating trace replay and constant propagation. It is susceptible to both false positives and negatives. The "Cvrg" column shows the coverage in percent, and the "FP" column shows the percentage of false positives in the total instructions reported.

We can see that using alternation improves coverage over purely under-approximate reconstruction in all cases, and that it drastically reduces the number of false positives compared to over-approximation. In fact, the number of false positives in over-approximation is prohibitive for realistic programs, therefore alternation is essential for applying control flow reconstruction in practice. We expect that these results can be significantly improved by either using more precise static analyses or directed test generation to generate additional traces.

6.3 Current Limitations and Future Work

Automated Trace Generation. Alternating control flow reconstruction could be effectively interleaved with automated test case generation directed at the locations of statically unresolved indirect jumps that have not yet been covered by a trace. The method for obtaining suitable test cases and thus traces is orthogonal to our approach. Indeed, the framework presented here could be combined with random testing, whitebox fuzz testing [10,17], or binary symbolic execution [6].

Divergences. If the over-approximate semantics is a sound abstraction of the concrete semantics, under-approximate states will always concretize to a subset of the concretization of the corresponding over-approximate states. In practice, however, unsoundness can be introduced by abstracting library calls or not handling parts of the instruction set. This can cause the over-approximation to diverge and not include the under-approximation. In our implementation, we give precedence to the concretization of the over-approximation in such cases to keep it consistent.

Concurrency. Our approach in its current form is limited to sequential programs. A simple way to apply it to multithreaded programs is to treat each thread separately, which can lead to unsoundness and possibly divergences from ignoring the actions of the other threads. A better solution would be to allow context switches in the under-approximation, e.g., by replaying one or more traces containing multiple threads arranged in a total order. To avoid state explosion, the over-approximation then only considers the schedules present in the under-approximation. We leave the implementation of such a strategy for future work.

7 Related Work

Several approaches use runtime control flow information to improve the results of analyzing binaries. Nanda et al. introduced *hybrid disassembly* in their tool BIRD [16]. They first use a heuristic disassembly algorithm to identify likely code regions in an executable. The code is then instrumented to check whether control transfers to a previously unexplored region, in which case the disassembler is invoked again. They rely on several heuristics for avoiding excessive instrumentation, and do not give a formal justification for their approach. In general, the exploration of code areas not covered at runtime suffers from the same limitations as regular heuristic disassembly strategies.

In recent work, Babic et al. [1] construct a CFG by folding a set of concrete traces and exploring the unexecuted branches of conditional jumps. In our own framework, this corresponds to using trace replay with a trivial static analysis that only knows a single $\top$ state and thus always enables both branches of conditional jumps. They do not provide a formal treatment of the reconstruction, only stating that the CFG "is, necessarily, an under-approximation of the complete interprocedural CFG". In fact, this statement is incorrect with respect to our definition of the concrete CFG, since there can be conditional jumps with only a single feasible branch.

Directed proof generation [4] combines over- and under-approximation in the form of predicate abstraction and directed test generation. Thakur et al. [18] lift this approach to binaries in their McVeto tool. As part of the analysis, the CFG is built through folding traces and connecting not yet fully explored branching points to the target surrogate, a special unknown node. The over-approximate data flow analysis is only performed on the folded trace. Therefore, the CFG can only be expanded by generating new test cases, which requires exhaustive exploration to achieve a complete CFG. In contrast, our method is able to perform over-approximation reconstruction of CFG parts not covered by traces. Their method would lend itself to generating traces towards statically unresolvable jumps in our framework, however.

Most work addressing disassembly relies on the use of heuristics to identify likely code regions [12,2,19]. Vigna [19] describes how to defeat anti-disassembly obfuscations by starting disassembly from every possible program location. In our framework, this amounts to performing purely over-approximate control flow reconstruction with again a trivial analysis that knows only one single $\top$ state.

Systematic, purely static approaches to control flow reconstruction from binaries have been scarce. De Sutter et al [8] described how to use data flow analysis in building a CFG, using unknown nodes for indirect jumps. Chang et al. [5] connect abstract interpreters at different language levels to achieve a form of decompilation. Bardin et al. [3] build on our own framework [15] to introduce iterative abstraction refinement.

8 Conclusion

This paper addresses a major weakness in static control flow reconstruction that arises when the possible targets of an indirect jump cannot be resolved precisely. The new reconstruction framework alternates between over- and under-approximation and skips over unresolvable jumps by substituting targets detected by an under-approximation.

Our framework is formalized as an abstract interpretation of a parameterized adapter semantics. It establishes a formal common ground for several approaches in control flow reconstruction from binaries, an area which has traditionally been dominated by ad-hoc solutions. By proving termination and relative soundness for the framework, we hope that this paper contributes to better understanding of static and dynamic approaches to the analysis of machine code.

Acknowledgments. We would like to thank Volodymyr Kuznetsov, Péter Bokor, and the anonymous reviewers for their insightful comments that greatly helped to improve the paper. The second author is supported by CASED (www.cased.de).

References

1. Babić, D., Martignoni, L., McCamant, S., Song, D.: Statically-directed dynamic automated test generation. In: Proc. Int. Conf. Soft. Testing and Analysis (ISSTA 2011). ACM (2011)
2. Balakrishnan, G., Reps, T.W.: Analyzing Memory Accesses in x86 Executables. In: Duesterwald, E. (ed.) CC 2004. LNCS, vol. 2985, pp. 5–23. Springer, Heidelberg (2004)
3. Bardin, S., Herrmann, P., Védrine, F.: Refinement-Based CFG Reconstruction from Unstructured Programs. In: Jhala, R., Schmidt, D. (eds.) VMCAI 2011. LNCS, vol. 6538, pp. 54–69. Springer, Heidelberg (2011)
4. Beckman, N.E., Nori, A.V., Rajamani, S.K., Simmons, R.J.: Proofs from tests. In: Proc. ACM/SIGSOFT Int. Symp. Soft. Testing and Analysis (ISSTA 2008), pp. 3–14. ACM (2008)
5. Chang, B., Harren, M., Necula, G.: Analysis of Low-Level Code Using Cooperating Decompilers. In: Yi, K. (ed.) SAS 2006. LNCS, vol. 4134, pp. 318–335. Springer, Heidelberg (2006)
6. Chipounov, V., Kuznetsov, V., Candea, G.: S2E: A platform for in-vivo multi-path analysis of software systems. In: Proc. 16th. Int. Conf. Architectural Support for Programming Languages and Operating Systems (ASPLOS 2011), pp. 265–278. ACM (2011)

7. Cousot, P., Cousot, R.: Abstract interpretation: A unified lattice model for static analysis of programs by construction or approximation of fixpoints. In: Conf. Rec. 4th ACM Symp. Principles of Programming Languages (POPL 1977), pp. 238–252 (January 1977)
8. De Sutter, B., De Bus, B., De Bosschere, K.: Link-time binary rewriting techniques for program compaction. ACM Trans. Program. Lang. Syst. 27(5), 882–945 (2005)
9. Godefroid, P., Klarlund, N., Sen, K.: Dart: directed automated random testing. In: Proc. ACM SIGPLAN 2005 Conf. Programming Language Design and Implementation (PLDI 2005), pp. 213–223. ACM (2005)
10. Godefroid, P., Levin, M.Y., Molnar, D.A.: Automated whitebox fuzz testing. In: Proc. Network and Distributed System Security Symp. (NDSS 2008). The Internet Society (2008)
11. Hex-Rays SA.: IDA Pro, `http://www.hex-rays.com/idapro/`
12. Kästner, D., Wilhelm, S.: Generic control flow reconstruction from assembly code. In: 2002 Jt. Conf. Languages, Compilers, and Tools for Embedded Systems & Software and Compilers for Embedded Systems (LCTES 2002-SCOPES 2002), pp. 46–55. ACM (2002)
13. Kinder, J., Veith, H.: Jakstab: A Static Analysis Platform for Binaries. In: Gupta, A., Malik, S. (eds.) CAV 2008. LNCS, vol. 5123, pp. 423–427. Springer, Heidelberg (2008)
14. Kinder, J., Veith, H.: Precise static analysis of untrusted driver binaries. In: Proc. 10th Int. Conf. Formal Methods in Computer-Aided Design (FMCAD 2010), pp. 43–50. FMCAD, Inc. (2010)
15. Kinder, J., Zuleger, F., Veith, H.: An Abstract Interpretation-Based Framework for Control Flow Reconstruction from Binaries. In: Jones, N.D., Müller-Olm, M. (eds.) VMCAI 2009. LNCS, vol. 5403, pp. 214–228. Springer, Heidelberg (2009)
16. Nanda, S., Li, W., Lam, L., Chiueh, T.: BIRD: Binary interpretation using runtime disassembly. In: 4th IEEE/ACM Int. Symp. Code Generation and Optimization (CGO 2006), pp. 358–370. IEEE Computer Society (2006)
17. Song, D.X., Brumley, D., Yin, H., Caballero, J., Jager, I., Kang, M.G., Liang, Z., Newsome, J., Poosankam, P., Saxena, P.: BitBlaze: A New Approach to Computer Security via Binary Analysis. In: Sekar, R., Pujari, A.K. (eds.) ICISS 2008. LNCS, vol. 5352, pp. 1–25. Springer, Heidelberg (2008)
18. Thakur, A.V., Lim, J., Lal, A., Burton, A., Driscoll, E., Elder, M., Andersen, T., Reps, T.: Directed Proof Generation for Machine Code. In: Touili, T., Cook, B., Jackson, P. (eds.) CAV 2010. LNCS, vol. 6174, pp. 288–305. Springer, Heidelberg (2010)
19. Vigna, G.: Static disassembly and code analysis. In: Christodorescu, M., Jha, S., Maughan, D., Song, D.X., Wang, C. (eds.) Malware Detection, Advances in Information Security, vol. 27, ch. 2, pp. 19–41. Springer, Heidelberg (2007)

Effective Synthesis of Asynchronous Systems from GR(1) Specifications*

Uri Klein[1], Nir Piterman[2], and Amir Pnueli[1]

[1] Courant Institute of Mathematical Sciences, New York University
[2] Department of Computer Science, University of Leicester

Abstract. We consider automatic synthesis from linear temporal logic specifications for *asynchronous* systems. We aim the produced reactive systems to be used as software in a multi-threaded environment. We extend previous reduction of asynchronous synthesis to synchronous synthesis to the setting of multiple input and multiple output variables. Much like synthesis for synchronous designs, this solution is not practical as it requires determinization of automata on infinite words and solution of complicated games. We follow advances in synthesis of synchronous designs, which restrict the handled specifications but achieve scalability and efficiency. We propose a heuristic that, in some cases, maintains scalability for asynchronous synthesis. Our heuristic can prove that specifications are realizable and extract designs. This is done by a reduction to synchronous synthesis that is inspired by the theoretical reduction.

1 Introduction

One of the most ambitious and challenging problems in reactive systems design is the automatic synthesis of programs from logical specifications. It was suggested by Church [3] and subsequently solved by two techniques [2,19]. In [15] the problem was set in a modern context of synthesis of reactive systems from Linear Temporal Logic (LTL) specifications. The synthesis algorithm converts a LTL specification to a Büchi automaton, which is then determinized [15]. This double translation may be doubly exponential in the size of φ. Once the deterministic automaton is obtained, it is converted to a Rabin game that can be solved in time $n^{O(k)}$, where n is the number of states of the automaton (double exponential in φ) and k is a measure of topological complexity (exponential in φ). This algorithm is tight as the problem is 2EXPTIME-hard [15].

This unfortunate situation led to extensive research on ways to bypass the complexity of synthesis (e.g., [11,7,13]). The work in [13] is of particular interest to us. It achieves scalability by restricting the type of handled specifications. This led to many applications of synthesis in various fields [1,5,24,8,10,6]. So, in some cases, synthesis of designs from their temporal specifications is feasible.

These results relate to the case of synchronous synthesis, where the synthesized system is synchronized with its environment. At every step, the

* Supported in part by National Science Foundation grant CNS-0720581.

V. Kuncak and A. Rybalchenko (Eds.): VMCAI 2012, LNCS 7148, pp. 283–298, 2012.

environment generates new inputs and the system senses all of them and computes a response. This is the standard computational model for hardware designs.

Here, we are interested in synthesis of asynchronous systems. Namely, the system may not sense all the changes in its inputs, and its responses may become visible to the external world (including the environment) with an arbitrary delay. Furthermore, the system accesses one variable at a time while in the synchronous model all inputs are observed and all outputs are changed in a single step. The asynchronous model is the most appropriate for representing reactive software systems that communicate via shared variables on a multi-threaded platform.

In [16], Pnueli and Rosner reduce asynchronous synthesis to synchronous synthesis. Their technique, which we call the Rosner reduction, converts a specification $\varphi(x; y)$ with single input x and single output y to a specification $\mathcal{X}(x, r; y)$. The new specification relates to an additional input r. They show that φ is asynchronously realizable **iff** $\mathcal{X}$ is synchronously realizable and how to translate a synchronous implementation of $\mathcal{X}$ to an asynchronous implementation of φ.

Our first result is an extension of the Rosner reduction to specifications with multiple input and output variables. Pnueli and Rosner assumed that the system alternates between reading its input and writing its output. For multiple variables, we assume cyclic access to variables: first reading all inputs, then writing all outputs (each in a fixed order). We show that this interaction mode is not restrictive as it is equivalent (w.r.t. synthesis) to the model in which the system chooses its next action (whether to read or to write and which variable).

Combined with [15], the reduction from asynchronous to synchronous synthesis presents a complete solution to the multiple-variables asynchronous synthesis problem. Unfortunately, much like in the synchronous case, it is not 'effective'. Furthermore, even if φ is relatively simple (for example, belongs to the class of $GR(1)$ formulae that is handled in [13]), the formula $\mathcal{X}$ is considerably more complex and requires the full treatment of [15].

Consequently, we propose a method to bypass this full reduction. In the invited paper [14] we outlined the principles of an approach to bypass the complexity of asynchronous synthesis. Our approach applied to specifications that relate to one input and one output, both Boolean. We presented heuristics that can be used to prove unrealizability and to prove realizability. It called for the construction of a weakening that could prove unrealizability through a simpler reduction to synchronous synthesis. This result is naturally extended to multiple variables, based on the extended Rosner reduction presented here, and is presented in an extended version [9]. In [14] we also outlined an approach to strengthen specifications and an alternative reduction to synchronous synthesis for such strengthened specifications. Here we substantiate these conjectured ideas by completing and correcting the details of that approach and extending it to multiple value variables and multiple outputs. We show that the ideas portrayed in [14] require to even further restrict the type of specifications and a more elaborate reduction to synchronous synthesis (even for the Boolean one-input one-output case of [14]). We show that when the system has access to the 'entire state' of the environment (this is like the environment having one multiple value variable) there are cases where a simpler reduction to synchronous synthesis can be applied. We give a conversion from the synchronous implementation to an asynchronous implementation realizing the original specification.

To our knowledge, this is the first 'easy' case of asynchronous synthesis identified. With connections to partial-information games and synthesis with nondeterministic environments, we find this to be a very important research direction.

Proofs, which are omitted due to lack of space, are available in [9].

2 Preliminaries

Temporal Logic. We describe an extension of Quantified Propositional Temporal Logic (QPTL) [21] with *stuttering quantification.* We refer to this extended logic as QPTL. Let X be a set of variables ranging over the same finite domain D. The syntax of QPTL is defined according to the following grammar.

$$\tau ::= x = d, \text{ where } x \in X \text{ and } d \in D$$
$$\varphi ::= \tau \parallel \neg\varphi \parallel \varphi \vee \varphi \parallel \bigcirc \varphi \parallel \ominus \varphi \parallel \varphi \mathcal{U} \varphi \parallel \varphi \mathcal{S} \varphi \parallel (\exists x).\varphi \parallel (\exists^{\approx} x).\varphi$$

where τ are *atomic formulae* and φ are *QPTL formulae* (formulae, for short).

We use the usual standard abbreviations as well as: $(\forall^{\approx} x).\psi$ for $\neg(\exists^{\approx} x).(\neg\psi)$, $\psi_1 \mathcal{B} \psi_2$ for $\psi_1 \mathcal{S} \psi_2 \vee \boxminus \psi_1$, $\psi_1 \Rightarrow \psi_2$ for $\square(\psi_1 \rightarrow \psi_2)$. For a set $\hat{X} = \{x_1, \ldots, x_k\}$ of variables, where $\hat{X} \subseteq X$, we write $(\exists \hat{X}).\psi$ for $(\exists x_1) \cdots (\exists x_k).\psi$ and similarly for $(\forall \hat{X}).\psi$. We sometimes list variables and sets, e.g., $(\exists \hat{X}, y).\psi$ instead of $(\exists \hat{X} \cup \{y\}).\psi$. Also, for a Boolean variable r we write r for $r = 1$ and $\overline{r}$ for $r = 0$.

LTL does not allow the $\exists$ and $\exists^{\approx}$ operators. We stress that a formula φ is written over the variables in a set X by writing $\varphi(X)$. If variables are partitioned to *inputs* X and *outputs* Y, we write $\varphi(X; Y)$. We call such formulae *specifications.* We sometimes list the variables in X and Y, e.g., $\varphi(x_1, x_2; y)$.

The semantics of QPTL is given with respect to computations and locations in them. A *computation* σ is an infinite sequence $a_0, a_1, \ldots$, where for every $i \geq 0$ we have $a_i \in D^X$. That is, a computation is an infinite sequence of value assignments to the variables in X. For an assignment $a \in D^X$ and a variable $x \in X$ we write $a[x]$ for the value assigned to x by a. If $X = \{x_1, \ldots, x_n\}$, we freely use the notation $(a_{i_1}[x_1], \ldots, a_{i_n}[x_n])$ for the assignment a such that $a[x_j] = a_{i_j}[x_j]$. A computation $\sigma' = a'_0, a'_1, \ldots$ is an *x-variant* of computation $\sigma = a_0, a_1, \ldots$ if for every $i \geq 0$ and every $y \neq x$ we have $a_i[y] = a'_i[y]$. The computation *squeeze*(σ) is obtained from σ as follows. If for all $i \geq 0$ we have $a_i = a_0$, then *squeeze*$(\sigma) = \sigma$. Otherwise, if $a_0 \neq a_1$ then *squeeze*$(\sigma) = a_0$, *squeeze*$(a_1, a_2, \ldots)$. Finally, if $a_0 = a_1$ then *squeeze*$(\sigma) =$ *squeeze*$(a_1, a_2, \ldots)$. That is, by removing repeating assignments, *squeeze* returns a computation in which every two adjacent assignments are different unless the computation ends in an infinite suffix of one assignment. A computation σ' is a *stuttering variant* of σ if *squeeze*$(\sigma) =$ *squeeze*(σ').

Satisfaction of a QPTL formula φ over computation σ in location $i \geq 0$, denoted $\sigma, i \models \varphi$, is defined as usual. We define here only the case of quantification.

1. We have $\sigma, i \models (\exists x).\varphi$ **iff** $\sigma', i \models \varphi$ for some σ' that is an x-variant of σ.
2. We have $\sigma, i \models (\exists^{\approx} x).\varphi$ **iff** $\sigma'', i \models \varphi$ for some σ'' that is a x-variant of some stuttering variant σ' of σ.

We say that the computation σ satisfies the formula φ, **iff** $\sigma, 0 \models \varphi$.

Realizability of Temporal Specifications. We define synchronous and asynchronous programs. While the programs themselves are not very different the definition of interaction of a program makes the distinction clear.

Let X and Y be the sets of *inputs* and *outputs*. We stress the different roles of the system and the environment by specializing computations to *interactions*. In an interaction we treat each assignment to $X \cup Y$ as different assignments to X and Y. Thus, instead of using $c \in D^{X \cup Y}$, we use a pair (a, b), where $a \in D^X$ and $b \in D^Y$. Formally, an interaction is $\sigma = (a_0, b_0), (a_1, b_1), \ldots \in (D^X \times D^Y)^\omega$.

A *synchronous program* P_s from X to Y is a function $P_s : (D^X)^+ \mapsto D^Y$. In every step of the computation (including the initial one) the program reads its inputs and updates the values of all outputs (based on the entire history). An interaction σ is called *synchronous interaction* of P if, at each step of the interaction $i = 0, 1, \ldots$, the program outputs (assigns to Y) the value $P_s(a_0, a_1, \ldots, a_i)$, i.e., $b_i = P_s(a_0, \ldots, a_i)$. In such interactions both the environment, which updates input values, and the system, which updates output values, 'act' at each step (where the system responds in each step to an environment action).

A synchronous program is *finite state* if it can be *induced* by a *Labeled Transition System (LTS)*. A LTS is $T = \langle S, I, R, X, Y, L \rangle$, where S is a finite set of *states*, $I \subseteq S$ is a set of *initial states*, $R \subseteq S \times S$ is a *transition relation*, X and Y are disjoint sets of *input* and *output* variables, respectively, and $L : S \mapsto D^{X \cup Y}$ is a *labeling* function. For a state $s \in S$ and for $Z \subseteq X \cup Y$, we define $L(s)|_Z$ to be the restriction of $L(s)$ to the variables of Z. The LTS has to be *receptive*, i.e., be able to accept all inputs. Formally, for every $a \in D^X$ there is some $s_0 \in I$ such that $L(s_0)|_X = a$. For every $a \in D^X$ and $s \in S$ there is some $s_a \in S$ such that $R(s, s_a)$ and $L(s_a)|_X = a$. The LTS T is *deterministic* if for every $a \in D^X$ there is a unique $s_0 \in I$ such that $L(s_0)|_X = a$ and for every $a \in D^X$ and every $s \in S$ there is a unique $s_a \in S$ such that $R(s, s_a)$ and $L(s_a)|_X = a$. Otherwise, it is *nondeterministic*. A deterministic LTS T induces the synchronous program $P_T : (D^X)^+ \mapsto D^Y$ as follows. For every $a \in D^X$ let $T(a)$ be the unique state $s_0 \in I$ such that $L(s_0)|_X = a$. For every $n > 1$ and $a_1 \ldots a_n \in (D^X)^+$ let $T(a_1, \ldots, a_n)$ be the unique $s \in S$ such that $R(T(a_1, \ldots, a_{n-1}), s)$ and $L(s)|_X = a_n$. For every $a_1 \ldots a_n \in (D^X)^+$ let $P_T(a_1, \ldots, a_n)$ be the unique $b \in D^Y$ such that $b = L(T(a_1, \ldots, a_n))|_Y$. We note that nondeterministic LTS do not induce programs. As nondeterministic LTS can always be pruned to deterministic LTS, we find it acceptable to produce nondeterministic LTS as a representation of a set of possible programs.

An *asynchronous program* P_a from X to Y is a function $P_a : (D^X)^* \mapsto D^Y$. Note that the first value to outputs is set before seeing inputs. As before, the program receives all inputs and updates all outputs. However, the definition of an interaction takes into account that this may not happen instantaneously.

A *schedule* is a pair (R, W) of sequences $R = r_1^1, \ldots, r_1^n, r_2^1, \ldots, r_2^n, \ldots$ and $W = w_1^1, \ldots, w_1^m, w_2^1, \ldots, w_2^m, \ldots$ of *reading points* and *writing points* such that $r_1^1 > 0$ and for every $i > 0$ we have $r_i^1 < r_i^2 < \cdots < r_i^n < w_i^1$ and $w_i^1 < w_i^2 < \cdots < w_i^m < r_{i+1}^1$. It identifies the points where each of the input variables is read and the points where each of the output variables is written. The order establishes that reading and writing points occur cyclically. When the distinction is not important, we call reading points and writing points *I\O-points.*

An interaction is called *asynchronous interaction* of P_a for (R, W) if $b_0 = P_a(\epsilon)$, and for every $i > 0$, every $j \in \{1, \ldots, m\}$, and every $w_i^j \leq k < w_{i+1}^j$:

$b_k[j] = P_a((a_{r_1^1}[1], \ldots, a_{r_1^n}[n]), (a_{r_2^1}[1], \ldots, a_{r_2^n}[n]), \ldots, (a_{r_i^1}[1], \ldots, a_{r_i^n}[n]))[j]$.

Also, for every $j \in \{1, \ldots, m\}$ and every $0 < k < w_1^j$, we have that $b_k[j] = b_0[j]$.

In asynchronous interactions, the environment may update the input values at each step. However, the system is only aware of the values of inputs at reading points and responds by outputting the appropriate variables at writing points. In particular, the system is not even aware of the amount of time that passes between the two adjacent time points (read-read, read-write, or write-read). That is, output values depend only on the values of inputs in earlier reading points.

An asynchronous program is *finite state* if it can be *asynchronously induced* by an *Initialized LTS (ILTS)*. An ILTS is $T = \langle T_s, i\rangle$, where $T_s = \langle S, I, R, X, Y, L\rangle$ is a LTS, and $i \in D^Y$ is an *initial assignment.* We sometimes abuse notations and write $T = \langle S, I, R, X, Y, L, i\rangle$. Determinism is defined just as for LTS. Similarly, given $a_1, \ldots, a_n \in (D^X)^+$ we define $T(a_1, \ldots, a_n)$ as before. A deterministic ILTS T asynchronously induces the program $P_T : (D^X)^* \mapsto D^Y$ as follows. Let $P_T(\epsilon) = i$ and for every $a_1 \ldots a_n \in (D^X)^+$ we have $P_T(a_1, \ldots, a_n)$ as before. As i is a unique initial assignment, we force ILTS to induce only asynchronous programs that deterministically assign a single initial value to outputs. All our results work also with a definition that allows nondeterministic choice of initial output values (that do not depend on the unavailable inputs).

Definition 1 (realizability). *A* LTL *specification* $\varphi(X;Y)$ *is* **synchronously realizable** *if there exists a synchronous program* P_s *such that all synchronous interactions of* P_s *satisfy* $\varphi(X;Y)$*. Such a program* P_s *is said to* synchronously realize $\varphi(X;Y)$. Synchronous realizability *is often simply shortened to* realizability. **Asynchronous realizability** *is defined similarly with asynchronous programs and all asynchronous interactions for all schedules.*

Synthesis is the process of automatically constructing a program P that (synchronously/asynchronously) realizes a specification $\varphi(X;Y)$. We freely write that a LTS realizes a specification in case that the induced program satisfies it.

Theorem 1 ([15]). *Deciding whether a specification* $\varphi(X;Y)$ *is synchronously realizable is 2EXPTIME-complete. Furthermore, if* $\varphi(X;Y)$ *is synchronously realizable the same decision procedure can extract a LTS that realizes* $\varphi(X;Y)$.

Normal Form of Specifications. We give a normal form of specifications describing an interplay between a *system* s and an *environment* e. Let X and Y be disjoint sets of input and output variables, respectively. For $\alpha \in \{e, s\}$, the formula $\varphi_\alpha(X;Y)$, which defines the allowed actions of α, is a conjunction of:

1. I_α (*initial condition*) – a Boolean formula (equally, an assertion) over $X \cup Y$, describing the initial state of α. The formula I_s may refer to all variables and I_e may refer only to the variables X.

2. $\square\, S_\alpha$ (*safety component*) – a formula describing the transition relation of α, where S_α describes the update of the locally controlled state variables (identified by being *primed*, e.g., x' for $x \in X$) as related to the current state (unprimed, e.g., x), except that s can observe X's next values.
3. L_α (*liveness component*) – each L_α is a conjunction of $\square \diamondsuit p$ formulae where p is a Boolean formula.

In the case that a specification includes temporal past formulae instead of the Boolean formulae in any of the three conjuncts mentioned above, we assume that a pre-processing of the specification was done to translate it into another one that has the same structure but without the use of past formulae. This can be always achieved through the introduction of fresh Boolean variables that implement temporal testers for past formulae [18]. Therefore, without loss of generality, we discuss in this work only such past-formulae-free specifications.

We abuse notations and write φ_α also as a triplet $\langle I_\alpha, S_\alpha, L_\alpha \rangle$.

Consider a pair of formulae $\varphi_\alpha(X;Y)$, for $\alpha \in \{e, s\}$ as above. We define the specification $Imp(\varphi_e, \varphi_s)$ to be $(I_e \wedge \square\, S_e \wedge L_e) \rightarrow (I_s \wedge \square\, S_s \wedge L_s)$. For such specifications, the *winning condition* is the formula $L_e \rightarrow L_s$, which we call $GR(1)$. Synchronous synthesis of such specifications was considered in [13].

The Rosner Reduction. In [16], Pnueli and Rosner show how to use synchronous realizability to solve asynchronous realizability. They define, what we call, *the Rosner reduction.* It translates a specification $\varphi(X;Y)$, where $X = \{x\}$ and $Y = \{y\}$ are singletons, into a specification $\mathcal{X}(x,r;y)$ that has an additional Boolean input variable r. The new variable r is called the *Boolean scheduling variable.* Intuitively, the Boolean scheduling variable defines all possible schedules for one-input one-output systems . When it changes from zero to one it signals a reading point and when it changes from one to zero it signals a writing point. Given specification $\varphi(X;Y)$, we define the *kernel formula* $\mathcal{X}(x,r;y)$:

$$\underbrace{\overline{r} \wedge \square \diamondsuit r \wedge \square \diamondsuit \overline{r}}_{\alpha(r)} \quad \rightarrow \quad \underbrace{\begin{pmatrix} \varphi(x;y) & \wedge \\ (r \vee \ominus \overline{r}) \Rightarrow (y = \ominus y) & \wedge \\ (\forall^{\approx} \widetilde{x}).[(r \wedge \ominus \overline{r}) \Rightarrow (x = \widetilde{x})] \rightarrow \varphi(\widetilde{x};y) & \end{pmatrix}}_{\beta(x,r;y)}$$

According to $\alpha(r)$, the first $I\backslash O$-point, where r changes from zero to one, is a reading point and there are infinitely many reading and writing points. Then, $\beta(x,r;y)$ includes three parts: (a) the original formula $\varphi(x;y)$ must hold, (b) outputs obey the scheduling variable, i.e., in all points that are not writing points the value of y does not change, and (c) if we replace all the inputs except in reading points, then the same output still satisfies the original formula.

Theorem 2 ([16]). *The specification $\varphi(x;y)$ is asynchronously realizable* **iff** *the specification $\mathcal{X}(x,r;y)$ is synchronously realizable. Given a program that synchronously realizes $\mathcal{X}(x,r;y)$ it can be converted in linear time to a program asynchronously realizing $\varphi(x;y)$.*

Pnueli and Rosner also show how the standard techniques for realizability of LTL [15] can handle stuttering quantification of the form appearing in $\mathcal{X}(x,r;y)$.

3 Expanding the Rosner Reduction to Multiple Variables

In this section we describe an expansion of the Rosner reduction to handle specifications with multiple input and output variables. The reduction reduces asynchronous synthesis to synchronous synthesis. Without loss of generality, fix a LTL specification $\varphi(X;Y)$, where $X = \{x_1, \ldots, x_n\}$ and $Y = \{y_1, \ldots, y_m\}$.

We propose the *generalized Rosner reduction*, which translates $\varphi(X;Y)$ into $\mathcal{X}^{n,m}(X \cup \{r\}; Y)$. The specification uses an additional input variable r, called the *scheduling variable*, that ranges over $\{1, \ldots, (n+m)\}$, which defines all reading and writing points. Variable x_i may be read by the system whenever r changes its value to i. Variable y_i may be modified whenever r changes to $n+i$. Initially, $r = n+m$ and it is incremented cyclically by 1 (hence, in the first $I\backslash O$-point x_1 is read). Let $i \oplus_k 1$ denote $(i \bmod k) + 1$.

We also denote $[r = (n+i)] \wedge \ominus[r \neq (n+i)]$ by $write_n(i)$ to indicate a state that is a writing point for y_i, $(r = i) \wedge \ominus(r \neq i)$ by $read(i)$ to indicate a state that is a reading point for x_i, $\bigwedge_{d \in D}[(z = d) \leftrightarrow \ominus(z = d)]$ by $unchanged(z)$ to indicate a state where z did not change its value, and $\neg \ominus \mathrm{T}$ by *first* to indicate a state that is the first one in the computation.

The kernel formula $\mathcal{X}^{n,m}(X \cup \{r\}; Y)$ is $\alpha^{n,m}(r) \rightarrow \beta^{n,m}(X \cup \{r\}; Y)$, where

$$\alpha^{n,m}(r) = \begin{pmatrix} r = (n+m) & \wedge \\ \bigwedge_{i=1}^{n+m} \Big[(r = i) \Rightarrow \Big[(r = i)\,\mathcal{U}[r = (i \oplus_{n+m} 1)]\Big]\Big] & \end{pmatrix}$$

$$\beta^{n,m}(X \cup \{r\}; Y) = \begin{pmatrix} \varphi(X;Y) & \wedge \\ \bigwedge_{i=1}^{m} \Big[[\neg write_n(i) \wedge \neg first] \Rightarrow unchanged(y_i)\Big] & \wedge \\ (\forall^{\approx} \tilde{X}).\Big[\bigwedge_{i=1}^{n}[read(i) \Rightarrow (x_i = \tilde{x}_i)]\Big] \rightarrow \varphi(\tilde{X};Y) & \end{pmatrix}.$$

There is a 1-1 correspondence between sequences of assignments to r and schedules (R, W). As r is an input variable, the program has to handle all possible assignments to it. This implies that the program handles all possible schedules.

Theorem 3. *The specification $\varphi(X;Y)$ ($|X| = n$, and $|Y| = m$) is asynchronously realizable* **iff** *$\mathcal{X}^{n,m}(X \cup \{r\}; Y)$ is synchronously realizable. Furthermore, given a program synchronously realizing $\mathcal{X}^{n,m}(X \cup \{r\}; Y)$ it can be converted in linear time to a program asynchronously realizing $\varphi(X;Y)$.*

Proof (Sketch): Suppose we have a synchronous program realizing $\mathcal{X}^{n,m}(X \cup \{r\}; Y)$ and we want an asynchronous program realizing $\varphi(X;Y)$. An input to the asynchronous program is stretched in order to be fed to the synchronous program. Essentially, every new input to the asynchronous program is stretched so that one variable changes at a time and in addition the new valuation of all input variables is repeated enough time to allow the synchronous program to update all the output variables. This is forced to happen immediately by increasing the scheduling variable r (cyclically) in every input for the synchronous program. This forces the synchronous program to update all output variables and this is the value we use for the asynchronous program. Then, the stuttering quantification over the synchronous interaction shows that an asynchronous interaction that matches these outputs does in fact satisfy $\varphi(X;Y)$.

In the other direction we have an asynchronous program realizing $\varphi(X;Y)$ and have to construct a synchronous program realizing $\mathcal{X}^{n,m}(X \cup \{r\};Y)$. The reply of the synchronous program to every input in which the scheduling variables behaves other than increasing (cyclically) is set to be arbitrary. For inputs where the scheduling variable behaves properly, we can contract the inputs to the reading points indicated by r and feed the resulting input sequence to the asynchronous program. We then change the output variables one by one as indicated by r according to the output of the asynchronous program. In order to see that the resulting synchronous program satisfies $\mathcal{X}$, we note that the stuttering quantification relates precisely to the possible asynchronous interactions. □

In principle, this theorem provides a complete solution to the problem of asynchronous synthesis (with multiple inputs and outputs). This requires to construct a deterministic automaton for $\mathcal{X}^{n,m}$ and to solve complex parity games. In particular, when combining determinization with the treatment of $\forall^{\approx}$ quantification, even relatively simple specifications may lead to very complex deterministic automata and (as a result) games that are complicated to solve.

Since the publication of the original Rosner reduction, several alternative approaches to asynchronous synthesis have been suggested. Vardi suggests an automata theoretic solution that shows how to embed the scheduling variable directly in the tree automaton [22]. Schewe and Finkbeiner extend these ideas to the case of branching time specifications [20]. Both approaches require the usage of determinization and the solution of general parity games. Unlike the generalized Rosner reduction they obfuscate the relation between the asynchronous and synchronous synthesis problems. In particular, the simple cases identified for asynchronous synthesis in the following sections rely on this relation between the two types of synthesis. All three approaches do not offer a practical solution to asynchronous synthesis as they have proven impossible to implement.

4 A More General Asynchronous Interaction Model

The reader may object to the model of asynchronous interaction as over simplified. Here, we justify this model by showing that it is practically equivalent (from a synthesis point of view) to a model that is more akin to software thread implementation. Specifically, we introduce a model in which the environment chooses the times the system can read or write and the system chooses whether to read or write and which variable to access. We formally define this model and show that the two asynchronous models are equivalent. We call our original asynchronous interaction model *round robin* and this new model *by demand*.

For this section, without loss of generality, fix a LTL specification $\varphi(X;Y)$, where $X = \{x_1, \ldots, x_n\}$ and $Y = \{y_1, \ldots, y_m\}$.

A *by-demand program* P_b from X to Y is a function $P_b : D^* \mapsto \{1, \ldots, n\} \cup (D \times \{n+1, \ldots, n+m\})$. We assume that for $0 \leq i < m$ and for every $d_1, \ldots, d_{m-1} \in D$, we have $P_b(d_1, \ldots, d_i) = (d, (n+i+1))$ for some $d \in D$.

That is, for a given history of values read\written by the program (and the program should know which variables it read\wrote) the program decides on the next variable to read\write. In case that the decision is to write in the next $I\backslash O$ point, the program also chooses the value to write. Furthermore, the program starts by writing all the output variables according to their order $y_1, y_2, \ldots, y_m$.

We define when an interaction matches a by-demand program. Recall that an interaction over X and Y is $\sigma = (a_0, b_0), (a_1, b_1), \ldots \in (D^X \times D^Y)$. An $I\backslash O$-*sequence* is $C = c_0, c_1, \ldots$ where $0 = c_0 < c_1 < c_2, \ldots$. It identifies the points in which the program reads or writes. For a sequence $d_1, \ldots, d_k \in D^*$, we denote by $t(P_b(d_1, \ldots, d_k))$ the value j such that either $P_b(d_1, \ldots, d_k) \in \{1, \ldots, n\}$ and $P_b(d_1, \ldots, d_k) = j$ or $P_b(d_1, \ldots, d_k) \in D \times \{n+1, \ldots, n+m\}$ and $P_b(d_1, \ldots, d_k) = (d, j)$. That is, $t(P_b(d_1, \ldots, d_k))$ tells us which variable the program P_b is going to access in the next $I\backslash O$-point. Given an interaction σ, an $I\backslash O$ sequence C, and an index $i \geq 0$, we define the *view* of P_b, denoted $v(P_b, \sigma, C, i)$, as follows.

$$v(P_b, \sigma, C, i) = \begin{cases} b_0[1], \ldots, b_0[m] & \text{If } i = 0 \\ v(P_b, \sigma, C, i-1), a_{c_i}[t(P_b(v(P_b, \sigma, C, i-1)))] & \\ \qquad \text{If } i > 0 \text{ and } t(P_b(v(P_b, \sigma, C, i-1))) \leq n & \\ v(P_b, \sigma, C, i-1), b_{c_i}[t(P_b(v(P_b, \sigma, C, i-1)))] & \\ \qquad \text{If } i > 0 \text{ and } t(P_b(v(P_b, \sigma, c, i-1))) > n & \end{cases}$$

That is, the view of the program is the part of the interaction that is observable by the program. The view starts with the values of all outputs at time zero. Then, the view at c_i extends the view at c_{i-1} by adding the value of the variable that the program decides to read\write based on its view at point c_{i-1}.

The interaction σ is a *by-demand asynchronous interaction* of P_b for $I\backslash O$ sequence C if for every $1 \leq j \leq m$ we have $P_b(b_0[1], \ldots, b_0[j-1]) = (b_0[j], (n+j))$, and for every $i > 1$ and every $k > 0$ such that $c_i \leq k < c_{i+1}$, we have

- If $t(P_b(v(P_b, \sigma, C, i-1))) \leq n$, forall $j \in \{1, \ldots, m\}$ we have $b_k[j] = b_{k-1}[j]$.
- If $t(P_b(v(P_b, \sigma, C, i-1))) > n$, forall $j \neq t(P_b(v(P_b, \sigma, C, i-1)))$ we have $b_k[j] = b_{k-1}[j]$ and for $j = t(P_b(v(P_b, \sigma, C, i-1)))$ we have $P_b(v(P_b, \sigma, c, i-1)) = (b_k[j], j)$.

Also, for every $j \in \{1, \ldots, m\}$ and every $0 < k < c_1$, we have $b_k[j] = b_0[j]$. That is, the interaction matches a by-demand program if (a) the interaction starts with the right values of all outputs (as the program starts by initializing them) and (b) the outputs do not change in the interaction unless at $I\backslash O$ points where the program chooses to update a specific output (based on the program's view of the intermediate state of the interaction).

Definition 2 (by-demand realizability). *A* LTL *specification* $\varphi(X; Y)$ *is* **by-demand asynchronously realizable** *if there exists a by-demand program* P_a *such that all by-demand asynchronous interactions of* P_a *(for all* $I\backslash O$*-sequences) satisfy* $\varphi(X; Y)$.

Theorem 4. *A* LTL *specification* $\varphi(X; Y)$ *is asynchronously realizable* **iff** *it is by-demand asynchronously realizable. Furthermore, given a program that asynchronously realizes* $\varphi(X; Y)$*, it can be converted in linear time to a program that by-demand asynchronously realizes* $\varphi(X; Y)$*, and vice versa.*

$$\left(\begin{array}{ll}\alpha^{n,m}(r) & \wedge \\ I_{\psi_e} \wedge \Box\, S_{\psi_e} & \wedge \\ \psi(X,r;Y) & \wedge \\ \bigwedge_{i=1}^{n} [\mathit{read}(i) \Rightarrow (x_i = \tilde{x}_i)] & \wedge \\ \bigwedge_{i=1}^{m} \left[[\neg \mathit{write}_n(i) \wedge \neg \mathit{first}] \Rightarrow \mathit{unchanged}(y_i) \right] & \end{array}\right) \rightarrow \varphi(\tilde{X};Y).$$

Fig. 1. Logical implication of asynchronous strengthening

Proof (Sketch): A round-robin program is also a by-demand program.

Showing that if a specification is by-demand realizable then it is also round-robin realizable is more complicated. Given a by-demand program, a round-robin program can simulate it by waiting until it has access to the variable required by the by-demand program. This means that the round-robin program may idle when it has the opportunity to write outputs and ignore inputs that it has the option to read. However, the resulting interactions are still interactions of the by-demand program and as such must satisfy the specification. □

5 Proving Realizability of a Specification, and Synthesis

As mentioned, the formula $\mathcal{X}^{n,m}$ does not lead to a practical solution for asynchronous synthesis. Here we show that in some cases a simpler synchronous realizability test can still imply the realizability of an asynchronous specification. We show that when a certain strengthening can be found and certain conditions hold with respect to the specification we can apply a simpler realizability test maintaining the structure of the specification. In particular, this simpler realizability test does not require stuttering quantification. When the original formula's winning condition is a $GR(1)$ formula, the synthesis algorithm in [13] can be applied, bypassing much of the complexity involved in synthesis.

We fix a specification $\varphi(X;Y) = \mathit{Imp}(\varphi_e, \varphi_s)$ with a $GR(1)$ winning condition, where $X = \{x_1, \ldots, x_n\}$, $Y = \{y_1, \ldots, y_m\}$, and $\varphi_e = \langle I_{\varphi_e}, S_{\varphi_e}, L_{\varphi_e}\rangle$. Let r be a scheduling variable ranging over $\{1, \ldots, (n+m)\}$ and let $\tilde{X} = \{\tilde{x} | x \in X\}$. We define the set of *declared output variables* $\tilde{Y} = \{\tilde{y} | y \in Y\}$. We assume that $r \notin X$, $\tilde{X} \cap Y = \emptyset$, and that $\tilde{Y} \cap X = \emptyset$. We re-use the notations $\mathit{write}_n(i)$, $\mathit{read}(i)$, $\mathit{unchanged}(x)$, and first.

We start by definition of a strengthening, which is a formula of the type $\psi(X,r;Y)$. Intuitively, the strengthening refers explicitly to a scheduling variable r and should imply the truth of the original specification and ignore the input except in reading points so that the stuttering quantification can be removed.

Definition 3 (asynchronous strengthening). *A specification* $\psi(X,r;Y) = \mathit{Imp}(\psi_e, \psi_s)$ *with a* $GR(1)$ *winning condition, where* $\psi_e = \langle I_{\psi_e}, S_{\psi_e}, L_{\psi_e}\rangle$, *is an* **asynchronous strengthening** *of* $\varphi(X;Y)$ *if* $I_{\psi_e} = I_{\varphi_e}$, $S_{\psi_e} = S_{\varphi_e}$, *and the implication in Fig. 1 is valid.*

Checking the conditions in Def. 3 requires to check identity of propositional formulae and validity of a LTL formulae, which is supported, e.g., by JTLV [17].

The formula needs to satisfy two more conditions, which are needed to show that the simpler synchronous realizability test (introduced below) is sufficient. Stuttering robustness is very natural for asynchronous specifications as we expect the system to be completely unaware of the passage of time. Memory-lessness requires that the system knows the entire 'state' of the environment.

Definition 4 (stuttering robustness). *A* LTL *specification* $\xi(X;Y)$ *is* **stutteringly robust** *if for all computations* σ *and* σ' *such that* σ' *is a stuttering variant of* σ, $\sigma, 0 \models \xi$ **iff** $\sigma', 0 \models \xi$.

We can test stuttering robustness by converting a specification to a nondeterministic Büchi automaton [23], adding to it transitions that capture all stuttering options [16], and then checking that it does not intersect the automaton for the negation of the specification. In our case, when handling formulae with $GR(1)$ winning conditions, in many cases, all parts of the specifications are relatively simple and stuttering robustness can be easily checked.

Definition 5 (memory-lessness). *A* LTL *specification* ξ *is* **memory-less** *if for all computations* $C = c_0, c_1, \ldots$ *and* $C' = c'_0, c'_1, \ldots$ *such that* $C, 0 \models \xi$ *and* $C', 0 \models \xi$, *if for some* i *and* j *we have* $c_i = c'_j$, *then the computation* $c_0, c_1, \ldots, c_i, c'_{j+1}, c'_{j+2}, \ldots$ *also satisfies* ξ.

Specifications of the form $\varphi_e = \langle I_e, S_e, L_e \rangle$ are always memory-less. The syntactic structure of S_e forces a relation between possible current and next states that does not depend on the past. Furthermore L_e is a conjunction of properties of the form $\Box \Diamond p$, where p is a Boolean formula. If the specification includes past temporal operators, these are embedded into the variables of the environment (c.f. [18]), and must be accessible by the system as well.

In the general case, memory-lessness of a specification $\varphi(X;Y)$ can be checked as follows. We convert both ξ and $\neg\xi$ to nondeterministic Büchi automata N_+ and N_-. Then, we create a nondeterministic Büchi automaton A that runs two copies of N_+ and one copy of N_- simultaneously. The two copies of N_+ 'guess' two computations that satisfy $\varphi(X;Y)$ and the copy of N_- checks that the two computations can be combined in a way that does not satisfy $\varphi(X;Y)$. Thus, the language of A would be empty **iff** $\varphi(X;Y)$ is not memory-less.

Note that if $\varphi(X;Y)$ has a memory-less environment then every asynchronous strengthening of it has a memory-less environment. This follows from the two sharing the initial and safety parts of the specification.

The kernel formula defined in Fig. 2 *under-approximates* the original. The formula $declare^{n,m}$ ensures that the declared outputs are updated only at reading points. Indeed, for every i, $\tilde{y}_i$ is allowed to change only when r changes to a value in $\{1, \ldots, n\}$. Furthermore, the outputs themselves copy the value of the declared outputs (and only when they are allowed to change). Thus, the system 'ignores' inputs that are not at reading points in its next update of outputs.

Theorem 5. *Let $\varphi(x;Y) = Imp(\varphi_e, \varphi_s)$, where $\varphi_e = \langle I_{\varphi_e}, S_{\varphi_e}, L_{\varphi_e}\rangle$, be a stutteringly robust specification with a $GR(1)$ winning condition and with a memoryless environment, where $|Y| = \{y_1, \ldots, y_m\}$ and where there is exactly one input - x. Let r be a scheduling variable ranging over $\{1, \ldots, (1+m)\}$, and let $\tilde{Y}$ be declared output variables.*

If $\psi(x, r; Y)$ is a stutteringly robust asynchronous strengthening of $\varphi(x;Y)$ and $\mathcal{X}_\psi^{1,m}(x, r; Y \cup \tilde{Y})$ is synchronously realizable then $\varphi(x;Y)$ is asynchronously realizable. Furthermore, given a program that synchronously realizes $\mathcal{X}_\psi^{1,m}$ it can be converted in linear time to a program that asynchronously realizes φ.

Proof (Sketch): The algorithm takes a program T_s that realizes ψ and converts it to a program T_a. The program T_a 'jumps' from reading point to reading point in T_s. By using the declared outputs in $\tilde{Y}$ the asynchronous program does not have to commit on which reading point in T_s it moves to until the next input is actually read. By ψ being a strengthening of φ we get that the computation on T_s satisfies φ. Then, we use the stuttering robustness to make sure that the time that passes between reading points is not important for the satisfaction of φ. Memoryless-ness and single input are used to justify that prefixes of the computation on T_s can be extended with suffixes of other computations. Essentially, allowing us to 'copy-and-paste' segments of computations of T_s in order to construct one computation of T_a. □

We note that restricting to one input is similar to allowing the system to read multiple inputs simultaneously.

In the case that φ has a $GR(1)$ winning condition then so does $\mathcal{X}_\psi^{1,m}$. It follows that in such cases we can use the algorithm of [13] to check whether $\mathcal{X}_\psi$ is synchronously realizable and to extract a program that realizes it. We show how to convert a LTS realizing $\mathcal{X}_\psi$ to an ILTS realizing φ.

For a LTS $T_s = \langle S_s, I_s, R_s, \{x, r\}, Y, L_s\rangle$, state $st_{es} \in S_s$ is an *eventual successor* of state $st \in S_s$ if there exists $m \leq |S_s|$ and states $\{s_1, \ldots, s_m\} \subseteq S_s$ such that the following hold: $s_1 = st$ and $s_n = st_{es}$; For all $0 < i < m$, $(s_i; s_{i+1}) \in R_s$;

$$
\begin{aligned}
\mathcal{X}_\psi^{n,m}(X \cup \{r\}; Y \cup \tilde{Y}) &= \alpha^{n,m}(r) \rightarrow \beta_\psi^{n,m}(X \cup \{r\}; Y \cup \tilde{Y}) \\
\beta_\psi^{n,m}(X \cup \{r\}; Y \cup \tilde{Y}) &= \begin{pmatrix} \mathit{declare}^{n,m}(\{r\}; Y \cup \tilde{Y}) & \wedge \\ \psi(X \cup \{r\}; Y) & \wedge \\ \bigwedge_{i=1}^{m} [[\neg \mathit{write}_n(i) \wedge \neg \mathit{first}] \Rightarrow \mathit{unchanged}(y_i)] & \end{pmatrix} \\
\mathit{declare}^{n,m}(\{r\}; Y \cup \tilde{Y}) &= \\
&\begin{pmatrix} \bigwedge_{i=1}^{m} [\mathit{write}_n(i) \Rightarrow (y_i = \tilde{y}_i)] & \wedge \\ \left[\left[(r = \ominus r) \vee \bigvee_{i=1}^{m} [r = (n+i)]\right] \Rightarrow \left[\bigwedge_{i=1}^{m} (\tilde{y}_i = \ominus \tilde{y}_i)\right]\right] & \end{pmatrix}.
\end{aligned}
$$

Fig. 2. The under approximation $\mathcal{X}_\psi^{n,m}(X \cup \{r\}; Y \cup \tilde{Y})$

For all $0 < i < m$, if $L(s_1)|_{\{r\}} = r_1$ then $L(s_i)|_{\{r\}} = r_1$, but $L(s_m)|_{\{r\}} \neq r_1$. If $L(s_m)|_{\{r\}} = 1$ we also call st_{es} an *eventual read successor*, otherwise an *eventual write successor*. Note that the way the scheduling variable r updates its values is uniform across all eventual successors of a given state.

Given a LTS $T_s = \langle S_s, I_s, R_s, \{x, r\}, Y, L_s \rangle$ such that $Y = \{y_1, \ldots, y_m\}$ the algorithm in Fig. 3 *extracts* from it an ILTS $T_a = \langle S_a, I_a, R_a, \{x\}, Y, L_a, i_a \rangle$. In the first part of the algorithm that follows its initialization, between lines 5 and 15, all reading states reachable from I_s are found, and used to build I_a (as part of S_a). In the second part, between lines 16 and 43, the $(m+1)$-th eventual successors of each reading state are added to S_a. This second part ensures that all writing states are 'skipped' so that R_a transitions include only transitions between consecutive reading states.

As T_s is receptive, so is T_a. In particular the algorithm transfers sink states that handle violations of environment safety or initial conditions to T_a.

6 Applying the Realizability Test

We illustrate the application of the realizability test presented in Section 5. To come up with an asynchronous strengthening we propose the following heuristic.

Heuristic 1. *In order to derive an asynchronous strengthening $\psi(X \cup \{r\}; Y)$ for a specification $\varphi(X; Y)$, replace one or more occurrences of atomic formulae of inputs, e.g., $x_i = d$, by $(x_i = d) \wedge \ominus(r \neq i) \wedge (r = i)$, which means that $x_i = d$ at a reading point.*

The rationale here is to encode the essence of the stuttering quantification into the strengthening. Since this quantification requires indifference towards input values outside reading points, we state this explicitly.

In [14] we showed how to strengthen the specification $\Box(x \leftrightarrow y)$ to an asynchronously realizable specification with the same idea: a Boolean output y copies the value of an input x.

$$\varphi_1(x; y) \quad = \quad [\neg(x \leftrightarrow y) \Rrightarrow (x \leftrightarrow \bigcirc x)] \rightarrow \begin{Bmatrix} x \Rrightarrow \Diamond y & \wedge \\ \overline{x} \Rrightarrow \Diamond \overline{y} & \wedge \\ y \Rrightarrow y \, \mathcal{S} \, \overline{y} \, \mathcal{S} \, x & \wedge \\ \bigcirc(\overline{y} \Rrightarrow \overline{y} \, \mathcal{B} \, y \, \mathcal{S} \, \overline{x}) & \end{Bmatrix}$$

This specification has a $GR(1)$ winning condition, it is stutteringly robust with a memory-less environment, and therefore it is potentially a good candidate to apply our heuristic. As suggested, we obtain the specification $\psi_1(x, r; y)$:

$$[\neg(x \leftrightarrow y) \Rrightarrow (x \leftrightarrow \bigcirc x)] \rightarrow \begin{Bmatrix} x \Rrightarrow \Diamond y & \wedge \\ \overline{x} \Rrightarrow \Diamond \overline{y} & \wedge \\ y \Rrightarrow y \, \mathcal{S} \, \overline{y} \, \mathcal{S} \, [x \wedge \ominus(r = 2) \wedge (r = 1)] & \wedge \\ \bigcirc\{\overline{y} \Rrightarrow \overline{y} \, \mathcal{B} \, y \, \mathcal{S} \, [\overline{x} \wedge \ominus(r = 2) \wedge (r = 1)]\} & \end{Bmatrix}$$

We establish that ψ satisfies all our requirements. We then apply the synchronous realizability test of [13] to the kernel formula $\mathcal{X}_{\psi_1}(x, r; y)$. This formula is realizable and we get a LTS S_1 with 30 states and 90 transitions, which is then minimized, using a variant of the Myhill-Nerode minimization, to a LTS S_1' with

Input: LTS $T_s = \langle S_s, I_s, R_s, \{x, r\}, Y, L_s \rangle$ such that $|Y| = m$, and an initial outputs assignment Y_{init}.
Output: The elements i_a, I_a, L_a, S_a and R_a of the extracted ILTS $T_a = \langle S_a, I_a, R_a, \{x\}, Y, L_a, i_a \rangle$.

```
i_a ← Y_init
I_a ← ∅, S_a ← ∅, R_a ← ∅
ST ← [EmptyStack]                ▷ a new states stack (for reachable unexplored 'read' states)
touched ← ∅                      ▷ a new states set (for states that were pushed to ST)
for all ini ∈ I_s do             ▷ find all reachable initial 'read' states
   for all succ ∈ S_s s.t. succ is an eventual (read) successor of ini do
      if succ ∉ touched then     ▷ add a new state to I_a and S_a
         push succ to ST
         touched ← touched ∪ {succ}
         I_a ← I_a ∪ {succ}
         S_a ← S_a ∪ {succ}
         L_a(succ)|_{x} ← L_s(succ)|_{x}, L_a(succ)|_Y ← L_s(succ)|_Ỹ
      end if
   end for
end for
while ST ≠ [EmptyStack] do       ▷ explore all reachable 'read' states
   st ← pop ST
   gen ← {st}
   for i = 1, ..., m do          ▷ find all m-th (last 'write') eventual successors of st
      nextgen ← ∅                ▷ a new states set
      for all st_gen ∈ gen do    ▷ find all i-th eventual successors of st
         for all succ ∈ S_s s.t. succ is an eventual (write) successor of st_gen do
            nextgen ← nextgen ∪ {succ}
         end for
      end for
      gen ← nextgen
   end for
   nextgen ← ∅                   ▷ a new states set
   for all st_gen ∈ gen do       ▷ find all 'eventual read successors' of st
      for all succ ∈ S_s s.t. succ is an eventual (read) successor of st_gen do
         nextgen ← nextgen ∪ {succ}
      end for
   end for
   for all st_ng ∈ nextgen do
      if st_ng ∉ touched then    ▷ add a new state to S_a
         push st_ng to ST
         touched ← touched ∪ {st_ng}
         S_a ← S_a ∪ {st_ng}
         L_a(st_ng)|_{x} ← L_s(st_ng)|_{x}, L_a(st_ng)|_Y ← L_s(st_ng)|_Ỹ
      end if
      R_a ← R_a ∪ {(st, st_ng)}  ▷ add a new transition to R_a
   end for
end while
return i_a, I_a, L_a, S_a, R_a
```

Fig. 3. Algorithm for extracting T_a from T_s

16 states and 54 transitions. The algorithm in Fig. 3 constructs an ILTS $A_{S_1'}$ with 16 states and 54 transitions. Using model-checking [4] we ensure that all asynchronous interactions of $A_{S_1'}$ satisfy $\varphi_1(x; y)$.

We devise similar specifications that copy the value of a Boolean input to one of several outputs according to the choice of the environment. Thus, we have a multi-valued input variable encoding the value and the target output variable and several outputs variables. The specification $\varphi_2(x; y_0, y_1)$ is given below.

$$\varphi_{2,e}(x; y_0, y_1) = \begin{pmatrix} ((x=0) \wedge y_1) \vee \\ ((x=1) \wedge \overline{y_1}) \vee \\ ((x=2) \wedge y_0) \vee \\ ((x=3) \wedge \overline{y_0}) \end{pmatrix} \Rightarrow \bigcirc\, \mathit{unchanged}(x)$$

$$\varphi_{2,s}(x; y_0, y_1) = \begin{pmatrix} (x=0) \Rightarrow \diamondsuit\, \overline{y_1} & \wedge \\ (x=1) \Rightarrow \diamondsuit\, y_1 & \wedge \\ (x=2) \Rightarrow \diamondsuit\, \overline{y_0} & \wedge \\ (x=3) \Rightarrow \diamondsuit\, y_0 & \wedge \\ y_0 \Rightarrow y_0\, \mathcal{S}\, \overline{y_0}\, \mathcal{S}\, (x=3) & \wedge \\ y_1 \Rightarrow y_1\, \mathcal{S}\, \overline{y_1}\, \mathcal{S}\, (x=1) & \wedge \\ \bigcirc[\overline{y_0} \Rightarrow \overline{y_0}\, \mathcal{B}\, y_0\, \mathcal{S}\, (x=2)] & \wedge \\ \bigcirc[\overline{y_1} \Rightarrow \overline{y_1}\, \mathcal{B}\, y_1\, \mathcal{S}\, (x=0)] & \end{pmatrix}$$

Using the same idea, we strengthen φ_2 to $\psi_2(x, r; y_0, y_1)$, which passes all the required tests. We then apply the synchronous realizability test in [13] to $\mathcal{X}_{\psi_2}(x, r; y_0, y_1)$ and get a LTS S_2 with 340 states and 1544 transitions, which is then minimized to 196 states and 1056 transitions. Our algorithm extracts an ILTS $A_{S'_2}$, which, as model checking confirms, asynchronously realizes φ_2.

From $\varphi_3(x; y_0, y_1, y_2)$ (similar to φ_2, with 3 outputs), we get a LTS with 1184 states and 8680 transitions.

7 Conclusions and Future Work

In this paper we extended the reduction of asynchronous synthesis to synchronous synthesis proposed in [16] to multiple input and output variables. We identify cases in which asynchronous synthesis can be done efficiently by bypassing the well known 'problematic' aspects of synthesis.

One of the drawbacks of this synthesis technique is the large size of resulting designs. However, we note that the size of asynchronous designs is bounded from above by synchronous designs. Thus, improvements to synchronous synthesis will result also in smaller asynchronous designs. We did not attempt to minimize or choose more effective synchronous programs, and we did not attempt to extract deterministic subsets of the nondeterministic controllers we worked with.

We believe that there is still room to explore additional cases in which asynchronous synthesis can be approximated. In particular, restrictions imposed by our heuristic (namely, one input environment and memory-less behavior) seem quite severe. Trying to remove some of these restrictions is left for future work.

Finally, asynchronous synthesis is related to solving games with partial information. There may be a connection between the cases in which synchronous synthesis offers a solution to asynchronous synthesis and partial information games that can be solved efficiently.

Acknowledgments. We are very grateful to L. Zuck for helping writing an earlier version of this manuscript.

References

1. Bloem, R., Galler, S., Jobstmann, B., Piterman, N., Pnueli, A., Weiglhofer, M.: Automatic hardware synthesis from specifications: A case study. In: DATE, pp. 1188–1193 (2007)
2. Büchi, J.R., Landweber, L.H.: Solving sequential conditions by finite-state strategies. Trans. AMS 138, 295–311 (1969)
3. Church, A.: Logic, arithmetic and automata. In: Proc. 1962 Int. Congr. Math., Upsala, pp. 23–25 (1963)
4. Clarke, E.C., Grumberg, O., Peled, D.: Model Checking. MIT Press (1999)
5. Conner, D.C., Kress-Gazit, H., Choset, H., Rizzi, A., Pappas, G.J.: Valet parking without a valet. In: IRSES, pp. 572–577. IEEE (2007)
6. D'Ippolito, N., Braberman, V., Piterman, N., Uchitel, S.: Synthesis of live behavior models for fallible domains. In: ICSE. ACM (2011)
7. Henzinger, T.A., Piterman, N.: Solving Games Without Determinization. In: Ésik, Z. (ed.) CSL 2006. LNCS, vol. 4207, pp. 395–410. Springer, Heidelberg (2006)
8. Kugler, H., Plock, C., Pnueli, A.: Controller Synthesis from LSC Requirements. In: Chechik, M., Wirsing, M. (eds.) FASE 2009. LNCS, vol. 5503, pp. 79–93. Springer, Heidelberg (2009)
9. Klein, U., Piterman, N., Pnueli, A.: Effective Synthesis of Asynchronous Systems from GR(1) Specifications. Tech Rep TR2011-944, Courant Inst of Math Sci, NYU
10. Kugler, H., Segall, I.: Compositional Synthesis of Reactive Systems from Live Sequence Chart Specifications. In: Kowalewski, S., Philippou, A. (eds.) TACAS 2009. LNCS, vol. 5505, pp. 77–91. Springer, Heidelberg (2009)
11. Kupferman, O., Vardi, M.Y.: Safraless decision procedures. In: FOCS (2005)
12. Piterman, N., Pnueli, A.: Faster solution of Rabin and Streett games. In: LICS, IEEE. IEEE Press (2006)
13. Piterman, N., Pnueli, A., Sa'ar, Y.: Synthesis of Reactive(1) Designs. In: Emerson, E.A., Namjoshi, K.S. (eds.) VMCAI 2006. LNCS, vol. 3855, pp. 364–380. Springer, Heidelberg (2005)
14. Pnueli, A., Klein, U.: Synthesis of programs from temporal property specifications. In: MEMOCODE, pp. 1–7. IEEE Press (2009)
15. Pnueli, A., Rosner, R.: On the synthesis of a reactive module. In: POPL, pp. 179–190 (1989)
16. Pnueli, A., Rosner, R.: On the Synthesis of an Asynchronous Reactive Module. In: Ronchi Della Rocca, S., Ausiello, G., Dezani-Ciancaglini, M. (eds.) ICALP 1989. LNCS, vol. 372, pp. 652–671. Springer, Heidelberg (1989)
17. Pnueli, A., Sa'ar, Y., Zuck, L.D.: JTLV: A Framework for Developing Verification Algorithms. In: Touili, T., Cook, B., Jackson, P. (eds.) CAV 2010. LNCS, vol. 6174, pp. 171–174. Springer, Heidelberg (2010)
18. Pnueli, A., Zaks, A.: On the Merits of Temporal Testers. In: Grumberg, O., Veith, H. (eds.) 25MC Festschrift. LNCS, vol. 5000, pp. 172–195. Springer, Heidelberg (2008)
19. Rabin, M.O.: Automata on Infinite Objects and Church's Problem. AMS (1972)
20. Schewe, S., Finkbeiner, B.: Synthesis of Asynchronous Systems. In: Puebla, G. (ed.) LOPSTR 2006. LNCS, vol. 4407, pp. 127–142. Springer, Heidelberg (2007)
21. Sistla, A.P., Vardi, M.Y., Wolper, P.: The complementation problem for Büchi autamata with application to temporal logic. TCS 49, 217–237 (1987)
22. Vardi, M.Y.: An Automata-Theoretic Approach to Fair Realizability and Synthesis. In: Wolper, P. (ed.) CAV 1995. LNCS, vol. 939, pp. 267–278. Springer, Heidelberg (1995)
23. Vardi, M.Y., Wolper, P.: Reasoning about infinite computations. I&C 115(1), 1–37 (1994)
24. Wongpiromsarn, T., Topcu, U., Murray, R.M.: Receding horizon control for temporal logic specifications. In: Johansson, K.H., Yi, W. (eds.) Proceedings of the 13th ACM International Conference on Hybrid Systems: Computation and Control, HSCC 2010, Stockholm, Sweden, April 12-15, 2010, pp. 101–110. ACM (2010) ISBN 978-1-60558-955-8

Sound Non-statistical Clustering of Static Analysis Alarms*

Woosuk Lee, Wonchan Lee, and Kwangkeun Yi

Seoul National University

Abstract. We present a sound method for clustering alarms from static analyzers. Our method clusters alarms by discovering sound dependencies between them such that if the dominant alarm of a cluster turns out to be false (respectively true) then it is assured that all others in the same cluster are also false (respectively true). We have implemented our clustering algorithm on top of a realistic buffer-overflow analyzer and proved that our method has the effect of reducing 54% of alarm reports. Our framework is applicable to any abstract interpretation-based static analysis and orthogonal to abstraction refinements and statistical ranking schemes.

1 Introduction

1.1 Problem

Users of sound static analyzers frequently suffer from a large number of false alarms. When we run a static analyzer for realistic software, false alarms often outnumber real errors. For example, in a case of analyzing commercial software, we have found only one error in 273 buffer-overflow alarms after a tedious alarm investigation work [10].

Although statistical ranking schemes [10][13] help to find real errors quickly, ranking schemes do not reduce alarm-investigation burdens. Statistical ranking schemes alleviate the false alarm problem by showing alarms that are most likely to be real errors over those that are least likely. However, the number of alarms to investigate is not reduced with ranking. We should examine all the alarms in order to find all the possible errors.

1.2 Our Solution

One way to reduce alarm-investigation burden is to cluster alarms according to their sound dependence information. We say that alarm A has (sound) dependence on alarm B if alarm B turns out to be false (true resp.), then so does

* This work was supported by the Engineering Research Center of Excellence Program of Korea Ministry of Education, Science and Technology(MEST) / National Research Foundation of Korea(NRF) (Grant 2011-0000971), the Brain Korea 21 Project, School of Electrical Engineering and Computer Science, Seoul National University in 2011, and a research grant from Samsung Electronics DMC R&D Center.

V. Kuncak and A. Rybalchenko (Eds.): VMCAI 2012, LNCS 7148, pp. 299–314, 2012.

alarm A as a logical consequence. When we find a set of alarms depending on the same alarm, which we call a dominant alarm, we can cluster them together. Once we find clusters of alarms, we only need to check whether their dominant alarms are false (true resp.).

In this paper, we present a sound alarm clustering method for static analyzers. Our analysis automatically discovers sound dependencies among alarms. Combining such dependencies, our analysis finds clusters of alarms which have their own a single or multiple dominant alarms. If the dominant alarms turn out to be false (true resp.), we can assure that all the others in the same cluster are also false (true resp.).

Example 1 through 3 show examples of alarm dependencies and how they reduce alarm-investigation efforts. These examples are discovered automatically by our clustering algorithm.

Example 1 (Beginning Example). Our analyzer reports 5 buffer-overflow alarms for the following code excerpted from NLKAIN 1.3 (Alarms are underlined).

```
1  void residual(SYSTEM *sys, double *upad, double *r) {
2    nx = 50;
3    u = &upad[nx+2];
4    ...
5    for (k = 0; k < ny; k++) {
6      u++;
7      for(j = 0; j < nx; j++) {
8        r[0] = ac[0]*u[0] - ax[0]*u[-1] - ax[1]*u[1] - ay[0]*u[-nx-2]
9          - ay[nx]*u[nx+2] - q[0];
10       r++; u++; q++; ac++; ax++; ay++;
11     }
12     u++; ax++;
13   }
14 }
```

Note the following two facts in this example:

1. If buffer access `u[-nx-2]` at line 8 overflows the buffer, so do the others since `-nx-2` is the lowest index among the indices of all the buffer accesses on `u`.
2. If buffer access `u[nx+2]` at line 9 does not overflow the buffer, neither do the others since `nx+2` is the highest index among the indices of all the buffer accesses on `u`.

Using these two facts, we can cluster alarms in two different ways: we can find a false alarm cluster which consists of all the alarms in the example and the dominant alarm is the one of the buffer access `u[nx+2]` at line 9. We can also find the true alarm cluster in the same way, except that the dominant alarm is the one of the buffer access `u[-nx-2]` at line 8. Instead of inspecting all the alarms, checking either the alarm of buffer access `u[-nx-2]` true or the alarm of buffer access `u[nx+2]` false is sufficient for users. □

Example 2 (Inter-procedural alarm dependencies). The following code excerpted from Appcontour 1.1.0 shows inter-procedural alarm dependencies. Our analyzer reports three alarms at line 3, 4, and 10. In the example, array `invmergerules` and `invmergerulesnn` have the same size 8.

```
1  int lookup_mergearcs(char *rule) {
2    ...
3    for (i = 1; invmergerules[i]; i++)
4      if (strcasecmp(rule, invmergerulesnn[i] == 0))
5        return (i);
6    ...
7  }
8  int rule_mergearcs(struct sketch *s, int rule, int rcount) {
9    if (debug)
10     printf("%s count %d", invmergerules[rule], rcount);
11   ...
12 }
13 int apply_rule(char *rule, struct sketch *sketch) {
14   ...
15   if ((code = lookup_mergearcs(rule)))
16     res = rule_mergearcs(sketch, code, rcount);
17   ...
18 }
```

Note the following two facts in this example:

1. If the alarm of the buffer access `invmergerules[i]` at line 3 is false, so are the others.
   – If alarm at line 3 is false, so is the one at line 4 because the buffer accesses at line 3 and 4 use the same index variable `i` and there is no update on the value between the two.
   – If alarm at line 3 is false, so is the one at line 10 because the value of index variable `i` at line 3 is passed to the index variable `rule` at line 10 without any change by function return and call ($5 \rightarrow 15 \rightarrow 16 \rightarrow 10$).
2. If the buffer access `invmergerules[rule]` at line 10 overflows, so do the others in a similar reason as the first fact.

We can find a false and true alarm cluster in the similar manner as in example 1. Instead of inspecting all the alarms, checking either the alarm at line 10 true or the alarm at line 3 false is sufficient. □

Example 3 (Multiple dominant alarms). The following code excerpted from GNU Chess 5.0.5 shows an example of a cluster with multiple dominant alarms. Three alarms are reported at line 3, 4, and 9. Array `cboard` and `ephash` have the same size 64.

```
1  void MakeMove(int side, int *move) {
2    ...
3    fpiece = cboard[f];
4    tpiece = cboard[t];
5    ...
6    if (fpiece == pawn && abs(f-t) == 16) {
7      sq = (f + t) / 2;
8      ...
9      HashKey ^= ephash[sq];
10   }
11 }
```

Since `sq` is the average of `f` and `t`, if both buffer accesses at line 3 and 4 are safe, buffer access at line 9 is also safe. In this example, we have a false cluster whose dominant alarms are the ones at line 3 and 4. □

Contributions

- We introduce a sound alarm clustering method for static analyzers that can reduce the alarm-investigation cost. Our framework is general in that it is applicable to any semantics-based static analysis. It is orthogonal to both refining approaches and statistical ranking schemes.
- We prove the effectiveness of our clustering method for the benchmark of 16 open-source programs. By our clustering method, we reduce the number of alarms to investigate by 54%.

Organization. Section 2 introduces our alarm clustering framework. Section 3 explains one practical algorithm which is a sound implementation of our alarm clustering method. Section 4 discusses the experiment results. We implemented our clustering algorithm on top of realistic buffer-overflow analyzer and apply it to the benchmark of 16 open-source programs. Section 5 discusses the related work and Section 6 concludes.

2 Alarm Clustering Framework

We describe our general framework of alarm clustering. In the rest of this section, we suppose basic knowledge of the abstract interpretation framework [3] and the trace partitioning abstract domain [16]. We begin by giving some definitions excerpted from [16].

2.1 Definitions

Programs. We define a program P as a transition system $(S, \to, S_\iota)$ where S is the set of states of the program, $\to$ is the transition of the possible execution elementary steps and S_ι denotes the set of initial states.

Traces. We write S^* for the set of all finite non-empty sequences of states. If σ is a finite sequence of states, σ_i will denote the (i+1)th state of the sequence, σ_0 is the first state and $\sigma_\dashv$ the last state. If τ is a prefix of σ, we write $\tau \preceq \sigma$.

A trace of program P is defined as a set $[\![P]\!] \triangleq \{\sigma \in S^* \mid \sigma_0 \in S_\iota \wedge \forall i.\sigma_i \to \sigma_{i+1}\}$. The set $[\![P]\!]$ is prefix-closed least fixpoint of the semantic function; i.e. $[\![P]\!] = \mathsf{lfp} F_P$ where F_P is the semantic function, defined as:

$$\begin{aligned} F_P &: 2^{S^*} \to 2^{S^*} \\ F_P(E) &= \{\langle s_\iota \rangle \mid s_\iota \in \mathcal{S}_\iota\} \\ &\quad \cup \{\langle s_0, \cdots, s_{n+1}\rangle \mid \langle s_0, \cdots, s_n \rangle \in E \wedge s_n \to s_{n+1}\}. \end{aligned}$$

Partitioned Reachable States. Using a well-chosen trace partitioning function $\delta : \Phi \to 2^{S^*}$, where Φ is the set of partitioning indices, one can model indexed collections of program states. Domain $\Phi \to 2^S$ is a partitioned reachable-state domain. The involved abstraction is $\alpha_0(\Sigma)(\varphi) \triangleq \{\sigma_\dashv \mid \sigma \in \Sigma \cap \delta(\varphi)\}$ and the concretization is $\gamma_0(f) \triangleq \{\sigma \mid \forall \tau \preceq \sigma . \forall \varphi .\ \tau \in \delta(\varphi) \Rightarrow \tau_\dashv \in f(\varphi)\}$. The pair of functions (α_0, γ_0) forms a Galois connection: $2^{S^*} \underset{\alpha_0}{\overset{\gamma_0}{\leftrightarrows}} \Phi \to 2^S$. We write concrete semantics $[\![P]\!]$ modulo partitioning function δ as $[\![P]\!]_{/\delta}$.

Abstract Semantics. We think of a static analyzer which is designed over an abstract domain $\hat{D} = \Phi \to \hat{S}$ with the following Galois connections:

$$2^{S^*} \underset{\alpha_0}{\overset{\gamma_0}{\leftrightarrows}} \Phi \to 2^S \underset{\alpha}{\overset{\gamma}{\leftrightarrows}} \Phi \to \hat{S}.$$

The galois connection of (α, γ) is easily derived from the one of (α_S, γ_S) between domains 2^S and $\hat{S}$: $2^S \underset{\alpha_S}{\overset{\gamma_S}{\leftrightarrows}} \hat{S}$.

The abstract semantics of program P computed by the analyzer is a fixpoint $\hat{T} = \mathsf{lfp}^{\#} \hat{F}$ where $\mathsf{lfp}^{\#}$ is a sound, abstract post-fixpoint operator and the function $\hat{F} : \hat{D} \to \hat{D}$ is a monotone or an extensive abstract transfer function such that $\alpha \circ \alpha_0 \circ F_P \sqsubseteq \hat{F} \circ \alpha \circ \alpha_0$. The soundness of the static analysis follows from the fixpoint transfer theorem [2].

Alarms. The static analyzer raises an alarm at trace partitioning index φ if $\gamma_S(\hat{T}(\varphi)) \cap \Omega(\varphi) \neq \varnothing$ where $\hat{T}$ is the abstract semantics of a program P and function $\Omega : \Phi \to 2^S$ specifies erroneous states at each partitioning index. In the rest of the paper, we use partitioning index and alarm interchangeably; alarm φ means the one at the trace partitioning index φ.

The alarm φ is false alarm (resp. true alarm) when the static analyzer raises the alarm and $[\![P]\!]_{/\delta}(\varphi) \cap \Omega(\varphi) = \varnothing$ (resp. $[\![P]\!]_{/\delta}(\varphi) \cap \Omega(\varphi) \neq \varnothing$).

Alarm Dependence. Our goal is to find concrete dependencies between alarms. Given two alarms φ_1 and φ_2, if alarm φ_2 is always false whenever alarm φ_1 is false; i.e.

$$[\![P]\!]_{/\delta}(\varphi_1) \cap \Omega(\varphi_1) = \varnothing \implies [\![P]\!]_{/\delta}(\varphi_2) \cap \Omega(\varphi_2) = \varnothing,$$

we say that alarm φ_2 has a concrete dependence on alarm φ_1. If we find this concrete dependence of alarm φ_2 on alarm φ_1, we also have another dependence as contraposition.

$$[\![P]\!]_{/\delta}(\varphi_2) \cap \Omega(\varphi_2) \neq \varnothing \implies [\![P]\!]_{/\delta}(\varphi_1) \cap \Omega(\varphi_1) \neq \varnothing$$

Since concrete dependence is not computable in general, we use abstract dependence which is sound with respect to concrete dependence. The idea is that if we can kill the alarm φ_2 from the abstract semantics refined under the assumption that alarm φ_1 is false, it also means that alarm φ_2 has concrete dependence on alarm φ_1. It is easy to see that this is correct because, even though the refined abstract semantics is smaller than the original fixpoint, it is still sound abstraction of concrete semantics if the assumption of alarm φ_1 false holds.

In the rest of the section, we define the notion of sound refinement by refutation and abstract dependence. We also prove the soundness of abstract dependence.

Refinement by Refutation. Using the assumption of alarm φ being false, we can get a sliced abstract semantics $\tilde{T}_\varphi$. The definition of $\tilde{T}_\varphi$ is,

$$\tilde{T}_\varphi = \mathsf{gfp}^{\#} \lambda Z.\hat{T}_{\neg\varphi} \sqcap \hat{F}(Z)$$

where $\mathsf{gfp}^{\#}$ is a pre-fixpoint operator and $\hat{T}_{\neg\varphi}$ is the same as the original fixpoint $\hat{T}$ except the erroneous states at partitioning index φ sliced out:

$$\hat{T}_{\neg\varphi} = \hat{T}[\varphi \mapsto \hat{T}(\varphi) \mathbin{\hat{\ominus}} \alpha_S(\Omega(\varphi))]$$

where $F[a \mapsto b]$ is the same as F except it maps a to b. The $\hat{\ominus}$ operator should be a sound abstract slice operator such that $\alpha_S \circ \ominus \sqsubseteq \hat{\ominus} \circ \alpha_{S\times S}$ where the operator $\ominus$ is a set difference and $\alpha_{S\times S}$ is an abstraction lifted for pairs. We assume that the abstract domain $\hat{S}$ has meet operator and abstract slice operator.

We can extend this refinement to the case of refuting multiple alarms. Suppose that we assume that set $\{\varphi_1, \cdots, \varphi_n\}$ of alarms is false. The refinement $\tilde{T}_{\{\varphi_1,\cdots,\varphi_n\}}$ of the fixpoint $\hat{T}$ with respect to these assumptions is,

$$\tilde{T}_{\vec{\varphi}} = \mathsf{gfp}^{\#} \lambda Z.\hat{T}_{\neg\{\varphi_1,\cdots,\varphi_n\}} \sqcap \hat{F}(Z)$$

where $\hat{T}_{\neg\{\varphi_1,\cdots,\varphi_n\}} = \bigsqcap_{\varphi_i \in \{\varphi_1,\cdots,\varphi_n\}} \hat{T}_{\neg\varphi_i}$.

Abstract Alarm Dependence. We now define abstract alarm dependence.

Definition 1 ($\varphi_1 \rightsquigarrow \varphi_2$). *Given two alarms φ_1 and φ_2, alarm φ_2 has abstract dependence on alarm φ_1, iff the refinement $\tilde{T}_{\varphi_1}$ by refuting alarm φ_1 kills alarm φ_2; i.e.*

$$\textit{iff } \gamma_S(\tilde{T}_{\varphi_1}(\varphi_2)) \cap \Omega(\varphi_2) = \varnothing.$$

We write $\varphi_1 \rightsquigarrow \varphi_2$ when an alarm φ_2 has abstract dependence on alarm φ_1. We prove the soundness of abstract alarm dependence as the following lemma.

Lemma 1. *Given two alarms φ_1 and φ_2, if $\varphi_1 \rightsquigarrow \varphi_2$, then alarm φ_2 is false whenever alarm φ_1 is false.*

As a contraposition of lemma 1, we also have a different sense of soundness of abstract alarm dependence.

Lemma 2. *Given two alarms φ_1 and φ_2, if $\varphi_1 \rightsquigarrow \varphi_2$, then alarm φ_1 is true whenever alarm φ_2 is true.*

We extend the notion of the abstract dependence for more than two alarms.

Definition 2 **($\{\varphi_1, \cdots, \varphi_n\} \rightsquigarrow \varphi_0$).** *Given set $\{\varphi_0, \cdots, \varphi_n\}$ of alarms, we write $\{\varphi_1, \cdots, \varphi_n\} \rightsquigarrow \varphi_0$, and say that alarm φ_0 has abstract dependence on set $\{\varphi_1, \cdots, \varphi_n\}$ of alarms, iff the refinement $\tilde{T}_{\{\varphi_1, \cdots, \varphi_n\}}$ by refuting set $\{\varphi_1, \cdots, \varphi_n\}$ of alarms satisfies*

$$\gamma_S(\tilde{T}_{\{\varphi_1, \cdots, \varphi_n\}}(\varphi_0)) \cap \Omega(\varphi_0) = \varnothing.$$

Lemma 3. *Given set $\{\varphi_0, \cdots, \varphi_n\}$ of alarms, if $\{\varphi_1, \cdots, \varphi_n\} \rightsquigarrow \varphi_0$, then alarm φ_0 is false whenever all alarms $\varphi_1, \cdots, \varphi_n$ are false.*

The contraposition of lemma 3 is not quite useful since it specifies only some alarms among set $\{\varphi_1, \cdots, \varphi_n\}$ of alarms are true when $\{\varphi_1, \cdots, \varphi_n\} \rightsquigarrow \varphi_0$ and alarm φ_0 is true.

In the rest of paper, we sometimes write $\vec{\varphi}$ to denote a set of alarms.

2.2 Alarm Clustering

Using abstract alarm dependencies, we can cluster alarms in two different ways.

Definition 3 (False Alarm Cluster). *Let $\mathcal{A}$ be set of all alarms in program P and $\rightsquigarrow$ be the dependence relation. A false alarm cluster $\mathcal{C}^F_{\vec{\varphi}} \subseteq \mathcal{A}$ with its dominant alarms $\vec{\varphi}$ is $\{\varphi \in \mathcal{A} \mid \vec{\varphi} \rightsquigarrow \varphi\}$.*

Definition 4 (True Alarm Cluster). *Let $\mathcal{A}$ be set of all alarms in program P and $\rightsquigarrow$ be the dependence relation. A true alarm cluster $\mathcal{C}^T_{\varphi} \subseteq \mathcal{A}$ with its dominant alarms φ is $\{\varphi' \in \mathcal{A} \mid \varphi' \overset{+}{\rightsquigarrow} \varphi\}$ ($\overset{+}{\rightsquigarrow}$ is the transitive closure of $\rightsquigarrow$ between only singleton alarms).*

Note that we cannot exploit dependencies like $\{\varphi_1, \cdots, \varphi_n\} \rightsquigarrow \varphi_0$ to make true alarm cluster. As we mentioned in 2.1, it does not tell us exactly which alarms among set $\{\varphi_1, \cdots, \varphi_n\}$ of alarms are true when alarm φ_0 is true.

The soundness of true and false alarm clusters directly follow the soundness of abstract alarm dependence.

Theorem 1. *Every alarm in $\mathcal{C}^F_{\vec{\varphi}}$ is false whenever all alarms $\vec{\varphi}$ are false.*

Theorem 2. *Every alarm in $\mathcal{C}^T_{\varphi}$ is true whenever alarm φ is true.*

For two reasons, we only focus on false alarm clusters. First, both type of clusters can be found from the same dependence relation $\rightsquigarrow$, so whether to make true or false alarm is simply the matter of interpretation. Second, in our current framework, true alarm clusters can exploit fewer dependencies than false alarm cluster, thus they cluster less alarms. In the rest of the paper, a cluster $\mathcal{C}$ means a false alarm cluster $\mathcal{C}^F$.

3 Alarm Clustering Algorithm

As we explain in section 2.2, we need to compute abstract dependence relation among all the alarms for clustering. A naive way to do this is to enumerate all possible subsets of all the alarms and find the others that are dominated by them. This naive algorithm requires 2^N times of re-computation where N is number of alarms, which is far from practical.

We present one practical alarm clustering algorithm, shown in algorithm 1, which clusters alarms based on a (not all) subset of possible dependencies. By one fixpoint computation, our algorithm finds the subset of possible dependencies. The idea is to slice the static analysis result as much as possible by refuting all alarms and track which dominant alarm candidate possibly kills which alarm. Then, we cluster the alarms which must be killed by the same dominant alarm candidate.

Our algorithm works in the following way: we start by assuming that each alarm is a dominant one of a cluster that clusters only itself. This can be expressed by slicing out the erroneous states at every alarm point but not propagating refinement yet. Then from an alarm point, say φ_1, we start building its cluster. We propagate its sliced, non-erroneous abstract state to another alarm point say φ_2 and see if the propagation further refines the non-erroneous abstract state at φ_2. If the propagated state is smaller than that at φ_2, it means refuting φ_1 will refute alarm φ_2, hence dependence $\varphi_1 \rightsquigarrow \varphi_2$ and thus we add φ_2 to the φ_1-dominating cluster. If the propagated state is larger than that at φ_2, then dependence $\varphi_1 \rightsquigarrow \varphi_2$ is not certain hence, instead of adding φ_2 to the φ_1-dominating cluster, we start building the φ_2-dominating cluster. If the propagated state is incomparable to that at φ_2, then we pick both alarms as dominant ones and start building the φ_1-and-φ_2-dominating cluster by propagating the slicing effect of simultaneously refuting (i.e., taking the meet of refuting) both alarms.

In the algorithm, we assume that Φ is the set of program points and every program point has several predecessors and successors specified by function pred and succ (line 2). For brevity, we also assume that an alarm can be raised at every program point; i.e. for all $\varphi \in \Phi$, $\hat{\Omega}(\varphi) \neq \bot$ where $\hat{\Omega}$ is abstract erroneous information (line 8).

From line 1 to 9, we give definitions used in the algorithm. Everything other than function R at line 7 is trivially explained by the comment on the same line. Function R keeps the information of dominant alarm candidate. As specified in the comment, if $R(\varphi) = \Delta$ for some program point φ and set Δ of dominant

Algorithm 1. Clustering algorithm

1: $w \in Work = \Phi \quad W \in Worklist = 2^{Work}$
2: $\mathsf{pred} \in Predecessors = \Phi \to 2^{\Phi} \quad \mathsf{succ} \in Successors = \Phi \to 2^{\Phi}$
3: $\hat{f} \in \Phi \to \hat{S} \to \hat{S}$ (* abstract transfer function for each program point *)
4: $T \in Table = \Phi \to \hat{S}$ (* abstract state indexed by program point *)
5: $\overrightarrow{\varphi} \in DomCand = 2^{\Phi}$ (* dominant alarm candidate. set of alarms. *)
6: $\Delta \in 2^{DomCand}$ (* set of dominant alarm candidates *)
7: $R \in RefinedBy = \Phi \to 2^{DomCand}$ (* $\{\varphi \mapsto \Delta\} \in R$: T(φ) is refined by $\overrightarrow{\varphi}$ in Δ *)
8: $\hat{\Omega} \in ErrorInfo = \Phi \to \hat{S}$ (* abstract erroneous state information *)
9: $\mathcal{C} \in Clusters = DomCand \to 2^{Partid}$ (* alarm clusters indexed by dominant alarms *)
10: **procedure** FixpointIterate(W, T, R)
11: **repeat**
12: $\varphi := \mathsf{choose}(W)$ (* pick a work from worklist *)
13: $\hat{s} := T(\varphi)$ (* previous abstract state *)
14: $\hat{s}' := \hat{f}(\varphi)(\bigsqcup_{\varphi_i \in \mathsf{pred}(\varphi)} T(\varphi_i))$ (* new abstract state *)
15: $\hat{s}_{new} := \hat{s}' \sqcap \hat{s}$
16:
17: $\Delta := R(\varphi)$ (* previous set of dominant alarm candidates *)
18: $\Delta' := \bigcup_{\varphi_i \in \mathsf{pred}(\varphi)} R(\varphi_i)$ (* new set of dominant alarm candidates *)
19: **if** $\hat{s} \sqsupset \hat{s}'$ **then** $\Delta_{new} = \Delta'$
20: **else if** $\hat{s} \sqsubseteq \hat{s}'$ **then** $\Delta_{new} = \Delta$
21: **else** $\Delta_{new} := \Delta \uplus \Delta'$
22: **if** $\hat{s}_{new} \sqsubset \hat{s}$ **then** (* propagate the change to successors *)
23: $W := W \cup \mathsf{succ}(\varphi)$; $T(\varphi) := \hat{s}_{new}$; $R(\varphi) := \Delta_{new}$
24: **until** W $= \varnothing$
25: **procedure** ClusterAlarms(T, R)
26: **for all** $\varphi \in \Phi$ **do**
27: **if** $T(\varphi) \sqcap \hat{\Omega}(\varphi) = \bot$ **then**
28: **for all** $\overrightarrow{\varphi} \in R(\varphi)$ **do**
29: $\mathcal{C} := \mathcal{C}\{\overrightarrow{\varphi} \mapsto \mathcal{C}(\overrightarrow{\varphi}) \cup \{\varphi\}\}$
30: **procedure** main()
31: $T := \hat{T}_{\neg\Phi}$ (* $\hat{T}$ is the original fixpoint *)
32: $R := \{\varphi \mapsto \{\{\varphi\}\} \mid \varphi \in \Phi\}$
33: FixpointIterate(Φ,T,R); ClusterAlarms(T,R)

alarms, it means that the abstract state at φ is refined by some dominant alarm candidate $\overrightarrow{\varphi}$ in Δ, thus alarm φ can be a member of the $\overrightarrow{\varphi}$-dominating cluster. We keep the set of dominant alarm candidates, not a single dominant alarm candidate, since there are branches where each branch takes different dominant alarm candidate. Line 32 shows that function R initially maps each program point φ to a set that only contains itself, which means that initially, alarm φ is the only member of the φ-dominating cluster.

Without considering gray-boxed parts, procedure FixpointIterate in the algorithm is a traditional fixpoint iteration to compute a pre-fixpoint of a decreasing chain. We pick a work from worklist (line 12), compute a new abstract state (line 14 and 15), and propagate the change to successors if the newly computed state is strictly less than the previous one (line 22). We repeat this until no work remains. To guarantee the termination or to speed up, we can integrate acceleration method (such as widening [4] in the decreasing direction). We start the fixpoint computation from the fixpoint refined by refuting all alarms (line 32).

Gray-boxed parts are to track which set of dominant alarm candidates refines the abstract state at program point φ. As specified from line 19 to line 21, there are three cases: 1) the new abstract state refines the previous one (line 19), 2) the previous abstract state is smaller than or equal to the new one (line 20), and 3) both abstract states are incomparable (line 21). For the first case, we change the set of dominant alarm candidates to the new one Δ' (line 18). For the second case, we do not change (line 19) since we cannot further refine the abstract state. For the last case, we pick both dominant alarm candidates from set Δ and Δ' (line 20). The new set of dominant alarm candidates is thus computed by the following lifted union $\Cup$:

$$\Delta_1 \Cup \Delta_2 = \{\vec{\varphi}_1 \cup \vec{\varphi}_2 \mid \vec{\varphi}_1 \in \Delta_1 \wedge \vec{\varphi}_2 \in \Delta_2\}.$$

For each dominant alarm candidate $\vec{\varphi}_1$ and $\vec{\varphi}_2$ in set Δ_1 and Δ_2 of alarm candidates, respectively, we union the two.

Finally, procedure ClusterAlarms validates the dominant alarm candidate information R based on the refined fixpoint T and clusters alarms. For each alarm at φ, we validate that the union of all dominant alarm candidates in $R(\varphi)$ really dominates alarm φ by checking that the refined abstract state $T(\varphi)$ kills the alarm (line 27). If the alarm is killed, we put alarm φ to the $R(\varphi)$-dominating cluster (line 28 and 29).

4 Experiments

4.1 Implementation

We have implemented our alarm clustering method on top of Airac [9,10,19,20,21], a realistic buffer-overflow analyzer for C programs. Our static analyzer is a sound, inter-procedural abstract interpreter with interval domain. Because of limited space, we do not explain our baseline analysis; See [20] for the details.

Three different alarm clustering analyses are implemented: 1) syntactic alarm clustering, 2) inter-procedural semantic clustering with interval domain, 3) intra-procedural semantic clustering with octagon domain. As we move from syntactic clustering to semantic clustering with octagon domain, we can cluster more alarms but need to pay more cost for the analysis. Thus, we initially use syntactic clustering to group alarms as many as possible and then apply the semantic clustering analyses to the rest of alarms that are not clustered yet.

In the rest of this section, we explain briefly about the implementation of each clustering analysis.

Syntactic Alarm Clustering. Syntactic alarm clustering is based on syntactically identifiable alarm dependencies. Two alarms are syntactically dependent iff 1) the expressions that raise the alarms are syntactically equivalent and 2) the variables inside the expressions have the same definition points in the definition-use chain [18].

We implement syntactic alarm clustering as a post-analysis phase. The first check for a syntactic dependence is trivial and the second check can exploit the definition-use chain already computed by our baseline analyzer. Once we find dependencies, the alarm clustering part is the same as algorithm 1.

Note that the syntactic alarm clustering can be explained in our clustering framework. Syntactic alarm dependence is a special type of abstract dependence such that the abstract transfer function between two alarm points is identity upto the alarm-related variables, thus the falsehood of one alarm makes the other also false trivially.

Example 4. Our static analyzer reports four alarms in the following code snippet excerpted from `ftpd.c` in `Wu-ftpd 2.6.2`:

```
1  /* extern char *optarg; */
2  while (*optarg && *optarg >= '0' && *optarg <= '9')
3    val = val * 8 + *optarg++ - '0';
```

We can easily find that three alarms at line 2 have syntactic dependencies on each other. We also find that two alarms in line 2 and 3 are also syntactically dependent; two expressions that raise the alarms are syntactically the same (`*optarg`) and the definitions of `optarg` at line 2 and 3 are always the same (either the one defined before the loop or newly defined at line 3). □

From a practical point of view, syntactic alarm clustering is beneficial for two reasons. First, syntactic alarm clustering is highly cost-effective. It requires only an additional definition-use analysis which does not cost a lot. Especially, our static analyzer has been performing definition-use analysis for its own use. Second, syntactic alarm clustering is precise because it does not involve any abstraction.

Alarm Clustering with Interval and Octagon Domain. We implement algorithm 1 for both interval and octagon domain. The algorithms work after syntactic clustering algorithm find alarm clusters. The octagon domain enables us to find dependencies that are visible only by relational analysis.

One difference between the implementation with interval domain and octagon domain is that we use more fine-grained "refined-by" information (R in algorithm 1) in the implementation with interval domain. We track set of dominant alarm candidates not per each program point, but per each variable. By tracking dominant alarm candidates in this way, we could find more dependencies.

For octagon domain-based analysis, which has not been supported by our baseline analyzer, we integrate a prototype using Apron octagon domain library [8] into our clustering system. We only implement intra-procedural analysis (for cost reduction) and paralleize it. For each function, we do dependence analysis [18] to find the set of alarm-related variables and pack only those variables to make octagons. We use the straightforward translation between the baseline, interval analysis results and their octagon representations.

Table 1. Alarm clustering results
B : baseline analysis, **S**: syntactic alarm clustering, **I** : semantic alarm clustering with interval domain, **O** : semantic clustering with octagon domain.

Program	LOC	# Alarms				% Reduction				Time(s)		
		B	S	S+I	S+I+O	S	+I	+O	S+I+O	B	I	O
nlkain-1.3	831	124	118	96	93	5%	18%	2%	25%	0.17	0.03	0.1
polymorph-0.4.0	1,357	25	19	13	13	24%	24%	0%	48%	0.12	0	0.06
ncompress-4.2.4	2,195	66	50	38	30	24%	18%	12%	55%	0.54	0.03	0.69
sbm-0.0.4	2,467	237	230	185	125	3%	19%	25%	47%	2.28	0.3	1.15
stripcc-0.2.0	2,555	194	165	143	127	15%	11%	8%	35%	2.76	0.07	25.44
barcode-0.96	4,460	435	386	329	302	11%	13%	6%	31%	3.23	0.1	2.59
129.compress	5,585	57	56	29	29	2%	47%	0%	49%	2.46	0.02	0.19
archimedes-0.7.0	7,569	711	342	215	132	52%	18%	12%	81%	6.48	0.27	16.11
man-1.5h1	7,232	276	226	189	165	18%	13%	9%	40%	11.65	0.28	1.86
gzip-1.2.4	11,213	385	341	278	263	11%	16%	4%	32%	10.03	0.3	2.92
combine-0.3.3	11,472	733	468	297	294	36%	23%	0%	60%	19.74	0.81	26.93
gnuchess-5.05	11,629	976	744	343	333	24%	41%	1%	66%	42.49	4.78	8.66
bc-1.06	12,830	593	330	320	198	44%	2%	21%	67%	33.75	7.04	27.23
grep-2.5.1	31,154	115	100	96	85	13%	3%	10%	26%	4.19	0.01	11
coan-4.2.2	22,414	461	350	332	291	24%	4%	9%	37%	126.66	1.91	6.14
lsh-2.0.4	110,898	616	387	319	264	37%	11%	9%	57%	115.13	2.12	204.12
TOTAL	245,861	6,004	4,312	3,222	2,744	28%	18%	8%	54%	381.68	15.94	335.19

4.2 Experiment Results

We apply our clustering analyzer on 16 packages from three different categories (Bugbench [14], GNU softwares, and SourceForge open source projects). Table 4 shows our benchmark.

Effectiveness. To evaluate how much our clustering can reduce the alarm-investigation effort, we measure the number of distinct dominant alarms of alarm clusters and compare it to the number of reported alarms. In table 4, the columns labeled "# Alarms" show the numbers of alarms reported by baseline analyzer (B), reduced by syntactic clustering (S), reduced further by semantic clustering with interval domain (S+I), and reduced further by semantic clustering with octagon domain (S+I+O), respectively. The next columns labeled "% Reduction" show the reduction ratios of each additional alarm clustering analysis (S, +I, and +O) and the total (S+I+O).

As shown in table 4, our alarm clustering reduces 54% of alarms on average. Note that even though the syntactic clustering reduces 28% of alarms, the semantic clustering reduces 26% additionally (18% by clustering with interval domain and 8% by the other). This means that semantic clustering analyses successfully find intricate alarm dependencies which can never be found by syntactic clustering.

We investigate the most effective and the least effective cases of the interval domain-based alarm clustering. Our interval domain-based algorithm turned out to be the most effective for gnuchess-5.05 and 129.compress (reduced by 41% and 47%) because of the following reasons. First, the sizes of almost all buffers in the programs are fixed. In this case, we can slice out erroneous state accurately, which is essential for refinement by refutation, even using interval domain. Second, there were many different buffers of the same size which are accessed using the same index variable. On the other hand, our interval domain-based clustering is least effective for grep-2.5.1 (reduced by 3%). It is because almost all buffers in the program are dynamically allocated, thus the sizes of them were hard to track accurately. Indeed, we found that the interval values of the sizes of buffers were, in most cases, $[0, \infty]$ which means the buffer can have arbitrary size. In this case, we cannot slice out the erroneous states at all.

For programs polymorph-0.4.0, 129.compress, combine-0.3.3, and gnuchess-5.0.5, octagon domain-based clustering is not effective. The reason of ineffectiveness for the first three programs is rather originated from our implementation, which has been only doing intra-procedural analysis. Indeed, program polymorph-0.4.0 has many library function calls between alarm points, so that they ruin the refinement. In the case of gnuchess-5.0.5, many buffers were accessed by indices with bit operations on them, which is beyond the reach of octagon domain.

We also investigate the most effective case of the octagon domain-based alarm clustering. The most effective case was program sbm-0.0.4. The program has long consecutive buffer accesses with the indexes having relationship of form $\pm i \pm j = c$. This type of relationship can be precisely expressed and handled by octagon domain.

Clustering Overhead. We measure the analysis time to assess the overhead of clustering analysis. All our experiments are performed on a PC with a 2.4 GHz Intel Core2 Quad processor and 8 GB of memory. In table 4, the columns labeled "Time" present times for the baseline analysis (B) and the additional alarm clustering with interval domain (I) and octagon domain (O). Note that we do not measure the cost of syntactic clustering since it exploits the definition-use chains already generated by the baseline analysis.

The overhead of interval domain-based alarm clustering is on average only 4% of the baseline analysis time. On the other hand, we find that the overhead of octagon domain-based clustering is almost close to, and even surpasses for some cases, the baseline analysis time. This is because octagon domain-based static analysis usually has higher cost than interval domain-based static analysis and our octagon domain-based abstract interpreter is prototypical and far less optimized than interval domain-based one which has been highly optimized [9,19,20].

5 Related Work

To our best knowledge, Le et al.'s work [23] is the first one that proposes non-statistical clustering method. They reduce the number of faults (alarms) by detecting correlations (dependencies) between them. By propagating the effects of the error state along the program path, they detect the correlation of pairs of alarms. They automatically construct a correlation graph which shows how faults are correlated. Based on the graph, we can reduce the number of faults to consider.

However, Le et al.'s method is not sound, while our method is sound. According to their experiment results, the dependencies they use to construct the correlation graph can be spurious (false positive), which means that it is not always safe to rule out faults even though they are correlated to the others.

Statistical ranking schemes [7,10,12,13] may help to find real errors quickly, but ranking schemes do not reduce alarm-investigation burdens as in our work. Since our technique is orthogonal to statistical ranking schemes, we might combine our technique with them for a more sophisticated alarm reporting interface.

Our work resembles to Rival's work [22] in the sense that both work refines the abstraction by exploiting the information about error state. In his work, Rival refines the abstraction by slicing out non-error states and sees if the initial state after refinement still insists that the erroneous states are reachable. If the initial state becomes bottom after refinement, the alarm turns out to be false. On the other hand, in our work, we refine the abstraction by slicing out erroneous states at one point and see if erroneous states at other points become non-reachable, which means that we found the dependence between alarms.

Our work is more general than error recovery technique that is used for reducing false alarms in many commercial static analysis tools [1,15,17]. For each alarm found, the commercial analyzers recover from those alarms; i.e. they assume that an alarm is false when they passed the alarm point. Because error recovery is done within the baseline analysis, possible refinements are bounded by the expressiveness of the abstract domain of the baseline. As we show in Section 4, we can use more expressive domain for clustering purpose than the one used in the baseline, which can be more cost-effective than using expensive abstract domain in the baseline. Additionally, our method can derive true clusters for which cannot be done by the error recovery technique.

Our clustering method can be integrated with other refinement approaches [5,6,11,22]. The goal of them is to remove false alarms by abstraction refinement, while our work is to reduce the number of alarms to investigate. Our work can reduce the number of targets to do the refinement.

6 Conclusion

We have presented a new, sound non-statistical alarm clustering method for semantic-based static analyzers. We propose a general framework of alarm clustering. Our technique is general enough to be applicable to any static analysis based on abstract interpretation. By experiment results, we show that our technique can considerably reduce the number of alarms to investigate manually.

Acknowledgment. The authors would like to thank Youil Kim, Daejun Park, Hakjoo Oh, Minsik Jin, and the anonymous referees for their comments in improving this work.

References

1. Blanchet, B., Cousot, P., Cousot, R., Feret, J., Mauborgne, L., Miné, A., Monniaux, D., Rival, X.: A static analyzer for large safety-critical software. In: PLDI, pp. 196–207 (2003)
2. Cousot, P., Cousot, R.: Abstract interpretation and application to logic programs. Journal of Logic Programming 13(2-3), 103–179 (1992)
3. Cousot, P., Cousot, R.: Abstract interpretation: A unified lattice model for static analysis of programs by construction or approximation of fixpoints. In: POPL, pp. 238–252 (1977)
4. Cousot, P., Cousot, R.: Comparing the Galois Connection and Widening/Narrowing Approaches to Abstract Interpretation. In: Bruynooghe, M., Wirsing, M. (eds.) PLILP 1992. LNCS, vol. 631, pp. 269–295. Springer, Heidelberg (1992)
5. Gulavani, B.S., Chakraborty, S., Nori, A.V., Rajamani, S.K.: Automatically Refining Abstract Interpretations. In: Ramakrishnan, C.R., Rehof, J. (eds.) TACAS 2008. LNCS, vol. 4963, pp. 443–458. Springer, Heidelberg (2008)
6. Gulavani, B.S., Rajamani, S.K.: Counterexample Driven Refinement for Abstract Interpretation. In: Hermanns, H. (ed.) TACAS 2006. LNCS, vol. 3920, pp. 474–488. Springer, Heidelberg (2006)
7. Heckman, S.S.: Adaptively ranking alerts generated from automated static analysis. Crossroads 14, 7:1–7:11 (2007)
8. Jeannet, B., Miné, A.: APRON: A Library of Numerical Abstract Domains for Static Analysis. In: Bouajjani, A., Maler, O. (eds.) CAV 2009. LNCS, vol. 5643, pp. 661–667. Springer, Heidelberg (2009)
9. Jhee, Y., Jin, M., Jung, Y., Kim, D., Kong, S., Lee, H., Oh, H., Park, D., Yi., K.: Abstract interpretation + impure catalysts: Our Sparrow experience. Presentation at the Workshop of the 30 Years of Abstract Interpretation, San Francisco (2008)
10. Jung, Y., Kim, J., Shin, J., Yi, K.: Taming False Alarms from a Domain-Unaware C Analyzer by a Bayesian Statistical Post Analysis. In: Hankin, C., Siveroni, I. (eds.) SAS 2005. LNCS, vol. 3672, pp. 203–217. Springer, Heidelberg (2005)
11. Kim, Y., Lee, J., Han, H., Choe, K.-M.: Filtering false alarms of buffer overflow analysis using smt solvers. Inf. Softw. Technol. 52(2), 210–219 (2010)
12. Kremenek, T., Ashcraft, K., Yang, J., Engler, D.R.: Correlation exploitation in error ranking. In: FSE, pp. 83–93 (2004)
13. Kremenek, T., Engler, D.R.: Z-ranking: Using Statistical Analysis to Counter the Impact of Static Analysis Approximations. In: Cousot, R. (ed.) SAS 2003. LNCS, vol. 2694, pp. 295–315. Springer, Heidelberg (2003)
14. Lu, S., Li, Z., Qin, F., Tan, L., Zhou, P., Zhou, Y.: Bugbench: Benchmarks for evaluating bug detection tools. In: Workshop on the Evaluation of Software Defect Detection Tools (2005)
15. MathWorks: Polyspace embedded software verification, `http://www.mathworks.com/products/polyspace/index.html`
16. Mauborgne, L., Rival, X.: Trace Partitioning in Abstract Interpretation Based Static Analyzers. In: Sagiv, M. (ed.) ESOP 2005. LNCS, vol. 3444, pp. 5–20. Springer, Heidelberg (2005)
17. Microsoft: Code contracts, `http://msdn.microsoft.com/en-us/devlabs/dd491992.aspx`
18. Muchnick, S.S.: Advanced compiler design and implementation. Morgan Kaufmann Publishers Inc., San Francisco (1997)

19. Oh, H.: Large Spurious Cycle in Global Static Analyses and Its Algorithmic Mitigation. In: Hu, Z. (ed.) APLAS 2009. LNCS, vol. 5904, pp. 14–29. Springer, Heidelberg (2009)
20. Oh, H., Brutschy, L., Yi, K.: Access Analysis-Based Tight Localization of Abstract Memories. In: Jhala, R., Schmidt, D. (eds.) VMCAI 2011. LNCS, vol. 6538, pp. 356–370. Springer, Heidelberg (2011)
21. Oh, H., Yi, K.: An algorithmic mitigation of large spurious interprocedural cycles in static analysis. Software: Practice and Experience 40(8), 585–603 (2010)
22. Rival, X.: Understanding the Origin of Alarms in ASTRÉE. In: Hankin, C., Siveroni, I. (eds.) SAS 2005. LNCS, vol. 3672, pp. 303–319. Springer, Heidelberg (2005)
23. Wei Le, M.L.S.: Path-based fault correlations. In: FSE (2010)

Automating Induction with an SMT Solver

K. Rustan M. Leino

Microsoft Research, Redmond, WA, USA
leino@microsoft.com

Abstract. Mechanical proof assistants have always had support for inductive proofs. Sometimes an alternative to proof assistants, satisfiability modulo theories (SMT) solvers bring the hope of a higher degree of automation. However, SMT solvers do not natively support induction, so inductive proofs require some encoding into the SMT solver's input.

This paper shows a surprisingly simple tactic—a rewriting strategy and a heuristic for when to apply it—that has shown to be useful in verifying simple inductive theorems, like those that can occur during program verification.

The paper describes the tactic and its implementation in a program verifier, and reports on the positive experience with using the tactic.

0 Introduction

Mathematical induction is an important element of just about any kind of formal proof. This paper concerns the use of induction in an automatic program verifier. More specifically, it is concerned with providing more automation for inductively proving some properties in the kind of program verifier that uses a satisfiability modulo theories (SMT) solver [10,22] as its reasoning engine.

Mechanical proof assistants have always provided support for inductive proofs, most famously starting with the Boyer-Moore prover whose powerful heuristics tried to determine which variables to use in induction schemes [5]. That work has been continued in proof assistants like PVS [23] and ACL2 [15]. Another technique for automatically trying to discover how to construct an inductive proof for a given property is *rippling* [6,14]. As is well known, it is frequently necessary to strengthen an induction hypothesis in order to make a proof go through, and techniques like rippling heuristically try to determine when it might be appropriate to strengthen or generalize a property to be proven. Whereas rippling is goal directed, the technique employed by Zeno [24] is more opportunistic in the way it proceeds.

Unsurprisingly, any system that reasons about infinitely many possible executions of a software program also makes use of induction, either explicitly or implicitly. For example, the KeY system [2] lets a user explicitly specify which induction scheme to apply when reasoning about the executions of a loop. Program verification (and theorem proving) in Coq [3] and VeriFun [25] also tend to make heavy use of induction. Other program verifiers, like Dafny [19], VCC [8], and VeriFast [12], implicitly rely on induction: the loop invariants used to reason about loop executions and the pre/-post specifications used to reason about recursive calls essentially play the role of an induction hypothesis.

V. Kuncak and A. Rybalchenko (Eds.): VMCAI 2012, LNCS 7148, pp. 315–331, 2012.

The implicit support of induction lets a user write programs whose correctness implies the validity of user-provided mathematical properties, essentially giving a manual way to write proofs using a program verifier [15,17,26,13]. In this paper, I go one step further, introducing a tactic that heuristically identifies programmer-supplied properties whose proof may benefit from induction, then automatically sets up the induction hypothesis, and finally passes the proof obligation to an SMT solver. I have implemented the technique in the Dafny program verifier [19][0] and have used it, for example, to automatically prove 45 of the first 47 problems in an evaluation corpus for automatic induction. The tactic is not nearly as powerful as what is used in provers like ACL2 or Zeno; indeed, it never strengthens or generalizes a property to be proved. Instead, the strong appeal of the present tactic lies in its simplicity and surprising effectiveness.

1 Background on Dafny

Before getting to the induction tactic, let me review two properties about program verifiers like Dafny. First, I will explain the verifier architecture, how to think about going from source-language semantics to SMT-solver input. Second, I will show how lemmas to be proved by induction arise in the context of a program verifier.

1.0 Verifier Architecture

A standard program-verifier architecture is to translate the source language of interest into an intermediate verification language (IVL) and then to pass the resulting IVL programs to a verification engine for the IVL [21,1,11]. In other words, the semantics of a given source-language program are encoded into an IVL program such that the correctness of the IVL program implies the correctness of the source program. The verification engine for the IVL attempts to establish the correctness of IVL programs by generating verification conditions that it passes to a reasoning engine, typically an SMT solver.

In this paper, the source language used is Dafny [19], the IVL is Boogie 2 [20], and the SMT solver is Z3 [9], but the tactic described is applicable to other program verifiers and reasoning engines as well. For the purpose of this paper, it is not necessary to understand the details of the Dafny-to-Boogie translation [18], and even less so the Boogie-to-Z3 translation [1,20]. It suffices to realize that the semantics of a given source-language program sometimes provides certain guarantees and sometimes dictates some proof obligations, and that the program verifier encodes these guarantees and proof obligations by translation into the IVL. Next, I will explain the form of this encoding.

A program verifier explicates source-language proof obligations by encoding them as *assert statements* in the IVL. Such proof obligations arise from the semantics of the executable constructs of the source language (for example, expressions used to index into an array must evaluate to a value within the bounds of the array) and from programmer-supplied specifications (for example, method postconditions). The program verifier also explicates source-language guarantees by encoding them as *assume statements* in the IVL.

[0] Dafny is available as open source and can also be used without installation in a web browser, see `research.microsoft.com/dafny`.

For example, the Dafny verifier translates the allocation statement `a := new int[E];` into the following Boogie code:

$$\textbf{assert}\ 0 \leqslant E;\quad \ldots\quad \textbf{assume}\ dtype(a) = array(type\_int());$$

where the assert statement encodes the proof obligation that the requested array size not be negative and the assume statement says that the dynamic type of a, after the assignment, is an array of integers (where $dtype$, $array$, and $type\_int$ are some functions defined elsewhere in the translation).

Semantically, $\textbf{assert}\ P;$ is equivalent to:

$$\textbf{assert}\ P;\ \textbf{assume}\ P; \tag{0}$$

(see [0]). Intuitively, this says that after proving P, one is entitled to assume it. This means that a proof obligation P arising in a source language can be translated into the intermediate verification language as the two statements (0). More generally, it is sound to translate a proof obligation P into:

$$\textbf{assert}\ Q;\ \textbf{assume}\ R; \tag{1}$$

where Q implies P and P implies R. This can be useful if, to the SMT solver, Q is easier to prove and R is easier to use.

1.1 Inductive Lemmas in a Program Verifier

On the way to proving the correctness of a program, it happens that one needs to state and prove lemmas about functions or data structures that are used by the program. When such a lemma requires an inductive proof, the induction tactic described in this paper can be useful.

Dafny is a programming language and a program verifier; it has no special constructs for stating and proving lemmas. Instead, a lemma can be stated as an inline assertion (via Dafny's `assert` statement) or as a call to a method whose postcondition is the statement of the lemma (*cf.* [13]). Such a method in Dafny is usually declared to be a *ghost* method; the Dafny verifier treats ghost methods and other ghost constructs like their non-ghost counterparts, but the Dafny compiler generates no code for ghost constructs [19].

For example, the Fibonacci function can be defined in Dafny as follows:

```
function Fib(n: nat): nat
{
  if n < 2 then n else Fib(n-2) + Fib(n-1)
}
```

A `function` in Dafny is a mathematical function and it denotes an expression (given in the body of the function). A `method`, on the other hand, denotes a behavior and is implemented by statements with possible control flow and mutations. To state a lemma about the `Fib` function, we introduce a (ghost) method with the desired lemma as the postcondition; for example:

```
ghost method FibLemma()
  ensures ∀ n: nat • Fib(n+1) + Fib(n+2) ≤ Fib(n+3);
{ }
```

Dafny will attempt to verify that the method terminates and that it terminates in a state where the postcondition holds. A successful verification thus implies that the property stated in the postcondition is a valid lemma. To use this lemma in some code, one simply invokes method `FibLemma`. Because the method is ghost, it is not included in the executable code, and thus the lemma has no effect on the run-time behavior of the program.

2 The Induction Tactic

The induction tactic builds on simple concepts working in concert. I will explain each concept in a separate subsection and then combine them to describe the tactic.

2.0 Induction Principle

The *Induction Principle* says that the formula

$$\forall n \bullet \; P(n) \tag{2}$$

where $P(n)$ is any expression that may have free occurrences of n, is equivalent to the formula

$$\forall n \bullet \; (\forall k \bullet \; k \prec n \implies P(k)) \implies P(n) \tag{3}$$

where $\prec$ is any well-founded order. The antecedent in (3) is known as the *induction hypothesis*. Thus, by the Induction Principle, to prove the validity of the formula (2), we may elect to proceed by proving the validity of the ostensibly weaker formula (3).

I feel compelled to make a remark, which for readers familiar with some mechanical proof assistants may clear up a point about what I refer to as induction. The fact that the induction hypothesis in (3) quantifies over all k smaller than n is known as *strong induction*. Many times, a weaker induction hypothesis suffices, namely the one that quantifies only over those k that are "one smaller" than n. For example, if n and k range over natural numbers, the weaker induction hypothesis can be stated as:

$$\forall k \bullet \; k = n - 1 \implies P(k)$$

Furthermore, by distinguishing those n that have a value "one smaller" and those n that do not, this condition is often formulated as:

$$n = 0 \;\;\vee\;\; (0 < n \wedge P(n-1))$$

Using this condition in place of the antecedent in (3) and simplifying, we get:

$$P(0) \;\;\wedge\;\; \forall n \bullet \; 0 < n \wedge P(n-1) \implies P(n)$$

or equivalently:

$$P(0) \quad \wedge \quad \forall n \bullet \ P(n) \implies P(n+1) \tag{4}$$

The two conjuncts in formula (4) are referred to as the *base case* and the *induction step*, which is how induction is used in some proof assistants and is probably how most of us learned about induction in our education. However, note that the formulation of the Induction Principle above (that is, (2) = (3)) does not necessitate bringing in the concept of a case distinction when defining induction. (This is somewhat analogous to the use of recursion in programming, where a conditional statement and a call statement are independent constructs that usefully come together in the body of a recursive procedure.)

2.1 Induction Translation

Here is why observation (1) in Sec. 1.0 is interesting for induction. If a proof obligation in a given source program takes the form (2), then the program verifier has the option to translate it into the IVL as:

$$\textbf{assert}\ (3);\ \textbf{assume}\ (2); \tag{5}$$

This *Induction Translation* has the effect that the SMT solver will be asked to establish the validity of (3), after which it is entitled to assume (2). Note that SMT solver does not need to know anything about induction. Instead, the (source-to-IVL translation of the) program verifier takes responsibility for the soundness of the translation into (5), and that soundness is justified by the Induction Principle.

2.2 Induction Heuristic

A program verifier has the option of translating proof obligation like (2) into the IVL statements (5), but when would that be a good idea? Always doing so can lead to bad performance, and always requiring the source-language programmer explicitly to say when to use the Induction Translation could be a nuisance. Better would be to use a good heuristic, possibly with a way to manually override the outcome of the heuristic.

A heuristic that is both simple and seems to work well, and which I will refer to as the *Induction Heuristic*, is to apply the Induction Translation if the bound variable n in (2) is used in $P(n)$ as part of an argument to a recursive function.

I tried and rejected a less discriminating heuristic, namely to apply the Induction Translation also if n is used in $P(n)$ as part of an index expression into an array or sequence. The Dafny test suite contains hundreds of methods and mentions more than 700 quantifiers, but most of the quantifiers can be proved without induction. I tried the less discriminating heuristic on the test suite. This resulted in out-of-memory failures for 8 of the method verifications and ten-minute timeouts for 2 others. Evidently, the additional induction hypotheses caused the SMT solver too much distraction.

The default heuristic used by Dafny is actually more discriminating than the Induction Heuristic, in two ways. First, n cannot be just any subexpression of an argument to a recursive function; the argument must *prominently* feature n. An expression prominently features n if the expression is n, or if the expression has the form $E + F$ or $E - F$ where E or F prominently features n. For example, in the postcondition of method `FibLemma` in Sec. 1.1, all three calls to `Fib` prominently feature `n` as an argument. Second, not all argument positions to recursive functions are considered; the formal parameter corresponding to the argument must contribute to the variant (which is used for proving termination) of the function. However, these two additional discriminating factors have not made any appreciable difference in the experiments I have run.

2.3 Well-Founded Orders in Dafny

The Induction Principle holds for any well-founded order $\prec$. Dafny fixes a well-founded order for each of its types and for lexicographic tuples. These are used in Dafny when reasoning about termination of loops and recursive calls [19]. The same ordering is used for $\prec$ in the Induction Translation.

The types most frequently used with induction are integers and inductive datatypes. For integers x and y, Dafny defines $x \prec y$ as:

$$x < y \quad \wedge \quad 0 \leqslant y$$

The lower bound 0 is somewhat arbitrary, and note that the order is not total when both x and y are negative; however, this simple order is easy for a programmer to remember and works well in practice.[1]

The ordering on inductive datatypes associates a *rank* with each datatype value and defines the rank of a constructed value to be strictly above the rank of each of its arguments. For example, given the definition:

```
datatype List = Nil | Cons(int, List);
```

Dafny defines $xs \prec Cons(x, xs)$ for any integer x and list xs.

2.4 Datatypes and Case Distinctions

The current version of Dafny does not use native SMT support for inductive datatypes. Instead, it encodes constructors and destructors of datatype values using suitably axiomatized functions. Every datatype value is generated by some constructor, but unrestricted use of this property can lead to expensive and unfruitful case distinctions in the SMT solver, so Dafny encodes this property only in certain places [19]. The property does tend to be useful when proving properties inductively, so Dafny makes the case distinction available to the SMT solver when applying the Induction Translation.

For example, suppose n in (2) is of the type `List` defined in Sec. 2.3. Then Dafny includes in the Induction Translation an additional antecedent:

$$n = Nil \quad \vee \quad \exists x, xs \bullet \ n = Cons(x, xs)$$

[1] For reasoning about termination of loops and recursive calls, the lower bound can be adjusted, because Dafny supports programmer-supplied variant expressions [19].

Actually, Dafny distributes these cases and produces one assert statement for each constructor, because this allows Dafny to give more precise error messages. So, the Induction Translation will produce the following 3 statements:

$$\begin{array}{l}\textbf{assert}\ \forall n \bullet\ (\forall k \bullet\ k \prec n \Longrightarrow P(k)) \wedge n = \mathit{Nil} \quad\Longrightarrow\quad P(n);\\ \textbf{assert}\ \forall n \bullet\ (\forall k \bullet\ k \prec n \Longrightarrow P(k)) \wedge (\exists x, \mathit{xs} \bullet\ n = \mathit{Cons}(x, \mathit{xs}))\\ \qquad\qquad \Longrightarrow\ P(n);\\ \textbf{assume}\ \forall n \bullet\ P(n);\end{array}$$

If the first assertion cannot be proved, Dafny reports that (2) might not hold for values constructed by `Nil`; if the second assertion cannot be proved, Dafny reports that (2) might not hold for values constructed by `Cons`.

2.5 Multiple Bound Variables

If a proof obligation has multiple bound variables, Dafny evaluates the Induction Heuristic for each one. If the Induction Heuristic applies to any of the bound variables, then Dafny applies the Induction Translation for all the bound variables to which the Induction Heuristic applies, combining these into a lexicographic tuple.

For example, consider a proof obligation:

$$\forall x, y, z \bullet\ Q(x, y, z)$$

and suppose the Induction Heuristic applies to x and z (that is, both x and z are prominently featured in $Q(x, y, z)$ as arguments to recursive functions). Applying the Induction Translation, Dafny thus produces:

$$\forall x, y, z \bullet\ (\forall k, m \bullet\ (k, m) \prec (x, z) \Longrightarrow Q(k, y, m)) \quad\Longrightarrow\quad Q(x, y, z)$$

where the definition of $(k, m) \prec (x, z)$ is the $\prec$ ordering on lexicographic pairs:

$$k \prec x \quad \vee \quad (k = x \wedge m \prec z)$$

Dafny only applies the Induction Translation to quantifiers that appear as positive top-level conjuncts of proof obligations. In particular, the Induction Translation is not applied to nested quantifiers. For example, if the proof obligation above had been formulated as:

$$\forall x, y \bullet\ \forall z \bullet\ Q(x, y, z)$$

then the Induction Translation would be:

$$\forall x, y \bullet\ (\forall k \bullet\ k \prec x \Longrightarrow \forall z \bullet\ Q(k, y, z)) \quad\Longrightarrow\quad \forall z \bullet\ Q(x, y, z)$$

2.6 Overriding the Induction Heuristic

As I report in Sec. 4, the Induction Heuristic seems to work well. However, there are times when one may wish to force or suppress the Induction Translation. Dafny has a general mechanism for hanging custom attributes in various places in the source code (akin to custom attributes in .NET and annotations in Java). One of those places is in quantifiers, just after the declaration of the bound variables. While use of such custom attributes is rare, it is sometimes a convenient feature to have.

Dafny supports an `:induction` attribute. Used with no arguments, this attribute says to apply the Induction Translation to all of the quantifier's bound variables. The `:induction` attribute can also be used by listing those bound variables to which the Induction Translation should apply. Finally, `:induction false` says not to apply the Induction Translation to the quantifier.

For example, consider the following method declaration:

```
ghost method AdjacentImpliesTransitive(s: seq<int>)
  requires ∀ i • 1 ≤ i < |s| ⟹ s[i-1] ≤ s[i];
  ensures ∀ i,j {:induction j} • 0 ≤ i < j < |s| ⟹ s[i] ≤ s[j];
{ }
```

The postcondition (keyword `ensures`) follows from the precondition (keyword `requires`), but proving that necessitates induction. Since this example does not involve any recursive functions, the Induction Heuristic does not apply. However, the custom attribute used in this example tells Dafny to apply the Induction Translation for bound variable `j`, which leads to a successful verification of the postcondition. Alternatively, using the attribute `{:induction i,j}` or simply `{:induction}` also leads to a successful proof. Note, however, that `{:induction i}` does not, since even proving the property for `i` being `0` requires induction on `j`.

3 Examples

In this section, I show four applications of the induction tactic in the program verifier: two are used to verify programs, one to verify a simple mathematical property, and one to verify properties of functions over inductive datatypes. I also show an application that exemplifies the operation of the SMT solver given the formula produced by the program verifier.

3.0 A Simple Program

The program in Fig. 0 shows a Dafny method. It takes an array `a` as an in-parameter and returns an integer `r` as an out-parameter. As specified by the postcondition, the method returns an index where the array is `0`, or returns `-1` if the array does not contain a `0`. As specified by the precondition, the array has non-negative elements and has the special property that an element `a[i]` is not much smaller than its preceding neighbor, `a[i-1]`. In particular, if `a[i]` is smaller than `a[i-1]`, then it is smaller only by `1`. This property allows the method implementation to do better than linear search, for if the array element at the current position `n` is non-zero, then the next possible zero occurs `a[n]` array elements later.

The correctness of the method implementation hinges on the fact that the update `n := n + a[n];` maintains the loop invariant, which in turn follows from the special property of the array. However, the special property needs to be applied repeatedly for the proof, which does not happen automatically. Instead, the programmer supplies

```
method FindZero(a: array<int>) returns (r: int)
  requires a ≠ null ∧ ∀ i • 0 ≤ i < a.Length ⟹ 0 ≤ a[i];
  requires ∀ i • 0 ≤ i-1 ∧ i < a.Length ⟹ a[i-1]-1 ≤ a[i];
  ensures 0 ≤ r ⟹ r < a.Length ∧ a[r] = 0;
  ensures r < 0 ⟹ ∀ i • 0 ≤ i < a.Length ⟹ a[i] ≠ 0;
{
  var n := 0;
  while (n < a.Length)
    invariant ∀ i • 0 ≤ i < n ∧ i < a.Length ⟹ a[i] ≠ 0;
  {
    if (a[n] = 0) { return n; }
    assert ∀ m {:induction} •
                  n ≤ m < n + a[n] ∧ m < a.Length ⟹ n+a[n]-m ≤ a[m];
    n := n + a[n];
  }
  return -1;
}
```

Fig. 0. A Dafny method that finds the index of a `0` in a given array `a`. Because the array has the special property that successive array elements do not decrease quickly (as stated by the second **`requires`** clause), the search is sub-linear (see the increase of `n`). The **`assert`** statement is proved by induction and then used to show the correctness of the program.

a lemma, here phrased as a Dafny **`assert`** statement. Since no recursive function is involved, the Induction Heuristic does not apply. Instead, the programmer uses the *`{:induction}`* attribute to indicate that the quantifier is to be proved using induction.

Feeding the program in Fig. 0 to the Dafny verifier proves the program (with no further user interaction) instantly (in 0.04 seconds on a single thread on a modern laptop with an Intel Core i7-M620 clocked at 2.67 GHz and running 64-bit Windows 7).

3.1 A Difficult Program

Floyd's "tortoise and hare" algorithm is a simple method for detecting whether a given linked-list node reaches a cycle or reaches **`null`** [16]. Its formal proof is not equally simple. One Dafny program for the algorithm, its specification (here shown slightly simplified)

```
method TortoiseAndHare() returns (reachesCycle: bool)
  ensures reachesCycle ⟺
    ∃ n • n ≠ null ∧ Reaches(n) ∧ n.next ≠ null ∧ n.next.Reaches(n);
```

and supporting definitions, and the lemmas needed for its verification is 233 (non white-space) lines long, of which 16 lines get compiled.[2] More than half of dozen of the quantified formulas given as lemmas require the Induction Translation to be verified. For example, one of them (slightly simplified) is:

[2] See the `FloydCycleDetect.dfy` program in the `Test/dafny2` folder of the `boogie.codeplex.com` source repository.

```
function Sum(n: nat): nat { if n = 0 then 0 else Sum(n-1) + n }
function CubeSum(n: nat): nat { if n = 0 then 0 else CubeSum(n-1) + n*n*n }
ghost method ArithmeticTheorem()
  ensures ∀ n: nat • CubeSum(n) = Sum(n) * Sum(n)  ∧  2*Sum(n) = n*(n+1);
{ }
```

Fig. 1. A Dafny encoding of the arithmetic theorem $\sum_{i=0}^{n} i^3 = (\sum_{i=0}^{n} i)^2$. Because of the induction tactic, the theorem is proved automatically.

```
assert ∀ j • 0 ≤ j ⟹ Nexxxt(x).Nexxxt(j) = Nexxxt(x + j);
```

where `Nexxxt(k)` returns the node obtained after `k` applications of the `.next` field. The program relies entirely on the Induction Heuristic and does not use any occurrence of the *{:induction}* attribute. The verification of the entire program takes just under 60 seconds.

3.2 Integers

Figure 1 states a familiar theorem about arithmetic. Functions `Sum` and `CubeSum` are defined recursively, and the theorem `CubeSum(n) = Sum(n) * Sum(n)` is stated as the postcondition of a method. Proving this arithmetic equality requires an additional fact about function `Sum`, which is also stated in the postcondition. Thus, the proof does what in mathematics is known as simultaneous induction.

The program in Fig. 1 is verified as shown (and with no further user interaction) in 0.09 seconds.

Remark: Alternatively, the closed-form property of `Sum` could have been given as a postcondition of function `Sum`:

```
function Sum(n: nat): nat
  ensures 2*Sum(n) = n*(n+1);
{ if n = 0 then 0 else Sum(n-1) + n }
```

The proof of this postcondition does not require the Induction Translation; the standard rules for postconditions and reasoning about (recursive) calls suffice.

3.3 Inductive Datatypes

Inductive datatypes are common in functional languages and in interactive proof assistants like Isabelle/HOL, Coq, PVS, and ACL2, which are based around functional languages. When proving properties of functions over such datatypes, it is natural to use induction. Dafny also supports inductive datatypes as well as user-defined recursive functions. Figure 2 defines two simple datatypes and three functions, the structure of whose definitions is representative of functions on inductive datatypes. Method `P19` states a theorem about these functions. The theorem is proved automatically (in 0.025 seconds), thanks to the induction tactic.

```
datatype Nat = Zero | Suc(Nat);
datatype List = Nil | Cons(Nat, List);
function minus(x: Nat, y: Nat): Nat {
  match x
  case Zero ⇒ Zero
  case Suc(a) ⇒ match y
    case Zero ⇒ x
    case Suc(b) ⇒ minus(a, b)
}
function len(xs: List): Nat {
  match xs  case Nil ⇒ Zero  case Cons(y, ys) ⇒ Suc(len(ys))
}
function drop(n: Nat, xs: List): List {
  match n
  case Zero ⇒ xs
  case Suc(m) ⇒ match xs
    case Nil ⇒ Nil
    case Cons(x, tail) ⇒ drop(m, tail)
}
ghost method P19()
  ensures ∀ n, xs • len(drop(n, xs)) = minus(len(xs), n);
{ }
```

Fig. 2. Two user-defined inductive datatypes in Dafny along with three functions defined on those datatypes. The postcondition of the method gives a theorem, which is proved automatically by Dafny's induction tactic.

3.4 Operation of the SMT Solver

As I have shown, the induction tactic is encoded in the translation from Dafny into Boogie, that is, the translation from the source language to the intermediate verification language. After that, Boogie and Z3 operate as usual. In other words, the induction tactic does not require any change to Boogie or Z3. Let us take a look at an example end to end, that is, from Dafny to Boogie to Z3 and let us also consider the operation of Z3 on its given verification condition.

Suppose we start with the following recursive function in Dafny:

```
function Fac(n: int): int { if n ≤ 1 then 1 else Fac(n-1) * n }
```

Dafny's translation of this function sets up proof obligations that will check that the function is well defined. Mimicking the Dafny function definition, the translation also includes the following Boogie declarations:

$$\begin{array}{l}\textbf{function}\ \mathit{Fac}(n\colon \textbf{int}) : \textbf{int};\\ \textbf{axiom}\ (\forall n\colon \textbf{int} \bullet\ \{\mathit{Fac}(n)\}\\ \qquad\qquad \mathit{Fac}(n) = (\textbf{if}\ n \leqslant 1\ \textbf{then}\ 1\ \textbf{else}\ \mathit{Fac}(n-1) * n));\end{array}$$

where the expression in curly braces specifies the *matching trigger* for the universal quantifier. The matching trigger tells the SMT solver how to select instantiations for the quantifier [10]. This definition of *Fac* in Boogie is a bit of a simplification, because Dafny also takes some measures that will reduce the chances of running into matching loops, where the SMT solver would keep instantiating universal quantifiers forever.

Suppose further that the proof obligation is to show that `Fac` only returns positive integers, as expressed in Dafny by the following lemma:

```
ghost method FacPos() ensures ∀ n • 1 ≤ Fac(n);  { }
```

The Dafny verifier detects in this postcondition proof obligation that the bound variable `n` in passed as an argument to a recursive function. So the Induction Heuristic applies and Dafny applies the Induction Translation, obtaining the following Boogie statements (in the Boogie procedure corresponding to the Dafny method `FacPos`):

$$\begin{array}{l}\textbf{assert}\ (\forall n{:}\,\textbf{int} \bullet\ (\forall k{:}\,\textbf{int} \bullet\ 0 \leqslant k \wedge k < n \Longrightarrow 1 \leqslant \mathit{Fac}(k)) \\ \qquad\qquad\qquad\qquad \Longrightarrow 1 \leqslant \mathit{Fac}(n)); \\ \textbf{assume}\ (\forall n{:}\,\textbf{int} \bullet\ 1 \leqslant \mathit{Fac}(n));\end{array}$$

Boogie then translates this into Z3 input, which essentially amounts to:

$$\begin{array}{l}(\forall n{:}\,\textbf{int} \bullet\ \{\mathit{Fac}(n)\}\ \mathit{Fac}(n) = (\textbf{if}\ n \leqslant 1\ \textbf{then}\ 1\ \textbf{else}\ \mathit{Fac}(n-1) * n)) \\ \Longrightarrow \\ (\forall n{:}\,\textbf{int} \bullet\ (\forall k{:}\,\textbf{int} \bullet\ 0 \leqslant k \wedge k < n \Longrightarrow 1 \leqslant \mathit{Fac}(k)) \Longrightarrow 1 \leqslant \mathit{Fac}(n))\end{array}$$

When Z3 tries to prove that this formula is valid, it negates it and starts looking for a satisfying assignment to the negation. The negation produces the following two conjuncts:

$$\begin{array}{l}(\forall n{:}\,\textbf{int} \bullet\ \{\mathit{Fac}(n)\}\ \mathit{Fac}(n) = (\textbf{if}\ n \leqslant 1\ \textbf{then}\ 1\ \textbf{else}\ \mathit{Fac}(n-1) * n)) \\ (\exists n{:}\,\textbf{int} \bullet\ (\forall k{:}\,\textbf{int} \bullet\ 0 \leqslant k \wedge k < n \Longrightarrow 1 \leqslant \mathit{Fac}(k)) \wedge \neg(1 \leqslant \mathit{Fac}(n)))\end{array}$$

Z3 then Skolemizes the existential, calling it, say, *Sk*. Since no matching trigger was indicated for the quantifier over k in the Z3 input, Z3 will at this time select a matching trigger for it; here, I show that selected trigger explicitly:

$$\begin{array}{l}(\forall n{:}\,\textbf{int} \bullet\ \{\mathit{Fac}(n)\}\ \mathit{Fac}(n) = (\textbf{if}\ n \leqslant 1\ \textbf{then}\ 1\ \textbf{else}\ \mathit{Fac}(n-1) * n)) \\ (\forall k{:}\,\textbf{int} \bullet\ \{\mathit{Fac}(k)\}\ 0 \leqslant k \wedge k < \mathit{Sk} \Longrightarrow 1 \leqslant \mathit{Fac}(k)) \\ \mathit{Fac}(\mathit{Sk}) < 1\end{array} \qquad (6)$$

At this time, the presence of the term $\mathit{Fac}(\mathit{Sk})$ will cause both quantifiers to be instantiated, with $n := k$ and $k := \mathit{Sk}$, yielding:

$$\begin{array}{l}\text{conjuncts (6)} \\ \mathit{Fac}(\mathit{Sk}) = (\textbf{if}\ \mathit{Sk} \leqslant 1\ \textbf{then}\ 1\ \textbf{else}\ \mathit{Fac}(\mathit{Sk}-1) * \mathit{Sk}) \\ 0 \leqslant \mathit{Sk} \wedge \mathit{Sk} < \mathit{Sk} \Longrightarrow 1 \leqslant \mathit{Fac}(\mathit{Sk})\end{array}$$

The last of these formulas will evaporate, since Z3 knows that $\mathit{Sk} < \mathit{Sk}$ is unsatisfiable. Z3 will now do a case distinction on the **if** expression.

For the **then** case, it gets:

$$\begin{array}{l}\text{conjuncts (6)} \\ \mathit{Sk} \leqslant 1 \\ \mathit{Fac}(\mathit{Sk}) = 1\end{array}$$

which (from $Fac(Sk) < 1$ and $Fac(Sk) = 1$) it will realize is unsatisfiable.

For the **else** case:

$$\begin{array}{l} \text{conjuncts (6)} \\ 1 < Sk \\ Fac(Sk) = Fac(Sk - 1) * Sk \end{array}$$

There is now a new term, $Fac(Sk - 1)$, which matches the given triggers, so Z3 will produce two more instantiations, namely with $n := Sk - 1$ and $k := Sk - 1$:

$$\begin{array}{l} \text{conjuncts (6)} \\ 1 < Sk \\ Fac(Sk) = Fac(Sk - 1) * Sk \\ Fac(Sk - 1) = (\textbf{if } Sk - 1 \leqslant 1 \textbf{ then } 1 \textbf{ else } Fac(Sk - 1 - 1) * (Sk - 1)) \\ 0 \leqslant Sk - 1 \wedge Sk - 1 < Sk \Longrightarrow 1 \leqslant Fac(Sk - 1) \end{array}$$

By $1 < Sk$, the antecedent $0 \leqslant Sk - 1 \wedge Sk - 1 < Sk$ simplifies to $true$, and thus the consequent $1 \leqslant Fac(Sk - 1)$ emerges as a fact. Z3 now realizes that the conjuncts:

$$\begin{array}{l} Fac(Sk) < 1 \\ 1 < Sk \\ Fac(Sk) = Fac(Sk - 1) * Sk \\ 1 \leqslant Fac(Sk - 1) \end{array}$$

are unsatisfiable, since the product of two positive numbers is not non-positive.

And that completes the proof.

4 Evaluation on a Test Suite for Induction

Theorem `P19` in Fig. 2 is part of a test suite for automatic induction, collected and used by the authors of the IsaPlanner system to evaluate their technique [14]. The suite contains 87 problems, of which IsaPlanner (which uses rippling [6] and an analysis of case statements) automatically solves the first 47. Beyond problem 47, the problems require various forms of abstraction, strengthenings, and new-lemma discovery. According to a paper on Zeno [24], ACL2s [7] automatically proves 74 of the 87 problems (with manually supplied type information) and the Zeno tool automatically proves 82 of them. The report on Zeno provides a detailed comparison of these tools on the test suite and some other problems [24].

Of the 47 problems that IsaPlanner can prove, Dafny can prove 45. For all the problems, the Induction Heuristic applies, so Dafny automatically uses the Induction Translation. For an induction tactic that is as simple as the one in Dafny, proving 45 of the 47 problems that IsaPlanner can solve seems surprisingly good.

Like the other tools, most of the proofs are instantaneous. Dafny spends 0.21 seconds on problem 39, 0.17 seconds on problem 45, and less than 0.10 seconds for each of the others.

Dafny cannot automatically prove problem 47 (and neither can ACL2s). However, problem 47 is verified using problem 23 as a lemma:

```
ghost method P47() ensures ∀ a • height(mirror(a)) = height(a); {
  P23(); // invoke the statement of problem 23 as a lemma
}
```

(I am unsure whether each problem in the test suite is allowed to use the preceding problems as lemmas. If so, Dafny also proves this one. Dafny proves each of the other 45 problems independently of each other.)

The other problem of the 47 that Dafny cannot automatically prove is problem 20. It requires the use of the preceding problem 15 as a lemma, and also requires an additional case distinction, which needs to be supplied manually:

```
ghost method P20()
  ensures ∀ xs • len(sort(xs)) = len(xs);
{
  P15(); // invoke the statement of problem 15 as a lemma
  // and manually introduce a case distinction:
  assert ∀ ys • sort(ys) = Nil ∨ ∃ z,zs • sort(ys) = Cons(z, zs);
}
```

The verification of this method requires 0.39 seconds.

5 Induction for Ghost Methods

The lemma expressed by the postcondition of method `P19` in Fig. 2 says something about all `n` and `xs`. Alternatively, the following method:

```
ghost method P19'(n: Nat, xs: List)
  ensures len(drop(n, xs)) = minus(len(xs), n);
{ }
```

states the same property, but just for the particular (but arbitrary) parameters `n` and `xs`. By universal generalization, the two methods express the same thing. Therefore, if the program verifier can prove `P19` automatically, we would expect it also to be able to prove `P19'` automatically.

Dafny's translation of the method makes this possible: at the beginning of the body of `P19'`, it effectively inserts recursive calls to `P19'` for all values of the parameters that satisfy the method's precondition (here, just **`true`**) and are smaller than the given `n,xs`. This *induction translation for methods* is analogous to the Induction Translation for quantifiers, and the heuristic for when to apply this method translation is also analogous to the Induction Heuristic for quantifiers. Two differences are noteworthy. One is that the "smaller" ordering on parameter values is determined by the method's (implicit or explicit) variant expression (see [19]), as required for the recursive calls to terminate. The other difference is that instead of inserting an induction-hypothesis antecedent, the induction translation for methods inserts code. Inserting that many calls could severely degrade the performance of a program, but Dafny performs this translation only for result-less effect-free ghost methods, so there is no impact on the program's run-time performance.

```
ghost method Lemma_RevConcat(xs: List, ys: List)
  ensures reverse(concat(xs, ys)) = concat(reverse(ys), reverse(xs));
{
  match (xs) {
    case Nil ⇒  assert ∀ ws • concat(ws, Nil) = ws;
    case Cons(t, rest) ⇒
      assert ∀ a,b,c • concat(a, concat(b, c)) = concat(concat(a, b), c);
} }
```

Fig. 3. A lemma about the list reversal and concatenation operations (whose standard recursive definitions are elided from the figure). Dafny automatically verifies the two assert statements and the postcondition, which altogether require 3 appeals to induction.

Thanks to the induction translation for methods, `P19'` verifies as given above (in 0.01 seconds). A more interesting example, which illustrates the induction translation for both quantifiers and methods, is shown in Fig. 3. First, the proof of the postcondition requires the properties that `Nil` is a right unit of `concat` (first **`assert`**) and that `concat` is associative (second **`assert`**), both of which are handled by the Induction Translation. Second, the proof of the postcondition requires induction on `xs` (in particular, it requires knowing the postcondition for `rest,ys` in the `Cons` case), which is handled by the induction translation for methods. Method `Lemma_RevConcat` is verified as given in the figure in 0.10 seconds.

6 Conclusion

In conclusion, the simple and straightforward (some may say brute force) approach of inserting induction-hypothesis assumptions at heuristically chosen points in the verification conditions passed to the SMT solver seems to be a win. Without unduly cluttering up the source program, it automatically sets up the induction for the SMT solver, and the SMT solver seems to do well at discharging the resulting proof obligations. The soundness of the approach is justified by a simple appeal to the Induction Principle.

The tactic performs on par with one serious participant in the quest for automatic induction, and yet is far simpler. The tactic introduces SMT solvers as a powerful workhorse in the arena of induction solvers.

I have described the induction tactic as used in a program verifier. However, the same tactic could be implemented in other settings, for example in a full-fledged proof assistant, perhaps as part of Isabelle's "sledgehammer" tactic [4].

Approaches to automatic induction are often accompanied by techniques for lemma discovery. It would be interesting to investigate how they could be incorporated in the context of an SMT solver or a program verifier like Dafny.

Acknowledgments. I am grateful to Will Sonnex, Sophia Drossopoulou, and Susan Eisenbach for their inspiring work on Zeno and for their encouraging comments. Thanks also to Bart Jacobs and Jan Smans who, during a recent visit of mine to Leuven, joined in a stint to learn more about automatic induction by rolling up their sleeves and coding up a little prototype solver. That effort led to me to wanting better support for induction in Dafny, which in turn led to the work presented in this paper. I appreciate the valuable comments by Jean-Christophe Filliâtre and the referees on an earlier version of this paper. Finally, I am indebted to Michał Moskal for serving as a sounding board for the ideas herein.

References

0. Back, R.-J., von Wright, J.: Refinement Calculus: A Systematic Introduction. Graduate Texts in Computer Science. Springer, Heidelberg (1998)
1. Barnett, M., Chang, B.-Y.E., DeLine, R., Jacobs, B., Leino, K.R.M.: Boogie: A Modular Reusable Verifier for Object-Oriented Programs. In: de Boer, F.S., Bonsangue, M.M., Graf, S., de Roever, W.-P. (eds.) FMCO 2005. LNCS, vol. 4111, pp. 364–387. Springer, Heidelberg (2006)
2. Beckert, B., Hähnle, R., Schmitt, P.H. (eds.): Verification of Object-Oriented Software. LNCS (LNAI), vol. 4334. Springer, Heidelberg (2007)
3. Bertot, Y., Castéran, P.: Interactive Theorem Proving and Program Development, Coq'Art: The Calculus of Inductive Constructions. Texts in Theoretical Computer Science. An EATCS Series. Springer, Heidelberg (2004)
4. Böhme, S., Nipkow, T.: Sledgehammer: Judgement day. In: Giesl, J., Hähnle, R. (eds.) IJCAR 2010. LNCS, vol. 6173, pp. 107–121. Springer, Heidelberg (2010)
5. Boyer, R.S., Moore, J.S.: A Computational Logic. ACM Monograph Series. Academic Press (1979)
6. Bundy, A., Basin, D., Hutter, D., Ireland, A.: Rippling: Meta-level Guidance for Mathematical Reasoning. Cambridge Tracts in Theoretical Computer Science, vol. 56. Cambridge University Press (2005)
7. Chamarthi, H.R., Dillinger, P.C., Manolios, P., Vroon, D.: The ACL2 Sedan Theorem Proving System. In: Abdulla, P.A., Leino, K.R.M. (eds.) TACAS 2011. LNCS, vol. 6605, pp. 291–295. Springer, Heidelberg (2011)
8. Cohen, E., Dahlweid, M., Hillebrand, M.A., Leinenbach, D., Moskal, M., Santen, T., Schulte, W., Tobies, S.: VCC: A Practical System for Verifying Concurrent C. In: Berghofer, S., Nipkow, T., Urban, C., Wenzel, M. (eds.) TPHOLs 2009. LNCS, vol. 5674, pp. 23–42. Springer, Heidelberg (2009)
9. de Moura, L., Bjørner, N.: Z3: An Efficient SMT Solver. In: Ramakrishnan, C.R., Rehof, J. (eds.) TACAS 2008. LNCS, vol. 4963, pp. 337–340. Springer, Heidelberg (2008)
10. Detlefs, D., Nelson, G., Saxe, J.B.: Simplify: a theorem prover for program checking. Journal of the ACM 52(3), 365–473 (2005)
11. Filliâtre, J.-C., Marché, C.: The Why/Krakatoa/Caduceus Platform for Deductive Program Verification. In: Damm, W., Hermanns, H. (eds.) CAV 2007. LNCS, vol. 4590, pp. 173–177. Springer, Heidelberg (2007)
12. Jacobs, B., Smans, J., Philippaerts, P., Vogels, F., Penninckx, W., Piessens, F.: VeriFast: A Powerful, Sound, Predictable, Fast Verifier for C and Java. In: Bobaru, M., Havelund, K., Holzmann, G.J., Joshi, R. (eds.) NFM 2011. LNCS, vol. 6617, pp. 41–55. Springer, Heidelberg (2011)
13. Jacobs, B., Smans, J., Piessens, F.: VeriFast: Imperative programs as proofs. In: VSTTE Workshop on Tools & Experiments (2010)
14. Johansson, M., Dixon, L., Bundy, A.: Case-Analysis for Rippling and Inductive Proof. In: Kaufmann, M., Paulson, L.C. (eds.) ITP 2010. LNCS, vol. 6172, pp. 291–306. Springer, Heidelberg (2010)

15. Kaufmann, M., Manolios, P., Moore, J.S.: Computer-Aided Reasoning: An Approach. Kluwer Academic Publishers (2000)
16. Knuth, D.E.: The Art of Computer Programming. Seminumerical Algorithms, vol. II. Addison-Wesley (1969)
17. Leino, K.R.M.: This is Boogie 2. Technical report, Microsoft Research (2008)
18. Leino, K.R.M.: Specification and verification of object-oriented software. In: Engineering Methods and Tools for Software Safety and Security. NATO Science for Peace and Security Series D: Information and Communication Security, vol. 22, pp. 231–266. IOS Press (2009); Summer School Marktoberdorf 2008 lecture notes
19. Leino, K.R.M.: Dafny: An Automatic Program Verifier for Functional Correctness. In: Clarke, E.M., Voronkov, A. (eds.) LPAR-16 2010. LNCS, vol. 6355, pp. 348–370. Springer, Heidelberg (2010)
20. Leino, K.R.M., Rümmer, P.: A Polymorphic Intermediate Verification Language: Design and Logical Encoding. In: Esparza, J., Majumdar, R. (eds.) TACAS 2010. LNCS, vol. 6015, pp. 312–327. Springer, Heidelberg (2010)
21. Leino, K.R.M., Saxe, J.B., Stata, R.: Checking Java programs via guarded commands. In: Formal Techniques for Java Programs, Technical Report 251. Fernuniversität Hagen (1999); Also available as Technical Note 1999-002, Compaq Systems Research Center
22. Nieuwenhuis, R., Oliveras, A., Tinelli, C.: Solving SAT and SAT modulo theories: From an abstract Davis-Putnam-Logemann-Loveland procedure to DPLL(T). Journal of the ACM 53(6), 937–977 (2006)
23. Owre, S., Rushby, J.M., Shankar, N.: PVS: A Prototype Verification System. In: Kapur, D. (ed.) CADE-11 1992. LNCS (LNAI), vol. 607, pp. 748–752. Springer, Heidelberg (1992)
24. Sonnex, W., Drossopoulou, S., Eisenbach, S.: Zeno: A tool for the automatic verification of algebraic properties of functional programs. Technical report, Imperial College London (2011), http://pubs.doc.ic.ac.uk/zeno/
25. Walther, C., Schweitzer, S.: About VeriFun. In: Baader, F. (ed.) CADE-19 2003. LNCS (LNAI), vol. 2741, pp. 322–327. Springer, Heidelberg (2003)
26. Zee, K., Kuncak, V., Rinard, M.: Full functional verification of linked data structures. In: PLDI 2008, pp. 349–361. ACM (2008)

Modeling Asynchronous Message Passing for C Programs

Everett Morse, Nick Vrvilo, Eric Mercer, and Jay McCarthy

Brigham Young University, Provo UT 84601, USA
{eamorse,nick.vrvilo}@byu.net,
{egm,jay}@cs.byu.edu
http://vv.cs.byu.edu

Abstract. This paper presents a formal modeling paradigm that is callable from C, the dominant language for embedded systems programming, for message passing APIs that provides reasonable assurance that the model correctly captures intended behavior. The model is a suitable reference solution for the API, and it supports putative what-if queries over API scenarios for behavior exploration, reproducibility for test and debug, full exhaustive search, and other advanced model checking analysis methods for C programs that use the API. This paper illustrates the modeling paradigm on the MCAPI interface, a growing industry standard message passing library, showing how the model exposes errors hidden by the C reference solution provided by the Multicore Association.

Keywords: Model Checking, Concurrency, Test, Debug, Validation.

1 Introduction

Asynchronous message passing for C is important in writing applications for embedded heterogeneous multicore systems. The Multicore Association (MCA), an industry consortium promoting multicore technology, is working to standardize message passing into a single API, MCAPI, for bare metal implementation and portability across platforms [26]. The MCAPI specification is a 169 page document in English. The inherent vagueness of such a description is valuable because implementation details are not micro-managed by API designers. In other words, high-level properties of the API such as "atomic", "blocking", or "non-overtaking" are specified without detailed explanation of internal API state nor how they should be provided. Correctness in implementing and using such an API, however, is difficult to reason about manually.

It is not unusual to provide an initial API implementation (production or otherwise) with a natural language description of the interface and MCAPI is no different, providing a C implementation of the interface. Unfortunately, there are two issues with it: i) it is implemented in a production language that is semantically distant from the natural language description so it is not clear which behaviors of the description it implements nor if it is correct; and ii) the reference is non-deterministic due to concurrency in the reference itself making test and

V. Kuncak and A. Rybalchenko (Eds.): VMCAI 2012, LNCS 7148, pp. 332–347, 2012.

debug activities difficult. A reference implementation needs to be semantically near the natural language description, while still being formal, and it needs to be deterministic for test, debug, and exploration. Programmers must have have a way to directly control API internals to expose or reproduce errors.

There are several formal modeling languages with mathematically defined operational semantics. A few languages such as TLA also provide a general runtime implementation of the operational semantics [14]; though most only provide tools to verify properties of models expressed in the formal language [11,17,13,22]. Regardless, the implementation of the operational semantics for these general languages is in a low-level language such as C introducing a significant gap between the mathematical expression of the semantics and the actual rendered implementation that is difficult to reason about. Additionally, for those that do implement a runtime for the formal language, there is no obvious way to connect that runtime to C programs written against the API. As such, these formal models are not suitable reference implementations for test and debug.

This paper presents a modeling language, 4M, for message passing APIs defined by natural language descriptions. The modeling language is sufficiently abstract to provide a reasonable assurance that the model correctly captures the intent of the natural language description. Furthermore, since 4M formally defines operational semantics, standard model checking or theorem proving techniques can be applied to prove the model implements the API specification (assuming such a specification exists). Novel to the 4M modeling language is a deterministic runtime, callable from C, derived from its operational semantics that is suitable for test, debug, scenario exploration, model checking, or other verification techniques. We demonstrate the methodology through a case study on the MCAPI communication library. The contributions of this work are

- a modeling language, 4M, implemented as a term rewriting system that is suited to natural language descriptions;
- a novel architecture to directly connect the C runtime to the 4M runtime to use the model as an instance of the API that is explorable, testable, and capable of model checking;
- an implementation of the rewriting system in Racket which a programming language based on PLT Scheme; and
- an MCAPI 4M model with running time results to measure overhead and bugs discovered from several C programs written against the MCAPI.

The result is that when an API is formally modeled in 4M, it is possible to use that model to explore system-wide program behavior that existing models and implementations cannot reason about.

Fig. 1 illustrates the methodology. 4M intuitively expresses the intent of the natural language API description (Fig. 1(a)). The core calculus describing the operational semantics of 4M is directly implemented by PLT Redex (Fig. 1(b)).[1] Programs using the API are developed in the C language as intended by the

[1] PLT Redex is a tool for creating and debugging language semantics defined as term rewriting systems, and it is part of the Racket runtime [7,8].

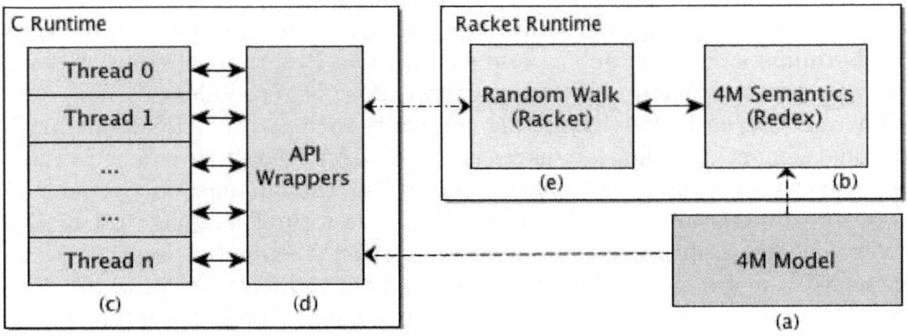

Fig. 1. Architecture for an API model callable from a native runtime

API (Fig. 1(c)). Such a program calls C function stubs that define the API interface and communicate with the runtime implementation of the 4M semantics through a pipe (Fig. 1(d)). Program execution proceeds in a normal fashion. As each thread enters the API, the corresponding thread is blocked. When all of the threads are blocked in the API, the API then communicates with a search strategy to choose a next state, and returns to the C runtime. In the case study on MCAPI presented in this paper, the search strategy is a random walk or an exhaustive search. The user can make both of these deterministic for debug or replay by setting the random seed to a known value (Fig. 1(e)).[2]

The following sections describe this process and our contributions in detail: Sec. 2 informally presents 4M on a toy message passing library;[3] Sec. 3 presents the novel client-server architecture that bridges the C runtime to the 4M core runtime; Sec. 4 presents our study on MCAPI; Sec. 5 addresses specific related work to this research; And Sec. 6 concludes and presents future work.

2 Modeling with 4M

Fig. 2(a) is the English description of a connectionless message passing API for multi-threaded applications. The specification defines four API functions to create mailboxes, get mailboxes, and then send and receive messages between mailboxes. The structure of the natural language specification defines transitions with their input, effects, and error conditions, which are helpful properties in understanding individual API behavior in isolation.

It is a challenge to explain intended behavior in simple scenarios consisting of a handful of calls when dealing with APIs for concurrent programs. Such scenarios are often created by adopters or implementers of the API to reason about the expected API behavior relative to its documentation. Most often these

[2] The random seed is provided as output from the tool and can be specified as part of the run configuration for a test.

[3] More details on the 4M language with its core operational semantics and programming framework are in [1].

```
mbox_t mbox(int id, status_t *s)
```
Description: Creates a mailbox for id, returns its reference, and sets *s to 1. If id already exists, *s is set to -1 and the return has no meaning.

```
mbox_t get_mbox(int id, status_t *s)
```
Description: Returns the reference for mailbox id and sets *s to 1. The call blocks if the mailbox has yet to be created.

```
void send(mbox_t frm, msg_t *msg, mbox_t to)
```
Description: Sends the message msg from the mailbox frm to the mailbox to. It is a blocking function and returns once the buffer msg can be reused by the application.

```
void recv(mbox_t to, msg_t *msg)
```
Description: Receives a message into msg from the mailbox to. It is a blocking function and returns once a message is available and the received data filled in msg. Messages from a common mailbox are non-overtaking.

(a)

Thread 0	Thread 1	Thread 2
to0 = mbox(0,&s)	to1 = mbox(1,&s)	from2 = mbox(2,&s)
	to0 = get_mbox(0, &s)	to0 = get_mbox(0, &s)
	from1 = mbox(3, &s)	to1 = get_mbox(1, &s)
recv(to0,&a)	recv(to1,&c)	send(from2,"Y",to0)
recv(to0,&b)	send(from1,"X",to0)	send(from2,"Z",to1)

(b)

Fig. 2. A simple message passing API. (a) The natural language description of the API. (b) A scenario written over the API.

scenarios assist in understanding the API behavior and are used to convey that understanding to the broader community. Consider the scenario in Fig. 2(b) that includes three threads using the blocking send (send) and receive (recv) calls from the API to communicate with each other. The declarations of the local variables (e.g., *to0*) are omitted for space. Picking up just after the mailboxes are defined, thread 0 receives two messages from the mailbox *to0* in variables a and b; thread 1 receives one message from the mailbox *to1* in variable c and then sends the message "X" to the mailbox *to0*; and finally, thread 2 sends the messages "Y" and "Z" to the mailboxes *to0* and *to1* respectively. After the scenario, we may ask: *"Which messages may be in which variables?"*

Intuitively, variable a should contain "Y" and variable b should contain "X" since thread 2 must first send message "Y" to mailbox *to0* before it can send message "Z" to mailbox *to1*; consequently, thread 1 is then able to send message "X" to mailbox *to0*. Such intuition is a correct program execution, but it is not the only execution, since the specification allows an alternative scenario where message "Y" is delayed in transit and arrives at mailbox *to0* after message "X".

The natural language description in Fig. 2(a) states that the send operation *"returns once the buffer* `msg` *can be reused by the application."* As such, the return of the send only implies a copy-out of the message buffer and not a delivery to the intended mailbox; thus, an additional program execution places the message "X" in variable a and the message "Y" in variable b.

Nuances like this are discovered in the process of concretizing internal API details, leading the modeler to engage in an iterative process with API designers which brings value to both by clarifying the semantics of the API. The specification in Fig. 2(a) is a simplified subset of a real communications API from the MCA (MCAPI). Conversations with the MCAPI designers confirmed the intended behavior of the API to include both program executions of the scenario. To date, there have been three published verification and analysis tools purpose-built for MCAPI and all of them omit the less intuitive program execution [23,6,5]. Naturally, our model does not omit it.

2.1 Formal Model of the API

There are several languages one might consider in modeling an API (see Sec. 5). Recent attempts to model MPI in the formal logic of TLA have shown the logic to be too low-level for practical application [14,20]. Alternatively, when considering a direct implementation such as one in C, not only is the gap between the natural language description and C extremely difficult to bridge, for example, the MCAPI reference solution includes 11776 lines of code to consider, it is not easy to test in the presence of concurrency because a user cannot readily control execution schedules. Moreover, C is unusually susceptible to bugs as evidenced by our experience with the MCAPI reference implementation which non-deterministically deadlocks.

We propose 4M, which matches the natural language description, as opposed to most existing modeling languages that do not. Furthermore, the intent of 4M is not to embed verification assertions such as guaranteed message delivery into the model. Rather, those types of correctness properties should be expressed in an appropriate logic and used to verify the correctness of the model. The goal is to capture the natural language description in an operational model. While 4M is yet another modeling language, it is domain specific, rather than general purpose, making it more amenable to the task at hand.

4M is a formal modeling language designed to keep the best things from the natural written style and remove the worst. To be specific, 4M keeps the structure of the natural language specification that defines transitions with their input, effects, and error conditions, but it replaces the statements such as *"message non-overtaking"* with effects described in first-order logic over a predefined and explicitly listed vocabulary of API state. Furthermore, all internal processing implied by statements such as "*it returns once the buffer can be reused by another application*" is made explicit by defining daemon transitions that operate on internal API state that are concurrently enabled with pending API transitions.

The 4M description for our toy API is given in Fig. 3. This model is the input in Fig. 1(a) of our proposed solution. The vocabulary for the API state is defined in lines 1–4 comprising mailboxes to track defined end points, modeled as a set (indicated by the braces {}), and queues, initialized with the value 0, to track outstanding message sends in the form of a list of tuples. The API interface is defined as a series of transitions given in lines 5–42 with always enabled daemon transitions in lines 43–53 to manage internal state.

Consider the mbox transition defined on lines 5–18. It takes three input parameters: a mailbox identifier id and references to result (resultAddr) and return status (statusAddr) which are used to communicate with the caller. The transition itself is divided into two sections: rules (lines 7–13) and errors (lines 14–17). Each section contains a set of guarded transitions.

The 4M language has a first order treatment of errors in any given transition. The language is designed for natural language description that presents a transition's normal behavior followed by a set of possible errors. An error or rule is enabled when its guard is true. The semantics of 4M block a transition until a guard becomes true (rule or error), and give preference to error rules. Any enabled error may be selected, and its corresponding transition is taken. In the mbox transition, the guard on the error in line 15 uses existential quantification (\E) over the set mailboxes to determine if the request duplicates an existing mailbox. The dot notation in box.0 of the guard implies that mailboxes is a set of tuples, and the notation is comparing the first member of each tuple to id. The effect of the error (indicated by the text following the ==> on line 16) is to set the memory referenced by statusAddr in the next state to the value -1. 4M does not support unbounded non-determinism so integers range over a bounded set using modular arithmetic. The '@' symbol is the dereference and the apostrophe indicates the next value. Evaluation of guards and application of the effect is one atomic step.

The rules section of mbox defines a single behavior on lines 8–12. This transition is always enabled in the absence of an error, and its effect is to (i) create an entry in the store and set the reference to be newAddr using the tmp command (line 9); (ii) set the next value of memory referenced by resultAddr to be newAddr (the content of resultAddr is the return value from the transition); (iii) update the set mailboxes with the tuple [id, newAddr] using the union operator \U (line 11); and (iv) set the memory referenced by statusAddr in the next state to 1 to indicate the successful completion of the transition as per the API specification. All of this occurs as one atomic step.

The other transitions get_mbox, send, and recv are defined like mbox. The transition recv, which blocks in the absence of a message, is protected by the guard on line 38 that is only satisfied if the memory referenced by variable to is not empty (i.e., when a message is pending). In the rule body, the variable to references a list (lines 39–40) where the first member is the message with the content copied into msg and the second member is the list of remaining messages.

Internal API housekeeping is managed by daemon transitions as illustrated by the pump transition defined on lines 43–53. Daemon transitions are invoked infinitely often in the API, executed as often as the guards are enabled, and represent a concurrent thread of execution. The pump daemon in the example

```
1  state
2   mailboxes = {}
3   queues = 0
4  end
5  transition mbox
6   input id, statusAddr, resultAddr
7   rules
8    true ==>
9     tmp newAddr;
10    @resultAddr' := newAddr;
11    mailboxes' := mailboxes \U {[id, newAddr]};
12    @statusAddr' := 1;
13   end
14  errors
15   (\E box in mailboxes: box.0 = id) ==>
16    @statusAddr' := -1;
17  end
18 end
19 transition get_mbox
20  input id, resultAddr
21  rules
22   (\E box in mailboxes: box.0 = id) ==>
23    let mailbox = (box in mailboxes: box.0 = id);
24    @resultAddr' := mailbox.1;
25  end
26 end
27 transition send
28  input from, msg, to
29  rules
30   true ==>
31    queues' := [from, queues];
32    @from' := [@msg, to, @from];
33  end
34 end
35 transition recv
36  input to, msg
37  rules
38   @to != 0 ==>
39    @msg' := (@to).0;
40    @to' := (@to).1;
41  end
42 end
43 daemon pump
44  rules
45   queues != 0 ==>
46    let from = queues.0;
47    let msg = (@from).0;
48    let to = (@from).1;
49    @to' := [msg, @to];
50    @from' := (@from).2;
51    queues' := queues.1;
52  end
53 end
```

Fig. 3. A simplified message-passing API in 4M

API is active anytime `queues` has a non-zero value, and its role is to transfer messages from sending mailboxes to receiving mailboxes. It does this transfer by (i) defining a local variable `from` holding the first element of the `queues` tuple with the `let` expression (line 46); (ii) defining `msg` to hold the actual message from the sender (line 47); (iii) defining `to` to hold the address of the destination mailbox (line 48); (iv) adding the message to the receiver mailbox (line 49);

(v) removing the message from the sender mailbox (line 50); and (vi) removing the pending send from `queues` (line 51). All of this occurs as one atomic step.

2.2 Semantic Implementation of 4M

4M is intended for human consumption with a form and semantics that are non-trivial to define. For example, 4M gives simultaneous update of all API state variables affected in a transition and allows calls to other transitions within an active transition. As such, it is possible to define a blocking send as a non-blocking send followed by a call to wait that blocks until the send completes. The nuances of this semantics are more easily realized by a simpler core calculus.

The operational semantics for the 4M core is given by a term rewriting system employing small-step semantics through continuations. The 4M core is mathematically defined in [1]. The novelty in the 4M semantics is the layering of machines to isolate non-determinism in a single machine. The 4M language itself is not terribly unique and rather its contribution lies more in the technique in creating a domain specific language to model a system.

The implementation of the semantics corresponds to Fig. 1(b) in our architecture for API modeling. Questions regarding API behavior over concurrent calls such as the scenario in Fig. 2(b) can be explored directly in the 4M core by iteratively presenting to the calculus the current API call of each participating thread and asking the calculus for all possible next states of the system. In such a manner, it is possible to evolve the API state from a known initial state to one of several possible end states allowed by the specification.

For example, consider the API state and the thread states shown in Fig. 4 for our scenario at the point where threads 0 and 1 are blocking on their first calls to `recv`, and thread 2 is blocking on its second call to `send`. The top portion of the figure shows the state of each thread with its local variables and the current program location indicated by the •-mark. The local variables hold references into the API state for each of the mailboxes created in the scenario.

The API state in the bottom portion of the figure is: `mailboxes`, that associates an ID with a memory reference that is the actual mailbox; `queues`, a list tracking undelivered messages; and the mailboxes themselves with their contents. From Fig. 4, the scenario has created four mailboxes, and mailbox 2, located at (addr 7), has the pending message "`Y`" to be delivered to (addr 5). The zero entry in the tuple indicates the end of the list (i.e., there is only one pending message). The `queues` variable indicates that the message from (addr 7) needs to be delivered (by the `pump` daemon in the 4M model of Fig. 3).

The semantics allows several next states from the state in Fig. 4 such as the `pump` transition moving the message out of the `from2` mailbox–(addr 7)–into the `to0` mailbox–(addr 5)–or adding the next send from thread 2 into the `queue` and the `from2` mailbox–(addr 7). A test is able to trace any possible execution from the current API state by randomly picking a transition allowed by the semantics.

Thread 0	Thread 1	Thread 2
`s`: 0 `to0`: (addr 5) `a`: `b`:	`s`: 0 `to0`: (addr 5) `to1`: (addr 6) `from1`: (addr 8) `c`:	`s`: 0 `to0`: (addr 5) `to1`: (addr 6) `from2`: (addr 7)
`•recv(to0,&a)` `recv(to0,&b)`	`•recv(to1,&c)` `send(from1,"X",to0)`	`•send(from2,"Z",to1)`
API Global State		
`mailBoxes`–*[id,ref]*	[0, (addr 5)] [2, (addr 7)]	[1, (addr 6)] [3, (addr 8)]
`queues`–*[ref,queues]*	[(addr 7), 0]	
(addr 5)–*mailbox 0*		
(addr 6)–*mailbox 1*		
(addr 7)–*mailbox 2*	("Y", (addr 5), 0)	
(addr 8)–*mailbox 3*		

Fig. 4. The state of the threads and API for Fig. 3 and Fig. 2(b) where the threads have run until thread 0 and thread 1 are blocking (indicated by the •-mark) at the receives and thread 2 is attempting its last send

3 4M Implementation

3.1 Reference Solution for Test, Debug, and Behavior Exploration

Manually writing the state of the API for the 4M core and manually stepping through the semantics definition is not feasible. Suppose instead that there exists an actual implementation of the 4M core that captures precisely the operational semantics. Naturally, it would be ideal to take a C program using the API, similar to the definition of thread 0 in Fig. 5(a), and connect it directly to the 4M core implementation to simulate the API behavior.

We provide such a connection. It is implemented by a role-based relationship between the C runtime and the 4M core implementation runtime, which we call the GEM (Golden Executable Model). Thin wrappers bridge the API calls to the actual C code as shown in Fig. 5(b). These correspond to Fig. 1(d) of our solution. The `gem_call` is the entry to the model of the API. The GEM implementation itself blocks waiting for all threads to invoke the API at which point it communicates with the 4M core implementation to send the states of the active threads. The component representing the search strategy corresponds to Fig. 1(e) of our solution. The search strategy determines priority in the search order of possible next states and can be customized by the user. The 4M implementation, corresponding to Fig. 1(b) of our solution, returns a possible next state, and the model releases the corresponding blocked `gem_call` for the stopped thread. The thread then continues until the next API entry occurs to repeat the process. The model stores a random seed from the execution for reproducibility.

Our architecture for a model replacement of APIs in C programs is divided into three different components: an implementation of 4M, a mechanism for capturing C API calls, and a strategy for exploring the possible system states (see Fig. 1). These components are connected as follows:

```
void t0() {
  msg_t a, b;    status_t s;
  mbox_t to0 = mbox(0, &s);
  recv(to0, &a);
  recv(to0, &b);
}
```

(a)

```
void send(mbox_t f,msg_t* b,mbox_t t) {
  gem_var bv;
  bv=init_var(b,buf_len(b),GEM_STRING);
  gem_call("send␣(%v␣%v␣%v)",f, bv,t);
  del_var(bv);
}
```

(b)

Fig. 5. An interface to connect the 4M core implementation to C programs. (a) The C implementation of thread 0 in the scenario. (b) The wrapper for the `send` API call.

1. A driver process spawns the GEM server and GEM client processes and creates their inter-process communication pipes.
2. As long as there are threads that are not terminated or blocked on API calls, the GEM client runs the user program using a cooperative threading model, executing threads one at a time.
3. As the GEM client makes API requests, the GEM server responds to each one and synchronizes its API state with that of the GEM client.
4. The 4M API model generates a list of possible next states given the information it has received about the threads and the blocked API call for each thread. A next state determines which blocking API call will finish. The GEM server randomizes the list of possible states and designates the first state as the one to be explored. To ensure deterministic behavior, the random seed used for the random walk can be set by the user.
5. Once a next state has been selected, the state change is synchronized with the GEM client and the corresponding threads are unblocked.
6. Steps 2 - 5 are repeated until program termination.

The underlying assumptions for correctness is that i) a thread eventually enters the API, even if it enters through an explicit call to exit the thread, at which point we can ignore it forever; and ii) there is no other non-determinism in the system (i.e., no I/O etc.). The first point (i) is needed to return control to the API model and indicate when it is time to compute a next state (i.e., all of the threads have arrived); otherwise, the model does not know if it should continue to wait for a thread to enter the API or compute a next state. The second point (ii) is important for replay.

The steps described represent the execution of a single pathway of the user program. In order to perform an exhaustive exploration, our tool implements a rewind and replay mechanism. When API calls are made by the GEM client on behalf of the user program, the responses returned by the GEM server and API are recorded in a file. This logging enables a zero-calculation replay of the user program up to the point where a new next state is to be explored. Again, we currently restrict out all other sources of non-determinism in the program in order for the replay to work correctly (i.e., I/O etc. must be deterministic for replay). The GEM client merely reads logged responses from the pipe rather than reading live responses. During the replay phase, the GEM server ignores any

```
1  mbox_t mbox(int id, status_t* s) {
2    mbox_t res;
3    gem_var sv, rv;
4    sv = reg_var(s, sizeof(int));
5    rv = reg_var(&res, sizeof(mbox_t));
6    gem_call("mbox␣(%d␣%v␣%v)",id,sv,rv);
7    del_var(sv); del_var(rv);
8    return res;
9  }
```

Fig. 6. An example wrapper for the `mbox` function

requests sent by the GEM client. The user program is not rerun in its entirety. It is instead run to a point decided by the GEM server (i.e., the point at which is new or different next state is to be considered).

The immutable and recursive characteristics of functional programs afford the GEM server some abilities not easily mirrored in the GEM client. In particular, they enable the server to "rewind" itself to an earlier program state by simply returning up the execution stack. We utilize this feature to exhaustively explore execution paths. Picking up just after step 6 above:

1. The GEM server checks if all possible paths have been explored.
2. If unexplored paths exist, the GEM server rewinds to the point where it last selected a next state from the list of next states given by the API model. If all states in the list have already been explored, the server is instead rewound to the latest point where there still exists unexplored next states.
3. The GEM client is told to replay the user program.
4. The GEM server waits for the GEM client to replay. The responses recorded from the last execution are sent to the client so it may replay to the execution point where the GEM server is waiting.
5. Normal execution continues, but this time the GEM server selects the first *unexplored* next state from the list.
6. When all paths have been explored, the tool terminates.

Following are some of the finer details of the C Wrappers. Fig. 6 shows an example wrapper that demonstrates the issues each wrapper must manage:

- The wrapper must match the API interface to be a suitable model. (Line 1)
- As the C runtime and 4M runtime communicate through a pipe, we must use an external representation of values. (Lines 2 and 3)
- Some parameters may be pointers to C memory (such as `s`), so the wrapper must allocate a 4M location (implemented by `reg_var`) for it. (Line 4)
- Similarly, 4M transitions do not have "return values"—instead a return is accomplished by passing a reference that gets updated. This encoding is managed by the wrapper by allocating a 4M location. (Lines 2 and 5)
- Since the 4M runtime simply waits for API calls to execute, the wrapper must marshal each call to 4M. This process entails encoding parameters as 4M values. Line 3 prepares references, then lines 4 and 5 use the function `reg_var` to associate the C memory references with 4M store locations. The `gem_call`

function (line 6) automatically expands its arguments to the correct 4M encoding based on the placeholders in the format string. More complicated data conversion may be necessary where C datatypes do not match the 4M core datatypes: C distinguishes between integer and floating-point numbers while 4M does not; C also allows arrays of bytes, while 4M has only strings. The details are important, but trivial and tedious.
- Inside `gem_call`, the 4M runtime takes over and can delay arbitrarily long until the result of the API call is computed by 4M and the search strategy.
- Once `gem_call` completes, the C memory locations associated with 4M store locations (as established in lines 4 and 5) are updated with their new values, and the result is returned (line 8).

In summary, the responsibility of the wrappers is to convert data types and parameters as needed, register memory shared by the C program and API, then communicate the call to the model where the state capture component takes over. Once the next state has been computed and reified into the C program, the model returns control to the wrappers.

Our 4M implementation is written in PLT Redex [7], a domain-specific language that ships with Racket [8] for encoding operational semantics as rewriting systems.[4] We employed PLT Redex for its development environment which provides a richer set of test and debug tools than say Maude, another term rewriting system. Further, PLT Redex is tightly integrated with Racket letting us embed arbitrary Racket code into the term rewriting system. Such integration is useful as some transformations over the machine state are more naturally expressed in Racket than in PLT Redex. As 4M is defined in machine semantics as a term rewriting system, the encoding in PLT Redex is obvious.

4 MCAPI Model Results

We validate our process on the connectionless message passing portion of the MCAPI communications library [26]. There are 43 API calls in the library registry, and 18 of those are related to the connectionless message passing. We implement the 12 most relevant calls that cover the bulk of the functionality. The 4M model comprises 488 lines of code utilizing 3 daemon transitions for internal processing which is quite small compared to the roughly 30 pertinent pages of the 169 page English description. The API state itself only contains 4 unique variables. The 4M model compiles into 284 lines of the 4M core calculus.

As there is no "formalism" of the MCAPI API to which we can relate our 4M model, we validate our model through empirical test. Specifically, we have developed a suite of API scenarios (i.e., regression tests) for which we have validated with the API designers the possible outcomes. We run each of these scenarios

[4] We use an unpublished compiler for PLT Redex that drastically improves performance by specializing Redex to deterministic reduction semantics where at most one reduction is applicable. With this new compiler, an exhaustive test that takes 12 minutes on the stock system completes in a few seconds.

Table 1. Benchmark Runtimes

Benchmark	Lines	API Calls	Paths	Run Time
Self Send	42	6	1	3.969s
Topher Scenario	128	18	27	6.595s
Leader	168	24	42	13.487s

through our API model ensuring that our model captures all the allowed behaviors specified in the scenarios. In the end, we have no definitive test that proves our model more correct than say the C reference implementation; however, as our model is not so semantically apart from the documentation as say the C reference implementation, we subjectively have a greater assurance (or at least we are more able to convince ourselves) that our model is correct. In other words, it is much easier to argue through inspection that our model implements the API than it is to argue similarly that the C reference solution implements the API.[5]

To quantify the overhead in the model, we report running times on several examples as measured with the Unix `time` command on an Intel Core 2 Quad 2.66 GHz machine with 8 GB of memory running Fedora 14 as well as the number of bytes sent through the pipes. Unfortunately, the tested examples are all in-house as there is no MCAPI code in the wild, to the knowledge of the authors, at the time of writing. Running the scenario in Fig. 2(b) directly in Racket (not through the C runtime) in single execution mode takes 1.6 seconds. The same single execution through the C runtime takes 3 seconds (2.6 of which is starting the Racket server). This overhead in starting the server is mitigated in longer running programs. In the C execution, ~2KB are communicated between the C runtime and the Racket server. The C runtime spends 403ms waiting for the Racket runtime (22ms on an average call). An insignificant amount of time is spent preparing, sending, and parsing IPC messages. Clearly this would grow with the size of the scenario and the size of the API state.

As a reference point, the running time for the MCAPI dynamic verifier MCC on a scenario with 3 threads, two performing parallel sends, and the third making two sequential receives is under 1 second [23], whereas in our implementation it takes 2.9 seconds total (2.6s to start the server and 0.3s to compute.) Recall that the MCC tool relies critically on a reference implementation that, as discussed previously, is buggy and does not include all the behavior allowed in the API. As a note, our 4M model can be a drop-in replacement for the reference implementation in the tool as our model provides the exact interface.

We implemented Dijkstra's self-stabilization algorithm [3] in C using MCAPI. This algorithm runs in 8.2 seconds at $n = 4$. Of this 8.2s, 5.5 was spent in the 4M implementation and 2.6 starting the Racket server. During the execution, ~14KB of data is communicated to Racket and ~3KB from Racket. This suggests that real programs do incur significant overhead using 4M but can still run feasibly. With $n = 6$, the algorithm completes in 35s. Table 1 summarizes the results obtained from other MCAPI benchmark programs with our tool.

[5] See [1] for the MCAPI 4M model and the 4M tool set.

As expected, the exhaustive search using our 4M model found both executions in the example scenario of Fig. 2(b) which is the *Topher Scenario* in the table. The non-intuitive scenario triggers an assertion violation in the test harness. In addition to these MCAPI benchmarks, we converted a control program for an amusement park used in an operating system class to MCAPI. The program is 1,192 lines of C code, creates 45 distinct threads, and issues thousands of MCAPI calls. The program has been run hundreds of times on the MCA reference solution and has never failed. When using the 4M model, the program immediately failed. Further inspection revealed three distinct race conditions latent in the code that can only be realized by specific message orderings allowed by the specification but not present in the MCA reference implementation.

5 Related Work

Verifying concurrent systems has long be a topic of active research. There are several modeling and specification languages with complete frameworks for analysis and model checking. These include Promela, Murphi, TLA+, Z, Alloy, and B, to name a few [11,4,14,25,12,2]. There are two differentiators as related to the proposed approach in this paper: first, the connection in other solutions between the mathematical semantic definition of the language and the runtime is not clear whereas the term rewriting systems expressed in PLT Redex are expressed naturally in mathematical notation; thus there is a reasonable assurance that the model runtime corresponds directly to the mathematical expression of the semantics. And second, the other solutions target analysis in the model's runtime whereas our work is intended as a model of the API that serves as a replacement for the actual API implementation when testing and debugging applications written against the API in the intended target language.

There have been attempts to model MPI in extant specification languages including conversion from C programs using MPI to the specification language [24,9,20,15]. Recent work takes CUDA and C to SMT languages [29,16,6,5]. Such implementations are only suitable to scenario evaluation and not drop-in replacement. They must also prove a correct translation to the analysis language.

Recent work in dynamic verification uses the program directly with the actual API implementation to perform model checking (i.e., the API implementation serves as the API model itself) [10,18,21,19,30,27,31,28]. Although search through continuations rather than repeated program invocation is similar to [18,21], the proposed work in this paper does not critically rely on an existing runtime implementation; thus, it is able to elicit all behaviors captured in the specification and directly control internal API behavior. Without such control, verification results are dependent on the chosen implementation, and even then, on just those implementation aspects that are controllable. For example, it is not possible to affect arbitrary buffering in MPI or MCAPI runtime libraries and as a result, behaviors such as those in our example scenario are omitted in the analysis [23]. Some recent work can test threaded or distributed libraries written against POSIX or Windows APIs, exploring all possible execution paths in the implementation itself, but they depend on a specific implementation [31,28].

6 Conclusion and Future Work

English specification of concurrent APIs catalog interfaces and list effects of correct and incorrect calls to those interfaces. Unfortunately, they provide no framework with which a programmer or designer might experiment to further understand the API in the presence of many concurrent calls. The work in this paper provides a replacement for concurrent APIs using a formal model by (i) creating the 4M language to intuitively model natural language API descriptions; (ii) defining a novel role-based architecture to directly connect the C runtime to 4M to use the model as an instance of the API that is explorable, testable, and capable of exhaustive search; (iii) building an implementation of 4M as a rewriting system in Racket; and (iv) validating the process in a portion of the MCAPI communication API. The result is that when an API is formally modeled in 4M, it is possible to use the same model with native programs written against the API to explore system-wide program behavior.

Future work includes (i) adapting reductions that leverage SMT technology from model checking to mitigate state explosion in data and scheduling non-determinism [29]; (ii) partial order reduction based on persistent sets; (iii) improving the communication between the different runtimes using search order and undo stacks; (iv) case study in other APIs and in particular the MCA API for resource allocation as it deals with shared memory; and (v) an implementation of the 4M core in Maude to improve running time performance.

References

1. The 4M modeling language, `https://github.com/ericmercer/4M`
2. Abrial, J.R.: The B-book: assigning programs to meanings. Cambridge University Press (1996)
3. Dijkstra, E.W.: Self-stabilizing systems in spite of distributed control. Communications of the ACM 17, 643–644 (1974)
4. Dill, D.L., Drexler, A.J., Hu, A.J., Yang, C.H.: Protocol verification as a hardware design aid. In: IEEE International Conference on Computer Design: VLSI in Computers and Processors, pp. 522–525 (1992)
5. Elwakil, M., Yang, Z.: CRI: Symbolic Debugger for MCAPI Applications. In: Bouajjani, A., Chin, W.-N. (eds.) ATVA 2010. LNCS, vol. 6252, pp. 353–358. Springer, Heidelberg (2010)
6. Elwakil, M., Yang, Z.: Debugging support tool for MCAPI applications. In: Parallel and Distributed Systems (2010)
7. Felleisen, M., Findler, R.B., Flatt, M.: Semantics Engineering with PLT Redex. The MIT Press (2009)
8. Flatt, M.: PLT: Reference: Racket. Tech. Rep. PLT-TR-2010-1, PLT Inc. (2010), `http://racket-lang.org/tr1/`
9. Georgelin, P., Pierre, L., Nguyen, T.: A formal specification of the MPI primitives and communication mechanisms. Tech. rep., LIM (1999)
10. Godefroid, P.: Model checking for programming languages using Verisoft. In: Principles of Programming Languages, pp. 174–186 (1997)
11. Holzmann, G.J.: The model checker SPIN. IEEE Transactions on Software Engineering 23, 279–295 (1997)

12. Jackson, D.: Software Abstractions: Logic, Language, and Analysis. The MIT Press (April 2006)
13. Jongmans, S.-S.T.Q., Hindriks, K.V., van Riemsdijk, M.B.: Model Checking Agent Programs by Using the Program Interpreter. In: Dix, J., Leite, J., Governatori, G., Jamroga, W. (eds.) CLIMA XI. LNCS, vol. 6245, pp. 219–237. Springer, Heidelberg (2010)
14. Lamport, L.: TLA - the temporal logic of actions, `http://research.microsoft.com/users/lamport/tla/tla.html`
15. Li, G., DeLisi, M., Gopalakrishnan, G., Kirby, R.M.: Formal specification of the MPI-2.0 standard in TLA+. In: Principles and Practices of Parallel Programming, pp. 283–284 (2008)
16. Li, G., Gopalakrishnan, G., Kirby, R.M., Quinlan, D.: A symbolic verifier for CUDA programs. In: Principles and Practice of Parallel Programming, pp. 357–358 (2010)
17. McMillan, K.L.: Symbolic Model Checking: An approach to the state explosion problem. Ph.D. thesis, Carnegie Mellon University (1992)
18. Mercer, E.G., Jones, M.: Model Checking Machine Code with the GNU Debugger. In: Godefroid, P. (ed.) SPIN 2005. LNCS, vol. 3639, pp. 251–265. Springer, Heidelberg (2005)
19. Musuvathi, M., Qadeer, S.: Iterative context bounding for systematic testing of multithreaded programs. In: Programming Language Design and Implementation (2007)
20. Palmer, R., DeLisi, M., Gopalakrishnan, G., Kirby, R.M.: An Approach to Formalization and Analysis of Message Passing Libraries. In: Leue, S., Merino, P. (eds.) FMICS 2007. LNCS, vol. 4916, pp. 164–181. Springer, Heidelberg (2008)
21. Păsăreanu, C.S., Mehlitz, P.C., Bushnell, D.H., Gundy-Burlet, K., Lowry, M., Person, S., Pape, M.: Combining unit-level symbolic execution and system-level concrete execution for testing NASA software. In: International Symposium on Software Testing and Analysis, pp. 15–26 (2008)
22. Roscoe, A.W.: Model-checking CSP, pp. 353–378. Prentice Hall International (UK) Ltd., Hertfordshire (1994)
23. Sharma, S., Gopalakrishnan, G., Mercer, E., Holt, J.: MCC: A runtime verification tool for MCAPI user applications. In: Formal Methods in Computer-Aided Design, pp. 41–44 (2009)
24. Siegel, S.F., Avrunin, G.: Analysis of mpi programs. Tech. Rep. UM-CS-2003-036, Department of Computer Science, University of Massachusetts Amherst (2003)
25. Spivey, J.M.: The Z notation: a reference manual. Prentice-Hall International Series In Computer Science, p. 155 (1989)
26. The Multicore Association, `http://www.multicore-association.org`
27. Vakkalanka, S., Gopalakrishnan, G., Kirby, R.M.: Dynamic Verification of MPI Programs with Reductions in Presence of Split Operations and Relaxed Orderings. In: Gupta, A., Malik, S. (eds.) CAV 2008. LNCS, vol. 5123, pp. 66–79. Springer, Heidelberg (2008)
28. Šimša, J., Bryant, R., Gibson, G.: dBug: Systematic Testing of Unmodified Distributed and Multi-threaded Systems. In: Groce, A., Musuvathi, M. (eds.) SPIN Workshops 2011. LNCS, vol. 6823, pp. 188–193. Springer, Heidelberg (2011)
29. Wang, C., Chaudhuri, S., Gupta, A., Yang, Y.: Symbolic pruning of concurrent program executions. In: The Foundations of Software Engineering, pp. 23–32 (2009)
30. Wang, C., Yang, Y., Gupta, A., Gopalakrishnan, G.: Dynamic Model Checking with Property Driven Pruning to Detect Race Conditions. In: Cha, S., Choi, J.-Y., Kim, M., Lee, I., Viswanathan, M. (eds.) ATVA 2008. LNCS, vol. 5311, pp. 126–140. Springer, Heidelberg (2008)
31. Yang, J., Chen, T., Wu, M., Xu, Z., Liu, X., Lin, H., Yang, M., Long, F., Zhang, L., Zhou, L.: MODIST: transparent model checking of unmodified distributed systems. In: Networked Systems Design and Implementation, pp. 213–228 (2009)

Local Symmetry and Compositional Verification

Kedar S. Namjoshi[1] and Richard J. Trefler[2,⋆]

[1] Bell Laboratories, Alcatel-Lucent
kedar@research.bell-labs.com
[2] University of Waterloo
trefler@cs.uwaterloo.ca

Abstract. This work considers concurrent programs formed of processes connected by an underlying network. The symmetries of the network may be used to reduce the state space of the program, by grouping together similar global states. This can result in an exponential reduction for highly symmetric networks, but it is much less effective for many networks, such as rings, which have limited global symmetry. We focus instead on the *local symmetries* in a network and show that they can be used to significantly reduce the complexity of *compositional reasoning*. Local symmetries are represented by a *symmetry groupoid*, a generalization of a symmetry group. Certain sub-groupoids induce quotient networks which are equivalent to the original for the purposes of compositional reasoning. We formulate a compositional reasoning principle for safety properties of process networks and define symmetry groupoids and the quotient construction. Moreover, we show how symmetry and local reasoning can be expoited to provide parameterized proofs of correctness.

"*Whenever you have to do with a structure-endowed entity try to determine its group of automorphisms*"
Hermann Weyl, ***Symmetry***, 1952

"*... there are plenty of objects which exhibit what we clearly recognize as symmetry, but which admit few or no nontrivial automorphisms. It turns out that the symmetry, and hence much of the structure, of such objects can be characterized algebraically if we use groupoids and not just groups.*"

Alan Weinstein, ***Groupoids: Unifying Internal and External Symmetry – A Tour through Some Examples***, Notices of the AMS, 1996.

1 Introduction

State-space explosion is the main obstacle to the scalability of model checking. In this work, we consider proofs of safety for programs structured as a network of processes, executing concurrently and asynchronously. The network is used to represent how state is shared between groups of processes. The model is expressive, allowing refined statements of sharing relationships, such as read-only, read-write and write-only. As an example, globally shared memory may

⋆ Supported by a Natural Sciences and Engineering Research Council of Canada grant.

V. Kuncak and A. Rybalchenko (Eds.): VMCAI 2012, LNCS 7148, pp. 348–362, 2012.

be represented by a hub-and-spoke network, with the memory at the hub and processes at the spokes; a dining philosophers network has processes arranged in a ring, with adjacent philosophers given read-write access to their shared fork.

A natural question is whether network symmetries can be exploited to reduce the complexity of model checking. Indeed, it is known that for networks which are highly symmetric, reducing the global state space by collapsing together symmetric states results in exponential savings [18,6,14]. On the other hand, many networks, such as rings, have limited global symmetry so this reduction is much less effective for those networks. We consider instead the *local symmetries* of a network and show that they can be used to significantly reduce the complexity of *compositional reasoning* methods.

The essence of compositional methods lies in using *local* reasoning as a substitute for *global* reasoning: each process of a concurrent program is analyzed separately along with an abstraction of its neighboring processes. The benefit is that local methods work in time polynomial in the number of processes, in contrast with the PSPACE-hardness of the model checking question. Efficiency comes, however, at the cost of incompleteness. (It is possible to overcome incompleteness by adding auxiliary state, at the cost of making the analysis less compositional.)

The intuition behind our results is that compositional methods, being local in their scope, benefit from purely local symmetries. Networks with little global symmetry can have significant local symmetry: in a ring network, for instance, any two nodes are locally similar, as they have identical left and right neighbors.

To illustrate these issues, consider a uniform ring network with N nodes. A program on this network may have a state space whose size is exponential in N – this is the case, for instance, of a simple token-based mutual exclusion protocol. The global symmetry group of the ring has N elements (the rotations), so the global state space can be reduced only by a factor of N. (The state space of a program could exhibit more symmetry than that of its underlying network, but that is not the case here.) We show that it is possible to automatically construct a compositional invariant which is strong enough to prove mutual exclusion, in time polynomial in N. Making use of the local symmetries of a ring, this calculation can be reduced to one on a fixed set of representative nodes, making the time complexity for computing the compositional invariant *independent* of N! Moreover, it is sometimes possible to pick the same set of representatives for all networks in a family. In such a case, the compositional invariant computed for a small instance forms a parameterized invariant which holds for all members of the family.

Technically, local symmetries are described by a *symmetry groupoid*, a generalization of a symmetry group (cf. the quotations at the start of this section). The main question tackled in this work is to determine precisely how the local symmetries of the network influence the symmetry of a compositional inductive invariant which is computed to prove safety properties. In the following sketch of the main results, a local invariant has the shape $(\forall i : \theta_i)$, where the quantification in i is over the nodes of the network and θ_i is an assertion which depends only on the neighborhood of node i.

1. Given an "balance" relation B on the network (a form of bisimulation defining local symmetries), if $(i, j) \in B$ then θ_i and θ_j are similar. I.e., the local symmetry of the network is reflected in the symmetry of the computed compositional invariant.
2. The orbit relation of the group of global automorphisms of a network forms a balance relation. I.e., global symmetries induce local symmetries.
3. A groupoid balance relation induces a quotient network which is equivalent to the original for the purpose of local reasoning.
4. If there is a single quotient for a family of networks, the compositional invariant computed for this quotient generalizes to a parameterized invariant which holds for all networks in the family.

The results point to deep connections between local symmetry, compositional methods and parameterized reasoning.

2 Networks and Their Symmetry Groupoids

A *network* is given by a pair (N, E) where N is a set of *nodes* and E is a set of *edges*. Each node is assigned a *color* by a function $\xi : N \to C$, with C a set of colors. Associated with each edge is a color, given by a function $\xi : E \to C$ (we use the same color set for simplicity); a set of input nodes, given by $ins : E \to \mathcal{P}(N)$; and a set of output nodes, given by $outs : E \to \mathcal{P}(N)$, where $\mathcal{P}(N)$ represents the power-set of N. The input and output sets of an edge may overlap.

There are several derived notions. The incoming edges for a node are given by a function $In : N \to \mathcal{P}(E)$, defined by $In(n) = \{e \mid n \in outs(e)\}$. The outgoing set of edges for a node is similarly defined by a function $Out : N \to \mathcal{P}(E)$, given by $Out(n) = \{e \mid n \in ins(e)\}$. The set of edges incident to a node is defined by the function $InOut : N \to \mathcal{P}(E)$, given by $InOut(n) = In(n) \cup Out(n)$.

Definition 1 (Points-To). *A node m points-to node n, denoted $m \in pt(n)$, if $m \neq n$ and $Out(m) \cap InOut(n)$ is non-empty.*

Informally, two nodes are locally similar if their immediate neighborhoods are identical up to a re-mapping.

Definition 2 (IO-Similarity). *Nodes m and n are (locally) similar, written $m \simeq_{IO} n$, if (1) the nodes have the same color, i.e., $\xi(m) = \xi(n)$, and (2) there is a correspondence between respective sets of incident edges, which preserves color and in/out status. I.e., there is a function $\beta : InOut(m) \to InOut(n)$ which is a bijection between $In(m)$ and $In(n)$, a bijection between $Out(m)$ and $Out(n)$ and for every e, $\xi(e) = \xi(\beta(e))$.*

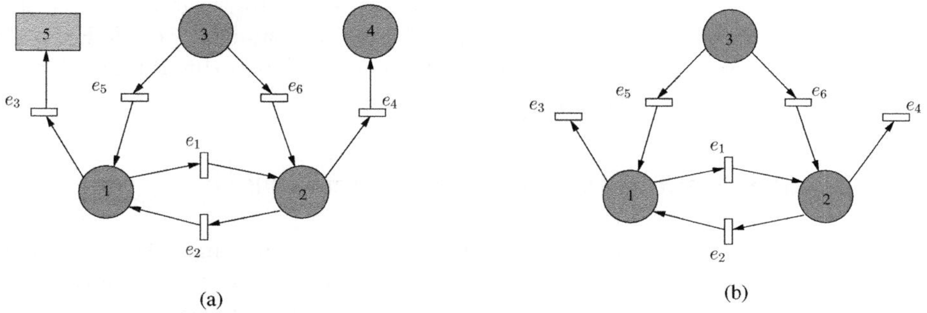

Fig. 1. Trivial Global Symmetry, Non-trivial Local Symmetry

Figure 1(a) an example network, based on one from [16]. Colors are also marked by shapes: node 5 has a different color from node 4. This network has only the identity as a global automorphism; however, nodes 1 and 2 are locally similar, as their neighborhoods – shown in Figure 1(b) – are related by the bijection β which maps input edges $e_2 \mapsto e_1; e_5 \mapsto e_6$ and output edges $e_1 \mapsto e_2; e_3 \mapsto e_4$. Nodes 3 and 2 point to node 1, while nodes 3 and 1 point to node 2.

2.1 Local Symmetry Groupoids

The set of tuples of the form (m, β, n) where β is a witnessing bijection for $m \simeq_{IO} n$ forms a *groupoid*. Following [16], we call this the symmetry groupoid of the network and denote it by $\mathcal{G}_{IO}$. A groupoid (cf. [3,26]) is (roughly) a group with a *partial* composition operation. It is defined by specifying a set of elements, E, a set of objects O, source and target functions $src : E \to O$ and $tgt : E \to O$ and an identity function $id : O \to E$. These must satisfy group-like conditions.

1. The composition ab of elements a, b is defined only if $tgt(a) = src(b)$, with $src(ab) = src(a)$ and $tgt(ab) = tgt(b)$
2. Composition is associative. If one of $a(bc)$ or $(ab)c$ is defined, so is the other, and they are equal
3. For every element a, the element $\lambda_a = id(src(a))$ is a left identity, i.e., $\lambda_a a = a$, and $\rho_a = id(tgt(a))$ is a right identity, i.e., $a\rho_a = a$
4. Every element a has an inverse (a^{-1}), such that $aa^{-1} = \lambda_a$ and $a^{-1}a = \rho_a$.

A groupoid can be pictured as a directed graph: the nodes are the objects, there is a directed edge labeled by element e from its source to its target object. Identities form self-loops. (A group is a groupoid with a single base object.)

In the network symmetry groupoid, the objects are the nodes of the network and the elements are all triples (m, β, n) where β is a bijection defining the similarity between nodes m and n. The identities are defined by $id(n) = (n, \iota, n)$, where ι is the identity map. For an element (m, β, n), $src(m, \beta, n) = m$, $tgt(m, \beta, n) = n$ and its inverse is (n, β^{-1}, m). The composition of (m, β, n) and (n, γ, o) is $(m, \gamma\beta, o)$.

A groupoid induces an *orbit relation*: objects a, b are related if there is a groupoid element e connecting them, i.e., if $src(e) = a$ and $tgt(e) = b$. From the groupoid properties, this is an equivalence relation. The orbit relation for the symmetry groupoid is just $\simeq_{IO}$.

3 Local Reasoning on a Process Network

In this section we develop an assume-guarantee rule for proving safety properties of process networks. It is similar to the rules from [15,23] which apply to the globally shared memory model. Each node in a network is assigned a process, with locally similar nodes being assigned similar processes. The proof rule results in an inductive invariant of the form $(\forall i : \theta_i)$ where θ_i is an assertion on the neighborhood of the process assigned to node i. We show that there is a strongest invariant of this form and that it can be computed as a simultaneous fixpoint.

3.1 Assignment of Variables and Processes

Given a network (N, E), we associate a variable l_n with each node n and a variable v_e with every edge e. The type of the variable is the color of the node or edge. Let $X_n = \{v_e \mid e \in In(n)\}$ be the set of input variables for node n; similarly, let $Y_n = \{v_e \mid e \in Out(n)\}$ be the set of output variables for n and let $L_n = \{l_n\}$. Let $V_n = X_n \cup Y_n \cup L_n$. Thus, V_n defines the variables in the immediate neighborhood of node n. The set V is defined as $(\cup\, n : V_n)$.

With each node n is associated a *transition condition* $T_n(V_n, V_n')$ which is constrained so that it leaves the variables in $X_n \backslash Y_n$ unchanged. The network as a whole has an *initial condition*, $\mathcal{I}$. The variables assigned to nodes and edges, the network initial condition and the transition conditions for each node define an *assignment* of processes to the network. We denote the process for node n as P_n. Let $\tilde{I}_n = (\exists V \backslash V_n : \mathcal{I})$ be the projection of the initial condition on to V_n.

Definition 3 (Valid Assignment). *An assignment is* valid *for $B \subseteq \mathcal{G}_{IO}$ if it respects the local symmetries in B: i.e., for every $(m, \beta, n) \in B$, it should hold that $[T_n \equiv \beta(T_m)]$ and $[\tilde{I}_n \equiv \beta(\tilde{I}_m)]$.*

In this definition, $\beta(f)$ is a predicate which holds for a valuation b over V if f holds for a valuation a over V where for every $e \in InOut(m)$, $a(v_e) = b(v_{\beta(e)})$ and $a(v_e') = b(v_{\beta(e)}')$, and $a(l_m) = b(l_n)$ and $a(l_m') = b(l_n')$. Informally, $\beta(f)$ is the predicate obtained by substituting in f variables from the neighborhood of m (i.e., those in V_m) with the variables which correspond to them by β.

The semantics of a valid program assignment is defined as the *asynchronous, interleaving* composition of the processes associated with each node. The initial condition is $\mathcal{I}$. The interleaved transition relation, $\mathcal{T}$, is defined as a choice between local transitions, $(\exists n : \tilde{T}_n)$, where $\tilde{T}_n$ is the transition relation which extends T_n so that all variables of nodes other than n are unchanged. Formally, $\tilde{T}_n \equiv T_n \wedge unch(V \backslash V_n)$.

3.2 Local Proof Rules

A rely-guarantee proof rule based on the Owicki-Gries method is given in [23] for shared-memory programs. We generalize this formulation to networks. The rely-guarantee conditions are expressed over vectors of the form $\theta = (\theta_1, \theta_2, \ldots, \theta_n)$, where each component, θ_i, is a state assertion local to process P_i. The proof conditions ensure that the conjunction $(\forall i : \theta_i)$ is a *global inductive invariant.*

Let $\theta_n(V_n)$ be a predicate on the neighborhood variables of node n. For $(\forall n : \theta_n)$ to be a globally inductive invariant, θ_n must include the initial states of P_n, it must be closed under transitions of P_n and it must be closed under interference from the nodes which point to n. We next express these conditions precisely. We use two convenient notational conventions, taken from the book by Dijkstra and Scholten [12]. The notation $[\varphi]$ expresses that φ is valid. The notation $(\exists X : r : \varphi)$, where $X = \{x_1, \ldots, x_k\}$ is a finite set of variables, is a shorthand for $(\exists x_1, \ldots, x_k : r \wedge \varphi)$. The predicate r constrains the type or the range of variables in X. If X is empty, the quantified expression is equivalent to *false*.

The first condition is expressed as

$$[\tilde{I}_n \Rightarrow \theta_n] \tag{1}$$

The second condition is expressed as follows, where SP_n is the strongest post-condition operator for node n. ($SP(T, \psi)$ is the set of successors of states satisfying ψ by transitions satisfying T. $SP_n(T, \psi)$ is the projection of states in $SP(T, \psi)$ on to V_n.)

$$[SP_n(T_n, \theta_n) \Rightarrow \theta_n] \tag{2}$$

Closure under interference is expressed as follows

$$[SP_n(intf^{\theta}_{mn}, \theta_n) \Rightarrow \theta_n] \text{ for every } m \in pt(n) \tag{3}$$

The transition term, $intf^{\theta}_{mn}$ (read *intf* as "interference") represents the effect of transitions at a node m on the values of variables in the neighborhood of node n. This is defined as

$$intf^{\theta}_{mn} \equiv (\exists V \backslash V_n, V' \backslash V'_n : \tilde{T}_m \wedge \theta_m) \tag{4}$$

The interference term is a function of (V_n, V'_n), and is thus a general transition term. The definition of $\tilde{T}_m$ implies, however, that the interference leaves all variables not in $V_n \cap Y_m$ unchanged.

The three implications can be gathered together to form a simultaneous system of implications $[F_n(\theta) \Rightarrow \theta_n]$, with F_n defined by

$$F_n(\theta) \equiv \tilde{I}_n \vee SP_n(T_n, \theta_n) \vee (\vee\, m : m \in pt(n) : SP_n(intf^{\theta}_{mn}, \theta_n)) \tag{5}$$

This is in pre-fixpoint form as $F_n(\theta)$ is monotone in the vector θ, ordered component-wise by implication. By the Knaster-Tarski theorem, this system has a least fixpoint. For finite-state systems, the fixpoint can be computed as the limit, say θ^*, of the iteration sequence given by $\theta^0_m = \tilde{I}_n; \theta^{k+1}_m = \theta^k_m \vee SP_n(T_n, \theta^k_n) \vee (\vee\, m : m \in pt(n) : SP_n(intf^{\theta^k}_{mn}, \theta^k_n))$. For infinite-state systems, the limit may be trans-finite. Component θ^*_n is defined over V_n, as can be seen by its equivalence to $F_n(\theta^*)$ and the definition of F_n.

Theorem 1. *(Soundness) The proof rules (1)-(3) imply that* $\theta = (\forall n : \theta_n)$ *is a globally inductive invariant.*

Proof: The base case, that $[\mathcal{I} \Rightarrow \theta_n]$, follows for all n by (1), as $\mathcal{I}$ is stronger than $\tilde{I}_n = (\exists V \backslash V_n : \mathcal{I})$. To show inductiveness, consider any state s satisfying θ and a transition by process P_m from state s to state t. As θ_m holds of s, the transition satisfies both T_m and $intf^{\theta}_{mn}$. By (2), θ_m holds of t. Now consider any other node n. If m points to n, as θ_n holds of s by assumption, it follows by (3) that θ_n holds of t. If m does not point to n, the transition does not change the values of any variables in the neighborhood of n, so that θ_n continues to hold. **EndProof.**

Complexity. Let L be the number of local states per process – i.e., the number of valuations to V_n, assuming all V_n's are identical. Let $|N|$ be the number of nodes in the network, which is also the number of components of the θ vector. Then, (1) the number of fixpoint rounds is at most $|N| * L$, as each round must strictly increase the set of states in at least one component; (2) the number of updates per round is $|N|$, as each component of θ is updated. The work for an update to θ_n is typically dominated by the interference term. Consider round k. For each m which points to n, this requires computing successors for all states in θ^k_n with respect to the transition relation $intf^{\theta^k}_{mn}$. For a state in θ^k, its successors can be found by looking up its association list in a table storing $intf^{\theta^k}_{mn}$. The cost of the successor computation is, therefore, bounded by $L * L$. The total cost is bounded by $(|N| * L) * |N| * (L^2 * D)$ where D is the maximum over all n of the size of $pt(n)$. This simplifies to $|N|^2 * L^3 * D$, which is polynomial in all parameters, whereas global model-checking is PSPACE-complete in $|N|$ which, in practice, implies time-complexity exponential in $|N|$.

Completeness. Owicki-Gries [25] and Lamport [20] recognized that local assertions may not always suffice to represent the global constraints needed for a valid proof. The resolution is to expose local state through auxiliary or history variables, a process which can be automated [8,9,17]. It was observed in [8] that for many protocols, constructing $(\forall ij)$ local invariants – described below – is a good alternative to adding auxiliary variables. We consider purely compositional proofs: auxiliary variables modify network symmetries in ways that will be explored in future work.

Pair-Indexed Properties. A similar simultaneous fixpoint scheme can be constructed for multi-indexed properties, such as $(\forall m, n : m \neq n : \theta_{mn})$. The proof rules for a pair (m, n) are as follows. The term $\tilde{I}_{mn}$ is defined as $(\exists V \backslash (V_n \cup V_m) : \mathcal{I})$ and SP_{mn} is the projection of SP on to variables $V_m \cup V_n$. We abbreviate $(\forall m, n : m \neq n : \theta_{mn})$ by θ.

$$[\tilde{I}_{mn} \Rightarrow \theta_{mn}] \tag{6}$$

$$[SP_{mn}(T_m \wedge unch(V_n \backslash V_m), \theta) \Rightarrow \theta_{mn}] \tag{7}$$

$$[SP_{mn}(T_n \wedge unch(V_m \backslash V_n), \theta) \Rightarrow \theta_{mn}] \tag{8}$$

$$[SP_{mn}(intf^{\theta}_{kmn}, \theta) \Rightarrow \theta_{mn}], \text{ for } k \in pt(m,n) \text{ where} \tag{9}$$

$$intf^{\theta}_{kmn} \equiv unch((V_n \cup V_m) \backslash V_k) \wedge (\exists V'_k \backslash (V'_m \cup V'_n) : T_k) \text{ and} \tag{10}$$

$$k \in pt(m,n) \text{ if } k \notin \{m,n\} \text{ and } Out(k) \cap (InOut(m) \cup InOut(n)) \text{ is non-empty} \tag{11}$$

For the rest of the paper we focus first on the simpler case of singly-indexed properties, returning to pair-indexed properties at the end.

4 Symmetry and Quotients

The equivalence $\simeq_{IO}$ induced by the local symmetry groupoid $\mathcal{G}_{IO}$ is not enough in itself to obtain the symmetry reduction results. While it ensures that nodes m, n related by $\simeq_{IO}$ have a similar neighborhood, it does not ensure that the nodes which point into m and n correspond in any way. Some correspondence is needed, as the processes on $pt(m)$ affect θ_m and those on $pt(n)$ affect θ_n. We define a bisimulation-like relationship which builds on (strengthens) the basic local symmetry relation. We call relations satisfying the stronger conditions "balance" relations, following [16], where a similar notion is defined.

Definition 4 (Balance). *A* balance *relation B is a subset of $\mathcal{G}_{IO}$ satisfying the following properties. For any (m, β, n) in B: (1) (n, β^{-1}, m) is in B, and (2) for any j in $pt(m)$, there must be k in $pt(n)$ and δ such that (2a) (j, δ, k) is in B and (2b) for every edge f in $InOut(j) \cap InOut(m)$, $\delta(f) = \beta(f)$.*

Condition (2a) ensures that any node which points to m has an equivalent node which points into n. Condition (2b) ensures that β and δ agree on edges that are common to m, j. The theorem below summarizes properties of balance relations.

Theorem 2. *(Balance Properties) For any network:*

1. *The union of two balance relations is a balance relation*
2. *The composition of two balance relations is a balance relation*
3. *There is a largest balance relation, which we denote by B^**
4. *B^* is a greatest fixpoint*
5. *B^* is a sub-groupoid of $\simeq_{IO}$.*

The final balance property implies that the orbit relation for B^* is an equivalence. The fixpoint property induces a partition-refinement algorithm for computing the orbit relation of B^* which is polynomial in the size of the network.

4.1 Automorphisms and Balance

Informally, an automorphism of a network is a permutation of the edge and node set which leaves the network structure unchanged. Formally, for a network (N, E), an *automorphism* is given by a function π which is a bijection from N to N and a bijection from E to E such that

1. (Color Preservation) For any node n, $\xi(n) = \xi(\pi(n))$, and for any edge e, $\xi(e) = \xi(\pi(e))$
2. (Link Preservation) For any node n and edge e, $n \in ins(e)$ holds iff $\pi(n) \in ins(\pi(e))$ and $n \in outs(e)$ holds iff $\pi(n) \in outs(\pi(e))$.

The global symmetry of the network is defined by its set of automorphisms, which forms a group under function composition. Given an automorphism group, G, of the network, define *Local*(G) as the set of triples (m, β, n) where, for some $\pi \in G$, $\pi(m) = n$ and β is π restricted to *InOut*(m). The following theorem shows that global automorphisms induce balance relations.

Theorem 3. *For any automorphism group G of a network, Local(G) is both a sub-groupoid of $\mathcal{G}_{IO}$ and a balance relation.*

The network of Figure 1 has a balance relation connecting 1 and 2 through the bijection β, even though the only automorphism is the identity.

4.2 Balance and Symmetry

The following theorem shows how a balance relation influences the symmetry of the computed invariant. We say that a vector θ *respects* a balance relation B if for all (m, β, n) in B, $[\theta_n \equiv \beta(\theta_m)]$.

Lemma 1. *Let B be a balance relation. Consider a program assignment which is valid for B. For any $(m, \beta, n) \in B$ and any transition condition $t(V_m, V'_m)$ and any predicate $p(V)$, it is the case that $[\beta(SP_m(t, p)) \equiv SP_n(\beta(t), \beta(p))]$.*

Lemma 2. *Let B be a balance relation. Consider a program assignment which is valid for B. For all $(m, \beta, n) \in B$, any θ which respects B, and $j \in pt(m), k \in pt(n)$ which correspond for (m, β, n) by B, $[\beta(intf^{\theta}_{jm}) \equiv intf^{\theta}_{kn}]$ holds.*

Theorem 4. *(Symmetry Reduction) Let B be a balance relation. For a program assignment which is valid for B, the computed local invariant θ^* respects B.*

Proof: The proof is by transfinite induction on the fixpoint stages. The inductive assumption at stage λ is that θ^S respects B for all stages S which precede λ.

(Basis) The initial values $\theta^0_m = \tilde{I}_m$ and $\theta^0_n = \tilde{I}_n$ are related as claimed by the validity of the assignment.

(Step ordinal) Suppose that the hypothesis is true at stage S. The definition of θ^{S+1}_m is $\theta^S_m \lor SP_m(T_m, \theta^S_m) \lor (\lor j : j \in pt(m) : SP_m(intf^{\theta^S}_{jm}, \theta^S_m))$. Applying β, which distributes over $\lor$, we get

$$\beta(\theta^S_m) \lor \beta(SP_m(T_m, \theta^S_m)) \lor (\lor j : j \in pt(m) : \beta(SP_m(intf^{\theta^S}_{jm}, \theta^S_m))) \quad (12)$$

The SP terms satisfy the conditions of Lemma 1. By the inductive hypothesis and Lemma 1, we get

$$\theta_n^S \vee SP_n(\beta(T_m), \theta_n^S) \vee (\vee j : j \in pt(m) : SP_n(\beta(intf_{jm}^{\theta^S}), \theta_n^S)) \quad (13)$$

By valid program assignment and Lemma 2, this is equivalent to

$$\theta_n^S \vee SP_n(T_n, \theta_n^S) \vee (\vee k : k \in pt(n) : SP_n(intf_{kn}^{\theta^S}, \theta_n^S)) \quad (14)$$

There is a slight subtlety in the last step. By the definition of B, every j has a corresponding $k \in pt(n)$. As B is closed under inverse, all k in $pt(n)$ are related to some $j \in pt(m)$. Hence, the interference terms for m map exactly to the interference terms of n. The final expression is just the definition of θ_n^{S+1}.

(Limit ordinal) Suppose that the hypothesis is true for all stages S below a limit ordinal λ. As β distributes over arbitrary unions, we obtain the chain of equivalences $\beta(\theta_m^\lambda) \equiv \beta(\vee S : S \prec \lambda : \theta_m^S) \equiv (\vee S : S \prec \lambda : \beta(\theta_m^S)) \equiv (\vee S : S \prec \lambda : \theta_n^S) \equiv \theta_n^\lambda$. **EndProof.**

4.3 Symmetry-Reduced Local Invariant Computation

The main symmetry theorem gives rise to the following symmetry-reduced fixpoint computation for the local invariant.

1. Fix a balance relation B which is a sub-groupoid of $\mathcal{G}_{IO}$. (B^* is one such relation.) Let $\simeq_B$ be its orbit relation; this is an equivalence.
2. Pick a representative from each equivalence class of $\simeq_B$. For a node n, let $rep(n)$ denote its representative.
3. For each non-representative node n fix a bijection β_n such that $(rep(n), \beta_n, n)$ is a triple in B. For a representative node r, fix β_r to be the identity.
4. Compute the fixpoint over the set of representatives. The fixpoint vector has a component θ_r for each representative r. To compute the update for representative r, use the formula for $F_r(\theta)$, except that the term θ_n for a node n which is not a representative node is replaced with $\beta_n(\theta_{rep(n)})$.

By induction on the fixpoint stages, we get the theorem below. The complexity of the symmetry-reduced calculation is given by the formula derived previously, with $|N|$ replaced by the number of representatives.

Theorem 5. *The symmetry-reduced computation computes the same least fixpoint as the original.*

4.4 Equivalent Networks and the Quotient Construction

A balance relation which is a groupoid (for instance, B^*) induces an orbit relation, which is an equivalence on the nodes. This partitions nodes into equivalence classes. We use the classes to define a quotient network, and show that it suffices to compute the local invariant on the quotient.

A quotient is an instance of the more general concept of an *equivalent network*. For networks W_1 and W_2 with valid assignments, W_2 is equivalent to W_1 via the relation $R \subset N_1 \times N_2$ if, for all $(i, j) \in R$, $[\theta_1^*(i) \equiv \theta_2^*(j)]$. Every network is equivalent to itself through the identity relation. A quotient construction produces a smaller assigned network which is equivalent to the original.

Given a network $W = (N, E)$ and a groupoid balance relation B, a *quotient* $\overline{W}$ is defined as follows.

1. The nodes of $\overline{W}$ are the equivalence classes of $\simeq_B$. Each class C has a defined representative, denoted $rep(C)$, chosen arbitrarily. We write the class for node n as $\overline{n}$. The color of a class is the (common) color of all nodes in it.
2. For a class C with representative r, there is an edge $\overline{e}$ for each edge e in $InOut(r)$. The edge $\overline{e}$ connects equivalence classes of nodes connected by e. In more detail, $m \in ins(e)$ iff $\overline{m} \in ins(\overline{e})$, and $m \in outs(e)$ iff $\overline{m} \in outs(\overline{e})$. The color of a quotient edge is the color of the edge which generates it.
3. A class C with representative r is assigned similarly to r; i.e., such that $[\tilde{I}_C \equiv \beta_r(\tilde{I}_r)]$ and $[T_C \equiv \beta_r(T_r)]$, where β is the bijection which relates each e in $InOut(r)$ to its corresponding edge $\overline{e}$.

The quotient is not unique, except under stronger conditions on the balance groupoid. (Non-uniqueness arises as the balance definition allows representatives x and y for a class C to have corresponding edges e and f such that e and f have inequivalent *outs* sets. This does not, however, influence the invariant computation, as only *ins* sets are relevant for the points-to definition.) The theorem below shows that local invariant computed on a quotient is identical to that on the original network for the representative nodes. Values for non-representative nodes are obtained by the transformation given in Theorem 4.

Theorem 6. *Any quotient* $\overline{W}$ *is equivalent to* W *via* $R = \{(r, C) \mid r = rep(C)\}$.

5 Pairwise Symmetry and Balance Relations

In this section, we turn to symmetry reduction for invariants of the form $(\forall i, j : i \neq j : \theta_{ij})$. The definitions of pairwise local symmetry and balance, given below, are analogues of the previous definitions for singly-indexed invariants.

For a pair of nodes (i, j), let $In(i, j) = In(i) \cup In(j)$ and let $Out(i, j) = Out(i) \cup Out(j)$. A node k is in $pt(i, j)$ if $k \notin \{m, n\}$ and $Out(k) \cap InOut(i, j)$ is non-empty. A *pairwise local symmetry* between (i, j) and (m, n) is possible if $\xi(i) = \xi(m)$ and $\xi(j) = \xi(n)$, and there is a a function β such that (i, β, m) and (j, β, n) are local symmetries. The set of all pairwise local symmetries $((i, j), \beta, (m, n))$ forms the pairwise symmetry groupoid of the network.

A *pairwise balance relation* B is a subset of the pairwise symmetry groupoid of the network which is closed under inverse, and such that for all $((i, j), \beta, (m, n))$ in B, and every k in $pt(i, j)$, there is l in $pt(m, n)$ such that

1. There is a function δ so that (k, δ, l) is a local symmetry, and
2. For all edges e in $InOut(k) \cap InOut(i, j)$, it is the case that $\beta(e) = \delta(e)$.

A program assignment is valid for B if for any $((i,j),\beta,(m,n))$ in B, $[\beta(T_i) \equiv T_m]$, $[\beta(T_j) \equiv T_n]$ and $[\beta(\tilde{I}_{ij}) \equiv \tilde{I}_{mn}]$. With a proof strategy similar to that for singly-indexed properties, we have the following analogue of Theorem 4.

Theorem 7. *(Pairwise Symmetry Reduction) Let B be a pairwise balance relation. For any program assignment valid for B: for any $((i,j),\beta,(m,n))$ in B, in the computed local pairwise invariant, θ^*, it is the case that $[\theta^*_{mn} \equiv \beta(\theta^*_{ij})]$.*

From a global automorphism group G, define $Local_2(G)$ as the set of triples $((i,j),\beta,(m,n))$ such that for a permutation π in G, $\pi(i) = m, \pi(j) = n$ and β is π restricted to $InOut(i,j)$.

Theorem 8. *For any automorphism group G of a network, $Local_2(G)$ is a pairwise groupoid balance relation.*

6 Consequences

Consider a simple token-passing protocol on a unidirectional ring network. Each process is in one of three states: thinking (T), hungry (H), and eating (E). It moves from T to H on its own; from H to E by removing a token from its left edge; and from E to T on its own, placing the token on its right edge. The predicate t_i expresses the presence of a token on the edge to the left of node i.

The singly-indexed local invariant for a ring is too weak to conclude safety (mutual exclusion). However, the pairwise local invariant suffices. It is given by $(\forall i,j : i \neq j : (t_i \Rightarrow \neg t_j) \wedge (E_i \Rightarrow \neg E_j \wedge \neg t_i \wedge \neg t_j))$.

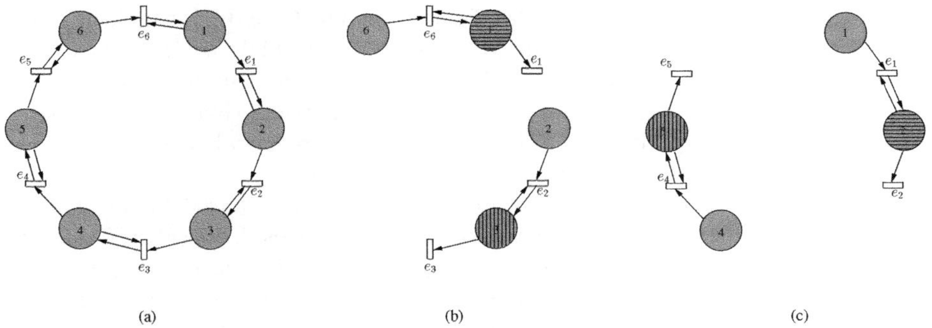

Fig. 2. Token-Ring Network and Neighborhood Views for $(1,3)$ and $(2,5)$

By Theorem 8, $Local_2(G)$ is a pairwise balance relation. Pairs (i,j) and (m,n) are related if the nodes in the pairs are the same distance apart (clockwise) on the ring. Thus, $(1,2)$ is a representative for spacing 1, and $(1,3)$ is a representative for spacing 2. It turns out that $(1,3)$ is also a representative for any larger spacing, as the relation between $(1,3)$ and (m,n) with spacing at least 2 is a balance relation. Figure 2 shows, for example, the similar local neighborhoods of $(1,3)$ and $(2,5)$ in a ring of size 6.

It suffices, therefore, to compute the pairwise invariant over the representative pairs $(1,2)$ and $(1,3)$ for a fixed ring network of size at least 3. Moreover, for a family of ring networks, each instance has the same pair of representatives. The following theorem establishes conditions under which a pairwise invariant generalizes to an invariant for any larger instance.

Theorem 9. *For a uniform ring network family where the processes and node and edge data types are independent of the size of the ring, the pairwise invariant computed for a ring of size 3 holds (by extending the range of node indices) for all larger ring sizes.*

For a dining philosophers protocol, mutual exclusion is required only between neighboring processes. For an abstract dining philosophers protocol, the singly-indexed invariant $(\forall i : E_i \Rightarrow fork_{i-1} = R \wedge fork_i = L)$ holds, where L, R represent left and right directions. Thus, the symmetry-reduced structure is a single node, which also proves that the invariant holds in a parameterized sense.

7 Related Work, Conclusions and Open Questions

There is a large body of work on compositional methods for verification of concurrent programs. Much of this work, the early examples of which are the Owicki-Gries method [25] and proof rules used by Lamport [20] and Jones [19], applies to a memory model where all processes share a common memory. The assume-guarantee method of Misra and Chandy [4] is based on a network model with processes communicating on unbounded queues. Compositional methods for CCS and CSP are described in [11,21]. Proof rules based on CCS/CSP synchronization have been automated using learning techniques [7]. In [24] and [1], for example, compositional proof rules are given that are sound (and semantically complete) for the full range of Linear Temporal Logic properties, thus including safety properties, liveness properties and fairness properties. Local reasoning has also been applied to synchronous computation [5,22].

Our network model is based on atomic actions and shared memory rather than CCS/CSP style synchronization or message queues. Using it, it is possible to represent, for instance, the sharing of forks among dining philosophers. The proof rules are assertion-based. The key idea of reduction with local symmetries should, we believe, carry over to other models of process communication.

Earlier work [23,10] on symmetry reduction for compositional reasoning applies to programs with a common shared memory. This paper significantly generalizes the scope of symmetry reduction to arbitrary networks of processes and fine-grained sharing relationships.

These results have been strongly influenced by the work of Golubitsky and Stewart on local symmetry in networks [16], but there are crucial differences in both the problem domain and the questions being addressed. The networks in [16] are clocked synchronous networks where the "program" at each node is given by an ordinary differential equation. The authors show that the local symmetries of the network influence the emergence of computations in which a group of nodes have completely synchronized (or phase-shifted) values. (In temporal logic terms, the network satisfies properties such as $\mathsf{EG}(x_1 = x_2)$ or $\mathsf{EG}(x_1' = x_2)$.) They identify balance as a necessary (and, in a sense, sufficient) condition for this behavior. Our results, on the other hand, are about interleaved process execution and universal rather than existential safety properties. We do make use of and adapt the groupoid formulation defined in their paper to describe local symmetries.

The results on parameterized verification build on the idea of generalizing from proofs of small instances that was explored in the work on "invisible invariants" [2]. This method was connected to compositional reasoning in [23]. The earlier papers used a globally shared memory model; the network model results in a strengthening of the results, especially for ring networks. The token-ring example from Section 6 falls into the decidable class from [13] but the result here is both more general in that it applies also to non-token-passing protocols and yet limited in that it applies only to inductive invariants. There is, of course, a variety of other methods for parameterized verification; these are, in general, incomparable. Our results do point to intriguing connections between local symmetry, compositional invariants and parameterized verification.

This work shows that striking reductions can be obtained by considering the combination of local symmetries with compositional reasoning. There are several intriguing open questions: the proper treatment of auxiliary variables, deriving similar results for CCS/CSP-style synchronization, extending the symmetry reduction theorems from safety to liveness properties and exploring the role of local symmetries in proofs of parameterized properties of irregular networks.

References

1. Amla, N., Emerson, E.A., Namjoshi, K.S., Trefler, R.J.: Visual Specifications for Modular Reasoning About Asynchronous Systems. In: Peled, D.A., Vardi, M.Y. (eds.) FORTE 2002. LNCS, vol. 2529, pp. 226–242. Springer, Heidelberg (2002)
2. Arons, T., Pnueli, A., Ruah, S., Xu, J., Zuck, L.D.: Parameterized Verification with Automatically Computed Inductive Assertions. In: Berry, G., Comon, H., Finkel, A. (eds.) CAV 2001. LNCS, vol. 2102, pp. 221–234. Springer, Heidelberg (2001)
3. Brown, R.: From groups to groupoids: A brief survey. Bull. London Math. Society 19, 113–134 (1987)
4. Chandy, K., Misra, J.: Proofs of networks of processes. IEEE Transactions on Software Engineering 7(4) (1981)
5. Cho, H., Hachtel, G.D., Macii, E., Plessier, B., Somenzi, F.: Algorithms for approximate FSM traversal based on state space decomposition. IEEE Trans. on CAD of Integrated Circuits and Systems 15(12), 1465–1478 (1996)
6. Clarke, E.M., Filkorn, T., Jha, S.: Exploiting Symmetry in Temporal Logic Model Checking. In: Courcoubetis, C. (ed.) CAV 1993. LNCS, vol. 697. Springer, Heidelberg (1993)
7. Cobleigh, J.M., Giannakopoulou, D., Păsăreanu, C.S.: Learning Assumptions for Compositional Verification. In: Garavel, H., Hatcliff, J. (eds.) TACAS 2003. LNCS, vol. 2619, pp. 331–346. Springer, Heidelberg (2003)

8. Cohen, A., Namjoshi, K.S.: Local Proofs for Global Safety Properties. In: Damm, W., Hermanns, H. (eds.) CAV 2007. LNCS, vol. 4590, pp. 55–67. Springer, Heidelberg (2007)
9. Cohen, A., Namjoshi, K.S.: Local Proofs for Linear-Time Properties of Concurrent Programs. In: Gupta, A., Malik, S. (eds.) CAV 2008. LNCS, vol. 5123, pp. 149–161. Springer, Heidelberg (2008)
10. Cohen, A., Namjoshi, K.S.: Local proofs for global safety properties. Formal Methods in System Design 34(2), 104–125 (2009)
11. de Roever, W.-P., de Boer, F., Hannemann, U., Hooman, J., Lakhnech, Y., Poel, M., Zwiers, J.: Concurrency Verification: Introduction to Compositional and Noncompositional Proof Methods. Cambridge University Press (2001)
12. Dijkstra, E., Scholten, C.: Predicate Calculus and Program Semantics. Springer, Heidelberg (1990)
13. Emerson, E., Namjoshi, K.: Reasoning about rings. In: ACM Symposium on Principles of Programming Languages (1995)
14. Emerson, E., Sistla, A.: Symmetry and Model Checking. In: Courcoubetis, C. (ed.) CAV 1993. LNCS, vol. 697. Springer, Heidelberg (1993)
15. Flanagan, C., Qadeer, S.: Thread-Modular Model Checking. In: Ball, T., Rajamani, S.K. (eds.) SPIN 2003. LNCS, vol. 2648, pp. 213–224. Springer, Heidelberg (2003)
16. Golubitsky, M., Stewart, I.: Nonlinear dynamics of networks: the groupoid formalism. Bull. Amer. Math. Soc. 43, 305–364 (2006)
17. Gupta, A., Popeea, C., Rybalchenko, A.: Predicate abstraction and refinement for verifying multi-threaded programs. In: POPL. ACM (2011)
18. Ip, C.N., Dill, D.: Better verification through symmetry. Formal Methods in System Design 9(1/2) (1996)
19. Jones, C.: Tentative steps toward a development method for interfering programs. ACM Trans. on Programming Languages and Systems, TOPLAS (1983)
20. Lamport, L.: Proving the correctness of multiprocess programs. IEEE Trans. Software Eng. 3(2) (1977)
21. Lamport, L., Schneider, F.B.: The "Hoare Logic" of CSP, and All That. ACM Trans. Program. Lang. Syst. 6(2), 281–296 (1984)
22. Moon, I.-H., Kukula, J.H., Shiple, T.R., Somenzi, F.: Least fixpoint approximations for reachability analysis. In: ICCAD, pp. 41–44 (1999)
23. Namjoshi, K.S.: Symmetry and Completeness in the Analysis of Parameterized Systems. In: Cook, B., Podelski, A. (eds.) VMCAI 2007. LNCS, vol. 4349, pp. 299–313. Springer, Heidelberg (2007)
24. Namjoshi, K.S., Trefler, R.J.: On the completeness of compositional reasoning methods. ACM Trans. Comput. Logic 11, 16:1–16:22 (2010)
25. Owicki, S.S., Gries, D.: Verifying properties of parallel programs: An axiomatic approach. Commun. ACM 19(5), 279–285 (1976)
26. Weinstein, A.: Groupoids: Unifying internal and external symmetry-a tour through some examples. Notices of the AMS (1996)

versat: A Verified Modern SAT Solver

Duckki Oe, Aaron Stump, Corey Oliver, and Kevin Clancy

Computer Science
The University of Iowa

Abstract. This paper presents versat, a formally verified SAT solver incorporating the essential features of modern SAT solvers, including clause learning, watched literals, optimized conflict analysis, non-chronological backtracking, and decision heuristics. Unlike previous related work on SAT-solver verification, our implementation uses efficient low-level data structures like mutable C arrays for clauses and other solver state, and machine integers for literals. The implementation and proofs are written in GURU, a verified-programming language. We compare versat to a state-of-the-art SAT solver that produces certified "unsat" answers. We also show through an empirical evaluation that versat can solve SAT problems on the modern scale.

1 Introduction

Several important recent works have applied powerful verification methods based on full-fledged inductive theorem proving to verify important systems artifacts. CompCert is an optimizing compiler for a subset of the C programming language, for which semantics preservation has been proved in the COQ proof assistant (see [12], and many other papers at the project web page, compcert.inria.fr). The seL4 microkernel verification effort uses the Isabelle theorem prover to prove that the microkernel implementation in C and assembly refines a high-level non-deterministic model expressing the desired system properties [10]. These impressive verification efforts show that the trustworthiness of practical systems artifacts can be raised to the highest levels currently known, using interactive theorem proving.

In a similar spirit, this paper presents versat, an efficient SAT solver for which we have verified correctness of "unsat" answers. SAT and SMT solvers are critical components of automatic verification tools like bounded model-checkers and k-induction provers [9,5], and are used for many other static analysis applications, such as symbolic execution [11]. However, just as any complex piece of software, SAT solvers do have bugs. Brummayer et al. reports crashes and incorrect answers from top-ranked solvers at the SAT competition 2007 and 2009 [4]. This paper represents a first step towards the development of verified high-performance analysis tools, by verifying correctness of "unsat" answers from a modern performant SAT solver. Just as operating systems and compilers are the foundations for computing systems generally, SAT and SMT solvers are increasingly the foundation for analysis and automatic verification tools. So we see SAT solvers as artifacts of fundamental interest, and hence natural targets for verification.

Specification. We have proved statically that whenever versat reports a set of input clauses unsatisfiable, then there exists a resolution proof of the empty clause from those

V. Kuncak and A. Rybalchenko (Eds.): VMCAI 2012, LNCS 7148, pp. 363–378, 2012.

input clauses. This proof (as a data structure) is not constructed at run-time. Rather, our verification confirms statically that it exists, for all formulas `versat` reports unsatisfiable. As our verification is itself constructive, the resolution proof could in principle be generated at run-time. But run-time proof-production imposes undesirable time and memory overhead on SAT solving. So it is preferable to have a static guarantee of soundness for the solver, at least for applications that do not need the actual proof artifact, but only require a trustworthy result.

Main Contribution. What makes our work distinctive is that it is, to the best of our knowledge, the first to statically verify soundness of a SAT solver implemented using efficient low-level data structures. These include 32-bit machine integers for literals and mutable C arrays for many solver data structures (e.g., clauses and look-up tables), which are manipulated using machine arithmetic/bitwise operations, and low-level pointer managements. In GURU, machine integers and their operations are precisely modeled as bit vectors and vector operations, including overflow situations. This does increase the burden of proof, but is necessary for performance. We demonstrate (Section 5) that `versat` can solve large benchmarks, including some on the order of those used in the SAT Competition. While further work would be required to achieve levels of performance closer to the current state of the art in SAT solving, `versat` is already valuable as being the first high-performance SAT solver that can deliver trustworthy results without the overhead of proof production (and subsequent proof checking). Furthermore, as `versat` already includes verified implementations of many of the standard modern solver data structures including those for watched literals and efficient conflict analysis, we hypothesize that our approach will scale to additional solver optimizations.

Verification Approach. This project also represents a major case study of a verification approach which is gaining importance, particularly within the Programming Languages community. The `versat` code has been developed and verified in a so-called *dependently typed* programming language called GURU [20]. The basic methodology of dependently typed programming is to express rich specifications through types, and include proofs (when needed) only internally, inside program code. Such proofs establish properties externally of functions used in expressing the specification. Such specificational functions are typically much smaller and more tractable than the programs they specify, thus reducing the burden of proof. GURU implements this approach to program verification, and also provides a static analysis for statically tracking memory. Thanks to this analysis, GURU does not require a garbage collector for memory management at runtime.

Paper Outline. We begin with a brief summary of dependent types for verified programming in GURU (Section 2). We then describe in more detail the specification we have statically verified for `versat` (Section 3). Next, we describe the actual implementation, and how we verify that it meets our specification (Section 4). We present empirical results supporting our claim that `versat`'s performance is within the realm of modern SAT solving (Section 5). We next cover important related work (Section 6), and then reflect a little on the experience of implementing an efficient verified SAT solver (Section 7), before concluding (Section 8).

2 Verified Programming in Guru

By way of background for the sections on the specification and implementation of versat below, we begin with a quick introduction to GURU. GURU is a functional programming language with rich types, in which programs can be verified both *externally* (as in traditional theorem provers), and *internally* (cf [1]).[1] For a standard example of the difference, suppose we wish to prove that the result of appending two lists has length equal to the sum of the input lengths.

External verification of this property may proceed like this. First, we define the type of append function on lists. In GURU syntax, the typing for this append function is:

```
append : Fun(A:type)(l1 l2 : <list A>). <list A>
```

This says that append accepts a type A, and lists l1 and l2 holding elements of type A, and produces another such list. To verify the desired property, we write a proof in GURU's proof syntax of the following formula:

```
Forall(A:type)(l1 l2:<list A>).
  { (length (append l1 l2)) = (plus (length l1) (length l2)) }
```

The equality listed expresses, in GURU's semantics, that the term on the left-hand side evaluates to the same value as the term on the right-hand side. So the formula states that for all types A, for all lists l1 and l2 holding elements of that type, calling the length function on the result of appending l1 and l2 gives the same result as adding the lengths of l1 and l2. This is the external approach.

With internal verification, we first define an alternative *indexed* datatype for lists. A type index is a program value occurring in the type, in this case the length of the list. We define the type <vec A n> to be the type of lists storing elements of type A, and having length n, where n is a Peano (i.e., unary) number:

```
Inductive vec : Fun(A:type)(n:nat).type :=
  vecn : Fun(A:type).<vec A Z>
| vecc : Fun(A:type)(spec n:nat)(a:A)(l:<vec A n>).
             <vec A (S n)>.
```

This states that vec is inductively defined with constructors vecn and vecc (for nil and cons, respectively). The return type of vecc is <vec A (S n)>, where S is the successor function. So the length of the list returned by the constructor vecc is one greater than the length of the sublist l. Note that the argument n (of vecc) is labeled "spec", which means specificational. GURU will enforce that no run-time results will depend on the value of this argument, thus enabling the compiler to erase all values for that parameter in compiled code.

We can now define the type of vec_append function on vectors:

```
vec_append : Fun(A:type)(spec n m:nat)
                (l1:<vec A n>)(l2:<vec A m>).<vec A (plus n m)>
```

[1] GURU is freely downloadable from http://www.guru-lang.org/.

This type states that `append` takes in a type `A`, two specificational natural numbers `n` and `m`, and vectors `l1` and `l2` of the corresponding lengths, and returns a new vector of length `(plus n m)`. This is how internal verification expresses the relationship between lengths which we proved externally above. Type-checking code like this may require the programmer to prove that two types are equivalent. For example, a proof of commutativity of addition is needed to prove `<vec A (plus n m)>` equivalent to `<vec A (plus m n)>`. Currently, these proofs must mostly be written by the programmer, using special proof syntax, including syntax for inductive proofs.

GURU supports memory-safe programming without garbage collection, using a combination of techniques [19]. Immutable tree-like data structures are handled by reference counting, with some optimizations to avoid unnecessary increments/decrements. Mutable data structures like arrays are handled by statically enforcing a readers/writers discipline: either there is a unique reference available for reading and writing the array, or else there may be multiple read-only references. The one-writer discipline ensures that it is sound to implement array update destructively, while using a pure functional model for formal reasoning. The connection between the efficient implementation and the functional model is not formally verified, and must be trusted. This is reasonable, as it concerns only a small amount of simple C code (less than 50 lines), for a few primitive operations like indexing a C array and managing memory/pointers.

3 Specification

The main property of `versat` is the soundness of the solver on top of the basic requirements of GURU, such as memory safety and array-bounds checking. We encoded the underlying logic of SAT in GURU to reason about the behavior of the SAT solver. That encoding includes the representation of formulas and the deduction rules. For a "UNSAT" answer, our specification requires that there exists a derivation proof of the empty clause from the input formula. Note that most solvers can generate a model with a "SAT" answer and those models can be checked very efficiently. So, we do not think there is a practical advantage for statically verifying the soundness of "SAT" answers. Also, it is important to note that the specification is the only part we need to trust. So, it should be clear and concise. The specification of `versat` is only 259 lines of GURU code. The rest of `versat` is the actual implementation and the proof that the implementation follows the specification, which will be checked by the GURU type system.

3.1 Representation of CNF Formula

The `formula` type is defined using simple data structures: 32 bit unsigned integers for literals and lists for clauses and formulas. The lower 31 bits of the literal represent the variable number, and the most significant bit represents the polarity. The GURU definitions of those types are listed below. The `word` type is defined in GURU's standard library, and represents 32 bit unsigned integers. We emphasize that these simple data structures are only for specification. Section 4 describes how our verification relates them to efficient data structures in the implementation.

```
Define lit := word
Define clause := <list lit>
Define formula := <list clause>
```

3.2 Deduction Rules

There may be different ways to specify the unsatisfiability of formula. One could be a model theoretic definition, saying no model evaluates a formula true or $\Phi \models \bot$. Another could be a proof theoretic one, saying the empty clause (False) can be deduced from the formula or $\Phi \vdash \bot$. In the propositional logic, the above two definitions are equivalent. In `versat`, we have taken a weaker variant of the proof theoretic definition, $\Phi \vdash_{res} \bot$ where only the resolution rule is used to refute the formula. Because $\vdash_{res}$ is strictly weaker than $\vdash$, $\Phi \vdash_{res} \bot$ still implies $\Phi \models \bot$. So, even though our formalization is proof theoretic, it should be possible to prove that our formalization satisfies a model theoretic formalization.

The `pf` type encodes the deduction rules of the propositional logic and `pf` objects represents proofs. Figure 1 shows the definition of `pf` type and its helper functions. `cl_subsume` is a predicate that means `c1` subsumes `c2`, which is just a subset function on lists defined in GURU's standard library. And `is_resolvent` is a predicate that means `r` is a resolvent of `c1` and `c2` over the literal `l`. Additionally, `cl_has` checks that the clause contains the given literal, and `cl_erase` removes all the occurrences of the literal in the clause. Also, `tt` and `ff` are Boolean values defined in the library. The `<pf F C>` type stands for the set of proofs that the formula `F` implies the clause `C`. Members of this type are constructed as derivation trees for the clause. Because this proof tree will not be generated and checked at run-time, the type requires the proper preconditions at each constructor. GURU's type system ensures that those proof objects are valid by construction.

The `pf_asm` constructor stands for the assumption rule, which proves any clause in the input formula. The `member` function looks for the clause C in the formula, returning `tt` if so. The `pf_sub` constructor stands for the subsumption rule. This rule allows to remove duplicated literals or change the order of literals in a proven clause. Note that the constructor requires a proof `d` of `C'` and a precondition `u` that `C'` subsumes `C`. Finally, `pf_res` stands for the resolution rule. It requires two clauses (`C1` and `C2`) along with their proofs (`d1` and `d2`) and the precondition `u` that `C` is a resolvent of `C1` and `C2` over the literal `l`.

3.3 The `answer` Type

In order to enforce soundness, the implementation is required to have a particular return type, called `answer`. So, if the implementation type checks, it is considered valid under our specification. Figure 2 shows the definition of the `answer` type. The `answer` type has two constructors (or values): `sat` and `unsat`. The `unsat` constructor holds two subdata: the input formula `F` and a derivation proof of the empty clause, `p`. The formula `F` is required to make sure the proof indeed proves the input formula. The term `(nil lit)` means the empty list of literals, meaning the empty clause. By constructing a value of the type `<pf F (nil lit)>`, we know that the empty clause is derivable

```
Define cl_subsume := fun(c1:clause)(c2:clause).
  (list_subset lit eq_lit c1 c2)

Define is_resolvent := fun(r:clause)(c1:clause)(c2:clause)(l:lit).
  (and (and (cl_has c1 (negated l))
            (cl_has c2 l))
       (and (cl_subsume (cl_erase c1 (negated l)) r)
            (cl_subsume (cl_erase c2 l) r)))

Inductive pf : Fun(F : formula)(C : clause).type :=
  pf_asm : Fun(F : formula)(C:clause)
              (u : { (member C F eq_clause) = tt }) .<pf F C>
| pf_sub : Fun(F : formula)(C C' : clause)
              (d : <pf F C'>)
              (u : { (cl_subsume C' C) = tt }) .<pf F C>
| pf_res : Fun(F : formula)(C C1 C2 : clause)(l : lit)
              (d1 : <pf F C1>)(d2 : <pf F C2>)
              (u : { (is_resolvent C C1 C2 l) = tt }) .<pf F C>
```

Fig. 1. The pf data type and helper functions

from the original formula. (Note that the proof p is marked as specificational using the spec keyword) The type checker still requires the programmer to supply the spec arguments. However, those arguments will be erased during compilation. We only care about the existence of such data, not the actual value. By constructing proofs only from the invariants of the solver, GURU's type system confirms that such proofs could always be constructed without fail. So, making them specificational, hence not computing them at run-time, is sound.

```
Inductive answer : Fun(F:formula).type :=
  sat : Fun(spec F:formula).<answer F>
| unsat : Fun(spec F:formula)(spec p:<pf F (nil lit)>).<answer F>
```

Fig. 2. The definition of the answer type

3.4 Parser and Entry Point

The formula type above is still in terms of integer and list data structures, not a stream of characters as stored in a benchmark file. The benchmark file has to be translated to GURU data structure before it can be reasoned about. So, we include a simple recursive parser for the DIMACS standard benchmark format, which amounts to 145 lines of GURU code, as a part of our specification. It might be possible to reduce this using a verified parser generator, but we judge there to be more important targets of further verification. Similarly, the main function is considered a part of the specification, as the outcome of the solve function is an answer value, not the action of printing "SAT" or "UNSAT". The main function simply calls the parser, passes the output to the solve function, and prints the answer as a string of characters.

4 Implementation and Proof

The specification in Section 3 does not constrain the details of the implementation very much. For a trivial example, a solver that just aborted immediately on every input formula would satisfy the specification. So would a solver that used the naive data structures for formulas, or a naive solving algorithm. Therefore, we have imposed an additional informal constraint on `versat`, which is that it should use efficient low-level data structures, and should implement a number of the essential features of modern SAT solvers. The features implemented in `versat` are conflict analysis, clause learning, backjumping, watched literals, and basic decision heuristics. Also, each of these features is implemented using the same efficient data structures that can be found in a C-language implementation like `tinisat` or `minisat`. However, implementing more features and optimizations make it more difficult to prove the soundness property.

Modern SAT solvers are driven by conflict analysis, during which a new clause is deduced and recorded to guide the search. Thus, the critical component for soundness is the conflict analysis module, which can be verified, to some extent, in isolation from the rest of the solver. Verifying that every learned clause is a consequence of the input clauses ensures the correctness of UNSAT answers from the solver, in the special case of the empty clause. Using the internal-verification approach described in the previous section, the conflict analysis module enforces soundness by requiring that with each learned clause added to the clause database, there is an accompanying specificational proof (the `pf` datatype described in Section 3). In this section, we explain some of the run-time clause data structure along with the invariants, and the conflict analysis implementation.

4.1 Array-Based Clauses and Invariants

In the specification, the data structure for clauses is (singly linked) list, which is easier to reason about. However, accessing elements in a list is not as efficient as an array. The elements of an array are more likely in the same cache line, which leads to a faster sequential access, as elements in a linked list are not. Also arrays will use less memory than lists, which need extra storage for pointers. So, at the implementation level, `versat` uses array-based clauses with invariants as defined in Figure 3. An `<array lit n>` object stands for an array of literals of size `n`. The variable `nv` represents the number of different variables in the formula `F`. It is also the maximum possible value for variable numbers as defined in the DIMACS file format (variables are named from 1 up to `nv`). The predicate `(array_in_bounds nv l)` used in the invariant `u1` means every variable in the array `l` is less than or equal to `nv` and not equal to zero. The invariant `u1` is used to avoid run-time checks for bounds when accessing a number of look-up tables indexed by the variable number, such as the current assignment, reference to the antecedent clauses, and decision level for the variable. It also implicitly states that the array `l` is null-terminated. In array-based clauses, the word value zero is used as the termination marker, instead of keeping a separate run-time variable for the length of the array. The second invariant `u2` states that the clause `c`, which is proved by `pf_c`, is the same as the interpretation of `l`, where `to_cl` is our interpretation of an array as a list. Again, this interpretation is only specificational and not performed at run-time.

```
Inductive aclause : Fun(nv:word)(F:formula).type :=
  mk_aclause : Fun(spec n:word)(l:<array lit n>)
                   (spec nv:word)(spec F:formula)
                   (u1:{ (array_in_bounds nv l) = tt })
                   (spec c:clause)(spec pf_c:<pf F c>)
                   (u2:{ c = (to_cl l) })
                  .<aclause nv F>
```

Fig. 3. The aclause type for the array-based clauses and invariants

At the beginning of execution, versat converts all input clauses into <aclause nv F> objects. In order to satisfy the invariants, the conversion function checks that every variable is within bounds and internally proves that the interpretation of the output array is exactly the same as the input list-based clause. Then, every time a new clause is learned, a new <aclause nv F> object is created and stored in the clause database. Remember the soundness of the whole solver requires a <pf F (nil lit)> object, which is a proof of the list-based empty clause. Assume we derived the empty array-based clause at run-time. From the invariant u2, we know that there exists an interpretation of the array clause. And we proved a theorem which states that the only possible interpretation of the empty array is the empty list, (nil lit). Now, we can conclude that the interpretation is indeed the empty list-based clause, which is proven valid according to another invariant pf_c. Thus, it suffices to compute the empty array-based clause to prove the empty list-based clause.

4.2 Conflict Analysis with Optimized Resolution

The conflict analysis is where a SAT solver deduces a new clause from the existing set of clauses by resolution. Usually, a series of resolutions are applied until the first unique implication point (UIP) clause is derived. In order to speed up the resolution step, advanced solvers like minisat use a number of related data structures to represent the intermediate conflict clauses and perform resolutions efficiently. In versat, we implemented this optimized resolution and proved the implementation is sound according to the simple definition of is_resolvent in the specification.

Figure 4 shows the data structure and invariants of intermediate conflict clauses, ResState, which are maintained after each resolution step over the course of conflict analysis. Those invariants are sufficient to prove the soundness of versat's conflict analysis. Figure 5 summarizes the variables used in the ResState type. The conflict clause is split into the literals assigned at the previous decision levels (c1) and the literals assigned at the current level (c2) according to the invariant u5. So, the complete conflict clause at the time is (append c1 c2). Notice that c2 is declared as a specificational data with the spec keyword. During conflict analysis, versat does not build each intermediate conflict clause as a single complete clause. Instead, the whole conflict clause is duplicated in a look-up table (vt), and it keeps track of the number of literals assigned at the current level, which is the c2l, as stated by the invariants u1, u2 and u3. The u2 and u3 ensure that the conflict clause and the table contain exactly the same set of literals. The look-up table vt enables a constant time check whether a literal is in the conflict clause, which makes duplication removal and other operations efficient. And it also enables a constant time removal of a literal assigned at the current level, which can be done by unmarking the literal on the vt and decrementing the value of c21 by one. That also requires all literals in the list c2 to be distinct (u4), so that removing all occurrences of a literal (as in the specification) will decrease the length only by one (in the implementation). Note that, although the type of c21 is nat (the Peano number), incrementing/decrementing by one and zero testing are constant time operations just like the machine integer operations. Also, note that, some invariants, i.e. all variables are within bounds, are omitted in the figure for clarity.

```
Inductive ResState : Fun(nv:word)(dl:word).type :=
  res_state : Fun
    (spec nv:word)
    (spec dl:word)
    (dls:<array word nv>)
    (vt:<array assignment nv>)
    (c1:clause)
    (spec c2:clause)
    (c21:nat)
    (u1:{ c21 = (length c2) })
    (u2:{ (all_lits_are_assigned vt (append c2 c1)) = tt })
    (u3:{ (cl_has_all_vars (append c2 c1) vt) = tt })
    (u4:{ (cl_unique c2) = tt })
    (u5:{ (cl_set_at_prev_levels dl dls c1) = tt })
    .<ResState nv dl>
```

Fig. 4. The datatype for conflict analysis state

For the resolution function, we have proved that the computation of the resolvent between the previous conflict clause and the antecedent clause follows the specification of is_resolvent, so that a new pf object for the resolvent can be constructed. At the end of the conflict analysis, versat will find the Unique Implication Point (UIP) literal, say l, and the ResState value will have one as the value of c21. Because the UIP literal must be assigned at the current decision level, it should be in c2 and the length of c2 is one due to the invariant u1. That means actually c2 is a singleton list that consists of l. Thus, the complete conflict clause is (cons lit l c1). Then, an array-base clause can be constructed and stored in the clause database, just as the input list-based clauses are processed at the beginning of execution. Finally, versat clears up the table vt by unmarking all the literals to recycle for the next analysis. Instead of sweeping through the whole table, versat only unmarks those literals in the conflict clause. It can be proved that after unmarking those literals, the table is clean as new using the invariant u3 above. Correctness of this clean-up process is proved in around 400 lines of lemmas, culminating in the theorem in Figure 6, which states that the efficient table-clearing code (clear_vars) returns a table which is indistinguishable from a brand new array (created with array_new).

Variable	Description
nv	the number of variables in the formula
dl	the current decision level
dls	a table of the decision levels at which each variable is assigned
vt	a look-up table for the variables in the conflict clause
c1	the literals of the conflict clause assigned at the previous decision levels
c2	the literals of the conflict clause assigned at the current decision level
c2l	the length of c2 (the number of literals assigned at the current decision level)
u1	the length of the list c2 is the same as the value of c2l
u2	all the literals in the conflict clause are marked on the table
u3	all the literals marked on the table are in the conflict clause
u4	all literals in the list c2 are unique
u5	all variables in c1 are assigned at the previous decision levels

Fig. 5. Summary of variables used in `ResState`

```
Define cl_has_all_vars_implies_clear_vars_like_new :
  Forall (nv:word)
         (vt:<array assignment nv>)
         (c:clause)
         (u:{ (cl_valid nv c) = tt })
         (r:{ (cl_has_all_vars c vt) = tt })
    .{ (clear_vars vt c) = (array_new nv UN) }
```

Fig. 6. The theorem stating correctness of table-clearing code

4.3 Summary of Implementation

The source code of `versat` totals 9884 lines, including proofs. It is hard to separate proofs from code because they can be intermixed within a function. Roughly speaking, auxiliary code (to formulate invariants) and proofs take up 80% of the entire program. The generated C code weighs in at 12712 lines. The C code is self-contained and includes the translations of GURU's library functions being used. The source and generated C code are available at `http://cs.uiowa.edu/~duoe/versat`. All lemmas used by `versat` have been machine-checked by the GURU compiler.

Properties Not Proved. First, we do not prove termination for `versat`. It could (*a priori*) be the case that the solver diverges on some inputs, and it could also be the case that certain run-time checks we perform (discussed in Section 7) fail. These termination properties have not been formally verified. However, what users want is to solve problems in a reasonable amount of time. A guarantee of termination does not satisfy users' expectations. It is more important to evaluate the performance over real problems as we show in Section 5. Second, we have not verified completeness of `versat`. It is (again *a priori*) possible that `versat` reports satisfiable, but the formula is actually unsatisfiable. In fact, we include a run-time check at the end of execution, to ensure that when `versat` reports SAT, the formula does have a model. But it would take substantial additional verification to ensure that this run-time check never fails.

5 Evaluation

We compared versat to picosat-936[2] with proof generation and checking for certified UNSAT answers. picosat is one of the best SAT solvers and can generate proofs in the RUP and TraceCheck formats. The RUP proof format is the official format for the certified track[3] of the SAT competition, and checker3 is used as the trusted proof checker. The TraceCheck format[4] is picosat's preferred proof format, and the format and checker are made by the developers of picosat. We measured the runtime of the whole workflow of solving, proof generation, and checking in both of the formats over the benchmarks used for the certified track of the SAT competition 2007. The certified track has not been updated since then.

Figure 7 shows the performance comparison. The "versat" column shows the solving times of versat. The "picosat(R)" and "picosat(T)" columns shows the solving and proof generation times of picosat in the RUP format and TraceCheck format, respectively. Since checker3 does not accept the RUP format directly, rupToRes is used to convert RUP proofs into the RES format, which checker3 accepts. The "rupToRes" column shows the conversion times, and the "checker3" column shows the times for checking the converted proofs. The "tracecheck" column shows the checking times for the proofs in the TraceCheck format. The "Total(R)" and "Total(T)" shows the total times for solving, proof generation, conversion (if needed), and checking in the RUP format and TraceCheck format, respectively. The unit of the values is in seconds. "T" means a timeout and "E" means a runtime error before timeout. The machine used for the test was equipped with an Intel Core2 Duo T8300 running at 2.40GHz and 3GB of memory. The time limits for solving, conversion, and checking were all 3600 seconds, individually.

versat solved 6 out of 16 benchmarks. Since UNSAT answers of versat are verified by construction, versat was able to certify the unsatisfiability of those 6 benchmarks. picosat could solve 14 of them and generated proofs in both of the formats. However, the RUP proof checking tool chain could only verify 4 of the RUP proofs within additional 2 hour timeouts (1 hour for conversion and 1 hour for checking). So, versat was able to certify the two more benchmarks that could not be certified using picosat and the official RUP proof checking tools. On the other hand, tracecheck could verify 12 of 14 TraceCheck proofs. Note that the maximum proof size was about 4GB and the disk space was enough to store the proofs.

When comparing the trusted base of those systems, versat's trusted base is the GURU compiler, some basic datatypes and functions in the GURU library, and 259 lines of specification written in GURU. checker3 is 1538 lines of C code. tracecheck is 2989 lines of C code along with 7857 lines of boolforce library written in C. Even though tracecheck is the most efficient system, the trusted base is also very large. One could argue that GURU compiler is also quite large (19175 lines of Java). However,

---

[2] picosat is available at http://fmv.jku.at/picosat/

[3] Information about the certified track, including the RUP/RES proof formats and checker3/rupToRes, is available at
http://users.soe.ucsc.edu/~avg/ProofChecker/

[4] TraceCheck is available at http://fmv.jku.at/tracecheck/

Benchmarks	versat	picosat(R)	rupToRes	checker3	Total(R)	picosat(T)	tracecheck	Total(T)
itox_vc965	1.74	0.18	0.88	0.36	1.42	0.18	0	0.18
dspam_dump_vc973	3565	0.57	2.32	0.99	3.88	0.55	0.01	0.56
eq.atree.braun.7.unsat	15.43	2.63	42.13	2.78	47.54	2.92	1.1	4.02
eq.atree.braun.8.unsat	361.11	24.11	642.35	E	E	26.47	9.11	35.58
eq.atree.braun.9.unsat	T	406.94	T		T	356.03	62.68	418.71
AProVE07-02	T	T			T	T		T
AProVE07-15	T	93.94	T		T	103.95	20.44	124.39
AProVE07-20	T	262.05	T		T	272.39	95.87	368.26
AProVE07-21	T	1437.64	T		T	1505.24	E	E
AProVE07-22	T	196.28	T		T	239.59	116.8	356.39
dated-5-15-u	T	2698.49	E		E	2853.12	E	E
dated-10-11-u	T	T			T	T		T
dated-5-11-u	T	255.06	E		E	266.6	23.36	289.96
total-5-11-u	1777.26	91.27	E		E	109.94	32.42	142.36
total-5-13-u	T	560.96	E		E	629.53	151.23	780.76
manol-pipe-c10nidw_s	772.68	25.46	7.38	1.37	34.21	25.54	0.1	25.64

Fig. 7. Results for the certified track benchmarks of the SAT competition 2007

because the GURU compiler is a generic system, it is unlikely to generate an unsound SAT solver from the code that it checked, and the verification cost of GURU compiler itself, if needed, should be amortized across multiple applications.

General Performance. We measured the solving times of `versat`, `minisat-2.2.0`, `picosat-936` and `tinisat-0.22` over the SAT Race 2008 Test Set 1, which was used for the qualification round for the SAT Race 2008. The machine used for the measurement was equipped with an Intel Xeon X5650 running at 2.67GHz and 12GB of memory. The time limit was 900 seconds. In summary, `versat` solved 19 out of 50 benchmarks in the set. `minisat` solved 47. `picosat` solved 46. `tinisat` solved 49. `versat` is not quite comparable with those state-of-the-art solvers, yet. However, to our best knowledge, `versat` is the only verified solver at the actual code level that could solve those competition benchmarks.

6 Related Work

Verifying the correctness of each individual result of a solver is generally believed to be easier than verifying the solver itself. For this reason, fields like SMT, where solvers are typically on the order of several tens of thousands of lines of code, have usually relied on result verification rather than solver verification. For example, there are many recent works on producing proofs from SMT solvers, and several solvers, including VERIT, Z3, and CVC3, can produce independently checkable proofs of the formulas they claim are valid [3,17,15,16,8]. Challenges in this area are devising a common proof format for SMT solvers, minimizing the overhead of proof production, and efficient proof checking.

There have been a number of works aimed at verifying automated reasoning algorithms. Lescuyer and Conchon verified a modern DPLL-based SAT solver in COQ and extraced OCAML code to compile into machine binary [13]. Also, Shankar and Vaucher's work verifying a modern SAT solver is a noteworthy example [18]. They concede, though, that while their model in PVS can be extracted to executable code, that code would not be as efficient as an implementation intended for high-performance use.

More closely related work is Marić's formal proof of correctness for a modern SAT solver implementing some low-level optimizations like watched literals in ISABELLE/HOL [14]. He proves soundness, completeness, and termination for a modern SAT solver written in ISABELLE's pure functional programming language. This is a major achievement, requiring around 25,000 lines of ISABELLE proof scripts. Marić proves much more about the solver than we do. In particular, proving termination would require extensive additional work for versat (see Section 7 below). But like Shankar and Vaucher, Marić verifies a functional model of a solver. This model uses pure-functional lists to represent clauses, and Peano naturals for variables. In contrast, versat uses mutable C arrays to represent clauses, and 32-bit machine words for literals. Also, Marić's resolution code is not optimized using a look-up table like versat and other modern solvers. Our work can thus be viewed as taking up Marić's concluding challenge to verify high-performance SAT solvers with efficient low-level data structures. To our knowledge, our work is the first to verify a deep property of a high-performance implementation of a modern solver.

Armand et al. extend COQ with support for more efficient data structures, including imperative arrays. They use their extended language to implement and verify an efficient checker for proofs produced by an external (to COQ) SAT solver [2]. In contrast, we have verified soundness of the efficient SAT solver itself. Both approaches use an inefficient functional model of arrays for formal reasoning, which is then replaced during compilation with a more efficient implementation. In our case, thanks to GURU's resource typing, this implementation is simply C arrays. Our readers/writers analysis ensures this is sound, even with destructive updates. Armand et al. use less efficient *persistent arrays* to combine destructive updating with persistence of old versions of the array [6]. Also, while GURU does not require run-time garbage collection, Armand et al. rely on compilation to OCAML (a garbage-collected language). GC overhead can be substantial in practice [21]. Also, it is noteworthy that Darbari et al. implemented an efficient TraceCheck proof checker in COQ [7].

7 Discussion

The idea for the specification was clear, and the specification did not change much since the beginning of the project. However, the hard part was formalizing invariants of the conflict analysis all the way down to the data structures and machine words, let alone actually proving them. Modern SAT solvers are usually small, but highly optimized as several data structures are cleverly coupled with strong invariants. The source code of minisat and tinisat does not tell what the invariants it assumes. As we discovered new invariants, we had to change our verification strategy several times along the development. Sometimes, we compromised and slightly modified our implementation. For example, the look-up table vt, used for resolution to test the membership of variable in the current conflict clause, could be an array of booleans. Instead, we used an array of `assignment`, which has three states of true, false, and unassigned. The other solvers assume the current assignment table already contains the polarity of each variable, which is an additional invariant. In `versat`, the table marks variables with the polarity, which duplicates information in the assignment table, avoiding the invariant above.

Unimplemented Features. Some features not implemented in `versat` includes conflict clause simplification and restart. Conflict clause simplification feature requires to prove that there exists a certain sequence of resolutions that derives the simplified clause. Although the sequence can be computed by topologically sorting the removed literals at run-time, additional invariants would be required to prove it statically.

Run-Time Checks. Certain properties of `versat`'s state are checked at run-time, like assert in C. We tried to keep a minimal set of invariants and it is simply not strong enough to prove some properties. Run-time checks makes the solver incomplete, because it may abort. Also, it costs execution time to perform such a check. In principle, all of these properties could be proved statically so that those run-time checks could be avoided. However, stronger invariants are harder to prove. Some would require a much longer development time and may not speed up the solver very much. Thus, the priority is the tight loops in the unit propagation and resolution. However, one-time procedures like initialization and the final conflict analysis are considered a lower priority. We did not measure how much those run-time checks cost, however, `gprof` time profiler showed that they are not bottlenecking `versat`.

Verified Programming in GURU. GURU is a great tool to implement efficient verified software, and the generated C code can be plugged into other programs. Optimizing software always raises the question of correctness, where the source code can get complicated as machine code. In those situations, GURU can be used to assure the correctness. However, some automated proving features are desired for general usage. Because `versat` heavily uses arrays, array-bounds checking proliferates, which requires a fair amount of arithmetic reasoning. At the same time, when code changes over the course of development, those arithmetic reasonings are the most affected and need to be updated or proved again. So, automated reasoning of integer arithmetic would be one of the most desired feature of GURU, allowing the programmer to focus on more higher level reasonings.

8 Conclusion and Future Work

`versat` is the first modern SAT solver that is statically verified to be sound all the way down to machine words and data structures. And the generated C code can be compiled to binary code without modifications or incorporated into other software. This paper has shown that the sophisticated invariants of the efficient data structures used in modern SAT solvers can be formalized and proved in GURU. Future work includes proving remaining lemmas and tuning the performance of `versat`. And we envision that the code and lemmas in `versat` can be applied to other SAT-related applications.

References

1. Altenkirch, T.: Integrated verification in Type Theory. Lecture notes for a course at ESSLLI 1996, Prague (1996); Available from the author's website
2. Armand, M., Grégoire, B., Spiwack, A., Théry, L.: Extending Coq with Imperative Features and Its Application to SAT Verification, pp. 83–98 (2010)
3. Bouton, T., de Oliveira, D.C.B., Déharbe, D., Fontaine, P.: veriT: An Open, Trustable and Efficient SMT-Solver. In: Schmidt, R.A. (ed.) CADE-22 2009. LNCS, vol. 5663, pp. 151–156. Springer, Heidelberg (2009)
4. Brummayer, R., Lonsing, F., Biere, A.: Automated Testing and Debugging of SAT and QBF Solvers. In: Strichman, O., Szeider, S. (eds.) SAT 2010. LNCS, vol. 6175, pp. 44–57. Springer, Heidelberg (2010)
5. Clarke, E.M., Biere, A., Raimi, R., Zhu, Y.: Bounded model checking using satisfiability solving. Formal Methods in System Design 19(1), 7–34 (2001)
6. Conchon, S., Filliâtre, J.-C.: A persistent union-find data structure. In: Proceedings of the 2007 Workshop on Workshop on ML, pp. 37–46. ACM (2007)
7. Darbari, A., Fischer, B., Marques-Silva, J.: Industrial-Strength Certified SAT Solving through Verified SAT Proof Checking. In: Cavalcanti, A., Déharbe, D., Gaudel, M.-C., Woodcock, J. (eds.) ICTAC 2010. LNCS, vol. 6255, pp. 260–274. Springer, Heidelberg (2010)
8. de Moura, L., Bjørner, N.: Proofs and Refutations, and Z3. In: Konev, B., Schmidt, R., Schulz, S. (eds.) 7th International Workshop on the Implementation of Logics, IWIL (2008)
9. Hagen, G., Tinelli, C.: Scaling up the formal verification of Lustre programs with SMT-based techniques. In: Cimatti, A., Jones, R. (eds.) Proceedings of the 8th International Conference on Formal Methods in Computer-Aided Design, Portland, Oregon, pp. 109–117. IEEE (2008)
10. Klein, G., Elphinstone, K., Heiser, G., Andronick, J., Cock, D., Derrin, P., Elkaduwe, D., Engelhardt, K., Kolanski, R., Norrish, M., Sewell, T., Tuch, H., Winwood, S.: seL4: Formal verification of an OS kernel. In: Matthews, J., Anderson, T. (eds.) Proc. 22nd ACM Symposium on Operating Systems Principles (SOSP), pp. 207–220. ACM (2009)
11. Kothari, N., Millstein, T., Govindan, R.: Deriving state machines from tinyos programs using symbolic execution. In: Proceedings of the 7th International Conference on Information Processing in Sensor Networks, IPSN 2008, pp. 271–282. IEEE Computer Society, Washington, DC (2008)
12. Leroy, X.: Formal certification of a compiler back-end, or: programming a compiler with a proof assistant. In: Morrisett, G., Peyton Jones, S. (eds.) 33rd ACM Symposium on Principles of Programming Languages, pp. 42–54. ACM Press (2006)
13. Lescuyer, S., Conchon, S.: A Reflexive Formalization of a SAT Solver in Coq. In: Emerging Trends of the 21st International Conference on Theorem Proving in Higher Order Logics, TPHOLs (2008)
14. Marić, F.: Formal verification of a modern SAT solver by shallow embedding into Isabelle/HOL. Theor. Comput. Sci. 411, 4333–4356 (2010)
15. McLaughlin, S., Barrett, C., Ge, Y.: Cooperating Theorem Provers: A Case Study Combining HOL-Light and CVC Lite. Electr. Notes Theor. Comput. Sci. 144(2), 43–51 (2006)
16. Moskal, M.: Rocket-Fast Proof Checking for SMT Solvers. In: Ramakrishnan, C.R., Rehof, J. (eds.) TACAS 2008. LNCS, vol. 4963, pp. 486–500. Springer, Heidelberg (2008)
17. Oe, D., Reynolds, A., Stump, A.: Fast and Flexible Proof Checking for SMT. In: Dutertre, B., Strichman, O. (eds.) Workshop on Satisfiability Modulo Theories, SMT (2009)
18. Shankar, N., Vaucher, M.: The mechanical verification of a dpll-based satisfiability solver. Electr. Notes Theor. Comput. Sci. 269, 3–17 (2011)

19. Stump, A., Austin, E.: Resource Typing in Guru. In: Filliâtre, J.-C., Flanagan, C. (eds.) Proceedings of the 4th ACM Workshop Programming Languages meets Program Verification, PLPV 2010, Madrid, Spain, January 19, pp. 27–38. ACM (2010)
20. Stump, A., Deters, M., Petcher, A., Schiller, T., Simpson, T.: Verified Programming in Guru. In: Altenkirch, T., Millstein, T. (eds.) Programming Languges meets Program Verification, PLPV (2009)
21. Xian, F., Srisa-an, W., Jiang, H.: Garbage collection: Java application servers' Achilles heel. Science of Computer Programming 70(2-3), 89–110 (2008)

Decision Procedures for Region Logic

Stan Rosenberg[1,⋆], Anindya Banerjee[2,⋆⋆], and David A. Naumann[1,⋆⋆⋆]

[1] Stevens Institute of Technology, Hoboken NJ 07030, USA
[2] IMDEA Software Institute, Madrid, Spain

Abstract. Region logic is Hoare logic for object-based programs. It features local reasoning with frame conditions expressed in terms of sets of heap locations. This paper studies tableau-based decision procedures for RL, the quantifier-free fragment of the assertion language. This fragment combines sets and (functional) images with the theories of arrays and partial orders. The procedures are of practical interest because they can be integrated efficiently into the satisfiability modulo theories (SMT) framework. We provide a semi-decision procedure for RL and its implementation as a theory plugin inside the SMT solver Z3. We also provide a decision procedure for an expressive fragment of RL termed restricted-RL. We prove that deciding satisfiability of restricted-RL formulas is NP-complete. Both procedures are proven sound and complete. Preliminary performance results indicate that the semi-decision procedure has the potential toscale to large input formulas.

1 Introduction

Frame conditions are an important part of procedure specifications. For procedures acting on shared mutable objects, frame conditions must designate the set of existing heap locations that may be updated —the footprint, in the terminology of separation logic. Following the lead of Kassios [12], the authors have developed a variant of Hoare logic, dubbed *region logic*, to explore the use of ghost state to express frame conditions in terms of explicit location sets [2]. We seek perspicuous specifications and effective local reasoning in automated verification based on SMT provers, for programs at the Java level of abstraction where heap locations are not integer addresses but rather are designated like $p.f$ where p is an object reference and f a field name. In region logic, frame conditions are designated in terms of *image* expressions[1] like $G`f$ where $G$ is a set of references (a *region*) and $G`f$ is the set of f fields of objects in G. Verification conditions typically involve operations on sets and predicates like containment and disjointedness.

Object sets are ubiquitous in functional specifications for object based programs (e.g., [28,19]). We are particularly interested in images, owing to their use in frame conditions. For example, in a state where $G_1 \# G_2$ holds (i.e., the regions are disjoint),

⋆ Partially supported by US NSF award CRI-0708330.

⋆⋆ Partially supported by CM Project S2009TIC-1465 Prometidos, MICINN Project TIN2009-14599-C03-02 Desafios, EU NoE Project 256980 Nessos.

⋆⋆⋆ Partially supported by US NSF awards CRI-0708330, CCF-0915611.

[1] A more conventional notation for images is $f[G]$, but this collides with array notation.

V. Kuncak and A. Rybalchenko (Eds.): VMCAI 2012, LNCS 7148, pp. 379–395, 2012.

a procedure that writes G_1‘f does not interfere with a formula that only depends on f fields of objects in G_2. Images are also useful to express closure conditions: if $p \in G$ and G‘$f \subseteq G$ then G contains the objects reachable from p via f. Using loop invariants that entail reachability properties but are expressed in pure first order logic, our prototype verifier performs well both for verifying data structure implementations and for local reasoning about data structure clients [22,25]. In addition to closure and disjointedness constraints, the assertion language of region logic features reference equality, points-to assertions, and type/subtype constraints (for Java's class types).

Previous experiments with automation of region logic [1,22] relied on axiomatization of region assertions, wherein regions are represented by ref $\rightarrow$ bool functions and the semantics is encoded by axioms using quantified formulas. However, automated reasoning about quantifiers is necessarily incomplete and typically ad-hoc. State-of-the-art SMT solvers perform E-matching [7] in order to limit the number of quantifier instantiations. Essentially, quantified formulas are annotated with syntactic patterns or triggers; typically the user supplies these annotations, otherwise default heuristics are used. Finding "good" patterns can drastically improve the performance of certain benchmarks. However, not all quantified formulas lend themselves to useful patterns. Furthermore, SMT solvers are typically not *refutationally-complete*; e.g., if a region assertion happens to be invalid, then its encoding using quantifiers may yield `UNKNOWN` which means that the solver did not find an unsatisfiable conjunction, although one must exist by Compactness of first-order logic.

Goal. Our ultimate goal in this work is to obtain an efficient decision procedure for the quantifier-free fragment of the region assertion language. Implicit in "efficient" is the requirement to integrate well within the SMT framework; i.e., decision procedures for region assertions must perform reasoning modulo theories such as partial order (for class types) and integers that arise in program verification conditions. In particular we want to decide verification conditions involving region assertions and heap updates. The latter requires reasoning modulo the theory of arrays.

Approach and contributions. There has been great progress in automated reasoning about sets and related theories, notably [26,24], but as we discuss in Sect. 6 prior work does not fully reach our goal.

Our approach is inspired by a tableau-based decision procedure for a simple language of sets of elements [27]. In that procedure, reasoning about sets is performed by tableau rules while reasoning about the elements of sets can be done entirely by an SMT solver.

We formalize a quantifier-free first-order language RL which is sufficiently expressive to accomodate the quantifier-free fragment of the region assertion language. We formalize a set of tableau-based rules collectively referred to as the RL-tableau calculus. Applying the rules has the effect of deriving a refutation proof in case the given formula is valid. If the formula is invalid, then a tableau obtained by saturating (i.e., exhaustively applying the rules) denotes a counterexample. RL-tableau rules contain only syntactic conditions, namely (subterm) occurence checks in their premises, so the rules are simple to implement. To check for saturation it suffices to ensure that every possible distinct rule instance has been applied.

We prove that the RL-tableau calculus is refutationally-complete. In general, for some invalid RL-formulas, the rules may be non-terminating. Thus, what we obtain is a semi-decision procedure for RL. We have implemented this procedure as a theory plugin inside Z3 [6]. Preliminary performance results are encouraging.

We conjecture that RL has a high complexity. If we consider only finite interpretations of RL, we can show that the resulting theory is NEXPTIME-hard (see [21]). This leads us to investigate a syntactic restriction of RL, called restricted-RL. The restriction amounts to disallowing assertions of the form $H \subseteq G`f$ but allowing assertions of the form $G`f \subseteq H$. We give a tableau calculus for restricted-RL and show that it provides a nondeterministic polynomial time decision procedure. We also prove that deciding conjunctions of restricted-RL literals is an NP-complete problem. Restricted-RL is sufficiently expressive to capture what we have found to be the most useful idioms of region logic, such as disjointedness and closure constraints.

Our main contributions can be summarized as follows.

- sound and complete tableau calculus for a theory RL which includes regions, reference subtyping, type-respecting functional images, arrays, etc.
- implementation of semi-decision procedure for RL as a theory plugin in Z3
- encouraging experimental results from synthetic benchmarks
- sound and complete calculus for an expressive fragment, restricted-RL
- NP-completeness of restricted-RL-tableau calculus

Full proofs and further details can be found in Rosenberg's dissertation [21].

2 Preliminaries

Throughout, we work with quantifier-free, many-sorted first-order logic with equality. We tacitly assume that each theory has the equality symbol always interpreted in the standard way. There are countably many variables of each of a theory's sorts.

Syntax. The language RL is boolean formulas over the signature Σ_{RL} defined by:

- sorts: $\mathsf{rgn}, \mathsf{ref}, \mathsf{arr}, \mathsf{fname}, \mathsf{cname}$
- constants:
  - **null**, of sort ref (*un-allocated reference*), **emp**, of sort rgn (*empty region*)
  - **alloc**, of sort rgn (*universal region*)
- function symbols:
  - $\cup, \cap, -$, of sort $\mathsf{rgn} \times \mathsf{rgn} \to \mathsf{rgn}$ (*union, intersection, difference*)
  - $\{\cdot\}$, of sort $\mathsf{ref} \to \mathsf{rgn}$ (*quasi singleton*)
  - img, of sort $\mathsf{arr} \times \mathsf{rgn} \times \mathsf{fname} \to \mathsf{rgn}$ (*image*)
  - read, of sort $\mathsf{arr} \times \mathsf{ref} \times \mathsf{fname} \to \mathsf{ref}$ (*field read*)
  - write, of sort $\mathsf{arr} \times \mathsf{ref} \times \mathsf{fname} \times \mathsf{ref} \to \mathsf{arr}$ (*field write*)
  - type, of sort $\mathsf{ref} \to \mathsf{cname}$ (*type of reference*)
  - dtype, of sort $\mathsf{fname} \to \mathsf{cname}$ (*enclosing type of field*)
- predicate symbols:
  - $\in$, of sort $\mathsf{ref} \times \mathsf{rgn}$ (*membership*), $\leq$, of sort $\mathsf{cname} \times \mathsf{cname}$ (*subtype*)

We use metavariables r, s, t for rgn-terms, u, v, w for ref-terms, h for arr-terms, f, g for fname-terms, K for cname-terms.

In region logic the heap is implicit: expressions like $x.f$ and $G`f$ are interpreted with respect to a program state. In that setting, an update to the heap, e.g., $x.f := y$, yields a new program state. We aim to decide verification conditions containing region assertions, so we represent heap updates explicitly. We use two-dimensional arrays to encode the heap. This representation is particularly useful for encoding frame conditions [4] and is used in `Verl` [25]. The heap is made explicit in *field read* and *image* expressions, $\mathsf{read}(h, u, f)$ for $u.f$ and $\mathsf{img}(h, r, f)$ for $r`f$. An update is encoded by a *field write* expression, e.g., $\mathsf{write}(h, u, f, v)$ for $u.f := v$. Note that function symbols are interpreted by total functions, yet field accesses are not defined everywhere.

To encode definedness of field accesses, we use type to encode the *runtime* class type of a reference, $\leq$ to encode subtyping (i.e., the subclass relation), and dtype to encode the class type enclosing a field (i.e., the class where a field is declared). For example, the RL formula $u \in \mathbf{alloc} \wedge \mathsf{type}(u) \leq \mathsf{dtype}(f)$ says that $u.f$ is defined. (Here, u denotes an allocated reference whose runtime type is a subclass of the class enclosing f's declaration; this is consistent with the semantics of field access in Java.) Because regions are untyped, i.e., may contain references of any class type, an image expression must account for references where a field access would be undefined. The semantics of RL reflects this constraint.

The syntax of RL is capable of expressing quantifier-free assertions of region logic (cf. [2,3]) with the exception of: field access expression $u.f$ in case f has type rgn, image expression $G`f$ in case f has type rgn, and type predicate $\mathsf{type}(K, x)$ where x has type rgn. See [21] for details on how to extend RL to handle these additional constructs.

Example. Following [2] we consider a finite binary tree with method *setLeftZero* whose body has a single command $x.left.item := 0$. The *item* field of parameter x's *left* node is set to 0. (Each node has fields *item*, *left* and *right*.) Specifications of the method, using region assertions, follow. The frame condition says that only the *item* field of objects in r may be written.

$$\begin{array}{l}
\textbf{requires } x \neq \textbf{null} \wedge x.left \in r \wedge x.right \in s \wedge r \# s \\
\textbf{requires } r`left \subseteq r \wedge r`right \subseteq r \wedge s`left \subseteq s \wedge s`right \subseteq s \\
\textbf{requires } \forall o : Node \in s \cdot o.item > 0 \\
\textbf{ensures } \forall o : Node \in s \cdot o.item > 0 \\
\textbf{writable } r`item
\end{array}$$

`Verl` works by translation to the intermediate form Boogie2 and uses the latter's VC generator, which is designed for performance rather than readability. To illustrate how the preceeding example is verified, we derived the following verification condition, for the **ensures** clause, by hand. It is a predicate on variables x and H, where H is a two-dimensional array that represents the current heap.

$$\begin{aligned}
&(1)\ (\forall h\colon \mathsf{arr}, o\colon \mathsf{ref} \cdot \mathsf{type}(o) \leq \mathit{Node} \wedge o \in \mathbf{alloc} \Rightarrow \mathsf{read}(h, o, \mathit{left}) = \mathbf{null} \\
&\qquad \vee (\mathsf{read}(h, o, \mathit{left}) \in \mathbf{alloc} \wedge \mathsf{type}(\mathsf{read}(h, o, \mathit{left})) \leq \mathit{Node})) \wedge \\
&(2)\ \ldots \text{ ditto, with } \mathit{right} \text{ for } \mathit{left} \ \ldots \wedge \\
&(3)\ \mathsf{type}(x) \leq \mathit{Node} \wedge (x = \mathbf{null} \vee x \in \mathbf{alloc}) \wedge \\
&(4)\ x \neq \mathbf{null} \wedge \mathsf{read}(H, x, \mathit{left}) \in r \wedge \mathsf{read}(H, x, \mathit{right}) \in s \wedge r \# s \wedge \\
&(5)\ \mathsf{img}(H, r, \mathit{left}) \subseteq r \wedge \mathsf{img}(H, r, \mathit{right}) \subseteq r \wedge \\
&(6)\ \mathsf{img}(H, s, \mathit{left}) \subseteq s \wedge \mathsf{img}(H, s, \mathit{right}) \subseteq s \wedge \\
&(7)\ (\forall o\colon \mathsf{ref} \cdot \mathsf{type}(o) \leq \mathit{Node} \wedge o \in s \Rightarrow \mathsf{read}(H, o, \mathit{item}) > 0) \\
\Rightarrow\ &(8)\ (\forall o\colon \mathsf{ref} \cdot \mathsf{type}(o) \leq \mathit{Node} \wedge o \in s \Rightarrow \mathsf{read}(H', o, \mathit{item}) > 0)
\end{aligned}$$

where $H' \mathrel{\widehat{=}} \mathsf{write}(H, \mathsf{read}(H, x, \mathit{left}), \mathit{item}, 0)$. Line (8) thus encodes the weakest precondition for the assignment $x.\mathit{left}.\mathit{item} := 0$ to establish the specified postcondition. Conjuncts (1)–(7) are essentially the translation of the **requires** clauses including additional assumptions. (The additional assumptions are conjuncts (1)–(3) which stem from the semantics of the programming language, namely definedness of field dereferences, type of x, whether x is allocated.) To prove the above VC is valid it suffices to prove unsatisfiability of its negation. The VC can be automatically proven using Z3 to reason about the quantifiers, types and arrays in conjunction with our (semi)decision procedure for quantifier-free region assertions.

Semantics. The semantics of RL is given by Def. 2. Therein we make use of the theory of arrays T_{A}, the theory of partial orders $T_{\leq}$, and the theory of equality T_{E}; the definitions are standard and therefore omitted (see [21, Sect. 4.2.2]). It is convenient to refer to the union of these theories as the *background-theory*.

Definition 1 (Background Theory)

- Let $T_{\mathsf{A}} \cup T_{\mathsf{E}} \cup T_{\leq}$ be called the *background-theory* with respect to RL.
- Let any literal from $\Sigma_{\mathsf{A}} \cup \Sigma_{\mathsf{E}} \cup \Sigma_{\leq}$ be called a *background-literal.*
- Let Φ be any conjunction of RL-literals. We say Φ is *background-satisfiable* iff all background-literals of Φ are satisfiable modulo the background-theory.

Each of T_{A}, T_{E}, $T_{\leq}$ admits a decision procedure, each theory is infinitely stable,[2] and no two signatures share any function or predicate symbol except the $=$ symbol. Thus, a decision procedure for the background-theory can be obtained by combining the decision procedures for T_{A}, T_{E}, and $T_{\leq}$ à la Nelson-Oppen [20].

Definition 2 (RL-**interpretation**)**.** An RL-*interpretation* is a Σ_{RL}-interpretation, $\mathscr{I}$, such that

- each sort $\tau \in \{\mathsf{ref}, \mathsf{rgn}, \mathsf{arr}, \mathsf{cname}, \mathsf{fname}\}$ is mapped to a non-empty set I_τ
- $I_{\mathsf{rgn}} = \mathscr{P}(\mathbf{alloc}^{\mathscr{I}})$, $\quad \mathbf{alloc}^{\mathscr{I}} \in \mathscr{P}(I_{\mathsf{ref}} \setminus \{\mathbf{null}^{\mathscr{I}}\})$, $\quad$ and $\mathbf{emp}^{\mathscr{I}} = \varnothing$
- symbols $\leq$ and read, write, are interpreted according to $T_{\leq}$, T_{A}, respectively
- symbols $\in, \cup, \cap, -$, are interpreted in the standard (set-theoretic) way
- $\{a\}^{\mathscr{I}} = \{a\} \cap \mathbf{alloc}^{\mathscr{I}}$, $\quad$ for every $a \in I_{\mathsf{ref}}$

[2] A theory T is *infinitely stable* if every T-satisfiable formula has an infinite model.

– For every $h \in I_{\mathsf{arr}}, r \in I_{\mathsf{rgn}}, f \in I_{\mathsf{fname}}$,

$$\mathsf{img}^{\mathscr{I}}(h,r,f) = \{\mathsf{read}^{\mathscr{I}}(h,a,f) \mid a \in r \wedge \mathsf{type}^{\mathscr{I}}(a) \leq^{\mathscr{I}} \mathsf{dtype}^{\mathscr{I}}(f)\} \cap \mathbf{alloc}^{\mathscr{I}}$$

The constant **alloc** is assigned any subset of the non-empty domain I_{ref} which excludes $\mathbf{null}^{\mathscr{I}}$. In region logic, **alloc** is implicitly updated following allocation so it contains the references to currently allocated objects, which serves to reason about freshness. The domain I_{rgn} is interpreted to be the set of all subsets[3] of $\mathbf{alloc}^{\mathscr{I}}$. Observe that I_{rgn} is non-empty since it contains at least the empty set. The quasi singleton is so named because $\{u\}^{\mathscr{I}}$ is empty if $u^{\mathscr{I}}$ is not in $\mathbf{alloc}^{\mathscr{I}}$. Note that **alloc** is not required to be finite; we return to this later.

The verification conditions generated by the `Verl` tool [25] impose additional constraints, in particular, heaps have no dangling references and object fields have values compatible with their types. For these constraints, quantifiers work well (e.g., see [17]), and they are not relevant in this paper.

The subset relation for regions can be expressed in more than one way; e.g., $r \subseteq s$ is equivalent to $r \cup s = s$ and to $r \cap s = r$. In the sequel, let $r \cup s = s$ be synonymous with $r \subseteq s$ unless otherwise noted. The membership predicate can encoded using other relations: $u \in r$ is equivalent to $\{u\} \subseteq r \wedge \{u\} \neq \mathbf{emp}$. We include $\in$ in the core syntax because membership is used directly by our decision procedure.

The image term $\mathsf{img}(h,r,f)$ is so called because its denotation is a region obtained by computing the (functional) *image* of r under f pointwise, for those points a where f is "defined", viz. the constraint $\mathsf{type}^{\mathscr{I}}(a) \leq \mathsf{dtype}^{\mathscr{I}}(f)$. To express it using the standard notion of images, $\mathsf{img}(h,r,f)$ is the image of r under $F\colon I_{\mathsf{ref}} \to I_{\mathsf{ref}}$, where F is the partial function obtained by restricting $\mathsf{read}^{\mathscr{I}}$ appropriately: $((h,a,f),b) \in F$ iff $a \in r$ and $\mathsf{read}^{\mathscr{I}}(h,a,f) = b$ and $\mathsf{type}^{\mathscr{I}}(a) \leq^{\mathscr{I}} \mathsf{dtype}^{\mathscr{I}}(f)$ and $b \in \mathbf{alloc}^{\mathscr{I}}$.

Definition 3 (RL-model). An RL-*model* of an RL formula Φ is an RL-interpretation that makes the formula **true**. We say $\mathscr{M} \models \Phi$ to denote that $\mathscr{M}$ is an RL-model for Φ.

Here and in the sequel, "satisfiable" typically denotes T-satisfiable. That is, Φ is satisfiable *modulo* theory T. We can say this concisely using the satisfaction relation: $\models_T \Phi$. When the theory is clear from the context, it can be elided (as in Def. 3).

3 RL-Tableau Calculus

Our aim is to decide whether a given *conjunction* of RL-literals is satisfiable. (An arbitrary formula is converted to CNF whence it suffices to guess a satisfiable conjunction of literals.) Our solution is based on the (refutational) proof method of *analytic tableaux* [23,8]. The tableau calculus we describe was inspired by the work of Zarba [27].

Given an arbitrary RL-conjunction Φ, RL-tableau calculus lets us infer all membership literals (literals of the form $u \in r$, $u \notin r$) as well as background-literals entailed

[3] This reflects the semantics in [2] that regions contain only allocated references, also implemented in Verl [25].

by Φ. We apply inference rules until either inconsistency is detected or every (applicable) rule has been applied. Some inference rules are *conjunctive*, meaning that they infer a conjunction of literals, while others are *disjunctive*, meaning that they infer a disjunction of (conjunctions of) literals —a case split.

A *tableau* is a rooted, finitely branching tree with literals as nodes. Following standard terminology, a *branch* is a path from the root that is maximal —i.e., it includes a leaf or is infinite. A tableau rule is applied to a branch. If applicable, a conjunctive rule adds one or more literals, extending the branch linearly. A disjunctive rule creates a fork, so the branch becomes several branches.

In a nutshell, the proof method works as follows. For the formula Φ to be decided, construct an initial tableau comprising a single branch whose nodes are the conjuncts of Φ. Repeatedly, non-deterministically choose an inference rule which when applied adds new nodes, possibly splitting the branch. The goal is to try to close each branch by determining that some of its nodes are contradictory. If we succeed in closing every branch then Φ is unsatisfiable. On the other hand, if there exists an *open* (i.e., not closed) branch and every rule instance has been applied, then Φ is satisfiable.

RL-tableau calculus comprises the rules in Figure 1. The premise of each rule is composed of a set of literals and possibly some subterm occurrence checks denoted by occurs predicate; occurs(t) holds whenever term t occurs as a (sub)term in any of the literals of a given branch. The conclusion of a conjunctive rule (such as the first of the $\cap$-rules and the second of the img-rules) is composed of a set of literals; for a disjunctive rule (such as the third of the $=$-rules, the second of the $\{\cdot\}$-rules, the $\in$-rules, and the first of the img-rules) each disjunct is associated with some set of literals.

Rules are applied within a branch. Thus for a given branch B, in order to apply a rule, we must find an applicable rule instance for B. A rule instance assigns terms to the free variables occurring in the corresponding rule. Subsequently, to check if the rule instance is applicable we must verify that the instantiated premise holds. E.g., let σ denote a rule instance in B for the first $\cap$-rule in Fig. 1 such that $\sigma(u) = u$, $\sigma(r) = r$, $\sigma(s) = r \cup s$. Then, σ is applicable iff $u \in r \cap (r \cup s)$ occurs in B. As a result of applying σ, we would add $u \in r$ and $u \in r \cap (r \cup s)$ to B.

The rules marked with $(*)$ create fresh variables denoted by w; freshness is enforced by negative occurrence checks. (While other rules may yield fresh terms, e.g., read(h, u, f) in the first img-rule in Fig. 1, these terms do not occur in antecedents; hence, only a bounded number of such terms can be created.) We preclude "dumb" rule applications—those rule applications which repeatedly apply the same rule instance—by tracking rule instances which already have been applied (see [21, Sect. 4.3]). E.g., for a given literal $r \neq s$ we can apply the third $=$-rule in Fig. 1 exactly once; the instantiation of w is irrelevant.

Definition 4 (Closed Branch). A branch B of an RL-tableau is *closed* iff it contains any of the following contradictory sets of literals

- any conjunction of background-literals *unsatisfiable* modulo the background-theory
- any two complementary $\in$-literals; i.e., literals of the form $u \in r$ and $u \notin r$
- any literal of the form $u \in \mathbf{emp}$

A tableau is *closed* iff all of its branches are closed. A branch/tableau which is not closed is *open*.

=-rules

$$\frac{r = s \quad u \in r}{u \in s} \qquad \frac{r = s \quad u \in s}{u \in r} \qquad \frac{r \neq s \quad \neg\mathsf{occurs}(w)}{w \in r,\ w \notin s \ \Big|\ w \in s,\ w \notin r}\ (*)$$

∩-rules

$$\frac{u \in r \cap s}{u \in r \quad u \in s} \qquad \frac{u \in r \quad u \in s \quad \mathsf{occurs}(r \cap s)}{u \in r \cap s}$$

{·}-rules

$$\frac{u \in \{v\}}{u = v} \qquad \frac{\mathsf{occurs}(\{u\})}{u \notin \mathbf{alloc} \mid u \in \{u\}}$$

∈-rules

$$\frac{u \in r \quad v \in s \quad \mathsf{occurs}(r \cap s)}{u \in s \mid u \notin s} \qquad \frac{u \in r \quad \mathsf{occurs}(r - s)}{u \in s \mid u \notin s}$$

$$\frac{u \in r}{u \in \mathbf{alloc}} \qquad \frac{u \in r}{u \neq \mathbf{null}} \qquad \frac{u \in r \quad v \notin r}{u \neq v}$$

img-**rules**

$$\frac{u \in r \quad \mathsf{occurs}(\mathsf{img}(h,r,f))}{\mathsf{type}(u) \not\leq \mathsf{dtype}(f) \mid \mathsf{read}(h,u,f) \notin \mathbf{alloc} \mid \mathsf{read}(h,u,f) \in \mathsf{img}(h,r,f)}$$

$$\frac{u \in \mathsf{img}(h,r,f) \quad \neg\mathsf{occurs}(w)}{w \in r \quad \mathsf{type}(w) \leq \mathsf{dtype}(f) \quad \mathsf{read}(h,w,f) = u}\ (*)$$

Fig. 1. Selected RL-tableau rules. (Omitting set union and difference, see [21, Fig. 4.1]).

The first condition in Def. 4 uses a decision procedure for the background-theory (see Sect. 2). The remaining conditions are purely syntactic. Intuitively, we need the first condition because the following rules propagate background-literals: the first {·}-rule, fourth and fifth ∈-rules and both img-rules.

A branch B of an RL-tableau is *satisfiable* iff there exists an RL-model for the conjunction of all literals in B. A tableau is *satisfiable* iff at least one of its branches is satisfiable.

If a branch is satisfiable, then by semantics (Def. 2) none of the conditions in Def. 4 can hold. Therfore, a satisfiable branch is open. The other direction—an open branch is satisfiable, may not hold. E.g., the branch corresponding to $u \in r \cap s$, $u \notin r$, is open by Def. 4. Yet, it is easily seen that an application of the first ∩-rule will yield a new branch, with the literals $u \in r$ and $u \in s$; this branch is closed owing to the second condition in Def. 4. Thus, a priori we cannot determine whether an open branch is satisfiable unless all rules in the branch have been exhaustively applied.

A branch B of a RL-tableau is *saturated* iff whenever a rule instance applies, and is not "dumb", the literals in its conclusion already occur in B. A tableau is *saturated* iff all of its branches are saturated.

Intuitively, a saturated branch is closed under all possible inferences. The notion of saturation plays a key role in establishing completeness (of the proof method). That is, if an RL-tableau for Φ yields an open and saturated branch, then Φ is satisfiable. Conversely, if the tableau is closed, then Φ is unsatisfiable.

A branch B of a RL-tableau is *completed* iff it is either saturated or closed. A tableau is *completed* iff all of its branches are completed. A completed tableau can be obtained by applying the rules until every branch either becomes closed or saturated.

Theorem 1 (Soundness). *Let Φ be a conjunction of* RL*-literals. If there exists a closed* RL*-tableau for Φ, then Φ is unsatisfiable.*

Theorem 2 (Completeness). *Let Φ be a conjunction of* RL*-literals. If Φ is unsatisfiable, then every completed* RL*-tableau for Φ is closed.*

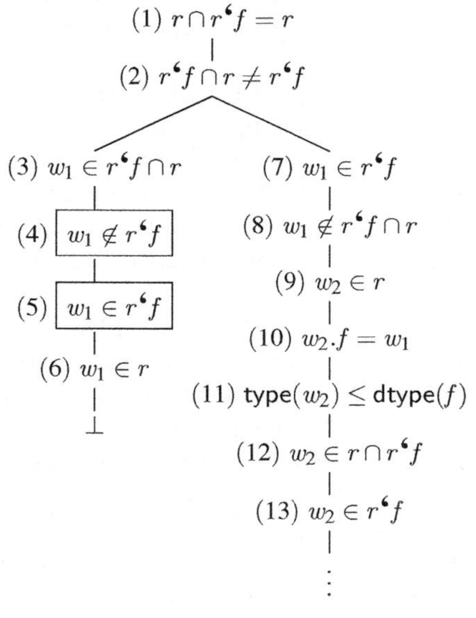

- (3), (4) *and* (7), (8) from (2) by third of =-**rules**
- (5), (6) from (3) by first of ∩-**rules**
- (9), (10), (11) from (7) by second of img-**rules**
- (12) from (1), (9) by second of =-**rules**
- (13) from (12) by first of ∩-**rules**

Boxed nodes are contradictory; right branch is infinite.

Fig. 2. RL-tableau for $r \subsetneq r^{\prime}f$, that is, $r \cap r^{\prime}f = r \wedge r^{\prime}f \cap r \neq r^{\prime}f$

Example. Several illustrative examples of RL-tableau are given in [21, Sect. 4.4]. Here, we describe one for which every completed RL-tableau must be infinite. Fig. 2 illustrates an RL-tableau for the conjunction $r \cap r^{\prime}f = r \wedge r^{\prime}f \cap r \neq r^{\prime}f$ which denotes: r is a *proper* subset of $r^{\prime}f$. (For brevity we use region logic notation $r^{\prime}f$ to stand for $\mathsf{img}(h,r,f)$ since the example only involves a single heap.) Observe that if the right branch is to be completed, then the branch must be infinite; the second img-rule will have been applied infinitely often. The tableau in Fig. 2 is not unique; e.g., we could swap the right and the left branches to obtain another RL-tableau. However, it is not difficult to see that every completed RL-tableau for the given conjunction is infinite. Intuitively, $r \subseteq r^{\prime}f$ expresses that there exists a function $f: r \to r \cup s$, for some s, such that f is surjective onto r, whereas $r^{\prime}f \not\subseteq r$ expresses that the range of f extends beyond r. No such function exists for any finite r.

4 Implementation of Semi-decision Procedure

Using the RL-tableau calculus we can construct a completed tableau $\mathscr{T}$ for any given RL-conjunction Φ. If $\mathscr{T}$ is closed, then owing to Theorem 1 Φ is unsatisfiable. If $\mathscr{T}$ is open, then owing to Theorem 2 Φ is satisfiable; indeed $\mathscr{T}$ determines a model. As witnessed by the previous example, some RL-conjunctions may yield completed RL-tableaux which are infinite. However, we can obtain a semi-decision procedure by ensuring that rules are applied in a systematic fashion.[4] Essentially, img-rules are applied in a lock-step fashion; i.e., apply exhaustively non-img-rules, apply img-rules for occurring terms, repeat.

The semi-decision procedure for RL has been implemented as a theory plugin in Z3; theory plugins are based on the DPLL(T) architecture [9]. In a nutshell, Z3 guesses a conjunction of literals, say L, which must hold. The plugin is notified with each asserted RL-literal $l \in L$ at which point it asserts new theory lemmas into Z3's context. (Z3's context represents the current tableau branch.)

The theory lemmas are nothing more than instances of the RL-tableau rules. Each rule is potentially applied to ensure saturation.[5] Reasoning modulo the background-theory is peformed entirely within Z3. (New background-literals are propagated by insantiating rules, e.g., first $\{\cdot\}$-rule.) Thus, to check if a branch is closed, we merely check if the literals $u \in r$ and $u \notin r$ have been asserted or the literal $u \in \mathbf{emp}$ has been asserted; both checks are purely syntactic. E.g., if $u \in \mathbf{emp}$ is asserted, then we simply assert $u \in \mathbf{emp} \Rightarrow \mathsf{false}$.

Our preliminary evaluation used synthetic benchmarks [21, Figs. 4.13, 4.14] to compare the performance of the semi-decision procedure versus an axiomatization of RL which relies on Z3's quantifier reasoning. The looping phenomenon (cf. Fig. 2) is observed in some cases, when the image rules are implemented directly as presented in Fig. 1. Our implementation includes an option to switch on certain heuristics described in [21, Sect. 4.4.1]. With that option all our benchmarks terminate, but there is no guarantee in general. The benchmarks include basic properties of boolean algebra and function images, as well as formulas, both valid and invalid, involving the full signature of RL except array writes. These capture typical verification conditions except for excluding literals involving integers or array manipulation, our goal being to focus evaluation on performance of the tableau procedure itself.

The procedure terminates fast (under 50ms) for valid formulas (i.e., `UNSAT` for their negations). For invalid formulas, it terminates fast with `UNKNOWN`, due to (potential) incomplete[6] quantifier reasoning in the theory of partial orders; partial order is typically axiomatized in Z3. For these benchmarks, however, it is sound to treat read, type, dtype, and $\leq$ as uninterpreted; then all the invalid benchmarks terminate under 50ms. Our results suggest that the semi-decision procedure has the potential to scale (see [21, Sect. 4.12]). Even on small benchmarks, its performance is much more predictable than the one that is reliant on quantifier instantiation. For example, out of 44 `UNSAT`

[4] The same idea is used in Smullyan's tableaux for first-order logic. For details see [21, Fig. 4.7].

[5] We describe how to do this efficiently in [21, Sect. 4.11].

[6] As of release 2.17, Z3 supports complete instantiation though it is not yet fully integrated with theory plugins.

benchmarks, Z3 timed out on 32 of them when using axioms for the region theory, while the theory plugin returned UNSAT in under 50ms for each of the 44 benchmarks. (Timeout was set to 100 seconds.) For the 8 UNSAT benchmarks on which Z3 terminated, its performance exhibited high variance (due to quantifiers).

5 Restricted-$\mathsf{RL_E}$-Tableau Calculus

Unrestricted RL appears to be of high complexity. In [21, Prop. 4.33] we show that it becomes NEXPTIME-hard if we change Def. 2 to require **alloc** to be interpreted as a *finite* set. (The proof builds on ideas of [10,26].) By imposing simple syntactic restrictions we obtain a theory for which satisfiability is NP-complete, yet which is expressive enough to encompass the verification conditions that arise from the specifications we have used in case studies [1,22]. We retain Def. 2 unchanged.

Definition 5 (restricted-$\mathsf{RL_E}$, restricted-RL). A restricted-$\mathsf{RL_E}$ literal is one such that

- there is no write symbol
- img symbol occurs only in the forms $\mathsf{img}(h,r,f) \subseteq s$ and $u \notin \mathsf{img}(h,r,f)$ where r,s are any img-free rgn-terms and h,f,u are any terms of the appropriate sort

A restricted-RL literal is one that satisfies the second of these restrictions.

The first restriction is only superficial since the theory of arrays can be reduced to the theory of equality by eliminating write terms. (See [21, Sect. 4.6] or [11].) The second restriction is key in establishing NP upper-bound; it essentially disallows literals of the form $s \subseteq \mathsf{img}(h,r,f)$ while allowing literals of the form $\mathsf{img}(h,r,f) \subseteq s$.

Our complexity result is the same for both restricted-RL and restricted-$\mathsf{RL_E}$. However, for technical [7] reasons our tableaux are formulated for restricted-$\mathsf{RL_E}$.

(R1)

$$\frac{u \in r \qquad \mathsf{occurs}(\mathsf{img}(h,r,f)) \qquad \mathsf{occurs}(\mathsf{read}(h,u,f))}{\mathsf{type}(u) \not\leq \mathsf{dtype}(f) \;\Big|\; \mathsf{read}(h,u,f) \notin \mathbf{alloc} \;\Big|\; \begin{array}{l} \mathsf{type}(u) \leq \mathsf{dtype}(f) \\ \mathsf{read}(h,u,f) \in \mathsf{img}(h,r,f) \end{array}}$$

(R2)

$$\frac{\begin{array}{cccc} u \in r & \mathsf{occurs}(\mathsf{img}(h,r,f)) & \neg\mathsf{occurs}(\mathsf{read}(h,u,f)) & \mathsf{occurs}(\mathsf{read}(h',u',f')) \\ & \models_{T_{\mathsf{BG}}} h' = h & \models_{T_{\mathsf{BG}}} u' = u & \models_{T_{\mathsf{BG}}} f' = f \end{array}}{\mathsf{type}(u') \not\leq \mathsf{dtype}(f') \;\Big|\; \mathsf{read}(h',u',f') \notin \mathbf{alloc} \;\Big|\; \begin{array}{l} \mathsf{type}(u') \leq \mathsf{dtype}(f') \\ \mathsf{read}(h',u',f') \in \mathsf{img}(h,r,f) \end{array}}$$

Fig. 3. img rules for restricted-$\mathsf{RL_E}$ tableau

[7] The background theory of restricted-$\mathsf{RL_E}$ is convex; not so for restricted-RL, due to arrays.

New rules. The restricted-$\mathsf{RL_E}$ tableau calculus has the img-rules in Fig. 3 which replace the img-rules in Fig. 1. The other rules are the same as in Fig. 1. The background-theory, T_{BG}, for restricted-$\mathsf{RL_E}$ is the union of the theory of equality, T_{E}, and the theory of partial orders, $T_{\leq}$. The rules in Fig. 3 provide complete reasoning about img literals for the restricted-$\mathsf{RL_E}$ theory. (R1) is nearly the same as the first img-rule in Fig. 1. The only difference is the addition of $\mathsf{type}(u) \leq \mathsf{dtype}(f)$ to the right-most disjunct. (R2), however, is an entirely new rule. (R2) deals with the case when $\mathsf{read}(h,u,f)$ does not occur in a branch (and hence not in the input conjunction). Intuitively, (R2) says that if some $\mathsf{read}(h',u',f')$ occurs in a branch, then we must guess if $\mathsf{read}(h',u',f') \in \mathsf{img}(h,r,f)$; the entailment conditions express that $\mathsf{read}(h',u',f')$ has the same denotation as $\mathsf{read}(h,u,f)$. That is, the equalities $h' = h$, $u' = u$, $f' = f$ are implied by the current branch, modulo the background-theory.

Checking implied equalities. One way to fulfill the semantic checks in (R2) is to compute all the implied equalities on all the background-terms in $\pi(\mathsf{B})$. To check if an equality $u = v$ is implied by the current branch modulo the background-theory, it suffices to check unsatisfiability of the conjunction $\pi(\mathsf{B}) \wedge u \neq v$ modulo T_{BG}. (Here $\pi(\mathsf{B})$ is the conjunction of all background-literals in the branch.)

Computing all implied equalities every time (R2) is considered would be inefficient. We describe one possible optimization. The optimization relies on the observation that fresh equality literals are added by the first $\{\cdot\}$-rule in Fig. 1; remaining rules can add background-literals of the form $u \neq v$, $u \neq \mathbf{null}$ and $\mathsf{type}(u) \not\leq \mathsf{dtype}(f)$, none of which could imply new equalities. Consequently, all implied equalities can be precomputed and updated whenever the first $\{\cdot\}$-rule is applied in the branch.

In practice, the implementation of (R2) may not need to query implied equalities. SMT solvers typically implement Nelson-Oppen combination method [18]. Z3 uses model-based theory combination [5]. In both frameworks, all implied equalities on mutually shared variables are eventually propagated to all other theories.

Theorem 3 (Soundness). *Let Φ be any conjunction of restricted-$\mathsf{RL_E}$-literals. If there exists a closed restricted-$\mathsf{RL_E}$-tableau for Φ, then Φ is unsatisfiable.*

Theorem 4 (Completeness). *Let Φ be any conjunction of restricted-$\mathsf{RL_E}$ literals. If Φ is unsatisfiable, then every completed restricted-$\mathsf{RL_E}$ tableau for Φ is closed.*

Complexity. Observe that the img-rules in Fig. 3 can create fresh terms only of the form $\mathsf{type}(u)$, $\mathsf{dtype}(f)$, both of sort cname, where neither u nor f is fresh; the number of such fresh terms is $\mathcal{O}(n^2)$ where n is the size of the input. This is in stark contrast to the img-rules in Fig. 1 which can create an unbounded number of fresh terms of sort ref (e.g., Fig. 2). We can derive the following branch bound for restricted-$\mathsf{RL_E}$ tableaux.

Lemma 1 (branch bound). *Let Φ be any restricted-$\mathsf{RL_E}$ conjunction. Let $\mathsf{size}(\Phi) = n$. Let B be any branch of a restricted-$\mathsf{RL_E}$ tableau for Φ. Then, $\mathsf{size}(\mathsf{B})$ is $\mathcal{O}(n^3)$.*

Conjunctions of resricted-$\mathsf{RL_E}$ literals suffice to encode arbitrary boolean clauses. Intuitively, non-determinism due to disjunctions can be encoded by singleton sets. Thus we have the following result ([21, Lemma 4.57]).

Lemma 2. *Deciding the satisfiability of a conjunction of restricted-*$\mathsf{RL_E}$ *literals is* NP-*hard.*

Owing to Lemma 1 and the fact that the premises in (R1) and (R2) of Fig. 3 can be checked in polynomial time,[8] we can formulate a non-deterministic decision procedure which runs in polynomial time. Given an arbitrary restricted-$\mathsf{RL_E}$ formula, Φ, we first transform it into CNF using Tseitsin's encoding, e.g., [13]. (The equisatisfiable CNF formula is linear in the size of Φ.) Next, we guess a conjunction of disjuncts and use it as the input to the tableau procedure; the tableau procedure merely applies all possible tableau rules in a non-deterministic fashion until each branch is complete.

Lemma 3. *Deciding the satisfiability of a restricted-*$\mathsf{RL_E}$ *formula is in* NP.

Theorem 5. *The satisfiability problem for restricted-*$\mathsf{RL_E}$ *is* NP-*complete.*

Recall that restricted-$\mathsf{RL_E}$ is obtained from restricted-RL by eliminating all array literals, i.e., literals containing write-terms. The reduction introduces only polynomially many fresh literals (see [21, Lemma 4.62]). Consequently, we can apply the reduction and appeal to Theorem 5 to obtain

Theorem 6. *The satisfiability problem for restricted-*RL *is* NP-*complete.*

6 Related Work

Our decision procedure extends the tableau-based decision procedure for the quantifier-free language **2LST**—*two-level syllogistic modulo* T [27]. **2LST** is an extension of **2LS**—a two-sorted language of sets of elements where the element sort is uninterpreted. Additionally, **2LST** has any number of constant, function and predicate symbols over the elem sort in some theory T, provided as a parameter. The function and predicate symbols are of the form: $F\colon \mathsf{elem} \times \cdots \times \mathsf{elem} \to \mathsf{elem}$, $P\colon \mathsf{elem} \times \cdots \times \mathsf{elem}$, of any arity. The interpretation of these symbols is dictated according to T. The decision problem is NP-complete assuming the decision problem for T is in NP. A tableau-based decision procedure for **2LST** was presented in [27]. It corresponds essentially to our Fig. 1, excluding the second $\{\cdot\}$, and the third and fourth $\in$-rules; in our setting, the background-theory plays the role of T. Note, if we keep the third $\in$-rule, we essentially obtain a decision procedure for **2LST** with a universal set, denoted by **alloc**. Consequently, RL can be seen as an extension of **2LST** with a universal set and images.

The tableau-based decision procedure is a combination method different from that of Nelson-Oppen. Notably, it does not perform the equality propagation between T and **2LS** in the sense of Nelson-Oppen. (Although, equalities amongst T-terms are propagated by tableau rules.) Furthermore, T need not be stably infinite. Intuitively, a decision procedure for T serves as a *black box*. After a rule is applied, a tableau simply asks the black box to determine if the new branch(es) remains open, i.e., whether a conjunction of elem-literals is T-satisfiable.

[8] This stems from the fact that T_{E}, $T_{\leq}$ are convex and can be decided in polynomial time.

Kuncak, et al. give a decision procedure for a quantified language of sets of uninterpreted elements with cardinality constraints [14]. The language is known as **BAPA**—boolean algebra with Presburger arithmetic. It permits quantification over sets and integers; quantification over elements is expressible in terms of set quantification. The decision procedure for **BAPA** admits quantifier-elimination. The restriction to quantifier-free formulas is called **QFBAPA**. This language has no separate syntax for element terms; elements are encoded by fresh set-variables whose cardinality is constrained to be 1. Remarkably, **QFBAPA**'s decision problem was shown to be NP-complete by Kuncak and Rinard [16].

Yessenov, et al. introduce a decidable language **QFBAPA**-Rel with image expressions under unary function symbols and predicate symbols of any arity [26]. As in **QFBAPA**, the element sort is un-interpreted. This language is very expressive and suited to verification of object based programs. It comes close to subsuming RL, indeed one of their examples is based on our specification for *setLeftZero*. Their functions are total whereas our images are not: region r in r‘f may contain some objects that lack field f. Perhaps this can be patched by introducing types.

For a function $f : A \rightarrow A$ and set $X \subseteq A$, the decision procedure of [26] eliminates terms of the form $f[X]$ by first rewriting X as a union of (disjoint) Venn regions, i.e., $X = \bigcup v_i$ and $f[X] = \bigcup f[v_i]$. Subsequently, each $f[v_i]$ is replaced by a fresh variable t_i with the cardinality constraints: $|t_i| \leq |v_i|$ and $|t_i| = 0 \Leftrightarrow |v_i| = 0$. The resulting formula is in **QFBAPA** which is NP-complete, thus the decision problem is in NEXPTIME. However, because the translation (to Venn regions) yields a **QFBAPA** formula of exponential size, the decision procedure does not seem practical.

Recently Suter et al. [24] have shown that it is possible to obtain an SMT-based decision procedure for **QFBAPA**. Their decision procedure has been implemented as a plugin in Z3. To reason about interpreted elements of sets, axiomatized predicate symbols singleton and element are added to **QFBAPA** subject to axioms $|\text{singleton(e)}| = 1$ (for singleton set) and $\text{element}(\text{singleton}(e)) = e$. The crux of the decision procedure is an algorithm that decomposes a formula such that the number of considered Venn regions is significantly reduced. Several experiments show that in practice the decomposition algorithm can handle formulas with a large number of set variables, despite exponential worst-case complexity. Suter et al. conjecture that their approach can be extended to **QFBAPA**-Rel.

7 Discussion

We conjecture that it is possible to devise a terminating tableau procedure to decide full RL, with respect to interpretations where **alloc** is finite; but this is unlikely to be of practical value because of its NEXPTIME-time complexity. (Our procedure is incomplete for finite **alloc**, as illustrated by the example in Fig. 2.) We conjecture that NEXPTIME-time complexity also holds for RL without the restriction to finite **alloc**. For typical verification condition generators, there is no need to explicitly require the heap domain to be finite. However, if **alloc** is fixed to be finite, then one can express cardinality constraints of the form $|r| \leq |s|$, for any rgn-terms r, s. Observe that under a finite interpretation of regions, $r \subseteq \mathsf{img}(h, s, f)$ implies the cardinality constraint $|r| \leq |s|$. (By cardinality, $r \subseteq \mathsf{img}(h, s, f)$ implies $|r| \leq |\mathsf{img}(h, s, f)|$; by image semantics and finiteness of regions, $|\mathsf{img}(h, s, f)| \leq |s|$, whence $|r| \leq |s|$ by transitivity.) The case of restricted-RL is simpler since every satisfiable formula has a finite model owing to Lemma 1 and Theorem 4.

In previous work we used a translation to the **BSR** fragment[9] inspired by [15]. For example a restricted-RL literal $r`f \subseteq s$ where r, s are variables, can be roughly encoded by a **BSR** formula $\forall u, v \cdot v \neq \textbf{null} \Rightarrow (r(u) \wedge f(u, v) \Rightarrow s(v))$, where r, s, f are predicate symbols. While the translation is possible for a language akin to restricted-RL, it breaks down when we encounter RL literals of the form $s \subseteq r`f$; such a literal would result in a formula with the quantifier prefix $\forall\exists$ which does not belong to **BSR**.

Although the procedures presented here seem promising, much more thorough performance evaluation is needed. The semi-decision procedure is not currently integrated with the `Verl` tool, but we have already instrumented `Verl` with the necessary hooks. We plan to complete that integration and also to implement the decision procedure for restricted RL. This will enable comparison between performance of the (semi)-decision procedures and the axiomatic implementation of RL already present in `Verl`. (And with **QFBAPA**-Rel, if an SMT-based implementation becomes available.) Ordinary use of `Verl` will assess performance on full VCs for a range of correct and incorrect programs, i.e., involving integers and other theories besides RL. From those VCs we may also extract benchmark formulas in the RL and restricted RL fragments, for more direct comparative evaluation of the procedures.

As presented here, RL reflects the semantics in the original paper on region logic [2]. Subsequently we streamlined the assertion language by allowing regions to contain null [3]; this validates a slightly different set of formulas (e.g., $x \in \{x\}$ becomes valid, whereas only $x \neq \textbf{null} \Rightarrow x \in \{x\}$ is valid according to Def. 2). It should be straightforward to adapt the tableau procedures to this semantics.

Acknowledgements. Thanks to Nikolaj Bjørner and Leonardo de Moura for help with Z3 integration and feedback on the implementation. Thanks to Clark Barrett for studying proofs of soundness and completeness of tableaux. Thanks to the anonymous referees for their comments.

References

1. Banerjee, A., Barnett, M., Naumann, D.A.: Boogie Meets Regions: A Verification Experience Report. In: Shankar, N., Woodcock, J. (eds.) VSTTE 2008. LNCS, vol. 5295, pp. 177–191. Springer, Heidelberg (2008)
2. Banerjee, A., Naumann, D.A., Rosenberg, S.: Regional Logic for Local Reasoning about Global Invariants. In: Ryan, M. (ed.) ECOOP 2008. LNCS, vol. 5142, pp. 387–411. Springer, Heidelberg (2008)
3. Banerjee, A., Naumann, D.A., Rosenberg, S.: Local reasoning for global invariants, part I: Region logic. Extended version of [2], available at [24] (July 2011)

[9] Bernays-Schönfinkel-Ramsey fragment.

4. Barnett, M., Chang, B.-Y.E., DeLine, R., Jacobs, B., Leino, K.R.M.: Boogie: A Modular Reusable Verifier for Object-Oriented Programs. In: de Boer, F.S., Bonsangue, M.M., Graf, S., de Roever, W.-P. (eds.) FMCO 2005. LNCS, vol. 4111, pp. 364–387. Springer, Heidelberg (2006)
5. de Moura, L., Bjørner, N.: Model-based theory combination. Electr. Notes Theor. Comput. Sci. 198(2), 37–49 (2008)
6. de Moura, L., Bjørner, N.: Z3: An Efficient SMT Solver. In: Ramakrishnan, C.R., Rehof, J. (eds.) TACAS 2008. LNCS, vol. 4963, pp. 337–340. Springer, Heidelberg (2008)
7. Detlefs, D., Nelson, G., Saxe, J.B.: Simplify: a theorem prover for program checking. J. ACM 52(3), 365–473 (2005)
8. Fitting, M.: First-Order Logic and Automated Theorem Proving. Graduate texts in Computer Science. Springer, Heidelberg (1996)
9. Ganzinger, H., Hagen, G., Nieuwenhuis, R., Oliveras, A., Tinelli, C.: DPLL(*T*): Fast Decision Procedures. In: Alur, R., Peled, D.A. (eds.) CAV 2004. LNCS, vol. 3114, pp. 175–188. Springer, Heidelberg (2004)
10. Givan, R., McAllester, D.A., Witty, C., Kozen, D.: Tarskian set constraints. Inf. Comput. 174(2), 105–131 (2002)
11. Kapur, D., Zarba, C.G.: A reduction approach to decision procedures. Technical report, University of New Mexico (2005)
12. Kassios, I.T.: Dynamic Frames: Support for Framing, Dependencies and Sharing Without Restrictions. In: Misra, J., Nipkow, T., Karakostas, G. (eds.) FM 2006. LNCS, vol. 4085, pp. 268–283. Springer, Heidelberg (2006)
13. Kroening, D., Strichman, O.: Decision Procedures: An Algorithmic Point of View. EATCS. Springer, Heidelberg (2008)
14. Kuncak, V., Nguyen, H.H., Rinard, M.C.: An Algorithm for Deciding BAPA: Boolean Algebra with Presburger Arithmetic. In: Nieuwenhuis, R. (ed.) CADE 2005. LNCS (LNAI), vol. 3632, pp. 260–277. Springer, Heidelberg (2005)
15. Kuncak, V., Rinard, M.C.: Decision procedures for set-valued fields. Electr. Notes Theor. Comput. Sci. 131, 51–62 (2005)
16. Kuncak, V., Rinard, M.C.: Towards Efficient Satisfiability Checking for Boolean Algebra with Presburger Arithmetic. In: Pfenning, F. (ed.) CADE 2007. LNCS (LNAI), vol. 4603, pp. 215–230. Springer, Heidelberg (2007)
17. Leino, K.R.M.: Dafny: An Automatic Program Verifier for Functional Correctness. In: Clarke, E.M., Voronkov, A. (eds.) LPAR-16 2010. LNCS, vol. 6355, pp. 348–370. Springer, Heidelberg (2010)
18. Manna, Z., Zarba, C.G.: Combining Decision Procedures. In: Aichernig, B.K. (ed.) Formal Methods at the Crossroads. From Panacea to Foundational Support. LNCS, vol. 2757, pp. 381–422. Springer, Heidelberg (2003)
19. Marron, M., Méndez-Lojo, M., Hermenegildo, M.V., Stefanovic, D., Kapur, D.: Sharing analysis of arrays, collections, and recursive structures. In: PASTE, pp. 43–49 (2008)
20. Nelson, G., Oppen, D.C.: Simplification by cooperating decision procedures. ACM Trans. Program. Lang. Syst. 1(2), 245–257 (1979)
21. Rosenberg, S.: Region Logic: Local Reasoning for Java Programs and its Automation. PhD thesis, Stevens Institute of Technology (June 2011); available at [25]
22. Rosenberg, S., Banerjee, A., Naumann, D.A.: Local Reasoning and Dynamic Framing for the Composite Pattern and Its Clients. In: Leavens, G.T., O'Hearn, P., Rajamani, S.K. (eds.) VSTTE 2010. LNCS, vol. 6217, pp. 183–198. Springer, Heidelberg (2010)
23. Smullyan, R.M.: First-Order Logic. Springer, Heidelberg (1968)

24. Suter, P., Steiger, R., Kuncak, V.: Sets with Cardinality Constraints in Satisfiability Modulo Theories. In: Jhala, R., Schmidt, D. (eds.) VMCAI 2011. LNCS, vol. 6538, pp. 403–418. Springer, Heidelberg (2011)
25. Verl: VErifier for Region Logic. Software distribution, at `http://www.cs.stevens.edu/~naumann/pub/VERL/`
26. Yessenov, K., Piskac, R., Kuncak, V.: Collections, Cardinalities, and Relations. In: Barthe, G., Hermenegildo, M. (eds.) VMCAI 2010. LNCS, vol. 5944, pp. 380–395. Springer, Heidelberg (2010)
27. Zarba, C.G.: Combining Sets with Elements. In: Dershowitz, N. (ed.) Verification (Manna Festschrift). LNCS, vol. 2772, pp. 762–782. Springer, Heidelberg (2004)
28. Zee, K., Kuncak, V., Rinard, M.C.: Full functional verification of linked data structures. In: PLDI, pp. 349–361 (2008)

A General Framework for Probabilistic Characterizing Formulae

Joshua Sack[1] and Lijun Zhang[2]

[1] Department of Mathematics and Statistics, California State University Long Beach
[2] DTU Informatics, Technical University of Denmark

Abstract. Recently, a general framework on characteristic formulae was proposed by Aceto et al. It offers a simple theory that allows one to easily obtain characteristic formulae of many non-probabilistic behavioral relations. Our paper studies their techniques in a probabilistic setting. We provide a general method for determining characteristic formulae of behavioral relations for probabilistic automata using fixed-point probability logics. We consider such behavioral relations as simulations and bisimulations, probabilistic bisimulations, probabilistic weak simulations, and probabilistic forward simulations. This paper shows how their constructions and proofs can follow from a single common technique.

1 Introduction

Probabilistic automata have been extensively used in systems involving both stochastic and nondeterministic choice. To combat the state space explosion problem, various reduction techniques have been introduced and applied to probabilistic automata. These techniques include bisimulation and simulation relations [21,20], partial order reductions [3,12], symbolic data structures [13], and game-based abstractions [15].

Bisimulation and simulation relations are particularly useful, because they enable us to use compositional minimization [21]. Briefly, each of the constituting components can be minimized first before being composed with other interacting components. This idea is extended to a probabilistic setting in [6]. Various logics have been considered to reason about probabilistic automata. In [5], a model checking algorithm is presented for probabilistic automata with respect to the logic PCTL, and in [9,14], Hennessy-Milner logics are used to characterize behavioral relations.

A characteristic formula for a behavioral relation is associated with each state in a model; the formula for a given state characterizes the set of states that the given state is related to according to the behavioral relation. In the case that the behavioral relation is simulation, one state is related to another if the first can be simulated by the other, that is, can be mimicked by the other. In effect, a characteristic formula allows us to reduce the problem of determining whether one state is simulated by another to the problem of model checking. Instead of directly checking whether the first state is simulated by the other, we check if the other state satisfies the characteristic formula of the first. In a more theoretical setting, some modal completeness and decidability theorems can be proved by constructing a finite satisfying model whose elements are normal forms, which are characteristic formulae for bisimulation or approximations to such formulae [18].

V. Kuncak and A. Rybalchenko (Eds.): VMCAI 2012, LNCS 7148, pp. 396–411, 2012.

This paper focuses on behavioral relations over probabilistic automata and their characteristic formulae. The semantics of our languages involve fixed-points, which provide us with a natural facility for expressing various kinds of infinite behavior, such as those that are infinite or have loops. We present a single method, adapted from [1], that allows one to easily obtain characteristic formulae of many behavioral relations, including simulations and bisimulations, probabilistic bisimulations, probabilistic weak simulations, and probabilistic forward simulations. The strength of this technique is its generality: we can construct a variety of characteristic formulae and prove their correctness using a single simple method.

Relation to Related Work: Our theory builds on a recent paper by Aceto et al. [1], where a general framework is introduced for constructing non-probabilistic characteristic formulae over transition systems. It allows one to directly obtain the characteristic formulae for many behavioral relations, which have traditionally involved technical – even if not difficult – proofs. Their main result (an earlier version of Theorem 1 in this paper), in its generality, can be used for all the behavioral relations we consider, except for probabilistic forward simulation. We thus provide a modest generalization of this theorem to address forward simulation.

A more universally relevant extension to the overall setting of [1] is to involve in its applications (previously developed) liftings of relations. Liftings are discussed in [10,23], and employed in [14] for fixed-point characterizations of (bi)simulations and probabilistic (bi)simulations. As they are central to probabilistic behavioral relations, liftings play a key role in adapting the framework of [1] to a probabilistic setting.

Another difference between our work and [1] is with the language used. The languages in [1] are fixed-point variants of Hennessy-Milner logic. For all our behavioral relations except the probabilistic forward simulation, we use a fixed-point variant of a two-sorted probability logic given in [16]. This allows us to interpret the characteristic formulae over states, as in [1], but to also have formulae over distributions that better fit with the setting of probabilistic automata. For probabilistic forward simulation, we involve a language, as in [19], only interpreted over distributions rather than states.

In [7], Deng and van Glabbeek study characteristic formulae for all the behavioral relations over probabilistic automata that we consider, though they restrict their automata to being finite. For all their behavioral relations, their characteristic formulae use a more complex one-sorted language over distributions than the one we use for probabilistic forward simulation, and the form of their formulae are different (reflecting their different but equivalent approach to lifting) and somewhat simpler (our characteristic formula for probabilistic bisimulation involve an infinitary disjunction). But the difference that we emphasize is that they use a separate technique for proving correctness of characteristic formulae for each preorder considered, while our framework provides characteristic formulae which are correct by construction.

Organization of the paper: In Section 2, we provide definitions to be used later in the paper. In Section 3, we present a slight adaptation of the framework developed in [1]. In Section 4, we recall the definition of probabilistic automata, the fixed-point characterization of bisimulation and simulation relations, and the weak bisimulations, and then we clarify the relationship between liftings used in [7] and in [14]. In Section

5, we present the language that we use for all our formulae except those from a language introduced in Section 6 that is defined specifically to characterize forward simulations. In Section 6, we illustrate how the characteristic formulae for all the behavioral relations that we consider can be constructed by applying the general framework. In Section 7, we describe some possible extensions of our work. Finally, Section 8 concludes the paper.

2 Preliminaries

Distributions. Let S be a set. A *distribution* over S is a function $\mu\colon S \to \mathbb{R}^{\geq 0}$ such that the *support* of μ, defined by $\mathrm{supp}(\mu) := \{s \mid \mu(s) > 0\}$, is countable, and $\sum_{s\in S}\mu(s) = 1$. We let $\mu(A)$ denote the sum $\sum_{s\in A}\mu(s)$, for all $A \subseteq S$. We denote by $\mathit{Dist}(S)$ the set of discrete probability distributions over S and, given an element $s \in S$, we denote by δ_s the *Dirac distribution* on s that assigns probability 1 to $\{s\}$.

Given a countable set of distributions $\{\mu_i\}_{i\in I}$ and a set $\{p_i\}_{i\in I}$ of real numbers in $[0,1]$ such that $\sum_{i\in I} p_i = 1$, we define the *convex combination* $\sum_{i\in I} p_i\mu_i$ of $\{\mu_i\}_{i\in I}$ as the probability distribution μ such that, for each $s \in S$, $\mu(s) = \sum_{i\in I} p_i\mu_i(s)$.

Given a distribution over distributions ($\mu \in \mathit{Dist}(\mathit{Dist}(S))$), define the flattening of μ by the function *flatten*, that maps μ to a distribution ν, defined by

$$\nu(s) = \sum_{\nu'\in\mathrm{supp}(\mu)} \mu(\nu')\nu'(s). \tag{1}$$

Complete lattices. A *partially ordered set* (poset) is a set A together with a relation $\sqsubseteq_A$ that is reflexive ($a \sqsubseteq_A a$ for every $a \in A$), anti-symmetric ($a \sqsubseteq_A b$ and $b \sqsubseteq_A a$ implies $a = b$), and transitive ($a \sqsubseteq_A b$ and $b \sqsubseteq_A c$ implies $a \sqsubseteq_A c$). We omit the subscript A when it should be clear from context. A *complete lattice* is a partially ordered set $(A, \sqsubseteq)$, such that every subset $B \subseteq A$ has a least upper bound in A, written $\sqcup B$, and consequently a greatest lower bound $\sqcap B$ in A as well.

A function $f : A \to B$ between lattices is *monotone* if $a \sqsubseteq_A a'$ implies $f(a) \sqsubseteq_B f(a')$ for each $a, a' \in A$. A function $f : A \to B$ is an *isomorphism* if it is bijective, monotone, and f^{-1} is monotone, and consequently maps least upper bounds to least upper bounds. We call a function f from A to itself an *endofunction*. We call a point $a \in A$ a *post-fixpoint* of f if $f(a) \geq a$, and a *fixed-point* of f if $f(a) = a$. By Tarski's fixed-point theorem [22], every monotone endofunction f on a complete lattice A has a least upper bound $\mathrm{gfp}\, f$ given by $\sqcup\{a \mid a \sqsubseteq f(a)\}$.

3 General Framework

In this section we present some background behind our technique for finding characteristic formulae for behavioral relations. We involve languages $\mathcal{L}$ consisting of a set of formulae with variables. We often use I for the index set of the variables. The formulae will be interpreted over a set P, such as a set of states or distributions. In [1], $I = P$. We find that in order to apply this general framework to forward simulations (Section 6.4), it is helpful to distinguishing the index set I from the set P over which formulas will be interpreted, in particular setting I to be the set of states and P the set of distributions.

Variables are interpreted by a function $\sigma : I \to \mathcal{P}(P)$, called a *variable interpretation*. Here $\sigma(i)$ is viewed as the set of elements of P where the variable is considered to be true. This is similar to a valuation of atomic propositions in modal logic. The variable interpretation can be extended to a full fledged semantics $\sigma^* : \mathcal{L} \to \mathcal{P}(P)$, using rules such as $\sigma^*(\varphi \wedge \psi) = \sigma^*(\varphi) \cap \sigma^*(\psi)$. For all formulae φ and $p \in P$, we generally write $p \in [\![\varphi]\!]\sigma$ or $(\sigma, p) \models \varphi$ for $p \in \sigma^*(\varphi)$.

We call a function $E : I \to \mathcal{L}$ a *declaration*. Such a function characterizes an equational system of formulae, equating the variable X_i with the formula $E(i)$. As formulae can contain variables, a declaration is effectively recursive. Involving recursive features of a language allows us to characterize some infinite or looping behavior without the need for infinitary formulae. Lanugages with recursion generally involve fixed-points of an endofunction.[1] Hence we extend a declaration E to an endofunction $[\![E]\!] : \mathcal{P}(P)^I \to \mathcal{P}(P)^I$ on variable intepretations (here we write $\mathcal{P}(P)^I$ for the set of functions that map I to $\mathcal{P}(P)$), given by

$$([\![E]\!]\sigma)(i) = [\![E(i)]\!]\sigma.$$

The endofunction $[\![E]\!]$ has a greatest fixed point if the language is monotone.[2] A language is monotone if whenever $\sigma_1 \sqsubseteq \sigma_2$ (pointwise set inclusion), then for all formulae φ and elements p, it holds that $(\sigma_1, p) \models \varphi \Rightarrow (\sigma_2, p) \models \varphi$.

Behavioral relations, such as bisimulation, are often defined as the greatest fixed-point of a monotone endofunction F on $\mathcal{P}(I \times P)$, where I and P are typically set to be the set of states. The following definition clarifies our formulation of a characteristic formula, which in our setting is really a declaration.[3]

Definition 1 (Declaration characterizing a relation). *A declaration* $E : I \to \mathcal{L}$ *characterizes the greatest fixed-point of an endofunction* $F : \mathcal{P}(I \times P) \to \mathcal{P}(I \times P)$ *if for all* $i \in I$ *and* $p \in P$*,*

$$\mathsf{gfp}[\![E]\!], p \models E(i) \text{ iff } (i, p) \in \mathsf{gfp}\, F \ .$$

[1] Although we do not involve fixed-points operators directly in the language, we make use of fixed-points of a function induced by the declaration. A fixed-point sematics based on this equational system is equivalent to a fragment of the μ-calculi. The equational system provides us with a more intuitive way of handling what is equivalent to multiple nestings of fixed-point operators.

[2] This is because variable interpretations form a complete lattice, ordered under pointwise set inclusion, and the function $[\![E]\!]$ is monotone if the language is. Hence we can apply Tarski's fixed-point theorem.

[3] As we do not involve fixed-point operators directly in the formulae of the language, our recursive features come from the equational system given by the declaration. A *formula together with a declaration* contains the information we would normally obtain from a formula in the sufficiently expressive fragment of μ-calculus. Given a declaration E and $i \in I$, we always set the formula component to $E(i)$ when providing a characteristic formula-with-declaration for i. With this convension, the declaration is all we need to specify.

We link variable interpretations with subsets of $I \times P$, using the function $\varphi : \mathcal{P}(I \times P) \to \mathcal{P}(P)^I$ given by

$$\varphi(R) = (i \mapsto R(i)) \tag{2}$$

where $i \mapsto R(i)$ is the function mapping element $i \in I$ to the set $\{p \mid iRp\}$.

Definition 2 (Declaration expressing an endofunction). *A declaration E expresses a monotone endofunction $F : \mathcal{P}(I \times P) \to \mathcal{P}(I \times P)$ if*

$$\varphi(R), p \models E(i) \textit{ iff } (i, p) \in F(R)$$

for every relation $R \subseteq I \times P$.

More formally, the theorem from [1] is as follows.

Theorem 1. *If a declaration E expresses a monotone endofunction F, then E characterizes its greatest fixed-point* $\mathsf{gfp}\, F$.

This theorem and the prior two definitions differ from the one in [1] in that they set $I = P$. Our generalization of distinguishing I from P does not affect the proof in [1] of the main theorem.

4 Probabilistic Automata, Simulations, and Bisimulations

We first discuss lifting of relations, followed by the definition of probabilistic automata and simulation relations.

4.1 Lifting of Relations

A relation lifting transforms a relation between two sets into a relation between two sets related to the first two. Having two levels of relations is central to definitions of probabilistic behavioral relations. Liftings of relations from $S \times Dist(S)$ to $Dist(S) \times Dist(S)$ were introduced by Jonssen & Larsen [17] using *weight functions* to define simulations for Markov chains. Later, Desharnais [8] gave a definition of liftings that did not involve weight functions. We prove (Theorem 2 below) that these characterizations of liftings are equivalent, by using recent key insights (Lemma 1 below) from [10,23].

First we present the following characterization [10,23] of the lifting of a relation $R \subseteq S \times P$ (with S and P both arbitrary sets) to a relation $\widehat{R} \subseteq Dist(S) \times Dist(P)$:

$$\mu \widehat{R} \nu \Leftrightarrow \forall (A \subseteq \operatorname{supp} \mu).\ \mu(A) \leq \nu(R(A)). \tag{3}$$

When $P = Dist(S)$, we can define from $R \subseteq Dist(S) \times Dist(P)$ a relation $\overline{R} \subseteq Dist(S) \times Dist(S)$ by flattening the elements (see Eq. (1)) of $Dist(P)$: for $\mu, \nu \in Dist(S)$,

$$\mu \overline{R} \nu \Leftrightarrow \exists \nu' \in Dist(P).\ \nu = \mathit{flatten}(\nu')\ \&\ \mu R \nu'. \tag{4}$$

We next present the following characterization, based on weight functions, of a lifting from $R \subseteq S \times Dist(S)$ to $\widetilde{R} \subseteq Dist(S) \times Dist(S)$, given by

$$\begin{aligned} \mu \widetilde{R} \nu \Leftrightarrow\ & \exists \{s_i\}_{i \in \mathbb{N}} \in S.\ \exists \{\nu_i\}_{i \in \mathbb{N}} \in Dist(S) \text{ such that} \\ & \mu = \textstyle\sum_{i=1}^{\infty} p_i \delta_{s_i} \text{ and } \nu = \sum_{i=1}^{\infty} p_i \nu_i, \text{ for} \\ & \text{some } p_i \geq 0, \textstyle\sum_{i=1}^{\infty} p_i = 1, \text{ and } s_i R \nu_i. \end{aligned} \tag{5}$$

Note that $\delta_x \xrightarrow{a} \mu$ if and only if $x \overset{a}{\rightsquigarrow} \mu$. We will, as in [14], use the lifting (3) in our formulations of behavioral relations. The form (5) was used in [7] to define weak transitions, and will be used by us in the corresponding section (Definition 6). The two characterizations of relation liftings are equivalent in the following sense.

Theorem 2. *Given a relation $R \subseteq S \times Dist(S)$, $\widetilde{R} = \overline{\widehat{R}}$.*

Before proving this, we define weight functions [17] and networks, which will be useful in the proof.

Definition 3 (Weight function). *Let S and P be arbitrary sets. Let $\mu \in Dist(S), \nu \in Dist(P)$ and $R \subseteq S \times P$. A* weight function *for (μ, ν) with respect to R is a function $\Delta : S \times P \to [0,1]$, such that*

1. $\Delta(s,p) > 0$ *implies* $s \; R \; p$,
2. $\mu(s) = \sum_{p \in P} \Delta(s,p)$, *for* $s \in S$ *and*
3. $\nu(p) = \sum_{s \in S} \Delta(s,p)$, *for* $p \in P$.

We only make sense of sums that have countably many non-zero terms. The conditions of Definition 3 ensure that $\Delta(s,p) = 0$ whenever either $s \notin \operatorname{supp} \mu$ or $p \notin \operatorname{supp} \nu$. Thus as an uncountable sum, only countably many terms would be non-zero, and hence it is safe to formulate this as an uncountable sum.

Definition 4 (The network for μ, ν and R). *Let $R \subseteq S \times P$, and let $\mu \in Dist(S), \nu \in Dist(P)$ be distributions. A* network *$\mathcal{N}(\mu, \nu, R)$ is a tuple (V, E, c), where*

1. $V = \{\nearrow, \searrow\} \cup \operatorname{supp}(S) \cup \operatorname{supp}(P)$, *with* $\nearrow, \searrow \notin S, P$,
2. $E = \{(s,p) \mid (s,p) \in R\} \cup \{(\nearrow, s) \mid s \in \operatorname{supp}(\mu)\} \cup \{(p, \searrow) \mid p \in \operatorname{supp}(\nu)\}$,
3. *c, the* capacity function, *is defined by:*
   (a) $c(\nearrow, s) = \mu(s)$ *for all* $s \in \operatorname{supp} \mu$,
   (b) $c(p, \searrow) = \nu(p)$ *for all* $p \in \operatorname{supp}(\nu)$, *and*
   (c) $c(s,p) = \infty$ *for all other* $(s,p) \in E$.

Lemma 1. *Let $R \subseteq S \times P$, and let $\mu_1 \in Dist(S), \mu_2 \in Dist(P)$. The following statements are equivalent:*

1. *There exists a weight function for (μ_1, μ_2) with respect to R.*
2. *The maximum flow of the network $\mathcal{N}(\mu_1, \mu_2, R)$ is 1.*
3. $\mu_1(A) \leq \mu_2(R(A))$ *for all* $A \subseteq S$.
4. $\mu_1(A) \leq \mu_2(R(A))$ *for all* $A \subseteq \operatorname{supp}(\mu_1)$.

The above lemma has been proposed in [10,23], and used in [14]. The formal proof for countable systems makes use of a recent result in [2]. Thus, for completeness, the proof of this lemma for countable systems is given below.

Proof. The equivalence between 1 and 2 is from Lemma 5.1 in [4]. The equivalence between 3 and 4 is straight forward. We will show that 1 implies 3 and that 4 implies 2.

($1 \Longrightarrow 3$): Let Δ denote the corresponding weight function for (μ_1, μ_2) with respect to R. Now we want to prove that for every $A \subseteq S$: $\mu_1(A) \leq \mu_2(R(A))$. First, letting $Dom(R)$ represent the set of first coordinates of the relation R, we have

$$\mu_1(A) = \sum_{u \in A} \sum_{v \in P} \Delta(u,v) = \sum_{u \in A} \sum_{v \in R(A)} \Delta(u,v) = \sum_{u \in A \cap Dom(R)} \sum_{v \in R(A)} \Delta(u,v),$$

which follows from the properties of a weight function (Definition 3), especially that $\Delta(u, v) = 0$ if $u \notin Dom(R)$ or $v \notin R(u)$. Similarly, from the first and third conditions of a weight function, we have that $\mu_2(R(A)) = \sum_{u \in R^{-1}(R(A))} \sum_{v \in R(A)} \Delta(u, v)$. From basic set theory, we see that $A \cap Dom(R) \subseteq R^{-1}(R(A))$. Thus by comparing $\mu_1(A)$ and $\mu_2(R(A))$, we have our desired result: $\mu_1(A) \leq \mu_2(R(A))$.

($4 \Longrightarrow 2$): Assume that the fourth clause is true. We show that the maximum flow of the network $\mathcal{N}(\mu_1, \mu_2, R)$ has value 1. To construct such a maximum flow, we borrow the proof idea of Theorem 7.3.4 from Desharnais [8]. According to the *Maximum Flow Minimum Cut Theorem* [2], the maximum flow equals the capacity of a minimal cut. Therefore, it suffices to show that there exists a minimal cut of capacity 1. Cut $\{\nearrow\}$ has capacity 1, but we still have to show that it is minimal. Let C be some minimal cut (not necessarily $\{\nearrow\}$). We let $B = C \cap S$. The capacity of C is the sum: $c(C) = \sum\{c(i, j) \mid i \in C, j \notin C\}$. Cut C has to fulfill $s \in B \implies R(s) \subseteq C$ because otherwise it would have infinite capacity. Hence the capacity of C is: $c(C) = \mu_1(S \setminus B) + \mu_2(R(B))$. By construction of the network $\mathcal{N}$, it holds that $B \subseteq \text{supp}(\mu_1)$. Since $\mu_1(B) \leq \mu_2(R(B))$, we have: $c(C) \geq \mu_1(S \setminus B) + \mu_1(B) = \mu_1(S) = 1$. Hence, the capacity of C is greater than or equal to 1, implying that the minimum cut has value 1. □

Proof. (Proof of Theorem 2)

Suppose that $\mu \widetilde{R} \nu$. Then $\mu = \sum_{i=1}^{\infty} p_i \delta_{s_i}$ and $\nu = \sum_{i=1}^{\infty} p_i \nu_i$, where $p_i \geq 0$, $\sum_{i=1}^{\infty} p_i = 1$, and $s_i R \nu_i$. Define $\nu' \in Dist(Dist(S))$, such that $\nu'(\nu_i) = p_i$. Then the p_i are the weights $\Delta(s_i, \nu_i)$ in the weight function for μ and ν' (Definition 3). By Lemma 1, $\mu(A) \leq \nu'(R(A))$, for all $A \in \text{supp}(\mu)$. Thus $\mu \widehat{R} \nu'$, and hence $\mu \overline{\widehat{R}} \nu$.

Suppose that $\mu \overline{\widehat{R}} \nu$. Then there is a $\nu' \in Dist(Dist(S))$, such that $\nu = \mathit{flatten}(\nu')$ and $\mu \widehat{R} \nu'$, i.e., for all $A \in \text{supp}\, \mu$, $\mu(A) \leq \nu'(R(A))$. By Lemma 1, there is a weight function Δ for μ and ν' with respect to R. Enumerate the pairs (s, ν), using a bijective function $f : (\text{supp}(\mu) \times \text{supp}(\nu')) \to \mathbb{N}$ (replace $\mathbb{N}$ with $\{1, 2, \ldots, N\}$ if $|\text{supp}(\mu) \times \text{supp}(\nu')| = N < \infty$). Let $g = f^{-1}$, $p_i = \Delta(g(i))$, $s_i = \pi_1(g(i))$ (where π_1 is the projection onto the first coordinate), and let $\nu_i = \pi_2(g(i))$. We then obtain the desired condition of (5) from the conditions of the weight function by plugging in an arbitrary s into the right hand side of the equation for μ in (5), and applying second condition of the weight function to see that we indeed get $\mu(s)$; and then note that the third condition of the weight function collapses the right hand side of the equation for ν in (5) into the right hand side of the equation for flattening of ν' into ν (recall that we used equation (4) to obtain ν'). □

4.2 Probabilistic Automata

Now recall the definition of probabilistic automaton [21], or PA for short.

Definition 5. *A* probabilistic automaton *is a triple $\mathcal{M} = (S, Act, Steps)$, where S is a countable set of* states, *Act is a countable set of* actions, *and the relation $Steps \subseteq S \times Act \times Dist(S)$ is the* transition relation.

Obviously, PAs comprise labeled transition systems (LTS) for the special case that for all $(s, a, \mu) \in Steps$, μ is a Dirac distribution. Denote a transition $(s, a, \mu) \in Steps$ by

$s \xrightarrow{a} \mu$, which is also referred to as an a-transition of s. We denote the set of distributions leaving a state s by action a by $Steps_a(s) = \{\mu \mid s \xrightarrow{a} \mu\}$.

Given a probabilistic automaton $(S, Act, Steps)$, we can augment the transition relation *Steps* (which maps states via actions to distributions) to another transition relation *Comb* (which also maps states via actions to distributions), such that each transition in *Comb* for any action corresponds to a convex combination of transitions in *Steps* for that action. Precisely, if $\{s \xrightarrow{a} \mu_i\}_{i\in I}$ is a set of transitions, then

$$s \overset{a}{\rightsquigarrow} \mu \text{ iff } \mu = \sum_{i\in I} p_i\mu_i \text{ for some } p_i \text{ where } \sum_{i\in I} p_i = 1. \tag{6}$$

The a transitions in *Step* are denoted by $\xrightarrow{a}$ and those in *Comb* are denoted by $\overset{a}{\rightsquigarrow}$. Note that as $\xrightarrow{a}$ may represent a finite relation over states, $\overset{a}{\rightsquigarrow}$ typically represents a relation that is uncountable.

4.3 Simulations and Bisimulations

In the following exposition, we fix some PA $\mathcal{M} = (S, Act, Steps)$ and observe that the set of relations over S, denoted by $2^{S\times S}$, is a complete lattice with set inclusion as the partial order. We review in this section how some notions of simulation and bisimulation can be presented in terms of suitable monotone functions over this lattice [14].

Simulation. Consider the function $F_{\precsim} : 2^{S\times S} \to 2^{S\times S}$ defined as follows:

$$R \mapsto \{(s,t) \in S \times S \mid \forall s \xrightarrow{a} \mu.\ \exists t \xrightarrow{a} \mu' : \mu\widehat{R}\mu'\} \tag{7}$$

We say that a relation $R \in 2^{S\times S}$ is a *simulation relation* if R is a post-fixpoint of $F_{\precsim}$, i.e. $R \subseteq F_{\precsim}(R)$. Note that the function $F_{\precsim}$ is monotone. Recall that Tarski's fixed-point theorem [22] says that the fixed-points of a monotone function form a complete lattice and that the greatest fixed-point is the union of all post-fixpoints. *Similarity*, denoted $\precsim$, is defined as the greatest fixed point of $F_{\precsim}$, and hence must be the union of all simulation relations, the greatest simulation relation.

Example 1. Let $\mathcal{M}$ be such that for every $(s, a, \mu) \in Steps$, μ is a Dirac distribution. Then

$$\begin{aligned} F_{\precsim} : R \mapsto & \{(s,t) \in S \times S \mid \forall s \xrightarrow{a} \delta_{s'}.\ \exists t \xrightarrow{a} \delta_{t'} : \delta_{s'}\widehat{R}\delta_{t'}\} \\ &= \{(s,t) \in S \times S \mid \forall s \xrightarrow{a} \delta_{s'}.\ \exists t \xrightarrow{a} \delta_{t'} : \delta_{s'}(\{s'\}) \leq \delta_{t'}(R(\{s'\}))\} \\ &= \{(s,t) \in S \times S \mid \forall s \xrightarrow{a} \delta_{s'}.\ \exists t \xrightarrow{a} \delta_{t'} : s'Rt'\}. \end{aligned}$$

By replacing the Dirac distributions δ_s by states s in the definition of $F_{\precsim}$ over the LTS $\mathcal{M}$, we obtain the same definition that is given in [1] for an endofunction, whose post-fixpoints are simulations.

A coarser relation, called *probabilistic simulation*, is defined in the same way by replacing transitions with combined transitions so that the greatest probabilistic simulation is the greatest fixed-point of the function $F_{\precsim^P} : 2^{S\times S} \to 2^{S\times S}$ defined by:

$$R \mapsto \{(s,s') \in S \times S \mid \forall s \xrightarrow{a} \mu.\ \exists s' \overset{a}{\rightsquigarrow} \mu' : \mu\widehat{R}\mu'\}\,. \tag{8}$$

A relation $R \subseteq S \times S$ is a probabilistic simulation if it is a post-fixpoint of $F_{\precsim^p}$. The greatest probabilistic simulation preorder $\precsim^p$ is defined as the greatest fixed-point of $F_{\precsim^p}$.

Bisimulation. The function corresponding to bisimulation is a symmetric variation of the function for simulation, such that $F_{\sim} : 2^{S\times S} \to 2^{S\times S}$ is defined by:

$$R \mapsto \left\{ (s,t) \in S \times S \,\middle|\, \begin{array}{l} \forall s \xrightarrow{a} \mu.\ \exists t \xrightarrow{a} \mu' : \mu \widehat{R} \mu' \\ \forall t \xrightarrow{a} \mu'.\ \exists s \xrightarrow{a} \mu : \mu \widehat{R} \mu' \end{array} \right\}$$

We say that a relation $R \in 2^{S\times S}$ is a *bisimulation relation* if R is a post-fixpoint of $F_{\sim}$, i.e. $R \subseteq F_{\sim}(R)$. The greatest bisimulation $\sim$ is defined as the greatest fixed-point *gfp* $F_{\sim}$.

Similarly, we introduce *probabilistic bisimulation*. The function $F_{\sim^p} : 2^{S\times S} \to 2^{S\times S}$ for probabilistic bisimulation is defined analogously, however using combined transitions:

$$R \mapsto \left\{ (s,t) \in S \times S \,\middle|\, \begin{array}{l} \forall s \xrightarrow{a} \mu.\ \exists t \overset{a}{\leadsto} \mu' : \mu \widehat{R} \mu' \\ \forall t \xrightarrow{a} \mu'.\ \exists s \overset{a}{\leadsto} \mu : \mu \widehat{R} \mu' \end{array} \right\}$$

A relation $R \subseteq S \times S$ is a probabilistic bisimulation if it is a post-fixpoint of $F_{\sim^p}$. The greatest bisimulation $\sim^p$ is defined as the greatest fixed-point *gfp* $F_{\sim^p}$.

It is easy to see that $\sim$ and $\sim^p$ are equivalence relations. It is not difficult to see that, restricting to LTSs, (bi-)simulation and probabilistic (bi-)simulation coincide.

Weak simulation. We say that an automaton $(S, Act_{\tau}, Steps)$ is divergent if there is an infinite sequence (s_i, μ_i), such that $s_i \xrightarrow{\tau} \mu_i$ and s_{i+1} is in the support of μ_i. An automaton that is not divergent is convergent.

Let *Act* be a non-empty set of actions, and let $Act_{\tau} = Act \cup \{\tau\}$, where τ is an element not appearing in *Act* and is regarded as an internal step. We define weak transitions similarly to those in [7,20]:

Definition 6 (Weak transitions). *Given a convergent countable probabilistic automaton $(S, Act_{\tau}, Steps)$, we define the following relations:*

- *define $x \xrightarrow{\hat{\tau}} \mu$ iff $x \xrightarrow{\tau} \mu$ or $\mu = \delta_x$, and define $x \xrightarrow{\hat{a}} \mu$ iff $x \xrightarrow{a} \mu$.*
- *define $\overset{\hat{\tau}}{\rightarrowtail}$ and $\overset{\hat{a}}{\rightarrowtail}$ from respectively $\xrightarrow{\hat{\tau}}$ and $\xrightarrow{\hat{a}}$ according to (5).*
- *for all $a \in Act_{\tau}$, define $\mu \overset{\hat{a}}{\Rightarrow} \nu$ iff there are μ' and ν', such that $\mu \overset{\hat{\tau}}{\rightarrowtail}{}^{*} \mu'$, $\mu' \overset{\hat{a}}{\rightarrowtail} \nu'$, $\nu' \overset{\hat{\tau}}{\rightarrowtail}{}^{*} \nu$, where $\overset{\hat{\tau}}{\rightarrowtail}{}^{*}$ is the reflexive transitve closure of $\overset{\hat{\tau}}{\rightarrowtail}$.*

A *weak simulation relation* is defined as a post-fixpoint of the endofunction $F_{\precapprox} : 2^{S\times S} \to 2^{S\times S}$ defined by:

$$R \mapsto \{(s,t) \in S \times S \mid \forall a \in Act_{\tau}.\ \forall s \xrightarrow{a} \mu.\ \exists t.\ \delta_t \overset{\hat{a}}{\Rightarrow} \mu' : \mu \widehat{R} \mu'\}\ .$$

Weak similarity, denoted $\precapprox$, is defined is the greatest fixed-point of $F_{\precapprox}$.

5 Hennessy-Milner Logic for Probabilistic Automata

Here we present our basic language $\mathcal{L}_{\mathsf{bas}}$, a two-sorted language, similar to one in [16], consisting of state formulae (interpreted over the states S of the automaton) and distribution formulae (to be interpreted over $Dist(S)$). It is suggested in [14] that such a two-sorted language could be useful for a coalgebraic approach, but we leave coalgebraic characteristic formulae for future work.

Of the two sorts, we are ultimately interested in the formulae over states, as the simulation and bisimulation relations we have seen so far are defined over states. Formally, given a set Act_τ of actions augmented with a silent action τ, we define the language $\mathcal{L}_{\mathsf{bas}}(Act_\tau)$ by the following two-sorted syntax. State formulae are given by:

$$\varphi ::= X_z \mid \top \mid \bot \mid \bigwedge_{k \in K} \varphi_k \mid \bigvee_{k \in K} \varphi_k \mid \langle T \rangle \psi \mid [T]\psi$$

where $T \in \{\xrightarrow{a}, \overset{a}{\rightsquigarrow}, \overset{a}{\Rightarrow} \mid a \in Act_\tau\}$, $k \in K$ for some cardinal K, and $z \in I$ for some index set I, which we will typically set equal to the set S of states; distribution formulae are given by:

$$\psi ::= \top \mid \bot \mid \bigwedge_{k \in K} \psi_k \mid \bigvee_{k \in K} \psi_k \mid \mathsf{L}_p \varphi$$

where $p \in [0, 1]$ and $k \in K$ for some cardinal K.[4]

Semantics. Let $\mathcal{M} = (S, Act, Steps)$ be a PA. The formula φ is interpreted on states and ψ on distributions over. Both will make use of a variable interpretation $\sigma : I \to \mathcal{P}(P)$, where P is the set of states S. Select components of the semantics are given by:

$\sigma, s \models X_z$	iff $s \in \sigma(z)$
$\sigma, s \models \langle T \rangle \psi$	iff $\sigma, \mu \models \psi$ for some μ such that $sT\mu$
$\sigma, s \models [T]\psi$	iff $\sigma, \mu \models \psi$ for all μ such that $sT\mu$
$\sigma, \mu \models \mathsf{L}_p \varphi$	iff $\mu(\{s \mid \sigma, s \models \varphi\}) \geq p$

where $T \in \{\xrightarrow{a}, \overset{a}{\rightsquigarrow}, \overset{a}{\Rightarrow} \mid a \in Act_\tau\}$. To be clear, we take $\xrightarrow{a}$ to be the primitive relation component in the probabilistic automaton, $\overset{a}{\rightsquigarrow}$ to be derived from $\xrightarrow{a}$ according to (6), and $\overset{a}{\Rightarrow}$ to be defined according to Definition 6.

We observe that this language is monotone:

Proposition 1. *if $\sigma_1 \sqsubseteq \sigma_2$ (pointwise set inclusion), then for all state formulae φ and states s, we have $\sigma_1, s \models \varphi \Rightarrow \sigma_2, s \models \varphi$ and for all distribution formulae ψ and distributions μ, we have $\sigma_1, \mu \models \psi \Rightarrow \sigma_2, \mu \models \psi$.*[5]

---

[4] It may be desirable to restrict p to rational numbers so as to have a countable language, but doing so would require we add a countable conjunction to many of our characteristic formulae.

[5] Note that this formulation of a monotone language is slightly stronger than the definition of a monotone language given in Section 3.

Proof. This is by induction on the structure of formulae:

IH suppose for every subformula ψ of φ, we have that whenever $\sigma_1 \sqsubseteq \sigma_2$, if ψ were a state formula, we have for each state s, $\sigma_1, s \models \varphi \Rightarrow \sigma_2, s \models \varphi$ and if ψ were a distribution formula, we have for each distribution $\sigma_1, \mu \models \psi \Rightarrow \sigma_2, \mu \models \psi$.

base case $\varphi = X_z$ immediate from definition.

Case booleans: these may be either state or distribution formulae, but the proof is straight forward.

Case $\varphi = \langle T \rangle \psi$, suppose that $\sigma_1, s \models \langle T \rangle \psi$. Then there is a μ such that $sT\mu$ and $\sigma_1, \mu \models \psi$. Then by the IH, $\sigma_2, \mu \models \psi$, and hence $\sigma_2, s \models \langle T \rangle \psi$.

Case $\varphi = [T]\psi$, this is almost identical to the $\langle T \rangle \psi$ case.

Case $\varphi = \mathsf{L}_p \psi$. Suppose that $\sigma_1, \mu \models \mathsf{L}_p \psi$. Then $\mu(\{s \mid \sigma_1, s \models \psi\}) \geq p$. But then by the IH, $\mu(\{s \mid \sigma_2, s \models \psi\}) \geq \mu(\{s \mid \sigma_1, s \models \psi\}) \geq p$. Thus $\sigma_2, \mu \models \mathsf{L}_p \psi$. □

6 Characteristic Formulae

In this section, we illustrate how the characteristic formulae for all the behavioral relations that we consider can be constructed by using our adaptation of the general framework of [1].[6]

6.1 Simulations

We express in $\mathcal{L}_{\mathsf{bas}}$ the endofunction $F_{\precsim}$ with the endodeclaration

$$E_{\precsim} : s \mapsto \bigwedge_{a \in Act} \bigwedge_{\mu : s \xrightarrow{a} \mu} \langle \xrightarrow{a} \rangle \bigwedge_{A \subseteq \mathsf{supp}\,\mu} \mathsf{L}_{\mu(A)} \bigvee_{z \in A} X_z .$$

Recall that $[\![E_{\precsim}]\!]$ is an endofunction on variable interpretations, and is monotone since the language is. Had we restricted our language to only allowing rational subscripts p in L_p, then we could replace $\mathsf{L}_{\mu(A)}$ by $\bigwedge_{p \in \mathbb{Q} \cap [0, \mu(A)]} \mathsf{L}_p$.

We see that $E_{\precsim}$ expresses $F_{\precsim}$ as follows:

1. $(s,t) \in F_{\precsim}(R)$
2. $\forall a \in Act,\ \forall s \xrightarrow{a} \mu,\ \exists t \xrightarrow{a} \mu',\ \mu \widehat{R} \mu'$
3. $\forall a \in Act,\ \forall s \xrightarrow{a} \mu,\ \exists t \xrightarrow{a} \mu', \forall A \subseteq \mathrm{supp}(A), \mu(A) \leq \mu'(R(A))$.
4. $\varphi(R), t \models \bigwedge_{a \in Act} \bigwedge_{\mu : s \xrightarrow{a} \mu} \langle \xrightarrow{a} \rangle \bigwedge_{A \subseteq \mathsf{supp}\,\mu} \mathsf{L}_{\mu(A)} \bigvee_{z \in A} X_z$.
5. $\varphi(R), t \models E_{\precsim}(s)$

To see the relationship between Items (3) and (4), note that $[\![\bigvee_{z \in A} X_z]\!]\varphi(R) = R(A)$, and hence the formula $\mathsf{L}_{\mu(A)} \bigvee_{z \in A} X_z$ holds whenever $\mu(A) \leq \mu'(R(A))$.

Then by Theorem 1, $E_{\precsim}$ characterizes gfp $F_{\precsim}$.

[6] The general framework in [1] should apply to most of the behavioral relations as presented in that paper; our adaptation is only needed for forward simulation.

Opsim: Toward investigating the opposite of simulation (which we abbreviate *opsim* or o), we express the endofunction

$$F_{\precsim^o} : R \mapsto \{(s,t) \in S \times S \mid \forall a \in \mathit{Act}.\ \forall t \xrightarrow{a} \mu'.\ \exists s \xrightarrow{a} \mu : \mu \widehat{R} \mu'\}$$

with the endodeclaration

$$E_{\precsim^o} : s \mapsto \bigwedge_{a \in \mathit{Act}} [\xrightarrow{a}] \bigvee_{\mu : s \xrightarrow{a} \mu} \bigwedge_{A \subseteq \mathrm{supp}\, \mu} \mathsf{L}_{\mu(A)} \bigvee_{z \in A} X_z .$$

We see that $E_{\precsim^o}$ expresses $F_{\precsim^o}$ as follows:

1. $(s,t) \in F_{\precsim^o}(R)$
2. $\forall a \in \mathit{Act},\ \forall t \xrightarrow{a} \mu',\ \exists s \xrightarrow{a} \mu,\ \mu \widehat{R} \mu'$
3. $\forall a \in \mathit{Act},\ \forall t \xrightarrow{a} \mu',\ \exists s \xrightarrow{a} \mu, \forall A \subseteq \mathrm{supp}(A), \mu(A) \le \mu'(R(A))$.
4. $\varphi(R), t \models \bigwedge_{a \in \mathit{Act}} [\xrightarrow{a}] \bigvee_{\mu : s \xrightarrow{a} \mu} \bigwedge_{A \subseteq \mathrm{supp}\, \mu} \mathsf{L}_{\mu(A)} \bigvee_{z \in A} X_z$.
5. $\varphi(R), t \models E_{\precsim^o}(s)$

Then by Theorem 1, $E_{\precsim^o}$ characterizes gfp $F_{\precsim^o}$. Note that $E_{\precsim} \wedge E_{\precsim^o}$ is the characteristic formula for bisimulation $\sim$.

6.2 Probabilistic Simulations and Probabilistic Bisimulation

Using the same argument as for simulation and opsimulation, we see that the endofunction

$$E_{\precsim^p} : s \mapsto \bigwedge_{a \in \mathit{Act}} \bigwedge_{\mu : s \xrightarrow{a} \mu} \langle \overset{a}{\rightsquigarrow} \rangle \bigwedge_{A \subseteq \mathrm{supp}\, \mu} \mathsf{L}_{\mu(A)} \bigvee_{z \in A} X_z .$$

expresses $F_{\precsim^p}$, and that the endofunction

$$F_{\precsim^{po}} : R \mapsto \{(s,t) \in S \times S \mid \forall a \in \mathit{Act}.\ \forall t \xrightarrow{a} \mu'.\ \exists s \overset{a}{\rightsquigarrow} \mu : \mu \widehat{R} \mu'\}$$

is expressed by the endodeclaration

$$E_{\precsim^{po}} : s \mapsto \bigwedge_{a \in \mathit{Act}} [\xrightarrow{a}] \bigvee_{\mu : s \overset{a}{\rightsquigarrow} \mu} \bigwedge_{A \subseteq \mathrm{supp}\, \mu} \mathsf{L}_{\mu(A)} \bigvee_{z \in A} X_z .$$

Hence $E_{\precsim^p}$ and $E^{\precsim^{po}}$ characterize gfp $F_{\precsim^p}$ and gfp $F_{\precsim^{po}}$ respectively. Note that $E_{\precsim^{po}}$ is typically infinitary, since the disjunction may be over an uncountable set. Similar to the case for ordinary bisimulation, $E_{\precsim} \wedge E_{\precsim^o}$ is the characteristic formula for probabilistic bisimulation $\sim^p$.

6.3 Weak Simulations

A weak simulation is defined as the greatest fixed-point of the endofunction $F_{\precapprox} : 2^{S \times S} \to 2^{S \times S}$ defined by

$$R \mapsto \{(s,t) \in S \times S \mid \forall a \in \mathit{Act}_\tau.\ \forall s \xrightarrow{a} \mu.\ \exists t.\ \delta_t \overset{\widehat{a}}{\Rightarrow} \mu' :\ \mu \widehat{R} \mu'\}\ .$$

Letting $s \overset{\hat{a}}{\rightrightarrows} \mu$ be defined by $\delta_s \overset{\hat{a}}{\Rightarrow} \mu$, we express this endofunction with the endodeclaration

$$E_{\precsim\!\!\approx} : s \mapsto \bigwedge_{a \in Act_\tau} \bigwedge_{\mu : s \xrightarrow{a} \mu} \langle \overset{\hat{a}}{\rightrightarrows} \rangle \bigwedge_{A \subseteq \mathrm{supp}\, \mu} \mathsf{L}_{\mu(A)} \bigvee_{z \in A} X_z.$$

Note that this is the same as for simulation, but with $\xrightarrow{a}$ replaced by $\overset{a}{\rightrightarrows}$. The proof that $E_{\precsim\!\!\approx}$ expresses $F_{\precsim\!\!\approx}$ is essentially the same as the proof for simulation. Thus by Theorem 1, $E_{\precsim\!\!\approx}$ characterizes gfp $F_{\precsim\!\!\approx}$.

6.4 Probabilistic Forward Simulation for Probabilistic Automata

Given a distribution $\mu \in Dist(S)$, we define $\breve{\mu} \in Dist(Dist(S))$ by

$$\breve{\mu}(\nu) = \begin{cases} \mu(s) & \nu = \delta_s \\ 0 & \text{otherwise} \end{cases}.$$

Note that $\mathit{flatten}(\breve{\mu}) = \mu$. In this section we consider the probabilistic forward simulation, defined by:

$$F_{\precsim\!\!\approx^f} : R \mapsto \{(s, \mu) \in S \times Dist(S) \mid \forall a \in Act_\tau.\ \forall s \xrightarrow{a} \nu.\ \exists \mu'.\mu \overset{\hat{a}}{\Rightarrow} \mu' : \nu \widehat{R} \breve{\mu}'\}$$

Note also that $F_{\precsim\!\!\approx^f}$ is monotone, as increasing the size of R will in turn increase the size of $\widehat{R}$, and hence $F_{\precsim\!\!\approx^f}(R)$ will not shrink.

As before, we want to express the endofunction $F_{\precsim\!\!\approx^f}$. We employ a "distribution" language $\mathcal{L}_{\mathsf{dst}}$, define as follows. Given a set *Act* of actions, the language $\mathcal{L}_{\mathsf{dst}}(Act_\tau)$ is given by:

$$\varphi ::= X_z \mid \top \mid \bot \mid \bigwedge_{k \in K} \varphi_k \mid \bigvee_{k \in K} \varphi_k \mid \langle \overset{\hat{a}}{\Rightarrow} \rangle \varphi \mid [\overset{\hat{a}}{\Rightarrow}] \varphi \mid \mathsf{L}_p \varphi$$

where $a \in Act_\tau$, $k \in K$ for some cardinal K, and $z \in I$ for some index set I, (which we will typically, or maybe always, make the set of distributions), $p \in [0, 1]$.

We interpret all formulae φ on distributions, and will use a variable interpretation $\sigma : I \to \mathcal{P}(P)$, where $P = Dist(S)$. Select components of the semantics are:

$\sigma, \mu \models X_z$	iff $\mu \in \sigma(z)$
$\sigma, \mu \models \langle \overset{\hat{a}}{\Rightarrow} \rangle \psi$	iff $\sigma, \nu \models \psi$ for some ν where $\mu \overset{\hat{a}}{\Rightarrow} \nu$
$\sigma, \mu \models [\overset{\hat{a}}{\Rightarrow}] \psi$	iff $\sigma, \nu \models \psi$ for all ν where $\mu \overset{\hat{a}}{\Rightarrow} \nu$
$\sigma, \mu \models \mathsf{L}_p \varphi$	iff $\breve{\mu}(\{\nu \mid \sigma, \nu \models \varphi\}) \geq p$

Note that $\mathsf{L}_p \varphi$ is defined differently here as it was in $\mathcal{L}_{\mathsf{bas}}$: in $\mathcal{L}_{\mathsf{dst}}$, we take the probabilities to be over sets of distributions, while in $\mathcal{L}_{\mathsf{bas}}$ we take them to be over sets of states. Also, although the variables are indexed by states in both languages, their interpretations are also different. One can check that $\mathcal{L}_{\mathsf{dst}}$ is monotone.

Then the endofunction

$$E_{\precsim\!\!\approx^f} : s \mapsto \bigwedge_{a \in Act_\tau} \bigwedge_{\nu : s \xrightarrow{a} \nu} \langle \overset{a}{\Rightarrow} \rangle \bigwedge_{A \subseteq \mathrm{supp}\, \nu} \mathsf{L}_{\nu(A)} \bigvee_{z \in A} X_z.$$

expresses $F_{\precsim_f}$, which can be seen as follows:

1. $(s, \mu) \in F_{\precsim_f}(R)$
2. $\forall a \in Act_\tau,\ \forall s \xrightarrow{a} \nu,\ \exists \mu \xRightarrow{\hat{a}} \mu',\ \nu \widehat{R} \breve{\mu}'$
3. $\forall a \in Act_\tau,\ \forall s \xrightarrow{a} \nu,\ \exists \mu \xRightarrow{\hat{a}} \mu', \forall A \subseteq \text{supp}(\nu), \nu(A) \leq \breve{\mu}'(R(A))$.
4. $\varphi(R), \mu \models \bigwedge_{a \in Act_\tau} \bigwedge_{\nu : s \xrightarrow{a} \nu} \langle \xRightarrow{\hat{a}} \rangle \bigwedge_{A \subseteq \text{supp}\, \nu} \mathsf{L}_{\nu(A)} \bigvee_{z \in A} X_z$.
5. $\varphi(R), \mu \models E_{\precsim_f}(s)$

Thus by Theorem 1, $E_{\precsim_f}$ characterizes gfp $F_{\precsim_f}$.

7 Extensions

For simplicity of presentation, we have chosen probabilistic automata, as they are one of the most important types of stochastic models studied in the literature. We want to note, however, that the general framework can be easily extended to other types of stochastic models.

Let us briefly discuss the model called continuous-time Markov chains (CTMC). In CTMCs, we do not have nondeterministic choices, whereas transitions are governed by a negative exponential distribution. Briefly, from each state s we have a unique transition of the form $s \xrightarrow{\lambda} \mu$, where λ is a positive constant characterizing the negative exponential distribution, and μ is the distribution (as in probabilistic automata). Then, starting from s, the probability of triggering the transition within time $t > 0$ is given by $1 - e^{-\lambda t}$, and once the transition is triggered, t is reached with probability $\mu(s')$.

As for probabilistic automata, the important preparation steps are to (i) provide a fixed-point based definition of bisimulation and simulation relations, and (ii) define appropriate logic and semantics, such as those in the Hennessy-Milner style. Indeed, both can be done for CTMCs in a straightforward way. The fixed-point based definition of simulation is based on the function: $R \mapsto \{(s,t) \mid E(s) \leq E(t) \wedge \mu \widehat{R} \mu'\}$where $E(s)$ is such that $s \xrightarrow{E(s)} \mu$ (which is unique as we mentioned), and similarly for $E(t)$. The only additional information is that the exit rate $E(t)$ from t is larger than that of s, meaning that t is *faster* than s. The logic is also simple because of the lack of nondeterministic choices: the only modal operator for state formulae is of the form $\langle \lambda \rangle \psi$, and the distribution formulae are the same as for PAs. The semantics for the modal operator is: s satisfies $\langle \lambda \rangle \psi$ if and only if $E(s) \geq \lambda$ and μ satisfies ψ with $s \xrightarrow{E(s)} \mu$ (as for probabilistic automata). In this way, characteristic formulae can be obtained for CTMCs, with respect to simulations, and also bisimulations. Moreover, further extensions to Markov automata [11], an orthogonal extension of CTMCs and PAs, can also be obtained along the same line.

8 Conclusion

This paper shows how the general theory in [1] for finding characteristic formulae can be adapted and applied to forward simulation and other behavioral relations in a setting for probabilistic automata. Although the characteristic formulae constructed using this method may differ from ones developed using other methods (such as those in [7]), it is helpful to see how a single method can be used to find characteristic formulae for these probabilistic behavioral relations in general, and that this technique can likely be used for far more probabilistic behavioral relations. Thus the main thrust of this paper is not in the results themselves, but in highlighting a method the research community should be aware of.

In [10], Desharnais et al. have considered a relaxation of (bi)-simulations in which the weight functions may differ by as much as ε. The case $\varepsilon = 0$ reduces to the traditional bisimulation relations considered in this paper, whereas the case $\varepsilon > 0$ is particularly useful for reasoning about systems that *nearly* match each other. Extending our results to such ε-bisimulations would be an interesting line of future work.

Acknowledgements. Joshua Sack was partly supported by the project "Processes and Modal Logic" (project nr. 100048021) of The Icelandic Research Fund. Lijun Zhang is partly supported by MT-LAB, a VKR Centre of Excellence.

We thank Luca Aceto, Holger Hermanns, Anna Ingolfsdottir and Björn Wachter for insightful discussions on an early version of the paper.

References

1. Aceto, L., Ingolfsdottir, A., Levy, P., Sack, J.: Characteristic formulae for fixed-point semantics: a general approach. To appear in Mathematical Structures in Computer Science (2010)
2. Aharonia, R., Bergerb, E., Georgakopoulosc, A., Perlsteina, A., Sprüssel, P.: The Max-Flow Min-Cut theorem for countable networks. Journal of Combinatorial Theory, Series B 101(1), 1–17 (2011)
3. Baier, C., D'Argenio, P.R., Größer, M.: Partial order reduction for probabilistic branching time. Electr. Notes Theor. Comput. Sci. 153(2), 97–116 (2006)
4. Baier, C., Engelen, B., Majster-Cederbaum, M.E.: Deciding bisimilarity and similarity for probabilistic processes. J. Comput. Syst. Sci. 60(1), 187–231 (2000)
5. Bianco, A., de Alfaro, L.: Model Checking of Probabilistic and Nondeterministic Systems. In: Thiagarajan, P.S. (ed.) FSTTCS 1995. LNCS, vol. 1026, pp. 499–513. Springer, Heidelberg (1995)
6. Boudali, H., Crouzen, P., Stoelinga, M.: A rigorous, compositional, and extensible framework for dynamic fault tree analysis. IEEE Transactions on Dependable and Secure Computing 99(1) (2009)
7. Deng, Y., van Glabbeek, R.: Characterising Probabilistic Processes Logically. In: Fermüller, C.G., Voronkov, A. (eds.) LPAR-17. LNCS, vol. 6397, pp. 278–293. Springer, Heidelberg (2010)
8. Desharnais, J.: Labelled Markov processes. Ph.D. thesis, McGill University (1999)
9. Desharnais, J., Gupta, V., Jagadeesan, R., Panangaden, P.: Weak bisimulation is sound and complete for pctl*. Inf. Comput. 208(2), 203–219 (2010)
10. Desharnais, J., Laviolette, F., Tracol, M.: Approximate analysis of probabilistic processes: Logic, simulation and games. In: QEST, pp. 264–273 (2008)
11. Eisentraut, C., Hermanns, H., Zhang, L.: On probabilistic automata in continuous time. In: LICS, pp. 342–351 (2010)
12. Giro, S., D'Argenio, P.R., Ferrer Fioriti, L.M.: Partial Order Reduction for Probabilistic Systems: A Revision for Distributed Schedulers. In: Bravetti, M., Zavattaro, G. (eds.) CONCUR 2009. LNCS, vol. 5710, pp. 338–353. Springer, Heidelberg (2009)

13. Hermanns, H., Kwiatkowska, M.Z., Norman, G., Parker, D., Siegle, M.: On the use of mtbdds for performability analysis and verification of stochastic systems. J. Log. Algebr. Program 56(1-2), 23–67 (2003)
14. Hermanns, H., Parma, A., Segala, R., Wachter, B., Zhang, L.: Probabilistic logical characterization. Inf. Comput. 209(2), 154–172 (2011)
15. Kwiatkowska, M.Z., Norman, G., Parker, D.: Game-based abstraction for markov decision processes. In: QEST, pp. 157–166 (2006)
16. Jonsson, B., Larsen, K., Yi, W.: Probabilistic Extensions of Process Algebras. In: Bergstra, J.A., Ponse, A., Smolka, S.A. (eds.) The Handbook of Process Algebra, pp. 685–710. Elsevier (2001)
17. Jonsson, B., Larsen, K.: Specification and Refinement of Probabilistic Processes. In: LICS, pp. 266–277 (1991)
18. Moss, L.: Finite Models Constructed from Canonical Formulas. Journal of Philosophical Logic 36, 605–740 (2007)
19. Parma, A., Segala, R.: Logical Characterizations of Bisimulations for Discrete Probabilistic Systems. In: Seidl, H. (ed.) FOSSACS 2007. LNCS, vol. 4423, pp. 287–301. Springer, Heidelberg (2007)
20. Segala, R.: Modeling and Verification of Randomized Distributed Realtime Systems. PhD thesis, MIT (1995)
21. Segala, R., Lynch, N.A.: Probabilistic simulations for probabilistic processes. Nord. J. Comput. 2(2), 250–273 (1995)
22. Tarski, A.: A Lattice-Theoretical Fixpoint Theorem and its Applications. Pacific Journal of Mathematics 5, 285–309 (1955)
23. Zhang, L.: Decision Algorithms for Probabilistic Simulations. PhD thesis, Universität des Saarlandes (2008)

Loop Invariant Symbolic Execution for Parallel Programs

Stephen F. Siegel and Timothy K. Zirkel*

Verified Software Laboratory, Department of Computer and Information Sciences
University of Delaware, Newark, DE 19716, USA
{siegel,zirkeltk}@udel.edu
http://vsl.cis.udel.edu

Abstract. Techniques for verifying program assertions using symbolic execution exhibit a significant limitation: they typically require that (small) bounds be imposed on the number of loop iterations. For sequential programs, there is a way to overcome this limitation using loop invariants. The basic idea is to assign new symbolic constants to the variables modified in the loop body, add the invariant to the path condition, and then explore two paths: one which executes the loop body and checks that the given invariant is inductive, the other which jumps to the location just after the loop. For parallel programs, the situation is more complicated: the invariant may relate the state of multiple processes, these processes may enter and exit the loop at different times, and they may be at different iteration counts at the same time. In this paper, we show how to overcome these obstacles. Specifically, we introduce the notion of *collective loop invariant* and a symbolic execution technique that uses it to verify assertions in message-passing parallel programs with unbounded loops, generalizing the sequential technique.

1 Introduction

1.1 Loop Invariant Symbolic Execution for Sequential Programs

Symbolic execution can be used to verify that assertions hold for all possible executions of a (sequential or parallel) program [10, 9]. The basic technique involves the exploration of a state-transition system in which *symbolic constants* $X_1, X_2, \ldots$ are used as inputs and/or initial values of variables. In each symbolic state, variables hold symbolic expressions in the X_i. A boolean-valued path condition variable pc is also included in the state. Control follows the usual program semantics, though at a branch on condition c, a nondeterministic choice is made, and pc is updated according to $\mathsf{pc} \leftarrow \mathsf{pc} \wedge c$ or $\mathsf{pc} \leftarrow \mathsf{pc} \wedge \neg c$, depending on the choice. The search is pruned whenever pc is seen to be unsatisfiable; automated theorem proving techniques are used for this purpose. When control reaches an

* Supported by the U.S. National Science Foundation grants CCF-0733035 and CCF-0953210, and the University of Delaware Research Foundation.

V. Kuncak and A. Rybalchenko (Eds.): VMCAI 2012, LNCS 7148, pp. 412–427, 2012.

assertion on expression e, the expression $\mathsf{pc} \Rightarrow e$ is evaluated to yield a boolean-valued symbolic expression, the validity of which is checked using the theorem prover. If all reachable states are explored and all claims have been established, one has proved that the assertions can never be violated. We will refer to this technique as *standard symbolic execution*.

Unfortunately, because of loops, there are usually an infinite number of reachable states. This is true even for programs in which all loops terminate after a finite number of iterations for any input—e.g., a program which takes as input an integer n and has a loop that iterates from 1 to n. One way to deal with this is to place bounds on the number of loop iterations and/or the values of variables (such as n) which determine loop iterations (see, e.g., [13,2,15]). In this approach, one sacrifices soundness for tractability: if the technique concludes no violations are possible for executions in which each loop iterates no more than B times, it is still possible that an assertion may be violated for some execution where a loop iterates $B+1$ times. Clearly, this is not satisfactory. Moreover, the number of states tends to blow up as the iteration bound increases, and in general there is no way to know how large the bound must be before one can conclude that the assertions hold for arbitrary numbers of iterations.

For sequential programs, one solution to this problem is a technique we call *loop invariant symbolic execution* (LISE) [8,14,1]. In this approach, we assume we are given a boolean expression e_l for each loop l. We also assume we are given a set of variables W_l which contains all variables that could be modified in the loop body. Additional symbolic constants are used to represent the values held by variables after an arbitrary number of loop iterations: call these $Y_{l,v}$, where $v \in W_l$. LISE explores a state-transition system which is similar to the system used in the standard technique, but modified in specific ways. When control reaches a loop location l, the validity of e_l is checked in the usual way. This establishes the base case for an inductive proof. Then, for each $v \in W_l$, v is assigned $Y_{l,v}$, discarding the old value for v. The expression e_l is then evaluated in this new environment and the result is added to the path condition, thereby encoding in the state the assumption that the invariant holds after an arbitrary number of executions of the loop body. Next, a nondeterministic choice is made between the *true* and *false* branches, as usual. For the *true* branch, control passes into the loop body and symbolic execution proceeds normally, except that the "back edges" which return control to the loop location are removed. In place of these is an assertion that again checks the validity of the invariant, establishing that e_l is inductive. Choosing the *false* branch moves control to the point just after the loop, from which the search proceeds normally.

Assuming there are a finite number of initial states, LISE, if applied to every loop in the sequential program, results in a transition system with a finite number of reachable states. (In the worst case, the number of such states is exponential in the size of the program.) The procedure is sound: if all of these states are explored and along the way each claim is proved, the result is a proof that the assertions (including the loop invariants) can never be violated on any execution of the program.

The limitations of the LISE approach are well-known. First, finding appropriate invariants is hard. Second, LISE can raise a "false alarm" for a number of reasons: (1) the theorem prover fails to prove a valid claim, (2) a claim is not valid because a previous loop invariant was too weak, and (3) a claim is not valid because the user-supplied expression is not actually a loop invariant, i.e., it does not hold upon reaching the loop or is not inductive. Finally, the technique only establishes partial correctness—it does not show that each loop will iterate only a finite number of times. On the other hand, there has been significant progress in finding loop invariants automatically (e.g., [5,14]). Automated theorem proving technology is also advancing steadily, and other techniques can be used to establish termination. All in all, LISE appears to be a promising approach for a very difficult problem.

1.2 Extending LISE to Parallel Programs: Challenges

The goal of this paper is to extend LISE to parallel programs. The main challenge concerns loops that span multiple processes, such as the `while` loop in Figure 1. The code is in C and is written in the typical "SPMD" style using the Message Passing Interface (MPI). Conceptually, each of the $n =$ `nprocs` processes executes its own copy of this code in its own address space, i.e., with no shared memory. Each process has a unique integer *rank* between 0 and $n-1$ (inclusive) and initializes its copies of `s` and `t` to $n(n-1)/2$. In each iteration of the loop, each process of positive rank sends its rank to the process of rank 0. Process 0 receives these messages in any order (using the *wildcard* `MPI_ANY_SOURCE`) and sums them, storing the result in `s`. The claimed invariant `s = t` holds trivially on all processes of positive rank (since neither variable is modified) and it seemingly holds on process 0, as $\sum_{i=1}^{n-1} i = n(n-1)/2$. However, the code contains a defect which can lead to a violation of the invariant on process 0: process 1, for example, could send its first message, race ahead to the next iteration and send its second message, and both messages could be received by process 0 in its first iteration. Hence any sound generalization of

```
int s = t = nprocs*(nprocs-1)/2;
#pragma TASS collective invariant I s == t;
while (true) {
  if (myrank == 0) {
   s = 0;
   for (j=1; j<nprocs; j++) {
    MPI_Recv(&x, 1, MPI_INT, MPI_ANY_SOURCE, 0, MPI_COMM_WORLD,
          MPI_STATUS_IGNORE);
    s+=x;
   }
  } else MPI_Send(&myrank, 1, MPI_INT, 0, 0, MPI_COMM_WORLD);
}
```

Fig. 1. `race.c`: the invariant may be violated when messages cross iteration boundaries. The pagma tells TASS to use LISE with the specified collective invariant when verifying that loop.

```
int n; /* input variable; assume n >= 0 */
int i = 0, x = 0;
#pragma TASS collective invariant I i==PROC[1-myrank]@main.i && \
    x==2*((i+1-myrank)/2);
while(i < 2*n) {
  if (myrank == 0 && i%2 == 0) {
    MPI_Recv(&x, 1, MPI_INT, 1, 0, MPI_COMM_WORLD, MPI_STATUS_IGNORE);
  } else if (myrank == 1 && i%2 == 1) {
    x = i+1;
    MPI_Send(&x, 1, MPI_INT, 0, 0, MPI_COMM_WORLD);
  }
  i++;
}
assert(x==2*n);
```

Fig. 2. `stagger.c`: a 2-process program in which messages sent on odd iterations are received in even iterations. The program is correct: the invariant and assertion hold on all executions. A synchronization at the loop location would cause deadlock. The notation `PROC[1-myrank]@main.i` references the variable `i` in the function `main` of process with rank `1-myrank`.

LISE to the parallel context must return a negative result (or at least, not return a positive result) on `race.c`.

If processes were required to synchronize at loop locations, a straightforward generalization of LISE might be possible. But as the example above shows, this is not the case: processes may enter or exit the loop at very different times and may be at different iterations at the same time. A *loop-synchronizing* technique—one which considers only the subset of executions in which processes synchronize at loop locations—cannot be sound: in `race.c`, for example, the invariant holds on all such executions, but, as we have seen, fails on other executions.

Figure 2 is an example of the dual problem: the code is correct, but imposing synchronization at the loop location would cause deadlock. This 2-process program takes as input a nonnegative integer n and iterates from 0 to $2n-1$. On odd iterations, process 1 sends a message to process 0, and on even iterations, process 0 receives. Note that the message is received in the iteration immediately preceding the one in which it is sent. This is not paradoxical; it simply requires process 1 to keep an iteration ahead of process 0. Again, a useful generalization of LISE should be able to verify the final assertion in this code.

In this paper, we present a sound generalization of LISE to parallel message-passing programs with a given, fixed number of processes (i.e., we are not dealing with the much harder problem of parametrized verification, which entails verifying correctness for all values of `nprocs`). Our approach builds on the notion of *collective assertions* [19]. A collective assertion is associated to locations in several processes and may refer to variables in all these processes. As control in a process passes through one of these locations, a snapshot of the process state is taken and inserted into a queue. Once there is a snapshot from every process, one snapshot from each process is dequeued and these snapshots are composed to form a global state at which the assertion is evaluated and checked. Violations are reported if an assertion fails, if any queue is nonempty at termination, or if assertions are not encountered in the same order in every process. Our generalization of LISE uses *collective loop invariants*, special collective assertions that play the role of ordinary loop invariants in sequential LISE. We have implemented the technique in the *Toolkit for Accurate Scientific Software* (TASS, [22, 21]), a symbolic execution-based verification framework for C/MPI programs. In addition to verifying assertions in a single program, TASS can verify the functional equivalence of two programs, and the LISE technique enables the equivalence verification to work with unbounded loops too.

2 Multiprocess Loop Invariant Symbolic Execution

2.1 Notation and Formal Framework

We use the notation and framework of [21]. For sets X and Y, let $\mathsf{Func}(X, Y)$ denote the set of all functions from X to Y. If $f \in \mathsf{Func}(X, Y)$, $x_0 \in X$ and $y_0 \in Y$, then $f[x_0 : y_0]$ denotes the function which maps x_0 to y_0 and otherwise agrees with f. X^* denotes the set of all finite sequences of elements of X. For $\xi \in X^*$ and $x \in X$, $\mathit{enqueue}(x, \xi) \in X^*$ denotes the sequence resulting from appending x to the end of ξ. For non-empty ξ, $\mathit{first}(\xi) \in X$ denotes the first element of ξ and $\mathit{dequeue}(\xi) \in X^*$ denotes the result of removing that element from ξ. Similarly, $\mathit{push}(x, \xi) \in X^*$ denotes the result of appending x to ξ, $\mathit{top}(\xi)$ denotes the last element, and $\mathit{pop}(\xi) \in X^*$ denotes the result of removing the last element.

We may give names $n_1, \ldots, n_r$ to the components of a Cartesian product of sets $X = X_1 \times \cdots \times X_r$. Given $x \in X$, $x.n_i$ denotes the ith component of x, and $x[n_i : v]$ is the element of X identical to x except at the component named n_i, where the value is v.

Let $\mathbb{B} \stackrel{\text{def}}{=} \{\mathit{true}, \mathit{false}\}$, $\mathsf{Val} \supseteq \mathbb{B}$ be a set of *values*, V a set of program *variables*, and $\mathsf{Eval}(V) = \mathsf{Func}(V, \mathsf{Val})$. Let $\mathsf{Expr}(V)$ denote the set of expressions over V. The semantics of expressions are defined by a function $\mathsf{eval}_V : \mathsf{Expr}(V) \times \mathsf{Eval}(V) \to \mathsf{Val}$. Let $\mathsf{BoolExpr}(V)$ be the subset of $\mathsf{Expr}(V)$ consisting of all expressions of boolean type: for any $g \in \mathsf{BoolExpr}(V)$ and $\eta \in \mathsf{Eval}(V)$, $\mathsf{eval}_V(g, \eta) \in \mathbb{B}$.

A *program graph* over V is a tuple $(\mathsf{Loc}, \mathsf{Act}, \mathsf{effect}, \mathsf{Tran}, \mathsf{Loc}_0, g_0)$ where

1. Loc is a set of *locations* and Act is a set of *actions*,
2. $\mathsf{effect} \colon \mathsf{Act} \times \mathsf{Eval}(V) \to \mathsf{Eval}(V)$ is the *effect function*,
3. $\mathsf{Tran} \subseteq \mathsf{Loc} \times \mathsf{BoolExpr}(V) \times \mathsf{Act} \times \mathsf{Loc}$ is the *conditional transition relation*,
4. $\mathsf{Loc}_0 \subseteq \mathsf{Loc}$ is a set of *initial locations*,
5. $g_0 \in \mathsf{BoolExpr}(V)$ is the *initial condition*.

Let SExpr denote the set of all symbolic expressions and $\mathsf{SBoolExpr}$ the set of boolean-valued symbolic expressions. A symbolic state includes the path condition (an element of $\mathsf{SBoolExpr}$), a location, and a function assigning a symbolic expression to each variable. Let $\mathsf{valid} \colon \mathsf{SBoolExpr} \to \mathbb{B}$ be a function with the property that for any ϕ, if $\mathsf{valid}(\phi) = \mathit{true}$ then ϕ is valid, i.e., any assignment of concrete values to the symbolic constants occurring in ϕ causes

ϕ to evaluate to *true*. This function models a conservative theorem prover. Let $\mathsf{seval}\colon \mathsf{Expr}(V) \times \mathsf{Func}(V, \mathsf{SExpr}) \to \mathsf{SExpr}$ denote the symbolic evaluation function.

A parallel program has a fixed number $n \geq 1$ of processes and is modeled as follows. The processes are identified with the set $\mathsf{Proc} = \{0, \ldots, n-1\}$. Each process p has a set of local variables V_p. In addition there is a set of shared variables V_{sh}. Shared variables may be used to represent the channels (buffered messages) when modeling a message-passing program. Process p is modeled as a program graph over $V_p \cup V_{\mathsf{sh}}$. We assume the location sets from two different processes are disjoint, as are the action sets.

The global program graph PG is the program graph over $V = V_{\mathsf{sh}} \cup \bigcup_{p=0}^{n-1} V_p$ defined as follows: the (initial) global location set is the Cartesian product of the local (initial) location sets; the initial condition is the conjunction of the local initial conditions; the global action set is the union of the local action sets; the effect function on an action in process p is extended to act trivially on variables that are not in V_p or V_{sh}; and each local transition $\langle l_p, g, \alpha, l'_p \rangle$ in process p introduces the set of all global transitions $\langle (l_0, \ldots, l_p, \ldots, l_{n-1}), g, \alpha, (l_0, \ldots, l'_p, \ldots, l_{n-1}) \rangle$ where l_j is any location in process j, for $j \in \mathsf{Proc} \setminus \{p\}$. Given any global transition t, define $\mathsf{proc}(t)$ to be the unique $p \in \mathsf{Proc}$ such that the action component of t is in Act_p. This is the standard interleaving model for a multiprocess program: each execution step consists of a single step in one process, while all other processes remain put.

2.2 Collective Assertions and Loop Invariants

We assume the program is annotated with *collective assertions*, which are identified with symbols in a set Id. Each $\mathsf{id} \in \mathsf{Id}$ determines (1) a nonempty set of processes $\mathsf{procs}(\mathsf{id}) \subseteq \mathsf{Proc}$, (2) a set of locations $\mathsf{dom}(\mathsf{id}) \subseteq \bigcup_{p \in \mathsf{procs}(\mathsf{id})} \mathsf{Loc}_p$, and (3) a function $\mathsf{assertion}_{\mathsf{id}}\colon \mathsf{dom}(\mathsf{id}) \to \mathsf{BoolExpr}(\bigcup_{p \in \mathsf{procs}(\mathsf{id})} V_p)$. Note that the expression associated to a location in process p may refer to variables in other processes, but not to shared variables. Without loss of generality, assume that every location is involved in at most one collective assertion. (No-ops may be inserted as necessary to meet this requirement.)

LISE requires some additional structure in the program graph for a process p. Specifically, we assume that certain locations in the program graph are designated as *LISE loop locations*. These have exactly two outgoing transitions: the *true* and *false* branches. Each acts as a no-op, i.e., the action associated to each is trivial. If the guard for the *true* branch is g, the guard for the *false* branch is $\neg g$. We further assume that g does not involve any shared variables. The set of LISE loop locations is denoted $\mathsf{LoopLoc}_p$, and the set of transitions emanating from them LTran_p. The function $\mathsf{isTrue}\colon \mathsf{LTran}_p \to \mathbb{B}$ tells whether a loop transition corresponds to the *true* or *false* branch.

The soundness of the multiprocess LISE technique does not require any further structural assumptions: if the technique reports that a property holds then the property must hold on every concrete execution of PG. However, it is unlikely to be effective (i.e., to converge and not return a spurious violation) unless

PG is generated from a program written in a language with structured "while" loops, without any jumps into or out of the loop bodies, and the loop locations correspond in the usual way to those loop statements. In a program graph generated in this way, there are certain restrictions on the sequence of loop operations that can occur along a control path through a process. Consider, for example, a process with two LISE loop locations, where t_i indicates the *true* branch for loop i and f_i the *false* branch. The sequence t_1, t_1, t_2, f_2, f_1 is possible: it can arise if the second loop is nested inside the first, and on some execution path the first loop is entered and then re-entered (without executing the second loop), while on the second iteration the second loop is executed once. A sequence such as t_1, t_2, f_1, on the other hand, cannot occur: the second loop would have to exit before the first could exit.

A *collective loop invariant* is a collective assertion id for which the elements of $\mathsf{dom}(\mathsf{id})$ are LISE loop locations. We assume every LISE loop location l_p participates in exactly one collective loop invariant $\mathsf{id}(l_p)$. This does not mean every loop in the program is required to participate in a collective invariant since there is no requirement that every node arising from a source-code loop be included in $\mathsf{LoopLoc}_p$.

2.3 Multiprocess LISE State

For $p \in \mathsf{Proc}$, let $\mathsf{ProcState}_p \stackrel{\text{def}}{=} \mathsf{Loc}_p \times \mathsf{Func}(V_p, \mathsf{Val})$. Call the first component $\mathsf{location}$ and the second eval. A *LISE record* is a structure used to record information about the state of a collective action. The components of a LISE record are as follows:

1. $\mathsf{id} \in \mathsf{Id}$, a symbol uniquely identifying a collective action,
2. $\mathsf{snapshots}$, a function which associates to each $p \in \mathsf{procs}(\mathsf{id})$ either the symbol null or an element of $\mathsf{ProcState}_p$, the snapshot of the process state,
3. $\mathsf{writeset}$, a function which associates to each $p \in \mathsf{procs}(\mathsf{id})$ a subset of V_p, the current estimate of the set of local variables modified in the loop body,
4. $\mathsf{isTrue} \in \mathbb{B}$, is this record for the execution of the *true* branch of a loop?,
5. $\mathsf{ppc} \in \mathsf{SBoolExpr}$, assumptions made during this loop iteration, and
6. $\mathsf{relation} \in \mathsf{SBoolExpr}$, a predicate relating new symbolic constants to values from the previous iteration.

The set of LISE records is denoted $\mathsf{LRecord}$. Components 1 and 2 are used for all collective actions. Components 3–6 are relevant only for loop actions; for non-loop actions, components 5 and 6 are *true*.

A *LISE state* is a structure with the following components:

1. $\mathsf{pc}_0 \in \mathsf{SBoolExpr}$, the permanent component of the path condition, used to record assumptions made when control is not inside a loop,
2. $\mathsf{location} \in \mathsf{Loc} = \mathsf{Loc}_0 \times \cdots \times \mathsf{Loc}_{n-1}$,
3. $\mathsf{eval} \in \mathsf{Func}(V, \mathsf{SExpr})$, a function giving the symbolic value of each variable,
4. $\mathsf{queue} \in \mathsf{LRecord}^*$, a FIFO queue of incomplete LISE records, and
5. $\mathsf{stack} \in \mathsf{LRecord}^*$, a stack of complete, *true*-branch, loop records.

The set of all LISE states is denoted LState. In initial LISE states, the queue and stack are empty. For $s \in \mathsf{LState}$, the *path condition* associated to s is

$$\mathsf{pc}(s) \stackrel{\text{def}}{=} s.\mathsf{pc}_0 \wedge \bigwedge_{r \in s.\mathsf{stack} \cup s.\mathsf{queue}} r.\mathsf{ppc} \wedge r.\mathsf{relation}.$$

This plays the same role as the path condition in standard symbolic execution: the search is pruned whenever $\mathsf{pc}(s)$ is determined to be unsatisfiable, and $\mathsf{pc}(s)$ is used as the assumption when checking assertions.

The $\mathsf{writeset}$ is used to determine the set of variables modified in the loop body. This is done dynamically, during exploration of the state space. The set is empty when control first reaches the loop, and a variable is only added to the set when it is actually modified. This allows a precise estimate of the set, especially in the presence of dynamically allocated memory and pointers. The set can grow with each loop iteration, but in most cases will converge after two or three iterations.

The queue stores information on incomplete collective actions: those for which at least one process involved in the action has reached that point, but at least one process has not. The stack is used for completed collective loop entry actions only. These are records for which all processes have entered the loop, but at least one has not yet exited the loop. If we think of the current location of the collective program as the location of the slowest process, the stack represents the loop nest the collective program is currently in.

A record is created when a process reaches a location for a collective assertion and is the first process to do so. The new record is enqueued at the end of the FIFO queue. It is dequeued once every process has reached the assertion. If it is a record for entering a collective loop, once the record is dequeued it is pushed onto the stack. It is eventually popped from the stack once every process has exited that loop. Hence at any time, the record for the oldest collective action is at the bottom of the stack, the actions become more recent as one moves up the stack, then to the beginning of the queue, and through to the end of the queue, which contains the most recent record.

The queue may have to record multiple consecutive iterations of the loop, due to the possible iteration lag between processes. The $\mathsf{relation}$ predicate is used to maintain a coherent relation between these successive iterations. It is discarded as soon as the record is complete and moved to the stack. This issue does not arise in sequential LISE, since no lag is possible.

It will be necessary to locate the records for the nest of loops a process p is inside in a given state s. This is computed using a stack T, initially empty. The algorithm iterates over the records r occurring in $s.\mathsf{stack}$ and $s.\mathsf{queue}$ from oldest to newest. For each such r, if $r.\mathsf{id}$ is a collective loop invariant and $r.\mathsf{snapshots}(p) \neq \mathsf{null}$, the following two steps are taken in order: (1) if T is nonempty and the top entry of T is a record for $r.\mathsf{id}$, pop T; (2) if $r.\mathsf{isTrue}$ is *true*, push r onto T. The resulting *loop nest stack* will contain the desired records, with the innermost loop at the top. We define $\mathsf{currentLoopRecord}(p, s)$ to be the top entry in this stack, or null if the stack is empty.

2.4 The Multiprocess LISE Next-State Function

We now describe the next-state function on LState. Let $s \in \mathsf{LState}$ and $t \in \mathsf{Tran}$ be a transition in process p. If $t \notin \mathsf{LTran}$, the update to the state proceeds as in standard symbolic execution, with the following exceptions: (1) a predicate that is to be added to the path condition is added instead to the ppc field for $\mathsf{currentLoopRecord}(p, s)$ (or to $s.\mathsf{pc}_0$ if that record is null), and (2) any variable modified is added to the sets $r.\mathsf{writeset}(p)$ for each r in the loop nest stack for p.

If the new location is annotated by a non-loop collective assertion, the usual collective assertion verification actions are taken: a snapshot of the local state is stored in the queue, and if the snapshot completes a record, the record is dequeued and the assertion checked. As these actions are a subset of those taken when executing a loop transition, we now turn to the more general situation.

So assume $t \in \mathsf{LTran}$. The next-state function is defined in Figure 3. The first task is to determine whether t represents an initial entry into the loop (from outside the loop body) or a re-entry, i.e., a return to the loop location after executing the loop body one or more times. This is determined by examining the current loop record r_0 for p: if r_0 is non-null and its identifier is the same as that of t, this is a re-entry, in which case W is assigned the writeset from the previous iteration; otherwise, W is assigned the empty set.

Next, we determine whether a record for this collective action already exists by checking if there is any record in the queue with a null snapshot for p. If there is, the oldest such record r_1 is selected and we check that the identifier of that record agrees with that of t. (If it does not agree, then p has encountered the collective assertions in a different order than another process, and an error is reported.) We further check that the isTrue flag of t agrees with that of r_1; if this fails then one process has exited the loop while another entered the loop on corresponding iterations, and an error is reported. If instead, p is the first to reach this collective action, a new record is instantiated with all snapshots null, writesets empty, and the ppc and relation predicates *true*.

The next step is the assignment of fresh symbolic constants to variables in W. The state is scanned to find the least m such that no Y_i occurs in the state for $i > m$. The new valuation eval' is equivalent to the old one, except that each variable in W has been assigned one of the Y_i. The guard for t is then re-evaluated using eval' and added to $r_1.\mathsf{ppc}$ to form the new ppc ϕ. The expression equating each new symbolic constant to the old value of the corresponding variable is added to the relational predicate to form the new relational predicate ψ. These predicates are used to create a new record r_2, which also incorporates the snapshot of the state of p. This new record either replaces the old one in the queue, or is inserted at the end of the queue. The new state s' is the same as s, except with the new location, valuation eval', and the modified queue.

We next deal with the case when the previous action completed the record r_3 at the front of the queue. If there is any snapshot still null in r_3, the record remains incomplete, and s' is returned. Otherwise, the snapshot valuations are united to form a single valuation which is used to evaluate the invariant

```
1  procedure execLoop(s : LState,  t : LTran) : LState is
2  │  let t = ⟨l, guard, α₀, l'⟩;  p ← proc(t);  r₀ ← currentLoopRecord(p, s);
3  │  if r₀ ≠ null ∧ r₀.id = id(lₚ) then W ← r₀.writeset; else W ← ∅;
4  │  if ∃i : s.queue[i].snapshots(p) = null then
5  │  │  let i₁ be the least such i;  r₁ ← s.queue[i₁];  isNew ← false;
6  │  │  if r₁.id ≠ id(lₚ) then error("out of order");
7  │  │  if r₁.isTrue ≠ isTrue(t) then error("conflicting loop exit");
8  │  else isNew ← true;  r₁ ← ⟨id(lₚ), λq.null, λq.∅, isTrue(t), true, true⟩;
9  │  let W = {v₁, . . . , v_k};
10 │  if ∃i : Yᵢ occurs in s then m ← the maximum such i;  else m ← 0;
11 │  eval' ← s.eval[v₁ : Y_{m+1}] · · · [v_k : Y_{m+k}];
12 │  φ ← r₁.ppc ∧ seval(guard, eval');
13 │  ψ ← r₁.relation ∧ s.eval(v₁) = Y_{m+1} ∧ · · · ∧ s.eval(v_k) = Y_{m+k};
14 │  r₂ ← ⟨id(lₚ), r₁.snapshots[p : ⟨lₚ, eval'|_{V_p}⟩], r₁.writeset[p : W], isTrue(t), φ, ψ⟩;
15 │  if isNew then queue' ← enqueue(s.queue, r₂); else queue' ← s.queue[i₁ : r₂];
16 │  s' ← ⟨s.pc₀, l', eval', queue', s.stack⟩;
17 │  r₃ ← first(queue');
18 │  if ∃q ∈ procs(r₃.id) : r₃.snapshots(q) = null then return s';
19 │  ξ ← ⋃_{q∈procs(r₃.id)} r₃.snapshots(q).eval;
20 │  claim ← seval(⋀_{q∈procs(r₃.id)} assertion_{r₃.id}(r₃.snapshots(q).location), ξ);
21 │  if ¬valid(pc(s') ⇒ claim) then error("Possible invariant violation");
22 │  r₄ ← r₃[ppc : r₃.ppc ∧ claim][relation ← true];
23 │  queue' ← dequeue(queue');
24 │  stack' ← s.stack;
25 │  if ¬empty(stack') ∧ top(stack').id = r₄.id then stack' ← pop(stack');
26 │  φ ← s.pc₀;
27 │  if r₄.isTrue then stack' ← push(stack', r₄);
28 │  else if empty(stack') then φ ← φ ∧ r₄.ppc;
29 │  else
30 │  │  r₅ ← top(stack');
31 │  │  stack' ← push(pop(stack'), r₅[ppc : r₅.ppc ∧ r₄.ppc]);
32 │  return canonic(⟨φ, l', eval', queue', stack'⟩);
```

Fig. 3. The next-state function for loop transitions in a multiprocess program

expressions and form the claim. The validity of claim (under the assumption of
the path condition) is then checked using the theorem prover.

A new record r_4 is now formed from r_3 by adding claim to the ppc field and
erasing the relational predicate. (The claim is no longer necessarily implied by
the path condition, since the relational predicate has been removed.) The first
record is now removed from the queue.

If the top entry on the stack is for a collective loop that matches the one
in the record just dequeued, the stack is popped, "forgetting" all information
from the previous iteration. There are now two cases: either r_4 represents a loop
exit (*false* branch), or (re-)entry (*true* branch). If an entry, r_4 is pushed onto
the stack. If an exit, r_4 is not inserted into the state, but the ppc field of r_4 is
recorded by adding it to the record r_5 now on the top of the stack (or to pc_0

if the stack is empty). As r_4 represents a *false* branch, r_4.ppc does not record any assumptions other than those arising from (1) the guards for the *false* loop branches from each process, and (2) the collective invariant claim. Hence, these are the only facts that are "remembered" when all processes exit the loop.

The function canonic, invoked before returning the new state, renames the Y_i involved in the state so that there are no gaps in the indexes. For example, if only Y_2, Y_3, and Y_7 are involved in s, then canonic might replace Y_2 with Y_1, Y_3 with Y_2, and Y_7 with Y_3, everywhere those symbols occur. The Y_i are also placed in a canonical order, determined by placing a total order on the variables, and on the traversal of all symbolic expressions. The process is analogous to "heap canonicalization" performed by many model checkers for transforming equivalent heap configurations into a single representative form. It is done for the same reason: to help determine that a new state is equivalent to one that has been seen before. This step is crucial for convergence in many cases.

2.5 Example

Consider the execution prefix of `stagger.c` (Figure 2) in which process 0 runs until it blocks at the receive, then process 1 runs until completing the send, then process 0 receives the message and proceeds to the top of the loop. Let $\mathtt{x}_0$ denote the copy of variable x in process 0, etc., use line numbers for locations, and ordered pairs for the values of a function at process 0 and 1. Then the state s arrived at has the form

$$\begin{aligned} s &= \langle X_1 \geq 0, \langle 4, 11\rangle, \{\mathtt{n}{:}\, X_1, \mathtt{i}_0{:}\, 1, \mathtt{x}_0{:}\, Y_1 + 1, \mathtt{i}_1{:}\, Y_1, \mathtt{x}_1{:}\, Y_1 + 1\}, r_1, r_0\rangle \\ r_1 &= [I,\ (\mathsf{null}, \langle 4, \{\mathtt{i}_1{:}\, Y_1, \mathtt{x}_1{:}\, 0\}\rangle),\ (\emptyset, \{\mathtt{i}_1, \mathtt{x}_1\}),\ \mathit{true},\ Y_1 < 2X_1,\ Y_1 = 1] \\ r_0 &= [I, \ldots,\ (\{\mathtt{i}_0, \mathtt{x}_0\}, \{\mathtt{i}_1, \mathtt{x}_1\}),\ \mathit{true},\ 0 < 2X_1,\ \mathit{true}]. \end{aligned}$$

Let us see what happens when process 0 executes the *true* loop branch from this state. The current loop record for process 0 is r_0, so $W = \{\mathtt{i}_0, \mathtt{x}_0\}$. We have $m = 1$, so $\mathtt{i}_0$ is assigned Y_2 and $\mathtt{x}_0$ Y_3, and

$$\begin{aligned} r_2 = r_3 = [I,\ (\langle 4, \{\mathtt{i}_0{:}\, Y_2, \mathtt{x}_0{:}\, Y_3\}\rangle, \langle 4, \{\mathtt{i}_1{:}\, Y_1, \mathtt{x}_1{:}\, 0\}\rangle),\ (\{\mathtt{i}_0, \mathtt{x}_0\}, \{\mathtt{i}_1, \mathtt{x}_1\}),\ \mathit{true}, \\ Y_1 < 2X_1 \wedge Y_2 < 2X_1,\ Y_1 = 1 \wedge Y_2 = 1 \wedge Y_3 = Y_1 + 1]. \end{aligned}$$

As this results in completing the first entry in the queue, we proceed to check that the path condition implies $\mathtt{i}_0 = \mathtt{i}_1 \wedge \mathtt{x}_0 = 2((\mathtt{i}_0 + 1) \div 2) \wedge \mathtt{x}_1 = 2(\mathtt{i}_1 \div 2)$ (where $\div$ denotes integer division), which reduces to checking $1 = 1 \wedge 2 = 2 \wedge 0 = 0$. The new record is

$$\begin{aligned} r_4 = [I,\ (\langle 4, \{\mathtt{i}_0{:}\, Y_2, \mathtt{x}_0{:}\, Y_3\}\rangle, \langle 4, \{\mathtt{i}_1{:}\, Y_1, \mathtt{x}_1{:}\, 0\}\rangle),\ (\{\mathtt{i}_0, \mathtt{x}_0\}, \{\mathtt{i}_1, \mathtt{x}_1\}),\ \mathit{true}, \\ Y_1 < 2X_1 \wedge Y_2 < 2X_1 \wedge Y_1 = Y_2 \wedge Y_3 = 2((Y_2 + 1) \div 2) \wedge 0 = 2(Y_1 \div 2),\ \mathit{true}] \end{aligned}$$

and the new state is $\langle X_1 \geq 0, \langle 5, 11\rangle, \{\mathtt{n}{:}\, X_1, \mathtt{i}_0{:}\, Y_2, \mathtt{x}_0{:}\, Y_3, \mathtt{i}_1{:}\, Y_1, \mathtt{x}_1{:}\, Y_1 + 1\}, \epsilon, r_4\rangle$, where ϵ is the empty sequence. Note how the original state s was still tied to the initial iteration of the loop, but those ties have been dropped in the new state. In two more iterations the essential inductive step will take place and the path will return to a state seen before.

2.6 Soundness

Multiprocess LISE is sound for very general reasons. A more formal proof is given in [20], but the ideas are simple. The LISE transition system is related to that of standard symbolic execution via the *projection map* ρ: $\mathsf{LState} \rightarrow \mathsf{SState}$, defined by $\rho(s) = \langle \mathsf{pc}(s), s.\mathsf{location}, s.\mathsf{eval}\rangle$. One must show that for any transition and $s \in \mathsf{LState}$, the projection of the image of s under the LISE next-state function subsumes the image of $\rho(s)$ under the standard next-state function. The soundness of LISE then follows from that of the standard technique.

While the LISE next-state function is complicated, its image under ρ is easy to understand. Control flow is exactly the same as in the standard technique (unlike sequential LISE, no back edges are removed). The differences are due to three types of transformations on SState: (1) replace every occurrence of symbolic constant X by symbolic constant Y, where Y does not occur in the original state; (2) if v holds value f, assign a new symbolic constant Y to v and add the constraint $Y = f$ to the path condition, and (3) weaken the path condition (by dropping some clauses from the conjunction). The first two result in equivalent states, the third in a state which subsumes the original.

3 Implementation and Experiments

We implemented multiprocess LISE by extending the TASS collective assertion facility. The invariants are encoded as pragmas immediately preceding a *while* or *for* loop. The syntax is the same as that for collective assertions (described in [19]) except that the keyword `invariant` is used in place of `assert`.

TASS supports various MPI-specific partial order reduction (POR) schemes. Used in conjunction with LISE, these are often key to obtaining convergence. Note that a necessary condition for convergence is that the maximum difference in iteration count between any two processes be bounded. In the *full* state space for `stagger.c` (Figure 2), this condition does not hold, since it is possible for all the messages from process 1 to be buffered. In the reduced space considered by the default POR, however, the send and receive always occur synchronously, and the two processes can get at most 2 iterations apart. (The POR theory guarantees that if an assertion violation occurs in the full space then a violation also occurs in the reduced space, so the reduction is sound.) By applying LISE to the reduced space, TASS reduces the problem to a finite number of states.

TASS uses *comparative symbolic execution* [18] to verify the functional equivalence of two programs. In its original form, this entails forming the sequential composition of the two programs and adding an assertion that the outputs from the two programs agree. We have modified this technique to use the parallel, instead of sequential, composition. If the first program has n processes, and the second m, the composite has $n + m$ processes and the two sets of processes just happen to never interact. With this modification, multiprocess LISE can be applied to the composite program. This is effective when the two programs have corresponding loops that can be related with a collective invariant, such as the programs of Figure 4. (Note "`joint`" is used for a collective invariant

```
#pragma TASS joint invariant LOOP true;
while (err>=tol) {
  i=j; j=k; k=i+j; tmp = k/j;
  if (tmp>=p) err=tmp-p; else err=p-tmp;
  p = tmp;
}
```

```
#pragma TASS joint invariant LOOP    \
  err==spec.err && p==spec.p && j>0 \
  && j==spec.j && k==spec.k && k>0;
while (err>=tol) {
  k=j+k; j=k-j; err=k/j-p; p=err+p;
  if (err < 0) err=-err;
}
```

Fig. 4. Fibonacci. Two functionally equivalent programs to compute ϕ. The program on the left is the specification. The notation `spec.k` indicates the variable `k` in the specification program.

spanning multiple programs). In such cases, the POR will effectively keep the two programs as close together as possible in their iteration counts, enabling convergence in many cases.

We applied multiprocess LISE to 9 examples. All (except `race`) take an integer input N and the goal is to verify a property for all N. The first two examples are discussed in Section 1; the others are (3) `matrix`, a sequential program for adding two $N \times N$ matrices in which we assert functional correctness, (4) `count`, a multiprocess program where each process loops from 1 to N and we check the loop variable equals N at termination, (5) `ring`, an MPI program where processes send right and receive left N times and we verify deadlock-freedom, (6) `mean`, two sequential programs computing the mean of an array of doubles, (7) `fib` (Figure 4), two sequential programs computing the limiting ratio of two consecutive terms in the Fibonacci sequence to within a given tolerance, (8) `nested`, two sequential programs, one computing $\sum_{i=1}^{n} \sum_{j=1}^{i^2} ij$, the other $\sum_{i=1}^{n} i \sum_{j=1}^{i^2} j$, (9) `diffusion`, two programs solving the 1d-diffusion equation, one sequential, one using MPI. In the last four, functional equivalence was verified.

In all cases except `race` (which contains a defect), we were able to formulate invariants enabling verification for all N. Performance data is given Fig. 5; all experimental artifacts can be obtained from [22]. For the most challenging example, `diffusion`, we also compare the performance of LISE with the standard

name	nprocs	trans	proofs	time
race*	10	823	1	0.9
stagger	2	201	51	2.1
matrix	1	30	103	5.2
count	10	138	55	3.7
ring	10	1521	70	4.3
mean	1+1	28	18	0.5
fib	1+1	60	29	1.4
nested	1+1	79	44	1.1
diffusion	1+10	3580	82	34.4

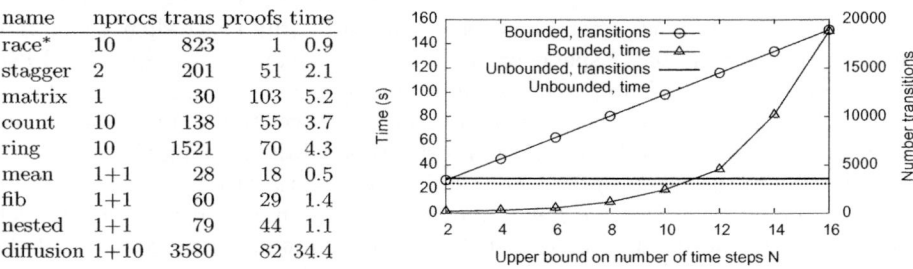

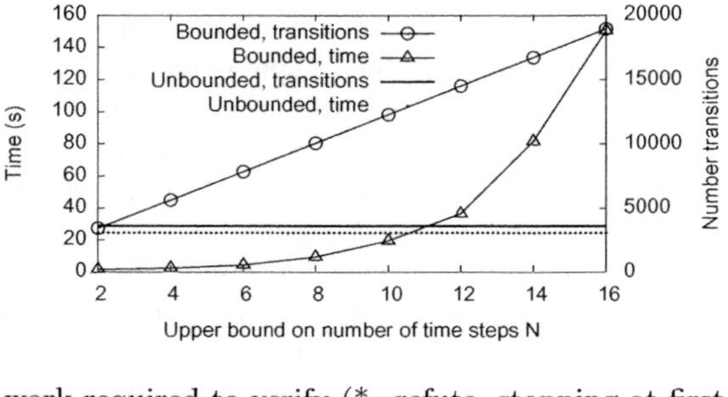

Fig. 5. Experimental results. Left: work required to verify (*=refute, stopping at first violation) using multiprocess LISE: number of processes (two numbers for equivalence verification), transitions, calls to theorem prover CVC3, and time (seconds). Right: verifying `diffusion` equivalence using upper bounds vs. using LISE to verify for all N.

technique using various upper bounds on N. Two facts stands out: (1) the number of transitions explored by LISE is usually comparable to that number for a very small bound, but (2) the time consumed per transition in LISE is very large. Inspection reveals that most of this time is due to the increased number and complexity of the theorem prover calls.

4 Conclusion

Related work. Related symbolic execution-based approaches, in addition to those discussed in Section 1, include [16], which presents a technique in which multiple control paths are combined and symbolically executed simultaneously. This eliminates the problem of loops in certain circumstances by combining multiple iterations into a single execution. However, some types of cyclic dependencies still require bounding the number of loop iterations, and it is not clear how to generalize the technique to parallel programs.

There have been other approaches to functional equivalence verification, but they tend to come with strong restrictions. For example, [24] presents a technique for verifying functional equivalence of affine programs with static control flow. It is fully automatic, requiring no invariants or other hints from the user, but does not apply when a loop condition is non-affine (e.g., `j<i*i`) or to programs with non-static branch conditions, or to multiprocess programs. Peggy [23] represents functions as *program expression graphs* and attempts to show two sequential functions are equivalent by transforming the graph of one into another using a library of axioms. *Translation validation* tools, such as TVOC [6], check that certain compiler transformations, including complex loop transformations, preserve equivalence. But this approach typically requires additional information from the compiler when dealing with loop transformations, and it is not clear if it could be extended to verify the equivalence of, say, a parallel program constructed by hand from a very different sequential version, such as our `diffusion` example.

Another family of verification approaches that can handle unbounded loops works by generating verification conditions to be discharged by a theorem prover. VCC [4] allows users to annotate loops with invariants, and supports multithreaded programs. It includes a notion of one- and two-state object invariants that cut across threads, but there does not appear to be a straightforward way to extend this notion to relate loop executions across different threads.

CBMC [3] is a bounded model checker for C programs. It handles loops by unrolling them a finite number of times, and so cannot verify the correctness of programs with unbounded loops (but may find bugs in them).

Loop-extended symbolic execution [17] reasons about all possible executions of a loop by introducing auxiliary variables to represent the number of times the loop has been executed. The loop body is then analyzed to find any linear relationships between program variables and the auxiliary variables. To the best of our knowledge, this approach has not been applied to concurrent programs.

Poirot [11] uses Corral [12] to analyze concurrent C and .NET programs by converting them to sequential programs. The conversion involves bounding the number of possible context switches. Loops are then replaced with recursive procedure calls. Corral checks for bugs by iteratively increasing the maximum recursion depth. At a given recursion bound, if a bug is found it will be reported and the process terminates. Otherwise, the recursion bound is incremented and the process repeats until a timeout is reached.

Future work. The main challenges now are to find ways to discover collective loop invariants automatically and to reduce the number and cost of theorem-prover invocations. Another limitation is that in the current framework, the collective invariants cannot reference the shared part of the state, so there is no way to express, for example, that the number of buffered messages is invariant. It will be interesting to see if the technique can be extended to express such properties.

Acknowledgment. We are grateful to the reviewers of CAV 2011 and VMCAI 2012 for their comments and suggestions.

References

1. Barnett, M., Leino, K.R.M.: Weakest-precondition of unstructured programs. In: PASTE 2005, pp. 82–87. ACM, New York (2005)
2. Cadar, C., Dunbar, D., Engler, D.: KLEE: Unassisted and automatic generation of high-coverage tests for complex systems programs. In: OSDI 2008 (2008)
3. Clarke, E., Kroning, D., Lerda, F.: A Tool for Checking ANSI-C Programs. In: Jensen, K., Podelski, A. (eds.) TACAS 2004. LNCS, vol. 2988, pp. 168–176. Springer, Heidelberg (2004)
4. Cohen, E., Dahlweid, M., Hillebrand, M., Leinenbach, D., Moskal, M., Santen, T., Schulte, W., Tobies, S.: VCC: A Practical System for Verifying Concurrent C. In: Berghofer, S., Nipkow, T., Urban, C., Wenzel, M. (eds.) TPHOLs 2009. LNCS, vol. 5674, pp. 23–42. Springer, Heidelberg (2009)
5. Godefroid, P., Luchaup, D.: Automatic partial loop summarization in dynamic test generation. In: ISSTA 2011. ACM, New York (2011)
6. Goldberg, B.: Translation Validation of Loop Optimizations and Software Pipelining in the TVOC Framework - in Memory of Amir Pnueli. In: Cousot, R., Martel, M. (eds.) SAS 2010. LNCS, vol. 6337, pp. 6–21. Springer, Heidelberg (2010)
7. Gopalakrishnan, G., Qadeer, S. (eds.): CAV 2011. LNCS, vol. 6806. Springer, Heidelberg (2011)
8. Hantler, S.L., King, J.C.: An introduction to proving the correctness of programs. ACM Comput. Surv. 8, 331–353 (1976)
9. Khurshid, S., Păsăreanu, C.S., Visser, W.: Generalized Symbolic Execution for Model Checking and Testing. In: Garavel, H., Hatcliff, J. (eds.) TACAS 2003. LNCS, vol. 2619, pp. 553–568. Springer, Heidelberg (2003)
10. King, J.C.: Symbolic execution and program testing. Comm. ACM 19(7), 385–394 (1976)
11. Lahiri, S., et al.: Poirot: The concurrency sleuth (2011), `http://research.microsoft.com/en-us/projects/poirot`
12. Lal, A., Qadeer, S., Lahiri, S.: Corral: A whole-program analyzer for Boogie. Tech. Rep. MSR-TR-2011-60, Microsoft Research (May 2011)

13. Păsăreanu, C., Rungta, N.: Symbolic PathFinder: Symbolic execution of Java bytecode. In: ASE 2010. ACM, New York (2010)
14. Păsăreanu, C.S., Visser, W.: Verification of Java Programs Using Symbolic Execution and Invariant Generation. In: Graf, S., Mounier, L. (eds.) SPIN 2004. LNCS, vol. 2989, pp. 164–181. Springer, Heidelberg (2004)
15. Ramos, D., Engler, D.: Practical, low-effort equivalence verification of real code. In: Gopalakrishnan and Qadeer [7], pp. 669–685
16. Santelices, R., Harrold, M.J.: Exploiting program dependencies for scalable multiple-path symbolic execution. In: ISSTA 2010. ACM, New York (2010)
17. Saxena, P., Poosankam, P., McCamant, S., Song, D.: Loop-extended symbolic execution on binary programs. In: ISSTA 2009, pp. 225–236. ACM, New York (2009), `http://doi.acm.org/10.1145/1572272.1572299`
18. Siegel, S.F., Mironova, A., Avrunin, G.S., Clarke, L.A.: Combining symbolic execution with model checking to verify parallel numerical programs. ACM TOSEM 17(2), Article 10, 1–34 (2008)
19. Siegel, S.F., Zirkel, T.K.: Collective Assertions. In: Jhala, R., Schmidt, D. (eds.) VMCAI 2011. LNCS, vol. 6538, pp. 387–402. Springer, Heidelberg (2011)
20. Siegel, S.F., Zirkel, T.K.: Symbolic execution for sequential and multi-process programs with unbounded loops. Tech. Rep. UD-CIS-2011/03, Univ. Delaware (2011)
21. Siegel, S.F., Zirkel, T.K.: TASS: The Toolkit for Accurate Scientific Software. Mathematics in Computer Science (2011), Special Issue on the Third International Workshop on Numerical Software Verification, to appear
22. Siegel, S.F., et al.: The Toolkit for Accurate Scientific Software (2011), `http://vsl.cis.udel.edu/tass`
23. Stepp, M., Tate, R., Lerner, S.: Equality-based translation validator for LLVM. In: Gopalakrishnan and Qadeer [7], pp. 737–742
24. Verdoolaege, S., Janssens, G., Bruynooghe, M.: Equivalence Checking of Static Affine Programs Using Widening to Handle Recurrences. In: Bouajjani, A., Maler, O. (eds.) CAV 2009. LNCS, vol. 5643, pp. 599–613. Springer, Heidelberg (2009)

Synthesizing Efficient Controllers*

Christian von Essen[1] and Barbara Jobstmann[2]

[1] UJF/Verimag, Grenoble, France
[2] CNRS/Verimag, Grenoble, France

Abstract. In many situations, we are interested in controllers that implement a good trade-off between conflicting objectives, e.g., the speed of a car versus its fuel consumption, or the transmission rate of a wireless device versus its energy consumption. In both cases, we aim for a system that efficiently uses its resources. In this paper we show how to automatically construct efficient controllers. We provide a specification framework for controllers in probabilistic environments and show how to synthesize implementations from them. We achieve this by reduction to Markov Decision Processes with a novel objective function. We compute optimal strategies for them using three different solutions (linear programming, fractional linear programming, policy iteration). We implemented and compared the three algorithms and integrated the fastest algorithm into the model checker PRISM.

1 Introduction

Synthesis aims to automatically generate a system from a specification. We focus on synthesizing reactive systems [17] from specifications given in temporal logics [12]. In this setting, specifications are usually given in a qualitative sense, i.e., they classify a system either as good (meaning the system satisfies the specification) or as bad (meaning the system violates the specification). Quantitative specifications assign to each system a value that provides additional information about the system. Traditionally, quantitative techniques are used to analyze properties like response time, throughput, or reliability (cf. [7,9,1,10]).

Recently, quantitative reasoning has been used to state preference relations between systems satisfying the same qualitative specification [2]. E.g., we can compare systems with respect to robustness, i.e., how reasonable they behave under unexpected behaviors of their environments [3]. A preference relation between systems is particularly useful in synthesis, because it allows the user to guide the synthesizer and ask for "the best" system. In many settings a better system comes with a higher price. E.g., consider an assembly line that can be operated in several modes that indicate the speed of the line, i.e., the number of units produced per step. We would prefer a controller that produces as many units as possible. However, running the line in a faster mode increases the power consumption and the probability to fail, resulting in higher repair costs. We are

* This work was supported by the EU project ASCENS, FP7-257414.

V. Kuncak and A. Rybalchenko (Eds.): VMCAI 2012, LNCS 7148, pp. 428–444, 2012.

interested in an "efficient" controller, i.e., a system that minimizes the power and repair costs per produced unit. The efficiency of a system is a natural question to ask; it has also been observed by others, e.g, Yue et al. [16] used simulation to analyze energy-efficiency in a MAC (Media Access Control) Protocol.

In this paper we show how to automatically synthesize a system that has an efficient average-case behavior in a given environment. We define efficiency as ratio between a given *cost* model and a given *reward* model. To further motivate this choice, consider the following example: assume we want to implement an automatic gear-shifting unit (ACTS) that optimizes its behavior for a given driver profile. The goal of our implementation is to optimize the fuel consumption per kilometer (l/km), a commonly used unit to advertise efficiency. In order to be most efficient, our system has to maximize the speed (given in km/h) while minimizing the fuel consumption (measured in liters per hour, i.e., l/h) for the given driver profile. If we take the ratio between the fuel consumption (the "costs") and the speed (the "reward"), we obtain l/km, the desired measure.

Given an efficiency measure, we ask for a system with an optimal average-case behavior. The average-case behavior with respect to a quantitative specification is the expected value of the specification over all possible behaviors of the systems in a given probabilistic environment [5]. We describe the probabilistic environment using Markov Decision Processes (MDPs), which is a more general model than the one considered in [5]. It allows us to describe environments that react to the behavior of the system (like the driver profile).

In the following we summarize our contributions[1] and outline the paper.

1. We present a framework to automatically construct a system with an efficient average-case behavior with respect to a reward and a cost model in a probabilistic environment. To the best of our knowledge, this is the first approach that allows synthesizing efficient systems automatically. After giving the necessary preliminaries in Section 2, we introduce our framework using a simple example in Section 3. In our framework, finding an optimal system corresponds to finding an optimal strategy in an MDP with ratio objective.
2. We introduce and study MDPs with ratio objectives (in Section 4). We present several algorithms to compute optimal strategies in MDPs under ratio objectives. All algorithms are based on decomposing the MDP into end-components [7]. The algorithms differ in the way they compute an optimal strategy for a single end-component. One algorithm uses fractional linear programming. The second one, a simple adaption of an algorithm presented in [7], is based on a reduction to linear programming. The third algorithm is based on policy iteration and a sequence of reductions to MDPs with long-run average-reward objective. This novel algorithm based on policy iteration is particularly interesting, since it can readily be applied to symbolically encoded MDPs and to large structures [15]. In Section 5, we compare our

[1] We presented preliminary results for ergodic MDPs in a workshop [14]. We refer to it to provide omitted details. The current paper presents, in addition, (i) the solution for the general case, (ii) a novel algorithm based on policy iteration, and (iii) an implementation.

framework based on MDPs with ratio objectives to related work and discuss the need for separating the cost and reward model.

3. We have implemented all algorithms in a stand-alone tool and compare them on our examples (see Section 6). In order to increase the scope of our approach, we also integrated the best-performing algorithm into the explicit-state version of PRISM [10], a well-known probabilistic model checker.

2 Preliminaries

Words, Quantitative Languages, and Specifications. Given a finite alphabet Σ, a *word* $w = w_0 w_1 \ldots$ is a finite or infinite sequence of *letters* in Σ. We use w_i to denote the $(i+1)$-th letter. The empty word is denoted by ϵ. We use Σ^* (Σ^ω) to denote the set of finite (infinite) words. Given two words $w \in \Sigma^*$ and $v \in \Sigma^* \cup \Sigma^\omega$, we write wv for their concatenation. A *(quantitative) language* [4] is a function $\psi : \Sigma^\omega \to \mathbb{R}^+ \cup \{\infty\}$ associating to each infinite word a value from the extended non-negative reals. A *qualitative language* is a special case mapping words to 1 or 0. We use qualitative and quantitative languages as *specifications* to describe the desired behavior of a system.

Labeled Transition Systems, Quantitative Automata and the Ratio Objective. A *Labeled transition systems (LTS)* is a tuple $\mathcal{A} = (Q, q_0, \Sigma, \delta)$ where Q is a finite or infinite set of states, $q_0 \in Q$ is the start state, Σ is a finite alphabet and $\delta : Q \times \Sigma \to Q$ is the *transition function*. We call an LTS finite if and only if Q is finite. We define δ^* as the usual extension of δ to finite words. The run of $\mathcal{A}$ on an infinite word $w = w_0 w_1 w_2 \ldots$ is the sequence of tuples $(q_0, w_0), (q_1, w_1), (q_2, w_2) \ldots$ where $q_{i+1} = \delta(q_i, w_i)$. Given finite LTS $\mathcal{A}$, a *cost or reward function* $c, r : Q \times \Sigma \to \mathbb{N}$ maps every transition of $\mathcal{A}$ to a natural number. We call a finite LTS with one or more cost/reward functions a *quantitative automaton*.

An *objective function* maps runs of a quantitative automaton to elements of $\mathbb{R}^+ \cup \{\infty\}$. Given a quantitative automaton $\mathcal{A} = (Q, q_0, \Sigma, \delta)$ with cost function c and reward function r, we define the *ratio objective function* [3] for each run $\rho = (q_0, w_0), (q_1, w_1), (q_2, w_2) \ldots$ of $\mathcal{A}$ as

$$\mathcal{R}^{\mathcal{A}}_{\frac{c}{r}}(\rho) := \lim_{m\to\infty} \liminf_{l\to\infty} \frac{\sum_{i=m}^{l} c(q_i, w_i)}{1 + \sum_{i=m}^{l} r(q_i, w_i)}. \quad (1)$$

We write $\mathcal{R}(\rho)$, if $\mathcal{A}$, c, and r are clear from the context. Intuitively, $\mathcal{R}(\rho)$ is the long-run ratio between the costs and rewards accumulated along a run. The first (left-most) limit allows us to ignore a finite prefix of the run, which ensures that we only consider the long-run behavior. The 1 in the denominator avoids division by 0 if the accumulated rewards are 0 and has no effect otherwise. We need the limit inferior here because the sequence of ratios might not converge. E.g., a run $q^1 p^2 q^4 p^8 \ldots$ with $c(q) = 0$ and $r(q) = c(p) = r(p) = 1$. Its value alternates between 1/6 and 1/3 and does not converge. The limit inferior of this run is 1/3. The ratio objective generalizes the long-run average objective (also known as mean-payoff objective, cf. [18]).

(Finite-)State Systems. A *(finite-)state system* is a tuple $\mathcal{S}=(S, s_0, L, A, \delta, \tau)$, where (S, s_0, L, δ) is a (finite) LTS, A is an *output alphabet*, and $\tau : S \to A$ is an *output function* mapping states to letters from A. The alphabet L is called the *input alphabet* of $\mathcal{S}$. We use $\mathcal{O}_\mathcal{S}$ to denote the function mapping input words $w \in L^\omega$ to the joint input/output word by applying τ to the run of $\mathcal{S}$ on w.

Given a quantitative language ψ over $(L \times A)^\omega$, the *value of the system $\mathcal{S}$ for a given input word $w \in L^\omega$ under ψ* is the value of the joint input/output word under ψ. We obtain the value by composing the functions ψ and $\mathcal{O}_\mathcal{S}$ and apply the composed function to w, i.e., $(\psi \cdot \mathcal{O}_\mathcal{S})(w)$.

Given a probability distribution μ over the input words L^ω, the *(average-case) value of a system $\mathcal{S}$ with respect to a specification ψ and the probability distribution μ* is the expected value $\mathbb{E}_\mu[\psi \cdot \mathcal{O}_\mathcal{S}]$. A system $\mathcal{S}$ is *optimal* with respect to ψ and μ if for every system $\mathcal{S}'$ the value of $\mathcal{S}'$ is smaller than or equal to the value of $\mathcal{S}$.

Markov Chains and Markov Decision Processes. Let $\mathcal{D}(S) := \{p : S \to [0,1] \mid \sum_{s \in S} p(s) = 1\}$ be the *set of probability distributions* over a finite set S. A *Markov decision process (MDP)* is a tuple $\mathcal{M} = (S, s_0, A, \tilde{A}, p)$, where S is a finite set of *states*, $s_0 \in S$ is an *initial state*, A is a finite set of *actions*, $\tilde{A} : S \to 2^A$ is the *enabled action function* defining for each state s the set of enabled actions in s, and $p : S \times A \to \mathcal{D}(S)$ is a probabilistic *transition function*. For technical convenience we assume that every state has at least one enabled action. If $|\tilde{A}(s)| = 1$ for all states $s \in S$, then $\mathcal{M}$ is called a *Markov chain (MC)*. In this case, we omit A and $\tilde{A}$ from the definition of $\mathcal{M}$.

An *L-labeled MDP* is a tuple $\mathcal{M} = (S, s_0, A, \tilde{A}, p, \lambda)$, where $(S, s_0, A, \tilde{A}, p)$ is an MDP and $\lambda : S \to L$ is a labeling function such that $\mathcal{M}$ is deterministic with respect to λ, i.e, $\forall s, a, s', s''$ if $p(s,a)(s') > 0$, $p(s,a)(s'') > 0$, and $s' \neq s''$, then $\lambda(s') \neq \lambda(s'')$. In Section 3, we use L-labeled MDPs to represent probabilistic environments that react to the actions chosen by the system. Since the environment does not know which action a system might choose, we require that in every state of an L-labeled MDP all actions are enabled, i.e., $\forall s \in S : \tilde{A}(s) = A$.

Sample Runs, Strategies, and Objective Functions. A *(sample) run* ρ of $\mathcal{M}$ is an infinite sequence of tuples $(s_0, a_0)(s_1, a_1) \cdots \in (S \times A)^\omega$ of states and actions such that for all $i \geq 0$, (i) $a_i \in \tilde{A}(s_i)$ and (ii) $p(s_i, a_i)(s_{i+1}) > 0$. We write Ω for the set of all runs, and Ω_s for the set of runs starting at state s.

A *strategy (or policy)* is a function $d : (S \times A)^* S \to \mathcal{D}(A)$ that assigns a probability distribution to all finite sequences in $(S \times A)^* S$. A strategy must refer only to enabled actions. An MDP together with a state s and a strategy d defines a probability space $\mathcal{P}^d_{\mathcal{M},s}$ that uniquely defines the probability of every measurable set of runs starting in s.

Given a measurable function $f : \Omega \to \mathbb{R}^+ \cup \{\infty\}$ that maps runs of $\mathcal{M}$ to values in $\mathbb{R}^+ \cup \{\infty\}$, we use $\mathbb{E}^d_{\mathcal{M},s}[f]$ to denote the expected value of f under the probability measure of $\mathcal{P}^d_{\mathcal{M},s}$ and call it the *value of s under strategy d wrt f*. Given an MDP $\mathcal{M}$ and a state s, a strategy d is called *optimal for objective f and state s* if $\mathbb{E}^d_{\mathcal{M},s}[f] = \min_{d'} \mathbb{E}^{d'}_{\mathcal{M},s}[f]$, where d' ranges over all possible strategies. Given an optimal strategy d for function f and state s, $\mathbb{E}^d_{\mathcal{M},s}[f]$ is called the *value of state s wrt f*. The *value of $\mathcal{M}$ wrt f* is the value of its initial state. If f is the ratio objective from Eqn. 1, then we call $\mathcal{M}$ with f a Ratio-MDP. If the domain of c is $\{1\}$, then the objective is equal to the classical *average-reward or mean-payoff objective* ([13]), and we call $\mathcal{M}$ with f an Average-MDP.

3 Specifying Efficient Controllers

We use a simple example to introduce our quantitative synthesis framework. Each part of the example is used to highlight one part of the framework.

Example. Assume we aim to synthesize an efficient controller for a reactor cooling system that controls the activation and maintenance of three pumps. The task of the pumps is to keep the reactor cool. If no pump is running, then the reactor cannot work. If all pumps are working, then the reactor can work at maximum effectivness. A pump that is working can break down, and a pump that is broken must be repaired. If a broken pump is not repaired immediately, then the cost of repairing increases. If two or more pumps are repaired at the same time, then there is a discount on repairing them. We aim for a system that is most efficient, i.e., it minimizes the maintenance costs per water-flow unit.

Modeling the Environment. We model the environment (i.e., the pumps) and its reaction to actions taken by the system using labeled MDPs. The model of a single pump is shown in Figure 1(a). A pump has two states: broken (↯) and ok (✓). In each of these states, the system can either turn a pump on to a slow mode with action `slow`, turn it on to a fast mode with action `fast`, switch it off with action `off`, or repair it with action `rep`. The failure of a pump is controlled by the environment. We assume a failure probability of 1% when the pump is running slowly and 2% when the pump is running fast. If it is turned off, then a failure cannot happen. Transitions in Figure 1(a) are labeled with actions and probabilities, e.g., the transition from state ✓ to ✓ labeled "`slow` 0.99" means that we go from state ✓ with action `slow` with probability 0.99 to state ✓. Note that the labels of the states (✓ and ↯) of this MDP correspond to decisions the environment can make. The actions of the MDP are the decisions the system can use to control the environment. The specification for n pumps is the synchronous product of n copies of the model in Figure 1(a), i.e., the state space of the resulting MDP is the Cartesian product, and the transition probabilities are the product of the probabilities; e.g., for two pumps, the probability to move from (✓, ✓) to (✓, ✓) on action (`slow`, `slow`) is 0.99^2.

System. Our systems are state machines that read the state of the environment and return actions to perform. The action affects the probability of the next state of the pump. A system $\mathcal{S}$ also represents a strategy $d_{\mathcal{S}}$ mapping finite sequences of environment states to actions. For example, a system that repairs the pump when it is broken would map the sequence ✓ ✓ ↯ to action `rep`. The strategy $d_{\mathcal{S}}$ together with the description of the environment (an MDP) induces a probability space over sequences of pairs of states and actions. E.g., if the

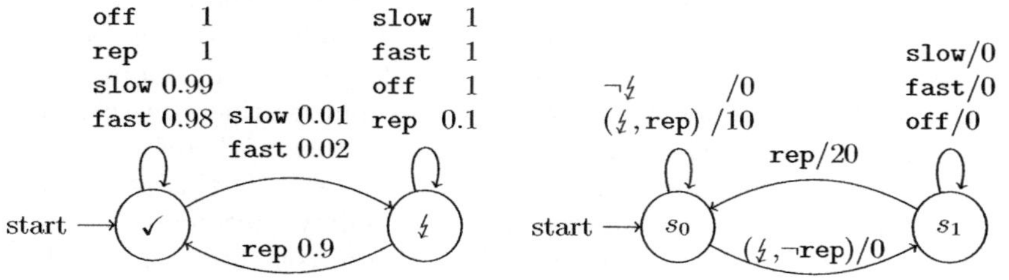

(a) A pump (b) Quantifying a pump

Fig. 1. Environment model and quantitative specification of the pumps example

system chooses action `slow` as long as the pump is ✓ and action `rep` as soon as the pump breaks down, then the sequence (✓, `slow`) (✓, `slow`) (↯, `rep`), which corresponds to transitions $✓ \overset{\texttt{slow}}{\to} ✓$ and $✓ \overset{\texttt{slow}}{\to} ↯$, has probability $0.99 \cdot 0.01$.

Specification. We use a quantitative specification, given by an automaton with a reward and a cost function, to evaluate a system with respect to a desired property. The automaton reads words over the joint input/output alphabet and assigns a value to them. For example, the specification automaton for the pump controlling system reads pairs consisting of (i) a state of a pump (input of the system) and (ii) an action (output of the system). We obtain this automaton by composing automata with a single cost function in various ways. In our example, we use for each pump two automata with a single cost function to express the repair costs and the water flow due to this pump. The automaton for the repair costs is shown in Figure 1(b). It assigns repair costs of 10 for repairing a broken pump immediately and costs 20 for a delayed repair. If we sum the numbers that the automaton outputs, we obtain the repair costs of a run. For example, sequence (✓, `slow`) (↯, `rep`) (↯, `rep`) has cost $0 + 10 + 10 = 20$. The water flow depends on the speed of the pump. The automaton describing the water flow assigns value 2 if a pump is running on slow speed, 4 if it is running on fast speed, and 0 if the pump is turned off or broken.

We extend the specification to multiple pumps by building the synchronous product of copies of the automata described above and compose the cost and reward functions in the following ways: we sum the rewards for the water flow and we take the maximum of repair costs of different pumps to express a discount for simultaneous repairs of more than one pump. The final specification automaton is the product of the water flow automaton and the repair cost automaton with (i) the repair cost as cost function and (ii) the water flow as reward function. We prefer behaviors with a small ratio between the accumulated repair costs and the accumulated water flow rewards and so we take Eqn. 1 as objective function $\mathcal{R}$.

We lift the specification from a single behavior to a system $\mathcal{S}$ (a set of behaviors) by computing the expected value of $\mathcal{R}$ under the probability distribution given by the environment model (an MDP) and the strategy $d_{\mathcal{S}}$ representing the system. This corresponds to averaging over all behaviors weighted by their probability. Our goal is to find a system that minimizes the maintenance costs and maximizes the water flow, i.e., a system that minimizes this expected value.

In the current specification a system that keeps all the pumps turned off has the (smallest possible) value zero, because pumps that are turned off do not break down and there is no need to repair them. Therefore, we require that at least one of the pumps is working. We can specify this requirement by using a qualitative specification described by a safety[2] automaton. This safety requirement can then be ensured by adapting the cost functions of the ratio objective [5,14]. For simplicity, we say here that any action in which not at least one pump is working has an additional cost of 10.

Synthesis Using MDPs. We build an MDP from the environment descriptions and the quantitative specifications by taking their product. The intuition is to run the environment MDP and the specification automaton in parallel. We get states of the form (s, q), where s is a state in the environment MDP and q is a state of the automaton. The set of actions enabled in this state is equal to the set of actions available in state s. The probability of moving from state (s, q) to state (s', q') when choosing action a is zero if there is no transition in the automaton from q to q' with input (s, a). Otherwise, the probability is equal to the probability of moving from s to s' in the MDP when choosing a.

The cost of an action is derived from the corresponding costs in the automaton. E.g., the probability of moving from $((\checkmark, \checkmark), (s_0, s_0))$ to $((\lightning, \lightning), (s_0, s_0))$ when choosing action $(\texttt{slow}, \texttt{slow})$ is 0.01^2, while the probability of moving to $((\lightning, \lightning), (s_1, s_1))$ is 0 because we cannot move from s_0 to s_1 with this action. The repair costs of choosing action $(\texttt{slow}, \texttt{slow})$ in state $((\checkmark, \checkmark), (s_0, s_0))$ is 0, while the water flow is 4 (2 for each pump).

The product of an MDP and an automaton with two cost functions is a Ratio-MDP. As we will show in Lemma 1, there is always a pure and memoryless optimal strategy for a Ratio-MDP. Such a strategy d corresponds to the following finite-state system with optimal behavior. The states of the system are the states of the MDP. The output function for state s is the action chosen by the strategy d for state s, i.e., $\tau(s) = d(s)$. The transition function of the system refers to the states of the MDP (or more precisely to their labeling function). The system moves from state s to s' with input label l, if s' is (labeled) l and the probability to reach state s' from state s under the action $d(s)$ given by the strategy d is strictly positive. In this way, the environment determines the next state of the system. The expected value of the system is equal to the expected value of the strategy it was constructed from.

Theorem 1. *Given an MDP $\mathcal{M}$ describing an environment and an automaton with ratio objective describing a quantitative specification, we can automatically synthesize an optimal finite-state system.*

[2] Our approach can also handle liveness specifications resulting in a Ratio-MDP with parity objective, which is then reduced to solving a sequence of MDP with mean-payoff parity objectives [5].

4 Solving MDPs with Ratio-Objectives

In this section we first recall well-known notions for MDPs and their strategies, then we prove some useful properties of Ratio-MDPs. Finally, we present three algorithms to compute the optimal value and an optimal strategy of a Ratio-MDP. We assume that an optimal strategy minimizes the ratio objective, the algorithms for maximizing the objective are analogous.

End-components [6,7]. Given an MDP $\mathcal{M} = (S, s_0, A, \tilde{A}, p)$, a set $C \subseteq S$ of states is an *end-component* if (i) C is p-closed (i.e., for all $s \in C$ exists $a \in A(s)$ such that $\forall s' \in S \setminus C : p(s,a)(s') = 0$) and (ii) the MDP obtained by restricting $\mathcal{M}$ to the states in C is strongly connected. An end-component is maximal, if it is not included in a strictly larger end-component.

Classification of MDPs and Strategies. Given an Markov chain $\mathcal{M} = (S, s_0, p)$, a state $s \in S$ is called *recurrent*[3] if the expected number of visits to s in the random walk starting from s_0 is infinite; otherwise s is called *transient.* A minimal set of recurrent states that is closed under p is called *recurrence class.* $\mathcal{M}$ is *unichain* if it consists of a single recurrence class and a (possibly empty) set of transient states; otherwise, $\mathcal{M}$ is called *multichain.*

A probability distribution π over S is a *stationary distribution* if all its entries satisfy $\pi(s) = \sum_{s' \in S} \pi(s')p(s,s')$. If $\mathcal{M}$ is unichain, then $\mathcal{M}$ has a unique stationary distribution. A strategy d is *pure* if for all sequences $w \in (S \times A)^*$ and for all states $s \in S$, there is an action $a \in A$ such that $d(ws)(a) = 1$. A *memoryless* strategy is independent of the history of the run, i.e., for all $w, w' \in (S \times A)^*$ and for all $s \in S$, $d(ws) = d(w's)$ holds. If a strategy is pure and memoryless, we represent it by a function $d : S \to A$. An MDP $\mathcal{M} = (S, s_0, A, \tilde{A}, p)$ together with a pure and memoryless strategy $d : S \to A$ defines an MC $\mathcal{M}^d = (S, s_0, A, \tilde{A}_d, p)$, in which only the actions prescribed in the strategy d are enabled, i.e., $\tilde{A}_d(s) = \{d(s)\}$. We call a pure and memoryless strategy d *unichain* (*multichain*) if the MC $\mathcal{M}^d$ is unichain (multichain, respectively). If $\mathcal{M}$ is associated with a cost function c, then we denote by c_d the corresponding cost-vector function[4], i.e., $c_d(s) = c(s, d(s))$ for all $s \in S$.

In the following, we discuss properties of Ratio-MDPs that are necessary for the correctness of the algorithms. Lemma 1 tells us that we need to consider only pure and memoryless strategies to compute the optimal value (see [14] for the proof). Lemma 2 strengthens this result to unichain strategies for MDPs that have a single end-component.

Lemma 1. *[14] Ratio-MDPs have optimal pure and memoryless strategies.*

Lemma 2. *Given a Ratio-MDP $\mathcal{M} = (S, s_0, A, \tilde{A}, p)$ such that S is an end-component of $\mathcal{M}$ and let d be a pure and memoryless strategy with value λ, then there exists a unichain strategy d' with value $\lambda' \leq \lambda$.*

---

[3] We do not distinguish null and positive recurrent states because we only consider finite MCs.

[4] We use vector and function notation interchangeably.It is well-known that every finite function can be represented by a vector and vice versa, given a total order on the domain elements.

Proof. This follows from prefix-independence of the ratio objective and the fact that for every pair of states s and s' in an end-component, there exists a strategy such that s can reach s' with probability 1. This allows us to construct from an arbitrary pure and memoryless strategy a unichain strategy with the same or a better value: d' fixes the recurrent class C with the minimal value induced by d; for states outside of C, d' plays a strategy to reach C with probability 1.

Next, we show how to compute the ratio value of an MDP with respect to a unichain strategy. Since the ratio objective is prefix-independent, the value of a state depends only on the rewards obtained in the (single) recurrence class induced by the unichain strategy. All states in a recurrence class have the same value, because they can reach each other with probability 1. Recall that the value of a state is the expected payoff over all runs starting in this state, and that the expected payoff is the Lebesgue integral over all runs. Every recurrence class has a stationary distribution π, in which the sth-entry $\pi(s)$ corresponds to the expected fraction of time spent in state s. We call a run *well-behaved* if, for each state s, the number of visits to the state s up to position n of the run divided by n converges with $n \to \infty$ to $\pi(s)$. The set of well-behaved runs has probability 1 (see [14] for more details). Every measurable set that is disjoint from the set of well-behaved runs has probability 0 and does not contribute to the value of a state. All *well-behaved* runs have the same value, which corresponds to the expected average reward with respect to the cost function divided by the expected average reward with respect to the reward function (if the corner cases of value zero and infinity are neglected). A classical result for MDPs with a cost function c and a unichain strategy d says that the expected average reward, i.e., $\mathbb{E}_d^{\mathcal{M}}[\lim_{n\to\infty} \frac{1}{n} \sum_{i=0}^{n-1} c(s_n)]$, is equal to $\pi \cdot c_d$, where π is the stationary distribution under strategy d. This gives the following lemma.

Lemma 3. *For a Ratio-MDP $\mathcal{M}$ and a unichain strategy d, let π be the stationary distribution induced by d and let c_d and r_d be the reward vectors under strategy d of the cost and the reward function, respectively, then we have*

$$\mathbb{E}_{\mathcal{M}}^{d}[\mathcal{R}] = \lim_{l\to\infty} \frac{\pi \cdot c_d}{1/l + \pi \cdot r_d}$$

The limit in Lemma 3 takes care of the case in which $\pi \cdot r_d = 0$. Lemma 4 addresses this and another corner case.

Lemma 4. *For every Ratio-MDP $\mathcal{M} = (S, s_0, A, \tilde{A}, p)$ such that S is an end-component of $\mathcal{M}$, we can check efficiently if the value of $\mathcal{M}$ is zero or infinity and construct corresponding strategies.*

Proof. $\mathcal{M}$ has value zero if there exists a strategy such that the expected average reward w.r.t. the cost function c is zero. We check this by removing all actions from states in $\mathcal{M}$ that have $c > 0$ and then recursively removing all actions that lead to a state without an enabled action. If the resulting MDP $\mathcal{M}'$ is non-empty, then there is a strategy with value 0 for the original end-component. It can be computed by building a strategy that moves to and stays in $\mathcal{M}'$.

$\mathcal{M}$ has value infinity iff (i) for every strategy the expected average reward w.r.t. cost function c is not zero, i.e., $\mathcal{M}$ has not value zero, and (ii) for all strategies the expected average reward w.r.t. the reward function r is zero. This can only be the case if for all actions in the end-component the value of cost function r is zero. In this case, any arbitrary strategy will give value infinity.

Since the ratio objective is prefix-independent and every run in a finite MDP reaches and stays in an end-component with probability 1, regardless of the strategy, we can compute the optimal value and a corresponding strategy for an arbitrary Ratio-MDP by decomposing it into end-components.

Lemma 5. *Given a Ratio-MDP $\mathcal{M}$ and an optimal pure and memoryless strategy d_i for every maximal end-component C_i in $\mathcal{M}$, we can compute the optimal value and construct an optimal strategy for $\mathcal{M}$.*

Proof. Let λ_i be the value obtained with d_i in the Ratio-MDP induced by C_i. Wlog we assume that every action is enabled in exactly one state. Let $\overline{\mathcal{M}}$ be the quotient MDP of $\mathcal{M}$ with respect to the equivalence relation induced by the partitioning into maximal end-components (i.e., $s \equiv s'$ iff $(s = s') \vee \exists i, s, s' \in C_i$). Note that in $\overline{\mathcal{M}}$ the probability of moving from some state $\overline{s}$ (representative of an equivalence class) with action a to another state $\overline{t}$ is $\sum_{t \in \overline{t}} p(s,a)(t)$. The actions enabled in $\overline{s}$ are all the actions enabled in any state equivalent to s. We modify $\overline{\mathcal{M}}$ to obtain an Average-MDP $\mathcal{M}'$ by removing all actions for which there is a state s such that $p(s,a)(s) = 1$. Furthermore, for all states s that represent an end-component C_i with value $\lambda_i < \infty$ we add a new action a_i with $p(s,a_i)(s) = 1$ and costs λ_i; all other actions have cost 0. We now recursively remove states without an enabled action and actions leading to removed states. If the initial state s_0 is removed, the Ratio-MDP has value infinity, because we cannot avoid to reach and stay in an end-component with value infinity. Otherwise, let d' be an optimal strategy for $\mathcal{M}'$. We define d by $d(s) = d'(\overline{s})$ for all states $s \notin \bigcup C_i$. For $s \in C_i$, if $d'(\overline{s}) = a_i$, we set $d(s) = d_i(s)$. Otherwise, let a be the action chosen in state $\overline{s}$, and let s' be the state in which a is enabled. Then, we set $d(s') = a$ and forall other states in C_i we choose d such that we reach s' with probability 1. We can choose the strategy arbitrarily in states that were removed from $\mathcal{M}'$, because these states will never be reached by construction of d.

4.1 General Shape

The general shape of the algorithms is shown in Algorithm 1. In Line 1 we decompose the Ratio-MDP into maximal end-components [7]. Then, we analyse each end-component separately: the predicates `isZero` and `isInfty` (Line 1 and 1, resp.) check if an end-component has has value zero or infinity using Lemma 4. If both checks fail, we use the function `solveEC` (Line 1), which implements one of the three algorithms presented in Section 4.2, 4.3, and 4.4 to compute the optimal value and an optimal strategy for this end-component. Finally, function `compose` (Line 1) takes these values and strategies from all the end-components and computes an optimal strategy for $\mathcal{M}$ using Lemma 5.

Input: Ratio-MDP $\mathcal{M}$, start state s_0
Output: Value λ and optimal strategy d

$ecSet \leftarrow$ `decompose`$(\mathcal{M})$;
foreach $i \leftarrow [0 \ldots |ecSet| - 1]$ **do**
    switch $ecSet_i$ **do**
        case `isZero` : $\lambda_i \leftarrow 0$; $d_i \leftarrow$ zero-cost strategy;
        case `isInfty` : $\lambda_i \leftarrow \infty$; $d_i \leftarrow$ arbitrary; ;
        otherwise : $d_i \leftarrow$ `solveEC`$(ecSet_i)$;
    endsw
end
$d \leftarrow$ `compose`$(\mathcal{M}, \lambda_0, \ldots, \lambda_{|ecSet|-1}, d_0, \ldots, d_{|ecSet|-1})$;

Algorithm 1. Finding optimal strategies for Ratio-MDPs

4.2 Policy Iteration

In this section we present a policy iteration algorithm for Ratio-MDPs and prove that it terminates and converges. Due to Lemma 5 we consider only Ratio-MDPs that are end-components and Lemma 4 allows us to assume that the value of the Ratio-MDP is neither zero nor infinity. The key idea is to construct a sequence of Average-MDPs $\mathcal{M}_i$ from the Ratio-MDP and a decreasing sequence of values λ_i. In every step, we search for an improved strategy in $\mathcal{M}_i$, which is mapped to an improved strategy in the Ratio-MDP leading to the next value λ_{i+1}.

Induced Average-MDP. Given a Ratio-MDP $\mathcal{M}$ and a value λ, we call an Average-MDP with the same structure as $\mathcal{M}$ and the cost function $c' = c - \lambda r$ the *Average-MDP induced by $\mathcal{M}$ and λ* and denote it by $\mathcal{M}_\lambda$.

Improvement. Given a Ratio-MDP $\mathcal{M}$ and a unichain strategy d with value λ and stationary distribution π, we use the Average-MDP $\mathcal{M}_\lambda$ induced by a value λ to improve strategy d. According to Lemma 3, d has ratio value $\lambda = \pi c_d / \pi r_d$, which is equivalent to $0 = \pi(c_d - \lambda r_d) = \pi c'_d$, showing that the average value g of d in $\mathcal{M}_\lambda$ is zero. Assume there exists a unichain strategy d' with an average value g' smaller than zero in $\mathcal{M}_\lambda$, then d' is also a better strategy in the original Ratio-MDP. To prove this, let π' be the stationary distribution of d'. Then, $0 > g' = \pi' c'_{d'} = \pi'(c_{d'} - \lambda r_{d'})$ by the definition of value in an Average-MDP. This is equivalent to $0 > \pi' c_{d'} - \pi' \lambda r_{d'}$ and $\lambda > \pi' c_{d'} / \pi' r_{d'} = \lambda'$ (the ratio value of d') and leads to the following lemma.

Lemma 6. *Given an MDP $\mathcal{M}$, let d and d' be two unichain strategies with values λ and λ', respectively. Then (1) $\lambda = \lambda'$ if and only if the value of d' in $\mathcal{M}_\lambda$ is 0 and (2) $\lambda' < \lambda$ if and only if the value of d' in $\mathcal{M}_\lambda$ is smaller than 0.*

Lemma 6 shows that we can use policy iteration on Average-MDPs to find an improved strategy for the original Ratio-MDP, provided we get a unichain strategy from the improvement. Since Average-MDPs are a special case of Ratio-MDPs, we can use Lemma 2 to convert a multichain strategy to a unichain strategy with a smaller or equal gain in the Average-MDP.

Input: End-component $\mathcal{M}$, unichain strategy d_0 (with $0 < \lambda_0 < \infty$)
Output: Optimal unichain strategy d_n
1 $n \leftarrow 0$;
2 **repeat**
3 $\quad \lambda_n \leftarrow \mathbb{E}^{d}_{\mathcal{M}}[\mathcal{R}]$;
4 $\quad d_{n+1} \leftarrow$ improved unichain strategy for $\mathcal{M}_{\lambda_n}$;
5 $\quad n \leftarrow n + 1$;
6 **until** $d_{n-1} = d_n$;

Algorithm 2. Policy iteration using Average-MDPs

Algorithm 2 searches for an improved strategy d of $\mathcal{M}_\lambda$ before updating λ and computing a new induced Average-MDP. Instead of asking for an improved strategy in Line 2, we can also ask for a strategy that is optimal with respect to the induced Average-MDP. In Section 6 we show a comparison of these options.

In order to use Algorithm 2 we need an initial unichain strategy d_0 with finite and non-zero value. Due to the case analysis in Algorithm 1, we know that the value of the analyzed end-component C is neither zero nor infinity. Therefore, (i) there is no strategy in C that has value zero and (ii) there exists at least one strategy with value $\lambda < \infty$. Strategy d_0 can be constructed as follows: (i) pick state s and action a such that $r(s, a) > 0$, (ii) set $d_0(s)(a) = 1$ and for all other states $s' \neq s$ pick a pure and memoryless strategy to reach s with probability 1 (such a strategy exists because we consider only end-components).

Termination and Convergence. In Line 2 we search for an improved strategy. According to Lemma 6 if such a strategy is found, then λ_n will decrease in the next step. There are only finitely many strategies and hence the algorithm terminates. It remains to show that we always find such a strategy if possible. Assume some non-optimal unichain strategy d_n with value λ_n, and assume that d^* is optimal and has value λ^*. We now show that d^* has value smaller zero in the MDP induced by λ_n. Let π be the stationary distribution of d^*. Let $v^* = \pi c_{d^*} - \lambda^* \pi r_{d^*}$ be the value of d^* in Average-MDP $\mathcal{M}_{\lambda^*}$ and let $v = \pi c_{d^*} - \lambda_n \pi r_{d^*}$ be the value of d^* in the Average-MDP $\mathcal{M}_{\lambda_n}$. From $\lambda^* < \lambda_n$ it follows that $v^* > v$ and from $v^* = 0$ it follows that $v < 0$. Hence, for each Average-MDP induced by a non-optimal strategy, there exists a strategy with a value smaller than zero.

4.3 Fractional Linear Program

The following fractional linear program also allows us to find an optimal solution for a Ratio-MDP that is an end-component with a finite ratio value. In [14], we provide a detailed explanation of the program in the case of recurrent Ratio-MDP, which can be extended to end-components with a finite ratio value by adapting the strategy construction. The fractional linear program minimizes

$$\frac{\sum_{s \in S} \sum_{a \in \tilde{A}(s)} x(s,a)c(s,a)}{\sum_{s \in S} \sum_{a \in \tilde{A}(s)} x(s,a)r(s,a)}$$

subject to the constrains $\sum_{a \in \tilde{A}(s)} x(s,a) = \sum_{s' \in s} \sum_{a \in \tilde{A}(s')} x(s',a)p(s',a)(s)$ for all states $s \in S$ and $\sum_{s \in S} \sum_{a \in \tilde{A}(S)} x(s,a) = 1$.

We construct a strategy from a solution for $x(s,a)$ as suggested by e.g. [13] for communicating Average-MDPs: we set $d(s) = a$ iff $x(s,a) > 0$. Using Lemma 2 we can construct unichain strategy from d with the same value.

4.4 Linear Program

We can also use the following linear program proposed in [7] to calculate an optimal strategy. We are presenting it here because we compare it to the other solutions in Section 6. The goal is to maximize λ subject to $h_s \leq c_s - \lambda r_s + \sum_{s' \in S} p(s,a)(s')h_{s'}$ for all states $s \in S$ and all actions $a \in \tilde{A}(s)$. To calculate a strategy from a solution h_s to the LP we choose the actions for the states such that the constraints are fulfilled when we interpret them as equations.

5 Related Work

In this section with discuss related work and give an example showing the difference between average and ratio objective. Our synthesis and experimental results are summerized in the next Section.

The related work can be divided into two categories: (1) work using MDPs for quantitative synthesis and (2) work on MDP reward structures. From the first category we first consider the work of Chatterjee et al. [5]. We generalize this work in two directions: (i) we consider ratio objectives, a generalization of average-reward objectives and (ii) we introduce a more general environment model based on MDPs that allows the environment to change its behavior based on actions the system has taken. In the same category there is the work of Parr and Russell [11], who use MDPs with weights to present partially specified machines in Reinforcement Learning. Our approach differs from this approach, as we allow the user to provide the environment, the specification, and the objective function separately and consider the expected ratio reward, instead of the expected discounted total reward, which allows us to ask for efficient systems.

Semi-MDPs [13] fall into the second category. Unlike work based on Semi-MDPs, we allow a reward of value 0. Furthermore, we provide an efficient policy iteration algorithm that works on our Ratio-MDPs as well as on Semi-MDPs. Approaches using the discounted reward payoff (cf. [13]) are also related but focus on immediate rewards instead of long-run rewards. Similarly related is the work of Cyrus Derman [8], who considered the payoff function obtained by dividing the expected costs by expected rewards. As shown later, we believe that our payoff function is more natural. Note that these two objective functions are in general not the same. Closest to our work is the work of de Alfaro [7]. In this work the author also allows rewards with value 0, and he defines the expected payoff over all runs that visit a reward with value greater than zero infinitely often. In our framework the payoff is defined for all runs. De Alfaro also provides a linear programming solution, which can be used to find the ratio value in an end-component (see Section 4.4). We provide two alternative solutions for end-components including an efficient policy iteration algorithm. Finally, we are the first to implement and compare these algorithms and use them to synthesize efficient controllers.

Average versus Ratio Objective. There are well-known techniques for finding optimal strategies for MDPs with average objective. A natural question to ask is, if the average objective would not suffice to describe our problem.

Recall the ACTS unit from Section 1. We want to optimize the relation of two measures: speed (km/h) and fuel consumption (l). In order to use the average objective, we have to combine these two measures. Two methods seem possible. First, we can subtract speed from consumption and minimize the average. When subtracting kilometers per hour from liters, the value of the optimal controller has no intuitive meaning. Furthermore, it can lead to non-optimal strategies as we will show in the next paragraph. Alternatively, we can divide consumption by speed in each step (leading to a measure $\lim_{n\to\infty}(c_1/r_1 + c_2/r_2 \dots)/n$). By this we obtain the correct unit but in general a different value for which the interpretation is not obvious. The same holds for the pumps example discussed in Section 3. We have two different measures: water flow and repair costs, with two different units: liter and dollar. With the ratio objective we can model the problem and its optimization criterion (efficiency) directly, and we can easily interpret the result (expected maintenance cost by liter).

We give a small example to show that simple reduction to subtraction can lead to strategies that differ from the optimal strategy of the ratio objective. Consider an MDP with 2 states, s_0 and s_1. There is one action enabled in s_1. It has cost 1 and reward 100 and leads with probability 1 to s_0. There are two actions in s_0: Action a_0 has cost 5 and reward 1 and leads with probability 1/9 to s_1 and with 8/9 back to s_0. Action a_1 has cost 10 and reward 1 and leads with probability 1/2 to s_1 and with 1/2 to s_0. The steady state distribution of the strategy choosing a_0 is $(9/10, 1/10)$, and so its ratio value is $(9/10\cdot 5+1/10\cdot 1)/(9/10\cdot 1+1/10\cdot 100) \approx 0.42$. For the strategy choosing a_1, the steady state distribution is $(2/3, 1/3)$ and the ratio value is $(2/3 \cdot 10 + 1/3 \cdot 1)/(2/3 \cdot 1 + 1/3 \cdot 100) \approx 0.634$, which is larger than the value for a_1. Hence choosing a_0 is the better strategy for the ratio objective. If we now subtract the reward from the cost and interpret the result as an Average-MDP, then we get rewards 4, 9, and -99 respectively. Choosing strategy a_0 gives us $9/10 \cdot 4 - 1/10 \cdot 99 = -6.3$, while choosing strategy a_1 gives us $2/3 \cdot 9 - 1/3 \cdot 99 = -27$. So, choosing a_1 is the better strategy for the average objective.

6 Synthesis and Experimental Results

Synthesis Results. We synthesized optimal controllers for systems with 2 to 5 pumps. They behave as follows: For a system with two pumps, the controller plays it safe. It turns one pump on in fast mode and leaves the other one turned off. If the pump breaks, then the other pump is turned on in slow mode and the first pump is repaired immediately. For three pumps, all three pumps are turned on in fast mode. As soon as one pump breaks, only one pump is turned on in fast mode, the other one is turned off. Using this strategy, the controller avoids the penalty of having no working pump with high probability. If two pumps are broken, then the last one is turned on in fast mode and the other two pumps are been repaired. In the case of four pumps, all pumps are turned on in fast mode if they are all working. If one pump breaks, then two pumps are turned on and the third working pump is turned off. The controller has one pump in reserve for the case that both used pumps break. If two pumps are broken, then only one pump is turned on, and the other one is kept in reserve. Only if three pumps are broken, the controller starts repairing the pumps. Using this strategy, the controller maximizes the discount for repairing multiple pumps simultaneously.

We also modeled the ACTS described in Section 1 using PRISM. The model has two parts: a motor and a driver profile. The state of the motor consists of revolutions per minute (RPM) and a gear. The RPM range from 1000 to 6000, modeled as a number in the interval (10, 60), and we have three gears. The driver is meant to be a city driver, i.e., she changes between acceleration and deceleration frequently. The fuel consumption is calculated as polynomial function of degree three with the saddle point at 1800 rpm. The final model has 384 states and it takes less than a second to build the MDP. Finding the optimal strategy takes less than a second. The resulting expected fuel consumption is 0.15 l/km. The optimal strategy is as expected: the shifts occur as early as possible.

Experiments. We have implemented the algorithms presented in this paper. Our first implementation is written in `Haskell`[5] and consists of 1500 lines of code. We use the Haskell package `hmatrix`[6] to solve the linear equation system and `glpk-hs`[7] to solve the linear programming problems. In order to make our work publicly available in a widely used tool and to have access to more case studies, we have implemented the best-performing algorithm within the explicit-state version of PRISM. It is an implementation of the strategy improvement algorithm and uses numeric approximations instead of solving the linear equation systems.

First, we will give mean running times of our `Haskell` implementation on the pump example, where we scale the number of pumps. The tests were done on a Quad-Xeon with 2.67GHz and 3GB of heap space. Table 1 shows our results. Column n denotes the number of pumps we use, $|S|$ and $|A|$ denote the number of states and actions the final MDP has. Note that $|S| = 3^n$ and $|A| = 12^n$. The next columns contain the time (in seconds) and the amount of memory (in MB) the different algorithms used. LP denotes the linear program, FLP the fractional linear program. We have two versions of the policy iteration algorithm: one in which we improve the induced MDP to optimality (Column Opt.), and one where we only look for any improved strategy (Column Imp.). The policy iteration algorithms perform best, and Imp. is slightly faster than Opt but uses a little more memory. For $n = 5$, the results start to differ drastically. FLP ran out

[5] `http://www.haskell.org`
[6] `http://code.haskell.org/hmatrix/`
[7] http://hackage.haskell.org/package/glpk-hs

Table 1. Experimental results table

n	$\|S\|$	$\|A\|$	LP		FLP		Opt		Imp.	
2	9	144	0.002	13	0.015	14	0.003	13	0.003	14
3	27	1728	0.043	14	0.642	20	0.027	13	0.009	14
4	81	20736	1.836	41	14.73	332	0.122	21	0.122	24
5	243	248832	67.77	505	n/a	n/a	1.647	162	1.377	166

of memory, LP needed about a minute to solve the problem, and both Imp. and Opt. stay below two seconds.

Using our second implementation, we also tried our algorithm on some of the case studies presented on the PRISM website. For example, we used the IPv4 zeroconf protocol model. We asked for the minimal expected number of occurrences of action `send` divided by occurrences of action `time`. If we choose $K = 5$ and `reset = true`, then the resulting model has 1097 states and finding the optimal strategy takes 5 seconds. For $K = 2$ and `reset = false`, the model has about 90000 states and finding the best strategy takes 4 minutes on a 2.4GHz Core2Duo P8600 laptop.

7 Conclusion

We have presented a framework for synthesizing efficient controllers. The framework is based finding optimal strategies in Ratio-MDPs. To compute optimal strategies we presented three algorithms based on strategy improvement, fractional linear programming, and linear programming, respectively. We have compared performance characteristics of these algorithms and integrated the best algorithm into the probabilistic model checker PRISM. As future work, we are planing to extend our implementation in PRISM to work with symbolically encoded MDPs. Developing a policy iteration algorithm was an important step in this direction, because it allows us to use semi-symbolic (known as symblicit) techniques, which can handle more than 10^{12} states for the long-run average case [15]. We expect that the ratio-case will scale to systems of similar size.

Acknowledgments. The authors would like to thank David Parker for his help with PRISM, and Hugo Gimbert and Luca de Alfaro for answering questions about their work.

References

1. Baier, C., Katoen, J.-P.: Principles of model checking. MIT Press (2008)
2. Bloem, R., Chatterjee, K., Henzinger, T.A., Jobstmann, B.: Better Quality in Synthesis through Quantitative Objectives. In: Bouajjani, A., Maler, O. (eds.) CAV 2009. LNCS, vol. 5643, pp. 140–156. Springer, Heidelberg (2009)
3. Bloem, R., Greimel, K., Henzinger, T.A., Jobstmann, B.: Synthesizing robust systems. In: FMCAD, pp. 85–92. IEEE (2009)

4. Chatterjee, K., Doyen, L., Henzinger, T.A.: Quantitative Languages. In: Kaminski, M., Martini, S. (eds.) CSL 2008. LNCS, vol. 5213, pp. 385–400. Springer, Heidelberg (2008)
5. Chatterjee, K., Henzinger, T.A., Jobstmann, B., Singh, R.: Measuring and Synthesizing Systems in Probabilistic Environments. In: Touili, T., Cook, B., Jackson, P. (eds.) CAV 2010. LNCS, vol. 6174, pp. 380–395. Springer, Heidelberg (2010)
6. Courcoubetis, C., Yannakakis, M.: Markov Decision Processes and Regular Events (Extended Abstract). In: Paterson, M. (ed.) ICALP 1990. LNCS, vol. 443, pp. 336–349. Springer, Heidelberg (1990)
7. de Alfaro, L.: Formal Verification of Probabilistic Systems. PhD thesis, Stanford University (1997)
8. Derman, C.: On sequential decisions and markov chains. Management Science 9(1), 16–24 (1962)
9. Haverkort, B.R.: Performance of computer communication systems - a model-based approach. Wiley (1998)
10. Kwiatkowska, D.P.M.Z., Norman, G.: PRISM: probabilistic model checking for performance and reliability analysis. SIGMETRICS Performance Evaluation Review 36(4), 40–45 (2009)
11. Parr, R., Russell, S.J.: Reinforcement learning with hierarchies of machines. In: Jordan, M.I., Kearns, M.J., Solla, S.A. (eds.) NIPS. The MIT Press (1997)
12. Pnueli, A.: The temporal logic of programs. In: FOCS, pp. 46–57. IEEE Computer Society (1977)
13. Puterman, M.L.: Markov Decision Processes: Discrete Stochastic Dynamic Programming. Wiley-Interscience (April 1994)
14. von Essen, C., Jobstmann, B.: Synthesizing systems with optimal average-case behavior for ratio objectives. In: Reich, J., Finkbeiner, B. (eds.) iWIGP. EPTCS, vol. 50, pp. 17–32 (2011)
15. Wimmer, R., Braitling, B., Becker, B., Hahn, E.M., Crouzen, P., Hermanns, H., Dhama, A., Theel, O.: Symblicit calculation of long-run averages for concurrent probabilistic systems. In: QEST, pp. 27–36. IEEE Computer Society (2010)
16. Yue, H., Bohnenkamp, H., Katoen, J.-P.: Analyzing Energy Consumption in a Gossiping MAC Protocol. In: Müller-Clostermann, B., Echtle, K., Rathgeb, E.P. (eds.) MMB&DFT 2010. LNCS, vol. 5987, pp. 107–119. Springer, Heidelberg (2010)
17. Manna, A.P.Z.: Temporal verification of reactive systems - safety. Springer, Heidelberg (1995)
18. Zwick, U., Paterson, M.: The complexity of mean payoff games on graphs. Theor. Comput. Sci. 158(1&2), 343–359 (1996)

Ideal Abstractions for Well-Structured Transition Systems

Damien Zufferey[1,⋆], Thomas Wies[2], and Thomas A. Henzinger[1,⋆]

[1] IST Austria
[2] New York University

Abstract. Many infinite state systems can be seen as well-structured transition systems (WSTS), i.e., systems equipped with a well-quasi-ordering on states that is also a simulation relation. WSTS are an attractive target for formal analysis because there exist generic algorithms that decide interesting verification problems for this class. Among the most popular algorithms are acceleration-based forward analyses for computing the covering set. Termination of these algorithms can only be guaranteed for flattable WSTS. Yet, many WSTS of practical interest are not flattable and the question whether any given WSTS is flattable is itself undecidable. We therefore propose an analysis that computes the covering set and captures the essence of acceleration-based algorithms, but sacrifices precision for guaranteed termination. Our analysis is an abstract interpretation whose abstract domain builds on the ideal completion of the well-quasi-ordered state space, and a widening operator that mimics acceleration and controls the loss of precision of the analysis. We present instances of our framework for various classes of WSTS. Our experience with a prototype implementation indicates that, despite the inherent precision loss, our analysis often computes the precise covering set of the analyzed system.

1 Introduction

One of the great successes in applying model checking techniques to the analysis of infinite state systems has been achieved by studying the class of *well-structured transition systems* (WSTS) [1, 12–16, 19, 20]. A WSTS is a transition system equipped with a well-quasi-ordering $\leq$ on its states that satisfies the following monotonicity property: for all states s, s', and t if $s \leq t$ and $s \rightarrow s'$ then there exists a state t' such that $t \rightarrow t'$ and $s' \leq t'$. In other words, $\leq$ is a simulation relation for the system. Interesting classes of WSTS include Petri nets [25] and their monotonic extensions [10], lossy channel systems [3], and dynamic process networks such as depth-bounded processes [22, 28].

Many interesting verification problems are decidable for WSTS. In particular, the verification of a large class of safety properties can be reduced to the *coverability problem*, which is decidable for WSTS that satisfy only a few additional mild assumptions [1]. The coverability problem asks whether, given a *bad state* s, there exists a reachable state s' of the system that covers the bad state, i.e., $s_0 \rightarrow^* s'$ and $s \leq s'$

⋆ This research was supported in part by the European Research Council (ERC) Advanced Investigator Grant QUAREM and by the Austrian Science Fund (FWF) project S11402-N23.

V. Kuncak and A. Rybalchenko (Eds.): VMCAI 2012, LNCS 7148, pp. 445–460, 2012.

where s_0 is an initial state $s_0 \in S_0$. In this paper, we are not just interested in solving the coverability problem, but in the more general problem of computing the *covering set* of a WSTS T. The covering set $Cover(T)$ is defined as the downward-closure of the reachable states of the system $Cover(T) = \downarrow \mathsf{post}^*(\downarrow S_0)$. With the help of the covering set one can decide the coverability problem, but also answer other questions of interest such as boundedness (which asks whether $Cover(T)$ is finite) and U-boundedness (which asks whether $Cover(T) \cap U$ is finite for some upward-closed set U). While coverability is decidable for most WSTS, boundedness is not [10], i.e., the covering set is not always computable. Therefore, our goal is to compute precise over-approximations of the covering set, instead of computing this set exactly. In this paper, we present a new analysis based on abstract interpretation [7, 8] that accomplishes this goal.

One might question the rational of using an approximate analysis for solving decidable problems such as coverability. However, in practice one often uses coverability to give approximate answers to verification problems that are undecidable even for WSTS (such as general reachability). Thus, completeness is not always a primary concern. Also, one should bear in mind that even though coverability is decidable, its complexity is non-primitive recursive for many classes of WSTS [27], i.e., from a practical point of view the problem might as well be undecidable. Nevertheless, the techniques that have been developed for solving the coverability problem provide important algorithmic insights for the design of good approximate analyses.

Among the best understood algorithms for computing the exact covering set of a WSTS are acceleration-based algorithms such as the Karp-Miller tree construction for Petri nets [20] or the more general clover algorithm [13]. These algorithms exploit the fact that every downward-closed subset of a well-quasi-ordering can be effectively represented as a finite union of order ideals [12, 17]. The covering set is then computed by identifying sequences of transitions in the system that correspond to loops leading from smaller to larger states in the ordering, and then computing the exact set of ideals covering the states reachable by arbitrary many iterations of these loops. This process is referred to as ω- or lub-acceleration. Since acceleration is exact, these algorithm compute the exact covering set of a WSTS, whenever they terminate. Since the covering set is not always computable, termination is only guaranteed for so-called *flattable* systems [13]. In a flattable WSTS the covering set can be obtained by a finite sequence of lub-accelerations of finite sequences of transitions. In particular, this means that every nested loop of transitions can be decomposed into a finite sequence of simple loops. Many WSTS of practical interest do not satisfy this property. We provide an example of such a system in the next section.

Contributions. We are the first to propose an abstract interpretation framework that computes precise approximation of covering sets for WSTS, captures the key insights of acceleration-based algorithms, yet is guaranteed to terminate even on non-flattable WSTS. The abstract domain of our analysis is based on the ideal completion of the well-quasi-ordering of the analyzed WSTS and an accompanying widening operator. The widening operator mimics the effect of acceleration, but loses enough precision to guarantee termination. Instead of accelerating loops that lead from sets of smaller to sets of larger states, our widening operator only accelerates the difference between these sets of states, independently of the actual sequence of transitions that produced

Equations:

$$\begin{aligned}
\text{client}(C, S) &= C().\text{client}(C, S) \oplus (\overline{S}(C).0 \mid \text{client}(C, S)) \\
\text{server}(S) &= S(C).(\overline{C}().0 \mid \text{server}(S)) \\
\text{env}(S) &= \text{env}(S) \mid (\nu\, C)\text{client}(C, S)
\end{aligned}$$

Initial state: $(\nu\, S)(\text{server}(S) \mid \text{env}(S))$

Fig. 1. A π-calculus process implementing a client-server protocol

them. We present instances of our framework for the WSTS classes of Petri nets, lossy channel systems, and depth-bounded process networks. Our experience with a prototype implementation indicates that, despite its inherent incompleteness, our analysis often computes the precise covering set of the analyzed system.

Further Related Work. We have already explained, in detail, the connection of our work with acceleration-based algorithms for computing the covering set. We discuss further connections with algorithms for solving the related coverability problem. The simplest algorithm for this problem is a backward analysis described in [1]. In practice, backward algorithms tend to be less efficient than forward algorithms, especially for dynamic process networks where the pre operator is expensive to compute [28]. Therefore, many attempts have been made at deriving complete forward algorithms for this problem. The most general solutions are described in [16] and [15]. The expand, enlarge, and check algorithm [16] decides the covering problem using a combination of an under-approximating and an over-approximating forward analysis. The over-approximating analysis relies on a so-called adequate domain of limits for the representation of downward-closed sets, which is actually the ideal completion of the underlying well-quasi ordering [12]. Ganty et al. propose an alternative algorithm [15] based on abstract interpretation. Unlike our approach, this algorithm uses a finite abstract domain that represents downward-closed sets by complements of upward-closed sets. The algorithm then relies on a complete refinement scheme to refine the abstraction for a specific coverability goal. Both algorithms [12, 15] compute an over-approximation of the covering set as a byproduct of the analysis, namely an invariant whose complement contains the coverability goal. To ensure completeness, the precision of this computed invariant is geared towards proving the specific instance of the coverability problem. Instead, our analysis computes a precise approximation of the covering set that is independent of any specific coverability instance.

An extended version of this paper with additional material (including proofs) is available as a technical report [30].

2 Motivating Example

We start with an example of a non-flattable system and illustrate how our analysis computes its covering set. Our example is given by the π-calculus process shown in Figure 1. The process models a concurrent system that implements a client-server protocol using asynchronous message passing. The process consists of one single server thread, an environment thread, and an unbounded number of client threads. Each type of threads is

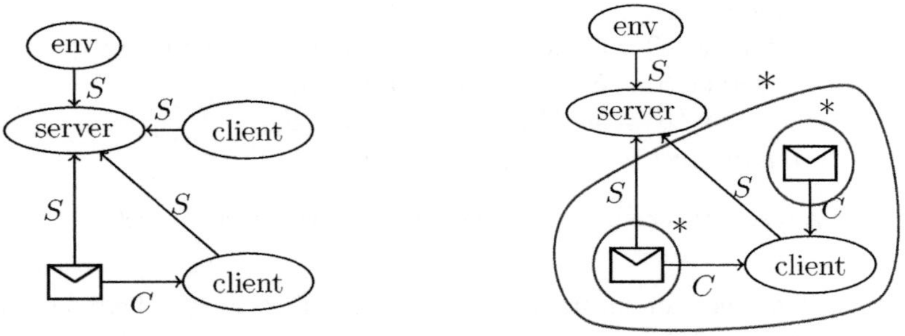

Fig. 2. Communication graph of the system in Figure 1 and the symbolic representation of the covering set of this system

defined by a recursive π-calculus equation. In each loop iteration of a client, the client non-deterministically chooses to either wait for a response from the server on its own dedicated channel C, or to send a new request to the server. Requests are sent asynchronously and modeled as threads that wait for the server to receive the client's channel name over the server's dedicated channel S and then terminate immediately. In each iteration of the server loop, the server waits for incoming requests on its own channel S and then asynchronously sends a response back to the client using the client's channel name C received in the request. The environment thread models the fact that new clients can enter the system at anytime. In each iteration of the environment thread, it spawns a new client thread with its own dedicated fresh channel name. The initial state of the system consists only of the server and the environment thread.

The states of a π-calculus process can be represented as a *communication graph* with nodes corresponding to threads (labeled by their id) and edges corresponding to channels (labeled by channel names). The left hand side of Figure 2 shows the communication graph representing the process:

$$\text{server}(S) \mid \text{client}(C_1, S) \mid \overline{S}(C_1).0 \mid \text{client}(C_2, S) \mid \text{env}(S)$$

The transition relation on processes is monotone with respect to the ordering on processes that is induced by subgraph isomorphism between their communication graphs, i.e., a process represented by a communication graph G can take all transitions of processes represented by the subgraphs of G. We call a set of graphs *depth-bounded*, if there exists a bound on the length of all simple paths in all graphs in the set. A *depth-bounded process* [22] is a process whose set of reachable communication graphs is depth-bounded. The subgraph isomorphism ordering is a well-quasi-ordering on sets of depth-bounded graphs, i.e., depth-bounded processes are WSTS. The process defined in Figure 1 is depth-bounded because the longest simple path in any of its reachable communication graphs has length at most 2. We now explain our analysis through this example.

Our analysis computes an over-approximation of the covering set of the analyzed WSTS, i.e., the downward-closure (with respect to the well-quasi-ordering) of its reachable set of states. The elements of the abstract domain of the analysis are the downward-closed sets. In our example, these are sets of communication graphs that are downward-closed with respect to the subgraph ordering. A finite downward-closed set of graphs can be represented by the maximal graphs in the set. The downward-closure of a single graph is an ideal of the subgraph ordering. Thus, any finite downward-closed set is a finite union of ideals. For well-quasi-orderings this is true for arbitrary downward-closed sets, including infinite ones. We symbolically represent the infinite ideals of the subgraph ordering by graphs where some subgraphs are marked with the symbol '*'. These markings of subgraphs can be nested. Such a symbolic graph represents the downward-closure of all graphs that result from (recursively) unfolding the marked subgraphs arbitrarily often. The right hand side of Figure 2 shows such a symbolic graph. It represents a downward-closed set of communication graphs of our example system that is also the covering set of the system. The covering set consists of all graphs that contain one server thread, one environment thread, and arbitrarily many clients with arbitrarily many unprocessed request and response messages each.

Our analysis works as follows: it starts with a set of symbolic communication graphs that represents the downward-closure of the initial states of the system. Then it iterates a fixed point functional that is composed of the following two steps: (1) compute the set of symbolic communication graphs that represent the downward-closure of the post states of the states represented by the current set of symbolic graphs, and (2) widen the resulting set of symbolic graphs with respect to the sequence of iterates that have been computed in the previous steps. The widening step compares the symbolic graphs in the new iterate pairwise to the symbolic graphs obtained in the previous iterates. If a symbolic graph in the new iterate is larger than some symbolic graph in a previous iterate then the larger graph must contain a subgraph that is not contained in the smaller one. This subgraph in the larger graph is then marked with a '*'. The intuition behind the widening is that, because of monotonicity of the transition relation, the sequence of transitions that lead from the smaller to the larger graph can be repeated arbitrarily often, which results in graphs with arbitrarily many copies of the new subgraph. Figure 3 shows a sequence of symbolic graphs obtained during the analysis of the client-server example. The final symbolic graph in the sequence represents the covering set of the system. This symbolic graph is also the fixed point obtained by our analysis, i.e., in this example the analysis does not lose precision.

Note that the covering set of our example system cannot be computed by a finite number of accelerations of finite sequences of transitions, i.e., the system is not flattable. This is reflected by the nesting of marked subgraphs in the symbolic graph that represents the covering set. To obtain this covering set via acceleration, one would need to compute the set of states reachable by a transfinite sequence of transitions resulting from ω-acceleration of a sequence of transition that is already infinite. The infinite sequence of transition that is to be accelerated corresponds to the creation of a client by the environment thread, followed by infinitely many exchanges of request and response messages between this client and the server. Since acceleration-based algorithms such as the clover algorithm [13] cannot accelerate infinite sequences of transitions, they do not terminate on our example system.

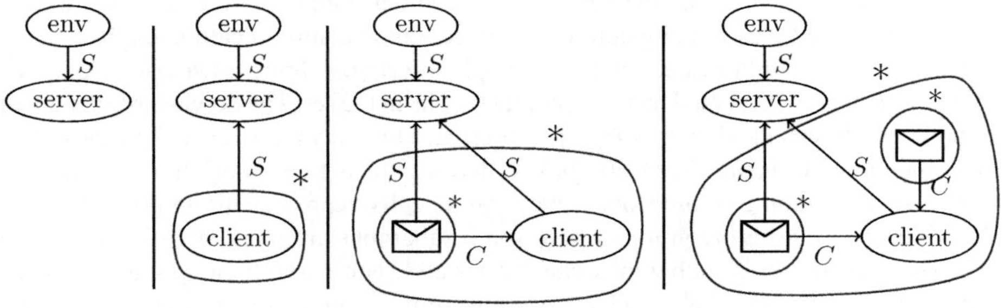

Fig. 3. Sequence of symbolic communication graphs produced by the analysis of the system in Figure 1

3 Preliminaries

Posets, lattices, wqos, and bqos. A *quasi-ordering* $\leq$ is a reflexive and transitive relation $\leq$ on a set X. In the following $X(\leq)$ is a quasi-ordered set. The *upward closure* $\uparrow Y$ of a set $Y \subseteq X$ is $\uparrow Y = \{\, x \in X \mid \exists y \in Y.\, y \leq x \,\}$. The *downward closure* $\downarrow Y$ of Y is $\downarrow Y = \{x \in X \mid \exists y \in Y. x \leq y\}$. A set $Y \subseteq X$ is *upward-closed* if $Y = \uparrow Y$ and *downward-closed* if $Y = \downarrow Y$. An *upper bound* $x \in X$ of a set $Y \subseteq X$ is such that for all $y \in Y$, $y \leq x$. The notion of *lower bound* is defined dually. A nonempty set $D \subseteq X$ is called *directed* if any two elements in D have a common upper bound in D. A set $I \subseteq X$ is an *ideal* of X if I is downward-closed and directed. We denote by $\mathit{Idl}(X)$ the set of all ideals of X and call $\mathit{Idl}(X)$ the *ideal completion* of X.

If a quasi-ordering $\leq$ on a set X is antisymmetric it is called a *partial ordering* and $X(\leq)$ a *poset*. A poset $L(\leq)$ is called a *complete lattice* if every subset $X \subseteq L$ has a least upper bound $\sqcup X$ and a greatest lower bound $\sqcap X$ in L. In particular, L has a least element $\bot = \sqcap L$ and a greatest element $\top = \sqcup L$. This lattice will be denoted by $L(\leq, \top, \bot, \sqcup, \sqcap)$. For a function $f : X \rightarrow Y$ and $X' \subseteq X$ we denote by $f(X')$ the set $\{\, f(x) \mid x \in X' \,\}$. A monotone function $f : L \rightarrow L$ on a complete lattice $L(\leq, \top, \bot, \sqcup, \sqcap)$ is called *continuous* if for every directed subset D of L, $\sqcup f(D) = f(\sqcup D)$. Recall Kleene's fixed point theorem which states that if $f : L \rightarrow L$ is continuous then its least fixed point $\mathit{lfp}^{\leq}(f) \in L$ exists and is given by $\sqcup \{\, f^i(\bot) \mid i \in \mathbb{N} \,\}$.

Let $L_1(\leq_1)$ and $L_2(\leq_2)$ be posets. A *Galois connection* between $L_1(\leq_1)$ and $L_2(\leq_2)$ is a pair of functions $\alpha : L_1 \rightarrow L_2$ and $\gamma : L_2 \rightarrow L_1$ that satisfy for all $x \in L_1, y \in L_2$, $\alpha(x) \leq_2 y$ iff $x \leq_1 \gamma(y)$. If γ is also injective then (α, γ) is called *Galois insertion*.

A quasi-ordering $\leq$ on a set X is called *well-quasi-ordering* (wqo) if any infinite sequence $x_0, x_1, x_2, \ldots$ of elements from X contains an increasing pair $x_i \leq x_j$ with $i < j$. We extend the ordering $\leq$ to an ordering $\leq$ on subsets of X as expected: for $Y_1, Y_2 \subseteq X$, we have $Y_1 \leq Y_2$ iff for all $y_1 \in Y_1$ there exists $y_2 \in Y_2$ such that $y_1 \leq y_2$. We will also refer to the notion of *better-quasi-ordering*. For all intents and purposes in this paper, it suffices to know that better-quasi-orderings are well-quasi-orderings that are closed under powerset construction, i.e., if $X(\leq)$ is a bqo then $\mathcal{P}(X)(\leq)$ is also a bqo. We refer to [23] for the precise (but rather technical) definition of bqos.

Well-structured transition system. A *transition system* is a tuple $T = (S, S_0, \rightarrow)$ where S is a set of states, $S_0 \subseteq S$ a set of initial states, and $\rightarrow \subseteq S \times S$ is a transition relation. We denote by $\mathsf{post} : \mathcal{P}(S) \rightarrow \mathcal{P}(S)$ the *post operator* of T defined by $\mathsf{post}(X) = \{ x' \in S \mid \exists x \in X. x \rightarrow x' \}$. Note that post is continuous on the complete lattice $\mathcal{P}(S)(\subseteq, S, \emptyset, \cup, \cap)$.

A *well-structured transition system* (WSTS) is a tuple $T = (S, S_0, \rightarrow, \leq)$ where $(S, S_0, \rightarrow)$ is a transition system and $\leq \subseteq S \times S$ a wqo that is upward-compatible with respect to $\rightarrow$, i.e., for all s_1, s_2, t_1 such that $s_1 \leq t_1$ and $s_1 \rightarrow s_2$, there exists t_2 such that $t_1 \rightarrow t_2$ and $s_2 \leq t_2$. The *covering set* of a well-structured transition system T, denoted $Cover(T)$, is defined by $Cover(T) = \downarrow lfp^{\subseteq}(\lambda X. \downarrow S_0 \cup \mathsf{post}(X))$.

4 Ideal Abstraction

We next describe our abstract interpretation framework for computing over-approximations of the covering sets of WSTS. For this purpose we fix a WSTS $T = (S, S_0, \rightarrow, \leq)$ throughout the rest of this section.

4.1 Concrete and Abstract Domain

Following the framework of abstract interpretation [7, 8], a static analysis is defined by lattice-theoretic domains and by fixed point iteration over the domains. The concrete domain $\mathcal{D}$ of our analysis is the powerset domain over the states S of WSTS T:

$$\mathcal{D} \stackrel{\text{def}}{=} \mathcal{P}(S)(\subseteq, \emptyset, S, \cup, \cap)$$

Since our analysis is to compute an over-approximation of the covering set of T, which is a downward-closed set, we define the abstract domain $\mathcal{D}_\downarrow$ as the set of all downward-closed subsets of S, again ordered by subset inclusion:

$$\mathcal{D}_\downarrow \stackrel{\text{def}}{=} \{ \downarrow X \mid X \subseteq S \} (\subseteq, \emptyset, S, \cup, \cap)$$

One can easily verify that $\mathcal{D}_\downarrow$ is a complete lattice. This choice of the abstract domain suggests the following abstraction function $\alpha_\downarrow : \mathcal{D} \rightarrow \mathcal{D}_\downarrow$ and concretization function $\gamma_\downarrow : \mathcal{D}_\downarrow \rightarrow \mathcal{D}$ defined as $\alpha_\downarrow(X) \stackrel{\text{def}}{=} \downarrow X$ and $\gamma_\downarrow(Y) \stackrel{\text{def}}{=} Y$.

Proposition 1. *The pair $(\alpha_\downarrow, \gamma_\downarrow)$ forms a Galois insertion between domains $\mathcal{D}$ and $\mathcal{D}_\downarrow$.*

According to [8], the Galois insertion $(\alpha_\downarrow, \gamma_\downarrow)$ defines the *best abstract post operator* $\mathsf{post}_\downarrow$ on the abstract domain $\mathcal{D}_\downarrow$:

$$\mathsf{post}_\downarrow \stackrel{\text{def}}{=} \alpha_\downarrow \circ \mathsf{post} \circ \gamma_\downarrow$$

We next show that we can effectively represent the elements of $\mathcal{D}_\downarrow$ and, for all practical purposes, effectively compute $\mathsf{post}_\downarrow$ on this representation. To obtain this representation, we exploit the fact that any downward-closed subset of a wqo-set $S(\leq)$ is a finite union of ideals of $S(\leq)$.

Denote by $\mathcal{P}_{\text{fin}}(\mathit{Idl}(S))$ the finite sets of ideals of $S(\leq)$ and define the quasi-ordering $\sqsubseteq$ on $\mathcal{P}_{\text{fin}}(\mathit{Idl}(S))$ as the point-wise extension of $\subseteq$ from the ideal completion $\mathit{Idl}(S)$ of $S(\leq)$ to $\mathcal{P}_{\text{fin}}(\mathit{Idl}(S))$:

$$L_1 \sqsubseteq L_2 \overset{\text{def}}{\iff} \forall I_1 \in L_1.\, \exists I_2 \in L_2.\, I_1 \subseteq I_2$$

Let $\mathcal{D}_{\mathit{Idl}}$ be the quotient of $\mathcal{P}_{\text{fin}}(\mathit{Idl}(S))$ with respect to the equivalence relation $\sqsubseteq \cap \sqsubseteq^{-1}$. For notational convenience we use the same symbol $\sqsubseteq$ for the quasi-ordering on $\mathcal{P}_{\text{fin}}(\mathit{Idl}(S))$ and the partial ordering that it defines on the quotient $\mathcal{D}_{\mathit{Idl}}$. We further identify the elements of $\mathcal{D}_{\mathit{Idl}}$ with the finite sets of maximal ideals, i.e., for all $L \in \mathcal{D}_{\mathit{Idl}}$ and $I_1, I_2 \in L$, if $I_1 \subseteq I_2$ then $I_1 = I_2$.

Now, define the function $\gamma_{\mathit{Idl}} : \mathcal{D}_{\mathit{Idl}} \to \mathcal{D}_{\downarrow}$ as $\gamma_{\mathit{Idl}}(L) \overset{\text{def}}{=} \bigcup L$.

Proposition 2. *The function γ_{Idl} is an order-isomorphism.*

Let $\sqcup$ and $\sqcap$ be the least upper bound and greatest lower bound operators on the poset $\mathcal{D}_{\mathit{Idl}}(\sqsubseteq)$. These operators exist because $\mathcal{D}_{\downarrow}$ is a complete lattice and $\mathcal{D}_{\downarrow}$ and $\mathcal{D}_{\mathit{Idl}}$ are order-isomorphic according to Proposition 2. The following proposition then follows immediately.

Proposition 3. *$\mathcal{D}_{\mathit{Idl}}(\sqsubseteq, \emptyset, \{S\}, \sqcup, \sqcap)$ is a complete lattice.*

Let $\alpha_{\mathit{Idl}} : \mathcal{D}_{\downarrow} \to \mathcal{D}_{\mathit{Idl}}$ be the inverse of γ_{Idl}. Since γ_{Idl} is an order-isomorphism, the pair $(\alpha_{\mathit{Idl}}, \gamma_{\mathit{Idl}})$ forms a Galois insertion between $\mathcal{D}_{\downarrow}$ and $\mathcal{D}_{\mathit{Idl}}$.

Let $\alpha = \alpha_{\mathit{Idl}} \circ \alpha_{\downarrow}$ and $\gamma = \gamma_{\downarrow} \circ \gamma_{\mathit{Idl}}$. Then (α, γ) forms a Galois insertion between concrete domain $\mathcal{D}$ and abstract domain $\mathcal{D}_{\mathit{Idl}}$. Let $\mathsf{post}_{\mathit{Idl}} = \alpha \circ \mathsf{post} \circ \gamma$ be the induced best abstract post operator on $\mathcal{D}_{\mathit{Idl}}$ and let F_{Idl} be the function $F_{\mathit{Idl}} = \lambda L.\, \alpha(S_0) \sqcup \mathsf{post}_{\mathit{Idl}}(L)$. The following proposition is then a simple consequence of Proposition 2.

Proposition 4. *The least fixed point of F_{Idl} on $\mathcal{D}_{\mathit{Idl}}$ is the covering set of T:*

$$\gamma(\mathit{lfp}^{\sqsubseteq}(F_{\mathit{Idl}})) = \mathit{Cover}(T)\ .$$

Can we compute $\mathit{lfp}^{\sqsubseteq}(F_{\mathit{Idl}})$? In general the answer is "no" for various reasons. First, we may not be able to compute the iterates of the abstract functional F_{Idl}, respectively, decide the fixed point test on the abstract domain. However, for the classes of WSTS that are of practical interest, this is not a problem: We say that the ideal completion $\mathit{Idl}(S)$ of a WSTS $T = (S, S_0, \to, \leq)$ is *effective* if (i) for all $I_1, I_2 \in \mathit{Idl}(S)$, checking $I_1 \subseteq I_2$ is decidable, and (ii) for all $I \in \mathit{Idl}(S)$, $\mathsf{post}_{\mathit{Idl}}(\{I\})$ is computable. It follows from [12, Theorem 3.4] that all WSTS with a so called *effective adequate domain of limits* [16] also have an effective ideal completion. Classes of WSTS with this property include, e.g., Petri nets and their monotone extensions [16], lossy channel systems [12], and depth-bounded processes [28].

Thus, assume that T has an effective ideal completion. Then, for any $L \in \mathcal{D}_{\mathit{Idl}}$ we can compute $F_{\mathit{Idl}}(L)$ and decide $F_{\mathit{Idl}}(L) \sqsubseteq L$. However, this is not yet sufficient for guaranteeing termination. In general, the covering set of a WSTS is not computable, i.e., we cannot expect that the sequence of iterates $(\bigsqcup_{i \leq n} F^i_{\mathit{Idl}}(\emptyset))_{n \in \mathbb{N}}$ stabilizes. In fact, even if the exact covering set $\mathit{Cover}(T)$ is computable for a particular WSTS, the sequence of fixed point iterates might not stabilize because the abstract domain $\mathcal{D}_{\mathit{Idl}}$ has (typically) infinite height. To ensure termination of our analysis, we next define an appropriate widening operator for the abstract domain $\mathcal{D}_{\mathit{Idl}}$.

4.2 Widening

Let us first recall the notion of set-widening operators [9]. A *set-widening operator* for a poset $X(\leq)$ is a partial function $\nabla : \mathcal{P}(X) \rightharpoonup X$ that satisfies the following two conditions:

- *Covering*: For all $Y \subseteq X$, if $\nabla(Y)$ is defined then for all $y \in Y$, $y \leq \nabla(Y)$.
- *Termination*: For every ascending chain $\{x_i\}_{i \in \mathbb{N}}$ in $X(\leq)$, the sequence $y_0 = x_0$, $y_i = \nabla(\{x_0, \ldots, x_i\})$, for all $i > 0$, is well-defined and an ascending stabilizing chain.

In the following, we define a general set-widening operator for the abstract domain $\mathcal{D}_{Idl}$. The reason for using a set-widening operator instead of the more popular pair widening operator is that we want to enable the widening operator to take into account the whole history of the previous iterates of the fixed point computation. This allows us to use widening to mimic the effect of acceleration for computing the exact covering set of flattable WSTS.

The set-widening operator on the abstract domain $\mathcal{D}_{Idl}$ is obtained by lifting a given set-widening operator for the ideal completion $Idl(S)$. This underlying widening operator on ideals is a parameter of the analysis because it is domain-specific for each class of WSTS. In the next section, we will describe several such widening operators for common classes of WSTS.

In general, extending a widening operator from a base domain to its finite powerset is non-trivial [5]. We can simplify this task by making a stronger assumption about the ordering $\leq$ on the base set S: we assume that $S(\leq)$ is not just a wqo, but a bqo. This ensures that the ideal completion $Idl(S)$ is itself a bqo with respect to the subset inclusion ordering. Using this fact we can then lift the set-widening operator on ideals to sets of ideals. From a practical point of view, requiring a bqo is not a real restriction, since all wqos of WSTS occurring in practice are actually bqos.

Assume that ∇_S is a set-widening operator on the poset $Idl(S)(\subseteq)$. Then define the operator $\nabla : \mathcal{P}(\mathcal{D}_{Idl}) \rightharpoonup \mathcal{D}_{Idl}$ as follows: for $C \subseteq \mathcal{D}_{Idl}$, if C is a finite ascending chain $C = \{L_i\}_{0 \leq i \leq n}$ in $\mathcal{D}_{Idl}(\sqsubseteq)$ let $\nabla(C)$ be defined recursively by

$$\begin{aligned}
\nabla(\{L_0\}) &= L_0 \\
\nabla(\{L_0, \ldots, L_i\}) &= \nabla(\{L_0, \ldots, L_{i-1}\}) \sqcup \\
&\qquad \{\, \nabla_S(\mathcal{I}) \mid \mathcal{I} \text{ maximal ascending chain in } \nabla(\{L_0, \ldots, L_{i-1}\}) \,\}
\end{aligned}$$

for all $0 < i \leq n$. In all other cases let $\nabla(C)$ be undefined.

Proposition 5. *If $S(\leq)$ is a bqo then ∇ is a set-widening operator for $\mathcal{D}_{Idl}(\sqsubseteq)$.*

We now define our analysis in terms of the widening sequence $\{W_i\}_{i \in \mathbb{N}}$ as follows:

$$W_0 = \emptyset \qquad \textit{and} \qquad W_{i+1} = \nabla(\{W_0, \ldots, W_i, F_{Idl}(W_i) \sqcup W_i\})$$

Note that for computing the image of ∇ in step $i+1$ we can reuse W_i. The properties of set-widening operators, Proposition 4, and Proposition 5 imply the soundness and termination of the analysis.

Theorem 6. *If $S(\leq)$ is a bqo then the sequence $\{W_i\}_{i\in\mathbb{N}}$ stabilizes and its least upper bound approximates the covering set of T, i.e., $Cover(T) \subseteq \gamma(\bigcup\{W_i\}_{i\in\mathbb{N}})$.*

Trace Partitioning. Note that, unlike acceleration, the widening operator ∇ does not take into account whether each widened chain of ideals is actually correlated by some sequence of transition in the system. This incurs an additional loss of precision that is not needed to ensure termination of the analysis. To avoid this loss of precision, we can refine the above analysis via combination with an appropriate trace partitioning domain [26]. The resulting analysis is a generalized Karp-Miller tree construction where acceleration has been replaced by widening.

5 Set-Widening Operators for Ideal Completions

We now discuss several instantiations of our analysis for different classes of WSTS by presenting the corresponding ideal completions and set-widening operators on ideals. We discuss, in turn, Petri nets, lossy channel systems, and depth-bounded processes.

5.1 Petri Nets

A *Petri net* is a tuple (S, T, W) where S is a finite set of places, T is a finite set of transitions, and $W : (S,T) \cup (T,S) \to \mathbb{N}$ is a (multi)set of arcs. A marking M is a map: $S \to \mathbb{N}$. We denote by $\mathcal{M}(S)$ the set of all markings over S. A transition $t \in T$ is fireable at M iff for all $s \in S$, $M(s) \geq W(s,t)$. Firing t at M gives M' defined as $M'(s) = M(s) - W(s,t) + W(t,s)$. The point-wise ordering of markings is a bqo [23]. The ideal completion $Idl(\mathcal{M}(S))$ of the markings of a Petri net can be represented by extended markings, which are functions $S \to \mathbb{N} \cup \{\omega\}$ [17]. The ordering on extended markings is given by $M \leq M'$ iff for all $s \in S$, $M'(s) = \omega$ or $M(s) \in \mathbb{N}$ and $M(s) \leq M'(s)$.

Widening for Petri Nets. The set-widening operator ∇_{PN} for a Petri Net corresponds to the usual acceleration used in the Karp-Miller tree construction for Petri nets. For a finite ascending chain $\{M_i\}_{0\leq i\leq n}$ we define $\nabla_{\mathsf{PN}}(\{M_i\}_{0\leq i\leq n}) = M$ where $M(s) = \omega$ if $M_n(s) > M_0(s)$ and $M_n(s)$ otherwise. Clearly this set-widening operator satisfies the covering condition. It also satisfies termination, since the set of places S is finite.

Precision of the Widening and Monotonic Extensions of Petri Nets. For standard Petri nets the above widening operator corresponds to the acceleration used in the Karp-Miller tree construction. In fact, for this class of WSTS our analysis does not lose precision. The reason is that in Petri nets sequences of firing transitions σ that increase the value of a marking M by some δ, $\sigma(M) = M + \delta$, do the same for all larger markings $M' \geq M$, i.e., $\sigma(M') = M' + \delta$.

For monotonic extensions of Petri nets, such as transfer nets and reset nets, the situation is more complicated. In a transfer net a transition can transfer all the tokens from one place to another place in a single step. In both cases we can use the same widening as for standard Petri nets, but the analysis may lose precision because neither transfer nets nor reset nets are flattable, in general. However, for a concrete net the loss of precision does not depend on the flattability of the net in consideration, i.e., there are non-flattable nets where the result of the analysis is exact and flat nets were the analysis over-approximates the actual covering set.

5.2 Lossy Channel Systems

A *lossy channel system* (LCS) [3] is a tuple (S, s_0, C, M, δ) where S is a finite set of control locations, s_0 is the initial location, C is a finite set of channels, M is a finite set of messages, and δ is a set of transitions. A state of an LCS is a tuple (s, w) where $s \in S$ and w is a mapping $C \to M^*$ denoting the content of the channels. A transition t is a tuple (s_1, Op, s_2) where $s_1, s_2 \in S$ and Op is of the form $c!/?\,m$ ($c \in C$,$m \in M$). The system can go from state (s_1, w_1) to (s_2, w_2) by firing transition t iff $Op = c!m \wedge w_2(c) \leq w_1(c)m$ or $Op = c?m \wedge mw_2(c) \leq w_1(c)$, the remaining channels are unchanged. The systems are called *lossy* because messages can be dropped from channels before and after performing a send or receive operation. The ordering on states $\leq$ is defined as $(s, w) \leq (s', w')$ iff $s = s'$ and for all $c \in C$, $w(c)$ is a subword of $w'(c)$. The subword ordering is a bqo [23] and thus so is the ordering $\leq$ on states. In the following we describe a widening on the content of individual channels. Its extension to states is defined as expected.

The downward-closed sets of the subword ordering are exactly the languages of simple regular expressions (SRE) [2], which are defined by the following grammar:

$$\begin{aligned} \mathit{atom} &::= (m + \epsilon) \mid (m_1 + \ldots + m_n)^* \\ \mathit{product} &::= \epsilon \mid \mathit{atom}\ \mathit{product} \\ \mathit{SRE} &::= \mathit{product}\ [\ +\ \mathit{SRE}] \end{aligned}$$

The ideals of the subword ordering are the languages denoted by the products in SRE. The ordering on the ideals is language inclusion.

Widening for LCS. The first step in defining the widening operator on channel contents is to define a notion of difference on the corresponding ideals. For a product p we denote by $|p|$ the number of atoms appearing in p and for $1 \leq i \leq |p|$ we denote by $p[i]$ the ith atom of p.

Let p, q be products. If $p \leq q$ then we can find a mapping $\iota : [1, |p|] \to [1, |q|]$ such that (i) ι is monotone, i.e., for all $i, j \in [1, |p|]$ if $i \leq j$ then $\iota(i) \leq \iota(j)$, (ii) for all $i \in [1, |p|]$ the language of $p[i]$ is included in the language of $q[\iota(i)]$, and (iii) for all $i, j \in [1, |p|]$ if $\iota(i) = \iota(j)$ and $q[\iota(i)]$ is of the form $(a + \epsilon)$ then $i = j$. We call ι an *inclusion mapping* for $p \leq q$. Note that we consider an interval $[l, r]$ to be empty if $l > r$, i.e., if $p = \epsilon$ then the inclusion mapping exists trivially.

Let p and q be atoms such that $p \leq q$ and let ι be an inclusion mapping for $p \leq q$. We define an extrapolation operator χ_{LCS} for p, q and ι as follows. If $p = \epsilon$ then $\chi_{\mathsf{LCS}}(p, q, \iota) = (\sum_i q[i])^*$. Otherwise, let $i_1, \ldots, i_n$ be the increasing sequence of indices in the range of ι. For each $j \in [1, n-1]$ define the interval $d_j = [i_j + 1, i_{j+1} - 1]$. Furthermore, define $d_0 = [1, i_1 - 1]$ and $d_n = [i_n, |q|]$. For all $j \in [0, n]$, define $s_j = \left(\sum_{i \in d_j} q[i]\right)^*$. Note that s_j is equivalent to ϵ if d_j is empty and, otherwise, s_j is equivalent to an atom of the form $\left(\sum_k m_k\right)^*$ where the m_k are the messages appearing in the atoms $q[i]$ for $i \in d_j$. Then define $\chi_{\mathsf{LCS}}(p, q, \iota) = s_0\, q[i_1] \ldots s_{k-1}\, q[i_k]\, s_k$.

Inclusion mappings are not necessarily unique. We therefore fix for each ascending sequence of products $p_1 \leq p_2 \ldots$ a corresponding sequence $\iota_1, \iota_2, \ldots$ such that (1) for all i, ι_i is an inclusion mapping for $p_i \leq p_{i+1}$, and (2) for every two ascending chains of products that share a common prefix, the corresponding sequences of inclusion mappings agree on this prefix.

Let $\pi = \{p_i\}_{0 \leq i \leq n}$ be an ascending chain of products with $n > 0$. The set-widening of π is then defined as $\nabla_{\mathsf{LCS}}(\pi) = \chi_{\mathsf{LCS}}(p_0, p_n, \iota_{0,n})$ where $\iota_{0,n}$ is the composition of the fixed sequence of inclusion mappings for π, $\iota_{0,n} = \iota_{n-1} \circ \cdots \circ \iota_0$.

Note that one cannot use the operator χ_{LCS} to define a standard pair widening operator ∇ on ideals of the subword ordering: $\nabla(p, q) = \chi_{\mathsf{LCS}}(p, q, \iota)$ where ι is an inclusion mapping for $p \leq q$. As a counterexample for termination of this operator consider the following sequence of ideals: $x_0 = \epsilon$, $x_1 = (a + \epsilon)$, $x_2 = a^*(b + \epsilon)$, $x_3 = a^*b^*(a + \epsilon)$, etc. Applying ∇ pairwise on consecutive elements of the sequence leads to the following diverging sequence: $y_0 = x_0 = \epsilon$, $y_1 = \nabla(y_0, x_1) = a^*$, $y_2 = \nabla(y_1, x_2) = a^*b^*$, $y_3 = \nabla(a^*b^*, x_3) = a^*b^*a^*$, etc. On the other hand, the set-widening operator ∇_{LCS} produces the stabilizing sequence: $y_0 = x_0 = \epsilon$, $y_1 = \nabla_{\mathsf{LCS}}(\{x_0, x_1\}) = a^*$, $y_2 = \nabla_{\mathsf{LCS}}(\{x_0, x_1, x_2\}) = (a + b)^*$, $y_3 = \nabla_{\mathsf{LCS}}(\{x_0, x_1, x_2, x_3\}) = (a + b)^*$, etc. For termination, it is crucial that the maximal length of the products provided as first argument of χ_{LCS} is bounded throughout all widening steps. This is for instance ensured by fixing the first argument of χ_{LCS} to one particular element of the widened sequence (e.g., the first element as in the definition of ∇_{LCS}). For a more detailed discussion and the proof of termination for the operator ∇_{LCS} we refer to the technical report [30].

5.3 Depth-Bounded Processes

Depth bounded processes (DBP) [22] form the largest known fragment of the π-calculus for which non-trivial verification problems are still decidable. In particular, we proved in [28] that the covering problem is decidable for this class. As for many other classes of WSTS, the coverability problem has non-primitive recursive complexity. This makes DBP a particularly interesting target for approximate analysis. We have already informally introduced DBP in Section 2 and explained how our analysis works for this class of WSTS. In the following, we explain the analysis of DBP in more detail. We outline an analysis that operates directly on process terms, instead of communication graphs.

We assume basic knowledge of the syntax and semantics of the π-calculus and refer the reader to [24] for a detailed introduction. We consider π-calculus processes that are described by finite systems of recursive π-calculus equations together with a process term denoting the initial state. We denote by $\equiv$ the usual syntactic congruence relation on π-calculus process terms.

The *nesting of restrictions* $nest_\nu$ of a process term is measured recursively as follows $nest_\nu(0) = nest_\nu(A(\boldsymbol{x})) = 0$, $nest_\nu((\nu x)P) = 1 + nest_\nu(P)$, and $nest_\nu(P_1 \mid P_2) = \max\{nest_\nu(P_1), nest_\nu(P_2)\}$. The *depth* of a process term P is the minimal nesting of restrictions of process terms in the congruence class of P: $depth(P) = \min\{\, nest_\nu(Q) \mid Q \equiv P \,\}$. A set of process terms $\mathcal{P}$ is called *depth-bounded* if there is $k_D \in \mathbb{N}$ such that $depth(P) \leq k_D$ for all $P \in \mathcal{P}$. A process is called *depth-bounded* if its set of reachable process terms is depth-bounded. As shown in [22], this definition is equivalent to the definition of depth-bounded processes that is given in Section 2 and refers to communication graphs.

We define the following natural quasi-ordering $\leq$ on process terms: let $P \equiv (\nu \boldsymbol{x})P'$ and Q be process terms then $P \leq Q$ if and only if $Q \equiv (\nu \boldsymbol{x})(P' \mid F)$ for some process term F. The ordering $\leq$ defines a bqo on sets of depth-bounded process terms. We have shown in [28] that the ideals of this bqo can be represented by extending process terms with a replication operator ! to encode that certain subprocesses may be repeated arbitrarily often. We call these terms *limit process terms*. For instance the covering set of the example discussed in Section 2 is denoted by the following limit process term:

$$(\nu S)(\text{server}(S) \mid \text{env}(S) \mid !(\nu C)(\text{client}(C, S) \mid !(\overline{S}(C).0) \mid !(C().0)))$$

The ordering $\leq$ is extended to limit process terms by extending the congruence relation $\equiv$ with additional axioms for replication. The resulting congruence relation (which we also denote by $\equiv$) corresponds to the *extended congruence relation* studied in [11], where it is also shown to be decidable.

Widening for Depth-Bounded Processes. We first describe an extrapolation operator χ_{DBP} on pairs of limit process terms, which is then lifted to a set-widening operator ∇_{DBP}. The extrapolation operator relies on a set of inference rules for checking validity of clauses of the form $P \leq Q$ where P, Q are limit process terms. The inference rules do not just prove $P \leq Q$ but do a bit more: given P and Q, the rules derive judgments of the form $\boldsymbol{x}, R, F \vdash P \leq Q$. The semantics of these judgments is that if $\boldsymbol{x}, R, F \rhd P \parallel Q \equiv$ can be derived then $(\nu \boldsymbol{x})R \equiv P$ and $(\nu \boldsymbol{x})(R \mid F) \equiv Q$. We call F an *anti-frame*[1] of $P \leq Q$. The anti-frame captures the difference between process terms P and Q. The basic idea of extrapolation is that if $\boldsymbol{x}, R, F \vdash P \leq Q$ can be derived then $\chi_{\mathsf{DBP}}(P, Q)$ is given by $(\nu \boldsymbol{x})(R \mid !F)$. The set-widening operator ∇_{DBP} then applies extrapolation recursively on the input chain. A detailed description of the operators χ_{DBP} and ∇_{DBP} can be found in the technical report [30].

The intuition behind the termination argument for the operator ∇_{DBP} is that for an infinite ascending chain of limit processes, ∇_{DBP} gradually saturates the finitely many nesting levels of restrictions in the elements of the chain. It is important to realize that the extrapolation operator χ_{DBP} is not a pair-widening operator for limit process terms. The recursion built into the set-widening operator ∇_{DBP} ensures that a sufficiently high nesting depth of the replication operator is achieved. Intuitively, this recursion approximates the acceleration of infinite traces that correspond to unfoldings of inner loops within nested loops of the analyzed system. This is crucial for the termination of the analysis on non-flattable WSTS, such as the example presented in Section 2.

6 Implementation and Evaluation

We have implemented a prototype tool called PICASSO and applied it to a set of example programs. PICASSO combines our ideal abstraction domain with a trace partitioning domain [26]. The resulting analysis is a generalized Karp-Miller tree construction with widening instead of acceleration. The implementation is parameterized by the concrete

[1] The term "anti-frame" refers to abduction in entailment provers for separation logic [6].

ideal completion and the widening operator on ideals that are used in the analysis. The tool PICASSO and the example programs are available on-line [29].

For the analysis of our examples we have implemented a generalization of the ideal abstraction domain and widening operator for depth-bounded processes that we described in Sec. 5.3. The representation of ideals used in the implementation more closely resembles the communication graphs with nested repeated substructures described in Sec. 2. This representation admits process nodes in communication graphs with arbitrarily many outgoing edges. Such nodes correspond to process identifiers in π-calculus process terms with unbounded (but unordered) parameter lists. To represent the limit elements we annotate the nodes in the graph with natural numbers indicating the nesting depth of the nodes. Testing the ordering on states is done by computing morphisms between the corresponding graphs. The morphisms take into account the nesting structure by allowing mappings to nodes of higher nesting depth to be non-injective. The actual test is encoded into a set of Boolean constraints and passed to a SAT solver. The morphisms are then reconstructed from the obtained satisfying assignments. The algorithm constructs a Karp-Miller tree using a depth-first search. When the tree is extended with a new node, widening is applied to the chains on the path to the root of the tree that contain the new node. Among the smaller ancestors of a node, not all are used for the widening. Instead, nodes are selected using an exponential back-off strategy. When the depth of the constructed tree becomes too large, the algorithm tends to slow down significantly. For such cases, we have implemented a restart policy. When a restart occurs, the leaves of the current tree are used as roots to construct new trees. The restart policy ensures that, for larger examples, the analysis terminates within reasonable time. The current implementation uses restart intervals of 5 minutes. The implementation exploits parallelism and makes use of multiple cores when possible.

We ran our experiments on a machine with two AMD Opteron 2431 processors and a total of 12 cores. We found that memory consumption was not an issue for the analysis of our examples. The examples that we have considered are depth-bounded processes, which are inspired by Scala programs. These Scala programs use the Scala actor library [18] for the implementation of dynamic process networks. Table 1 summarizes the results of our experiments. The `ping-pong` example is the "*Hello World*" of actor programming and is taken from the tutorial for the Scala actor library. All remaining examples follow a client-server type of communication with an unbounded number of clients. These examples cover common patterns that arise in message passing programs. The second and third program are variations of the example presented in Section 2. In the third program, we added a timeout to the receive operations of clients. We model the timeout by letting the clients send `Timeout` messages to themselves. This pattern is often used in programs based on the Scala actor library. The `genericComputeServer` example is the message passing skeleton of a tutorial for remote actors [4]. The example implements a compute server that accepts computation tasks from clients and then executes them. The second version uses actors to model the closures that are sent to the server. This model is obtained using the usual reduction of high-order π-calculus to the standard π-calculus. The `liftChatLike` example is the message-passing skeleton extracted from a chat application based on the lift web framework [21]. Since our implementation does not yet support collections, the broadcast pattern that is used in the

Table 1. Experimental results: the columns indicate the number of nodes in the Karp-Miller tree, the number of ideals in the covering set, and the running time

Name	tree size	cov. set size	time
`ping-pong`	17	14	0.6 s
`client-server`	25	2	1.9 s
`client-server-with-TO`	184	5	12.8 s
`genericComputeServer`	57	4	4.6 s
`genericComputeServer-fctAsActor`	98	8	14.8 s
`liftChatLike`	1846	21	1830.9 s
`round_robin_2`	830	63	48.8 s
`round_robin_3`	3775	259	737.8 s

original implementation has been changed into a polling pattern. The `round_robin_`k example is a load balancer that routes requests to a pool of k workers. Increasing the value of k greatly increase the number of interleavings that the analysis has to consider. With added support for collections, we can analyze a generic `round_robin_`k, which should also reduce the symmetry in the model.

Our experiments indicate that our analysis produces sufficiently precise approximations of the covering set to be useful for program verification and program understanding. The main bottle neck of our analysis is the explosion caused by interleavings of the transitions of individual processes. We did not yet explore techniques such as partial order reduction to tackle this problem.

7 Conclusion

We proposed a novel abstract interpretation framework to compute precise approximations of the covering set of WSTS. Our analysis captures the essence of acceleration-based algorithms that compute the exact covering set but only terminate on flattable systems. By replacing acceleration with widening we ensure that our analysis always terminates. We discussed several concrete instances of our framework including the application to depth-bounded process networks, which are typically non-flattable. Our experience with a prototype implementation shows that the analysis is often precise, which makes it a useful tool for verification and program analysis.

References

1. Abdulla, P.A., Cerans, K., Jonsson, B., Tsay, Y.-K.: General decidability theorems for infinite-state systems. In: LICS, pp. 313–321 (1996)
2. Abdulla, P.A., Collomb-Annichini, A., Bouajjani, A., Jonsson, B.: Using forward reachability analysis for verification of lossy channel systems. FMSD 25(1), 39–65 (2004)
3. Abdulla, P.A., Jonsson, B.: Verifying programs with unreliable channels. In: LICS, pp. 160–170 (1993)
4. Azzopardi, T.: Generic compute server in Scala using remote actors (2008), `http://tiny.cc/yjzva` (accessed November 2011)
5. Bagnara, R., Hill, P.M., Zaffanella, E.: Widening operators for powerset domains. Software Tools for Technology Transfer 8(4/5), 449–466 (2006)

6. Calcagno, C., Distefano, D., O'Hearn, P.W., Yang, H.: Compositional shape analysis by means of bi-abduction. In: POPL, pp. 289–300 (2009)
7. Cousot, P., Cousot, R.: Abstract interpretation: a unified lattice model for static analysis of programs by construction or approximation of fixpoints. In: POPL, pp. 238–252 (1977)
8. Cousot, P., Cousot, R.: Systematic design of program analysis frameworks. In: POPL, pp. 269–282. ACM (1979)
9. Cousot, P., Cousot, R.: Abstract interpretation frameworks. Journal of Logic and Computation 2(4), 511–547 (1992)
10. Dufourd, C., Finkel, A., Schnoebelen, P.: Reset Nets Between Decidability and Undecidability. In: Larsen, K.G., Skyum, S., Winskel, G. (eds.) ICALP 1998. LNCS, vol. 1443, pp. 103–115. Springer, Heidelberg (1998)
11. Engelfriet, J., Gelsema, T.: Multisets and structural congruence of the pi-calculus with replication. Theor. Comput. Sci. 211(1-2), 311–337 (1999)
12. Finkel, A., Goubault-Larrecq, J.: Forward Analysis for WSTS, Part I: Completions. In: STACS. Dagstuhl Sem. Proc., vol. 09001, pp. 433–444 (2009)
13. Finkel, A., Goubault-Larrecq, J.: Forward Analysis for WSTS, Part II: Complete WSTS. In: Albers, S., Marchetti-Spaccamela, A., Matias, Y., Nikoletseas, S., Thomas, W. (eds.) ICALP 2009, Part II. LNCS, vol. 5556, pp. 188–199. Springer, Heidelberg (2009)
14. Finkel, A., Schnoebelen, P.: Well-structured transition systems everywhere! Theor. Comput. Sci. 256(1-2), 63–92 (2001)
15. Ganty, P., Raskin, J.-F., Van Begin, L.: A Complete Abstract Interpretation Framework for Coverability Properties of WSTS. In: Emerson, E.A., Namjoshi, K.S. (eds.) VMCAI 2006. LNCS, vol. 3855, pp. 49–64. Springer, Heidelberg (2005)
16. Geeraerts, G., Raskin, J.-F., Van Begin, L.: Expand, Enlarge and Check: New algorithms for the coverability problem of WSTS. J. Comput. Syst. Sci. 72(1), 180–203 (2006)
17. Goubault-Larrecq, J.: On noetherian spaces. In: LICS, pp. 453–462. IEEE Computer Society (2007)
18. Haller, P., Odersky, M.: Scala actors: Unifying thread-based and event-based programming. Theor. Comput. Sci. 410(2-3), 202–220 (2009)
19. Joshi, S., König, B.: Applying the Graph Minor Theorem to the Verification of Graph Transformation Systems. In: Gupta, A., Malik, S. (eds.) CAV 2008. LNCS, vol. 5123, pp. 214–226. Springer, Heidelberg (2008)
20. Karp, R.M., Miller, R.E.: Parallel program schemata. J. Comput. Syst. Sci. 3(2), 147–195 (1969)
21. Lift. Lift web framework, `http://liftweb.net/`
22. Meyer, R.: On boundedness in depth in the pi-calculus. In: IFIP TCS. IFIP, vol. 273, pp. 477–489. Springer, Boston (2008)
23. Milner, E.C.: Basic wqo- and bqo-theory. Graphs and order (1985)
24. Milner, R.: The polyadic pi-calculus: A tutorial. In: Logic and Algebra of Specification. Computer and Systems Sciences. Springer, Heidelberg (1993)
25. Petri, C.A., Reisig, W.: Scholarpedia 3(4), 6477 (2008), `http://www.scholarpedia.org/article/Petri_net`
26. Rival, X., Mauborgne, L.: The trace partitioning abstract domain. ACM Trans. Program. Lang. Syst. 29(5) (2007)
27. Schnoebelen, P.: Revisiting Ackermann-Hardness for Lossy Counter Machines and Reset Petri Nets. In: Hliněný, P., Kučera, A. (eds.) MFCS 2010. LNCS, vol. 6281, pp. 616–628. Springer, Heidelberg (2010)
28. Wies, T., Zufferey, D., Henzinger, T.A.: Forward Analysis of Depth-Bounded Processes. In: Ong, L. (ed.) FOSSACS 2010. LNCS, vol. 6014, pp. 94–108. Springer, Heidelberg (2010)
29. Zufferey, D., Wies, T.: Picasso Analyzer, `http://ist.ac.at/~zufferey/picasso/`
30. Zufferey, D., Wies, T., Henzinger, T.A.: On ideal abstractions for well-structured transition systems. Technical Report IST-2011-10, IST Austria (November 2011)

Author Index

GPSR Compliance

The European Union's (EU) General Product Safety Regulation (GPSR) is a set of rules that requires consumer products to be safe and our obligations to ensure this.

If you have any concerns about our products, you can contact us on ProductSafety@springernature.com

In case Publisher is established outside the EU, the EU authorized representative is:

Springer Nature Customer Service Center GmbH
Europaplatz 3
69115 Heidelberg, Germany

Batch number: 09490872

Printed by Printforce, the Netherlands